# HISTORY OF
# THE SECOND WORLD WAR
## UNITED KINGDOM MILITARY SERIES
#### Edited by J. R. M. BUTLER

A

The authors of the Military Histories have been
given full access to official documents. They and the
editor are alone responsible for the statements
made and the views expressed.

The three Commanders-in-Chief: Admiral Sir Andrew Cunningham, Air Chief Marshal Sir Arthur Longmore, General Sir Archibald Wavell.

# THE MEDITERRANEAN
## AND
# MIDDLE EAST

## VOLUME I

## The Early Successes against Italy

### (to May 1941)

BY

### MAJOR–GENERAL I. S. O. PLAYFAIR
C.B., D.S.O., M.C.

WITH
### COMMANDER G. M. S. STITT, R.N.
### BRIGADIER C. J. C. MOLONY
### AIR VICE–MARSHALL S. E. TOOMER
C.B., C.B.E., D.F.C.

This edition of The Mediterranean and Middle East: Volume I
first published in 2004
by The Naval & Military Press Ltd

Published by
**The Naval & Military Press Ltd**
Unit 10 Ridgewood Industrial Park,
Uckfield, East Sussex,
TN22 5QE England
Tel: +44 (0) 1825 749494
Fax: +44 (0) 1825 765701
www.naval–military–press.com

Printed and bound by Antony Rowe Ltd, Eastbourne

# CONTENTS

# APPENDICES

# MAPS AND DIAGRAMS

# PHOTOGRAPHS

Most of the photographs are Crown Copyright and are repro-
duced by courtesy of the Imperial War Museum and the
Ministries concerned. Nos. 4 and 7 are from paintings by
Rowland Langmaid; Nos. 1, 39, 42 and 43 were taken by
Lt.-Col. J. E. B. Barton, and No. 34 by W. P. Thesiger. These
are reproduced with their kind permission.

# EDITOR'S PREFACE

THE MILITARY series of the United Kingdom History of the Second World War has been planned in accordance with a Government decision announced to the House of Commons on 25th November 1946. The purpose of the history, said the then Prime Minister, was 'to provide a broad survey of events from an inter-Service point of view rather than separate accounts of the parts played by each of the three Services'. The historians have thus felt themselves under no obligation to tell the story of operations in the same detail as was thought appropriate in the case of the war of 1914–1918. For such detailed narratives the student must turn to the unit or formation histories of which many have already appeared. We have set ourselves to present a single series of volumes in which the whole military story, and every part of it, is treated from an inter-Service aspect. Here and elsewhere throughout our work the word 'military' is used to cover the activities of all three fighting Services, as distinct from the other sides of the national war effort which are treated in the Civil Histories edited by Sir Keith Hancock.

Even on the military side, however, it seemed that a 'broad survey' which confined itself to a description of campaigns and operations would fail to give a satisfactory account of how the war of 1939–45 was waged. The vast area over which operations were progressively extended, the number and the variety of the campaigns being fought simultaneously, the constant need of co-ordinating policy and strategy with governments overseas, together with the centralization of command rendered possible by modern systems of communication—all these increased the range and importance of the part played by the supreme authority at home and seemed to demand that a fuller treatment of the higher direction of the war should be attempted than has been usual in military histories. It was accordingly decided to allot several volumes to Grand Strategy as devised in Whitehall and at Washington, including one volume on developments prior to the actual outbreak of war in September 1939.

For the rest, the history has been planned to cover the following themes or theatres: the defence of the United Kingdom, the maritime war viewed as a whole, the two campaigns of the early period in Norway and in north-west Europe, the strategic air offensive, and the three epic series of military operations on the grand scale in the Mediterranean and Middle East, in the Far East, and again in the north-west of Europe in 1944 and 1945. Additional volumes have been allotted to the history of Civil Affairs or Military Government in view of the novelty and importance of the problems involved in this field of military responsibility.

In order to avoid undue detail, the standpoint from which campaigns have been viewed is that of the theatre commander. The intention has been to treat all the campaigns on the same scale; but it must be confessed that in some cases when the total forces involved were small, as in Norway in 1940 and in the Western Desert in the early phases, the narrative has descended to describe the operations of detached units in greater detail than their size would normally justify.

No doubt the proposed dual treatment of strategic problems, at the Whitehall level and at the level of theatre headquarters, involves a risk, indeed a certainty, of some overlapping. This would be the case even if it were not our aim, as it is, to make each group of volumes intelligible by itself and to that extent self-contained. We cannot unfortunately assume that the general reader, for whom as much as for military students our history is intended, will be prepared to buy or read the whole of our twenty or thirty volumes. We think that a moderate amount of overlapping is excusable and may even be welcomed if it avoids the necessity of constant reference to other volumes.

The description of a war waged by Allies, in which 'integration' was successfully carried to lengths unattempted in previous campaigns, raised further problems. Granted that our commission is to write the history not of the Second World War as a whole but of the military effort of the United Kingdom, on what principle ought we to handle campaigns or actions in which men from the United Kingdom and from other nations fought side by side? Where United Kingdom forces served under foreign or Dominion command, or vice versa, it seems clear that decisions or actions of our fellow combatants must be described with sufficient fullness to preserve a proper balance in the story. On the other hand it is not desirable to duplicate the accounts given in the histories sponsored by our Allies and by the other nations of the British Commonwealth, especially when the primary sources are under their control. Arrangements have indeed been made with them for mutual information on points of special interest and for an exchange of drafts; it is hoped that these arrangements will at least reduce the likelihood of controversy due to ignorance of another nation's point of view, though they will not, of course, eliminate differences of interpretation. It has not been possible to make such arrangements in the case of the U.S.S.R.

With regard to German military records, however, the Allied historians are fortunate, to an unprecedented degree, in having access to a mass of original documents, some of them of the highest importance, which were captured during the occupation of Germany and are now held under joint Anglo-American control. In the case of the other enemy Powers both the volume and the value of the documents captured are considerably less and details of their military plans and operations have of necessity been obtained from more conventional sources of information.

To the official United Kingdom records we have been allowed full access, and we have done our best to supplement them by reference to unofficial accounts, published and unpublished, written and oral. We have felt bound, however, to respect the requirements of military 'security', and in some cases cipher telegrams have been paraphrased, though not in such a way as to affect the sense. In accordance with the recognized British constitutional principle we have not held ourselves free to reveal individual differences of opinion within the War Cabinet nor, as a rule, to lift the veil of Civil Service anonymity.

We have taken it as our prime duty to present an accurate narrative of events. But events, properly speaking, include plans and intentions as well as actions, and it is the duty of a historian, as opposed to a mere annalist, to say why, as well as how, things happened as they did. He must interpret, not merely narrate, and interpretation implies a personal judgement. In any case the need to select from the vast mass of material implies a personal judgement of what is most relevant and important.

We all share the contemporary outlook, and some of us are laymen in military matters; it would be unbecoming in us to attempt to pronounce what a commander should have done or should not have done in a particular situation. Our ideal would be to let the facts speak for themselves, to point out how such a decision led to such a result, and to leave speculation and moralising to the strategists; but the facts can only speak to our readers as we have selected and presented them, and we have not shrunk from stating what seemed to us the lessons that emerged from a particular course of events.

It is normally the duty and desire of a historian to support his assertions and arguments by detailed references to his authorities. Such references serve partly as an indication of his sources, partly as a challenge to his readers to verify his statements. Where, however, the main authorities are official documents which are not at present, and for some time are not likely to be, open to public inspection, published references have comparatively little point, since the challenge cannot be taken up. The nature of the material used can, we think, in most cases be sufficiently indicated in the prefaces or bibliographical notes to the several volumes. Accordingly our normal practice has been that explained by Sir Keith Hancock in his introduction to the Civil Histories. 'It has been decided not to clutter the published pages with references to official files which are not yet generally available to students. In the published series, footnotes have been confined to material that is already accessible. The completed documentation has been given in confidential print. There it will be immediately available to critical readers within the government service. No doubt it will become available in due time to the historians of a future generation. The official historians of this generation have consciously submitted their work to the professional verdict of the future.'[1]

In the use of the enemy documents the historians' labours have been immensely lightened by the help of their colleagues charged with the collection, collation and interpretation of this vast mass of material. Work on the German and Italian documents has been directed by Mr. Brian Melland; Colonel G. T. Wards has advised with regard to the Japanese. Valuable assistance in this matter has also been rendered by Commander M. G. Saunders, R.N., of the Admiralty Historical Section and by Squadron Leader L. A. Jackets of the Air Historical Branch.

The maps have been prepared under the experienced direction of Colonel T. M. M. Penney of the Cabinet Office Historical Section. The spelling of the place-names follows in the main the system approved at an informal conference of the British and American experts in October 1947, but current usage has been adhered to where not to do so would be pedantic. In the representation of Allied and enemy troops the conventional symbols and colours, where used, are those officially recognized during the war. Apart from the fact that work on some of our maps had begun before November 1950, when the British Army changed its system, it seemed natural to follow the convention used in contemporary maps.

The appointment of a civilian editor to be responsible for the production of the military histories made it desirable that on general questions as well as special points he should be able frequently to consult authorities whose opinions on Service matters would command respect; I am fortunate to have had so helpful a panel of advisers as Vice-Admiral Sir Geoffrey Blake, Lieutenant-General Sir Henry Pownall, Air Chief Marshals Sir Douglas Evill and Sir Guy Garrod, and Lieutenant-General Sir Ian Jacob. These distinguished officers not only have given me the benefit of their experience and judgement in the planning of the history and the selection of writers but have read and commented on the volumes in draft; in all these matters, however, responsibility rests with the Editor alone.

The history could not have been written without the constant assistance of the Service Historical Sections, and the historians would express their gratitude to Rear-Admiral R. M. Bellairs,

---

[1] *History of the Second World War: British War Economy*, p. xii.

Brigadier H. B. Latham and Mr. J. C. Nerney, and also to Lieutenant-General Sir Desmond Anderson, of the War Office, and their staffs. The monographs, narratives and summaries produced by the Service Departments have greatly reduced the labours, though not the responsibilities, of the historians, and the staffs concerned have been lavish of their help in supplying information and comment. Similar acknowledgements are due to the authors of the Civil Histories, and we are grateful to Mr. Yates Smith of the Imperial War Museum and to other librarians for the loan of books.

Finally, the historians in general and the Editor in particular are deeply indebted to Mr. A. B. Acheson of the Cabinet Office. His advice and help have been of the greatest service to us in many ways; indeed, without the relief provided by Mr. Acheson in administrative matters, a part-time editor could hardly have performed his task.

J. R. M. B.

# INTRODUCTION

THIS IS the first of six volumes which are to cover the campaign in the Mediterranean and Middle East from 1939 to 1945, so that on the average each volume will deal with one crowded year of war by sea, land, and air. The account is a joint one, which is particularly appropriate to this theatre because the activities of the three Services were closely interlocked from the first.

'The War in the Mediterranean and Middle East' includes the struggle for control of the communications in the Mediterranean and Red Seas; the ebb and flow of the enemy's attempts to invade Egypt; the campaigns in Greece, Crete, Iraq, and Syria; the destruction of Italy's East African Empire; the defeat of the German and Italian forces in North Africa; the capture of Sicily; the campaign on the mainland of Italy; and the operations in the Aegean, the Adriatic, and the Balkans. Every variety of ground was fought over from desert to mountain, in conditions ranging from extreme heat to bitter cold, and with every discomfort from sandstorms to snow. The forces of every Dominion and almost every colony in the Commonwealth took part at one time or another, as well as contingents from ten of the other Allied nations.

The term 'Middle East' is not used in its geographical sense of a region lying between the Near East and India, but as meaning the area included in the army and air commands. These areas were not identical, nor did they remain constant, but expanded and contracted with the progress of the war. In November 1942, a separate (Allied) high command created for the landings in French North Africa comes upon the scene, and thereafter has a large share in the 'Mediterranean and Middle East' story. Prior to that date the title applies to that part of the war which took place mainly within the areas of responsibility of the naval Commander-in-Chief, Mediterranean Station, and the army and air Commanders-in-Chief, Middle East. This is the first example of a campaign directed by three Commanders-in-Chief jointly responsible for carrying out the policy of His Majesty's Government.

The writing of a joint story means that to the usual difficulty of selection from a mass of detailed information is added the problem of maintaining a just and reasonable balance—a problem which obviously cannot be solved by any rule of thumb. We have tried to relate it to our broad task of telling the story generally at the level of the High Command, and we have therefore included many matters which, though small in themselves, affected the views of the Commanders-in-Chief, or which serve to illustrate the process of translating into action the decisions they took. In general we have steered a middle course between two extreme opinions: namely, that on the one hand all space not devoted to fighting is wasted, and on the other that military history would be quite interesting were it not for the battles. More positively, we have tried, whenever possible, to give 'the reason why', rather than simply what happened.

The vast size of the Mediterranean and Middle East theatre makes a number of changes of scene unavoidable. In order to present the course of events as coherently as possible we have dwelt on each 'front' for as long as we could without interfering too much with the general chronology, but it must be remembered that the whole theatre did not appear to the Commanders-in-Chief as a number of neatly separated areas of operations; in spite of the distances it was all one.

It may seem a long time before the first shot is fired. (Indeed, we felt that some readers might, like the Gryphon, want the adventures first.) But it seemed only right to give a broad indication of how the strategic situation in the Mediterranean and Middle East had developed, for without this a reader could not help being puzzled by much that happened. It must be remembered that, apart from the unending struggle at sea, the scene of decisive operations in autumn 1939 was Poland; in early 1940 it was Norway; then France; then came the Battle of Britain, which might have been a prelude to invasion. All this time the stage in the Middle East was being set with whatever players and properties could be spared.

We make no apology for referring so often to administrative matters. It is now widely understood that administration is not the drab servant of the art of war, unworthy of mention in the same breath as a battle, but that it is rather of war's very essence. Armies and air forces can operate only with what the lines of communication succeed in delivering. The influence of equipment, also, can hardly be too strongly emphasized. The arrival of a new weapon or a new piece of mechanism could have tremendous consequences: examples in the present volume are the Hurricane fighter, the Matilda tank, and the introduction of radar on land, at sea and in the air. During the war the development of equipment received a great stimulus; brains and money were applied to it to an extent unheard of in peace. As a result, the equipment of the Services was being improved all the time. So also was the enemy's, and it is impossible to understand the course of events without taking into account the state that both had reached. The material factors therefore require frequent mention because they were constantly changing.

The human factor is of course no less important, for the usefulness of guns, ships, aircraft and all the other aids to success in battle lay in the hands of the men and women who served and tended them. We have found it impossible to be consistent in singling out individuals and units for mention by name. The principal reason is that, quite apart from the difficulty of choosing equivalent standards between the Services, the scale of events on one front was often quite different from that on another, and it varied greatly from time to time on the same front. It is not that the action of a small unit was any less meritorious if the unit happened to form part of a large force than if it was acting more on its own; but in a broad and general account it is obvious that the sense justifies the mention of names in some cases to an extent which is impossible in others. Where we have thought it right to particularize it has not been because of any hard and fast rules but because we felt that the story required it. There are, of course, regimental, squadron, divisional and other Service histories in which units and names are given in great detail.

No attempt has been made to give a complete list of the forces in the theatre; for one thing it was constantly changing and for another it was so big. At the beginning of 1941, for example, there were over 1,000 Army units alone, apart from the 400 or so which formed part of the Divisions. A list of the Commanders and Staff Officers who held high appointments during the period covered by this volume is given in Appendix 9.

A careful comparison of British records with those of the German and Italian Air Forces has shown that claims for the aircraft destroyed in air combat were usually over-estimated by both sides, especially when large numbers of aircraft were engaged. Air combats took place at high speeds, usually at high altitudes and often above clouds, which made the ultimate fate of an opponent difficult, if not impossible, to determine. When formations of aircraft were engaged it was quite possible for more than one pilot or air gunner to fire at, and claim, the same aircraft. Great care was taken at the time to eliminate errors of this sort, but inaccuracies still remain. In this book the method adopted has been to assess the enemy's losses at the end of an operation, or phase of an operation, by using his own official records—which are, of course, not necessarily the same as his published figures. When it has not been possible to do this or when, for any special reason, inaccurate or suspect figures are quoted, attention is drawn to the fact in the text.

The methods of assessing the results of our own air attacks improved greatly as the war went on. During the period of this volume the assessment depended mainly on the reports of the aircrews and on the limited number of photographs they were able to take. From high or medium altitudes, particularly at night, or when flashing low over the target, the aircrews could at best gain only a general idea of the damage done to such targets as buildings and their contents, ships and harbours, aircraft on the ground, and motor transport. Only the enemy knew what the real damage was. The immense amount of research involved in trying to trace the results of hundreds of small attacks—even if the records exist—has not seemed to us worth-while. Each attack was usually made on a small scale, and it was only the cumulative effect of many which brought about the results desired. In general, therefore, we have not attempted in this volume to give the damage caused by individual raids; as with the air combat losses the method we have adopted has been to assess achievements at the end of an operation or phase of an operation.

Our principal sources of information have been: Chiefs of Staff's and other Government records; diaries of ships, units, formations and staffs; current orders, appreciations and reports; intelligence summaries; official despatches; captured documents; records of meetings; and files of correspondence and signals between the Commanders-in-Chief, their subordinates, and their Ministries. We have based every statement of fact upon the best evidence we have been able to obtain. All official documents are not, however, equally reliable; for instance, a particular report may have been made in all good faith but in ignorance of certain important facts. In examining matters of this sort we have been helped by the many individuals specially qualified to comment, at home and in the other nations of the Commonwealth, who have been good enough to read our drafts. This has been of great value to us not only by setting us right over occasional matters of detail, but by helping to recapture the atmosphere of the time, which in turn has often led to an understanding of what was otherwise obscure. We wish to express our gratitude to all who have helped us in this way.

The Editor has expressed the debt we all owe to the Service Historical Branches, to the Mapping Section, and to the Librarians and Keepers of the various records in the Cabinet Office and Ministries and the Imperial War Museum. We wish to add our thanks to those who have helped us particularly with the present volume: Commanders G. A. Titterton and M. G. Saunders, both of the Admiralty Historical Section; Brigadier W. P. Pessell, Lieutenant-Colonel G. R. Johnston and Lieutenant-Colonel J. E. B. Barton of the Cabinet Office Historical Section; Squadron Leader L. A. Jackets, Mr. F. L. Roberts and Miss H. Raven of the Air Historical Branch. Much of the work on German and Italian documents has been done by Mrs. J. M. Hamilton, and general research work has been done, at one time or another, by Miss R. P. G. Gee, Mrs. G. F. Oakley, Miss Jean Burt and Miss Anthea Vincent. Miss Sheila

Kinnear has typed all the drafts. To all these and to Mr. A. J. Charge, Keeper of Photographs, Imperial War Museum, we are most grateful.

Commander G. M. S. Stitt, R.N., died before work on the present volume was finished. His place has been taken by Captain F. C. Flynn, R.N.

Fighting in the Mediterranean and Middle East began in June 1940 when Italy decided to enter the war. It went on for five years—which was longer than in any other theatre. It was of course here that Italy was defeated, and for nearly two years this was the only theatre with a land front on which British and German troops were in contact. So it was mainly here that the techniques of land warfare were kept constantly up-to-date, the intimate tactical co-operation of land and air forces evolved and perfected, and the conduct of large and intricate landing operations put to the practical test. Thus the Mediterranean and Middle East was the workshop in which the weapon of invasion was forged and the trial ground on which it was proved; it was here that the highest commanders learned their business of handling it.

But it was a long time before forces and equipment were available on such a scale as this, and the story is one of humble beginnings, for, as is usual in the opening stages of their wars, the British had to be adept in the art of doing without. Inevitably there were set-backs, failures, and disappointments, making heavy demands on the moral no less than on the physical courage of leaders and led. But from the outset there were successes too. The early encounters may seem insignificant if measured only by the numbers engaged, but they show what resolute and confident commanders and men can do. And had the Eastern Mediterranean arena not been successfully held during the lean years (in which case, for want of bases, no British fleet or air forces could have even disputed the control of the Mediterranean sea communications) the task of the Allies in gaining a foothold in Europe would have been rendered immensely more difficult; indeed, it might well have proved to be beyond their powers.

I. S. O. P.
F. C. F.
C. J. C. M.
S. E. T.

IN 1884 Ferdinand de Lesseps, builder of the Suez Canal, was elected to the French Academy. In the course of a speech of welcome Ernest Renan said: 'Hitherto the Bosphorus has provided the world with embarrassment enough; now you have created a second, and more serious, source of anxiety. For this defile not only connects two inland seas, but it acts as a channel of communication to the oceans of the world. So great is its importance that in a maritime war everyone will strive hard to occupy it. You have thus marked the site of a future great battlefield'.

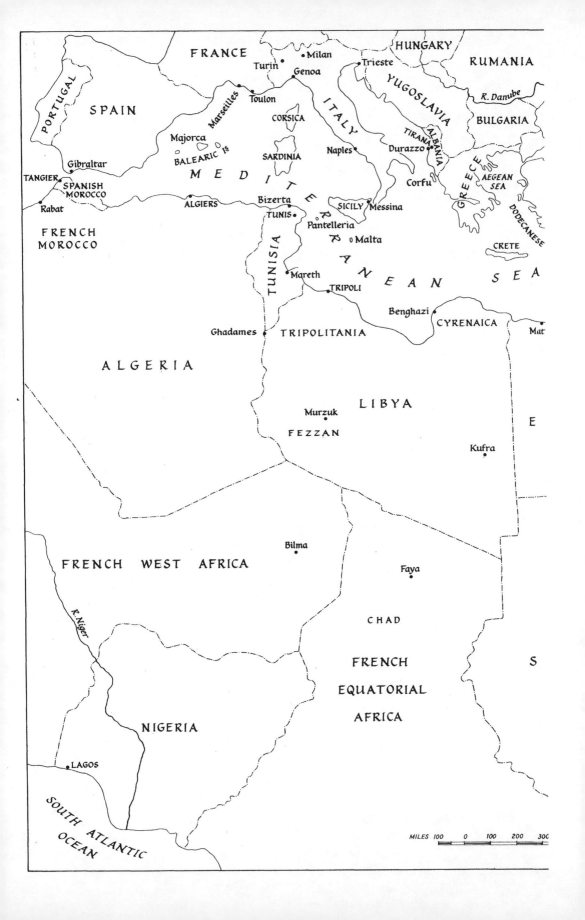

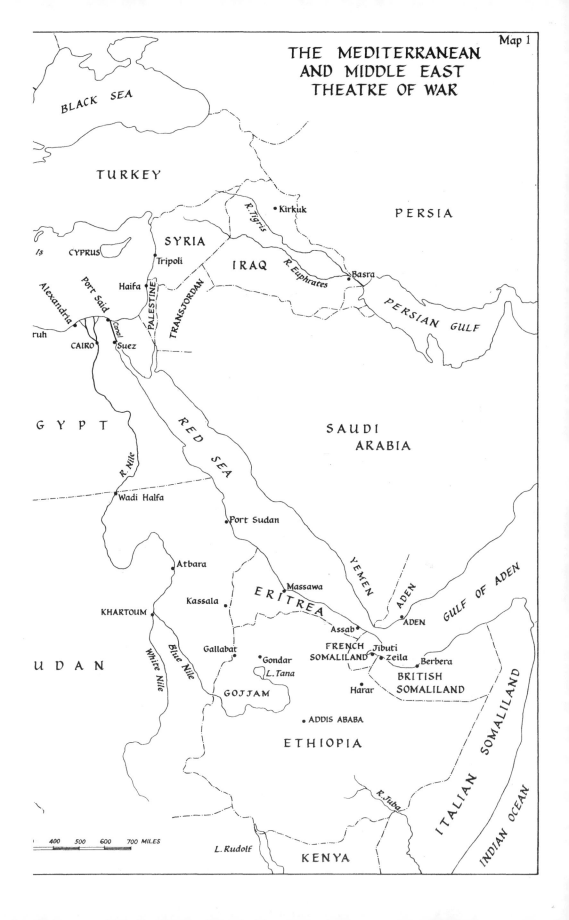

Map 1

THE MEDITERRANEAN
AND MIDDLE EAST
THEATRE OF WAR

BLACK SEA

TURKEY

PERSIA

• Kirkuk

SYRIA

Is CYPRUS

Tripoli

IRAQ

R. Tigris

R. Euphrates

Basra •

PERSIAN GULF

Haifa •

PALESTINE

TRANSJORDAN

Port Said

Alexandria

ruh

CAIRO • Suez

Canal

GYPT

R. Nile

RED SEA

SAUDI
ARABIA

Wadi Halfa •

• Port Sudan

Atbara •

YEMEN

Massawa •

ERITREA

ADEN

Kassala •

KHARTOUM •

GULF OF ADEN

Assab •

ADEN •

UDAN

White Nile

Blue Nile

Gallabat •

FRENCH
SOMALILAND

Jibuti
Zeila

Berbera •

• Gondar

L. Tana

Harar •

BRITISH
SOMALILAND

GOJJAM

• ADDIS ABABA

ETHIOPIA

ITALIAN SOMALILAND

R. Juba

INDIAN OCEAN

400  500  600  700 MILES

L. Rudolf

KENYA

# CHAPTER I

# THE GROWING TENSION IN
# THE MIDDLE EAST

*See Maps 1 and 2 and Chronology on page 21.*

UPON TWO of the Mediterranean countries in particular the First World War left a deep mark. Turkey lost her empire, and Italy fought on the winning side only to be bitterly disappointed at the Peace Conference.

Turkey had enjoyed a nominal suzerainty over Egypt, but when she entered the war the British announced that they intended to defend Egypt themselves, and declared a Protectorate. The Turks were encouraged by their German allies to keep up an overland threat to the Suez Canal, the most sensitive point on the British artery of sea communication with the East. The Germans hoped that large British forces would be devoted to the protection of this waterway, as in fact they were. In the ensuing campaigns in Palestine and Mesopotamia the Turkish armies were totally defeated. The Peace treaties left Turkey with only a small foothold in Thrace, and from the ruins of her Arabian Empire emerged the states of Syria, Iraq, Palestine, and Transjordan.

British interest in the security of the Suez Canal remained undiminished after the war, and the region from Egypt to the head of the Persian Gulf gained greatly in importance with the growth of aviation, for it became an essential link in the air route to India and beyond. The Anglo-Iranian oilfield at the eastern end of this area was still the principal source of British-owned oil, but by 1931 the new Kirkuk field in northern Iraq had been connected by pipelines to the Mediterranean ports of Haifa in Palestine and Tripoli in Syria, and in this field the British had a large interest also. For these reasons alone it was clearly to Great Britain's strategic advantage that Egypt, Palestine, and the new Arab States should be stable, peaceful, and friendly. To this end she made great efforts in the years between the wars, with the results that are referred to later in this chapter.

Italy, after nine months of indecision, had joined Great Britain and France in 1915 in return for certain promises which, when the time came for making the Peace settlements, those countries were unable to honour to their full extent. Italy was resentful and hurt;

C

it seemed to her that she had made heavy sacrifices for nothing. Yet it was not Italy but militarist Japan who first defied the newly created League of Nations, which she did by resorting to aggression in the Chinese province of Manchuria in 1931. The next year a Conference in accordance with the Covenants of the League met to discuss the reduction of national armaments. It was still in being, though making little progress, when, in January 1933, Adolf Hitler became Chancellor of the German Reich. The following October Germany rejected the idea of disarmament, withdrew from the League, and began to rearm. From that moment Germany was a potential enemy, but not, as yet, an immediate menace. Although Japan had successfully defied the League there still remained the hope that, in future, the undertaking of the member Nations to sever all trade and financial relations with an aggressor State would act as a sufficient deterrent. It was Italy who put this undertaking to the test.

The British view of Italy at the end of 1933, when the first rearmament programme was being drawn up, was that she was friendly, in the sense that she need not be considered as an enemy; consequently no expenditure was to be incurred or any steps taken exclusively on her account. This was still the British attitude when, early in October 1935, after a long and active period of preparations that were impossible to conceal, Italian forces from Eritrea and Somalia invaded and bombed the territory of Ethiopia, a country whose admission to the League had been sponsored by Italy herself. This was a flagrant breach of the Covenant of the League. Six weeks later a policy of limited economic sanctions was adopted by the League Council against the declared aggressor. Of the fifty states in the Assembly who supported the policy, Great Britain alone showed any signs of readiness to adopt the extreme measures which in the last resort might be necessary to make it effective.[1] At the end of September the British Mediterranean Fleet, having been powerfully reinforced, was at Alexandria, Port Said, and Haifa. There were British troops and air forces in Egypt. Signor Mussolini was therefore taking a great risk in electing to fight a war in an under-developed country to which his sole means of access was by sea—either through the Suez Canal or all the way round the Cape. Nevertheless, the gamble succeeded; for apart from making a few promises to provide facilities at certain Mediterranean harbours for the British Fleet the other nations stood aside and awaited events. The Suez Canal, in accordance with the Constantinople Convention, remained open to

---

[1] 'Not a ship, not a machine, not a man had been moved by any other member state'—Sir Samuel Hoare in the House of Commons, 19th December 1935. Austria, Germany and Albania did not support the policy, and Switzerland pleaded her time-honoured neutrality.

the passage of Italian ships, so that warlike stores of all kinds continued to pass freely on their way.[1]

The British Commanders most directly concerned were the Naval Commander-in-Chief, Mediterranean Station; the Air Officer Commanding, Royal Air Force, Middle East; and the General Officer Commanding, British Troops in Egypt. These officers were warned that if war broke out with Italy, not as the result of deliberate military action in furtherance of League policy but owing to some hostile act by Italy, the British might have to bear the brunt for some time. They reacted by asking for certain reinforcements from the United Kingdom, and the situation in western Europe made it possible to meet the most pressing of their needs. Their plan disclosed—in miniature, as it were—many of the characteristics of the campaigns that were to follow. For instance: the need for adequate, secure bases; the limiting effect of logistics upon operational planning; and the dependence of each Service upon the action of the others.

Communications between Italy and Eritrea would, of course, be interrupted, but the only other way in which pressure could be applied was by naval action against the sea routes by which supplies reached Italy, and against the sea communications between Italy and Libya. The fleet must therefore expect retaliatory action, and here entered the unknown factor of attack from the air. Whatever might be in store for warships at sea, it would be most unwise to allow the fleet at anchor to be exposed to air attack without doing everything possible to make the conditions difficult for the attacker. But the fleet itself had virtually no reserves of anti-aircraft ammunition, and the other forms of air defence were extremely weak. In fact the only way of lessening the danger to the fleet at its base at Alexandria would be for the Royal Air Force to attack the Italian airfields and maintenance organizations in Cyrenaica. It happened that the Italians had recently introduced their Savoia 81 bomber, believed to possess a top speed greater than that of our fighters and to be able to operate some 200 miles farther afield than any of the British light bombers stationed in the Middle East. This meant that advanced landing-grounds would have to be made available to the Air Force very close to the western frontier of Egypt, and that even then our bombers would have to work at the limit of their effective range. The hard flat surfaces in this area made the actual construction of landing-grounds an easy matter, but to be of any use the landing-grounds would have to be stocked with fuel and other essential requirements.

---

[1] By the Constantinople Convention of 1888 the Canal was to be open in war or peace to all vessels including warships. No act of war was to be committed in the Canal or within three miles of its ports of access.

The problem facing the Army was how to protect these landing-grounds. Obviously it involved the ability to operate to westward of them, but to be drawn forward in this way was by no means an ideal way of defending the Delta area of Egypt; far better to meet the advancing enemy farther to the east, where our problems of supply would be more easily solved and where the enemy's would be greatly increased. The coastal railway from Alexandria ended at Fuka. Forty miles further west is the small port of Matruh. Everything required by the army and air force in the Western Desert would have to be carried either by train to the one or by sea to the other. Unfortunately Matruh had a low capacity for handling cargo and could not be relied upon in winter. Nor were there enough lorries to lift and distribute everything from the railhead at Fuka. A much better port than Matruh was Tobruk, but the forces required for an advance as far as this were beyond our means. It was accordingly decided to make the advanced base and base airfields in the Matruh area and to extend the railway thither as soon as possible. (By February 1936 it was completed, as a single line.) Sidi Barrani would also be held; a small detachment would be at Siwa Oasis; and a mobile force would be based on Matruh, ready to attack hostile columns and cover the temporary use of forward landing-grounds.

The Canal and Delta regions of Egypt contained the supply and maintenance installations on which the British forces depended. The presence of some 80,000 Italian residents was therefore a cause of no little anxiety. Egypt alone of the states who were not members of the League had been prepared to apply the policy of sanctions; Egyptian opinion generally was anti-Italian, pro-Ethiopian, and to some extent (as the lesser of two evils) pro-British. Nevertheless, Italian propaganda was active and recent rioting had shown some anti-British bias. The Nessim Government had recently been weakened by the withdrawal of Wafdist support, and it was feared that if it should fall and be replaced by a popular government still more British troops would have to be allotted to internal security duties. An appreciable proportion of the reinforcements were in fact to be used in this way. As for the Canal itself, the Italians could make no use of it during a war with the British, but they might try to interfere with its working and even to block it. Forces had therefore to be stationed where they could guard against blocking, sabotage, and low-flying air attacks.

Finally there was the Red Sea. With the Mediterranean closed to through traffic, as it might be, our main means of access to Egypt would be by the Red Sea. The danger was that this narrow route would be liable to attack from the air and possibly by sea as well. Our own naval forces would be based on Aden, while the air forces that we could use to afford some protection to the route by attacking enemy submarine and air bases would operate from Aden and the Sudan. The security of Aden was clearly of great importance; as for the Sudan, an Italian advance into this country seemed unlikely while the Ethiopian campaign was still in progress.

Nor, for the present, did there seem to be any particular likelihood of an invasion of Egypt from Libya. In fact, the only immediate causes of anxiety were the threat of air attack on the Fleet in harbour and the vulnerability of our sea communications with Egypt. But the long-term possibilities of the new situation were plain enough, and without waiting for the outcome of the war the Chiefs of Staff gave their Three Power Enemy warning to the Government: the danger of the simultaneous hostility of Germany, Japan and Italy, they said, emphasized the need for allies, and especially for friendship with France. It was necessary, in their view, not to be estranged from any Mediterranean power that lay athwart our main artery of communication with the east. In view of the growing menace of Germany it was materially impossible to make provision against a hostile Italy and therefore it was important to restore friendly relations with her. The Cabinet agreed: Germany and Japan constituted far likelier threats, and it was hoped that relations with Italy could be improved by diplomatic means. On 7th March 1936 German troops marched into the Rhineland, and early in May, just in time before the rains, the Italians completed their remarkable campaign in Ethiopia and annexed the country. The Emperor fled and was taken off at Jibuti in a British warship. The League of Nations had not resorted to force, nor even imposed sanctions on oil. The Italians had confined their warlike acts to Ethiopia. The British had risked more than any other power in furtherance of the League's principles, and in so doing they had conducted a useful dress-rehearsal which showed up clearly the strength and weakness of their position in Egypt.

It was not surprising that both Great Britain and Egypt felt that the time had come to place their diplomatic relations upon a more satisfactory footing. Negotiations to try to reconcile British interests and Egyptian sovereignty had been in progress for several years. It is true that in 1922 the Protectorate had been formally abolished, but the recognition of Egypt's rights as an independent sovereign state was qualified by certain reservations, and the differences arising from these reservations proved difficult to resolve. However, by the beginning of 1936 the Egyptians, though no less anxious than before to put an end to the military occupation of their country, had seen what acts of violence could be done to a member of the League by an aggressive fellow-member. Moreover, this particular aggressor had acquired an appreciably greater strategical interest in their country than ever before. To the British the recent events had emphasized the importance of a stable Egypt and served as a reminder —if any were needed—that any settlement must contain such military provisions as would assure the future defence of the country and of the Imperial communications through it. After it had more than once seemed that the negotiations would break down over the military clauses, and in spite of ceaseless Italian propaganda, agreement was reached with Nahas Pasha's Wafdist Government and the treaty was signed on 26th August 1936.

In essence, the effect was that in war Egypt would be our ally. The military occupation of the country was to cease forthwith, but the security of the Suez Canal would require the presence of limited British forces for some time to come. Their presence in the country was, however, to be rendered less obtrusive, and accommodation would accordingly be built for them within a narrow zone stretching along the Canal, slightly expanded so as to include the air station at Abu Sueir. It was expected that British forces would be withdrawn from Cairo in four years time, but permission was given for them to remain in the neighbourhood of Alexandria for eight years.

In the meantime the British would help to train and equip the Egyptian army and air force and the Egyptian Government would improve the communications within the Canal zone and thence to Cairo and across the Delta to Alexandria and the Western Desert. For this purpose essential roads were to be constructed or improved to comply with up-to-date military specifications. The capacity of the railways was to be improved, notably across the Delta and on the coastal line between Alexandria and Matruh. Unloading facilities would remain available at Port Said and Suez, and in the Geneifa area would be built the principal entraining platforms, depot areas, and marshalling and locomotive yards. Army training would be permitted to the east of the Canal and in a large clearly defined area to the west also, while staff exercises might be carried out in the Western Desert. Aircraft were to be allowed to fly wherever necessary for training purposes; adequate landing-grounds and seaplane anchorages might be provided, and in some cases might be stocked with fuel and stores. An important provision was that not only would the King of Egypt give us all the facilities and assistance in his power, including the use of his ports, airfields and means of communication in time of war, but that these facilities would be accorded if there was an imminent menace of war or even an apprehended international emergency. Moreover, the Egyptian Government would take all the measures necessary to render their assistance effective; they would introduce martial law and would impose an adequate censorship. In an agreed note of the same date the right to strengthen the British forces in any of the above-mentioned eventualities was specifically recognized.

The treaty was ratified on 22nd December 1936. On 26th May 1937, sponsored by the United Kingdom, Egypt was elected a member of the League of Nations.

On 15th July 1936 the economic sanctions so half-heartedly imposed upon Italy for her action against Ethiopia were formally lifted by the League. Three days later the Spanish Civil War broke out, thus transferring the storm-centre westwards.

The Chiefs of Staff again emphasized the need for a peaceful Mediterranean and hoped that nothing would prejudice the restoration of friendly relations with Italy. This hope did not look like being fulfilled, for Benito Mussolini, under the pretext of helping to arrest the spread of Communism, proceeded to give General Franco his active support. Whether or not his object was to secure concessions that would give him strategic advantages over the British in the Western Mediterranean, it was not long before the Balearic Islands, and Majorca in particular, were being developed by large numbers of Italians. It seemed that here, at least, the intention might be to establish a permanent base.

A further cause for concern was the recognition in November of the Franco régime by both Germany and Italy, whose unity of interest was expressed by the formation of the Rome-Berlin Axis. And apart from the rivalries provoked by the civil war several minor causes of friction between Great Britain and Italy had arisen since the conclusion of the Ethiopian campaign. The Anglo-Egyptian Treaty was greeted with the comment that the British forces for the Canal zone were greater than any employment in that locality would warrant, and the *Giornale d'Italia* had observed that a policy of strengthening Great Britain's influence in a sea in which Italy had such interests must inevitably cause irritation. The tension was momentarily eased by the signing in Rome on 2nd January 1937 of the Anglo-Italian Joint Declaration, popularly and perhaps hopefully known as the Gentlemen's Agreement. Freedom of movement in the Mediterranean was recognized as a vital interest to both the British Empire and Italy. Both parties disclaimed any desire to modify or see modified the national sovereignty of any country in the Mediterranean area, and agreed to discourage any activities liable to impair mutual relations. No mention of Spain was made in the Declaration, but in an exchange of notes Signor Mussolini confirmed that Italy had no territorial ambitions in Spain or in the Balearics and would preserve unchanged the position in the Western Mediterranean.

The signature of the Gentlemen's Agreement did not in fact prove to be the signal for the improvements hoped for. On the contrary, many events occurred in the next few months that seemed inconsistent with Italy's specified purpose of furthering the ends of peace or with a desire for friendship with Great Britain. For example, there were hostile references to the United Kingdom in the government-controlled Press; derogatory broadcasts in Arabic; and reference by the Fascist Grand Council to increased military expenditure and a greater measure of economic self-sufficiency. There were also the decisions to set up a High Command in North Africa, with control over land, sea, and air forces, and to form a metropolitan army corps in Libya; and there was the announcement that the Italian Navy must add to their battleships and other types so as to be capable of operating on the high seas. The Chief of the Air Staff declared in the Senate that great changes had taken place in the strategical employment of the Italian Air Force: the centre of gravity had moved towards the Mediterranean, the Red Sea, and the Indian Ocean; consequently all air bases in those zones had been strengthened—Sicily, Sardinia, the Aegean Islands, Pantelleria, and Tobruk. Massawa and Assab were further developed and the native army in Ethiopia continued to expand. The campaign of anti-British propaganda and intrigue was particularly violent in the Middle East and the Levant, and in a proclamation by Marshal Balbo to the Arabs of Libya it was claimed that the Duce was now the protector of Islam, and as such exalted the Muslim people.

It is of course possible that these steps were taken in genuine apprehension of the threat to the security of the position in which Italy had placed herself. There were signs that the Italian people had no wish to go to war with their traditional friends. But because the Italian people were not in control of their own destinies it was impossible to ignore such ominous activities. The Cabinet considered the whole situation in July 1937 and decided that Italy could not now be regarded as a reliable friend; the ban on expenditure on measures to provide against attack by her was to be lifted; and a start was to be made towards bringing the defences of the Mediterranean and the Red Sea ports up-to-date. In defensive preparations in Europe first place was to be given to providing a deterrent to aggression by Germany, and the Prime Minister emphasized the importance of doing nothing which could arouse Italian suspicions or be construed as provocative.

Meanwhile the Spanish Civil War was providing ample cause for

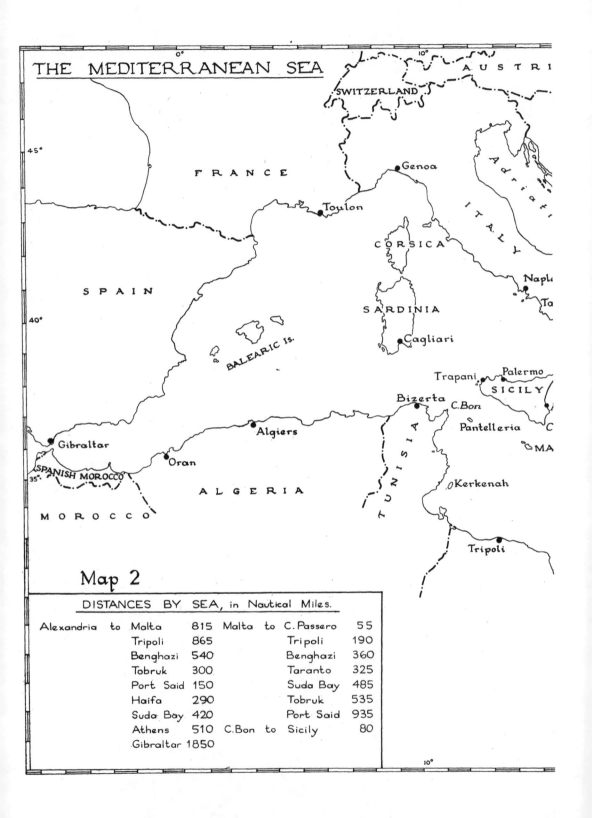

# THE MEDITERRANEAN SEA

AUSTRI...
SWITZERLAND

45°

FRANCE

Genoa

Toulon

CORSICA

ITALY

SPAIN

BALEARIC Is.

SARDINIA

40°

Cagliari

Napl...

Ta...

Trapani

Palermo

SICILY

Bizerta

C.Bon

Pantelleria

C

MA...

Algiers

Gibraltar

Oran

SPANISH MOROCCO

35°

TUNISIA

Kerkenah

ALGERIA

MOROCCO

Tripoli

## Map 2

| DISTANCES BY SEA, in Nautical Miles. | | | | |
|---|---|---|---|---|
| Alexandria to | Malta | 815 | Malta to C. Passero | 55 |
| | Tripoli | 865 | Tripoli | 190 |
| | Benghazi | 540 | Benghazi | 360 |
| | Tobruk | 300 | Taranto | 325 |
| | Port Said | 150 | Suda Bay | 485 |
| | Haifa | 290 | Tobruk | 535 |
| | Suda Bay | 420 | Port Said | 935 |
| | Athens | 510 | C.Bon to Sicily | 80 |
| | Gibraltar | 1850 | | |

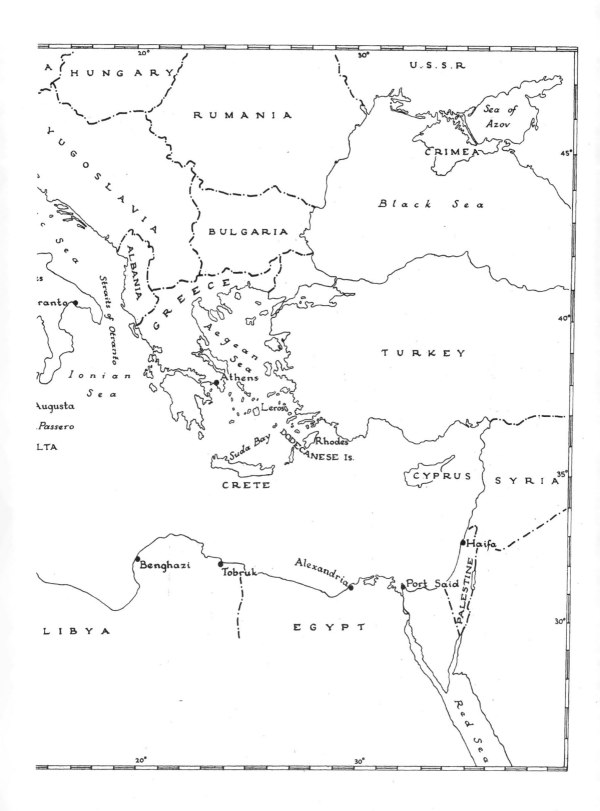

anxiety. Not only was British shipping being attacked from the air in Spanish territorial waters, but merchant vessels bound for Spain began to be subjected to torpedo attacks by submarines which it was presumed could only be Italian. This was nothing less than piracy, and the British and French Governments quickly initiated a plan for dealing with it. Merchant ships were to follow certain defined routes, to be patrolled by destroyers and aircraft of the two navies, with orders to 'fire and sink'. With the institution of these patrols the attacks ceased abruptly. Italy had declined to take part in the conference at Nyon on 10th September at which the plan was adopted, but three weeks later she allowed her navy to partake in the patrols. This appearance of the suspect among the ranks of the police suggested that there was a limit beyond which Signor Mussolini was not prepared to go. Apart from this, the situation in the Mediterranean gave little cause for complacency.

Now that Italy could no longer be regarded as a reliable friend, the question of a base for the Mediterranean Fleet became acute. Hitherto, the Royal Navy had counted upon using Gibraltar and Malta, so that no other docking or repair facilities in the Mediterranean would be needed. But if a hostile Italy was to be taken into account the problem became very different. Naval forces would obviously have to operate in the Eastern Mediterranean and for this purpose even Malta was too far away. Moreover, the extent to which Malta would be usable, if at all, under the heavy air attack that must be expected was impossible to assess in advance. Therefore another base, where docking and repairs could be carried out, would clearly be necessary.

Before the signing of the Anglo-Egyptian Treaty the principal objection to Alexandria as a main fleet base was the uncertainty of our position in Egypt. It was thought for a time that a better solution would be to develop the British island of Cyprus, with Famagusta as the naval base. But its distance from Egypt, over 300 miles, meant that no matter what provision was made at Cyprus it would still be necessary to use Alexandria as an advanced operational base, and it would have to be defended. The protection and control of the Suez Canal depended upon our power to defend Egypt, so that any development of Cyprus would add to, and not lessen, the tasks of the army and the air force. Again, the wisdom of making a base so close to the mainland of Turkey was questionable; the work would take several years to carry out and the estimated cost was very high. The conclusion was reached in April 1937 that it would be best to concentrate all the main base facilities at Alexandria: light naval forces operating in the eastern basin of the Mediterranean could be based at Haifa. The Egyptian Government would be asked to consent to the provision of means for docking and repair at Alexandria, where, with a comparatively small amount of dredging, the berthing could be much improved. Even so, if the place was to serve as a repair base for a fleet containing heavy ships it would want a suitable graving dock. This would entail the deepening of the Great Pass channel to allow a damaged capital ship to pass through, incidentally reducing the delay in entering and leaving harbour in certain weather conditions.

Much had been done while the Fleet had been based at Alexandria during the Ethiopian crisis to improve the harbour and its defences by dredging and by laying mooring buoys, booms and nets, but nothing had been done for two years to improve the docking and repair facilities either at Alexandria or anywhere else in the eastern basin, so that in this respect the position was rather worse than during the 1935 crisis, when French harbours would have been available had we wanted to use them. The extension of the dock at Gibraltar to take heavy ships would require another two years to complete, while the coast defences there and at Malta were still in process of being modernized. The situation in the air was far worse. Italian aircraft in Libya were greatly superior in number and performance to any that we could concentrate in Egypt, while their proximity to their metropolitan bases would make further reinforcement an easy matter. Yet in Egypt there were no fighter aircraft and no ground anti-aircraft defences whatever, and this situation could only be put right at the expense of the air defences of Great Britain. Highly vulnerable targets, besides Alexandria and Cairo, would be the oil refinery and storage installations at Suez; the port, docks and oil storage at Port Said; the port facilities and shipping in the Canal; and the advanced base at Matruh. Plans for air raid precautions were far from complete, and there was therefore a risk of heavy civilian casualties. Finally, the outlook for the army was by no means bright. The reinforcements sent from the United Kingdom during the winter of 1935–36 had been withdrawn. Many of the British units were well below their war strength, and their peace-stations were far removed from the Western Desert. The Egyptian Army was still in the early stages of re-equipping and training. The Italians, on the other hand, had recently established two corps of metropolitan troops in Libya—four divisions in all, of which two were fully motorized.

Thus, while our ultimate aim would be the defeat of Italy, the immediate task must be to defend Egypt. Much would depend upon the amount of warning received, but it was always possible that there would be little or none. In that event, it would be no easy matter to forestall the Italians at Matruh—the obvious first objective for their motorized troops. It was clear that the army might require the fullest assistance of the other two Services in holding up the expected Italian advance, and, even so, was likely to be severely taxed. An elaborate scheme existed for the reinforcement of Egypt by convoys from the United Kingdom partly through the Mediterranean but mainly round the Cape and from India. However, His Majesty's Ambassador in Cairo, Sir Miles Lampson, and the local Commanders were far from satisfied with these tentative arrangements, since the reinforcements round the Cape might not arrive in time and those through the Mediterranean might not arrive at all.

Two events occurred before the end of 1937 which added to the general tension. First, Italy announced in November that she had joined Germany and Japan in their Anti-Comintern Pact. The British Chiefs of Staff took the opportunity to renew their Three Power Enemy warning, insisting that our interests lay in a peaceful Mediterranean and that we ought to return to a state of friendly relations with Italy. Without overlooking the help we should hope to receive from France and from other possible allies, they could not foresee the time when our defence forces would be strong enough to safeguard our territory, trade, and vital interests against Germany, Italy, and Japan simultaneously. They therefore emphasized the importance, from the point of view of Imperial Defence, of any diplomatic action that would reduce the number of our potential enemies and give us allies.

No sooner had this warning been given than Italy announced her withdrawal from membership of the League. The British Chiefs of Staff, with the prospect of three major enemies ever in mind, recorded their opinion that the military situation then facing the British Empire was 'fraught with greater risk than at any time in living memory, apart from the war years' and that an immediate acceleration of the armament programme was essential.

Whatever might be the outcome of these suggestions, it was plainly advisable to try to improve the situation in Egypt without delay. Many of the necessary measures would involve the active co-operation of the Egyptian Government, who had recently shown some concern regarding the state of preparedness of their country to resist attack. It had even been suggested in the Egyptian Parliament that there should be a treaty of reinsurance with Italy. The Ambassador strongly supported the view that the Royal Air Force should be strengthened and anti-aircraft units provided. As a possible alternative to the further increase of the garrison—assuming that it was not desired to invoke the 'apprehended international emergency' clause of the treaty—he suggested that reinforcements for Egypt should be stationed in Palestine, where they would be handy if required.

In December the decision was taken to despatch from the United Kingdom an anti-aircraft brigade and a light tank battalion to

Egypt forthwith, and to authorize the General to move troops to Matruh when he thought necessary. The Air Force in the Middle East was to be rearmed. Two months later, in February 1938, the Cabinet approved further measures: British army units in Egypt were to be brought up to strength and provided with more transport; an infantry brigade was to go to Palestine, where it would be available as a reserve. The Royal Air Force was to be increased by a squadron of 21 Gladiator fighters from the meagre resources of the air defences of Great Britain. Twelve medium bombers were to be sent out at once to increase the existing first-line strength of the Wellesley squadrons. As soon as possible, two squadrons of light bombers (24 Hinds—already obsolescent) were to follow. If these figures are remarkable only for their smallness, it must be remembered that Germany was now the most serious enemy, and that it was the Government's policy to put first the creation at home of forces which might deter her from aggression. To send even small reinforcements overseas delayed the growth of the forces in the United Kingdom: for example, to provide even these few bombers for the Middle East would reduce the strength of Bomber Command by the equivalent of three squadrons for at least twelve months.

The Führer did not think it necessary to inform his Axis partner of his intention to annex Austria. It was a surprise, therefore, to the Italians, and not a particularly welcome one, when in March 1938 German troops appeared on the Brenner. Meanwhile, His Majesty's Government was taking diplomatic action to improve relations with Italy, and an Agreement was concluded in April in which the Declaration of January 1937 was reaffirmed. In addition, the two Governments agreed to exchange information annually about any major prospective changes in the British and Italian forces in the neighbourhood of the Mediterranean, Red Sea, and Gulf of Aden. Each would notify the other of any intention to build new naval or air bases in the Red Sea area, or in the Mediterranean to the east of longitude 19° East, which is just west of the meridian of Benghazi. Both undertook not to seek any privileged position in territory belonging to Saudi Arabia or the Yemen, nor to encourage any other Power to do so, and not to fortify the former Turkish islands in the Red Sea. British interests in Italian East Africa would be protected and natives would be recruited only for local policing and defence. A second agreement expressing a desire for friendly relations in East Africa generally—the *Bon Voisinage* Agreement—was signed also by the Egyptian Government. The free use of the Suez Canal at all times as laid down in the Convention of 1888 was reaffirmed.

In an exchange of notes Italy stated that she had already begun to reduce her Libyan garrison to its peace time strength. She repeated her assurance that she had no political or territorial aims in Spain or the Balearic Islands and that she would adhere to the British plan for the gradual withdrawal of foreign volunteers from Spain. Britain for her part undertook to facilitate the recognition by the League members of Italian sovereignty over Ethiopia, and in May His Majesty's Government announced that they regarded the Ethiopian incident as closed. But they insisted that the Spanish question must be settled before the present agreement could come into force, and it was on that account delayed until the following November. However, the Spanish Civil War was by no means the only disturbing factor during the intervening months, for the Czechoslovakian crisis and the Munich settlement gave a foretaste of what was in store for Europe; and as if this were not enough Great Britain found herself with a major rebellion on her hands in Palestine.

By 1936, the British policies of simultaneously supporting the creation of a national home for the Jews and encouraging Arab aspirations for independence had produced a crisis in the affairs of Palestine. The Palestinian Arabs had seen the growth of nationalist movements all round them—in Iraq, Syria and Egypt. They viewed with indignation and alarm the continued purchase of Arab lands by Jews and the increasingly high figures approved for Jewish immigration. The Arab world in general had been shocked and not a little alarmed by the invasion of the virtually defenceless Ethiopia. Nevertheless, the fact that direct action had succeeded and the restraining influences had failed did not escape the notice of the discontented Palestinian Arabs. Matters came to a head when, in April, amid a chorus of Italian propaganda about the waning power and prestige of Britain, the Arabs declared a general strike. Within a few weeks there were disturbances throughout the country. A few troops were called in from Egypt and Malta, but in September it was decided to despatch a whole division from the United Kingdom in a determined attempt to restore order. In October, after an appeal to the Palestinian Arabs by the rulers of the Arab States of Saudi Arabia, Iraq, Transjordan and the Yemen, the general strike was. called off, though acts of violence continued to occur.

In November a Royal Commission arrived in Palestine to investigate the whole problem. During the succeeding months it was. possible to reduce the garrison gradually to about two brigades, while the country awaited the Commission's report—expectant, but on the whole comparatively quiet. The recommendation was not published until the following July.[1] Palestine was to be divided into

---

[1] The Peel Report. Cmd 5479 of 1937.

three parts—a suggestion that was quite unacceptable to the Arabs though it attracted some support from the Zionist Congress, inasmuch as it envisaged the creation of a Jewish state, albeit a small one.

The conflict between Jewish Zionism and Arab Nationalism had now come to a head and His Majesty's Government found itself in a difficult position. If partition was the only way of establishing a Jewish National Home, and if every form of partition was to be rejected by the Arabs, what was to be done? The international atmosphere in the autumn of 1937 was already tense, and to make things worse there began again in September acts of violence and sabotage in Palestine. As time went on the action of the Arab gangs became more organized and co-ordinated, and by April 1938 there was a state of open rebellion. In July it was again necessary to call upon Egypt for troops and aircraft, but the Munich crisis in September made their return to Egypt imperative. During October large forces arrived from the United Kingdom and by the end of the month the whole country was under military control, though the process of restoring order was to be long and difficult.[1] An event which certainly tended to restrain Arab opinion at this juncture was the finding by a second (or technical) Commission that partition was impracticable.[2] The next step towards a settlement was the announcement that a conference would be held in London early in 1939, for which invitations were sent, not only to the Jewish Agency and the Palestine Arabs, but also to the neighbouring states of Egypt, Iraq, Saudi Arabia, Transjordan, and the Yemen. All these states had diplomatic ties of one kind or another with Great Britain, and all were highly sensitive to events in Palestine. It is therefore appropriate to review briefly their main strategic features.

Iraq had been the first of the former Turkish provinces to obtain her independent sovereignty, her treaty of alliance and mutual support with Great Britain having been signed in 1930. In 1932, sponsored by Great Britain, she joined the League of Nations as the first Arab member. By the terms of the treaty she would, in the event of war, come to our help as an ally. Her aid would consist in furnishing us with all the facilities and assistance in her power, including the use of railways, rivers, ports, airfields and means of communication. At any time she would, on request, afford all facilities for the passage of British forces through the country. After 1937 there would be no British troops in Iraq, but the Royal Air

---

[1] Three British battalions had also arrived from India. By mid-November the General Officer Commanding in Palestine and Transjordan had under his command two horsed cavalry regiments and the infantry of about two divisions, with a few ancillary troops. Operating under his orders were also two squadrons and an armoured car company of the R.A.F. based in Transjordan. Considerable naval forces, including a battle-cruiser, were based on Haifa.

[2] The Woodhead Report. Cmd 5854 of 1938.

Force would be allowed to remain at their bases at Shaibah near Basra and Habbaniya. They had the double role of protecting our oil interests and of maintaining an important link in the air route between Egypt and India. For the protection of these air bases there was a force of native Levies and armoured cars. Internal security and the protection, within Iraqi territory, of the pipelines which ran from the northern Iraq oilfields to Haifa and Tripoli (Syria) respectively were the responsibility of the Government of Iraq.

The strategic importance of Iraq was further enhanced by the existence of the oilfield at Maidan-i-Naftun, in Persia, operated by the Anglo-Iranian Oil Company. The pipeline, over 150 miles long, ended at the port of Abadan, close to the Iraq frontier. Here were located the refinery and loading wharves for the tankers. So important to the British was this supply that the provision of a force for the security of the southern Persian oilfield area had already been accepted as a potential commitment by the Indian Government.

Lastly there was the overland route from the head of the Persian Gulf to Palestine, which, although very long and under-developed, had to be considered as an alternative approach to Egypt in case enemy aircraft in Italian East Africa should make the passage of the Red Sea too precarious. Basra and Baghdad were linked by a single-line metre-gauge railway, by two roads (which became unserviceable after heavy rain), and by river-vessels along the Tigris. From Baghdad there was a road to near Ramadi; thereafter the hard surface of the desert made a road unnecessary to a point near Rutba. The next section was soft, requiring a road, and through Transjordan the surface was variable, mostly rough, and impassable in wet weather. In Palestine there was a good road to Haifa, which was connected by standard-gauge railway through Gaza to the Sinai Railway and so to Kantara on the Suez Canal. The whole distance from Basra to Kantara was some 1,200 miles. To use such a route for the passage of men, equipment and stores in any quantity would obviously need a great deal of preparation, and everything would depend upon the attitude of the Iraqi Government. It was therefore a matter for satisfaction when, during the crisis of September 1938, this Government spontaneously informed His Majesty's Government that they were fully prepared to carry out their treaty obligations.

The Arab state of Transjordan was included in the original mandate for Palestine but since 1923 had enjoyed virtual autonomy. The administration was in Arab hands, under the sovereignty of the Emir Abdullah Ibn Hussein (brother of King Feisal of Iraq) who was assisted by a British Resident and a number of advisers. The country was in fact entirely dependent upon Great Britain. Strategically, together with Palestine, it was well situated to afford depth for the defence of the Suez Canal against attack from the north-east. The airfields at Ramleh in Palestine and at Amman and the landing-grounds further east along the pipeline marked stages on the air route between Egypt and Iraq. Some 250 miles of the overland route lay within the frontiers of Transjordan. The Transjordan Frontier Force was the local force at the disposal of the High Commissioner for Palestine, and was available for military duty in Palestine and Transjordan. The Arab Legion was the police force of Transjordan, responsible to the Transjordan Government.

King Ibn Saud of Saudi Arabia was the most powerful of the independent Arab rulers. With Great Britain he had a treaty of friendship and good understanding—but not an alliance. Soon after the Italian conquest of Ethiopia he made a treaty of Arab brotherhood and alliance with Iraq, followed a month later by a treaty of friendship with Egypt. There was therefore some evidence of a common leaning towards Great Britain and even of a measure of Arab solidarity. Ibn Saud's friendship was particularly important because Saudi Arabia's frontier with Transjordan ran only some 50 miles from the Kirkuk–Haifa pipeline and the overland route; further to the east its frontier with Iraq approached within 100 miles of the air station at Shaibah; while away to the south the territory of Saudi Arabia marched with that of the British Protectorate of Aden.

The Yemen had been bound to Great Britain by a treaty since 1934, and had made a 'moral alliance' with Saudi Arabia the same year. By the Anglo-Italian Agreement of 1938 Great Britain and Italy had undertaken not to seek political privileges in either country. This was obviously a considerable concession on Great Britain's part, but if it meant that the Italians would not be able to acquire facilities for stirring up trouble or for attacking Aden from this direction, it would be worth while. The importance of Aden was apparent during the Ethiopian War and nothing had occurred to lessen it.

Such, then, was the main strategic significance of each Arab country invited to the London Conference on Palestine. Before the Conference met, the Chiefs of Staff emphasized the need to convince Egypt and the Arab States that it was to their interest to observe their treaty obligations and, where there was no treaty, to maintain friendship with Great Britain.[1] On this depended the security of our forces and of our lines of communication. The retention of our hold on the Middle East was essential to our whole scheme of Imperial Defence. There was ample evidence, they added, that the Axis would welcome our fall from the predominant position that we held

---

[1] Along the western shores of the Persian Gulf His Majesty's Government had treaty relations also with Kuwait, Bahrein and the Sheikhs of Qatar and the Oman Coast.

in the eyes of the Muslim world. Already Germany was actively supporting the subversive influences that were ranged against us.

The Conference began early in February, and by the middle of March agreement was found to be unattainable. The British Government decided therefore to impose its own solution, which accordingly appeared in a White Paper.[1] Palestine was not to be converted into a Jewish State against the will of the Arab population. Within ten years an independent sovereign state was to be created, bound by treaty to the United Kingdom, in the government of which both Jews and Arabs would take part. Meanwhile, Jewish immigration was to be severely restricted for five years and thereafter would be subject to Arab consent. Transfers of land were to be regulated. This plan was received with hostility by the Arab extremists, especially those who followed the lead of the former Mufti of Jerusalem, now in exile in the Lebanon.[2] The suspicion that Great Britain would not fully implement the White Paper policy was sedulously fostered by hostile elements. The Jews were still more dissatisfied, and acts of violence attributed to them began to increase. The German press and broadcasts took the opportunity to denounce British cruelty and atrocities.

Two strong restraining influences were, however, at work. On the Arab side, the Egyptian and Iraqi delegates continued to press for acceptance of the British scheme, while, as war approached, the Jews, although intensely disappointed with the White Paper, could scarcely do otherwise than give immediate support to the enemies of their German persecutors, and hope for better things in the future.


March 1938 saw the German invasion of Austria, and the question was: when would it be the turn of Czechoslovakia? During August and September it was clear that events were moving to a climax, and with the breakdown of the Godesberg meeting between Mr. Chamberlain and Herr Hitler on 23rd September it seemed likely that Great Britain would shortly be involved in war. Precautionary measures were adopted at home and overseas and remained in force until after the tension had been relieved by the Munich settlement. The Mediterranean Fleet assembled at Alexandria, and defence precautions were put in hand there and at the other ports. In the Western Desert British troops occupied Matruh while Royal Air Force squadrons in Egypt moved to their war

---

[1] Cmd 6019 of May 1939.

[2] Hajj Amin Effendi al Husseini had been sentenced for inflammatory speeches in 1920. He was pardoned, and became Mufti (or interpreter of the canonical law) of Jerusalem and President of the Supreme Islamic Council. In October 1937 the Arab Higher Committee of which he was also President was declared illegal; he thereupon fled from Palestine but continued to intrigue against the British, notably in connexion with the Iraq rebellion of 1941.

stations, and the scheme for the reinforcement of Egypt from other overseas Air Commands was put into operation. The whole episode constituted another valuable rehearsal which drew attention to many weaknesses and shortcomings.

The Commander-in-Chief, Mediterranean, Admiral Sir Dudley Pound, found that insufficient stores of all kinds, including ammunition, had been accumulated. His war complements of men had not arrived in time. Local defences had not been given enough notice to come to full readiness. As regards the French, he was aware of the rough division of the Mediterranean into areas of responsibility, but he had no knowledge of any French naval dispositions or plans. He emphasized that the effort of all three Services in the Mediterranean could only be really effective if some joint plan were made for eliminating the enemy in North Africa very soon after the outbreak of war. The mere cutting of Italian sea communications would only result in a steady attrition of our own sea forces which would be difficult to make good with our limited repair facilities. He gave an estimate of the naval strength[1] he thought necessary, and emphasized that defensive tasks (such as escorts) must be reduced to a minimum; for this reason he hoped that troops coming from India would use the overland route. Lastly, the situation at Malta was extremely unsatisfactory: was the place to be defended properly or not?

The Admiralty's reply to these proposals was that the forces considered necessary by the Commander-in-Chief would probably·be available, except for the submarines, of which he might receive 13 instead of 21. Regarding the possibility of an offensive strategy, the army and air forces would be quite inadequate; resources would therefore have to be devoted initially to the security of Egypt, and the Fleet must harass the Italian lines of communication as much as possible. As for the overland route, the state of affairs in Palestine made it impossible to guarantee its use; a division of destroyers must therefore be detailed in readiness for escort work in the Red Sea. Malta was still the subject of a special investigation.

The Inter-Command air reinforcement scheme referred to above was a plan for offsetting local weakness by developing the ability to concentrate. The existing programme for the expansion of the Royal Air Force was still a long way from completion, and the measures for hastening the production of aircraft had not made themselves fully felt. The rise of Germany to the position of the most likely and the most dangerous enemy meant that the Air Forces overseas would have to be largely self-sufficient; if war came soon there would be no early flow of men, aircraft or stores from the United Kingdom.

---

[1] 3 battleships, 1 aircraft carrier, 4 eight-inch and 5 six-inch cruisers, 40 destroyers and 21 submarines. This represented an increase of 2 six-inch cruisers, 11 destroyers and 14 submarines.

Squadrons already overseas would therefore have to be ready to move and re-deploy at very short notice.

These plans involved a great deal more than the moving of aircraft, although for this to be done quickly and efficiently the air route had to be secure and provision made in advance for fuelling and maintenance and for communication and meteorological facilities. But in addition to arriving quickly in an emergency, squadrons had to be able to operate at once from their new stations— and be prepared to go on operating. Therefore the necessary operational airfields must be stocked with fuel, bombs and ammunition. Behind them there must be bulk reserves of all these, while the salvage and repair organization would have to be capable of dealing with greatly increased numbers. In addition, a proportion of heavy stores and spares, with the necessary motor transport, would have to be held in the receiving areas. Beside all this there would of course be the problem of receiving a sudden large influx of officers and men.

As a result of a thorough examination of the working of the plan in practice, many improvements were made. Even so, the fact remained that the scheme, when fully executed, could not produce sufficient forces for the simultaneous defence of Egypt, the Sudan and Kenya borders, and the shipping route through the Red Sea. Approval was obtained for some essential increases, but there was no immediate prospect of getting them. The moves which were in fact carried out on the eve of war with Germany are given on page 41.

An important step in army organization was taken by forming a number of units already in Egypt into a Mobile Division.[1] The value of good communications between Egypt and Palestine was shown by the move of one armoured car regiment and two infantry battalions to Palestine when the local situation became serious, and back again to Egypt for the September crisis. Soon afterwards, as has been seen, large forces assembled in Palestine for the purpose of restoring order, and it was hoped that some of these would be available for moving to Egypt if another emergency arose there.

The official Egyptian attitude during the September crisis was correct and helpful. The Government co-operated in putting the precautionary measures into force and on 26th September proclaimed *état de siège*, to enable emergency powers to be taken under the Law of 26th June 1923. But after the crisis had passed there seemed to be a more lively appreciation of what war might mean. In some quarters a weakening of purpose was apparent: there was talk

---

[1] The units were a Cavalry Brigade of a light tank regiment, a light car regiment, and an armoured car regiment; a Tank Group of two tank battalions; and a Pivot Group of one Royal Horse Artillery regiment and one motor battalion. The Mobile Division, with changes in composition and organization, later became the Armoured Division and later still the 7th Armoured Division.

of neutrality and of the advantage of making a *bon voisinage* agreement with Italy. Difficulties arose over the lack of progress on some of the treaty roads and railways, and the task of inducing the Egyptians to continue to prepare for the defence of their country became more arduous. After much discussion, it was agreed to set up various committees to work with the British in such matters as the supply and distribution of oil, food, and resources generally. The Defence Co-ordination Committee, originally set up during the Ethiopian War, was revived for the purpose of bringing the most urgent British needs to the notice of the appropriate government departments. Thus, in one way or another, the 1938 crisis served to clarify many issues which were of vital interest to the British and Egyptians alike.


Three years had now passed since Signor Mussolini had seized Ethiopia and had given Italy an empire beyond a defile which the British could close at any moment. This might seem to be a good reason for remaining on good terms with the British, particularly as the empire was proving to be a heavy drain on Italy's limited economy. On the other hand, Italian aspirations towards expansion of power and influence were undoubtedly hard to reconcile with a situation in which the control of the empire's life-line was in British hands. It was no longer a case of a solitary Italy against a sanctionist world: she had proudly become the junior partner in the Axis and had allowed her name to be linked with Germany and Japan in the Anti-Comintern Pact. She was known to be in no position to risk a long war, but if the Germans were to make good her worst deficiencies the risk would be less. Consequently a war started by Germany in which Great Britain and France were heavily involved might give Italy just the chance she wanted.

Yet it was obvious that her real interests lay, as they did in 1914, somewhere between the opposing camps; for the prospect of seeing the whole of central Europe succumb to Hitler cannot have been an agreeable one. Therefore there was still a chance that Italy might remain neutral—at any rate during the early stages of a war, but it had to be recognized that she might decide to throw in her lot with Germany even with the certainty of becoming completely subservient to that hardest of taskmasters.

And if Italy were to see her opportunity, might not Japan see hers and so create the very situation that the Chiefs of Staff were so anxious to avoid? In February 1939 the Cabinet decided to approach the French Government with the suggestion that staff conversations should take place on the basis of war against Germany and Italy in combination—possibly joined later by Japan—and that their scope should include all likely fields of operations, especially the Mediterranean and Middle East.

# Chronology 1933-1938

| | | |
|---|---|---|
| 1933 | 30th January | Hitler becomes Chancellor of the German Reich |
| | October | Breakdown of the Disarmament Conference |
| 1935 | 2nd October | Italy invades Ethiopia |
| 1936 | 7th March | German Troops enter the Rhineland |
| | 18th July | Outbreak of Spanish Civil War |
| | 26th August | Anglo-Egyptian Treaty signed |
| | 25th October | Rome-Berlin Axis announced |
| 1937 | 2nd January | Anglo-Italian Joint Declaration ('The Gentlemen's Agreement') signed |
| | 8th July | China and Japan at war |
| 1938 | 13th March | Germany annexes Austria (The '*Anschluss*') |
| | April | Open rebellion in Palestine |
| | 16th April | Anglo-Italian Agreement signed |
| | 29th September | The Munich Settlement |

# CHAPTER II

# 1939: PLANS AND PREPARATIONS
# IN CASE OF WAR

*See Chronology on page* 40

THE CONVERSATIONS between the French and British Staffs began in London at the end of March, just before the announcement of the guarantees to Poland. The first step was to formulate a common policy, and the general conclusion was that Anglo-French strategy should be adapted to a long war. The warlike preparations of Germany and Italy were well advanced, but these countries could not hope to add appreciably to their resources in the course of a war, and would therefore be likely to stake their chances on a knock-out blow. Great Britain and France, on the other hand, though less well prepared, were in a position to increase their war potential steadily, provided they could protect their war industries and sea communications from air and submarine attack. Germany would most probably attack on land via Belgium and Holland, combining this with air attacks on a large scale against France or Britain or both. Italy would be more likely to undertake major offensive operations by land from Libya and Ethiopia than across the barrier of the Alps. Widespread submarine and raider activity in the Atlantic and Mediterranean would aim at depriving the Allies of their sea-borne supplies.

The Allied staffs therefore envisaged a war in three phases. The first would be one of preserving as far as possible the integrity of Allied territory and of defending vital interests. The second would be one of holding Germany and dealing decisively with Italy; meanwhile, Allied military strength would be built up until such time as a major offensive strategy became possible. Command of the sea would enable economic pressure to be applied from the outset, and would later confer freedom of choice in striking at the enemy's most vulnerable points. Italy was so obviously the weaker partner that counter-offensive operations against her in North Africa were expected early in the war. The final phase of the war would be the defeat of Germany. This policy was accorded ministerial approval and the agreed strategic objects in the Mediterranean and Middle East were made the basis of meetings between French and

British Commanders in North Africa, Aden, and Palestine, at which the operational implications were examined.

The French and British staffs did not take many days to reach agreement on broad lines, but no sooner had they done so than a fresh crisis arose—this time in the Balkan quarter of the Mediterranean. On Good Friday, 7th April 1939, Italian troops disembarked at Durazzo and other ports on the Albanian coast. There was practically no opposition. By Easter Sunday they had occupied the capital, Tirana, and King Zog had fled to seek refuge in Greece. Within a few days King Victor Emmanuel had accepted the Albanian crown and Italy had assumed direction of Albania's external affairs.

There had been indications that something of the sort was contemplated, but the British policy was to preserve normality, so much so that on 7th April the Commander-in-Chief and ships of the Mediterranean Fleet were paying routine visits to Italian ports. They were at once withdrawn and, when it was rumoured that the Greek island of Corfu was about to be attacked, the fleet at Malta was brought to instant readiness for war. On 8th April Signor Mussolini gave a formal assurance that he had no designs on Greece and that he was anxious to maintain the Anglo-Italian Agreement. In spite of this the fleet was moved unostentatiously to Alexandria, where it began to establish itself.

It was a little difficult to reconcile the Duce's assurances with his actions, for the invasion of Albania could hardly be regarded as a contribution to the general cause of peace, which was the declared object of the Agreement. Worse still, it obviously constituted a change in the *status quo*, which both parties had specifically undertaken to maintain. The attitude of His Majesty's Government was conditioned by the hope that Italy might yet act as a brake on Germany. With the 'Three Power Enemy' warning still in mind they refrained from tearing up the Anglo-Italian Agreement but tried to make it clear that they would not accept any further forcible disturbances of the *status quo* in the Mediterranean or the Balkan peninsula. At this juncture the Germans took up the running and sent a naval force on a cruise in Spanish waters. Whatever the precise object of this gesture was—and it was no doubt intended to be provocative—the result was to produce a concentration of the British Fleet at the eastern end of the Mediterranean, while a strong French force went to Gibraltar to supplement the British units already there. Having evoked this display of allied unity the German force withdrew.

Within a week of the Italian landings in Albania, the British and French Governments announced that they had promised to give all the help in their power if Greek or Rumanian independence were threatened and if the Greek or Rumanian Government considered it vital to resist. The rejoinder to this was the announcement on 7th May of a political and military pact between Italy and Germany, to be known as the Pact of Steel. Five days later a Joint Declaration was announced by Great Britain and Turkey—the outcome of long negotiations into which the sudden appearance of Italian forces on the Balkan mainland had no doubt infused a sense of urgency. Pending the conclusion of a definite agreement, the British and Turkish Governments would, in the event of an act of aggression leading to war in the Mediterranean area, co-operate effectively and lend each other all the aid and assistance in their power. After a further month of discussion about the cession of the Hatay (Alexandretta) to Turkey a similar declaration was made by the French and Turkish Governments. These were highly significant developments, for Turkey occupied a geographical position of great importance. Not only had she land frontiers with Iraq and Syria, but she commanded the third gateway to the Mediterranean—the Dardanelles. The closing of this route would be a severe blow to the Italian war effort. Largely self-sufficient in foodstuffs, Italy was deficient in raw materials; her petroleum products, in particular, would have to come mainly from the Black Sea. In addition, if Turkey were hostile, the Italian Dodecanese Islands, most of which lie within twenty-five miles of the Turkish coast, would become hostages to fortune. The naval and air base at Leros, in particular, would be a liability for defence instead of a vantage-point for the attack of shipping. And on a wider issue it was possible that Turkey as a prominent member of the Balkan Entente might succeed in promoting some measure of solidarity in the Balkans, in the face of which the usual Axis technique of piecemeal destruction might fail.[1]

The regional meetings between French and British Commanders in the Mediterranean and Middle East were held in May and June at Rabat, Aden, and Jerusalem. The general objects were to render the Italian position in Libya, and eventually in Ethiopia, untenable. Operations were to be designed to cut sea communications between Italy and Libya, and to retain control of the Red Sea and the entrances to the Mediterranean. In view of the importance of Tripoli to the Italians the French would undertake a large-scale

---

[1] The Pact between Turkey, Greece, Yugoslavia, and Rumania was signed in 1934. It provided for the mutual guarantee of existing frontiers; Bulgaria, who was dissatisfied with hers, declined to join.

offensive from Tunisia into Tripolitania, provided that Spain were clearly neutral. If, however, Egypt were seriously attacked, the French would carry out an offensive on a reduced scale, whatever the situation in Morocco. Meanwhile, the British aim would be to defend Egypt and try to contain as many Italian forces as possible on the Egyptian front. The air forces would operate in defence of Egypt and join with the Royal Navy in attacking Italian communications with Cyrenaica.

In the East African area the agreed Allied object at sea would be to secure the Red Sea route and isolate Italian territories, so as to deprive their armed forces of reinforcements and supplies. The task of controlling the sea communications in the Gulf of Aden and Red Sea would clearly fall to the British, as the French had no naval forces and only one squadron of obsolete aircraft. The initial object on land would be to defend Allied territory and foster rebellion in Italian East Africa; later, when resources became available, the Allies would pass to the offensive. The part of Italian East Africa which it would then be necessary to occupy was the general area Eritrea—Harar—Addis Ababa, and by far the best base for an offensive against this area would be French Somaliland, with its port of Jibuti. In the early stages of the war, the security of French Somaliland would therefore be of great importance to the Allies.

In the Levant, where there were no adjoining Italian territories, the strategic objects would be to maintain the security of important Allied interests and, subject to this, to release forces from Syria and Palestine for service elsewhere. Syria, for which the French held the mandate, had great significance for the British largely because of its geographical position. It filled the gap between Iraq and the Mediterranean; its territory flanked and partially blocked the lines of advance from the north towards the Persian Gulf; and through it ran all the rail and road communications from Turkey towards Palestine and Egypt, as well as nearly 500 miles of the northern branch of the Iraq oil pipeline.

It was realized that the attitude of the Iraqi Government would have an important bearing on the military problems that were likely to arise. For instance, there would no doubt be some difficulty in dealing with the tribes on the eastern borders of Syria and Transjordan if the Iraqi Government did not adopt a genuinely friendly attitude. In particular there was the problem of protecting the oil pipelines. The oilfield area and much of the pipe itself were in Iraq, and therefore vulnerable, but it was hoped that the recent Anglo-Turkish Declaration would encourage the Iraqi Government to take action against anti-British influences in the country.

As regards the terminal oil ports of Haifa and Syrian Tripoli, the position in peace time was that France drew about three-quarters of the combined output of these ports. The French now said that they did not intend to draw any Iraq oil in time of war. Interest therefore centred mainly on Haifa, where a refinery was under construction, due to be completed in June 1940. The crude oil, unrefined as delivered by the pipeline, was not suitable as naval fuel; the storage tanks at Haifa on the Bay of Acre offered a most conspicuous target for air or sea bombardment; and these factors coupled with a certain amount of anxiety as to the safety of the pipeline itself resulted in the Admiralty's decision not to count for the present upon the output of Haifa in war time. Instead they would use part of the storage accommodation for a reserve stock of naval fuel oil, brought from elsewhere. Haifa was, however, to be used as a base for light naval forces in the eastern basin, though the seaward defences were incomplete and no anti-aircraft defences had as yet been installed.

The French were anxious to use Cyprus as an advanced base for aircraft on seaward patrols, especially towards the Italian Dodecanese Islands, and for giving depth to the air defences of Beirut. The British, on the other hand, did not wish Cyprus to grow into a defensive commitment involving forces that could ill be spared. They agreed, however, that the airfields at Nicosia and Larnaca should be improved and that refuelling and rearming facilities should be installed and made available to the French. Nevertheless, for the purpose of attacking the Dodecanese Islands it seemed that sites in south-western Anatolia would be much more suitable, if the Turks would consent to their use.

Finally the French agreed that a small expeditionary force might be required to move from Syria through Palestine to Egypt.[1] The British, too, were able to regard a proportion of their forces in Palestine as potential reinforcements for other areas, although the excitement that had greeted the announcement of His Majesty's Government's plan for the new Palestinian state had not entirely died down. Thus, a skeleton division of six battalions became the 'Middle East reserve', with the probable role of moving to Egypt; one of them was earmarked for the Sudan; and two for Habbaniya in case of local necessity. The troops that would still be allotted to internal security duties amounted to the equivalent of a skeleton division of eight battalions. The Air Force squadrons in Palestine and Transjordan were regarded as available to reinforce Egypt.

Allied naval co-operation in the Mediterranean had hitherto been discussed between the staffs of the Admiralty and the Ministry of

---

[1] The total armed forces in Syria comprised 11 battalions and ancillary troops of Colonial regulars, and 9 battalions of locally enlisted troops under French officers, with a high proportion of light cavalry and 'desert' (i.e., camel and light car) squadrons. The two groups of air forces were roughly equivalent to three R.A.F. squadrons.

Marine. French forces were to control the Western Mediterranean almost as far west as Gibraltar and British forces the eastern basin. The line of demarcation passed through the Strait of Messina and then curved to include Malta in the British area and the port of Tripoli in the French. The French were to protect British merchant ships (except when in convoy) as well as their own as far east as Algiers. Both naval forces would try to interrupt Italian communications with Libya in their respective areas. If Japan were to enter the war —and the possibility of this had to be taken into account—His Majesty's Government intended to send a fleet to the Far East. The strength and composition would have to be decided in the light of events and would depend, among other factors, upon the progress of operations already in hand against Italy, since these would offer the best prospects of speedy results. There would also be the effect upon Egypt, Greece and Turkey to be considered. Nevertheless, it would be largely at the expense of the Mediterranean that a fleet for the Far East would be created; British naval forces would remain for the local defence of Malta, Egypt and the Canal, but the main task of restraining Italian naval activity would fall upon the French.

At the end of July 1939 Vice-Admiral Ollive, Commander-in-Chief, *Flotte de Haute Mer*, (*Med.*),[1] paid a visit to Admiral Cunningham at Malta.[2] The agreed naval objects were to cut all Italian sea communications; retain control of the entrances to the Mediterranean; and exert any other pressure on Italy that might be possible by naval means. One ally was to take advantage of any dispersion caused by the action of the other. Plans of action on the outbreak of war were exchanged. They included plans for air reconnaissance, and the action of submarines. Provisional plans had been made for the bombardment by sea or air of several ports and harbours in North Africa, Sicily and Italy. The intention was to be ready to deliver some of these attacks directly war began, but the French and British Governments had by now agreed to restrict bombardment to purely military objectives in the narrowest sense of the word, and as far as possible to avoid making any attacks which would involve

---

[1] The *Flotte de Haute Mer* consisted of 3 battleships of the *Provence* class, 7 eight-inch and 3 six-inch cruisers, 1 cruiser/minelayer, 25 fleet destroyers, and 12 smaller destroyers. In addition, under V.A.C.-in-C. *Force Maritime du Sud* there were at Toulon 18 submarines, 3 fleet destroyers and 4 smaller destroyers; at Bizerta 23 submarines and 4 small destroyers; at Oran 12 submarines and 1 seaplane carrier. 2 submarines were based on Beirut with orders to co-operate with British forces in the Eastern Mediterranean.

[2] Admiral Sir Andrew Cunningham had been Rear-Admiral Destroyers in the Mediterranean during the Ethiopian crisis 1935/36 and later Vice-Admiral Second-in-Command 1937/38 flying his flag in H.M.S. *Hood*. In 1938/39 he was Deputy Chief of Naval Staff at the Admiralty. In June 1939 he became C.-in-C. Mediterranean in succession to Sir Dudley Pound who became First Sea Lord and Chief of Naval Staff.

loss of civil life.[1] This meant that the intended plans could not be carried out, and that the initial operations by the Fleet would have to be limited to anti-submarine operations and sweeps—a very tame alternative.

The small historic island of Malta, the headquarters of the Mediterranean Fleet in peace, was to play a vital part in Mediterranean strategy. Its importance was due mainly to its geographical position, for it contained the only British harbour between the eastern and western entrances to the Mediterranean—just midway between the two. It possessed dock and repair facilities, reserves, and resources, which had been built up at great cost over many years. It was also an important air base, both as a stepping stone on the air route and as a centre for air reconnaissance over the Central Mediterranean. There were therefore strong reasons for wishing the island to be secure.

Unfortunately the size and proximity of the Italian Metropolitan Air Force made the air defence of Malta extremely difficult. The island is less than half the size of the Isle of Man and the most important objectives were crowded together in an area round the harbour. They made ideal targets for air attack, which, delivered by strong air forces working from well-established shore bases only half an hour's flight away, could be both heavy and sustained. There was no effective warning system prior to March 1939, and the radar then installed gave only limited cover. There was no possibility of adding any depth to the warning system, and in consequence the defending fighters would be severely handicapped. But the number of airfields that could be made would not permit the use of more than a very few squadrons, and the protection of the grounded aircraft— a vitally important matter under these conditions—would involve a large dispersal project with the possible alternative of an elaborate programme of tunnelling. Then again, ground taken over for airfields would be lost for growing food, and as it was the island imported nearly three-quarters of its needs. Other essential imports were fuel, machinery and most war materials. Since the expenditure of resources, especially ammunition, in conducting an active defence would entail a heavy commitment for replacements, the whole problem of keeping the island supplied would be a serious one. However desirable it might be, for reasons of prestige and strategy, not only to prevent the island's capture but also to retain the ability to use it for offensive purposes, it was clearly going to be no easy

---

[1] Detailed instructions were drawn up which were much more restrictive than the rules for Naval bombardment (*Hague Convention No. IX of 1907*) and Air Force bombardment (*Draft Hague Rules of Aerial Warfare 1922/23*).

matter to do so. In 1935 the weak state of the anti-aircraft defences had made it advisable to withdraw the Mediterranean Fleet to a safer anchorage. But although the Royal Navy accepted this at the time, they had no intention of being permanently deprived of the use of Malta without the fullest investigation into the possibilities of providing adequate defence.

It was in July 1937, when Italy ceased to be regarded as a reliable friend, that the Cabinet decided to make a start with modernizing the defences of ports in the Mediterranean and the Red Sea. No very large expenditure was to be incurred, and nothing was to be done which could be construed by the Italians as provocative. So far as this decision affected Malta, it meant that a great deal of work could be done that was essential for security, such as boom defence, underground storage, work on splinter- and gas-proofing and air raid precautions generally, cable burying, and work on the new Luqa airfield.

In the summer of 1939 the broad policy for Malta was still undecided. The Admiralty urged that everything possible should be done to ensure its effective use in war. Without it the Fleet might be unable to fulfil its object of severing Italian sea communications and even the position in the Eastern Mediterranean might be endangered. There would be great advantages in being able to work in combination with the French without having to make the 900 mile passage from Alexandria, and the consequent saving would mean that naval forces could, if required, be more readily made available for despatch to the Far East. Finally, the naval facilities at Malta could not be transferred elsewhere, and neither Bizerta nor Toulon offered a satisfactory alternative. The Admiralty therefore wanted to see Malta so strong that it would not be worth attacking. The Air Ministry, on the other hand, were convinced that whatever scale of defence was provided could not prevent the Italian Air Force from rendering Malta unusable as a Fleet base. As an alternative plan they were greatly attracted by the idea of basing a strong bomber force in Tunisia, with the particular object of reducing the effectiveness of Italian attacks on Malta, but this could not be done for some time. A thorough technical investigation of the anti-aircraft problem of Malta was carried out, after which the Committee of Imperial Defence decided to approve increases of guns and searchlights, together with the addition of four fighter squadrons. The new total was to be 112 heavy guns; 60 light guns; 24 searchlights. By way of comparison, the numbers actually present in Malta on the eve of Italy's entry into the war were 34 heavy guns; 8 light; 24 searchlights; and no fighter squadrons. But it had to be recognized that it would be a long time before the anti-aircraft equipments and the men to man them could be available, and perhaps longer still before the fighter squadrons could be found. Half measures would be of no avail. A small consignment of anti-aircraft guns already on its way to Malta was accordingly diverted, 8 heavy guns to Alexandria and 8 light to Aden, for it was now fully realized that the Fleet would have to be based initially at Alexandria.

By the summer of 1939 there seemed to be a distinct possibility that Italy might be contemplating a challenge to Allied interests in the Mediterranean and in North and North-East Africa. This possibility, coupled with the difficulties arising from the Palestine problem, meant that the British sea and air communications to India and the Far East were to some extent threatened. Moreover, our guarantees to Greece and Rumania and our agreement with Turkey had added to our commitments in the Eastern Mediterranean. The defence of British interests in the Mediterranean and Middle East was clearly one strategic problem; it was important therefore to make some central British authority responsible for the co-ordination of war plans in the whole area, and for collaborating with the French Commanders and possibly with those of the Greek and Turkish forces as well. To see what was involved it is necessary to review briefly the situation of each Service.

The Royal Air Force had had a 'Middle East Command' since the First World War. It comprised Egypt, the Sudan, and Kenya, with administrative (but not operational) responsibility for Palestine and Transjordan. There were independent Air Commands in Iraq, Aden, and Malta—the last being known as the Mediterranean Command—all directly under the Air Ministry. In April 1938, it was decided that the A.O.C. Middle East should in war time exercise higher control and direction over all the air forces in the Palestine-Transjordan, Iraq, Aden, and Malta Commands in addition to those in the 'Middle East Command' proper. In peace he was to co-ordinate the preparations for the reinforcement of Egypt, the Sudan, Kenya, and Aden. This therefore was a step towards ensuring the best use of the forces available, dispersed as they necessarily were. In March 1939 the status of the post was raised, and Air Marshal Sir William Mitchell became Air Officer Commanding-in-Chief.[1]

The position of the army was more complicated. There were three separate Commands: Egypt, the Sudan, and Palestine-Transjordan. Control over the forces of the East African territories—notably the King's African Rifles—was exercised by an Inspector-General responsible to the Colonial Office. In peace this officer was also

---

[1] Air Marshal Mitchell had served in the Middle East as Air Officer Commanding Iraq during 1935/37. From 1937 until he became A.O.C.-in-C., Middle East, he was Air Member for Personnel at the Air Ministry.

Inspector-General of the Royal West African Frontier Force; in war he was to command the troops in East Africa. Then there were army garrisons at the naval and air bases of Malta and Aden. It was realized that it would be necessary to centralize the control of most of the army forces in the area under one Commander in war, but there were objections to doing so in peace. The question was when to install him. At the time of Munich a senior General had been sent to Cairo in readiness to assume the post of General Officer Commanding-in-Chief Middle East, but after a few weeks he was withdrawn to Gibraltar, where he became Governor and Commander-in-Chief. For a time it was hoped that he might again be available to go to Cairo in an emergency. But the ominous events of April and May 1939 suggested that war might not be very far off. In fact, the time had come to appoint a General Officer Commanding-in-Chief so that he might start at once to study the situation in conjunction with his colleagues in the other Services. The post was accordingly created in June, and Lieut.-General Sir Archibald Wavell was selected to fill it.[1] Briefly, he was to take command forthwith of the troops in Egypt, the Sudan, Palestine, Transjordan, and Cyprus. He was to prepare plans for them and for any troops in Iraq, Aden, British Somaliland, and the Persian Gulf. He was to collaborate as necessary with the French, the Egyptians and any other allies.[2] Thus, two 'Middle East' Commands—army and air—now existed; not identical, but very similar in scope.

The position of the Royal Navy was different. The naval Commanders-in-Chief of the Mediterranean and East Indies Stations were both concerned in Middle East affairs. In peace the East Indies Station included the Gulf of Aden and the Red Sea as far north as the port of Suez, and it was intended that this should be the same in war. There were good reasons. In conducting the war at sea against Italy, in conjunction with the French, the Commander-in-Chief Mediterranean was likely to have his hands full; it was therefore not practicable to place the other naval Commander-in-Chief under his orders. But the main reason was geographical. The security of trade and the protection of convoys in the Indian Ocean were the responsibility of the Commander-in-Chief East Indies and must obviously remain so. The timing, routeing, and escorting of convoys were all matters for him to decide: they would depend—as would any naval support for operations in East Africa—largely upon the raider situation in the Indian Ocean, in which connexion it must be remembered that Japan was a potential enemy. Thus there were grounds at this time for leaving the important base and convoy-assembly-

---

[1] General Wavell had served in the Middle East under Lord Allenby. He had commanded the forces in Palestine during the troubles of 1937. In 1939 he held the Southern Command in England.

[2] The Charter for the G.O.C.-in-C. is reproduced in Appendix 1.

port of Aden in the charge of the Commander-in-Chief East Indies, and although the army and air Chiefs viewed the security of the Suez Canal and Red Sea as one problem and would have preferred to deal with only one naval Chief, the Admiralty could not see its way to agree.

On 22nd June the Committee of Imperial Defence, when creating the post of General Officer Commanding-in-Chief, took the decision that the Commanders-in-Chief of the three Services should be responsible for co-ordinating the defence policy in the Middle East. Both naval Commanders-in-Chief were mentioned in this connexion, but the Commander-in-Chief Mediterranean became in effect the third member of the triumvirate, while a permanent representative in Cairo acted for the Commander-in-Chief East Indies in the latter's absence. This triumvirate formed the High Command. Each Commander-in-Chief was to remain responsible to his Ministry for matters affecting his own Service; jointly they would be answerable to the Chiefs of Staff.[1] They were to take as a basis for their consultations the Chiefs of Staff's latest appreciation. Their decisions would have to be reached by discussion, since no member of the triumvirate was supreme; none was even *primus inter pares*. This was not an entirely haphazard arrangement, but was thought to be the best in the circumstances. Indeed, in no theatre of the war was a Supreme Commander appointed over the three British Services only. The term came into being shortly after the entry of the United States into the war; it involved command over *allied* forces and was finally replaced by the title 'Supreme Allied Commander'.

The weakness of the triumvirate arrangement was that the three Commanders-in-Chief were unable to form a combined headquarters in which constant contacts at all levels would be possible. The Commander-in-Chief Middle East and the Air Officer Commanding-in-Chief felt obliged to place their headquarters in the capital, Cairo, the centre of communications with their vast geographical commands and of their political responsibilities. The naval Commander-in-Chief, however, felt the need to be at Alexandria, in order to keep in close touch with his Fleet, which naval tradition demanded that he should lead in action. In his opinion this outweighed the obvious advantages to be derived from the close association of the three headquarters. But it meant that for meetings either he and his staff had to go to Cairo or the other two Chiefs and their staffs to Alexandria. Moreover, the gap between formal meetings could not be bridged by frequent, if informal personal contacts.

---

[1] The Chiefs of Staff in London were in a comparable position. Individually they were the professional heads of their Services; collectively they formed the body which was to give professional advice to the War Cabinet; in peace they reported to the Committee of Imperial Defence, which in war was due to lapse.

E

To lessen these difficulties and to represent the naval point of view, an additional Naval Chief of Staff was appointed with an office in the same building as the Army and Air Headquarters in Cairo.

To serve the Commanders-in-Chief in their joint capacity they were provided with a Joint Planning Staff and a Joint Intelligence Centre.[1] The three senior members of the Joint Planning Staff also held operational positions in their own Service headquarters, for it was felt that plans should be made by people who would have to bear some of the responsibility for carrying them out. The main function of the Joint Intelligence Centre was to collate information from all sources about the countries of the Middle East, including Syria, East Africa, the Persian Gulf and Persia—some twenty countries in all. The sources that were to feed the Centre included the Ministries and Departments in London; H.M. Ambassadors, Ministers and Consuls; Colonial Governors and Residents; various Service Commanders, and so on. The Centre was to compile summaries and broad appreciations and disseminate them among some sixty addressees. Much of the subject-matter would inevitably be political and it was therefore proposed that the Centre should contain representatives of the Foreign and Colonial Offices; but this suggestion looked like causing so much delay that the Chiefs of Staff, in their anxiety to see a centre of some sort started as soon as possible, obtained approval for a joint Service Staff to be set up forthwith, its composition to be perhaps widened at a later date. In this way the Middle East Intelligence Centre was born on 1st August 1939. It was at first somewhat out of balance, for whereas the Navy and Air Force possessed their own Service operational intelligence staff, the newly created Middle East Headquarters of the Army had none, and had to rely largely upon the Centre, which had not been designed for the purpose.

Such were the origin and structure of the High Command. It began to function formally on 18th August when the three Commanders-in-Chief met on board H.M.S. *Warspite* to consider the strategical situation. They recorded that they felt the lack of a comprehensive plan to govern the action of the three Services. They were of course familiar with the broad policy for the conduct of the war which had been approved by the Allied Governments. They were also aware of the conclusions of the regional meetings with the French, but these had not yet been put together into the form of a broad plan. The Commanders-in-Chief decided to examine the possibilities of taking action against the Italians in Libya, but recognized that

---

[1] The word 'joint' in this connexion implied naval, army and air. The word 'combined' was later used to denote British and American; as in the term 'Combined Chiefs of Staff' which meant the British (Joint) Chiefs and the American Joint Chiefs together.

before anything appreciable could be done in this respect the Red Sea passage might prove not to be sufficiently secure; if so, their first task must be to try to improve the situation in that area.


Three years had now elapsed since the signing of the Anglo-Egyptian Treaty, but in many respects the situation in Egypt was still far from satisfactory. Allowance must be made for the political instability of a country so recently freed from military occupation; the wish to be secure and the wish to be quit of the British were both understandable, but they would nevertheless continue to be incompatible until such time as Egypt should be strong enough to defend herself. It was easy to sympathize with those Egyptians who felt that for the present there could hardly be too many British troops at hand, but who, on a longer view, looked forward to a happy condition in which there would be none. There was indeed yet another possible choice, and that was to discount the decadent British and turn instead to the conquerors of Ethiopia and Albania. There was no lack of counsellors among King Farouk's intimate circle ready to advocate this course. The Wafdists by the summer of 1939 had themselves been out of office for eighteen months; during this time they had lost no opportunity of decrying the treaty—which they themselves had negotiated—and of hampering its execution in every way. The Cabinet of Mohamed Mahmoud Pasha enjoyed little popular support, and their fear of the Wafdist opposition no doubt accounted for much of the procrastination and evasion that characterized their attitude to many of their commitments under the treaty. Anyhow, there was by now a long list of items on which progress had been very disappointing: the landing arrangements at Matruh; work on communications throughout the country generally; and improvements to the water supplies and camp sites in the desert. Worst of all no work had been done on the promised graving dock at Alexandria; improvements to the harbour facilities were proceeding very slowly; and no dredging had been done to deepen the Great Pass.

All this was made worse by the anti-aircraft situation. Early in 1938, in response to strong representations, the War Office had sent out an anti-aircraft brigade to Egypt consisting of twenty-four 3-inch guns and twenty-four searchlights. But trained men were urgently needed for the rapidly expanding air defences of Great Britain, and an agreement was therefore made with the Egyptian Government by which Egyptian troops should replace the British as soon as possible, consistent with a reasonably efficient state of anti-aircraft defence. The Egyptian target-practice showed considerable promise, but, as time went on, the British commanders in Egypt viewed the process of replacement with growing concern. The Naval Commander-in-Chief, especially, was by no means content that the ground anti-aircraft defence of his anchorage and base should be in other than British hands. Alexandria was also of importance in other respects. It was the second largest city in Egypt and the largest commercial port, with large stocks of coal, oil and petrol.[1] It was the only Egyptian port equipped to handle heavy lifts of cargo. The R.A.F. Aircraft Depot was only a few miles away at Aboukir and through Alexandria passed the principal road and rail communications from the Delta to the west. A Flag Officer (Liaison), Rear-Admiral F. Elliott, had been appointed to co-ordinate matters of local defence, and he was already the Fortress Commander in all but name. In war he was to be responsible to the General Officer Commanding British Troops in Egypt for the security of the Fortress, but was to meet the requirements of the Commander-in-Chief, Mediterranean, in every possible way.

The Chiefs of Staff were impressed by these considerations and proceeded to scrape up what they could to improve the anti-aircraft position.[2] First, they tried unsuccessfully to coax a battery out of India. Then it was decided that four 3·7-inch guns, with their crews, from Gibraltar and eight earmarked for Malta should be sent to Alexandria, the latter to be manned by the Royal Marines. In addition, twelve light guns were allotted to Egypt and it was stipulated that six of them were to be deployed at Alexandria.

Over and above this local problem was the vital one of air defence generally. The total resources were still woefully small, it is true, but by the summer of 1939 the fighter strength had risen to three squadrons, besides one Egyptian squadron in being and another forming. At Alexandria there would be a number, varying from time to time, of disembarked fighters of the Fleet Air Arm. There were Egyptian-manned observer posts in the desert, and there was one mobile radar set, which gave limited cover to Alexandria. In June it was strongly represented by the Air Staff and agreed between the Services that the time had come to unify the control of all these resources on the general pattern of the Air Defence of Great Britain. Only in this way could the necessary flexibility be obtained for dealing with attacks that might develop at one or more points over a very wide area. This area comprised the zone of the forces in the desert and their communications; Alexandria; Cairo and the Delta; and the Canal with its terminal ports. Any scheme for collecting and broadcasting warnings and for centralizing the control of operations

---

[1] Population 573,000; including 14,300 British, 9,400 French, 2,400 Italians and 3,700 Greeks.

[2] Of the guns then in Egypt, namely, thirty-eight 3-inch, four 3·7-inch, and four light (Bofors) all were manned by Egyptians, except eight of the twenty-two guns at Alexandria. All the searchlights—24 at Alexandria and 16 at Cairo—were manned by Egyptians.

naturally depended upon good telecommunications and these would take time to install. It also meant building up staffs for group and sector operation rooms and report centres. It was therefore important to make an early start and the Commanders were told to seek the collaboration of the appropriate Egyptian authorities.

The principal danger to the Suez Canal was thought to be that of blocking by specially prepared vessels, before or soon after the declaration of war. Or there might be sabotage or low-flying air attack. The local land defence was under the Commander of the Canal Brigade Area, while to keep touch with the Canal authorities over such matters as the control of shipping a Vice-Admiral was appointed as Naval Liaison Officer, later to be called Senior British Naval Officer, Canal Area. The question of mounting guns at the terminal ports had been under consideration for some months, but approval had been withheld in case the Italians should react unfavourably to what might be regarded as an infringement of the Canal Convention. Delay might mean locking up four destroyers at a critical moment, so the Chiefs of Staff returned to the charge and at the end of March 1939 the Cabinet agreed to invite the Egyptian Government to take the necessary steps. No objections were made; the guns were accordingly mounted, and were ready at both Suez and Port Said by 13th April.

The equipment of the Egyptian Army was of British pattern and in many respects it was better and more plentiful than in some of the British units. Training had made progress and officers and men had shown themselves keen to learn. The proposed employment of the Egyptian Army, approved in August by the Minister of National Defence, was that it should provide the following: patrols for the western frontier, for reporting any hostile movements; a contribution (including field, medium, anti-aircraft and anti-tank artillery) to the Matruh garrison; a small mobile force to operate in the desert south-west of Cairo; detachments for the protection of the railway between Alexandria and Matruh; certain units for the defence of Alexandria; and nine battalions for anti-sabotage duties. There were also the anti-aircraft units already referred to, and certain coast defence units. It was thought that these tasks would strain the Egyptian Army to the utmost. Its value in war remained to be seen, but had it not been available at this moment the alternatives would have been to distribute the British troops among a large number of additional tasks, at the expense of the force available to strike at the enemy, or else leave many vulnerable points unguarded and run considerable risks in respect of internal security.

The British forces available for active operations consisted in the main of the Armoured Division (as the Mobile Division formed during the previous year was now called) and the Cairo Brigade.

Towards the end of July the situation in Palestine allowed of the move of one infantry brigade, the 18th, to the Abbassia area, and a second remained ready to follow when required. Finally, in the middle of August, the 11th Indian Infantry Brigade arrived in Egypt, the first of India's invaluable contributions to the defence of the Middle East. In 1938 the Chatfield Committee had reported on India's defence policy, recommending that Indian forces should contribute to the defence of certain strategic areas outside India; among these were Egypt and the Persian Gulf. Forces for these tasks would have to be suitably equipped according to modern standards. By August 1939 this state had not been reached, but India neverthe-less began to despatch her External Defence Troops; the new equipment was to join them at their destination as soon as it could be provided from the United Kingdom. The 11th Indian Infantry Brigade accordingly moved to Fayid on the Great Bitter Lake, and began to train with its new weapons and vehicles.

In Europe the sands were running out. Herr Hitler had rejected President Roosevelt's appeal to him and Signor Mussolini to give an assurance of their non-aggressive intentions; he had denounced the naval agreement with Great Britain and the Non-Aggression Pact with Poland. A measure of compulsory military training had been introduced in Great Britain. The situation in Danzig was being exploited along grimly familiar lines. On 21st August the Soviet-German Non-Aggression Pact was announced, and the next day Mr. Chamberlain made it clear beyond all doubt that Britain's guarantee to Poland would be fulfilled by force if necessary. On 25th August the Anglo-Polish Treaty of mutual assistance was signed. War with Germany was thus becoming increasingly probable; and was not Italy bound to Germany by a Pact of Steel?

Italy, however, was engaged in a struggle against difficult economic conditions for which her government's foreign policy was largely responsible. She had been living on a war basis since 1935. Her adverse trading balance was very large and the Budget for 1939–40 forecast a heavy deficit. It was difficult to see how she could be in any condition for war; a further armaments race at this juncture was likely to be disastrous.

In the Army a major reorganization was taking place, involving the reduction of the infantry of a division from three regiments to two; the process was still far from complete, and would be a serious handicap to operations of any size. It is true that between January and April there had been some spectacular calling up of conscripts and reservists; morale was thought to be high; and the Army had admittedly had some recent experience of campaigning. On the other hand, there were known to be shortages of weapons and equipment, and of officers and instructors. The conclusion was that the Italian Army was not ready for war on a large scale.

The morale of the Fleet was known to have improved under the Fascist régime and Italian ships were well built, well armed, and fast. But in 1914–18 the Italian Navy had had only small running fights with the Austrians in the Adriatic, and since then the Fleet appeared to have carried out insufficient exercises for full efficiency. The submarine fleet, however, deserved respect by its very size.

The Air Force had probably reached the peak of its readiness for a major war at the end of 1936. Since then the war potential had been running down and reserves were now low. The deduction was that the Air Force was not fit to enter a war of the first magnitude with any hope of pursuing it successfully once the initial blow had spent itself.

So there were grounds for doubting whether Italy could be genuinely desirous of entering a war at all. But if she did decide to do so—and her policy would of course be determined by Signor Mussolini, and by him alone—her geographical position would enable her to cause the Allies considerable embarrassment. In the first place her naval and air forces, operating from their home bases, might close the Mediterranean to through shipping. The Suez Canal would therefore be the normal means by which reinforcements would reach the Mediterranean Fleet; it would be an essential internal waterway of the Middle East Base; and it would be the means of exit if the Mediterranean Fleet had to go to the Far East. Unfortunately, the Red Sea itself was liable to attack from bases in Italian East African territory, and the Italian naval and air units in this area would no doubt be encouraged to act with determination against Allied shipping in the narrow waters.

So, in the last week of August, on the eve of war with Germany, the Chiefs of Staff repeated once more their opinion that Italy's neutrality would be decidedly preferable to her active hostility, and urged that no attempt should be made to compel her to declare her position if this would be likely to bring her in against us. Their estimate of Italian unreadiness to wage a serious war was quite correct, and, in the event, Italy entered the war only when it seemed to Mussolini that nothing but a little token fighting would be required. Indeed, during the negotiations for the Pact of Steel of May 1939 Mussolini informed Hitler that Italy could not take part in a European war before 1942. When suddenly told in August 1939 that Germany was about to invade Poland, he presented the Germans with a long list of requirements—in which coal, steel, oil, and wood were prominent—that would have to be provided before Italy could join in. On learning from Hitler that his demands could not be met, Mussolini decided to adopt an attitude of neutrality favourable to Germany, and to move and deploy Italian troops in such a way as to pin down French and British forces. So began the period of nine months' 'non-belligerency', during which the Italian capacity to wage war for any length of time increased but little. To the British Commonwealth, on the other hand, it afforded a most valuable breathing-space.

# Chronology: March–August 1939

| | |
|---|---|
| 15th March | Germany invades Czechoslovakia |
| 29th March | Anglo-French Staff Conversations begin |
| 31st March | British and French guarantees to Poland announced |
| | End of Spanish Civil War |
| 7th April | Italy invades Albania |
| 12th April | Anglo-Turkish Joint Declaration of Mutual Aid |
| 13th April | Announcement of British and French guarantees to Rumania and Greece |
| 7th May | Announcement of the 'Pact of Steel' between Germany and Italy |
| 9th May | End of the war in Ethiopia |
| 23rd June | Franco-Turkish Declaration of Mutual Aid |
| 21st August | Soviet-German Non-Aggression Pact announced; signed 23rd August |
| 25th August | Anglo-Polish Alliance signed |

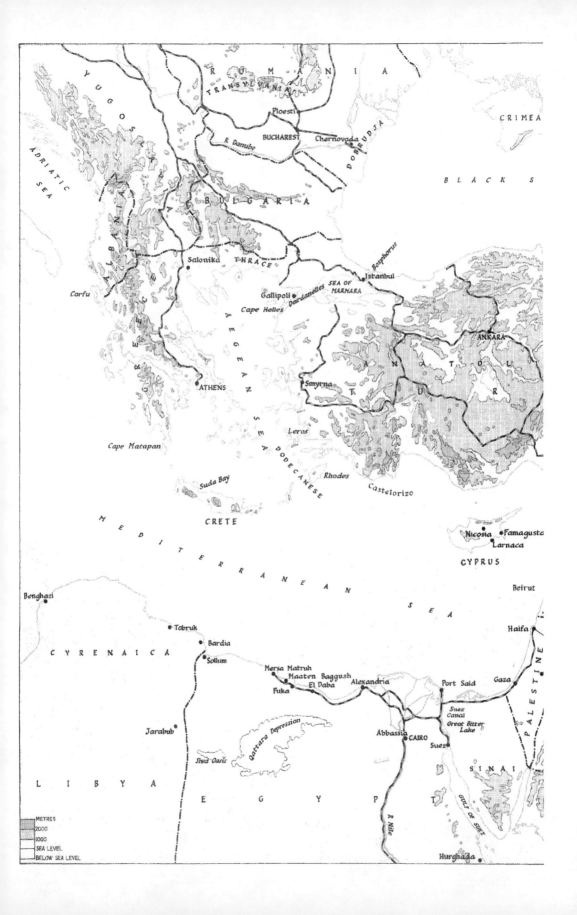

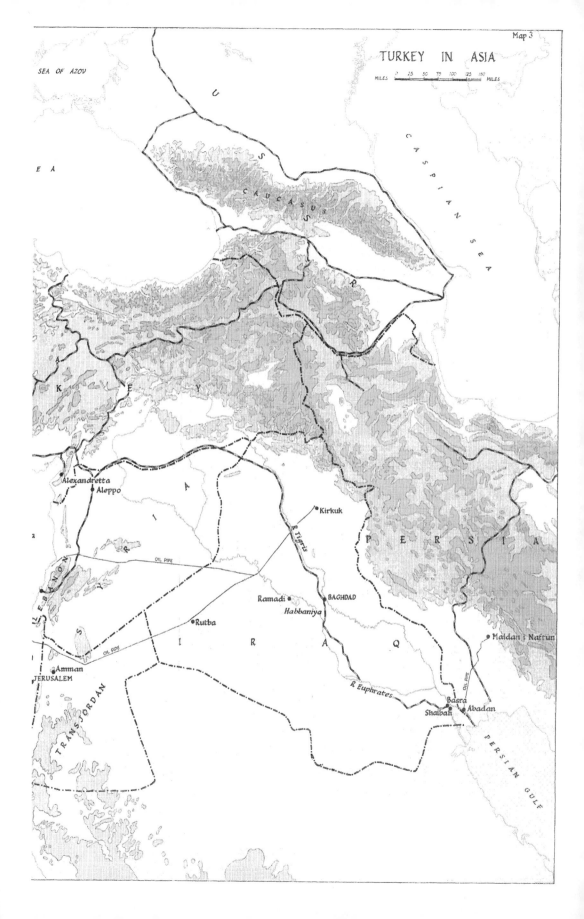

Map 3

TURKEY IN ASIA

MILES 0 25 50 75 100 125 150 MILES

SEA OF AZOV

U.S.S.R.

CASPIAN SEA

SEA

CAUCASUS

TURKEY

Alexandretta

Aleppo

Kirkuk

R. Tigris

PERSIA

OIL PIPE

SYRIA

BAGHDAD

Ramadi

Habbaniya

Rutba

Maidan i Naftun

IRAQ

OIL PIPE

Amman

JERUSALEM

R Euphrates

Basra

Abadan

TRANSJORDAN

Shaibah

PERSIAN GULF

LEBANON

# CHAPTER III

# AT WAR WITH GERMANY:
# UNEASY CALM IN THE
# MEDITERRANEAN
## (September 1939-February 1940)

*See Maps 2 and 3 and Chronology on page 58*

ON 30TH AUGUST the Commanders-in-Chief received from the Chiefs of Staff an instruction to the effect that should they receive a formal telegram warning them to adopt a state of instant readiness for war, and should this telegram specify both Germany and Italy as possible enemies, the defensive precautions taken against attack by Italy were to be as far as possible non-provocative. By this time a number of moves had already been completed or were in progress. On 23rd August the air reinforcement scheme was put into operation in a slightly modified form: three bomber squadrons and one bomber transport squadron moved to Egypt from Iraq and Palestine; the flying-boat squadron from Iraq moved to Aden; and in Kenya a squadron of the Southern Rhodesian Air Force relieved a bomber squadron of the Royal Air Force for service in the Sudan. By 28th August these moves were practically complete, bringing the bomber strength in Egypt to a total of 90 first-line aircraft. The total fighter strength of 75 included one Egyptian Gladiator squadron, which it was hoped would acquit itself well if Cairo were attacked. No aircraft were called forward from India, where rearmament was in progress; one bomber squadron was accordingly retained in Iraq for the time being.

The Italian air forces in Libya were not thought to have any great superiority in numbers over the Royal Air Force in Egypt, and many of them would no doubt remain on the Tunisian front, but their proximity to the metropolitan air bases made it an easy matter for either front, or even both, to be reinforced. The aim of the Air Officer Commanding-in-Chief was to reduce this potential superiority at the outset by an immediate offensive against aircraft, fuel, supplies, air bases, and maintenance facilities.

Meanwhile the British and Egyptian army units were moving into position. By 28th August the Armoured Division was disposed in the

41

area Matruh—Maaten Baggush; the Cairo Brigade had taken over the defence of Matruh itself; troops for the defence of Alexandria and of the Canal area were in position; while the 18th Infantry Brigade and attached troops were in Command reserve at Abbassia. The 11th Indian Infantry Brigade was continuing its training at Fayid, and there was still one infantry brigade in Palestine, in general reserve.

Egyptian army units assumed the dispositions agreed upon by the G.O.C. British Troops in Egypt, Lieut.-General H. Maitland Wilson, with the Minister of National Defence.[1] Two squadrons of the Frontier Force were at Siwa and Sollum for reporting movements of hostile land or air forces. One armoured car squadron of the 11th Hussars was at Sidi Barrani, with a detachment temporarily at Sollum; thus the patrolling of the Egyptian frontier was almost entirely in the hands of Egyptian troops, which the Italians could hardly look upon as a provocative arrangement.

British intentions in the Western Desert were governed by the probability that the initiative would be with the enemy. The most important task was the defeat of any attempt to capture Matruh, but if the enemy's advance should prove to be more formidable than expected it might be necessary to allow Matruh to be invested, or even to evacuate it, and fall back to the vicinity of El Daba. In this event the force of five battalions which the French had agreed to make available in emergency for the defence of Egypt would be called upon. If, on the other hand, the enemy did not attack on land, a forward movement to the vicinity of the frontier was contemplated; alternatively, this might be the sequel to a successful defensive engagement. The administrative aspects of these plans were of great importance and are considered in the following chapter.

The Navy, also, had made its preparations. At this time there were concentrated at Alexandria three battleships, one aircraft carrier, one anti-aircraft cruiser, three 8-inch and three 6-inch cruisers, 26 destroyers and a number of auxiliaries. From 20th August steps had been taken to prepare for war and to guard against sudden attack. On 23rd August the Admiralty assumed control of merchant ships and requisitioned a number for naval service. Dawn and dusk air patrols by the Fleet Air Arm were instituted off Alexandria, and the channels were swept for mines.

On 31st August the British Ambassador in Rome was informed by Count Ciano that Italy would not fight against England or France 'whatever Berlin says'. The next day Germany attacked Poland, and the Italian Government announced that Italy would not take the initiative in military operations, which was regarded as tantamount

---

[1] See page 37.

to a declaration of neutrality. The same day the Commanders-in-Chief received a formal warning telegram, in which both Germany and Italy were named as possible enemies.

A start was at once made in laying the first minefield off Malta. Next day a patrol was set up between Crete and Cape Matapan to intercept German shipping from the Aegean and to cover our own. On 3rd September the 3rd Destroyer Flotilla was ordered to Gibraltar on instructions from the Admiralty to prevent the entry of German U-boats into the Mediterranean. It thus passed out of Admiral Cunningham's command.

During the days which preceded the statement of Italy's attitude it was of course necessary to reduce the risks to which British merchant shipping might be exposed. On 26th August there were no less than 270 of these vessels in the Mediterranean, at sea or in port. The Admiralty therefore ordered those in the Mediterranean to continue their voyages, while any others entering were to be held at the terminal ports. As a large volume of British shipping was also to be found at any time in the Red Sea, orders were issued on 26th August that ships making for the Red Sea from the Indian Ocean were to be held at Aden. Eight destroyers from the Mediterranean were sent into the Red Sea, and all available warships on the East Indies Station were ordered to proceed to Aden.

Ships could not be held at the terminal ports indefinitely, however, and by 31st August the congestion had become serious. It was therefore decided that ships on government charter, and those with a speed of 15 knots, should be allowed through the Mediterranean; all other traffic was to be diverted round the Cape. On 1st September the tension was eased by the Italian announcement of non-belligerency, and the declaration of war with Germany on the 3rd evoked no sign that Italy had changed her mind. Diversions round the Cape were accordingly cancelled, though certain ships whose first or last port of call lay east of Rangoon would continue to use the Cape route. Convoys began to assemble at Gibraltar and Port Said for escort through the Mediterranean; these were a British responsibility, but air reconnaissance off the North African coast was provided for them by the French, who also assumed responsibility for the Algiers—Marseilles convoys instituted at the same time.

The only danger to shipping in the Mediterranean would now be from German U-boats, for it was feared that the heavy losses sustained from this cause during the First World War might be repeated. It was later learned that the Italians did not accede to German requests for submarine supply stations in the Mediterranean, and that in fact only one German submarine paid a short visit to the Mediterranean in November 1939. As nothing happened, precautions were relaxed. Independent sailings were resumed on 16th October, although ships bound for the United Kingdom from Port Said continued to sail in convoy until 2nd December. In order to reduce the risk of unfortunate incidents with Italian submarines, of which the consequences might have been very dangerous, escort vessels were only to be allowed to attack a submerged submarine (except within British or Allied territorial waters) if it committed a hostile act or 'was in a position to do so'—a restriction which greatly increased the difficulty of providing adequate protection to shipping. It was therefore a matter for satisfaction when on 21st September the Italian Government agreed that any of their submarines when outside their own exercise areas (which were to be notified), would remain on the surface and under escort.

On the outbreak of war there were some 45 German merchant vessels dispersed among neutral ports in the Mediterranean. Most of them happened to be in Italian waters, where they remained until Italy entered the war. Some succeeded in making the passage to the Dardanelles, almost entirely through neutral territorial waters, and so filtered through to the Black Sea, where, by the Montreux Convention of 1936, warships of a belligerent could not follow. All of them were later to be of considerable value to the Axis. In the meantime, those that remained in the Mediterranean were prevented from moving by the French Fleet in the western basin and by the British in the eastern.

The agreed Allied policy for the conduct of the war against Germany and Italy aimed at reducing the enemies' powers of resistance by the steady and rigorous application of economic pressure from the outset, and plans had been made accordingly. They included measures for controlling contraband traffic bound directly or indirectly for the enemy under a neutral flag, in furtherance of the right of a belligerent to proclaim as contraband any commodity or article which is of use for the prosecution of the war. By the outbreak of war with Germany the British contraband control bases at Gibraltar, Malta, Haifa, and Port Said were ready to function, though they were not fully staffed. The French had established similar bases at Algiers, Oran, and Marseilles. Vessels intercepted at sea and suspected of carrying goods destined for Germany were to be brought to these bases under armed guards found by the intercepting ships; after examination, their cargoes were liable to be confiscated. British naval officers had been posted to Algiers, Salonika, Volos, Istanbul, Piraeus, Smyrna, Famagusta and Suez, where they gave advice to shippers on contraband procedure and helped with the issue of navicerts—a form of certificate introduced in December 1939, enabling a ship carrying no contraband to be passed quickly by the intercepting control vessels.

It was obviously a matter of great importance that contraband should be prevented from reaching Germany; this was in fact the only means of bringing pressure to bear upon her at the time. But the interruption of her sea-borne imports would force her to try to increase her trade wherever she could—with Italy, for example. It was the policy of the British Government to secure as much Italian trade as possible, and negotiations were set on foot in Rome for a comprehensive war trade agreement between the two countries, which was to include the provision by Italy of a certain amount of aircraft and armaments. Meanwhile, the strong desire to see Italy remain neutral was reflected in a number of attempts to minimize the inconvenience to the Italians caused by the enforcement of contraband control. Although the Allies had every intention of respecting the rights of all neutrals, and of inflicting no unnecessary hardships, a certain amount of dissatisfaction was inevitable. In the circumstances it was obvious that special care would be required not to present Mussolini, who had never forgotten the economic sanctions of 1935, with a very plausible excuse for taking offence. It is not surprising that this aim came into frequent conflict with the policy of making the economic pressure on Germany as severe as possible.

The Chiefs of Staff had made it clear to the Commanders-in-Chief that no action was to be initiated against Italy that would be likely to bring her in against us. Admiral Cunningham therefore gave orders that Italian shipping in the Eastern Mediterranean was not to be molested. In reporting this action to the Admiralty on 3rd September he expressed the view that Italy's attitude required to be more clearly defined before the risk of offending her by contraband control could be taken. As it was undesirable to discriminate between Italy and other neutrals, the order meant that there was practically no control in this area; neutral ships were to be boarded only if their identity was in doubt. This attitude could obviously not be maintained for long without resulting in considerable benefit to Germany, and on 6th September the Admiralty gave orders that contraband control was to be applied to all neutral flags without discrimination; they made the special proviso, however, that ships in the Mediterranean, the Straits of Gibraltar, and the Suez Canal should not be sent in for examination unless found to be openly carrying contraband consigned to Germany, or unless they were suspected of un-neutral service. Copies of ships' manifests were to be obtained whenever possible, subject to the overriding consideration of not provoking incidents with Italian ships. Two days later these orders were put into effect, and patrols were established in the

Aegean, in the approaches to the Adriatic, and to the south of the Messina Straits. Operations connected with the imposition of contraband control were placed under Vice-Admiral J. C. Tovey, who at the time was Vice-Admiral, Destroyers.

It seemed that individual Italians did not really object to the restrictions imposed, but they were anxious to avoid giving any appearance of voluntary submission. The difficulty was that at Port Said submission could not be made compulsory, because the exercise of belligerent rights in the Canal area was expressly forbidden by the Suez Canal Convention. Egypt was, moreover, strictly speaking a neutral country, as she had broken off diplomatic relations with Germany without declaring war. Consequently, if ships refused examination, the alternative was to board them outside the three-mile limit, place a guard on board if the cargo was suspect, and steam to Haifa. This procedure commended itself to the Italians as being preferable to voluntary submission, but it caused a great deal of delay which gave rise to further complaints. To placate them on this point a control base was eventually established at Aden to deal with ships making for the Mediterranean from the east.

Another concession was that only in special circumstances were vessels plying between Italy and her colonies to be diverted for examination. Again, Italian ships outward bound from the Mediterranean were to be boarded only for identification. Nevertheless causes for complaint arose; for instance, dual examination sometimes occurred although examination by either a French or a British authority was supposed to exempt a ship from any further control. Another difficulty arose from the different interpretations of the term 'territorial waters'; the Italians recognized a six mile limit, the British only three; in the Aegean it often happened that Italian ships were boarded between three and six miles from shore.

In November 186 ships were intercepted in the Aegean alone and 83 of them were boarded and sent to the nearest control base for examination. There were no bases in the Aegean, since neutral territory could not be used for the purpose; those that were available were so far away that patrols in the Aegean could not be maintained at full efficiency. Moreover, a large volume of shipping was able to move long distances within territorial waters, which the existence of a control base in the Aegean could not have prevented.

It soon became apparent that the controls were far from achieving their full purpose. There was evidence that Piraeus was being used as an *entrepôt* for German imports and that the Salonika railway was being used for forwarding them, but there was little doubt that the principal leakages were through Italy. It was known in October that the Germans were making efforts to obtain goods through Italian ports, and several large contraband cargoes were believed to have reached the free port of Trieste. Other ports were used also, notably Genoa, where a trade in Spanish and Portuguese products had sprung up. Italian firms, as well as others in Greece and Yugoslavia, were found to be helping German imports on their way by various ingenious methods.

Even so, the exercise of contraband control did not justify the retention of a large fleet in the Mediterranean. The battleships and modern cruisers were accordingly withdrawn for service elsewhere, to provide raider-hunting groups and additional cover for convoys in the Atlantic and Indian Oceans and to supply a force of cruisers for the North Sea. Relations with Italy were reasonably good at this moment, and the reduction of the Mediterranean Fleet may incidentally have done something to improve them. The intention was, of course, notified to the Italians in accordance with the agreement, still in force, to exchange information on major military movements. On instructions from the Admiralty Admiral Cunningham transferred his flag ashore at Malta on 1st November, and in the middle of the month the battleships *Barham* and *Warspite* returned to the United Kingdom, followed later by destroyers, depot and repair ships, and M.T.Bs; the *Malaya* and *Glorious* had been sent to operate from Aden against enemy raiders in the Indian Ocean, and the 1st Cruiser Squadron (*Devonshire, Suffolk, Norfolk*) had joined the Home Fleet. By the end of December the Mediterranean Fleet was reduced to four small cruisers (*Arethusa, Penelope, Galatea, Capetown*), one Australian flotilla leader (*Stuart*), four Australian destroyers (*Vampire, Vendetta, Voyager, Waterhen*) and two submarines. In the absence of any naval reserves, armed guards for ships brought in under contraband control were supplied by the Malta garrison, and from time to time a French squadron co-operated in sweeps of the Aegean.

For the first twelve weeks of the war German exports sailing under neutral flags passed unmolested. On 18th November the Germans played straight into British hands by laying magnetic mines without providing for the safety of peaceful navigation, as required by the Hague Convention of 1907, either by declaring dangerous areas or by arranging for the mines, if drifting, to become harmless. On 21st November the War Cabinet decided that German exports would be seized as a reprisal for this serious breach of international law. This was a measure that would hit Italy particularly hard in respect of the deliveries of German sea-borne coal, and in order to soften the blow the British Government offered to make good the loss with British coal, as an item in the trade agreement. Wishing to be reasonable, they would allow German coal to continue to sail to Italy while the trade agreement was still under negotiation.

Mussolini had, on several previous occasions, shown himself to be extremely irritated by contraband control. The embargo on German coal imports was the signal for a particularly violent outburst by the Italian press: they spoke of Britain's provocative gesture; of the interruption of Italy's imperial communications; of being threatened with strangulation; and of having to tighten their belts so that the British could resume their five meals a day in the interests of humanity. Although by the end of January the Ambassador was able to report that the situation was not quite as bad as it appeared, the trade negotiations were nevertheless becoming increasingly difficult. On 8th February Mussolini put an end to all immediate hope of securing a comprehensive agreement by declining to discuss further the suggestion that Italy should sell certain armaments to the United Kingdom. Nor would he give any guarantee as to the destination of raw material imported by Italy from the British Empire. For some time the Italian negotiators persisted in their attempts to find a basis for a more limited economic agreement, but the breakdown of the formal negotiations meant the withdrawal of the steadying influence which had been felt while they lasted—largely because they provided a means of settling disputes arising from the incidence of contraband control.


The strategic situation in the Mediterranean and Middle East had for the past few years been conditioned largely by the attitude of Italy. The German invasion of Poland now disclosed a danger from a different direction. In little more than a month from the signing of the Soviet-German Pact of Non-Aggression on 23rd August 1939 Poland had been overrun and partitioned, and it was the turn of Rumania to feel anxious. She had good reason: Germany would derive great advantages from possession of the Rumanian oilfields; Russia was known to covet her lost province of Bessarabia; Bulgaria wished to regain the southern Dobrudja; and Hungary had her eyes on Transylvania. Nor was there anything effective that the Allies could do to help.

The full implications of this strange association of Nazi Germany with Bolshevik Russia were extremely difficult to assess. To Italy it must have come as an unpleasant surprise, and she might take a little time to recover her bearings. Russia would be sure to view with disfavour the prospect of German penetration to the Black Sea and the Straits, and although she might give her new partner some economic assistance, thus retarding the effect of the Allies' pressure, she would be most unlikely to co-operate to an extent that might restrict her own military activities. On the whole it seemed probable that she would take the opportunity to increase her own influence, while incidentally helping the Germans, by embarrassing the Allies

—and especially the British—in secondary theatres. She might confine herself to a campaign of propaganda, which would require vigorous counter-action. Or she might penetrate into Persia; if so, the British would have to provide for the internal security and air defence of the Anglo-Iranian oilfields and the port of Basra. Or she might decide to annex the northern provinces of Afghanistan, for which there were ample Russian forces on the spot. This would bring the cities of northern India within range of Russian bombers and would lead to demands for fighters and anti-aircraft guns, as India was virtually defenceless against air attack. It might lead also to a call for troops to help to deal with the disturbances likely to occur in the tribal territory of the North-West Frontier and in India herself. Unless Italian neutrality was assured there would be no possibility of meeting these demands.

It had been the British policy to encourage the neutrality not only of Italy but also of the Balkan Entente. It was now evident that there existed a threat of penetration into the Balkans by Germany and possibly Russia. Germany in particular, with her central position and her ample resources on land and in the air, would be able to operate in the Balkans at comparatively short notice. Such a disturbance would be likely to implicate Italy—who was so sensitive to events in the Balkans—but it was impossible to predict exactly what her attitude would be. One thing, however, was quite clear: Rumania was likely to be Germany's next objective, but she might not be the final one, and a threat to British strategic interests in the Middle East might well be about to develop from the direction of the Balkans.

Herein lay the military importance of Turkey and Iraq, for their territories were capable of providing depth for the defence of the Suez Canal, the Anglo-Iranian oilfields, and the route between Basra and Palestine. The British had consistently held the view that in Turkey lay the key to the security of the whole Allied position; as the first line of defence against aggression from the north she would be invaluable. She alone of the Balkan Powers was capable of offering serious resistance to Germany, though she had by no means all the arms and equipment that she would need. The more she could be helped in this respect, the greater would be her chances of holding on in Thrace; but even if the Turkish forces were thrown back to Anatolia they should be able to make an effective barrier of the Straits, for by the time the Germans had advanced as far as this they would have behind them a long and probably insecure line of supply. It was to Turkey, therefore, that war material should be sent; and, provided that Italy's neutrality made it possible to reduce the British forces in Egypt, consideration might be given to supporting Turkey if she were attacked. The significance of her geographical position

F

had of course been recognized at the time of the Anglo-Turkish Declaration in May, but in the light of the Pact between Germany and Russia it stood out with greater clarity than ever.

The Declaration itself had taken some time to negotiate, and it was the signal for further activity, especially in the financial and economic fields, with the object of concluding a definite agreement. A Turkish technical mission came to London to support the demands for war material, while a British delegation in Turkey sought to elicit the Turkish views on strategical questions. If greater progress was made towards the establishment of friendly relations than in reaching agreement on specific matters, it was due to a certain caution on both sides. The British had no armaments to waste and were interested in the use that would be made of any they might supply; the Turks, on the other hand, wanted to know what benefits would accrue from an alliance before they disclosed their own plans. All this time the French approaches to Turkey were proceeding independently, with a somewhat similar exchange of missions. The atmosphere was friendly, and when in August H.M.S. *Warspite* paid an official visit to Istanbul, Admiral Cunningham was invited to Ankara for a discussion with the Turkish Chief of Staff.

This insistence upon the importance of Turkey did not mean that the Allies regarded an attack upon her as inevitable. They realized that much would depend upon the attitude of Bulgaria, who was making no secret of her territorial claims against the Balkan Entente, but their main concern was how to prevent any form of German domination of the Balkans. Could these countries be induced to sink their many differences and present a united front pledged to neutrality? Past history offered little encouragement, but if no attempt were made it was unlikely that anything would be done. The French considered that some visible token of support would be required in order to strengthen the will of the Balkan states to resist aggression; an Allied force should therefore be installed at Salonika before the crisis occurred. Naturally, the consent of Greece would first be necessary. The British view was that the suggested action would involve a most undesirable diversion of effort and that in any case the arrival of military forces would be regarded as a breach of neutrality; therefore far from calming and unifying the Balkans it might have the opposite effect. Salonika was anyhow most unsuitable as a base for operations; the communications with the interior were indifferent; the climate was bad, and malaria was rampant. The force which could be spared and maintained there was likely to be so small that it was hard to see what advantages there would be to offset the many drawbacks.

The two governments had not reached agreement on this point before the Commanders-in-Chief in Cairo were visited on 31st

August by General Weygand, who had just been appointed to command the French forces in the Eastern Mediterranean in the event of war.[1] The arrival of such a distinguished colleague, of proved ability and of wide experience in the field of allied co-operation, was most welcome, although it soon became clear that in him the Salonika project had a spirited advocate. He did not question the need for Egypt to be secure, and a force would accordingly be held in Syria to move to Egypt if the situation demanded. He also appreciated the importance of Turkey, but he considered that Salonika might well be the key point and that its defence would be vital to the conduct of the war. He therefore intended to build up in Syria two divisions, which, he hoped, would not be depleted by the needs of Egypt, but which would be available to be sent to Salonika by sea: the problem of transporting the force was one for the British. At this juncture the attitude of Italy was of course uncertain, and Admiral Cunningham could not accept this heavy additional commitment, even if Smyrna and not Beirut were used as the port of embarkation, because there would be great risks from the air and from submarines. In the early days of hostilities with the Italians he could not agree to tie up his forces on escort duties; their task was to seek out the enemy. If troops had to be moved, he thought they had better go overland. Thus attention was focused back on Turkey.

Early in October a definite stage was reached when the War Cabinet was informed that, following an examination by the two staffs, the French were convinced that the proposals they had made for Salonika were not practicable. An Allied force might be sent there only if Greece was in danger of being overrun, and if she made a request, and if Italy agreed. On 11th October the Commanders-in-Chief were told that as a result of study of the various combinations of possibilities it had been decided to give the utmost support to Turkey, and build up an Allied reserve to be available to meet whichever of the threats arose. It would be based on Egypt and the Levant.

On 19th October, after a period of uncertainty while the Turkish Foreign Minister paid a visit to Moscow, the Treaty of Mutual Assistance between the United Kingdom, France, and Turkey was signed. Briefly, it required the signatories to collaborate effectively and to lend all the aid and assistance in their power if they should

---

[1] General Maxime Weygand was for several years Chief of Staff to Marshal Foch, notably during 1918 when the latter was Allied Generalissimo. In 1920, when Warsaw was threatened by Bolshevik forces, Weygand was placed in control of the Polish armies and conducted a successful offensive. In 1923–24 he was High Commissioner in Syria, and later was Inspector General of the French Army, a post equivalent to Commander-in-Chief. On retirement in 1935 he became Vice-President of the Suez Canal Company and was elected a member of the French Academy. When recalled to duty in 1939 he was 72 years old. He took over command of the French forces in the Middle East on 2nd September 1939. Earlier in the year he had visited Turkey.

become involved in war in the Mediterranean area as a result of aggression by a European Power or in consequence of the guarantees to Greece and Rumania. A suspensive clause absolved Turkey from fulfilling her obligations until certain loan and credit conditions had been complied with, and until supplies of war material for the effective defence of her Thracian frontier had been provided for her. A protocol stipulated that Turkey could not be compelled to take any action which would involve her in armed conflict with the U.S.S.R.

The questions of supply, which were clearly of such importance, were handled not by the Commanders-in-Chief but by the Allied governments, for they had to be viewed in the light of other re-armament programmes and the needs of the western front and the defence of Great Britain. General Wavell, who was at Ankara for the signing of the Treaty, reported to the War Office that questions of material were uppermost in the minds of the Turks; and in his opinion the sooner we could see Turkey well equipped and confident, the better. In order to decide what was to constitute the effective collaboration required by the Treaty it would of course be necessary for staff talks and meetings between the Commanders to be held. The Turks were in no hurry to begin, but a great deal of exploratory work was done by the British, involving much detailed recon-naissance, to examine the possible ways in which the Middle East forces could, in various circumstances, move to the help of the Turks. These studies took eventual shape as plans, known from their code-names as the 'Jungle' plans, worked out in great detail, for sending contingents varying from a few special units to a large force of all arms, and strong air forces, to various destinations in Thrace and Anatolia. The issues turned largely upon such essential pre-liminaries as the improvement and defence of the ports, the develop-ment of communications, and the construction of airfields.

The broad statement of policy given to the Commanders-in-Chief on 11th October had by no means left them clear as to what might be required of them. Towards the end of November Admiral Cunningham represented to the Admiralty that he and his colleagues were feeling the need of guidance as to the ways in which the war was likely to develop. He wanted to know which theatres the Allies were expecting to fight in, and with what forces. Without this information he could not have a workable plan ready for the rapid assembly of shipping of the right quantity and types. General Wavell had been called home apparently to discuss preparations for the expansion of the army, and the Admiral wanted to be able to give the earliest possible attention to the naval aspects of any strategy that was being contemplated. In particular, he commented on the fact that according to the Montreux Convention Allied ships could not enter the Dardanelles until an act of aggression had taken place, which might well be too late. An instance occurred a few months later when Turkish permission was sought for the passage of two British gunboats through the Straits. The intention was for them to enter the Danube in furtherance of preparations being made to interfere with Germany's oil supplies from Rumania, and also to withdraw a large number of tugs, tankers and other valuable craft of the Allied river transport fleet. The Turks adhered to the Convention, and, as a non-belligerent, refused the request.

Towards the end of December it seemed to the Allied governments that the time might be propitious for offering encouragement to the Balkan Powers, as there was some reason for supposing that a determination among them to resist attack by Germany or Russia was taking shape. It was essential that Italy should not regard such an offer as a move against herself; she was therefore to be consulted in advance, after which the approaches would be made through Turkey. However, the Italian reaction was not encouraging, and there was no apparent likelihood of her committing herself. Allied efforts thereupon became directed towards co-operation with Turkey, a course which the British had favoured all along.

The Commanders-in-Chief were accordingly authorized to begin discussions with the Turkish staff on the clear understanding that Italy was presumed neutral, but it not was until March that the many preliminaries were satisfactorily settled. The British and French met beforehand at Cairo to review the state of the 'Jungle' plans and to draw up a concerted report for use as a basis of discussion with the Turks. Finally, on 15th March, senior officers of all three countries met at Aleppo, the British being represented by the chief staff officers of each Service.

The conference nearly foundered at the outset, as the Turks wanted particularly to consider the defence of Thrace with Italy hostile, a situation which the British and French delegates were not empowered to discuss. However, by the exercise of much patience, the conference was kept in being for the full seven days, and some useful exchanges of information and views took place, during which it became evident that the Turks had some exaggerated ideas of the scale of attack they might have to meet and of the help that the Allies might be able to provide. The situation was eased by the arrival of authority from London and Paris to discuss in general terms the hypothesis of a hostile Italy, with a view to holding a meeting on this basis at the Commanders-in-Chiefs' level at a later date.

The outbreak of war found Egypt recovering from a major political crisis. After six months of ceaseless bitter criticism by the Wafdist opposition, Mohamed Mahmoud Pasha had resigned and had been replaced by the Chief of the Royal Household, Aly Maher Pasha. This was an indication that the Government might not fully represent the undoubtedly anti-German feeling of the people. Diplomatic relations with Germany were broken off, but war was not declared. *Etat de siège* was proclaimed, but its confirmation by Parliament was not sought until a month later, a delay which naturally gave rise to indecision and doubts, for *état de siège* was the authority for the nomination of British commanders in the Alexandria, Canal, and Western Desert areas, enabling them to issue orders to Egyptian troops; it was also the legal basis of the regulations for censorship, and of the requisitioning of civilian property, labour, buildings, land, and transport. Disquieting tendencies soon showed themselves: the Wafd increased its anti-British activities, making much play with the difficult economic situation; bitterness was engendered over British political intentions in Palestine; and in circles close to the Throne there were some obvious pro-Axis leanings. The attitude of the forces, by contrast, was co-operative and correct, and on 28th August General Wilson wrote to the Minister of National Defence expressing his appreciation of the speed and smoothness with which the Egyptian Army had carried out its moves, and of the arrangements made by the Egyptian State Railways in connexion with the despatch of the British troops to their war stations.

As September and October went by with no signs of any aggressive intentions on the part of the Italians, it became possible to relax the state of readiness in Egypt and to withdraw a proportion of units into more congenial surroundings. Training exercises and artillery practice camps began to be held in the desert, and at the end of November the Armoured Division was withdrawn to Abbassia and there continued to train intensively. Matruh remained fully garrisoned.

If there was much necessary training to be carried out there was also plenty of thinking to be done. General Wavell had been struck, as soon as he took over his command, by the defensive outlook that the policy of non-provocation and the general shortages had brought about. Within a week of the outbreak of war he ordered his subordinate commanders to work out their requirements six months ahead on the supposition that we should be at war with Italy. In Egypt, General Wilson was to plan operations for the capture of Jarabub and Bardia, for which he could assume a corps of two divisions and an armoured division available. He was to examine the possibility of using a small body of specially trained men transported by air, or even of parachute troops. At the same time he was to be prepared to receive in Egypt six divisions of a possible general reserve.

General Barker was to estimate his minimum requirements for the internal security of Palestine, based on certain assumptions as to the state of affairs in the neighbouring countries. He was not to consider a major threat to Palestine from the north, but he was to be prepared to send a brigade to reinforce the Iraqi army.

The commanders in Kenya and the Sudan were to begin to examine operations to destroy and disperse Italian forces and to support local risings, in order to assist the main Allied effort which would be made from French Somaliland. From the Sudan, too, General Platt was to consider an operation towards the Italian post at the oasis of Kufra, with the object of assisting a French effort against southern Libya from the Chad region.

Reporting these steps to the War Office General Wavell pointed out that it was important for him to be told what the policy was to be. If defensive, the forces that he expected to have ought to be just about sufficient, when a few of the worst shortages, notably anti-aircraft units, were made good. But if the policy was to be offensive, then apart from the requirements in land forces the Air Force would have to be capable of establishing local air superiority in the Western Desert, and extensive administrative developments would be necessary, which would take much time and material. He recalled that the French at Rabat in May had referred to their intended offensive against Tripolitania. If Spain were neutral and if the Spanish forces in Morocco were at least partially demobilized, the French had agreed to use six divisions in this offensive, which was all that could be maintained in southern Tunisia. If Egypt were seriously attacked, however, the French had said they would undertake an offensive with two divisions, whatever the situation in Morocco might be. General Wavell's latest information was that the whole question of an offensive was in abeyance until the French could be reinforced with air forces and heavy artillery. This was confirmed when, in December, he paid a personal visit to General Noguès, the Commander-in-Chief in French North Africa.

On 14th October General Wavell received the reply that a defensive policy was to be maintained in the Western Desert and that his demands for forces and for administrative developments were to be based on that assumption. This did not rule out such offensive operations as could be carried out within the limit of these resources. In the Sudan, military operations were to be confined to what was necessary to assist the main immediate object of reopening the Red Sea route. They would be primarily defensive, but it was also intended, when the time was ripe, to foster rebellion in Ethiopia and support it by the operation of small columns. General Platt was accordingly told to keep a close watch on the rebel activities then in progress, and to be prepared to help the active chiefs with arms and money. Rebel activity had revived during the previous rainy season and, if the Italians found themselves at war with us before they had stamped it out, it should be capable of extension.

The inability of the French to mount their intended offensive into Tripolitania was emphasized by the changes taking place in their air forces. It had been agreed in May that it would be to the advantage of both Allies if the French air forces in Tunisia could be increased, so that strong attacks could be made upon Italian air bases, especially in Sicily, and upon the terminal ports used by shipping on the Libyan run. The Royal Air Force in the Middle East was too weak to make any contribution, even for this worthy purpose. However, the overriding aim of both Governments had been to build up their home defences against the German threat, and the more modern French bombers had been withdrawn to France and were being replaced by obsolescent types. After this there would be a period of rearming and training with American aircraft, which would not be completed before April 1940, at the earliest; meanwhile the French would have little or nothing with which to counter the Italians effectively. This would of course have its effect on the ability of the Air Force in Egypt to carry out its tasks of neutralizing the enemy air forces, of attacking ports, bases, and supply centres, and of supporting the Army and Navy. Unfortunately there was at this time no prospect of any increase in the strength of the Air Force in the Middle East, while the Air Officer Commanding-in-Chief had to report in January that his general administrative situation was 'becoming worse than ever'.

On land, however, the winter of 1939–40 saw some additions to the British strength. A second Indian infantry brigade arrived early in October to join the 4th Indian Division, a formation which, being on the Indian establishment, had yet to receive much of the equipment necessary for fighting a European enemy in desert conditions.[1] From the United Kingdom the only formation that could be spared was the 1st Cavalry Division, comprised of horsed Yeomanry units, and this was sent to Palestine by March 1940, to release some regular units from internal security duties and to continue its training. Here again the low standard of equipment severely limited the roles for which the reinforcing troops were fitted. The fact was that the output of the United Kingdom had not reached a size even approximating to the many demands upon it. This caused delay in the equipping and training not only of British and Indian troops but also of the various contingents from countries which could provide willing men but no weapons; it was a handicap in the negotiations with Turkey, and it was a ruling factor in the availability of Dominion formations for service in the Middle East.

---

[1] See page 38.

Australia and New Zealand both declared war on the same day as Great Britain, and began at once to expand their defence forces. They both wished to send contingents overseas to wherever they were needed most, provided always that the situation in the Far East allowed this to be done with safety. But although they could raise troops, their ability to equip them was very limited. Australia could supply many of the simpler items, but New Zealand could produce little more than rifles. Australian arsenals were well adapted for expansion, but it would take time. The principle was quickly adopted that the troops of these Dominions should do their elementary training in their own countries and then move to the Middle East, where modern equipment on a suitable scale for training would come to them from the United Kingdom, to be followed later by a full provision as for British troops. This could only be done by giving them a higher priority in the existing armaments programme than that of some of the British units. It was a commitment for which no provision had been made, as no Dominion was prepared to commit itself in advance.

In December 1939 General Wavell was told that he might expect one Australian division by April 1940, and one New Zealand division by the following August. In February the first units began to arrive—one brigade from each country—accompanied by a proportion of their divisional troops and a few base units. Mr. Eden, the Secretary of State for Dominion Affairs, flew out to Suez to greet them, and they moved to their training areas—the Australians to Palestine and the New Zealanders to Maadi near Cairo.

The position in the Union of South Africa was somewhat different: the armed forces could be required to serve in defence of the Union outside its borders, but only within 'South Africa'—a term which was undefined. The Union declared war on Germany on 6th September, and shortly afterwards General Smuts, the new Prime Minister, notified London of his government's intention to expand their land and air forces and asked whether weapons and aircraft could be supplied by the United Kingdom. Nothing approaching the full demand could be met. The outcome was an offer in December of a brigade group for service in Kenya, and the question whether this could correctly be treated as service within South Africa was answered by the decision to send none but volunteers. The offer was not immediately accepted, partly because the necessary equipment was not yet available and partly because of the policy of giving Italy no grounds for provocation. In March 1940, General Wavell visited General Smuts, who shortly afterwards informed the British Government that the brigade group, to be equipped and maintained by the Union, would be ready to leave by the end of June. In addition, an anti-aircraft brigade and up to three air force squadrons would be made available if the United Kingdom could equip them.

Thus by March 1940, a start had been made on the immense task of assembling, equipping, and training an Empire and Commonwealth army in the Middle East. The early arrivals were welcome indeed, and of a quality that held out high promise of excellence. But in immediate fighting value they did little to offset the reputed strengthening of the Italians in Libya or the weakening of the French in North Africa. It remained to be seen whether they would be in all respects fit for war and whether their numbers could be added to before war came: how long, in fact, the uneasy calm in the Mediterranean and Middle East was destined to last.

# Chronology: September 1939-March 1940

| | | |
|---|---|---|
| 1939 | 1st September | Germany invades Poland |
| | 3rd September | Great Britain and France declare war on Germany. Australia and New Zealand declare war on Germany |
| | 6th September | South Africa declares war on Germany |
| | 10th September | Canada declares war on Germany |
| | 17th September | Russia invades Poland |
| | 27th September | Polish resistance ends. Poland is partitioned between Russia and Germany on 29th September |
| | 19th October | Anglo-French-Turkish Treaty of Mutual Assistance signed |
| | 4th November | President Roosevelt signs Neutrality Act inaugurating the Cash and Carry Scheme and proclaiming Combat Areas |
| | 30th November | Russia invades Finland |
| 1940 | 12th February | First Australian and New Zealand contingents reach Egypt |
| | 15th March | Franco-British Staff Conference with Turks at Aleppo |

Map 4

# THE EGYPT – PALESTINE BASE

## Showing principal communications
### Legend

Installations existing in 1939 shown in Blue
Planned expansion at new sites shown in Red

| | | |
|---|---|---|
| ◉ ...Airfields | 1....Supply depots | 6...Vehicle depots & stores |
| O...Landing grounds | 2....Ammunition & bomb depots | 7...Engineer stores |
| ⊕...Flying boat bases | 3...Bulk petrol | 8...Personnel camps |
| ⊥ ...Flying boat alighting areas | 4...Ordnance depots | 9...Hospital areas |
| | 5...Ordnance workshops | 10...RAF maintenance units |

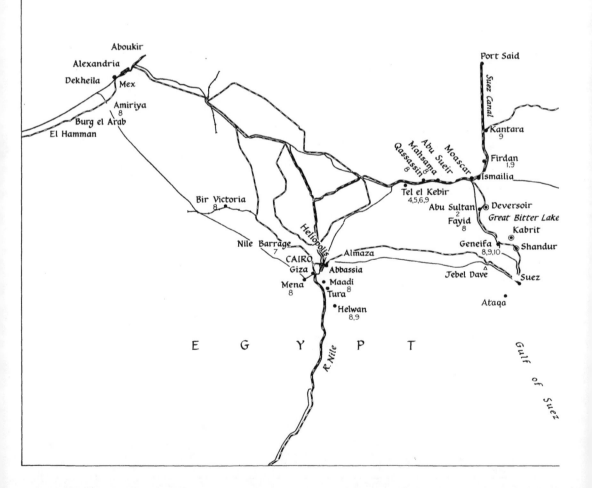

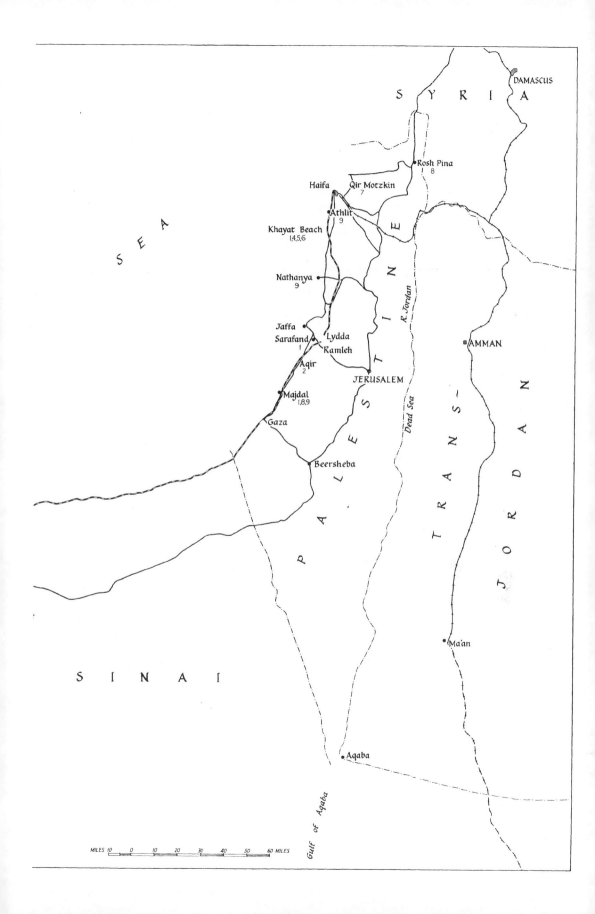

SYRIA

DAMASCUS

Rosh Pina
8

Haifa
Qir Motzkin
7

Athlit
9

Khayat Beach
1,4,5,6

Nathanya
9

Jaffa
Sarafand
1

Lydda
Ramleh

Aqir
2

JERUSALEM

Majdal
1,8,9

Gaza

Beersheba

AMMAN

PALESTINE

R. Jordan

Dead Sea

TRANS-

JORDAN

SEA

SINAI

Ma'an

Aqaba

Gulf of Aqaba

MILES 10   0   10   20   30   40   50   60 MILES

# CHAPTER IV

# THE LOGISTIC FOUNDATIONS

# (1939-40)

*See Map 4*

> 'Military history means the survey of
> administrative in at least as great a degree
> as strategical and tactical genius. . . . People
> who have never studied military history do
> not realize that a campaign is a gigantic
> picnic, and that, unless careful arrangement
> be made long beforehand for every detail
> of food, forage, clothing and carriage, an
> army may perish. . . .'
>
> *(From a lecture on 'Military History'*
> *delivered at Trinity College, Cambridge, in*
> 1913 *by the Hon. John Fortescue.)*

THE TERM 'administration' was used by the Army and
the Royal Air Force alike to mean the whole process of
providing forces with what they require or of performing
some service for them. The fact that land and air forces would often
be operating from the same area had led the Air Force to adopt a
system very similar to the Army's. Briefly this was for the officer in
chief command to exercise control of administration through his
staff and thence through the heads of the administrative services.
The latter were suitably represented at the various subordinate
headquarters, so that policy could be centrally controlled and
executive functions decentralized. In 1939 the administrative
services were as follows: medical, chaplains, pay, provost, graves,
supplies and transport, transportation, ordnance, works, engineer
stores, remount, veterinary, canteen, postal, labour, hirings, salvage,
printing and stationery. In respect of several of these services the
requirements of the Air Force in the Middle East were handled
wholly or in part by the Army, while their own maintenance
organization included the supply, repair and salvage of aircraft,
and the supply of equipment and motor transport.

The Army Council's instructions to General Wavell (Appendix 1)
entrusted him, amongst other things, with the control of high policy,
the preparation of war plans, and, in the event of war, the

co-ordination of the action of the land forces and the distribution of available resources between them. For his immediate tasks he was provided with a modest staff of five officers, of whom one was to be 'administrative'. It was not to be expected that this staff could do more than serve as a peace time nucleus; indeed, it had not been in existence more than a few weeks when the outbreak of war with Germany and the negotiations for the Treaty with Turkey convinced General Wavell that the administrative side in particular must be strengthened at once, so that considerations of movement and maintenance could be given full weight in the earliest stages of planning. Early in October Brigadier B. O. Hutchison was accordingly transferred from Palestine to take charge of the administrative side.

The alternative to a planning staff would have been a complete General Headquarters, but to establish this was hardly feasible.[1] The British Army was in a state of rapid expansion, so that trained and experienced officers were scarce, and the needs of the French front, which were considerable, naturally took priority. The administration of the troops in Egypt, the Sudan, Palestine and Transjordan, and East Africa could, for the present, continue to be directed from the War Office. The disadvantage was that General Wavell had to lean heavily upon the staffs and heads of services of the existing Commands for the detailed and specialist work required in the preparation of his plans, and much of this work fell outside the purview of the Commanders to whom these officers were primarily responsible. This was an anomalous situation, which had to be accepted for the time being. If, however, the war were to spread to the Middle East, a more rational system, with administrative responsibility taking its proper place as part of the function of command, would clearly be necessary.

It was also clear to General Wavell that the land forces in the Middle East would sooner or later have to be appreciably strengthened if their contribution to the war was not to be confined to trying not to lose it. He therefore initiated a preliminary survey for the creation of a base for a force of fifteen divisions—say 300,000 men. This figure was no more than an estimate based on a consideration of possible roles, for by the end of October, when the survey of ports, railways, roads and sites was completed, the long-term policy for the Middle East was still being considered in London.[2] At the beginning

---

[1] The War Establishment of G.H.Q. Middle East issued in October 1940 provided for 1,061 officers and men, of whom over 700 were for administrative duties.

[2] The objects for which British forces might be required in the Middle East were not unlike those for which troops had been concentrated in Egypt towards the end of 1915. On that occasion there was a 'Force in Egypt' under one general, a 'Mediterranean Expeditionary Force' under another, and a separate 'Levant Base' for dealing with Salonika, Gallipoli, and Mesopotamia.

of December General Wavell accompanied by Brigadier Hutchison and Air Commodore Drummond flew to London to join in the discussions.

The investigations being made by the Army led Air Chief Marshal Mitchell to enquire of the Air Ministry in October whether a large increase of air forces was also contemplated, for he was under no illusions as to the magnitude of the administrative preparations that would be necessary. He was told in reply that the main problem for the time being was to expand the Royal Air Force into a force capable of gaining and maintaining superiority on the western (European) front. There could be no question of reinforcing the Middle East in the near future. Nevertheless, his dissatisfaction at his want of men and equipment, coupled with the knowledge that the Chiefs of Staff were seriously considering the operation of Air Force units in Turkey, prompted the Air Officer Commanding-in-Chief to send his senior administrative officer, Air Vice-Marshal A. C. Maund, to London early in January to represent the difficulties under which his Command was already labouring. If the worst deficiencies were not made good it would be quite impossible to maintain an air force in Turkey or anywhere else. A few days later the War Cabinet's policy became known.

In their review of military policy in the Middle East dated 5th December 1939 the Chiefs of Staff estimated that in view of the weakness of the Allied air forces and anti-aircraft artillery it could not be said that British interests were secure against Italian attack. If Germany or Russia were to begin determined offensive operations in the Middle East it would be necessary to provide additional land and air forces to defend our interests and to prevent the defeat of Turkey. If Italian hostility were added to German or Russian aggression, we should have to deal with the Italian fronts before we could give any assistance to Greece or Turkey. Apart from the salutary political effect of a show of force there were therefore good reasons for building up our forces, but this ought not to be done at the expense of essential requirements in Western Europe or of the ability to defend Singapore. Moreover it would be useless to add considerably to the forces without first developing the bases and communications which would sustain their operations. This administrative development, it was realized, would—particularly in respect of the land forces—be a more lengthy process than the actual concentration of troops and air forces. It ought therefore to be put in hand at once, so that if the strategical situation were to require the despatch of additional forces these would be able to function with the least possible delay.

The War Cabinet agreed with these views on 15th January 1940. The policy for the land forces was to be as follows. Only those formations already under orders for the Middle East should be sent there; namely, one Australian division and the 1st Cavalry Division to Palestine, and one New Zealand division to Egypt. The base organizations in Egypt and Palestine were to be put in hand at once, and the gradual accumulation of material reserves for a force of nine divisions, including the present garrisons, was to be begun. One division, which the Government of India had already offered to provide, should be made ready in India for the defence of the Anglo-Iranian oilfields. Reserves of material should be accumulated in India for a force of three divisions which might be employed in Iraq and Persia. Basra should be developed as a base port for a force of this size. In case of interruption to traffic in the Red Sea the overland route Baghdad—Haifa was to be further improved, but the capacity of the route Mombasa—Cairo was likely to be so small that no great effort was to be devoted to it. The existing figure of 90 days for war reserves would also apply to any additional forces sent to the Middle East.[1] It was also decided that an additional battalion of the Sudan Defence Force should be raised, and that one brigade, and later a second, of the Royal West African Frontier Force should be transferred from West Africa to Kenya, where the necessary reserves for them should be built up. Finally it was decided that the Turks should be induced to develop their air facilities and communications in Thrace and western Anatolia, for which purposes technical advice and help should be made available to them.

The policy for the Royal Air Force was to be: to increase the mobility of the existing squadrons to enable them to operate from Turkey or Greece; to build up the strength gradually to a total of 4 heavy and 8 medium bomber squadrons, 10 fighter, and 5 army co-operation squadrons; to make certain provisions on shore for the Fleet Air Arm and for the Royal Air Force co-operating with the Royal Navy; and to plan base facilities for operating twelve additional heavy bomber squadrons. The implications of these decisions are referred to later in this chapter, but it will be understood that they could not be pursued as isolated projects. The Army and the Air Force were obliged to take each other's expansion into account, for the Army was the joint provider of a great many services (of which transportation was one)[2] and of common-user stores (including

---

[1] The figure for the number of days of war reserves, multiplied by the estimated daily rates of expenditure, produces the total quantities of reserve stocks to be held. Over and above this estimated reserve is a working margin allowance—in this case anything up to 60 days—varying with the commodity. The reserve is an insurance against a possible period of interrupted sea communications; the working margin is intended to cover the intervals in the arrival of shipments.

[2] The term transportation includes the construction and working of docks, railways, and inland waterways.

food and building materials) and it was obviously desirable that sites, resources, and facilities should be allotted to the best advantage. As regards construction, the arrangement was broadly for the Air Force to retain responsibility for all work at their stations in the Canal and Delta areas and for the Army to undertake new airfields west of the Delta, and in general to be responsible for electric power, water, and bulk petrol supply.

The immediate effect of the War Cabinet's decisions, as far as General Wavell was concerned, was to add to his responsibilities. He was now to take command of British land forces in East Africa and British Somaliland, and any that might be sent to Turkey or the Balkans including Greece.[1] If major land operations occurred in or near Iraq, Aden, or the shores of the Persian Gulf, he was to command the land forces involved. As he had not the staff to enable him to exercise all these functions forthwith, he was to be free to assume administrative control in the several areas of his Command in accordance with the situation and the means at his disposal. Heads of the principal services were appointed to act as technical advisers during planning and to prepare for the assumption of administrative control. To clarify his own position, his title was changed on 15th February 1940 to 'Commander-in-Chief Middle East'.[2] His area of responsibility was a very large one, involving a great deal of tedious travelling. Much of his time, and that of the Air Officer Commanding-in-Chief and other senior officers of both Services, would have been saved if suitable long range communication aircraft had been provided. The matter was repeatedly referred to London, but the first really suitable type—the Lockheed—combining reasonable speed and comfort did not reach the Middle East until November 1940.

Egypt was of course admirably situated as the main location of a central reserve. The populated and cultivated Delta and valley of the Nile are unsuitable for large military installations, but elsewhere all is desert, which although barren, shadeless, and inhospitable is capable of carrying railways, roads, runways, and buildings amply dispersed against air attack. Of still greater importance was the existence of the three deep-water ports, linked with each other and with Cairo and the Delta by the standard-gauge Egyptian railway system. The bulk of the commercial traffic was carried by Alexandria,

---

[1] He already commanded in Egypt, the Sudan, Palestine and Transjordan, and Cyprus. See Appendix 1 for his original instructions.
[2] This title was the traditional one for a Commander of higher status than a General Officer Commanding-in-Chief. It was open to some criticism in this instance on the ground that as the Middle East was a joint command the title should have been 'Army (or Land) Commander-in-Chief'.

which was now to be used as a naval base. Port Said was a useful transhipment port. Suez, though only partly developed and scarcely used, except for pilgrim traffic, possessed great possibilities for expansion. The flexibility thus provided in Egypt was further increased by the existence of a railway link between the Suez Canal and Palestine's deep-water port of Haifa. Thus the whole area possessed the essential attributes of a large overseas base, but even so its development was a very different matter from the establishment of bases in France, separated from the industries and resources of the United Kingdom by no more than the width of the Channel.

The region is one of the driest in the world: the sun is hot, and the wind is dust-laden. Egypt depends for its water supply, and hence for its very existence, upon the river Nile, and even from this plentiful source the water is unsafe for drinking, and even for washing, without treatment. This, in outlying areas, involved the erection of much plant, so that the time required to prepare a camp or depot was often governed by the installation of a safe water supply. But the Nile gives life to the soil and by intensive cultivation Egypt is able to export cotton, corn, and vegetables. In 1939 her industries of war time importance were very few, and all her iron, steel, coal, timber, and machinery were imported. There was a small oilfield near Hurghada but no other mineral deposits of any consequence. In Palestine, too, there was a general lack of raw materials, but this essentially agricultural country was nevertheless rapidly developing its industries. There was a valuable production of cement, and an appreciable quantity of motor transport was in use. An all-weather road from Beersheba to Ismailia was nearing completion, providing yet another important link between Palestine and Egypt.

Six divisions were to be based on Egypt and three on Palestine, with Egypt holding rather more than its share of ammunition, reserve vehicles, and transportation stores. The divisional 'slice' was to be taken at 25,000 men with a sixty per cent. surplus of vehicles.[1] In Palestine, the plan was to expand the existing depots at Sarafand and supplement them by further construction at Khayat Beach near Haifa. In Egypt, the main depots were to be in the Tel el Kebir-Qassassin area along the railway and sweet-water canal to the west of Ismailia. Others were to be sited beside the Suez Canal and the Great Bitter Lake, e.g., the supply depot at Firdan and the ammunition depot at Abu Sultan. A few installations were to be in the

---

[1] During the early stages of planning it is convenient to assume an inflated figure, or 'slice', for the strength of a division, in order to allow for a proportion of overheads, that is to say, the units, whether combatant or not, which do not normally belong to a division but which are a necessary component of a larger balanced force. The number and type of these units depend upon many factors. The figure for the slice steadily grew as the war went on, not because the divisions themselves became larger but because the proportion of non-divisional units, and especially of labour, was constantly being increased.

1. Entrance to workshops and explosive stores in the Tura caves. The Nile is in the distance.

*Facing p. 64*

2. Observation Hill, at the southern end of the Tug Argan Gap, British Somaliland. View looking almost due east.

3. Takoradi: landing a Hurricane fighter brought by
H.M.S. *Argus*.

*Facing p. 65*

4. H.M.S. *Illustrious* parts company with the 3rd Cruiser Squadron before the attack on Taranto
(From the painting by Rowland Langmaid.)

neighbourhood of Cairo. The extensive caves at Tura and Massara (from which the stone for the Pyramids at Giza was quarried) were already being adapted to receive ammunition, aircraft bombs, and other explosives.[1] In the hills to the west of Suez large petrol storage installations, part Army, part Air Force, were being erected. Suez was likely to become an important port of entry and would have to be enlarged; the first step was to build wharves for lighters at points in the Gulf of Suez and along the Canal.

Before these plans could be acted on, General Headquarters Middle East had a fundamental difficulty to overcome. Work was already proceeding as quickly as possible on preparations for the troops who were expected shortly, but local stocks of materials were practically exhausted. Everything depended upon how quickly essential supplies could be obtained from overseas. In these circumstances General Headquarters Middle East, to their credit, acted with great promptitude and acumen. They placed orders, for quickest possible delivery, wherever they could, and did their best to cut down the demands on the United Kingdom. They made direct approaches to South and East Africa, India, Burma, Malaya, and Australia, and in addition contrived to save time and shipping space by tapping some of the nearer sources. Local production of cement, bitumen, bricks, and so on, was increased as much as possible. Although there were delays and disappointments, it was not long before a flow of stores, in addition to shipments from the United Kingdom, began to arrive from these eastern markets. Timber (notably from Rumania until the Dardanelles were closed); steel, fabricated ready for use and in sheets for making anti-tank mines and containers for oil, petrol and water; tin; gelignite; defence stores; tools; pumps; pipes and fittings; machinery for road work; workshop plant; cargo handling gear; and so on. A large quantity of machinery, pumps and pipes was even ordered in Italy, but when the German Ambassador heard of this transaction it was quickly stopped. However, there was a pleasant windfall of German-made pipes in Palestine, which enabled a water pipeline in the Western Desert to be started. This policy of converting the available money into tangible assets as quickly as possible was amply justified by results. It enabled General Headquarters Middle East to remain one move ahead, which was indeed fortunate, for when the final approval from London for the completion of the nine-division base was given it was soon followed by an increase in the planning figure to 14 divisions to arrive by June 1941, and 23 by March 1942.[2] The slice was now to be 35,000.

---

[1] See Photo. 1.

[2] The Treasury had granted sums to the Army and to the R.A.F. for immediate use; beyond these amounts their method was to give sanction to projects in principle and then to subject the various items to scrutiny in detail. Final approval was consequently given piecemeal.

G

Even so this large programme did not represent by any means the whole problem. The installations had not only to be built, but to be manned in such a way as to function reliably in all conditions. Egypt could provide ample unskilled labour, but a strong framework of trained and disciplined units would clearly be necessary. Of these base and lines-of-communication units there were practically none, owing to the general shortage and the low priority given to the Middle East. The base installations in Egypt in 1939 were about adequate for the existing forces and no more. Later, when the Middle East suddenly became the centre of activity, there was a pressing need to make good these deficiencies, and this came into violent conflict with the urge to build up the fighting troops. Thus began a long, and at times violent, tug-of-war between the Teeth and the Tail.

The outlying base at Basra presented a special problem. The first troops to land would come from India, and would have to be maintained from there. But if the force became involved in major operations it was to be under General Wavell's command, and therefore the administrative control at Basra should be exercised by General Headquarters Middle East. As a working arrangement, therefore, the detailed planning for the lay-out at Basra (Shaibah) was begun by India on a basis agreed with Middle East.

A further question concerning Iraq was that of the overland route between Haifa and Baghdad. In September 1939 General Wavell reported that the road seemed to him to be reasonably satisfactory as a reinforcement route—east to west—although there were some particularly bad stretches in Iraq which would be impassable for several days in bad weather. He regarded this situation as unacceptable because the road might be wanted at short notice for military movement from west to east; if, for instance, the garrison at Habbaniya were threatened by revolt. (This is precisely what happened in May 1941.) Moreover, if the Air Force made extensive use of their aircraft depot at Habbaniya, they would require the road to be fit for regular traffic. By arrangement with the Government of Iraq (who would not agree to bear a portion of the cost) work on this portion was begun under British supervision in May 1940, and by the end of the year it was ready except for winter use.

Yet another administrative commitment arose over the 'Jungle' forces. Detailed plans had to be made for organizing, moving, and maintaining them, treating the Middle East for this purpose as the base from which advanced bases would have to be thrown off as necessary. To operate the advanced bases and the often primitive lines of communication would require many administrative units, the lack of which has already been referred to. Some of the projects were pursued beyond the planning stage: for instance, technicians and construction parties and plant, all badly wanted elsewhere, were sent to Gallipoli and Anatolia for work on anti-malarial measures, jetties, roads, and airfields.

Yet all this time there remained the possibility that it was Italy with whom the first clash would occur; therefore there could be no relaxation of the efforts to improve the defensive arrangements— many of them administrative—in Kenya, British Somaliland, and the Sudan. As a general precaution, and particularly on behalf of the Royal Air Force in the Sudan, it was thought wise to develop the Mombasa—Nile Valley route to a capacity of 300 tons a day. But the fact remained that the first direct threat to the security of the main Middle East bases—naval, army, and air—would probably be from Libya, and this issue was likely to be decided in the Western Desert. Unfortunately the position here was most unsatisfactory, for what was administratively possible fell a long way short of what was tactically desirable.

The problem of supply has naturally loomed very large in every campaign conducted in undeveloped countries, but as a cavalry officer who took part in Lord Kitchener's Nile campaign wrote in 1899: 'Victory is the beautiful, bright-coloured flower. Transport is the stem without which it could never have blossomed. Yet even the military student, in his zeal to master the fascinating combinations of the actual conflict, often forgets the far more intricate complications of supply.'[1] Forty years on—to 1939—and almost all the army's horses had been replaced by internal combustion engines; its equipment had become far more elaborate and its weapons more varied and powerful. Mechanized forces had now the ability to strike far and strike hard, if only they could be kept provided with the means to live, move, and fight. But in each of these respects the problems of administration had become more complex than ever; and nowhere more so than in the Western Desert. In one way or another they seldom failed to give cause for anxiety to commanders on both sides. As far as the British were concerned in 1939 the most serious feature of the situation was the lack of motor transport.

At the outbreak of war there were three channels of supply from the Delta to the advanced base at Matruh: the railway, the road, and the sea. The railway had been hurriedly completed, as a single line, during the emergency caused by the Italian invasion of Ethiopia. Since then the traffic capacity and the railhead facilities had been somewhat increased. Provision for water storage had been made at many points, but the water found along the coast was largely unfit for use in locomotives and it was necessary to allot one train in every eight to carry water for them. Work on a pipeline to deliver water

---

[1] Winston S. Churchill: *The River War.* (1899.) Vol. I, p. 276.

from Alexandria to points along the railway was therefore begun.

The scarcity of fresh water was, of course, a very serious matter. Scattered over the Western Desert were a number of large rock cisterns made for catching the rainfall, but their chief use was to store water brought by other means. Tube-wells were sunk in large numbers, but the water from them was often too saline. The principal sources in 1939 were the Roman aqueducts at Matruh and Baggush. These were horizontal passages, or adits, tunnelled into a layer of comparatively sweet water only a few feet above sea level. Attempts to increase the yield by enlarging the passages or by pumping at a higher rate were apt to do more harm than good, as the salinity would increase and the aqueduct would have to be rested to recover.[1] Nevertheless the yield at Matruh was appreciably increased, and was supplemented by water-boats from Alexandria and by distillation plant on shore. None of these devices, however, altered the fact that water had to be strictly rationed, and transported by vehicles over considerable distances.

The vehicle situation in the autumn of 1939 was the cause of much concern. In the first place, the total number of available load-carriers was quite unequal to the heavy demands, even after full use had been made of hirings. Every military unit in Egypt and Palestine was short of some of its authorized vehicles, but efforts had first to be concentrated upon trying to provide the Armoured Division with an improvised rearward link or 'second line' of transport. The other difficulty was that, although any wheeled vehicle could use the coastal road between Alexandria and Matruh, none that was not desert-worthy could safely leave it.

This desert-worthiness was to some extent a relative condition, but in general it required a high engine clearance above ground; a large ratio of power to weight; convenient gear ratios; strong springs; large low-pressure tyres; and a condensing arrangement to conserve the cooling water. Even after Egypt and Palestine had been combed for desert-worthy vehicles the Armoured Division was some 200 load-carriers short. Extra mileage was thus thrown on the tracked (fighting) vehicles, adding to their wear and tear, already a matter of great concern owing to the lack of maintenance units. The result was that the mobile troops in the Western Desert were tethered to their railhead by a very short administrative rope. Thus they were placed at a disadvantage tactically, which was one of the reasons why it might not prove practicable to hold Matruh against a determined attack.

---

[1] Outside the Nile basin all the subsoil water is more or less saline. The presence of common salt in moderation may actually have been beneficial, since the health of troops in the desert was generally good. It probably reduced the incidence of heat exhaustion. Other salts had other effects.

Throughout the early months of 1940 great efforts were made to improve the situation. Desert-worthy vehicles of the newly-arrived 1st Cavalry Division and transport units of the 4th Indian Division were lent to the Armoured Division. Some vehicles that had been in reserve were manned by newly recruited Jews, Arabs, Maltese, and Cypriots. The capacity of the workshops to deal with overhauls had been increased. Stocks of spare parts had grown. A motor ambulance convoy and a water-tank company had been raised. The road between Matruh and Sidi Barrani had been improved. By the summer of 1940 the 7th Armoured Division, although still deficient of over 100 vehicles, was able to support the operations of its foremost troops right up to the Cyrenaican frontier—a distance from railhead of 140 miles as the crow flies.

At the outbreak of the war in September 1939 there were only five permanent airfields in Egypt, three in Palestine, two in Iraq, two in Malta, one in the Sudan, two at Aden and one in Kenya, none of which would accommodate more than one squadron. With the exception of one airfield in Egypt and another in Palestine which had runways, all were unsuitable for the operation of modern bombers and fighters. In Egypt there were also a number of desert airfields as far west as Matruh and southwards to Luxor and Wadi Halfa. Living quarters were usually tents, while cook houses and dining rooms were built of prefabricated sectional hutting, and the technical accommodation was in a similarly constructed type of hangar. In Palestine there were some 40 prepared emergency landing grounds, without accommodation, scattered throughout the country. Facilities also existed at the civil airports of Lydda and Haifa which were subsequently taken over and developed for operational purposes.

By the terms of the Anglo-Egyptian Treaty of 1936 new airfields for the Royal Air Force were to be built by the Egyptian Government in the Canal Zone. Three years later discussions with the Egyptian Government were still going on, and practically the only work the Egyptians had done was on the important strategic roads in the Canal Zone. There was now no more time to waste, and the responsibility for building the new airfields was transferred to the British. Work was started immediately on six new stations near the Canal. Each airfield was designed to take two heavy bomber squadrons, with four runways and the normal dispersal points and protective pens for aircraft. In Palestine the construction of a new two-bomber station at Aqir (near Lydda) had begun in July 1939. Other work involved in airfield construction was to provide accommodation for men and technical stores; administrative buildings; sick quarters; bomb and fuel installations; mechanical and electrical installations; airfield lighting and control systems; wireless systems; water supply; drainage; and approach roads.

Temporary landing strips could be made almost anywhere in the desert with very little work. In most places the natural ground provided a satisfactory foundation for permanent runways also. It was decided not to make these of concrete, for which the materials, plant, and experienced labour were not readily available, but to use instead the comparatively quick process of mix-in-place with bitumen. Runways of this type stood up satisfactorily to intense traffic during the whole campaign with very little maintenance. Some of the airfields in Palestine and the Sudan had to be constructed on cotton soil, which becomes like glue when wet and opens up in deep cracks when dry; here it was necessary to lay a thick soling of stone below the bitumen surface of the runways.[1]

At Malta the only air establishments existing before the war were the seaplane base and engineering workshops and two small grassed airfields. One of these airfields was used mainly by the Fleet Air Arm and the other by Italian civil air lines. Work on a third airfield was begun in October 1939, and completed with four runways by May 1940. But apart from the building of certain underground installations for aviation fuel, bombs, and wireless equipment, nothing was done to plan or provide for the accommodation of further units, or to build an aircraft depot. When aircraft began to operate from Malta in June 1940, the workshops had to be gradually expanded in no properly planned manner into a parent repair and equipment depot to cope with many different types of aircraft and engines. These included Flying-Boats, Swordfish, Walrus, Magisters, Queen Bees, Gladiators, Hurricanes, Hudsons, Glenn Martins, Wellingtons, Blenheims and Fulmars. It says much for this unit that in spite of the shortage of skilled men and most types of spare parts it was able to keep aircraft flying by improvisation and by manufacturing spare parts from whatever materials could be obtained locally.

The policy in force in September 1939 was for each squadron in the Middle East to be responsible as far as possible for maintaining its own aircraft, work beyond its capacity being sent back to the depot at Aboukir. Although this depot had been in existence since the First World War its expansion had not kept pace with the growing needs of the Command. Its position rendered it vulnerable to air and sea attack; its workshop layout did not meet modern requirements; and its airfield was unsuitable for the latest types of aircraft. Plans

---

[1] In 1939 the heaviest bomber in the Service—the Wellington—had an all-up weight of 30,000 lb. and a wing span of 86 feet. With the introduction of heavier aircraft such as the Lancaster, Liberator, and Fortress, with their higher tyre pressures, it became necessary to strengthen and lengthen some of the runways, and modify hangars and handling facilities.

had therefore been made to build an up-to-date depot at Geneifa under the terms of the Anglo-Egyptian Treaty, but apart from some work on the airfield very little had been done by September 1939. Long discussions followed between the Air Ministry and Headquarters Middle East as to whether it would be better to continue with the Geneifa depot and accept the long delay before it was ready, or to arrange for workshop and other facilities at certain of the stations to be extended—a quicker but an unsatisfactory and inefficient alternative. In spite of the pressing need for increased maintenance facilities it was not until June 1940 that a decision was reached, which was a compromise between the two alternatives; but by this time an increase in the strength of the Royal Air Force in the Middle East was being planned, calling for yet another expansion of the maintenance facilities.

The visit of Air Vice-Marshal Maund to the United Kingdom in January 1940 was a timely one, coinciding as it did with the Cabinet's decision to increase the strength of the air forces in the Middle East. His visit convinced the Air Ministry, when other means had failed, that there was a serious lack of men and equipment in the Middle East, and that urgent action must be taken if the Command was to be in a fit state either to send an expedition to Turkey or to fight Italy. On examination it was found that most of the deficiencies could be met from existing stocks at home; many items in fact could be sent out immediately without upsetting the priorities governing supplies to units in the United Kingdom and France. Other items, particularly aircraft operational equipment, of which there was a shortage everywhere, would have to be divided among units in Great Britain, France, and the Middle East. The main causes of the shortage of men were the ban which had been placed immediately war broke out on sending any airmen overseas, and the fact that the Middle East Command still remained, for the most part, on peace establishments. Indeed, for some of the new administrative units no establishments at all had been authorized. With the removal of the ban on trooping and the issue of war establishments, a start was made to meet the more serious deficiencies, but the situation after Dunkirk caused a further hold-up in the despatch overseas of certain classes of skilled tradesmen.

The Cabinet's decisions on air force policy had far-reaching administrative implications. First there was the need to increase the mobility of existing squadrons to enable them to operate from Turkey or Greece by the spring of 1940. This was largely a matter of motor transport. The situation in 1939 was better than it had been during the 1938 emergency, when the moves of squadrons to their war stations had been greatly delayed by the shortage of vehicles, but it was not yet satisfactory. Steps were therefore taken to send out urgently from the United Kingdom enough additional men and vehicles to meet the barest essential needs.

The decision to increase the strength of the air forces in the Middle East involved the formation of one new heavy bomber squadron, seven new fighter squadrons, and one or more new army co-operation squadrons, depending upon the strength and dispositions of the army. It entailed also the rearming of the two bomber transport squadrons and one medium bomber squadron with heavy bomber aircraft. Most of these squadrons were to be based on airfields under construction in Egypt, but additional airfields would be required west of the Delta for the new fighter squadrons. In Palestine, in the Sudan, and at Aden additional airfields would be required.

For the reception of the reinforcing group of twelve heavy bomber squadrons detailed plans could not be made, as it was impossible to say where they might, in the event, be sent. They might operate from Egypt or Palestine; from Tunisia or Turkey; or even from Kenya. To prepare realistically for these possibilities would have meant the building of some 50 new airfields—a project obviously quite out of the question. The only practical solution would be to provide airfield equipment, mechanical transport (including specialist vehicles), aircraft spares, and reserves of bombs, and store them at convenient places within the theatre ready for immediate use should the need arise.

Until 1939 the policy had been to hold reserve stocks to last about two months at the estimated war time rates of consumption. During 1939 financial approval was obtained for raising this to three months, in addition to a working margin. As it normally took about a year in peace time to obtain delivery of major items of equipment, the new programme was very incomplete when the war with Germany began. Moreover, new types of aircraft were being introduced into the Middle East for which there had been no time to build up any reserve stocks at all. The war with Germany resulted in an embargo on the despatch of any items required by the Royal Air Force at home or by the Air Component in France. Generally speaking, in September 1939, the aircraft reserves in the Middle East were about 140% of the first line strength, and the reserves of explosives and aviation fuel were equal to about three months estimated requirement.

Finally there were the preparations for the squadrons intended for maritime operations. It had been agreed with the Admiralty that four general reconnaissance squadrons should be based in the Central Mediterranean (at Malta, with alternative sites in Tunisia over which discussions with the French were in progress) and two squadrons at the Eastern end (at Alexandria and Haifa). The provision of these squadrons would entail some increase in airfield and slipway facilities, in addition to which the complements of two aircraft carriers, amounting to six Fleet Air Arm squadrons, would require airfield and maintenance facilities ashore.

The proposal to increase the number of flying units had other implications than the development of airfields. It meant the formation of a fighter group, three wing headquarters, and at least two operational training units, together with many new ancillaries such as maintenance and equipment units, ammunition depots and parks, meteorological stations, and an additional communication squadron. It also involved the provision of more storage capacity for bulk fuel. Not that there was as yet any prospect of the additional squadrons becoming available, and the most that could be done to implement the Cabinet's policy was to put in hand whatever preparations were possible without drawing upon the resources of the United Kingdom or of the western front. By the time that Italy entered the war and France collapsed, this had not amounted to very much.

But even the operation of the existing squadrons had already stretched the maintenance organization to its utmost. In the Western Desert, in particular, the conditions gave rise to many special problems. For example, there was no air filter that would satisfactorily resist the all-pervading sand and dust, with the result that day-to-day serviceability was seriously affected, while the change to coarse pitch of the variable-pitch air screw was often made impracticable. Instruments, too, were so badly affected that it was necessary to form a special mobile section to service the instruments in the squadron aircraft. Another serious inconvenience was the blowing-out and cracking of the perspex panels of the Blenheim aircraft, due to distortion from the heat of the sun. All these difficulties, and many others, involved so much additional maintenance work that it was found necessary, soon after the war began, to form an advanced repair and salvage section in the Western Desert and to augment the maintenance organization in the Canal Zone.

There is no doubt that more use might have been made of the quiet period before Italy entered the war to develop local resources and build up a stronger repair organization. There were in Egypt many hundreds of civilians with some engineering experience, and a great many more who were capable of being trained as mechanics; as the war went on full use was made of them. Later, too, many garages and small engineering works were brought into the maintenance organization and large numbers of tradesmen were thereby released to meet deficiencies in skilled men elsewhere. But it was not generally realized at the time what an immense amount of maintenance was going to be required, nor how elaborate would the local organization have to be in order to keep a high proportion of aircraft serviceable in a theatre where the conditions were so difficult and which was so distant from the United Kingdom and all its resources. And, as with the Army, it was to prove easier to obtain recognition of weaknesses in the Teeth than in the Tail.

The fact that Malta might no longer be available as a fleet base during a war with Italy presented the Royal Navy with a new problem. In previous wars ships had been able to proceed to properly equipped and protected bases for repairs and docking. From these bases stores, victuals, and ammunition had been supplied to vessels, and it had not been difficult to arrange for any unit to be within reasonable reach of an established base. Thus the Navy was not accustomed to dealing with administrative problems on a large scale, and as the naval supply services—unlike those of the Army—were almost entirely in the hands of civilians, few naval officers had ever been directly concerned with such matters. But a fleet in the Mediterranean, deprived of the use of Malta and possibly not in control of the passage through the central basin, would be called upon to operate without a fully established base. The only port in the Eastern Mediterranean that could berth a fleet of moderate size was Alexandria, where many commercial facilities existed. It would have to serve both as an operational and a main base; it had the disadvantage of being over 800 miles from the Italian mainland; and, not being land-enclosed, was difficult to protect from seaward.

Up to the time of Munich it was believed that sufficient stores of all kinds and ammunition could be carried afloat in special supply ships which would themselves be able to replenish at Malta, and, as the ports of Egypt would be at the disposal of the Royal Navy in the event of an apprehended international emergency, no undue concern was felt on this score. So far as victualling stores were concerned, it had been found during the Ethiopian crisis that shore facilities were important, but those that had been temporarily acquired on a small scale at Port Said, and to an even lesser extent at Haifa and Alexandria, had been given up in 1936.

· There remained the questions of oil fuel supply, of repairs, and, above all, of docking. Adequate storage of oil fuel ashore was of course desirable. At Port Said the Shell Company's storage tanks were suitably situated and were sufficient to meet the requirements of ships there; but at Alexandria the oil tanks were so close to the quayside that, if they received bomb damage, their contents would spill over into the harbour where they might cause a conflagration. It was therefore planned to keep at least 25,000 tons of furnace oil stored afloat and dispersed in tankers; this arrangement would not be entirely satisfactory, for apart from the danger of having so much oil fuel in the harbour it was wasteful in tanker tonnage. These tankers would replenish at Haifa where there was first class storage accommodation, of which the Admiralty had decided as early as September 1938 to take up 60,000 tons, to be filled with oil fuel shipped from the Abadan refinery. They considered that the desert pipeline could not be relied on in time of war. Besides, the oil which it delivered was crude, and the Haifa refinery was unlikely to be working before the middle of 1940. There was the possibility of course that the enemy would succeed in blocking the Canal and would menace the route through the Red Sea, but Admiral Cunningham did not expect that the Canal would be closed for any appreciable period and there was every confidence that, after a few weeks, the Navy could establish command of the Red Sea. Nevertheless, it was clearly wise to concentrate as much oil as possible in the Eastern Mediterranean in case the Canal should be closed.

To meet the normal requirements for repairs the repair ship H.M.S. *Resource* was to be berthed in Alexandria harbour. In addition there would be repair and depot ships for destroyers and submarines. But there still remained the problem of docking, for in the Eastern Mediterranean there was only one graving dock capable of taking warships up to a 6-inch cruiser of the *Arethusa* class. This was the Gabbary graving dock, owned and operated by the Egyptian Ports and Lights Administration but later absorbed into Admiralty dockyard control. This question of docking was of great importance, not only for repairs, but also for the cleaning of ships' bottoms, for the growth that was known to accumulate in Alexandria harbour would so reduce the speed of our ships as to give the Italians a still greater advantage in this respect. As far back as 1937 proposals had been accepted by the Egyptian Government for the construction of a 1,000 ft long graving dock, together with other improvements such as the extension of certain breakwaters and quays, dredging in the harbour, and the deepening of the Great Pass Channel from 34 to 40 feet; this was required to enable capital ships to return to harbour even if their draft were increased by damage received in action. But beyond a certain amount of dredging in the harbour nothing was done.[1]

This, then, was the position during the Munich crisis of 1938. It emphasized the necessity for the development of naval base facilities in the Eastern Mediterranean and prompted the Commander-in-Chief, Admiral Sir Dudley Pound, to forward a number of proposals for making good the glaring deficiencies which the crisis had brought to light. By March 1939 the most pressing question was still the docking of ships, and the Admiralty suggested that the Malta floating dock, which was capable of accommodating the most modern battleship, should be transferred to Alexandria. To this the

---

[1] Even by the middle of 1944 the Great Pass had only been dredged to a minimum depth of 36 feet.

Commander-in-Chief raised the strongest objections, pointing out the disadvantages of losing the facilities of a floating dock at Malta and rejecting the idea of surrendering altogether the use of Malta as a base.[1] In deference to his wishes the Admiralty decided to move the Portsmouth floating dock to Alexandria; after a passage causing no little anxiety it arrived only three weeks before the outbreak of war with Germany. This dock (A.F.D.5) had been built in 1912 and during the 1914–18 war had served the Grand Fleet in Scottish waters. It was later moved to Portsmouth, where the greatest care had been taken to preserve the life of its boilers, generators and pumps. On arrival at Alexandria the boilers had to be steamed and the machinery run continuously throughout the whole period of the war, and at no time was it necessary to modify the docking programme on account of mechanical defects. But the fact that it was only capable of taking vessels up to 31,500 tons, which included *Queen Elizabeth* and *Royal Sovereign* Class battleships in a specially lightened condition but not any more modern battleship, was to impose definite limitations on the composition of the Eastern Mediterranean Fleet.

It was realized that to provide naval stores and victuals by means of supply ships replenishing at Malta might not be possible during a war with Italy. Accordingly, in January 1939, store depots, regarded as extensions of the Malta Yard, were set up at Alexandria and Port Said. By the outbreak of war the main depot had spread to cover nearly three acres, which eventually became more than thirty, and the difficulty was to find suitable buildings. The excellent dockside sheds were soon required for the transit handling of the great volume of war material for all three Services. The Navy had to adapt such premises as cotton warehouses, an old church, and a disused racehorse stable, and accept the inconvenience and delay, not to mention the security difficulty, of having its stores scattered over a wide area. This led to a requirement for further transport, which the Army helped to provide and operate.

After Munich a small reserve victualling depot was established at Alexandria; it was brought into use when the fleet concentrated there after the Italian invasion of Albania. Since then the Army had held a reserve of frozen meat for naval requirements, and arrangements had been made for its replenishment by frozen meat ships from Colombo. The total naval ration strength at Alexandria in October 1939, ashore and afloat, was about 12,000.

If the Fleet had become involved in hostilities in 1935 it would

---

[1] The Malta floating dock was damaged in some of the first air raids and was finally put out of action and sunk on 21st June 1940.

have been seriously handicapped by the shortage of reserve ammunition. To remedy this situation the Admiralty requisitioned a number of merchant vessels to act as both Armament Store Carriers (ASC) and Armament Supply Issuing Ships (ASIS) and sent them to the Eastern Mediterranean early in August 1939. A scheme was prepared and a site chosen for a naval armament depot ashore near Dekheila, where natural cover existed in caves from which stone had been quarried for over 3,000 years. On the outbreak of war this scheme was still in the planning stage and it was decided that, initially at least, all reserve ammunition should be stored afloat. As it was clearly undesirable for it all to be concentrated in Alexandria harbour, three ASIS were berthed in the Great Bitter Lakes. A further dispersal was arranged in Alexandria harbour by the use of a number of cotton lighters, of which eventually 84 were taken up and moored in a specially protected area. Apart from the additional security, this arrangement provided a ready means of replenishing ships as they entered harbour; while they were berthing, tugs would bring the lighters alongside. Armament offices and non-explosive stores were established on Mahmoudieh Quay.

Thus, by September 1939, action was well in hand to create naval base facilities at Alexandria. But as the days passed and an uneasy peace settled over the Mediterranean, progress was arrested. Ships, including all the repair and depot ships, left the Mediterranean station for active operations in the war against Germany. Under orders from the Admiralty the Commander-in-Chief transferred his flag ashore at Malta on 1st November. Here, in addition to the operational staff, he was followed by the large proportion of the stores, armament, and victualling staff who had been drafted to build up the Alexandria base. Stores started filtering back to Malta, where the ASIS also off-loaded a quantity of their ammunition. The ASC were paid off for employment on more general service. The Bitter Lakes organization was closed down, and early in 1940 the special ammunition lighters at Alexandria were returned to their owners. Only victualling stores continued to be built up, but at a very slow rate.

Concerned at the situation, Admiral Cunningham appealed to the Admiralty in January for stores, ammunition, and other war material to be maintained in the Mediterranean at a level that would suffice for a considerable fleet. The Admiralty agreed, but it was not until May, when Italy's entry into the war seemed imminent and the fleet once again began to concentrate in the Eastern Mediterranean, that activities were resumed. Stores of all kinds were transferred from Malta, and labour was recruited locally and trained for specialized duties. Armament Stores Carriers and Issuing Ships reappeared, embarked their outfits at Malta, and took up their berths in the Eastern Mediterranean. By June 1940 the situation was substantially the same as it had been in September 1939, with one important difference. Previously the fleet had included four 8-inch cruisers and only three 6-inch. Now there were eight 6-inch cruisers and none of the larger type. This meant a shortage of 6-inch reserve ammunition, which was temporarily relieved in July by taking advantage of H.M.S. *Liverpool's* trip to Aden with 2nd Bn The Black Watch to bring back to the Mediterranean much of the reserve 6-inch ammunition held there for the East Indies Station.

No further progress had been made with the naval armament depot near Dekheila and it was still the policy for ammunition reserves to be stored afloat. The danger of this was soon emphasized when an ASC was hit by a bomb in Alexandria harbour and set on fire. Fortunately the carrier was empty at the time. On the other hand Egypt was liable to invasion and plans had even to be made for a temporary withdrawal of the Fleet from Alexandria; it was therefore not considered opportune to disperse naval ammunition ashore where it might be overrun by the enemy and lost. Some depth charges were, however, stored at Aboukir, and spare torpedoes, eventually amounting to several hundreds, were dispersed ashore at Alexandria and Port Said.

Airfields from which naval aircraft could operate and to which carrier aircraft could be flown on their parent ship's return to harbour were an essential requirement of a fleet base. At Alexandria this was particularly important because, in the early days, the Fleet Air Arm fighters provided a valuable contribution to the air defence. For this purpose the Egyptian air station at Dekheila had been taken over by the Royal Navy and, as H.M.S. *Grebe*, provided accommodation for four naval air squadrons. Further facilities were soon needed, and in August 1940 the construction began at Lake Mariut (Alexandria) of an airfield to take six disembarked squadrons, but it was not ready until the middle of 1941. The Air Officer Commanding-in-Chief undertook the provision of a separate reserve, storage, and repair station for the Fleet Air Arm at Fayid (H.M.S. *Phoenix*) in the Canal area, and, in addition, a special depot to meet the growing demands for naval aircraft stores was established in the Jebel Massara, near Tura.

It soon became clear that, for various reasons, the *Resource* was unable to meet all the requirements of a dockyard, and that a repair organization would have to be established ashore. Starting with an office on Mahmoudieh Quay, an organization was built up which eventually employed a labour force of 2,500. But, although the local unskilled labour was plentiful and efficient, the lack of skilled labour, which was in such demand at home and so rare in Egypt, was a serious handicap, and the fact that British, Maltese, and local employees all received different rates of pay was not conducive to smooth working.[1] But the most serious difficulties arose from shortage of plant and machine tools. There were, of course, a number of private firms in Alexandria, and they were used to the full, but their ship-repairing facilities were poor, their machinery was obsolete and in bad condition, and their ability to carry out structural repairs was limited.[2] But by improvisation and with the use of machine tools provided by the Army, supplemented later by captures from the enemy, difficulties were largely overcome, so that vessels could be taken in hand for conversions, refits, and repair of damage received in action.

The Gun Mounting Depot was another important branch of dockyard activity which grew to an unexpected extent. The maintenance of the armament and fire-control instruments of ships demanded no little ingenuity, especially in the early days; for example, if new gun-barrels were not available, barrels had to be taken from damaged ships. Much was done, too, to improve the inadequate anti-aircraft armament in H.M. ships, before the Oerlikon guns became available, by mounting Italian guns captured by the Army.

It was, of course, unfortunate that so much had to be concentrated at Alexandria, but it was only possible for minor ports, such as Haifa and Port Said, to relieve this congestion in some small degree. A few destroyers and submarines could be taken in hand for boiler cleaning and refit at Port Said, but it was not until very much later that facilities, mostly supplied by the Army, were available at Haifa for this purpose. The oil refinery at Haifa began production in June 1940, and soon became the principal source for the supply of oil fuel to the fleet, but it was liable to air attack from the Dodecanese, and an air raid in July destroyed one tank and damaged others. The Commander-in-Chief represented to the Admiralty that with only one heavy anti-aircraft battery and no fighter aircraft or up-to-date warning system it would only be a matter of time before the refinery was put out of action. Fortunately the Italians did not persist with their attacks. Haifa had also been earmarked as the principal mine depot for the fleet, and this—with the Army's help —it eventually became. But rather than store mines in such a vulnerable spot the Commander-in-Chief decided to keep his mine

---

[1] In the United Kingdom it was impossible to obtain skilled volunteers for Alexandria and, without a special Act of Parliament, none but established men—nearly all of whom were over 50 and therefore too old—could be compelled to go. Eventually a special category of rating, known as Special Repair Rating (D) was instituted consisting of men called up for dockyard work and put into naval uniforms. But this scheme was not approved until June 1942 and it was of no help in the early development of Alexandria.

[2] Over 20,000 job contracts were placed with them between 1939–45.

carriers in the Canal area until Haifa should be reasonably safe from air attack.

Broadly speaking, then, in spite of some satisfactory features, there was much in the base situation to cause Admiral Cunningham grave concern. There seemed little likelihood that the deepening of the Great Pass, for which he had pressed, would ever be achieved; the repair organization was a sketchy improvisation; the lack of an adequate reserve of 6-inch and anti-aircraft ammunition was a constant anxiety. Worse still, the defences of Alexandria, especially against air attack, inspired little confidence. Yet upon the safety of the floating dock virtually depended the ability of the fleet to operate; if the dock was destroyed the effect upon our whole position in the Middle East would be incalculable. That these difficulties and dangers were successfully overcome was due to ingenuity and enterprise in making full use of the facilities available, to good luck, to the ready co-operation of Egyptian officials at Alexandria, animated by the Director-General of the Ports and Lights Administration (a retired Rear-Admiral, Sir Gerard Wells), and to the help of the other Services.

# CHAPTER V

# ITALIAN HOSTILITY
# INCREASES
## (March - June 1940)

*See Chronology on page* 100

ON 10TH MARCH 1940 the Reich Foreign Minister, von Ribbentrop, arrived in Rome, apparently to inform Mussolini of Germany's future plans. His visit was followed on the 18th by a meeting at the Brenner Pass between the two dictators themselves. The Duce seems to have been much impressed and to have come away convinced of Germany's military supremacy, though Count Ciano assured the British Ambassador a few days later that there would be no change in Italy's foreign policy. The reports reaching London at the time were somewhat conflicting, but the general inference was that Mussolini would not initiate any violent action unless the Germans first gained a military success. It is true that there had been some calling-up of Italian reservists; that the army in Libya was being strengthened; and that Italian propaganda was becoming increasingly anti-British in tone. As against this, the Italian people were, on the whole, opposed to war, and, although the Duce was strong enough to impose his will in the last resort, he was so well aware of his country's weaknesses and un-readiness that he would be unlikely to bring her in deliberately—except to join the winning side.

In September 1939 the Allies had found themselves ill-prepared to undertake a war against Germany; now, seven months later, they were still dangerously short of many of their essential require-ments for defence, let alone those that would be needed for major offensive operations. Yet if the Germans, with or without Russian help, were to extend the war to the Balkans, the Allies would want to move to the help of Turkey. But in the Middle East, as General Wavell had pointed out, British preparations for war were very far from complete, partly because of the delays in meeting his demands for men and material, and partly because of the ban on taking any action that might annoy the Italians. At the same time the air forces were quite inadequate to meet serious and prolonged air attacks and could not provide the normal support expected for land and sea operations. It was therefore clear that the Allies' difficulties would be greatly increased by Italian intervention.

This naturally led to further consideration in London of the attitude that ought now to be adopted towards Italy. Was it wise to adhere to the policy of non-provocation? If the Duce was really awaiting a suitable moment to intervene, would it not be better to speak to him in a language easily understood by dictators, and confront him with a show of force? This might have the effect of making him hesitate, but on the other hand it might provoke him into unreasonable action, and the danger was that this might occur before we were ourselves in a satisfactory position to meet the consequences.

The deterrent steps that could be taken on land did not amount to very much, being confined to a few internal movements and activities indicating a general closing up towards the frontiers of Cyrenaica and Italian East Africa. Two or three air force squadrons could be set in motion towards Egypt and Palestine from Kenya and the Far East. By far the most effective action open to us would be to reconstitute a strong naval force in the Eastern Mediterranean and Red Sea. This would threaten Italy's communications with her African empire and the Black Sea trade routes, and would help to stiffen the attitude of Egypt, Turkey, and the Levant States towards Italy. Moreover it would result in adequate naval forces being in position should Mussolini suddenly decide to take the plunge. Finally, in order to play upon his fear that the war might be carried into his own country, it should be easy to arrange for information to reach Italy that preparations were being made to bomb the industrial areas of Northern Italy from airfields in the south of France. For most of these suggested measures French acquiescence and collaboration would of course be essential.

While the question of policy was being considered by the Allied Governments, some preliminary steps were taken. On 27th March the Admiralty ordered certain depot and repair ships to sail for Alexandria and ten submarines to leave the China and East Indies Stations for the Mediterranean. Naval Commanders-in-Chief were told that it might be necessary to reassemble a large force at short notice in the Eastern Mediterranean. India was warned that she might be asked to send two bomber squadrons to the Middle East. However on 9th April the Commanders-in-Chief in the Middle East were informed that, although relations with Italy had become more uncertain, it was felt that no important moves by them were necessary at the moment.

On this very day the German invasion of Norway and Denmark began. The Royal Navy became at once heavily committed in northern waters and was now in no position to spare forces for the

Mediterranean. In the circumstances it was decided to approach the French, who had strong forces already concentrated in the western basin, with a view to their assuming responsibility for the whole of the Mediterranean. With the German operations making successful progress it was inevitable that the Duce should become restive. Would he decide that this was the moment to enter the war? It seems that he was only restrained on 17th April by the emphasis laid by his military advisers, especially Marshal Badoglio, on the unpreparedness of the army and the general lack of armaments. He made a short public speech on 21st April from the balcony of the Palazzo Venezia with 'work and weapons' as its theme, and told an assembly of Fascist officials in the course of a tirade against the blockade that Italy must be ready to take part in the events of which she was at present a spectator. Reports reaching the Allies at the time indicated that the Italians might be contemplating an attack, possibly on Greece, but much more probably on Yugoslavia. The Allied Governments were thus faced with another difficulty. They had given no guarantee to Yugoslavia, but if she were invaded and they took no action the result would probably be a collapse of all Allied political influence in south-east Europe. The Balkan States, and possibly even Turkey, might be driven to come to an understanding with Germany and Italy as quickly as they could.

On 23rd April the Allied Governments re-affirmed that it was still their policy not to provoke Italy but that they must be ready to act if she became an aggressor. They gave further consideration to the implications of Italian aggression, but on the Yugoslavian issue they decided not to commit themselves in advance. On 29th April the War Cabinet agreed to a number of precautionary measures. All British merchant ships sailing to or from the Indian Ocean, other than mail steamers, were routed round the Cape. One regular British battalion was to go from France to Gibraltar, and subject to the concurrence of the Indian Government two bomber squadrons were to be sent from India to Egypt, and one Indian battalion to Aden. The defences of Alexandria, Haifa, Malta and Gibraltar were to be manned. The 7th Armoured Division was to move unobtrusively into the Western Desert. The transfer to Kenya of two brigade groups of the Royal West African Frontier Force had already been approved, and the South African Government had agreed to send a brigade and an air contingent, but the ships for these moves were not yet available. One battalion of the Northern Rhodesia Regiment was to move from Kenya to British Somaliland.

The French were informed of these measures and were asked to take similar action. British and French naval Commanders-in-Chief were keeping in close touch with each other, but it was not necessary to pursue the suggestion that the French should assume naval responsibility for the whole Mediterranean, since the operations of the past three weeks in northern waters had resulted in such serious losses to the German Fleet that it was now possible for the Royal Navy to release considerable forces for the Eastern Mediterranean. On 3rd May the battleships *Royal Sovereign* and *Malaya* arrived from convoy duties in the Atlantic, to be followed towards the end of the month by the *Ramillies* and the aircraft carrier *Eagle* from similar duties in the Indian Ocean. On 14th May the *Warspite*, fresh from operations at Narvik, re-hoisted the flag of Admiral Cunningham which had been temporarily worn by the *Malaya*. Of the cruisers assembling in May and early June the *Orion* came from the American and West Indies Station, the *Neptune* from the South Atlantic, the *Gloucester* from the East Indies, H.M.A.S. *Sydney* from Australia, and the *Liverpool* from China. In addition, two anti-aircraft cruisers, destroyers, and minor war vessels came from the Home Fleet. Also under Admiral Cunningham's command was a French squadron, consisting of the battleship *Lorraine*, three 8-inch cruisers, one 6-inch cruiser, three destroyers, and six submarines. In the Red Sea a naval concentration to form what was known as the Red Sea Force, consisting of four cruisers, four destroyers and four sloops, followed by the necessary auxiliaries, assembled at Aden early in May.

A difficult problem now arose over the passage of convoys bound for Suez containing the second and third contingents of troops from Australia and New Zealand. The Dominion Governments were naturally extremely anxious lest hostilities with Italy should break out before their convoys had passed through the Red Sea. Their anxiety was fully shared by the Admiralty, and it was only after very careful consideration that the leading convoy was allowed to continue. It reached Suez safely on 17th May with about 7,000 Australian troops, the second brigade group of the 6th Australian Division. The next convoy left Fremantle on 12th May, but on the 15th the Admiralty decided, in consultation with the Dominion Governments, that its passage through the Red Sea would involve an unjustifiable risk. The convoy, carrying some 15,000 Australian and New Zealand troops, the second brigade group of the New Zealand Division, and the third of the 6th Australian Division, was therefore diverted round the Cape and reached the Clyde on 16th June. The arrival of this fine body of Dominion troops just as France collapsed was a welcome occurrence as far as the defence of Great Britain was concerned, but the Governments of Australia and New Zealand viewed with some dismay the splitting of their contingents between probable battle-fields as far apart as the United Kingdom and the Middle East, not merely on account of the administrative difficulties that would arise but because of their very natural desire to see their contingents take the field as complete Dominion formations.

The conference at Aleppo in March[1] had made it clear to the Commanders-in-Chief that before any further discussions could usefully be held with the Turks it was necessary to receive more information about the general Allied plans in the event of war with Italy. They wanted to know, for example, what were the plans for attacking Italy; whether it was the intention of the French to invade Libya from Tunisia; at what stage would operations be undertaken to neutralize or capture the Dodecanese, particularly Rhodes; and what additional forces might they expect to receive to meet their increasing commitments. These questions were put to the Chiefs of Staff on 9th April, and as this was the day on which the invasion of Denmark and Norway began it is not surprising that no conclusive answers were forthcoming. In fact it was not until the middle of May that the Commanders-in-Chief received a directive based on the views of the British and French High Commands. One point in it was quite clear: no resources could now be spared from France or the United Kingdom.

There was agreement that at the outset of war with Italy Allied major strategy would be generally defensive, with the objects of securing Allied territories, together with Egypt, Palestine, and Syria; of controlling the Straits of Gibraltar and the Suez Canal and the sea communications to French North Africa; and of maintaining the Red Sea route. Although defensive, this strategy would automatically cut Italy's communications with East Africa and the outer seas and would impose economic pressure on her. The French no longer intended to carry out a large-scale offensive from Tunisia in the early stages, and even local offensive operations would now be conditional on direct British air support, which was obviously not available.

Both High Commands recognized the strategical importance of Crete and agreed that provision should be made to deny it to the Italians. The only certain way of ensuring this would have been to send a small force to stiffen and support the Greek garrison, but this would have compromised the neutrality of Greece and might well have provoked Mussolini into declaring war. The only acceptable course was to hold a small force in readiness to sail for the island immediately it was learned that Italy had violated Greek territory or was on the point of doing so. It was agreed that this force should consist of French troops, transported from Syria in French men-of-war. Responsibility for the safe passage would rest upon Admiral

[1] See page 53.

Cunningham. Aircraft and guns for air defence would have to be provided by the British.

The defensive nature of the general strategy threw into relief the British proposals for bringing pressure to bear on Italy quickly, and it was hoped effectively, by air attacks on the concentration of war industry in the area Milan-Turin-Genoa. If carried out in sufficient strength this action might have important and far-reaching results and would probably cause the Italian High Command to bring back some of their air forces that might otherwise be employed elsewhere, and so relieve the pressure in the Mediterranean theatre. The ruthless and indiscriminate bombing in Holland by the *Luftwaffe*, beginning on 10th May, had caused the Allies to relax the restrictions which they had imposed on air bombardment. Accordingly all preparations were made for squadrons of the Royal Air Force, operating from airfields in the south of France, to attack this area immediately Italy entered the war. Fresh instructions were issued to Commanders-in-Chief on 4th June confining naval and air bombardment as before to military objectives, but interpreting this term as including such targets as shipyards, oil installations, factories, and other establishments engaged in the manufacture, assembly or repair of military material. As the intentional bombing of civilian populations as such was illegal, objectives were to be identified and reasonable care was to be taken to avoid undue loss of civil life in the vicinity of the target.[1]

It was clear from the directive that in the Aegean area the French High Command had much more ambitious ideas than the British. They had made proposals for occupying, subject to Greek consent, Milos and possibly also Salamis, Navarino, and Argostoli, not only to prevent the Italians from getting these key points, but also as a first step in the encirclement and subsequent reduction of the Dodecanese. The French were prepared to provide the necessary troops, which they estimated at three battalions, and to transport them in French cruisers, but again expected the British to provide the air and anti-aircraft cover. The French realized that if Italy were in the war there could be no question of sending a large expeditionary force to Salonika, but they were anxious to send something, and now proposed a token force of a few thousand men, mainly to demonstrate to the Greeks that the Allies were not deserting them. They accepted the fact that such a force could not be maintained in the orthodox manner, and were quite prepared to see their troops live on the country and fight under the same conditions as the Greek army. This was an entirely different project from the proposals discussed previously, but the Chiefs of Staff thought that militarily it was equally unsound. They recognized that it

---

[1] Cf. page 29.

would be mainly a French commitment, but the responsibility for transporting and landing the force in the face of an Italian air threat would fall upon the Commander-in-Chief, Mediterranean, and the French were counting once more upon the British to contribute aircraft and anti-aircraft guns.

In view of the heavy responsibility carried by the British for the defence of Egypt, the French had agreed to provide from Syria the initial land support for Thrace, which, until control of the Aegean had been secured, would be limited by the capacity of the Anatolian railway to about one division. They were again counting on the British to provide artillery, tanks and anti-tank units. A German thrust against Thrace, coupled with Italian hostility, constituted perhaps the greatest danger to which Allied interests in the Mediterranean were likely to be exposed, but without adequate air defence it was extremely doubtful whether the Turks would be able to maintain their positions or any Allied help arrive in time to be of use. The Commanders-in-Chief were accordingly urged to give special attention to the provision of air security for the Turkish front.

Finally there was the question of the Dodecanese. Under the military convention with Turkey the Allies were committed to assist with naval and air forces in the reduction of these islands. The French were anxious to do this as early as possible. The importance of having Turkey as an ally in a war with Italy needed no stressing. In particular, with Turkey on our side the Bosphorus would be open to us and closed to Italy, whose communications with the Black Sea would be cut. The French felt that the best way of making certain that the Turks would come in on our side would be to show our determination to reduce the Dodecanese at an early stage. Moreover they regarded this as an essential preliminary to any other operation in the Eastern Mediterranean.

In theory there was much to be said for the various French proposals; the objection to them was that they bore little relation to actualities. The recent Norwegian campaign had shown all too clearly that operations to throw forces ashore and maintain them without adequate air defence imposed a great strain on the navy and were liable to be extremely costly. Yet the Chiefs of Staffs had no option but to warn the Commanders-in-Chief that no aircraft or anti-aircraft guns could be spared from France or the United Kingdom at this juncture. They felt, moreover, that the French proposals involved so much dispersion of the limited resources that, if they were carried out in full, the security of the whole Allied position in the Middle East would be jeopardized. The Chiefs of Staff felt that the Allied Commanders on the spot, who were now obliged to rely upon their own resources, were in the best position to judge what risks could be accepted and to assess how the available resources could best be used. They therefore instructed the Commanders-in-Chief to concert plans with General Weygand and report what they proposed to do. It happened that General Weygand had met the Commanders-in-Chief for discussion on 10th May on board H.M.S. *Malaya*, and had been made aware of the serious shortages in aircraft, weapons, and essential equipment for the types of operation under consideration. This was the day on which Germany invaded Holland, Belgium and Luxembourg; on this day also Mr. Winston Churchill became Prime Minister.

By the middle of May it was known that Italy had been busily preparing for war for some weeks. The navy was fully prepared; the air force was ready so far as its resources permitted; the army had been mobilized since 10th May and the troops in Libya, Albania, and the Dodecanese had all been reinforced. It was recognized that the decision rested entirely with the Duce. For a time it had been thought possible that he intended to satisfy German demands, and perhaps gain his own ends in the Mediterranean, by all means short of going to war. The Ambassador in Rome reported in April that Italy was losing strength month by month. Stocks of all raw materials were low, and few emergency war stocks were believed to exist; only in respect of petroleum was the country any better equipped for war than she had been six months earlier.[1] Nevertheless, the balance of evidence pointed to the conclusion that Mussolini had made up his mind, in spite of the shortages of material in the fighting services and the economic vulnerability of his country, that Italy was to enter the war at Germany's side. In view of the successes that the Germans were having in France, this might be very soon.

Nor could the local situation be regarded as entirely satisfactory. Throughout the countries of the Middle East doubts had arisen, and were becoming more widespread with every new German success, whether the Allies could win the war. In Persia the general feeling was that Germany was the stronger, and there was much dissatisfaction in government circles at the failure of Great Britain to fulfil her orders for armaments as promptly as had been hoped. In Iraq public opinion was noticeably turning against the British, and in such a politically unstable country there was always the danger of the establishment by *coup d'état* of a government hostile to the Allies' interests. The Mufti had fled to Iraq from the Lebanon and had begun to be politically active. In Saudi Arabia there was strong sympathy with the Arab cause in Palestine and Syria, although Ibn Saud himself remained friendly. In Transjordan the Emir's confidence

---

[1] It now appears that the Italians had accumulated nearly one and three quarter million tons of oil by June 1940. Tankers bound for Italy carrying 116,000 tons passed through the Straits of Gibraltar as late as 13th May. In his diary for 29th May 1940 Ciano wrote: 'We are literally without some metals. On the eve of war—and what a war!—we have only 100 tons of nickel.' (*Ciano's Diary*: ed. Malcolm Muggeridge, 1947.)

in Great Britain never wavered. In short, while there were those who realized that an Allied victory offered the best guarantee of such independence as the Middle Eastern countries had already achieved, there was also a body of more envenomed opinion which regarded Allied influence as the main hindrance to the achievement of full independence. The undercurrent of discontent created conditions favourable to propaganda, intrigue, and misrepresentation.

The situation in Egypt was the principal cause of concern to the Commanders-in-Chief. The Egyptians viewed the possibility of becoming involved in war with apprehension which might very easily be turned into panic. Under the pressure of Axis propaganda, backed by German successes, this would in all probability take an anti-British direction. While there was no immediate cause for alarm, it had to be recognized that irresponsible politicians and excitable mobs were liable to create a dangerous situation. To protect the large European population, safeguard the Canal, and keep open the essential but very vulnerable communications within Egypt and with the Sudan and Palestine might require the use of all the available British resources, though perhaps not for long. Fortunately there seemed to be no immediate threat of land attack on Egypt or the Sudan, nor for that matter on Kenya or Aden either. There was, however, evidence that a large-scale operation was being prepared against Somaliland, and, although the French defences in this area were strong, the British were without any anti-tank or anti-aircraft guns and might be hard pressed. This estimate of Italian intentions has been shown to be substantially correct. On 31st March Mussolini told his Chiefs of Staff that if the war continued it would be impossible for Italy to stay out of it. He intended to remain on the defensive on both fronts of Libya, on the Kenya front, and in the Aegean; in East Africa there would be strictly limited offensives towards Kassala and Gedaref, and an offensive against Jibuti.

Such, then, was the general background to the conference which was to take place with the French and Turkish commanders at Beirut—the first occasion on which the British were empowered to enter into detailed discussions with the Turks on the hypothesis of a hostile Italy[1]. The circumstances were not encouraging. The news from France was daily becoming worse, and on 18th May it was learned that General Weygand would not be present; he was being recalled to France to replace General Gamelin in command of the French land forces. His place was taken by General Massiet, the commander of the French mobile forces in the Levant.

If nothing very constructive emerged from the Beirut conference it did at least clear the air. General Massiet's instructions were to insist on the necessity for a concentration of the maximum Allied air

---

[1] See page 53.

strength in an immediate attempt to reduce the Dodecanese Islands. He reiterated the argument that until the threat from them had been eliminated no other operations in the Eastern Mediterranean would be possible. The British Commanders-in-Chief agreed that the Staffs should examine the problem, but felt it necessary to state the British attitude in terms which allowed of no ambiguity. In a war against Italy the decisive factor would be Allied sea-power in the Mediterranean. It was therefore of primary importance to ensure the security of the naval base at Alexandria, of Egypt as the main military and air base, and of the Red Sea line of communication. This composite task would absorb the whole British effort at the outset, the Royal Air Force in particular being barely strong enough for its primary role. The British could therefore offer very little help to the French and Turks at present, but when the bases were secure they could take greater risks. Meanwhile, the Italian position in the Dodecanese would gradually deteriorate as the result of naval pressure. Marshal Chakmak, for his part, was not prepared to see the Turkish Air Force weakened by losses in operations against the Dodecanese, since its full strength might be needed in defence of Thrace.

Discussion of 'the worst possible case'—Germany, Italy, Bulgaria, and Russia all hostile—elicited a French undertaking to send one division to Thrace, although it would take more than a month to arrive; one division would assist the Turks, preferably against the Dodecanese; and one was tentatively earmarked for Salonika. No progress was made in a discussion on a possible offensive against Russia, but in the event of a Russian invasion from the Caucasus it was hoped that the British plans for the defence of the Mosul oilfields in conjunction with Iraqi forces would be of some indirect assistance to the Turks. The main point of interest of the whole conference was that the Turks showed no disappointment at the meagreness of the help which was offered to them, though they were naturally non-committal. The line taken by the British Commanders-in-Chief was fully endorsed by the Chiefs of Staff, and it is quite possible that Marshal Chakmak was favourably impressed by the candour with which the British views were stated. He realized no doubt that the Allies were fighting for their lives in Western Europe, and even if the conference did nothing else it showed clearly that the British in the Middle East were badly in need of much of the equipment which they had been supplying to the Turks.

A comparison of naval strength at the end of May shows that British and French surface forces in the whole Mediterranean were together superior to those of the Italians.[1] With the two *Littorios* (nine

---

[1] For the organization of the British forces see page 101.

15-inch, 31 knots), which were expected to join the fleet in about July, the Italians would have a force of six battleships, seven 8-inch and twelve 6-inch cruisers and some fifty fleet destroyers. They had no aircraft carriers, for they relied on shore-based aircraft to provide all their air support.

In the western basin, the French Mediterranean Fleet based on Toulon, Bizerta, Algiers and Oran included the two modern battle-cruisers *Dunkerque* and *Strasbourg* (eight 13-inch, 29½ knots), as well as two battleships, four 8-inch and six 6-inch cruisers and thirty-five fleet destroyers of a very powerful type. At Gibraltar, under the Flag Officer, North Atlantic, were one British battleship, one 6-inch cruiser and nine destroyers.

The Allied forces in the Eastern Mediterranean consisted of the British Mediterranean Fleet of four battleships, eight 6-inch cruisers, twenty fleet destroyers and the aircraft carrier *Eagle*, and a French squadron, under Vice-Admiral R. E. Godfroy, of one battleship, three 8-inch cruisers, one 6-inch cruiser and three destroyers.

With the exception of the Italian *Littorio* battleships and the French battlecruisers, the capital ships on both sides were vessels completed just before or at the beginning of the First World War. Of these, Admiral Cunningham's own flagship, the *Warspite*, and two of the Italian battleships had been extensively modernized. Similar altera-tions to the other two were nearly completed. The 12·6-inch guns of all four would then out-range the 15-inch guns of every British battleship except the *Warspite*.

Thus, although the Italians by virtue of their central position might be able to concentrate superior force in the area of their choice, they had to be prepared for attacks from both directions at once by forces whose combined strength was superior to their own. Type for type the speed of Italian warships was higher than that of the British, and this could give the Italian Fleet an advantage in determining when and where to seek action, when to break it off, or when to avoid it altogether. They had a further advantage in possessing 108 submarines in the Mediterranean against 46 French and 12 British. The influence that air power would have on these comparative strengths was still unknown and estimates were very varied. In train-ing and morale the British were confident of their own superiority.

Admiral Cunningham had not the same advantage as the Italians of possessing additional destroyers for meeting the many commit-ments, apart from fleet duties, for which these craft were needed. This meant he would be unable to take his whole battlefleet to sea at the same time without temporarily stopping all other activities, but it would not prevent him from being able to operate with suf-ficient force to retain command of the Eastern Mediterranean so long as there was a French fleet in the western basin to co-operate with his own movements and deter the Italians from making a serious challenge in either area. In Tunisia the French were well placed to cut Italian communications with Libya by surface ships, aircraft and submarines; of the last, as has been seen, they possessed four-fifths of the total Allied strength in the Mediterranean.

In the Red Sea the principal danger lay in the eight Italian submarines and seven fleet destroyers which were based at Massawa, in addition to other vessels for local defence. Properly handled they could inflict serious initial losses on Allied shipping in that area, since the Red Sea Force could only just provide essential escorts for convoys. On the other hand, Massawa would be cut off from seaborne supplies and reinforcements, so that the enemy's naval effort in the Red Sea might be expected to grow progressively weaker.


The Italian land forces in Libya in early June were estimated, with reasonable accuracy considering the difficulty of obtaining intelligence, to be nine metropolitan (or regular) divisions, four (in reality three) Blackshirt divisions, two Libyan native divisions, and a number of Army and Corps troops, besides various other Libyan units and Frontier Guards. A metropolitan division consisted of about 13,000 men, including both conscripts and volunteers, while Blackshirt and Libyan divisions numbered about 8,000 men each. These forces, under North Africa Supreme Headquarters, were organized as the 5th Army in Tripolitania and the 10th Army in Cyrenaica. It was thought on the eve of war that the 10th Army, consisting of one metropolitan and one Blackshirt Corps, each of two divisions, and a group of two Libyan divisions, was moving up towards the Cyrenaican frontier, which was weakly held by Frontier Guards.

While these formations were thought (correctly) to be complete in men, certain deficiencies were either known or suspected. The heavier weapons, for example tanks and artillery, were in general below modern standards of efficiency, while there was a shortage of medium artillery, and a diversity of types in other natures. Rather more than half the regular troops in Libya had received a fair amount of training, offset by the lower efficiency of the remainder who were recruits. Morale was low owing to poor food and living conditions, and it seemed that only the politically enthusiastic Blackshirts were eager for war. It was known that the Italians lacked the transport to make their formations fully mobile, but stores and ammunition were considered to be enough for three months and food for ten.

As regards the Allied forces, the French had in Tunisia six divisions, a fortress division, and a light cavalry division; a force which, as General Noguès had predicted, would be capable only of local operations with limited objectives. In Syria there was an expeditionary force of three divisions, inadequately armed and trained, in addition to some forty thousand troops organized for frontier duties and tribal control.

In Egypt General Wavell had some 36,000 men; they were not however organized in complete formations. Equipment was seriously short throughout, especially artillery of all natures, ammunition, fighting vehicles, and transport. The two armoured brigades of the 7th Armoured Division had each two regiments, instead of three, and these were only partly equipped.[1] The 4th Indian Division also had but two brigades and part of its artillery. Of the New Zealand Division there was as yet one infantry brigade, a cavalry regiment less a squadron, a machine-gun battalion, and a field regiment of artillery. There were also fourteen battalions of British infantry and two artillery regiments. There was, in addition, the Egyptian Army, which was in some respects better equipped than many of the British units; but as Egypt had not declared war on Germany the amount of support to be counted on from the Egyptian Army was doubtful. In Palestine there were about 27,500 troops consisting of an incomplete horsed cavalry division, two cavalry regiments, two Australian brigades with two field regiments of artillery and some divisional troops, and a British infantry brigade and two other battalions. Of these troops the cavalry and the Australians were unlikely to be fully equipped and trained before the end of the year. From Palestine one brigade might have to be provided for service in Iraq, while certain other units were earmarked for internal security duties.

Over Italian East Africa as a whole it had been very difficult to obtain accurate information about the armed forces. There were thought to be: upon the Sudan frontier eleven brigades of native troops and twelve Blackshirt battalions—or 20,000 men with 200 guns; in southern Ethiopia about 7,000 native and 1,000 white troops; in Italian Somaliland 7,000 native troops and 4,000 levies. A metropolitan division was at Addis Ababa and six native brigades at Diredawa and Harar. The estimated total was 30,000 white and 100,000 native troops, with 400 guns, 200 light tanks, and 20,000 lorries.[2]

---

[1] For outline organization see page 105.

[2] Five weeks after war began the revised estimate was: white troops 95,000, native troops 160,000; total 255,000, including services and reserves. The difficulty was to keep pace with the constantly changing strength of the irregulars. The actual figures of the *Ministero dell' Africa* were: on 1st June, white 91,203, native 199,273, total 290,476; on 1st August, 112,731 and 258,322, total 371,053. These include the navy and air force which the British figures do not. On 30th May Mussolini informed Hitler that there were 350,000 Italian and native troops.

British forces in this theatre were few, scattered, and lightly equipped. In the Sudan, with a frontier against the enemy of 1,200 miles, were three British battalions and the Sudan Defence Force, which with police and sundry irregular detachments totalled about 9,000 men. In Kenya, whose frontier was 850 miles long, were two East African brigades and two light batteries, or some 8,500 men. British Somaliland had one battalion of the King's African Rifles and the five companies of the Somaliland Camel Corps; in all 1,475 strong. Aden was garrisoned by two Indian battalions.

There is no doubt, therefore, that the Italians, both in Libya and East Africa, had the advantage over the British in numbers. But against this must be set two important factors: a generally lower morale and some weaknesses in material. The British troops were certainly few in numbers for their many possible tasks, while they were of necessity dispersed in widely separated areas, so that there was little chance of offsetting the disparity in numbers by a rapid transfer from one area to another. Yet numbers were almost the least of General Wavell's anxieties: what he lacked was any complete formation—fully equipped and trained as such—and without this his force could not be regarded as being in a high state of preparedness for war.

On 13th May 1940 Air Chief Marshal Sir Arthur Longmore assumed command of the Royal Air Force in the Mediterranean and Middle East in place of Sir William Mitchell.[1] All Royal Air Force units stationed or operating in Egypt, the Sudan, Palestine and Transjordan, East Africa, Aden and Somaliland, Iraq and adjacent territories, Cyprus, Turkey, the Balkans, Malta, the Red Sea and Persian Gulf came under his command. His directive defined the primary role of these forces as the defence of Egypt, the Suez Canal, and the maintenance of communications through the Red Sea. He was responsible, in conjunction with the Commanders-in-Chief Mediterranean, East Indies, and Middle East, as appropriate, for the preparation of plans for the employment of air units within his Command.[2]

He was to be responsible for the general administrative control of his Command so far as operational requirements dictated, but the Air Officers Commanding Aden, Iraq, and Mediterranean (Malta) were to exercise local administrative control under the Air Ministry.

---

[1] Air Chief Marshal Longmore had had varied experience in Commands at home. He was Commandant of the Imperial Defence College during 1936–38. He was a member of the Air Mission to Australia and New Zealand in 1939. Air Chief Marshal Mitchell became Inspector General of the Royal Air Force.

[2] The directive to the Air Officer Commanding-in-Chief is reproduced in full at Appendix 2.

This arrangement was made to avoid overloading the staff of Air Head-quarters with local administrative detail, but it soon proved to be unworkable, and it was not long before the Air Officer Commanding-in-Chief was given a free hand to assume whatever degree of adminis-trative control of his subordinate commands he deemed necessary.

On reviewing the state of his forces, Sir Arthur found the situation far from reassuring. He had no modern fighters or long-range bombers. He was short of aircraft spares and other equipment. The strength of his squadrons in Egypt and Palestine amounted only to 96 bombers and bomber transports (mainly Blenheim Mark I and Bombay); 75 fighters (Gladiator)—including a fighter squadron of the Royal Egyptian Air Force—24 army co-operation aircraft (Lysander) and 10 flying-boats (Sunderland): a total of 205 aircraft. If Italy should enter the war there would be little prospect of receiving any reinforce-ments or replacements for some time to come. Any strengthening of the air forces in Egypt or East Africa would depend upon such re-shuffling within the Command as circumstances would permit. Resources would have to be strictly conserved from the outset, for with this meagre force the Air Officer Commanding-in-Chief would have to neutralize the enemy air forces in Cyrenaica and the Dodecanese; attack lines of supply and ports within range; provide support for naval and land operations; and give fighter protection to such important targets as the Fleet Base at Alexandria, Cairo, Port Said, and the Suez Canal. Furthermore, he knew that in certain circumstances he might be pressed to send squadrons to the aid of the Turks in Thrace. On the other hand, the French had in North Africa about 65 fighters and 85 bombers—the latter in the course of being replaced by American Douglas and Glenn Martin aircraft—and it was hoped that their activities would be co-ordinated with those of the Royal Air Force in neutralizing the Italian Air Force in Libya. In Syria the French had a weak force of some 95 aircraft (13 bombers, 26 fighters, and 56 of other types).

Towards the end of May it was estimated that the strength of the Italian Air Force in Libya, exclusive of reserves was approximately 84 modern bombers (S.79, S.81) and 56 of Colonial types (Ghibli); 144 fighters of which about half were C.R.32 or C.R.42; and 57 other aircraft of various types. Of these approximately half the bombers and fighters, it was believed, were based in Cyrenaica. It was estimated that a further 84 aircraft (36 bombers, 12 fighters, and 36 other aircraft) were stationed in the Dodecanese: a total of 425 aircraft in Libya and the Dodecanese. The true figures for the Italian strength, when war broke out, were 140 bombers, 101 fighters, and 72 other types—a total of 313 aircraft disposed in Libya and the Dodecanese. It was thought at the time that the balance of forces as between Tripolitania, Cyrenaica, and the Dodecanese could be altered by switching squadrons from one to the other, and that a still greater advantage lay in the ability to reinforce any of these theatres from the Metropolitan Air Force. The Allies could do nothing to interfere with the flow of such reinforcements except in so far as the French in Tunisia might be able to attack any airfields in Sicily and Pantelleria used by the Italians as staging posts.

In East Africa it was believed that, exclusive of reserves, the Italians had 36 modern bombers and 114 of Colonial types; 45 modern fighters; and 18 others: a total of 213 aircraft. In fact, they had 325 aircraft of which 142 were in reserve. Bomber reinforcements could be flown in from Italy via Libya, but the numbers would be governed by the ability to maintain and operate them. So long as the blockade by land and sea was complete, the stocks of fuel, bombs, ammunition, and aircraft spares, already believed to be below requirements, could not be replenished.

At Aden the Royal Air Force had one bomber squadron armed partly with Blenheim Mark Is and Vincents; one Blenheim Mark I squadron recently arrived from India at reduced establishment; a fighter squadron (Gladiator) at half strength; and one flight of a land-based G.R. squadron (Blenheim IV). In the Sudan there were three bomber squadrons (Wellesley) and one fighter flight (Gladiator). Until the end of May, British air units in Kenya consisted only of a Rhodesian squadron armed with obsolete aircraft and three flights of the Kenya Auxiliary Air Force. By the end of May, units of the South African Air Force had begun to arrive with a mixed collection of obsolete aircraft amounting to the equivalent of two bomber squadrons and one fighter squadron. The latter was immediately brought to Egypt, and rearmed and trained on Gladiators. Excluding the aircraft of the Rhodesian squadron and the Kenya Auxiliary flights, there were by the outbreak of war some 85 Wellesleys and Blenheims, 9 Vincents, 24 Hartbeests, 15 Junkers 86, and 30 Gladiators and Furies in Aden, Kenya and the Sudan.

The Italian fighter (C.R.42) had a slightly better performance than the Gladiator. Their bomber (S.79) could carry a heavier bomb load than the Blenheim Mark I and had an advantage in range that would enable it to operate from airfields in Cyrenaica out of the Blenheims' reach. As against this, the Italian maintenance organization was not considered to be very efficient; the average proportion of serviceable aircraft in Libya was estimated to be about 70%, and in East Africa it was put as low as 30%. About one-third of the Italian pilots were thought to be up to Royal Air Force standard, and some had had recent experience of active service in Spain.[1]

---

[1] For particulars of British and Italian aircraft see Appendix 8.

Thus on the one hand the Italian air forces were numerically superior to those of the British opposed to them, and were in general better armed, in addition to which they were capable of being appreciably reinforced—except in East Africa. On the other hand the Italians were short of aircraft spares, equipment, and reserves of fuel, while their maintenance organization was poor. Air Chief Marshal Longmore felt confident that what he lacked in quantity would be largely offset by the high morale and better training and experience of his air and ground crews. He came to the conclusion that the Italians' effective fighting strength might deteriorate rapidly in the face of a determined air offensive.

By the end of May all three services were at the alert and ready for war to break out at any moment. The Libyan frontier was being patrolled by squadrons of the Egyptian Frontier Force. The 7th Armoured Division (less the 7th Armoured Brigade) had assembled in the neighbourhood of Matruh, with the Support Group of two regiments of Royal Horse Artillery and two motor battalions disposed as a covering force between the main body and the frontier. Lines-of-communication troops had been reinforced. On 1st June the 14th Infantry Brigade from Palestine reached Egypt, where its presence would do something to stiffen Egyptian morale, and where it would be available for internal security duties if needed.

Although no major changes had been made in the general plans for war outlined in Chapter III, General Wavell intended to launch immediate attacks to clear the enemy from the frontier posts and to dominate the country as far west as possible. On 8th June Major-General R. N. O'Connor, with the headquarters of the 6th Division, arrived from Palestine to assume command of all troops in the Western Desert, thus relieving General Wilson of responsibility for the direct control of operations which had been his in addition to the command of all troops in Egypt. On 17th June H.Q. 6th Division was re-designated H.Q. Western Desert Force.

Shortly after taking over command, Air Marshal Longmore decided to concentrate his entire bomber force—less one squadron retained in reserve—in the Western Desert, placing the whole of the air forces there under the command of Air Commodore Collishaw. As it was important that the Italian air force should be hit hard as soon as possible after the declaration of war, Collishaw was given authority to begin operations without waiting for further orders directly he was satisfied that a state of war existed.

In the Sudan and Kenya it was not possible to cover the long and vulnerable frontiers with the few troops available. Small mobile forces were therefore placed at the principal frontier posts to delay

I

any enemy advance, a policy which was considered preferable to abandoning them without action. By the middle of May British Somaliland had been reinforced by one battalion of the King's African Rifles, which was moved up to defend an important defile on the Italian approach road to Berbera. The British force in Somaliland was placed under the orders of General Legentilhomme who had permission to withdraw the force towards Jibuti if the situation made this necessary.

The exposed position of Malta made it very likely that the Italians would attempt its early capture. During May the garrison was reinforced by a British battalion from Gibraltar, making five British battalions in all, in addition to The King's Own Malta Regiment. But against the air attacks which were expected on a large scale the island was quite inadequately defended. Owing to the calls for defence of vital areas elsewhere it had not been possible to provide any of the four fighter squadrons approved for the air defence of the island.[1] Nor had any of the additional anti-aircraft guns arrived. Malta was of supreme importance to Admiral Cunningham as a base from which to operate against the Italian lines of communication to Libya, and the fact that the island was so weakly defended against air attack caused him the greatest concern, which he constantly represented to Whitehall. Chance came to the rescue where foresight had failed. Four packing cases consigned to the carrier *Glorious*—by now in home waters—were found to contain four Sea Gladiators. The Air Officer Commanding, Air Commodore F. H. M. Maynard, obtained permission to erect them and form them into a local fighter defence unit flown by pilots from his headquarters staff and from flying-boat units. One unfortunately crashed soon afterwards, but the other three—'Faith', 'Hope', and 'Charity'—survived to demonstrate Malta's determination to overcome difficulties and show fight. If the idea was impudent it was also inspiring, with the added attraction of being, like so many British achievements, entirely impromptu.

On 27th May the Admiralty approved Admiral Cunningham's definition of his initial object, which was to secure control of sea communications in the Eastern Mediterranean and Aegean and to cut off the enemy's supplies to the Dodecanese Islands. In the Prime Minister's view this was not a sufficiently aggressive object; the fleet ought to sally forth to ensure an early collision with the Italian forces, whose fighting quality could thus be judged. No one was more eager for this than Admiral Cunningham himself, whose intentions were anything but defensive. Naval action against the Italian communications with the Dodecanese would not only encourage the Turks, but might well have the effect of drawing

---

[1] See page 30.

Italian heavy units eastwards. There were, however, certain factors that the Commander-in-Chief could not ignore. He felt that his long-range air reconnaissance was quite inadequate. He was short of light forces and could spare none to work from Malta. He had already reported his intention of carrying out an extensive sweep into the Central Mediterranean, but in this he would be seriously handicapped by the lack of adequate means of reconnaissance and of retaining contact with the enemy when located—disadvantages from which the enemy did not suffer. He was therefore unlikely to gain contact with much more than Italian aircraft and submarines. He felt it necessary to get the measure of these before attempting prolonged operations in the Central Mediterranean, but if Malta were attacked from the sea he intended to move with the whole fleet to its relief. There was also the need to hold ships in instant readiness to carry troops to Crete in order to gain the use of Suda Bay, a base farther to the west where his fleet could refuel and replenish ammunition. If adequate air reconnaissance could eventually be established from Tunisia or Malta he hoped to keep a force of cruisers and destroyers operating almost permanently in the central area to prey on the traffic to Libya.

The Chiefs of Staff agreed with these views. They had already told the Commanders-in-Chief that there was little hope of adding to their resources, as was anyhow evident from the disasters taking place in France. The outcome was the despatch of a telegram on 4th June to each Commander-in-Chief reminding him that, although the Mediterranean forces had at first to be strategically on the defensive, it was important, in view of the serious situation in the west, that local offensive action should be taken against the Italians whenever possible.

In a last attempt to avoid provocation the Admiralty gave orders, received on 23rd May, that no Italian ship in the Mediterranean was to be stopped or diverted by any contraband control. But as May drew to a close Italy's hostile intentions were no longer in doubt. On 1st June orders were issued for Italian cargoes to be seized in the event of war and, on 4th June, for Italian shipping in colonial ports to be delayed on devious pretexts. Precautions were intensified against possible sabotage in the Suez Canal. Two days later Italy announced that all waters within 12 miles of her coasts were dangerous to navigation.

Events were now moving rapidly to the climax. At 4 a.m. on 10th June the 2nd Destroyer Flotilla, with two flying-boats from No. 201 Group, left Alexandria for an anti-submarine sweep westwards. The Mediterranean Fleet was at two hours notice; merchant ships were ordered to keep more than three miles from the coasts of Malta, Cyprus, and Palestine between sunset and sunrise; the lights of the Suez Canal were extinguished and navigation during darkness was suspended. In the Western Desert No. 202 Group and the Western Desert Force were preparing to get their blows in first.

# Chronology: March-June 1940

| | |
|---|---|
| 12th March | Russo-Finnish war ends |
| 18th March | Hitler and Mussolini meet at the Brenner |
| 9th April | Germany invades Denmark and Norway |
| 15th April | First British forces land in Norway |
| 10th May | Germany invades Holland, Belgium and Luxembourg |
| 10th May | Mr. Churchill becomes Prime Minister and Minister of Defence |
| 14th May | Commanders-in-Chief in Middle East receive policy for war with Italy |
| 15th May | Dutch resistance ends |
| | German troops enter France |
| 27th May | Belgian resistance ends |
| 28th May | British forces begin evacuation from Dunkirk |
| 8th June | Withdrawal of French and British forces from North Norway completed |
| 10th June | Italy declares war on Great Britain and France as from 11th June: Canada declares war on Italy |
| 11th June | Australia, New Zealand and South Africa declare war on Italy |

# The Organization of the three Services in 1940, with particular reference to the Mediterranean and Middle East

## THE ROYAL NAVY

The word FLEET is a loose term, officially defined as meaning a number of vessels working in company. When reference is made to a specific Fleet, such as the Mediterranean Fleet, it includes all H.M. Ships and Vessels operating in that area—known as the STATION—under the command of the Commander-in-Chief.

Ships and Vessels of His Majesty's Fleets are organized in SQUADRONS for cruisers and above, or FLOTILLAS for destroyers and below. Unlike the First World War, when the Grand Fleet was composed of numerous Battle Squadrons, there was normally only one Battle Squadron with each of the main fleets during the Second World War. Squadrons and Flotillas, if numbers of ships permit, are further sub-divided into two DIVISIONS and four SUB-DIVISIONS. The term BATTLEFLEET includes not only the Battle Squadron but also those ships screening it and manoeuvring with it.

Squadrons of Battleships, Aircraft Carriers, and Cruisers consisted of two or more ships, each squadron being under the command of a Flag Officer, e.g. 1st Battle Squadron, 3rd Aircraft Carrier Squadron, 7th Cruiser Squadron. In the Mediterranean there was usually only one Aircraft Carrier, which normally operated with the Battleships at sea; it was regarded as forming part of the Battle Squadron for manoeuvring purposes. The Carrier(s), together with the Fleet Air Arm in general, came under the administrative command of the Flag Officer Aircraft Carriers.

The aim of the Eastern Mediterranean Fleet during the early part of the war was to maintain the Battle Squadron at a strength of four Battleships (two Divisions) under the administrative command of a Rear- or Vice-Admiral, who also assumed operational command when the Commander-in-Chief was not afloat. The strength of Cruiser Squadrons varied from two to six cruisers. These squadrons, as far as possible, were composed of ships of the same class, as cruisers varied in size from the 4,200-ton 25-year old 'C' class cruisers carrying 6-inch guns to the 10,000-ton County class carrying 8-inch guns. Some of the 'C' class had all their 6-inch guns replaced by modern anti-aircraft weapons.

A Flotilla of destroyers consisted of not more than eight boats— as far as possible of the same class—together with a Flotilla Leader, which is a larger type of destroyer to accommodate the Captain (D) and his staff. Very often, owing to casualties and defects, a flotilla consisted of only three or four boats, in which case it was sometimes commanded by a Commander (D). Whereas Divisions of Battleships and Cruisers were numbered as integral parts of the Squadron to which they belonged, e.g. 2nd Division of 1st Battle Squadron, Destroyer Divisions were not.

All the Destroyer Flotillas belonging to a Fleet came under the administrative and operational command of a Rear-Admiral (D) who generally flew his flag in a small cruiser. As explained in the text, the Mediterranean cruisers and destroyers, in the autumn of 1940, for a time all came under the operational control of a Vice-Admiral who was known as the Vice-Admiral Light Forces (V.A.L.F.). This was a purely local arrangement. Minesweeping Flotillas were organized on similar lines to Destroyer Flotillas, but were administered by the local Admiral of the port from which they were operating, e.g. the Fortress Commander, Alexandria, or the Vice-Admiral, Malta.

Any number of Submarines formed a Flotilla for administrative purposes, but as the boats operated independently they were not organized into Divisions like destroyers. Flotillas were normally administered and operated by a Captain (S) who commanded the depot ship or shore establishment which happened to be their operational base.

Squadrons of the Fleet Air Arm were organized on similar lines to those in the Royal Air Force, but they were smaller. Twelve aircraft (without reserves, which could not be carried) were the normal complement of a Squadron, which was divided into flights and sub-flights. In earlier and smaller Carriers the strength of a squadron of the Fleet Air Arm was governed by the capacity of the Carrier. The *Eagle*, for example, could only carry eighteen aircraft, which were divided into two Squadrons of nine each. Conditions under which squadrons were disembarked naturally varied with circumstances. When, for instance, the Carrier was present—e.g. at Alexandria, with the Squadrons disembarked at Dekheila—only the minimum number of maintenance ratings were landed with the aircraft, while the workshops and headquarters staff remained on board. The type of aircraft embarked in Carriers varied according to the tasks and the aircraft available; it is mentioned, where appropriate, in the text. An old Carrier like the *Eagle* had no stowage for fighters; if embarked, they had to be kept ranged on deck.

The distance a ship of a given design can steam depends not only upon how much fuel she can carry but on the speed, the weather, and the cleanliness of the ship's bottom. The old battleship *Royal Sovereign* had an endurance of about 2,500 miles at 20 knots in calm weather. This meant that ships of this class, if taking part in operations in the Central Mediterranean, had to refuel at Malta, since it was desirable to keep a wide margin of fuel in hand for eventualities. The modernized *Warspite*, on the other hand, had almost twice the fuel endurance of the *Royal Sovereign*. Although on some occasions destroyers were fuelled from battleships at sea in the Mediterranean, the danger from air and submarine attack made the operation very risky, apart from which it was generally impossible to provide special escort for oilers to meet the Fleet at sea. Operational endurance depended also on the supply of ammunition, particularly anti-aircraft. As described in the text, there was more than one occasion on which operations had to be abandoned or modified owing to the anti-aircraft ammunition having been expended. The ammunitioning of ships at sea in the Mediterranean, as developed later in the Pacific, was obviously impracticable. An advanced base for fuel and ammunition, nearer to the main operational area, would have naturally increased the ability of ships to remain operating in that area.

The Supply Services in the Navy, unlike those in the Army and the Royal Air Force, were largely run by civilians. Thus, the Naval Store, Armament, and Victualling Officers, besides various dockyard officers associated with the supply and refitting of ships, were not subject to the Naval Discipline Act although the Commander-in-Chief naturally controlled the movements of Store Ships once they were on his Station.

## THE ARMY

The organization of the British Army for a major war was centred round the DIVISION, in which the basic arm was the infantry. There was also the CAVALRY DIVISION and the ARMOURED DIVISION, in which the basic arms were the cavalry and the tank arm respectively. All three types were represented in the Middle East.

### The division

The division was the smallest formation to contain, as an integral part, a proportion of arms other than infantry.

The unit of infantry was the BATTALION. An INFANTRY BRIGADE was a permanent grouping of three battalions, together with a headquarters through which the Brigadier exercised control.

The division, commanded by a Major-General, consisted of a headquarters, three infantry brigades, and certain units of other arms collectively known as the DIVISIONAL TROOPS: e.g. three field regiments and an anti-tank regiment of artillery; three field companies and a field park company of engineers; divisional signals, and so on.

Occasionally a portion of the divisional troops would be attached temporarily to an infantry brigade for some special purpose; this improvised formation was known as a BRIGADE GROUP.

### Non-divisional units

Many types of fighting units existed (mostly on paper) which did not form part of a division; such as medium, heavy, and anti-aircraft artillery, machine-gun battalions, and various engineer, signal, and infantry tank units. These NON-DIVISIONAL UNITS were intended for allotment to formations as the situation might demand. Thus, if two or more divisions were grouped for purposes of command into a CORPS, a proportion of non-divisional units would become the CORPS TROOPS. Similarly, if two or more corps were grouped as an ARMY, there would be an appropriate allotment of ARMY TROOPS. It will be seen, therefore, that an increase in the total strength of a force implied a decrease in the proportion of infantry to the whole. As the war progressed it became increasingly necessary to apply the bulk of the corps troops, and even army troops, to support first one and then another of the divisions. The first corps formed in the Middle East was the 13th, which grew out of the Western Desert Force, in January 1941. The first army was the 8th, formed in September 1941.

Many other types of non-divisional units were required for administrative and maintenance purposes, principally at the base and on the lines of communication. In the Middle East their activities covered a very wide range, since the more undeveloped the country the more varied the work to be done. The need for units of this type is referred to on pages 61, 66.

### Cavalry division

A horsed cavalry division arrived in Palestine in the spring of 1940. Most of its divisional troops were taken from it for service in Egypt during 1940. Two of its three cavalry brigades went to form the 10th Armoured Division in 1941.

### Armoured formations

The tank was a British invention of the First World War, but the urge for economy in the inter-war years resulted in the British losing their lead. Very few tanks were built, and work on design and research was severely restricted. The result was that in 1939 the armoured arm was in a very backward state. The latest tanks naturally went to France.

British tanks in the Middle East were of three types:

(*a*) light tanks, for reconnaissance work; fast, lightly armoured, and armed with machine-guns.

(*b*) medium or cruiser tanks; more heavily armoured, capable of a fair speed, armed with a gun and machine-guns.

(*c*) 'I' tanks; still more heavily armoured, but slower; intended for working with infantry; armed with a gun and machine-guns.

An armoured division was intended to consist of two armoured brigades, each of three regiments (or battalions) of medium and light tanks; a SUPPORT GROUP of two motor-borne infantry battalions and field and anti-tank regiments of artillery; and certain divisional troops. In the Middle East the one embryo armoured division—the 7th—could only be very gradually provided with up-to-date replacements for its existing vehicles. The growth of this division is referred to on pages 19, 68, 93, 186, 188, 200.

An 'I' tank battalion was a non-divisional unit, allotted according to circumstances. The despatch of the first Matilda 'I' tanks to the Middle East is referred to on page 190.

It must be stressed that the value of an armoured formation could not be judged merely by comparing the numbers of tanks with those of the enemy. Apart from morale and training, it depended upon mechanical reliability, armour, relative speed, efficiency of inter-communication, and—above all—fire power.

## Dominion forces

The Dominions had decided to organize any forces they might raise on the same lines as the British, with only minor differences; and to equip and train them similarly.

## The Indian Army

The Indian Army requires special mention. It was a standing regular army of long-service volunteers, organized and trained on the same lines as the British Army. Units were habitually up to strength and a large part of the army had seen active service in small expeditions. Most of the regimental officers were British, and the formation commanders and staff officers were appointed from either the British or the Indian service. A number of British regular units also served in India in peace time, and it had long been the custom for an infantry brigade to consist of one British battalion and two Indian battalions.

Reference has been made on page 38 to the readiness of the Indian Government to send its troops overseas if they could be supplied with the modern weapons and equipment appropriate to the conditions, their own scale being quite unsuitable against a first class Power.

The proportion of artillery to infantry was comparatively low; it was mostly British, but armed with obsolescent guns. There were no anti-aircraft guns, few anti-tank weapons, and there was a lack of modern light machine-guns, mortars, and carriers. A start had been made with mechanization, but most of the cavalry was still horsed, and animals provided the greater part of the army's transport.

*Strengths*

Even without comparing particulars of weapons—which is of course a matter of fundamental importance—it will be seen that the counting of heads in any theatre of war can by itself give only a very rough and possibly quite erroneous picture of the fighting power of a force. But in order to give some idea of the size of some of the principal British-type units and formations the following extracts are given from authorized establishments for men and guns. The actual strengths in the Middle East in 1940 were often well below these figures. Details of transport and other weapons and equipment are omitted.

| Unit or formation | Officers and men | Field guns | Anti-tank guns |
|---|---|---|---|
| Infantry battalion  .    .    . | 780 | — | — |
| Infantry brigade    .    .    . | 2,525 | — | 9 |
| Field regiment, R.A.    .    . | 583 | 24 | — |
| Anti-tank regiment, R.A.    . | 543 | — | 48 |
| Divisional engineers    .    . | 916 | — | — |
| Divisional signals    .    . | 491 | — | — |
| Divisional R.A.S.C.    .    . | 1,124 | — | — |
| Infantry division    .    .    . | 13,659 | 72 | 75 |
| Cavalry division    .    .    . | 11,220 | 48 | — |
| Armoured regiment or battalion | 580 | — | — |
| Armoured brigade .    .    . | 1,896 | — | — |
| Support Group    .    .    . | 2,864 | 24 | 56 |
| Armoured division .    .    . | 9,634 | 24 | 56 |

The establishment of tanks in an armoured regiment or battalion was 52.

As a rough guide, the terms SQUADRON, BATTERY, or COMPANY may be taken as denoting a unit or sub-unit of between 100 and 300 strong. For example: a rifle company of an infantry battalion had 127 officers and men; a squadron of an armoured regiment, 170; a field company of engineers, 242; a divisional petrol company, 255; a battery of field artillery, 267.

For explanation of the term DIVISIONAL SLICE, see page 64n.

# THE ROYAL AIR FORCE

The Mediterranean and Middle East Command of the Royal Air Force was organized into a number of smaller Commands, (see pages 31, 94), GROUPS, STATIONS, and WINGS. Under these formations were the fighting units—the SQUADRONS; the maintenance units responsible for the maintenance and supply of all equipment; signal and radar units; the training units for both air and ground crews; hospitals; and special units such as armoured car, and balloon barrage squadrons.

Command was normally exercised by Air Headquarters through the medium of a Group or, if there was no Group, direct through the Station or the Wing. The number of Stations and Wings and the types of units under command of a Group varied according to circumstances and the tactical requirements, but as a general rule Groups were composed of units of the same type.

When a number of units were together they were described as a Station and came under the control of the Station Commander. On the other hand when squadrons operated together as a mobile formation they were known as a Wing.

Squadrons were armed with fighter, bomber, reconnaissance, or transport types of aircraft and, broadly speaking, their functions came within these main classifications. But as the war progressed they were to be given many different roles, which necessitated modifications to aircraft, armament, and equipment, and special training for aircrews.

Squadrons were sub-divided into two, or in certain cases three, flying FLIGHTS and a headquarters flight. The headquarters flight was composed of engine and aircraft repair sections, and signals, armament, photographic, transport and administrative sections. But when two or three fighter or bomber squadrons were controlled by a Station or Wing Headquarters the sections of the headquarters flight would be established as part of the formation headquarters, in order to economize manpower and material. This was generally satisfactory for squadrons based in the United Kingdom, but was not flexible enough for moving warfare, as in the Western Desert.

The first line strength of a squadron consisted of a number of initial equipment (I.E.) aircraft. An immediate reserve (I.R.) of up to 50 per cent of the I.E. was usually—but not always—held by each squadron. Further reserves were kept at air stores parks and maintenance units. The following are examples of the established strengths of squadrons in the Middle East soon after the fall of France:-

| Role of Squadron | Type of aircraft | I.E. | I.R. | Approximate strength, Officers and Airmen |
|---|---|---|---|---|
| Fighter    .    .    . | Gladiator or Hurricane | 16 | 8 | 250 |
| Bomber    .    .    . | Blenheim | 16 | 8 | 400 |
| „    .    .    . | Wellington | 16 | 8 | 490 |
| General Reconnaissance, Flying-Boat | Sunderland | 6 | 2 | 250 |
| Army Co-operation    . | Lysander | 12 | 6 | 290 |

With a few exceptions all the airmen of a squadron or a technical unit were tradesmen. For example, in a Wellington bomber squadron there were electricians, fitters, instrument makers, wireless and electrical mechanics, fabric and metal workers, photographers and armourers and so on. To reach the required standard of skill in the majority of these trades much training and experience were needed, so that the expansion of the Air Force was not only a matter of numbers of aircraft and airmen and of flying training.

When war broke out with Italy the squadrons in the Middle East were, for the most part, armed with obsolescent aircraft. Particulars of the performance of these and of the enemy's aircraft, their armament and functions, are given at Appendix 8. It should be borne in mind that both sides were constantly introducing new types or improving existing ones.

The numbers of squadrons or of aircraft at any time do not, therefore, give a true picture of the offensive or defensive power of an Air Force. The value of a serviceable aircraft depends upon the morale and skill of the aircrew, but an aircraft which cannot be flown is of no fighting value at all. Much depends, therefore, upon the ground crews and upon the repair and salvage organizations, in keeping the number of serviceable aircraft as high as possible. In 1940, and indeed in 1941, the Repair and Salvage Organization of the Royal Air Force in the Middle East had many short-comings; even so it proved to be much better than that of the Italians.

# CHAPTER VI

# ITALY DECLARES WAR

## (June 1940)

AT 4.45 P.M. on 10th June the Italian Minister for Foreign Affairs informed the British Ambassador in Rome that at one minute past midnight the King of Italy would consider himself to be at war with the United Kingdom. Count Ciano added that this was a declaration of war and not a pre-announcement. For some little time it had been expected almost daily, and when the Commanders-in-Chief received the news they lost no time in putting into effect their plans for striking at the enemy by sea, air, and land.

The 2nd Destroyer Flotilla had already sailed in the early hours of 10th June for an anti-submarine sweep to westward of Alexandria. Just before 10 o'clock that night H.M.S. *Decoy* located a submarine to the south of Crete and attacked it, for it was presumed to be hostile because submerged.[1] At one o'clock in the morning of the 11th Admiral Cunningham took his fleet to sea with the object of gauging the Italian submarine and air activity, and in the hope of encountering surface forces that he could attack. Even for this first operation he was unable to take the two *Royal Sovereign* class battleships on account of their lack of speed and the shortage of destroyers. His force therefore consisted of the battleships *Warspite* and *Malaya*, the aircraft carrier *Eagle*, five cruisers and nine destroyers. Two more cruisers from Port Said were to join the fleet at sea, and the French force of four cruisers and three destroyers was ordered to sail from Beirut, sweep into the Aegean, and then steam to Alexandria.

Sweeping to the westward the fleet remained for twelve hours off the Libyan coast, during which time one division of cruisers appeared off Benghazi and another engaged small craft off Tobruk. Off Derna an Italian cruiser escaped owing to tardy transmission of her position and poor visibility. The sweep was carried to within 120 miles of the heel of Italy but no important enemy forces were met, and the fleet returned to Alexandria on the evening of 14th June. Although no less than fifty Italian submarines had been at sea in the Mediterranean, with strong patrol lines off Alexandria and between Crete and Tobruk, the only loss sustained by the fleet was the cruiser *Calypso* torpedoed by a submarine. She was the fleet's first casualty, and sank after an hour and a half with the loss of one

---

[1] See page 44 for the agreement with the Italians of 21st September 1939.

officer and 38 ratings. This loss was partly offset by the damaging of the old Italian cruiser *San Giorgio* which was set on fire in Tobruk harbour by aircraft of No. 202 Group co-operating with the British cruisers.

His first fleet operation was a disappointment to Admiral Cunningham, but it was not without its results. The enemy's inaction at sea suggested no great desire to seek battle, and his air reconnaissance seemed to be not fully developed. On the other hand, the operation showed clearly that the *Eagle's* aircraft were insufficient for the many tasks required of them. It gave, in Admiral Cunningham's opinion, practical proof of the impossibility of establishing effective control over the Central Mediterranean without some such fuelling base as Suda Bay.

Italian reactions were also being tested in other directions. On 14th June French cruisers from Toulon bombarded military objectives at Genoa in conjunction with attacks by No. 767 Fleet Air Arm Squadron from Hyères, while French aircraft bombed the oil tanks at Venice. On the 17th an Italian submarine was sunk by the French in the Western Mediterranean. On the 21st a force of British cruisers and a French battleship bombarded military installations at Bardia —the first of many operations of this type and one from which much useful experience was gained.

British submarines had meanwhile begun their long, arduous, often monotonous, and always hazardous vigil. Patrols off Crete had in fact been established, on the Admiralty's instructions, since 20th May, but from 10th June all available boats from Alexandria and Malta went to sea and patrols were thereafter continuous. The initial losses were heavy; of the four boats operating from Malta three failed to return—the *Grampus*, *Odin* and *Orpheus*. Believing that they were lost on minefields off Italian ports, the Commander-in-Chief forbade submarines in future to cross the 200 fathom line unless pursuing an important enemy unit: in fact, all three vessels were sunk by Italian anti-submarine craft. Control of submarine operations, other than minelaying, to the west of 20°E (the longitude of Benghazi) was at this time under Rear-Admiral Ven at Bizerta. Similarly, the seven French submarines based at Beirut were under the operational control of the British Commander-in-Chief. On the first patrols no major units were encountered, but on 20th June the *Parthian* sank the Italian submarine *Diamante* off Tobruk.

The first two days of war had seen the loss of some 130,000 tons of Italian merchant shipping by capture, self-destruction, or internment. Enemy ships on passage, even when carrying troops or stores, were protected from attack by submarines, because these could not give the warning prescribed by international law. This provision was not observed by the Germans, and was modified by the Italians in their announcement that within a distance of 30 miles from any hostile coast they intended to sink shipping on sight. Even this did not cover the sinking without warning on 12th June of the Norwegian tanker *Orlanger* 40 miles off the coast of Egypt. In retaliation Admiral Cunningham ordered all Italian tankers to be sunk on sight, but was immediately told by the Admiralty that his order was contrary to Government policy and must be cancelled. He protested repeatedly about the handicaps under which he was labouring, and gradually the restrictions were relaxed. Thus on 14th July he was authorized to attack without warning any Italian shipping within 30 miles of the Libyan coast, and on the 18th this was extended to cover Italian shipping within 30 miles of any Italian territory in the Mediterranean, and ships of any nationality within the same distance of the coast of Libya. But until as late as January 1941 it was possible for ships flying even the German flag to sail with impunity off the coasts of Italy, Sicily, or the Dodecanese.

There remained the difficult problem of interfering with Italian trade in the Aegean, especially the important tanker traffic from the Black Sea. Some measure of control by the Turks would have been a great help, but Turkey, not being a belligerent, preferred to adhere strictly to the article of the Montreux Convention by which merchant ships of any nationality, carrying any kind of cargo, enjoyed freedom of passage through the Dardanelles. From here onwards they were able to find safe passage by way of Greek territorial waters and the Corinth Canal.

In the Red Sea there were few naval forces, but the fact that this was now the main British supply route made it important that it should be secure. One ship was safely sailed under escort from Suez to Aden, and one from Aden to Suez. Though this produced no reaction by the enemy, it did not alter the fact that the eight Italian submarines and seven fleet destroyers based on Massawa could, if skilfully handled, be a serious danger to Allied shipping. On 16th June an Italian submarine sank a Norwegian tanker south of Aden. Little did she know what was to be the outcome of this act. For two days she was hunted by warships and aircraft, and was believed to have been damaged. The main forces then withdrew to other tasks, leaving the trawler *Moonstone* on patrol. On 19th June the submarine surfaced, intending to sink her small enemy and escape. The *Moonstone*, however, opened fire at once with her machine-guns, and her single gun, and although assailed by gunfire and torpedoes, obtained two hits on the conning-tower. With her captain killed the submarine surrendered. She was the *Galileo Galilei*, and her capture brought a valuable haul of documents, including the sailing orders of four other submarines.[1] Dispositions were then

---

[1] Captain M. A. Bragadin in *Che ha fatto la Marina? 1940-45* (Milan 2nd. ed., 1950) p. 42, attributes this loss to the fact that submarine crews in the Red Sea suffered severely from heat-stroke and gas intoxication, and states that the *Galileo Galilei* was found by the British adrift with the crew overcome by poison fumes.

made which resulted in two of these being sunk, one as far away as the Persian Gulf. A third was wrecked near Port Sudan. Four out of eight submarines were thus accounted for, a loss which effectively discouraged the others, which were recalled in February 1941 and reached German-occupied Bordeaux the following May. The *Galileo Galilei* was ultimately berthed at Port Said, to serve as a generating station to charge the batteries of British submarines.

The Italian surface forces in the Red Sea also remained inert, so that the Allied convoys which had now been instituted proceeded without any interference from them. It could not be assumed that this happy state of affairs would continue, so that in fact there was no respite for the British naval forces. Convoy duty was incessant and was made particularly severe by the trying combination of Red Sea climate and active service conditions.

*See Map* 5.

The principal tasks for which the Royal Air Force had to be prepared were briefly: reconnaissances for all three Services, air defence, and offensive action. Particular importance was attached to the offensive action, because it was likely that the Italian air force in Libya would be appreciably reinforced. It was therefore decided to strike rapidly and as hard as possible at aircraft and airfield installations and ports. The pity was that the means available would not permit of a much stronger blow, and that the main supply port of Benghazi was out of reach of the Mark I Blenheims. The subsidiary port of Tobruk and the nearby airfields thus became the main objective area.

The decision to use No. 202 Group to command all the air forces in the Western Desert has already been referred to. The Headquarters arrived at Maaten Baggush on 10th June: just in time. The force was brought to the alert, aircraft made ready for immediate operations, and details of tasks decided. A few minutes after midnight Air Commodore Collishaw received word of the declaration of war; he was told to carry out reconnaissances as arranged and to use bomber formations to accompany them so as to attack favourable targets observed, especially concentrations of aircraft.

The first attack was made on the airfield at El Adem by 26 Blenheims of Nos. 45, 55 and 113 Squadrons: some success was achieved but three bombers were lost. The enemy's aircraft were not dispersed and there was every sign of unreadiness. The attack was repeated during the day and in all 18 aircraft were destroyed or damaged on the ground.[1] At dawn next day nine Blenheims of Nos. 45, 113 and 211 Squadrons attacked shipping at Tobruk in

---

[1] Generale di Squadra Aerea G. Santoro: *L'Aeronautica Italiana nella II^a Guerra Mondiale* (Rome, 1950), p. 394.

conjunction with the operations of the cruisers; this was the attack which damaged the *San Giorgio*. Tobruk was attacked three times during the next two days and nights, with some damage to shipping and oil tanks. On 14th June Gladiators of No. 33 Squadron and Blenheims of No. 211 Squadron supported the army's operations for the capture of Fort Capuzzo. The Air Officer Commanding-in-Chief would have liked nothing better than to continue on this scale, but uncertainty about his own replacements and reinforcements compelled him to husband his resources. From 17th to 21st June the comparative lull was broken by night attacks by single aircraft of No. 216 Squadron on the airfields of El Adem and Tobruk.

Throughout the month the Lysanders of No. 208 Squadron, operating from advanced air strips close to Western Desert Force headquarters, carried out regular reconnaissances of the enemy's forward area; the more distant tasks were allotted to Blenheims of No. 113 Squadron. Cover in these various operations was provided by the Gladiators of No. 33 Squadron by offensive sweeps and close escort. On the 21st fighter cover was given to the naval forces bombarding Bardia while bombers attacked shipping in the harbour. Further attacks were made on Tobruk and, at the request of the army, on enemy troop concentrations at Bir el Gubi. In general, for the rest of the month the air offensive was directed at the Tobruk airfields, and it was during one of these attacks that Marshal Balbo, Governor-General and Commander-in-Chief of the Armed Forces in Libya, arriving over Tobruk, was shot down by his own anti-aircraft guns. The Marshal had enjoyed the regard of the whole air world, and his death led to one of those courteous exchanges so rare in modern war as to deserve record: Sir Arthur Longmore caused a note of respectful regret to be dropped, which was acknowledged with gratitude.

The enemy was altogether slower off the mark than the Royal Air Force and was evidently much less ready. Some attacks by formations of not more than a dozen bombers were made on targets in the forward area, but the expected heavy attacks on Alexandria did not occur. Nor until the night of 21st/22nd June were Alexandria and the aircraft depot at Aboukir raided at all, and then the bombing was inaccurate and the damage slight. Towards the end of the month the enemy made determined attacks on the advanced airfields at Sidi Barrani and Matruh. If these caused little loss, they nevertheless made two things quite clear: that the Gladiator was too slow for the effective interception of the Italian bombers, and that the primitive warning system, which was all that it had been possible to provide in the forward area, rarely gave the fighters time to get into position. Of the four Hurricanes in Egypt only one could be spared for Air

K

Commodore Collishaw; but this one managed to multiply itself in Italian eyes by operating from different landing grounds and by its opportune appearances in unexpected places. The similar device of using single aircraft to attack widely separated targets was often successful in causing Italian commanders to appeal for air support, which resulted in a tendency to disperse their fighter effort and in a general over-estimate of the strength of the Royal Air Force.

Meanwhile, in the East African theatre the policy was to neutralize the enemy's air force by destroying his reserves, which he could not replace, of aircraft, spares, fuel and ammunition. Installations and the airfields flanking the Red Sea were accordingly struck as hard as possible. On 11th June No. 14 Squadron scored a notable success by destroying 780 tons of aviation fuel at Massawa, and during the next four days eight attacks were made on an airfield near Assab by Nos. 8 and 39 Squadrons, causing damage to aircraft and installations. Similar results were achieved at Diredawa, where in addition an ammunition dump was destroyed. Anti-submarine patrols by Nos. 8 and 94 Squadrons over the Red Sea contributed to the capture of the *Galileo Galilei* and the enemy's other submarine losses.

Although these operations had begun with great vigour and no little success, Sir Arthur Longmore had nevertheless to weigh his forces against some unpleasant possibilities. His own reinforcements were uncertain, but the Italian air offensive from Libya must be expected to grow heavier and German air forces might arrive to add weight to it. This threatening prospect in Egypt and the Mediterranean made it all the more important that the Red Sea line of communications should be secure, particularly from air and submarine attacks. The good results of the early British attacks in East Africa suggested that a greater effort against the hostile air force in this theatre might pay a rapidly growing dividend.[1] Sir Arthur Longmore decided therefore to increase the effort by sending one of his Bomber Squadrons (No. 45 Squadron) from the Western Desert to the Sudan, and to divert to Aden No. 11 (Blenheim) Squadron then on its way from India to Egypt. In Egypt more fighters were needed to meet the expected air offensive, and these he found by converting a Blenheim Bomber Squadron (No. 30) into a Fighter Squadron, thereby reducing still further the small striking force in the Western Desert. Of modern fighters there were, by the end of June, only seven Hurricanes in Egypt and five in Malta. In these circumstances it was imperative to husband resources with great care, for not only were aircraft scarce but spares of all kinds

---

[1] The Italian Air General Pinna, in a report dated 17th June, stated that in the first week the R.A.F. had destroyed a large quantity of food, tyres, engines, spare parts, fuel, and 15 aircraft; if the attacks were to continue with the same regularity the air force would be in a critical condition within a month.

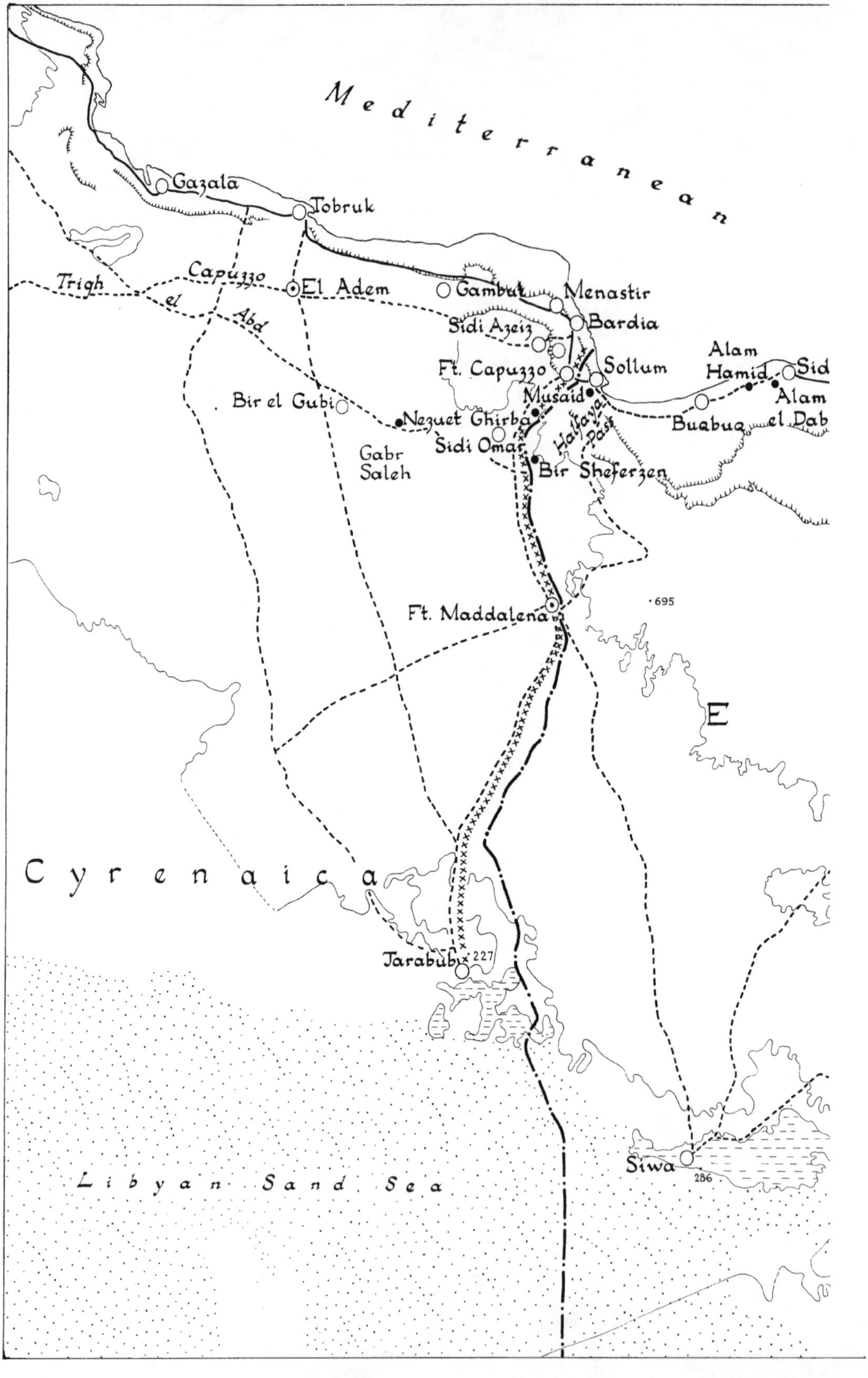
Mediterranean
Gazala
Tobruk
Trigh Capuzzo
Trigh el Abd
El Adem
Gambut
Menastir
Bardia
Sidi Azeiz
Ft. Capuzzo
Sollum
Alam Hamid
Alam el Dab
Musaid
Bir el Gubi
Nezuet Ghirba
Sidi Omar
Halfaya Pass
Buqbuq
Gabr Saleh
Bir Sheferzen
695
Ft. Maddalena
E
Cyrenaica
Jarabub
227
Libyan Sand Sea
Siwa
286

# Map 5
## The Western Desert of Egypt 1940

MILES 10    0    10    20    30    40    50    60    70    80 MILES

SPOT   HEIGHTS   IN   FEET
CONTOURS   AT   100   METRES
AIRFIELDS                                ⊙
LANDING   GROUNDS              ○

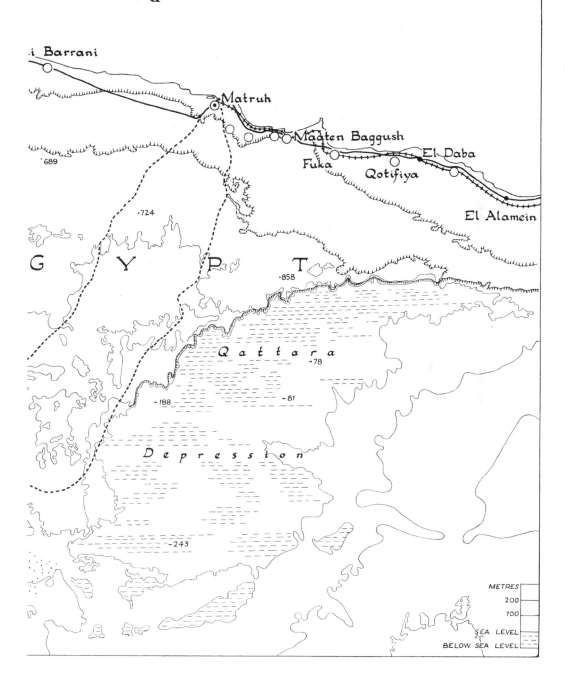

*S e a*

.i Barrani

Matruh

Maaten Baggush

Fuka                El Daba

Qotifiya

El Alamein

·689

·724

G        Y        P        T

·858

*Q a t t a r a*

·78

·188        ·81

*D e p r e s s i o n*

·243

| METRES |
|---|
| 200 |
| 100 |
| SEA LEVEL |
| BELOW SEA LEVEL |

for every type were short also; indeed, for the Hurricanes and Blenheim IVs there were none.

The part of the desert in which operations were to be carried on during 1940, soon to become familiar as the Western Desert, was a rough rectangle some 240 miles long and 150 miles across at the widest point. Strictly speaking the name means the Western Desert of Egypt, and therefore applies only to the tract lying east of the Libyan frontier. Popular usage soon applied the name to the desert west of the frontier as well. On the north of the boundary is the coast, where Mersa Matruh, Sidi Barrani, Bardia, Tobruk and Gazala became well-known names. On the west an imaginary boundary must be drawn from Gazala southward into the desert; the southern limits are marked by the oases of Jarabub and Siwa, lying on the fringe of the forbidding Sand Sea.[1] North-east from Siwa runs the ragged lip of the almost impassable Qattara Depression. Along the Libyan frontier, from the coast to Jarabub, stood a triple fence of barbed wire which had been erected by the Italians as a means of controlling Bedouin migrations. Along it were scattered a number of small block houses—the sole frontier defences.

The area thus outlined consists of two layers of country: a coastal strip of varying width, and then, at an average height of more than 500 feet above, the Libyan plateau. The ascent from the coast to the plateau forms the Escarpment, a feature which was to have an important influence on operations, because from Sofafi westwards it was impassable by wheels or track vehicles save at a few points; to the eastward also it restricted movement, though to a lesser extent. While the whole region is desert, it is not the waste of sand which the name suggests. Except in the sandy coastal strip there is limestone rock lying close below the surface of clay or fine sand, often breaking through in irregular patches. Pebbles, small boulders, and low scrub are frequent, and give a distinctive blackish colour to the desert at a distant view. Water is scarce, and the wells lie mostly in the coastal belt, though here and there inland are found deep wells and those cisterns known in service Arabic as 'birs', which date from Roman times and are marked by mounds of excavated rubble at their mouths. Many of these inland wells and cisterns are ruined, or dry, or hold a store of water which is scanty and foul.

The climate of the desert is variable. In summer the days are very hot, but the nights usually cold; in winter it is extremely cold, and heavy rain may fall. In spring and summer a frequent hot wind

---

[1] The Sand Sea, which is part of the Inner Desert, is described in connexion with the exploits of the Long Range Desert Group in Chapter XV.

from the Sahara brings with it clouds of fine sand which fills the eyes and lungs, clogs machines, and smothers food and equipment, while reducing visibility to a matter of yards. Amongst other irritations of life are scorpions and vipers amid stones and scrub, and, wherever men collect, sudden myriads of flies.

As a theatre of operations, the main characteristic of the desert was that it produced nothing for the support of armies: every article required for life and war had to be carried there. The climate was not in itself inimical to operations or to existence, and the desert was on the whole healthy, although the conditions imposed no little bodily and mental strain on the troops.

There were no roads except that running along the coast, but there were some recognized tracks which followed the easier ground or the pattern of wells. Such were the Trigh Capuzzo from Fort Capuzzo to El Adem and the west; the Trigh el Abd from Bir Sheferzen through Bir el Gubi to the north-west; and others less well known. Movement across the desert was possible in any direction subject to the limitations imposed by the Escarpment, the nature of the surface, and the ability of the individual to find the way. The Escarpment was an obstacle to mechanical movement north and south except where road cuttings had been made, or were later made as the campaign developed. Natural gaps did of course exist but could not be relied upon to afford passage to numbers of vehicles without improvement. All over the plateau there were large areas where the surface offered no obstacles to wheels or tracks, but within this general freedom were many restrictive types of 'going'. There were stretches of sand which would bring a vehicle to a halt while its wheels or tracks spun, becoming each instant more deeply embedded; rocky outcrops, sudden hollows, and seamy fissures which were difficult to thread; stony areas destructive to tracks and springs; and large tracts which became impassable after rain. Skilled driving could overcome these difficulties, but good navigation was necessary for keeping direction in a featureless country whose main landmarks, before artificial ones were added, were the mounds of rubble excavated from the 'birs'. Sun, stars, and compass were the instruments essential to navigation, and the ability to use them was an indispensable attribute: but to move confidently and freely, and generally to feel at home, something more was wanted—an acuteness of perception hard to define but commonly called 'desert sense'. And even then it was possible to become bewildered or lost.[1]

The desert concealed its tactical features. Observation points were few save on the Escarpment, and places of concealment were equally

---

[1] A notable example of faulty reconnaissance or navigation, or both, occurred during the Italian advance in September. General Maletti's Group, which had been given a flanking role, lost its way to the starting point at Sidi Omar, and had to be searched for by aircraft. See page 208.

scarce. But the practised eye could recognize the undulations, depressions, and other accidents of ground which afforded covered approaches or hull-down positions for tanks and cover for men and guns, though it was not possible, save in some conditions of light or weather, to be certain of escaping observation from the air.[1] On the ground there might be haze, dust and tricks of light to make observation and recognition difficult. Finally, the rocky foundation of the desert often made it necessary to use power tools and explosives for the construction of satisfactory defences; but this same firm foundation made the preparation of temporary landing strips an easy matter.[2]

Before June 1940 the Army and Air Force had both carried out such exercises in the Western Desert as were possible in the circumstances, and much had been learnt about the movement of small mechanized forces and about the operation of aircraft from desert landing grounds. There was however a great deal still to learn about the desert and its ways before its peculiarities, especially in relation to a war of machines, could be said to be generally understood. Gradually the techniques were evolved and the methods perfected, the essential instruments being the desert-wise man and the desert-worthy vehicle.

At the outbreak of war the strength and general condition of the Italian forces in Cyrenaica and Tripolitania was known with some accuracy, but their detailed dispositions had not been discovered. In fact the enemy's intentions and dispositions were broadly these. They expected the French to attack Tripoli from Tunisia, while the British, whose strength they over-estimated, carried out a limited offensive into Cyrenaica. The 5th Italian Army was suitably disposed to meet the French attack, and at the beginning of June the 10th Army was concentrating in Cyrenaica. It was intended that the 1st Libyan Division should defend the frontier from Jarabub to Sidi Omar, while the 21st Corps was to be responsible from there to the coast, and for the defence of Bardia and Tobruk. The 22nd Corps would be stationed south-west of Tobruk to co-operate with the 21st Corps, and to counter-attack any British advance round the formation's southern flank. As a first stage in the concentration the Frontier Guard was reinforced by a Blackshirt brigade, divided between Bardia and Tobruk, and a smaller regular garrison was placed in Jarabub. As the 1st Libyan Division moved eastward part of the 62nd (Marmarica) Division was to be sent to Bardia to reinforce the

---

[1] 'Hull-down' meant that the tank's hull was behind cover and only the turret exposed.

[2] For the effects of desert conditions in general upon the maintenance of aircraft see page 73.

garrison. Marshal Balbo hoped to defeat any attempt to capture
Bardia or Tobruk, which were thought to be the probable British
objectives, and then, somewhat vaguely, to pass to the offensive
himself.

The British assessment of the available information was that the
Frontier Guard posts from Bardia to Jarabub were weak but were
being reinforced, and that the 21st Corps was concentrating in the
area of Bardia and Fort Capuzzo. The extent of the reinforcement
and the degree of concentration achieved were not known when war
broke out. To meet this situation the British Western Desert Force
was ordered to dominate the frontier and to cut the enemy's land
communications with Jarabub. Objectives were to be as varied as
possible in order to puzzle and harass the enemy, but men, vehicles,
and materials were to be husbanded. For this task General O'Connor
threw out a covering force, controlled by the 7th Armoured Division,
and consisting of part of one armoured brigade and the Support
Group.

By the evening of 11th June the 11th Hussars (save for a squadron
at Sidi Barrani) with their Morris and elderly Rolls Royce armoured
cars had reached the frontier wire on a broad front. Between thirty
and forty miles to the east were the headquarters of the covering
force and of the 4th Armoured Brigade, which had with it only one
regiment—the 7th Queen's Own Hussars, in light and cruiser tanks.
The Support Group lay to the north-east, about Sidi Barrani and
Buq Buq. During the night the 11th Hussars crossed the wire, and
what were the first shots of the desert war were drawn from enemy
posts at Sidi Omar by patrols of A and B Squadrons. It soon became
clear that the enemy had been surprised; in fact his troops on the
frontier were unaware of the outbreak of war. Patrolling continued
all day, and 70 prisoners were taken.

The next step was for the patrolling of the frontier to be taken over
by a squadron of the 7th Hussars and a company of 1st Battalion,
The King's Royal Rifle Corps, while the 11th Hussars pushed
farther afield, thus beginning a phase in which the covering force
settled down to dominate the desert along and on the enemy's side
of the frontier. On 14th June the 7th Hussars captured Fort Capuzzo,
and the 11th Hussars took Maddalena. Next day the 11th Hussars
placed an ambush on the coast road between Bardia and Tobruk
and on 16th June killed 21 of the enemy and captured 88 including
General Lastucci, Engineer-in-Chief of the 10th Army.[1] On the
same day a squadron of the same regiment discovered an enemy
force of some 17 light tanks, 4 guns and 400 infantry near Nezuet

---

[1] The Duce wrote to the King on 17th June as follows: 'Affairs on the Egyptian
frontier did not turn out too brilliantly. Our losses in the past few days have been
2 redoubts, 24 armoured cars, and 2 Libyan—I repeat Libyan—companies. I believe
Balbo will restore the situation.'

Ghirba. This discovery was reported to 4th Armoured Brigade, who sent forward a cruiser squadron of 7th Hussars and a troop of J Battery R.H.A. The squadron of the 11th Hussars had meanwhile taken action to hold the enemy. When the reinforcements arrived a concerted attack was made which routed the Italian force with the loss of more than 100 killed and captured, all their guns and light tanks and several lorries. There were no British casualties.

During the remainder of the month vigorous patrolling spread over an area which extended in the north to the coast road between Bardia and Tobruk, in the west to Bir el Gubi, and in the south to Jarabub. These operations did not indeed prevent the enemy continuing to concentrate between Bardia and Tobruk and further to the westward, nor yet from recapturing Fort Capuzzo, but in these opening weeks the units of the covering force acquired invaluable experience. Their exploits had been largely successful, and the results went far beyond the immediate gains. For it had been clearly demonstrated that British troops could learn to use, and not to fear, the desert; with the desert for an ally there were great opportunities for enterprise and initiative. The enemy had not shown that he realized this; he seemed reluctant to venture far from his roads and tracks. Here was an advantage to be pressed.


Malta received the first of its many air attacks towards 5 o'clock in the morning of 11th June, when ten Italian aircraft bombed the dockyard and Hal Far airfield. Of the 112 heavy and 60 light anti-aircraft guns approved by the Committee of Imperial Defence a year before, only 34 heavy and 8 light were present; the 24 searchlights had all arrived.[1] There was only one radar set, which could not be expected to be permanently in action. It is true that there were the three Gladiators, but what were they, however gallantly flown, against the relays of Italian aircraft that were expected to appear?

The second attack—this time by 25 aircraft—followed late in the afternoon. In the remaining days of June there were 36 attacks, by day and night, of varying intensity, the heaviest being made by 60 bombers escorted by fighters. The early targets were clearly meant to be the dockyard and airfields, but the bombs usually fell over a large area. The damage was not so great as had been feared, although it was bad enough. Hits occurred on the naval establishment at Fort St. Angelo, on various workshops and dockyard installations, on the naval hospital, and on a submarine in dry dock, while on 21st June the floating dock, already damaged on three occasions, received a direct hit and sank. This was enough to make Admiral Cunningham abandon Malta as a submarine base for the time being.

[1] See page 30.

The situation would have been immeasurably worse had not the morale of the civilian population proved equal to the strain. At the outset a general exodus took place from the Three Cities area, which added a food-distribution problem to the many difficulties facing the civil authorities. But under the inspiring leadership of Lieutenant-General Sir William Dobbie, the Governor and Commander-in-Chief, confidence was soon restored and with it grew a determination to overcome hardship and a strong will to resist. As a result of the impetus given to the A.R.P. arrangements by these early attacks the organization was in a much better condition when the time came for it to be severely tested by the *Luftwaffe* seven months later. Seventy civilians were killed in June.

It stood to reason that civilian morale could not be expected to remain high unless the people could see that the air defence was being strengthened and that steps were being taking to ensure the provision of at least the bare essentials of life, for this small island could never support its population of 270,000. It was obviously necessary to achieve a proper balance between civil and military supplies of all kinds, and the first step was the creation of an authority for the Co-ordination of Supplies—COSUP—responsible for preparing the island's consolidated demands. A complementary body was later established in Egypt, known as the Malta Shipping Committee, whose duty it was to arrange for the loading of convoys bound for Malta.

The most urgent requirement was of course to increase the number of fighter aircraft, but Malta was not the only place where they were wanted and during the month only a modest reinforcement was received. On 4th June six Hurricanes flew from England for Egypt, via France, Tunis, and Malta. The Governor, supported by the naval and air Commanders-in-Chief, urged that these should be allowed to remain at Malta. The answer was that the Fleet base at Alexandria must have priority; one Hurricane, however, delayed in Tunis for repairs, did remain in Malta. On 18th June the Air Ministry despatched a further twelve, of which Malta was authorized to keep six. Owing to bad weather and other mishaps only the latter number arrived at Malta, and two of them were ordered on to Egypt. The outcome was that in the last week of June Malta had four serviceable Hurricanes besides two of the three original Gladiators, fast wearing out. There was one other reinforcement. On 21st June twelve Swordfish of No. 767 Fleet Air Arm Squadron were transferred at the instigation of Admiral Cunningham from Hyères to Malta, where they came under the operational control of the A.O.C. for the purpose of attacking Italian shipping.

These additional aircraft, welcome though they were, did not by any means solve all Air Commodore Maynard's problems; in fact

5. A British 60-pdr gun in action under its camouflage net.
Taken from below the escarpment, September 1940.

*Facing p. 120*

6. A patrol of Gladiators returning to its desert base.

7. 'There is no spot more naked': four-barrelled .5 machine-
gun in action. (From the painting by Rowland Langmaid.)

8. An operation in a hospital tent in the desert.

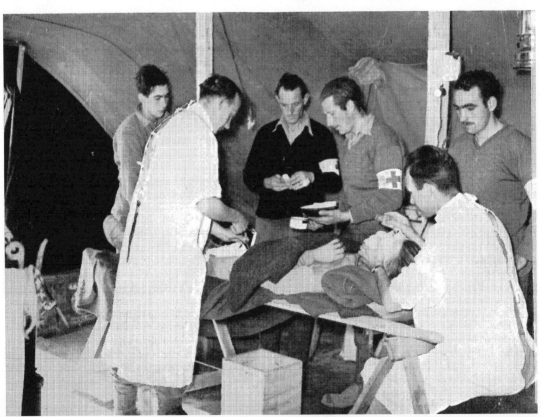

9. A Hurricane flying over the coastal strip of the Western Desert. The sea is on the left; then a belt of sand and scrub; clear of this is the thin ribbon of the main road to Matruh.

10. Dust! The effect of a flight of Hurricanes taxi-ing across the landing ground.

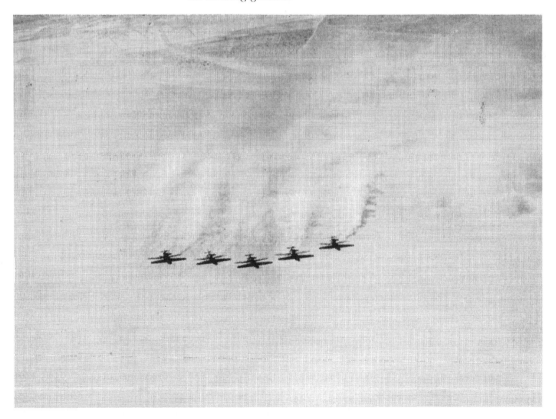

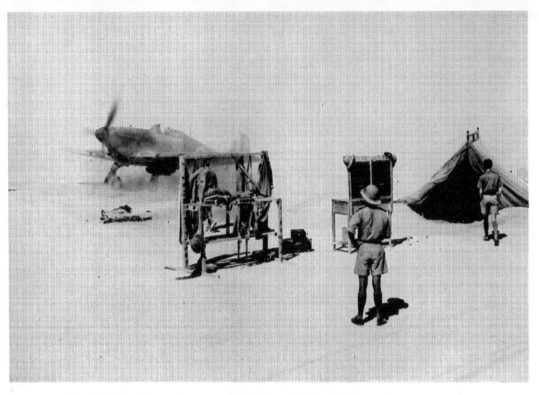

11. Dust! A Hurricane about to take off from its 'base'. The operations room is in the tent.

12. The desert is not always dry. Airmen literally bailing out after a sudden rainstorm.

they increased them, for not only was his air defence organization entirely improvised but his small peace time establishment of officers and men was quite insufficient for undertaking so many new activities. Nor had he any reserves to call upon. It was indeed fortunate, and very surprising, that the attacks had not been heavier and the damage greater. Italian civil aircraft had been flying over and landing regularly on Malta right up to the outbreak of war and there had of course been consular officials on the island. In one way or another the Italian Air Staff should have been well informed about the island's weaknesses. If they were, they did not admit it: on the contrary, they described the defences as formidable and paid an unconscious compliment to the pilots of the three Gladiators by crediting the island with twenty-five fighters on the outbreak of war.

In Egypt the King and Aly Maher Pasha had been showing themselves to be increasingly opposed to the interests of the Allies. It had been strongly put to the Prime Minister that, if Italy should declare war upon the Allies, Egypt should declare war upon Italy. In the event this was not done. On 12th June the Prime Minister declared in Parliament that Egypt would not join in hostilities unless Italian troops invaded Egyptian territory, or unless Egyptian towns or military objectives were attacked by Italian aircraft. Diplomatic relations with Italy had, however, been broken off. The announcement received the almost unanimous approval of the Egyptian Parliament. From the British point of view, too, there was much to be said for this attitude which seemed likely to ensure that Egyptian defence forces, especially anti-aircraft guns and searchlights, would come into action if their collaboration were required. And if Egypt was to be drawn into the war it was perhaps better that it should be as the result of Italian attack than of Allied pressure. The position was therefore accepted for the time being, but, as the days passed and the Italian Minister did not leave, and the Italian suspects were not interned, and Allied interests continued to be obstructed, it was difficult to avoid the conclusion that the King and the Prime Minister were leaning towards a policy of re-insurance with Italy. Their reasoning no doubt was that if France collapsed the position of Great Britain in the Mediterranean would become untenable and the predominant Mediterranean Power would then be Italy. The situation became so intolerable that the War Cabinet approved of strong pressure being applied to King Farouk. As a result, Aly Maher Pasha resigned office on 23rd June. Four days later the King appointed Hassan Sabry Pasha, a man personally favourable to British interests but politically too weak to promote them. The King had yielded, it is true, but his policy had not changed. Nevertheless it was thought better to accept the position than to bring about an even worse crisis at this juncture.

The Beirut conference had shown Turkey how little she could expect from the Allies in the way of military assistance; since then her supplies of war materials had fallen below expectations and there had been the resounding German success in France. One of the Allies seemed unlikely to be able to fulfil her obligations under the Treaty, but by Article 7 the provisions remained binding on Turkey as bilateral obligations. In these circumstances it is hardly to be wondered at that Turkey chose to invoke the protocol by which she was absolved from any action that might involve her in armed conflict with the Soviet Union. In other words she remained non-belligerent though benevolent.

Iraq's reaction was to do nothing. The Palestine question was still a cause of anti-British agitation, aggravated by the presence in Baghdad of the Mufti, under lax restraint. Feeling against the British was running high, particularly among the younger army officers. The attitude of the Iraqi Government had seemed to be one of impotence or possibly of connivance, though towards the end of May they had shown signs of greater resolution. There was ample evidence of the mingled fear and admiration that Germany's successes had instilled; there was a suspicion of the existence of a 'fifth column' organization; and there was doubt of the loyalty of the Iraqi Army in an emergency.

Such, then, was the attitude of the three countries with whom Great Britain had worked so hard to negotiate treaties of alliance or mutual assistance, a policy which was to be amply justified although the results had so far not been spectacular. As for the attempts to solidify opposition to the Axis in the Balkans, there seemed to be no longer any prospect of success in this direction. The Commanders-in-Chief might well feel that much of their labours of the past year had been in vain, but worse was in store for them. On 14th June they were warned that France might seek a separate peace. Three days later they learned that she had asked for an armistice. His Majesty's Government, they were told, were determined to continue the war until victory was won.

The attitude of the French authorities in North Africa, Syria, and Somaliland to the collapse in Metropolitan France varied from time to time and place to place. On 17th June General Noguès rejected a suggestion that he should break with the Bordeaux Government, and for a few days his official attitude was reserved. He disapproved of making public announcements of future intentions while there remained a French Government which had not laid down its arms. A factor which added to the uncertainty was that, although the armistice with Germany was signed on 22nd June, it was not to take effect until the armistice with Italy, requested by the French Government on June 20th, should be signed also. There were indications however that Noguès might be privately resolved to fight on, to which colour was lent by Admiral Darlan's orders of 17th June for operations in North Africa to continue, and by a message sent by Noguès to Mittelhauser on 22nd June in the same sense.[1] The morale of the French forces and population also appeared to be unshaken. But by 23rd June doubts had begun to appear, and there was a tendency in military circles to regard resistance as conditional upon some form of assistance from Britain. On June 24th the armistice with Italy was signed; on the same day General Noguès again rejected a suggestion of a break with Bordeaux, and that evening he proclaimed 'The armistice is signed', and declared that for the moment the integrity and defence of North Africa seemed assured. He recommended calmness, unity, discipline, and confidence in the future of France as the policy to be followed.

In Syria reactions were sharper. General Mittelhauser and the High Commissioner, although deeply affected by the collapse of 17th June and left without precise information or instructions, expressed their determination to fight on. This resolution was supported in all quarters. General Mittelhauser was convinced that the Mediterranean basin must, and could, be defended by Anglo-French forces, and General Wavell and Air Chief Marshal Longmore, visiting him on 20th June, found him ready to discuss ways and means. He was eager to launch an air attack upon Rhodes, for which he asked some assistance, and in return expressed his readiness to provide a division for the defence of the Suez Canal, and later two bomber squadrons and some fighters to add to the air defence of Egypt. He suggested that a joint Anglo-French planning staff should be set up. 'Morale in Syria is good', wrote General Wavell, 'and there is no intention of abandoning the struggle'.

Certain anxieties, however, underlay this determination. There was a keen desire to know the attitude of General Noguès, about which the information was scanty though reassuring, and coupled with this was the wish for a French Government to be set up in Algiers. In spite of this uncertainty General Mittelhauser, after consultation with the High Commissioner, broadcast on 23rd June his decision to fight on. He admitted in confidence that he expected to be chastised for this declaration, and the strain upon him was evidently great.

In French Somaliland the resolute General Legentilhomme, who was now in command of both French and British forces, declared at once that he would continue to fight. And when the Governor said that if he received instructions to surrender Jibuti he would obey, the General said that he would use force to prevent him. This was

---

[1] General Mittelhauser had arrived in Beirut on 28th May, in place of General Weygand.

uncompromising enough, but Legentilhomme also expressed a wish to see formed somewhere a fresh French Government. Characteristically he desired this not so much to provide a legal basis for his own actions as to stiffen the wills of civilian administrators.

On 18th June the Chiefs of Staff felt bound to consider whether, with France dropping out of the war, the British Mediterranean Fleet ought not to be withdrawn altogether: for one thing it did not lie between the Italian Fleet and the vital Atlantic trade routes. But the effects of withdrawal would have been so serious that it was decided not to force this grave issue until the fate of the French Navy 'had been settled, and the question was submerged in the clash of events. On the 20th Admiral Cunningham was able to report that Admiral Godfroy's squadron was full of fight, and was about to take part in a sweep by the fleet into the Central Mediterranean planned to begin on the 22nd. The fleet had just begun to leave harbour when this operation was cancelled on the Admiralty's order—a vivid reminder of the general uncertainty about the French Navy. Godfroy was still without official notice of the armistice terms, but his attitude was unchanged; in Syria too, the naval morale was high. But on the 24th Godfroy received an order from his Admiralty to cease hostilities and proceed to French ports upon the armistice being ratified. Admiral Cunningham thereupon made it clear that he would not allow the French ships to leave Alexandria in any circumstances. Thus began a state of tension, but more than a week was to pass before the crisis was reached.

During these bitter days the French were not without British encouragement and support. It had not been possible to supply North Africa with arms and equipment nor to land there a small force to stimulate resistance, as had been advocated by the Governor of Gibraltar, but on a higher plane there had been the British Government's offer of union and common citizenship. In Syria, at any rate, this proposal was well received, but the Council of Ministers in France did not accept it. Further strenuous efforts, as will shortly be described, were to be made to arouse or foster the will to resist of Frenchmen overseas. It is difficult for anyone but a Frenchman to realize the intensity of the doubts and fears with which they were beset at this time, or the severity of the conflict in which their honour and their loyalties were so deeply involved. To side openly with the British must have been a difficult decision to take; but the consideration that probably weighed least with those who took it was the fact that they laid themselves open by the terms of the armistice to be treated, if captured, as *francs-tireurs*.[1] Great as was the strain on individuals, that on the leaders was greater still, and their decisions were anxiously awaited.

---

[1] A provision which was contrary to accepted international law.

# CHAPTER VII

# THE FRENCH COLLAPSE

FOR MORE than a year the British had worked hard to concert plans and preparations with the French. They had been at great trouble to prevent the additional weight of Italy being thrown into the scale, for it had long been realized that this would impose a very severe strain on their combined resources. And now, not only had Italy declared war, but within a fortnight the British Commonwealth had found itself facing the consequences single-handed.

With the signature of the armistice with Italy, the German armistice came into force also. The full implications of the terms could not be judged in England immediately, nor, indeed, were the precise terms known. One thing however was quite clear: that while no one could tell what would eventually be saved from the wreckage of France's armed strength, large enemy forces were immediately available for employment elsewhere and could not be expected to remain idle. Broadly, the Germans had the choice between invading England and turning to the Balkans. Either of these courses, whether accompanied or not by direct intervention in the Mediterranean area, would profoundly affect the military situation in the Middle East, for, as has been seen, the prospect of a German invasion of the Balkans was unwelcome enough even when France was an active ally, while if the United Kingdom was to be threatened with invasion there would be little chance of sparing the men and material now needed in the Middle East.

As far as was known in London on 27th June, the armistice terms provided for the transfer of a large part of France to German control; for the demobilization and disarming of all French armed forces other than those required to keep order; and for the recall of the ships of the fleet (except those left free for safeguarding French interests in the Colonial Empire) to their home ports, there to be demobilized and disarmed under German or Italian control. Frontier zones in Tunisia and Algeria and the whole of French Somaliland were to be demilitarized, as also were the naval bases of Toulon, Bizerta, Ajaccio, and Oran. The Italians were to have full use of the port of Jibuti, and the French section of the Addis Ababa railway. All these proceedings would be supervised by German or Italian commissions.

At sea the whole balance of strength had been upset at a stroke: the British would now be obliged to retain sufficient naval forces in

European waters to match both the German and Italian fleets. Hitherto, the Western Mediterranean had been the French zone of responsibility, and the British had intended to abandon the Eastern Mediterranean if they felt it necessary to send a fleet to the Far East, in which event the French would have assumed the task of containing the Italian fleet.[1] The Australian and New Zealand Governments had now to be told that in the new situation no fleet could be sent to the Far East. Within the Mediterranean the British had lost the co-operation of three French battleships, two battlecruisers and fourteen cruisers, besides numerous destroyers, submarines and small craft; the only coasts remaining open to them were those of Egypt and Palestine, the islands of Cyprus and Malta, and the Rock of Gibraltar. Italian naval and air forces would be able to move freely in the central and western basins. This led to some anxiety about Gibraltar, where the existing British forces were inadequate even for giving due warning of enemy approach. All this was bad enough, but a recent move by Spain suggested worse to come. On 14th June she had exchanged her neutrality for non-belligerency and occupied the international zone of Tangier on the pretext of guaranteeing its neutrality. It seemed possible that, following the example of Italy, she was preparing to come to the help of the winning side.

In order that the Italian fleet should not be entirely unopposed in the western basin, nor the front door of the Mediterranean be left unguarded, a British force—to be known later as Force H—had already begun to assemble at Gibraltar. It was directly under the Admiralty, and not under the command of Admiral Cunningham. The nucleus of the force consisted of the battlecruiser *Hood* and the aircraft carrier *Ark Royal* (No. 800 Squadron—12 Skuas; No. 803 Squadron—12 Skuas; Nos. 810, 818 and 820 Squadrons—30 Swordfish), which arrived at Gibraltar on 23rd June. But even when the force was formed it would not restore the balance, nor could enemy ships be prevented from moving in comparative safety between Italy and the North African ports.

While the services of the French fleet had unquestionably been lost, it was equally certain that the territory of France itself would no longer be accessible, so that British aircraft would be unable to land and refuel on their way from the United Kingdom to the Middle East. The provision of an alternative route was therefore an urgent necessity, which led to the development of the Takoradi air route between West Africa and the Sudan, described in Chapter X. It was always possible that in the French overseas possessions the enemy might have difficulty in enforcing the armistice terms, so that something might yet be saved from the land and air forces in North Africa, French Somaliland, and Syria. If, on the other hand,

---

[1] Referred to on page 28.

the terms could be successfully enforced, the Italians in Libya would no longer need to concern themselves with Tunisia, but would be free to devote their whole attention to Egypt. A greatly increased scale of air attack on the naval base at Alexandria would then have to be expected and an invasion of Egypt regarded as distinctly probable. If, in addition, the Germans intended to use French North Africa themselves, and succeeded in doing so, they would acquire air bases conveniently situated for attacking Malta and Gibraltar. As for French Somaliland, this was the intended starting point for the eventual offensive against the Italians in Ethiopia, so that the loss of the territory and its port of Jibuti would necessitate a completely new plan; for the present the ability to hold British Somaliland would be greatly reduced and the threat to British shipping slightly increased. There remained Syria, where the French had been preparing forces for various agreed tasks: one to occupy Crete, another to assist Turkey, and another to move to Egypt in case of emergency. With Italy already at war it was most disconcerting to think that these and all the other plans for mutual co-operation might now be so much waste paper. It was clearly necessary to do everything possible to encourage the French at this juncture.

Accordingly, French officials everywhere were informed that, in the British view, the signature of the armistice had been obtained under duress. Metropolitan France had been occupied by the enemy, but the overseas empire was intact and had still a vital part to play. Civil and military authorities overseas were therefore called upon by the British Government and people to fight on to the end for victory, which would mean the restoration of the greatness of France. To this appeal was added the voice of General de Gaulle. As early as 18th June he had invited Frenchmen on British soil to put themselves in touch with him: now, on the 24th, he called upon all servicemen and technicians overseas to join with those who still wanted to fight.[1] A Provisional French National Committee and a French Volunteer Legion were to be formed in the United Kingdom. On the 27th the General addressed himself to North Africa in particular, as it was to Algiers that Frenchmen overseas were inclined to look for a lead. They had not long to wait, for in Algeria there was a surge of anti-British feeling and defeatism, and on the 25th General Noguès refused to see Mr. Duff Cooper, the Minister of Information, and General Lord Gort, who had flown to Rabat in Morocco. By the next day it was evident to the British military mission in Algiers that Noguès had no further intention of resisting. As there was nothing more that the mission could do it left the country on 28th June.

[1] One French submarine, the *Narval*, entered Malta on 26th June to place herself under the authority of de Gaulle. After carrying out several patrols she was destroyed by an Italian torpedo boat off Benghazi.

On this day His Majesty's Government formally recognized de Gaulle as the leader of all free Frenchmen, wherever they might be, who rallied to him in support of the Allied cause.

In Syria opinion was sharply divided, and it was soon evident that General Mittelhauser was feeling the great burden of his responsibilities, and that his initial resolution was being undermined by the difficulties of his position. When he heard that Noguès intended to obey the order to capitulate, Mittelhauser decided that he must do the same. The Commanders-in-Chief in the Middle East were authorized to announce that all French forces who continued to fight could count on the full political and financial support of the British Government, and that such forces would be welcome if at any time they wished to join the British. So far as this affected Syria General Wavell was inclined to doubt the wisdom of encouraging the wholesale disintegration of the French forces that seemed likely to occur, as it might give rise to a state of confusion and disorder on Palestine's hitherto secure northern flank. He was told, however, that the Government's policy was to accept the services of all Frenchmen who would continue to fight, and that local considerations were of secondary importance. Having consulted the Turkish Government, His Majesty's Government announced on 1st July that they could not allow Syria or the Lebanon to be occupied by any hostile power or to be used as a base for attacks on those countries which the British were pledged to defend or to become the scene of such disorder as to constitute a danger to those countries. They therefore held themselves free to take whatever measures might be necessary.

In French Somaliland the attitude of General Legentilhomme towards General Wavell remained one of frankness and loyalty, even after he had been ordered by his own Government to cease hostilities and relinquish his authority over British troops. Both he and the Governor declared their intention of continuing to fight by the side of the British. On 28th June the locally appointed Italian armistice commission tried to get in touch with Legentilhomme, who reported to Cairo that he intended to temporize, and added that he expected to be attacked before long. 2nd Battalion The Black Watch was accordingly sent in H.M.S. *Liverpool* from Egypt to Aden, there to be held ready to support Legentilhomme, who meanwhile continued to fob off and mislead the Italians with protestations of ignorance, and seems to have enjoyed himself immensely in the process.

The doubts and uncertainties which attended the collapse of France were naturally not confined to French territory. One very important question was: what would be the reaction of Turkey? The defection of the French in Syria had deprived her of her nearest source of military aid and had severed her land communications with the British; and this at a moment when ominous clouds were appearing on the Balkan horizon. For the armistice had only been in force for two days when Rumania renounced the Anglo-French guarantee and aligned herself with Germany—not that this availed her anything when she received a peremptory demand from the U.S.S.R. to give up Bessarabia and Northern Bukovina. Germany advised her to submit, and by the end of June these provinces were in Russian occupation. This meant that Turkey's hereditary enemy was drawing unpleasantly near, perhaps with an eye upon the Straits, while there was always the danger that Bulgaria might be the next country on Germany's list. It was already obvious to the Turks that the help they had hoped for under the Tripartite Treaty would not be forthcoming; in fact, one of the signatories was now in no position to fulfil any obligations. In these circumstances it might not be easy to persuade the Turks that alliance with the United Kingdom was still the best policy for them to pursue. It was obvious that they were going to be faced with a difficult decision, which the artful and experienced von Papen, recently appointed German Ambassador in Ankara, would do his utmost to influence. In the opinion of the British Ambassador at Ankara, much would depend upon the fate of the French Mediterranean Fleet. If this were to fall into Axis hands it would become very difficult, he thought, to hold Turkey where she was, in view of her growing fear of Russia.

This was clearly the moment for a pronouncement on military policy, and on 3rd July the Chiefs of Staff telegraphed their appreciation of the new situation. It was more reassuring in its tone than in its content. Most of it was already familiar—a restatement of the factors which contributed to the security of the Middle East. Our policy had necessarily to continue to be generally defensive. The Chiefs of Staff recognized the necessity for strengthening the forces in the Middle East at the earliest possible moment, but the governing factor was the probability of heavy air action against the United Kingdom, followed perhaps by invasion. Shortage of equipment would severely handicap us in meeting these threats. The policy would be to concentrate on the defence of the United Kingdom and start to release equipment for the Middle East when the situation following the impending trial of strength could be more clearly judged. This might not be for two months; meanwhile, everything that could be spared would be sent, including, if possible, modern fighters to rearm the squadrons in Egypt, and bombers to replace wastage. The situation in Syria was having disturbing effects in Iraq and even in Persia; subject, therefore, to the consent of the Iraqi Government, it was proposed to send a division from India to secure the Anglo-Iranian oilfields.[1]

Hardly had this dispassionate survey been made when a matter

---

[1] The 5th Indian Division.

L

which had been causing anxiety ever since France had shown signs
of collapse came sharply to a head. The direct issue was the future
of the French capital ships, and it was destined to darken and
imperil to a dangerous extent the friendship and understanding
between Great Britain and France.


The departure of French warships from ports on the north and
west coasts of France during June was in keeping with the assurances
given by Admiral Darlan, Marshal Pétain, and others, that in no
circumstances would the French Fleet be allowed to fall intact into
enemy hands. Two old battleships, with other vessels, proceeded to
Plymouth and Portsmouth. The recently completed battleship
*Richelieu* sailed from Brest for Casablanca on the 18th, followed next
day by the partially completed *Jean Bart* from St. Nazaire. But the main
portion of the fleet was in the Mediterranean, having been based on
North African ports since April. Admiral Godfroy's Force X was
at Alexandria; six cruisers were at Algiers; a few units remained at
Toulon; while at Mers-el-Kebir, the naval port adjacent to Oran, was
Admiral Gensoul with the two modern battlecruisers *Dunkerque* and
*Strasbourg*, two battleships, a seaplane carrier, and six fleet destroyers.
At Oran itself were four submarines and a number of torpedo boats.

The War Cabinet was deeply concerned lest the most powerful
ships should become available to the enemy, for it was thought that
this might alter the whole course of the war. The armistice conditions
as known to the British on 23rd June stipulated that the French Fleet
was to be demobilized under German or Italian supervision in its
normal home ports, to which ships were to be recalled. The Germans
(and later the Italians) declared that they had no intention of using
French ships for their own ends except for coastal protection and
minesweeping. The French were known to have protested against
the recall of their ships to home ports, but with what success the
British Admiralty was as yet unaware.

There was of course ample reason for placing no reliance on any
undertaking given by the Germans. The advice of the Chief of Naval
Staff was that if the French capital ships fell into enemy hands it
would be some two months before the Germans could efficiently
employ them and some three months before the Italians could do so.[1]

---

[1] A view held by many naval officers is that this was an understatement of the
difficulties with which the enemy would be faced; that the handing over of a ship
intact was very unlikely; and that it was more unlikely still that French officers and
men would actively co-operate with the enemy. The German Foreign Office's minutes
of a talk between Hitler and Mussolini at Munich on 18th June 1940 contain no
reference to the use of the French Fleet by the Axis powers, but record some anxiety
lest it should become available to the British; in particular, the large accretion of
destroyers might make it impossible for German submarines to attack convoys. It was
agreed that the French Fleet would have to be neutralized, and the Führer observed
that scuttling would be a good solution.

The War Cabinet felt bound to assume that if the Germans wanted to get possession of any of the French ships they would succeed; no one knew better how to devise and enforce methods of compulsion. However resolute the French might intend to be, it was more than likely that events would pass beyond their control; so long, therefore, as these powerful ships remained afloat within reach of the Germans they constituted a very great potential menace. Accordingly, on 27th June the War Cabinet decided that, if necessary, they must be prevented from returning to their metropolitan ports.

On 28th June Vice-Admiral Sir James Somerville was appointed to the command of Force H, with the initial task of securing the transfer, surrender, or destruction of the French warships at Oran and Mers-el-Kebir. Next day Admiral Cunningham was warned that all French warships were likely to be recalled to their home ports for demilitarization under German or Italian control; he was also told of Somerville's orders and of the drastic action that would probably have to be taken against the ships at Oran. He was to send two submarines to co-operate. He replied expressing the strongest disapproval of the suggested action, which he thought would have serious consequences in the Middle East. It is easy to understand his interest and concern in the fate of any French ships—particularly those in the Mediterranean—for Admiral Godfroy's squadron was an integral part of the Eastern Mediterranean Fleet, and the two Admirals were friends and respected colleagues.

On arrival at Gibraltar Admiral Somerville was able to consult several officers who were singularly competent to advise on French naval matters. Admiral Sir Dudley North, Commanding the North Atlantic Station, had paid a special visit on 24th June to Admiral Gensoul, who had assured him that his ships would be fought by Frenchmen or not at all; he gave his word of honour that in no circumstance whatever would they fall intact into German or Italian hands. Captain C. S. Holland of the *Ark Royal* had recently been Naval Attaché in Paris; he spoke French fluently, and among his many personal acquaintances in the French Navy was Admiral Gensoul himself. In addition, there were present two officers who had recently held liaison posts at the French naval base at Bizerta.

Early on 1st July Somerville received orders to be ready to act on the 3rd, and to make his preparations on the basis that the French would be given four choices: first, to bring their ships to a British harbour and fight on; second, to steam to a British port whence the crews would be repatriated; third, to demilitarize their ships immediately to our satisfaction; fourth, to sink them. A few hours later the Admiral signalled to say how impressed he was by the consensus of advice that the threat of force should be avoided at all costs, and that no French Admiral, faced with an ultimatum, would do other than resist. For this reason he proposed to use Holland as an emissary to arrive some hours ahead of Force H. Later, in the belief that the French ships might soon be sailing for metropolitan ports, he altered his plan and proposed to the Admiralty that Force H should arrive one hour after Holland, whose duty it would be to explain and discuss the British proposals. If the first alternative were refused Admiral Somerville would propose that the French should proceed to sea with a minimum steaming party and allow themselves to be captured by Force H. The third and fourth alternatives would be put forward as invitations. It was Admiral Somerville's own belief at the time that Gensoul would accept the first choice.

Early on the 2nd Somerville received his final instructions from the Admiralty, together with the terms of the communication to be made to Gensoul. The third alternative had been amended so as to give preference to demilitarization taking place at some French port in the West Indies, though if Gensoul suggested doing it at Mers-el-Kebir Somerville was authorized to agree, provided he was satisfied that the measures taken could be carried out under his supervision within six hours and would prevent the ships being brought into service for at least one year even at a fully equipped dockyard port—a proviso which in effect ruled out anything short of immediate scuttling. The idea of sending Captain Holland ahead was objected to on the ground that it would be most undesirable to have to deal with the French fleet at sea. 'Hence you should arrive in the vicinity of Oran with your force at whatever time you select and send your emissary ashore subsequently taking any action you consider fit with your force in the period before the time limit expires.' In the last resort Somerville was to endeavour to destroy the ships at Mers-el-Kebir, particularly the *Dunkerque* and *Strasbourg*.

At 6.30 a.m. on 3rd July H.M.S. *Foxhound* with Captain Holland on board duly requested permission to enter the harbour of Mers-el-Kebir, and then made the following signal, the text of which Admiral Somerville had approved and had communicated to the Admiralty on 1st July: 'The British Admiralty has sent Captain Holland to confer with you. The British Navy hopes their proposal will enable you and your glorious French Navy to range yourself side by side with them. In these circumstances your ships would remain yours and no one need have any anxiety for the future. A British fleet is at sea off Oran waiting to welcome you.'[1]

At 8.10 the French Admiral's barge drew alongside the *Foxhound* for the Flag Lieutenant to present the Admiral's compliments. He returned to the *Dunkerque* to say that Holland was on such an important mission that he wished to see the Admiral in person. But by this

---

[1] Force H consisted of *Hood* (Flag), *Ark Royal, Valiant, Resolution*, two cruisers and eleven destroyers.

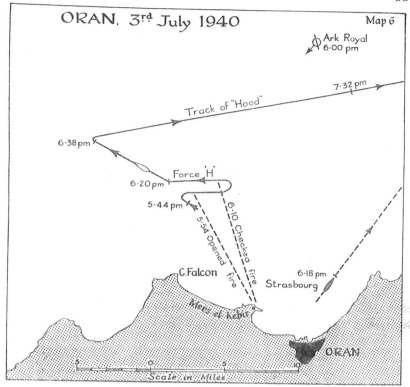

ORAN, 3rd July 1940     Map 6

time Gensoul had learnt of the *Foxhound's* signal and had grasped the significance of the presence of Force H. Indignation at the underlying threat coloured all his subsequent actions. At 8.47 he ordered the *Foxhound* to leave, whereupon Captain Holland started on his way to the *Dunkerque* by motor-boat. As Gensoul declined to see him, he could do no more than hand over to the Flag Lieutenant the written communication which he had hoped to explain verbally point by point. It was in French, the English text being as follows:

To Monsieur l'Amiral Gensoul from Admiral Somerville.

His Majesty's Government have commanded me to inform you as follows:

They agreed to the French Government approaching the German Government only on condition that, if an armistice was concluded, the French Fleet should be sent to British ports. The Council of Ministers declared on 18th June that, before capitulating on land, the French Fleet would join up with the British or sink itself.[1]

---

[1] This sentence, alone, is misleading. The information given to the British Ambassador in Bordeaux on 18th June was that the Council of Ministers had been discussing the action they would take if presented with terms requiring the French Fleet to be surrendered. This contingency did not arise, so the 'declaration' never became operative.

Whilst the present French Government may consider the terms of the Armistice with Germany and Italy are reconcilable with these undertakings, H.M. Government finds it impossible from their previous experience to believe that Germany and Italy will not at any moment which suits them seize French warships and use them against Britain and Allies. Italian Armistice prescribes that French ships should return to metropolitan ports, and under armistice France is required to yield up units for coast defence and minesweeping.

It is impossible for us, your comrades up to now, to allow your fine ships to fall into the power of the German or Italian enemy. We are determined to fight on until the end and, if we win, as we think we shall, we shall never forget that France was our Ally, that our interests are the same as hers, and that our common enemy is Germany. Should we conquer, we solemnly declare we shall restore the greatness and territory of France. For this purpose we must be sure that the best ships of the French Navy will not be used against us by the common foe.

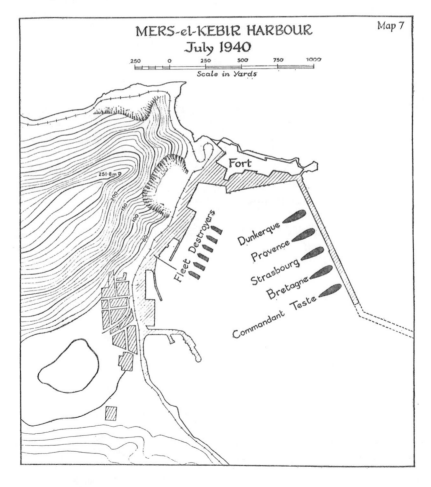

MERS-el-KEBIR HARBOUR
July 1940

Map 7

Scale in Yards

In these circumstances, H.M. Government have instructed me to demand that the French Fleet now at Mers-el-Kebir and Oran shall act in accordance with one of the following alternatives:

A. Sail with us and continue to fight for victory against the Germans and Italians.

B. Sail with reduced crews under our control to a British port. The reduced crews will be repatriated at the earliest moment. If either of these courses is adopted by you we will restore your ships to France at the conclusion of the war, or pay full compensation if they are damaged meanwhile.

C. Alternatively, if you feel bound to stipulate that your ships should not be used against Germans or Italians, since this would break the Armistice, then sail them with us with reduced crews to some French port in the West Indies—Martinique, for instance—where they can be demilitarized to our satisfaction, or perhaps be entrusted to the United States of America, and remain safely until the end of the war, the crews being repatriated.

If you refuse these fair offers, I must with profound regret require you to sink your ships within six hours. Finally, failing the above, I have the orders of His Majesty's Government to use whatever force may be necessary to prevent your ships from falling into German or Italian hands.

This communication, which was not drafted by Admiral Somerville but came to him with the authority of the War Cabinet, reached Gensoul shortly after 9.30. At 9.45 he signalled to the French Admiralty saying that a British force—whose size was accurately stated—was off Oran; that he had been given an ultimatum to sink his ships in six hours; and that he intended to reply to force with force. It is remarkable that he made no reference to any of the alternatives offered to him.

Meanwhile Captain Holland was waiting in the *Foxhound's* motor-boat at the harbour mouth. He reported that he could see the French ships furling awnings and raising steam. This information drew from the First Sea Lord a personal signal to Admiral Somerville suggesting that he should consider mining the harbour. At 10 o'clock Somerville received a message from Admiral Gensoul that the assurances given by him to Sir Dudley North still held good, but in view of what amounted to a veritable ultimatum the French warships would meet force with force. Thereafter Holland did his best in conversations with the Flag Lieutenant and Chief of Staff, and finally at 4.15 p.m. Admiral Gensoul received him. This seemed an encouraging development, but what Gensoul was really doing was to play for time. The interview was not made any easier by the Admiral's indignation at the mining of his harbour entrance, which had been done shortly after 1 p.m. by aircraft. How was it possible for him now to accept any of the first three proposals?

At times it seemed to Holland as if some measure of agreement was in sight, but the truth is that the discussions were all to no purpose, for matters were already beyond local control. Gensoul's hasty and misleading signal of 9.45 a.m. had reached the French Chief of Staff, Admiral Le Luc, at about noon. In the absence of Darlan—now Minister of Marine—Le Luc ordered all French forces in the Western Mediterranean to prepare for battle and rally to Oran under the orders of Gensoul. The naval air arm was to prepare for service with the fleet. Gensoul was to inform the British of these steps.

But Somerville knew of them already, for the British Admiralty had picked up Le Luc's order and passed it on, adding: 'Settle matters quickly or you will have reinforcements to deal with.' This prompted Somerville to signal to Gensoul: 'If none of the British proposals are acceptable by 17.30 it will be necessary to sink your ships.' The receipt of this at 5.15 p.m. put an end to all discussion. Captain Holland's feelings as he took his leave are best left to the imagination. As he went over the side at 5.25 'Action stations' was sounded. As he passed the *Bretagne* the officer of the watch saluted smartly. A few minutes later Force H opened fire. There was a sheet of flame as one of the first salvoes struck the *Bretagne*; it rose to a great height as the battleship blew up, and covered the harbour in a pall of smoke. Of her crew, 37 officers and 940 ratings were killed. There was another explosion as the stern of the destroyer *Mogador* was blown off by a 15-inch shell. The flagship *Dunkerque*, also hit, managed to fire 40 rounds at the *Hood* before being put out of action. The *Provence* succeeded in getting under way and also opened fire, but was herself badly damaged, burst into flames, and ran aground. In all, 1297 French lives were lost.

Signals were flashing from the shore begging Somerville to cease fire, and at 6.10 he did so, in order to give the French the opportunity to abandon their ships and save further loss of life. Signalling 'Unless I see your ships sinking I shall open fire again,' he turned Force H to the westward in order to avoid undue exposure to the fire of the shore batteries, and to reduce the risk of injuring men proceeding ashore in boats if it should be necessary to reopen fire. Knowing that the French were aware of the mines in the harbour entrance, he felt sure that none of their ships would try to put to sea.

In this he was mistaken, for as soon as the firing began Gensoul ordered his ships to proceed to sea. Through the thick pall of smoke with which the harbour was covered the *Strasbourg* started to move. Skilfully handled in a visibility of only a few yards she escaped the mines, passed through the boom, and reached the open sea. At 6.20 she was reported by one of the *Ark Royal's* aircraft to be moving east. This seemed unlikely, but ten minutes later it was confirmed. Altering course to the east Somerville followed in pursuit and diverted a striking force of six Swordfish from the task of attacking ships in harbour. But by 8.20 the *Strasbourg* was 25 miles ahead and apparently undamaged. The chase was abandoned; another air attack was made, but again without success. With the cruisers from Algiers she reached Toulon on the evening of 4th July, followed later by the *Commandant Teste* and other ships from Oran.

Doubts about the extent of the damage to the *Dunkerque* led to a dawn attack by torpedo-carrying aircraft from the *Ark Royal* on 6th July. An explosion was caused in a tug alongside the battlecruiser, which tore a long rent in her hull. She, at any rate, would be out of action for a year.

There remained the *Jean Bart* at Casablanca and the *Richelieu* at Dakar. As it was known that the *Jean Bart* was without her main armament it was decided to take no action against her. In the case of the *Richelieu* similar proposals to those offered to Admiral Gensoul were made by signal on 7th July from the flagship of Admiral Onslow, the officer in charge. They were ignored, and the time limit duly expired at 8.5 p.m. At 2.15 a.m. next morning four depth charges were cast under the *Richelieu's* stern from the motor-boat of the carrier *Hermes*. Owing to the shallowness of the water they failed to explode, and the motor-boat made a hazardous passage among adjacent merchant ships and so out to sea. At dawn on the 8th an attack was made by six torpedo-carrying aircraft from the *Hermes* and, although only one torpedo exploded, it apparently set off the depth charges also and caused enough damage to take a year to repair at Dakar.


There is one aspect of Oran about which there can be no two opinions. As the Prime Minister wrote in his message to Admiral Somerville, 'You are charged with one of the most disagreeable and difficult tasks that a British Admiral has ever been faced with. . . .' The message went on to say that there was complete confidence in him and that he was relied upon to carry out his task relentlessly. This instruction, and the others that he received, were entirely consistent with the decision to which the British Government had come for reasons which, in the light of the known facts, seemed to them good and sufficient.

They did not know that the Italians had agreed on 30th June that certain ships could be demilitarized at Toulon or in African ports; though here, of course, they would be under the eye of the Italian Armistice Commission. The French Admiralty tried to transmit this news to London, but although it was sent by two routes only a corrupt version reached the British Admiralty. Nor did the

British know before July 3rd that Admiral Darlan had on 24th June issued a last message to his Fleet, in which he stated his wish that French warships should remain French, under the French flag, with reduced French crews. Should the Armistice Commission try to prevent this, at the very moment that they did so, and without further orders, ships were to proceed to the United States or sink themselves if they could not otherwise be prevented from falling into the hands of the enemy. In no case was a ship to fall into enemy hands intact.[1]

What effect the possession of this information would have had upon the attitude of His Majesty's Government, in all the anxiety and uncertainty of the moment, is impossible to assess. It certainly cannot be assumed that they would have considered intervention by British forces to be unnecessary. They were convinced of the vital necessity of ensuring that the French capital ships were placed beyond the reach of German or Italian compulsion or treachery. At Mers-el-Kebir this would have meant departure for a secure port or being scuttled under British supervision. The French Government, for their part, were anxious not to bring still further hardship upon their country by breaking the conditions of the armistice. It is hard to see how these divergent views could have been reconciled.

The circumstances at Alexandria were entirely different from those at Oran and—thanks to the patience and understanding shown by Admiral Cunningham—so was the result. The cordial understanding between the two Admirals was an important factor from the outset. In fact the first move was made by Godfroy on 27th June when he offered to discharge all oil fuel from his ships so as to save the British the embarrassment of having to keep a large force in harbour to look after them. All he required was an assurance that there was no intention of seizing his ships by force. This was referred to the Admiralty, who directed that no such assurance was to be given. The next day the Commander-in-Chief reported that Godfroy had given his word that he would make no attempt to leave Alexandria, but that if Darlan ordered him to break out he would first ask permission to withdraw his parole and would then request to sail with a British unit in company, with the object of scuttling all his ships outside. So far, so good.

On 29th June the Admiralty asked the Commander-in-Chief for his views on a proposal that he should seize Godfroy's ships simultaneously with Admiral Somerville's approach to Gensoul at Oran. Admiral Cunningham replied opposing it strongly. The French ships at Alexandria were in no danger of falling into the enemy's

---

[1] The French text of this signal is given in Appendix 3.

hands, and a forcible attempt to seize them would only result in their being scuttled at their moorings, causing unnecessary casualties and fouling the harbour with wrecks. This would have a deplorable effect in the Middle East, and would be particularly likely to antagonize the French Suez Canal officials, whose co-operation was essential to us. He therefore pleaded for matters to be allowed to pursue their present course, and took the opportunity to repeat that he was very much against the proposed use of force at Oran.

The reply to this was that, if the use of the French ships could be obtained without bloodshed, well and good; if not, there were two alternatives which were to be presented to the French Admiral on 3rd July. Either the ships were to be placed in a non-seagoing condition with skeleton crews, the British Government being responsible for pay and upkeep, or they were to be sunk at sea. After due reflection Admiral Godfroy wrote to say that he had no choice but to sink his ships. He was accordingly told officially to prepare to sail at noon on 5th July, but Admiral Cunningham wrote privately saying that he quite understood that Godfroy might regard the reduction of his crews as incompatible with his duty; would he therefore be prepared to order the oil fuel to be discharged from his ships and the warheads from his torpedoes to be landed? To this suggestion Godfroy agreed without demur, in spite of his having received a signal from the French Admiralty ordering 'Weigh immediately and leave Alexandria with all your ships, using force if necessary'. By 5.30 p.m. the French ships were discharging their fuel.

To Admiral Cunningham's surprise and indignation the report of this apparently satisfactory progress drew a reply from the Admiralty noting that the French ships were discharging oil, but ordering 'crews to commence being reduced at once by landing or transfer to merchant ships, especially key ratings, before dark tonight. Do not fail'. This signal was despatched at a time when it was after sunset at Alexandria. It struck the Commander-in-Chief as being a rather unusual signal to emanate from their Lordships, and as he was unable to comply with it he reported in due course that he had ignored it.

It was at this juncture that Godfroy became aware that ultimatums were in the air. 'Admiral', he wrote to Cunningham, 'I have just learnt that an ultimatum has been addressed to our Atlantic Fleet by the British Admiralty. My Admiralty has ordered me to sail, though I have requested assurance that the order is authentic. I realize that sailing is impossible, but in order not to incur reproach for having discharged oil fuel after receiving orders to sail I have stopped the discharge pending events. But that alters nothing. I give you my word as to my intentions which remain unchanged from those I expressed to you in writing this morning.'

By the time that Cunningham's Chief of Staff arrived to remonstrate, Godfroy had heard of the engagement at Mers-el-Kebir. Thereafter he declined to continue discharging oil or to remove any of his men. He also refused to sink his ships at sea, adding that if he were allowed out of harbour he would run for it, even though this would probably lead to a battle. He would agree to remain at Alexandria with full crews, but if faced by any demand backed by force he would scuttle his ships in the harbour.

The Commander-in-Chief thereupon decided that he must face Godfroy with a demand to be interned or surrender. He informed the Admiralty accordingly, adding that he did not propose to take this action until the morning of 5th July, so that arrangements could be made for the disposal of the French crews. During the night Godfroy learned more details of the action at Mers-el-Kebir, and at 7 a.m. Cunningham received another letter from him repudiating each and every undertaking he had given and reserving to himself complete liberty of action. From the upper deck of the *Warspite* the French ships could be seen raising steam and clearing their armament for action. It seemed that Godfroy was now determined to fight his way to sea, and that a battle in Alexandria harbour was inevitable.

One unusual course remained. It would take six to eight hours for the French warships to raise steam, and Admiral Cunningham decided to use the time available to appeal to officers and ships' companies over Godfroy's head and suborn them from allegiance to him. A message in French was composed explaining the helplessness of their situation, our sincere desire not to fight, and the generous terms which could be accepted without loss of dignity or honour. This was flashed to every ship, and was also written on large blackboards and exhibited from boats steaming slowly round the French ships. In addition, Captains of British ships visited their opposite numbers to reason with the French Captains, being received in most cases with cordiality and nowhere with hostility. (In accordance with the usual custom, British warships had been detailed to act as hosts to particular French vessels during their stay in port.) All this appeared to have an excellent effect and it was soon evident that many French officers disagreed with their Admiral.

Meanwhile the Admiralty, strongly desirous of avoiding a battle in Alexandria harbour, suggested that British ships should be taken to sea and engage the French from seaward after a suitable ultimatum. But Admiral Cunningham refused to be hustled and replied that he did not want to force matters to a head but wished to wait 'for contacts on lower planes to have effect'.

Throughout the morning meetings were held on the foc's'les of the French ships at which ratings harangued their shipmates, while a number of visits of French captains to Godfroy took place. The French Minister in Cairo had also been prevailed upon to use his influence and arrived at an opportune moment. Early in the afternoon all French commanding officers were seen to go on board their flagship and, an hour later, Godfroy signalled his desire to see Admiral Cunningham. The upshot of this meeting was that Godfroy 'yielded to overwhelming force', and agreed to continue the discharge of oil fuel forthwith and to the placing of his ships in a condition in which they could not fight. The discharge of ships' companies was to be a matter for further discussion. The immediate danger was thus over, for which the credit is primarily due to the men on the spot.[1]

The decision that, if all else failed, the French capital ships were to be attacked was as serious as it was repugnant, seeing that it might have driven France to war against us. Had this occurred, the naval situation, especially in the Mediterranean, would have become graver still. In all there remained under the Vichy Government's control one battlecruiser, one aircraft carrier, four 8-inch and ten 6-inch cruisers, thirty destroyers and seventy submarines. Numerous bases would have become available to the Axis. French air forces had flown in large numbers to North Africa, where there were now believed to be 180 French bombers and 450 fighters. Attacks could have been made on Malta and Gibraltar and any of our naval forces that might be in the Central or Western Mediterranean. Malta would have become more isolated than ever. Shipping bound for the Middle East by the Cape route would have been liable to attacks from naval and air bases on the west coast of Africa and from Madagascar, while the defences of the important convoy assembly port of Freetown would have required strengthening urgently. Various other defence commitments would have arisen in consequence of threats from neighbouring French territories, while in Egypt a large number of hostile French residents and officials would have been an embarrassment. Finally, if German and Italian action had compelled the withdrawal of the fleet from the Eastern Mediterranean, the transport of Axis forces to Syria could no longer have been prevented and this might have produced a very serious situation indeed.

In weighing up these risks it was realized in London that the French were already so stunned and disorganized by their defeat as to be incapable of any fully co-ordinated action for the present, but

---

[1] In *A Sailor's Odyssey*, 1951, p. 255, Lord Cunningham records that no subsequent success of the British Fleet passed without Admiral Godfroy's congratulations; no loss without his sympathy.

Dr. Goebbels had been presented with some first-class material and might be expected to make good use of it. The principal danger would naturally be from the French Navy itself, which could hardly be blamed if it became embittered and vindictive.

To the world in general the action against the French ships served as an indication of Britain's relentless determination, which was of greater significance than the purely material results, especially as one of the intended victims—the battlecruiser *Strasbourg*—had escaped undamaged. The British Ambassadors in the Mediterranean countries reported that reactions were on the whole very favourable. Turkish official opinion was said to be in sympathy with the British action. In Greece it was generally thought to have been fully justified, though officially there was some alarm at the worsening of Anglo-French relations. In Yugoslavia the news was well received and led to the conviction that the British meant to win the war. In the United States the Secretary of State informed the British Ambassador that, when the French Ambassador had conveyed the Pétain Government's protest, he had been told that the whole of American opinion supported Great Britain's action.

In French Somaliland the gallant General Legentilhomme continued to obstruct the enforcement of the armistice and even stopped the Vichy emissary, General Germain, when he arrived on the frontier. But on 19th July he found himself opposed by his naval and air colleagues at the Governor's Council, and desiring above all to avoid civil war he came to the conclusion that those Frenchmen who wished to continue the struggle should do so elsewhere. He managed to temporize for a little longer and finally departed for Aden on 5th August, leaving Germain engaged in trying to obtain the best local terms that he could, under pressure from Vichy to break off all relations with the British.

In the Chad Province of French Equatorial Africa, which lies between Nigeria and the Sudan, the French Government's capitulation was widely resented. Touch was established with General de Gaulle, and the attitude of the military authorities and officials seemed very promising. In the Cameroons, too, there was a strong Free French element. By the end of August both provinces had declared their adherence to General de Gaulle.

In West Africa, on the other hand, the authorities were apathetic and generally unwilling to cut themselves off from the Home Government, and there was a strong and embittered naval element.

On 4th July the French broadcast an order forbidding British ships and aircraft to approach within twenty miles of any French territory, and on the following day French warships still at sea were ordered to intercept British merchant vessels. In the early hours of 5th July French aircraft appeared over Gibraltar, but their bombs fell harmlessly into the Bay, which suggested that the attack had been carried out with little enthusiasm. The same day the French Government announced their intention of breaking off diplomatic relations, and on the 8th they did so. In order to ease the tension the Admiralty broadcast an order on 12th July directing that no further action against French ships in Colonial or North African ports was to be taken, but the right was reserved to take action against French warships proceeding to enemy-controlled ports. Merchant ships were to be stopped by force, if necessary, from entering any port in French territory where British merchant vessels were being detained. In repeating this signal to the Mediterranean Fleet Admiral Cunningham added that H.M. ships were not to open fire on French warships met at sea unless the latter fired first.

Force H was still to be based at Gibraltar in order to prevent Italian ships from breaking out into the Atlantic and to act offensively against Italian naval forces and coasts; it had also to be prepared to operate in the Atlantic. Within the Mediterranean its activities were to be co-ordinated with those of the Mediterranean Fleet; this meant that many of the Mediterranean operations carried out by Force H came under the general control of Admiral Cunningham. The force had no sooner returned to Gibraltar from Oran than it was called upon to take part in the operations against the Italians with which a very promising start had already been made.

# CHAPTER VIII

# ENCOURAGING START OF THE STRUGGLE AT SEA

WITH THE collapse of France and the consequent loss of the French Fleet it became quite clear that the whole position in the Middle East would depend upon the retention of the British Fleet in the Eastern Mediterranean. Admiral Cunningham's fundamental aim remained unchanged: it was to seek out and destroy Italian naval forces. He had always realized, from what was known of the enemy, that it might not be easy to bring about the encounters he sought, and, as has been seen, his first attempts, made immediately after the entry of Italy into the war, were unsuccessful. It was quite possible, however, that the attitude of the Italian Fleet had at that time been governed by Mussolini's desire to secure the fruits of victory without any unnecessary fighting; but now that the elimination of the French had altered the balance to such a marked extent Admiral Cunningham had some reason for hoping that he would be more successful in bringing the Italians to action.

It is now apparent that only in the Central Mediterranean was this at all likely to occur. On the day of the birth of the Italian High Command, 31st March 1940, the Duce announced that the general policy of the Navy would be 'offensive at all points in the Mediterranean and outside'. The Service Chiefs of Staff—Graziani, Cavagnari, and Pricolo—met ten days later and discussed how this directive was to be interpreted. Marshal Badoglio, the Duce's Chief of Staff, held that it should not be taken to mean that they should throw themselves 'with lowered head' against the French and English fleets, but rather that they should assume dispositions aimed at interrupting the enemy's sea communications, especially by the use of submarines.

On April 14th Admiral Cavagnari submitted to Mussolini an *aide-mémoire* expressing the view that, in the absence of any definite strategic objective to be achieved by the combined operations of the three Services, the task of the fleet should be to engage the enemy's forces. It must be assumed that he had no offensive action in mind, and certainly did not intend to 'seek out and destroy'. He visualized only two possibilities: the Allied fleets would either be content to maintain their hold in the eastern and western basins and rely on economic pressure to exhaust Italy, or else would act aggressively with the object of rapidly neutralizing her. In the latter event the Italian naval attitude would continue to be defensive, because the French and British could quickly make good their losses from other forces outside the Mediterranean whereas Italian losses could not be replaced.

The collapse of France completely altered the balance of naval power, but the Italian naval staff adhered to their views on the question of losses. Their policy was to remain on the defensive at each end of the Mediterranean; only in the centre were they prepared, so long as their forces did not become engaged with greatly superior forces of the enemy, to act offensively or counter-offensively.[1] To fulfil this condition it was very desirable that the Navy should be particularly well served by air reconnaissance. The Italian policy had been to refrain from building aircraft carriers because there was no part of the Mediterranean which could not be reached by aircraft from shore bases on Italian soil. With the exception of the recon-naissance aircraft carried by warships and the few which operated under local naval Commanders, all the aircraft which would be used for supporting naval operations were under Italian Air Force command. From the frequency with which shadowing aircraft were observed by the British Fleet it seemed that the Italian air reconnais-sance was reasonably good, especially as it was seldom long before a force of bombers appeared on the scene. It will be seen, however, that the percentage of hits obtained by the customary high-level attacks was very small.

The fact that the Italian Navy was to be supported mainly by aircraft not under its own command would seem to have been a strong argument for insisting upon the closest collaboration with the Air Force. This was evidently not fully appreciated, for it was certainly not done. The failure must be attributed primarily to those who were responsible for high policy and for making practical arrangements for training and operational control.

Apart from Admiral Cunningham's aim of coming to grips with the Italian surface forces, there were many other tasks demanding his immediate attention, of which the most important was to throttle the supply line from Italy by which the Italian forces in Libya were being built up. Bombardment of concentrations of troops and stores near the coast would contribute to this aim, but attack on the sea-borne traffic was of far greater importance. Apart from the limited means

---

[1] This attitude is confirmed by Vice-Admiral Weichold, who became chief German Naval Liaison Officer at Italian Headquarters in June 1940. In his opinion the opera-tional aim of the Italian Navy was limited to maintaining a strong defence in the Central Mediterranean and keeping open the sea route to Libya. He considers that this cautious outlook was partly due to their being totally untrained in night operations at sea, for which they had not developed the necessary fire-control and searchlight apparatus.

at the Commander-in-Chief's disposal for doing this, his hands were still tied by the convention which prevented submarines and aircraft from attacking vessels other than warships and troop transports. Even in the process of identifying the latter a submarine would run great risk of detection, besides possibly losing a favourable opportunity to fire torpedoes. The same restriction seriously hampered the achievement of a further objective, which was the denial of sea-borne trade to Italy; for example, the bauxite traffic from Yugoslavia and the tankers which came from the Black Sea via the Corinth Canal or the Kithera Channel. While a measure of control could still be applied in the Aegean by surface forces, these were severely handicapped by the lack of an Aegean base.

An essential requirement for carrying out successful offensive operations at sea was extended vision, and this could only be supplied by ample air reconnaissance. With all his other commitments the Air Officer Commanding-in-Chief had the greatest difficulty in providing the Navy with more than a fraction of the air reconnaissance it needed, as there were only two squadrons of flying-boats (with a combined first line strength of nine aircraft) at his disposal for the Mediterranean. For reconnaissance in the Mediterranean to be effective it was necessary that many of the aircraft employed on it should be able to work from Malta, but the constant air raids during June and the lack of defence against them had made it hazardous to refuel even flying-boats except during darkness. In a signal of 1st July Admiral Cunningham therefore urged once more that fighters should be sent to Malta and that more air reconnaissance should be made available. He explained that as he could not even refuel light forces at Malta, it was only possible to take intermittent action against Italian transport and supply ships on their way to Libyan ports. His further representations in the light of operational experience and the steps taken to strengthen Malta are referred to later in this chapter.

Another task that was always present was the protection of British and Allied merchant shipping in the Eastern Mediterranean. On June 27th Admiral Cunningham informed the Admiralty of the shipping policy he intended to pursue. Trade convoys in the Aegean would be run periodically to connect with Red Sea convoys; convoys would be organized for oilers, transports, and armament supply ships moving between Haifa, Port Said and Alexandria, but other local shipping for Eastern Mediterranean ports outside the Aegean would be allowed to sail independently; and when occasion demanded he would run a convoy to Malta. In response to his request for a representative of the Ministry of Shipping in the Middle East, Sir Henry Barker was appointed on June 29th.

All this shipping had of course to be protected against surface vessels, submarines, and aircraft. Distant cover by the battlefleet could provide against raids by the Italian Fleet; destroyers could provide reasonable protection against submarines; but there was little with which to counter the air menace from the Dodecanese. The anti-aircraft armament of ships themselves was inadequate; protection by fighters was not possible at such a distance from their bases; and the weight of bombing attacks that could be made on airfields in the Dodecanese was nothing like enough to neutralize them and was little more than a cause of irritation to the Italians.

Just as the Commander-in-Chief was informing the Admiralty of his policy, an operation was actually in progress to cover a large movement in the Eastern Mediterranean, and it illustrates very clearly the interdependence of the various naval tasks at this time. Admiral Cunningham had planned to run two convoys, one fast and one slow, from Malta to Alexandria while the first of the Aegean convoys (A.S.1) was being escorted from the Dardanelles to Egyptian ports. For the latter, which originally consisted of seven ships but was subsequently joined by four more from Salonika, Piraeus and Smyrna, the two old 6-inch cruisers *Capetown* and *Caledon* with four destroyers were detailed as escort with orders to sail the convoy from Cape Helles on the morning of June 28th. Five destroyers were to sail from Alexandria at daylight on the 27th, carry out an anti-submarine sweep in the neighbourhood of Kithera and then proceed to Malta as close escort for the convoys to Alexandria. A covering force of the 7th Cruiser Squadron under the command of Vice-Admiral Tovey in the *Orion* would operate to the west of Crete, and a supporting force of two battleships, the *Eagle* and the 2nd Destroyer Flotilla would cruise south-west of Crete and act as the situation demanded.

Information about Italian submarine movements led to the five destroyers being routed instead through the Kaso Strait for an anti-submarine hunt to the north of Crete, and thence past Kithera to Malta. Barely half way between Alexandria and Crete an Italian submarine, *Console Generale Luizzi*, was sighted on the surface. It dived, was heavily attacked and damaged, surfaced again and was finally destroyed. The sweep passed without further incident until dawn on the 29th by which time the destroyers had passed through the Kithera Straits and were in position about 150 miles to the west of Crete. Another Italian submarine was then sighted on the surface. The attacks made upon it after it dived were unsuccessful, but meanwhile a third submarine, the *Uebi Scebeli*, was observed, also on the surface. As on the first occasion the vessel resurfaced on being damaged by depth charges, but when fire was opened the crew came on deck to surrender. The weather permitted boarding, and some valuable confidential books and papers were seized. Prisoners from the two submarines amounted to 10 officers and 85 ratings. Flying-boats on patrol also had a number of encounters with submarines, and one of No. 230 Squadron had the good fortune to sink two—the *Argonauto* on the 28th and the *Rubino* on the 29th. From the latter she picked up four survivors.

The encounter with the *Uebi Scebeli* had taken place in almost the exact spot where, the evening before, the 7th Cruiser Squadron in its general covering role had engaged three enemy destroyers, now known to have been proceeding from Taranto to Tobruk. They had first been reported by a flying-boat of No. 228 Squadron at 12.10 p.m. on 29th May, when they were in a position about 50 miles west of the Ionian island of Zante and were believed to be steering towards Kithera. A later report from another flying-boat indicated that the destroyers were continuing to the south, so course was altered to intercept.

At 6.30 p.m. the enemy was at last sighted and fire was opened at a range of 18,000 yards. The course of the action was to the south-west, with the 1st division (*Orion, Neptune, Sydney*) on the starboard quarter of the enemy and the 2nd division (*Liverpool, Gloucester*) on the port quarter. Clever use of smoke by the Italians made ranging and spotting difficult for the British cruisers and shortly after 8.0 p.m. the Vice-Admiral broke off the action. By this time one of the enemy destroyers, the *Espero*, had been disabled, but continued to fire until 8.40 p.m. when she was sunk by the *Sydney*. Forty-seven survivors were rescued and an empty cutter with oars, provisions and water was slipped for any others. The action of the Italian destroyers in attempting to engage on a steady course in a duel with twelve 4·7-inch guns against forty-eight 6-inch was admittedly gallant, but with their turn of speed it would have been better tactics to turn away at once, then shadow, and attack with torpedoes during the night. As it was, the remaining destroyers *Zeffiro* and *Ostro* reached Benghazi the following morning.

Owing to the small amount of ammunition now remaining in the cruisers and to a report that numerous Italian submarines were at sea, the Commander-in-Chief postponed the sailing of the Malta convoys, directed the destroyers to return to Alexandria, and ordered the cruisers to afford support to the Aegean convoy. That night the 7th Cruiser Squadron swept up the west coast of Greece to Cephalonia, then turned and overhauled the convoy next day off the south-west corner of Crete. The ships had been subjected to a considerable amount of bombing and were re-routed past Kithera instead of through the Kaso Strait, though the attacks continued until they were well south of Crete. At least 85 bombs fell round the ships, without doing any damage. Meanwhile, the battle squadron had patrolled without incident and all forces returned to Alexandria by July 2nd.

On July 5th it was the turn of the Fleet Air Arm to strike the enemy. No. 813 Squadron, armed with torpedoes, had moved from Dekheila to Sidi Barrani. Nine Swordfish launched their torpedoes against shipping at Tobruk while No. 211 Squadron R.A.F. provided reconnaissance and eleven of its aircraft attacked the airfield. Twelve fighters of No. 33 Squadron R.A.F. maintained patrols over the target. Seven torpedoes dropped inside the harbour and, according to an Italian report, the destroyer *Zeffiro* was sunk and another, the *Euro*, holed forward. Two merchant vessels, the *Manzoni* (4,000 tons) and *Serenitas* (5,000 tons), were also sunk and the Lloyd Triestino liner *Liguria* (15,000 tons) damaged. All aircraft returned safely. In his report the Commander-in-Chief stated that the success of this operation was due to the co-operation provided by the Air Force.[1] While the attack was in progress the 3rd Cruiser Squadron (*Capetown*, *Caledon*) with four destroyers sailed as far as Bardia to bombard enemy shipping in that port and to render assistance to any returning aircraft in distress. Fire was opened at a range of 9,000 yards at dawn on July 6th and two military supply ships were hit. The force, though attacked by enemy aircraft, returned without damage. On the same evening as the attack was being carried out on Tobruk, No. 830 Squadron from Malta bombed hangars and workshops at Catania.

All this time there was the urgent question of the two convoys from Malta whose sailing had been postponed on 28th June; they carried men and stores required for the naval base at Alexandria, where their arrival was anxiously awaited. As it was expected that the Italians would dispute the passage of these ships, it was decided that the movement should take place under cover of a fleet operation. As a diversion Force H was to cruise in the Western Mediterranean and carry out an air attack on Cagliari.

The fleet sailed from Alexandria on the evening of 7th July in three groups. Ahead was Vice-Admiral Tovey in the *Orion* with the remainder of the 7th Cruiser Squadron—*Neptune*, *Sydney*, *Gloucester*, *Liverpool*—and the Australian flotilla leader *Stuart*. The central group consisted of the Commander-in-Chief in the *Warspite* screened by five destroyers; some miles astern were the slower battleships *Malaya* and *Royal Sovereign*, the carrier *Eagle* (Nos. 813 and 824 Squadrons—seventeen Swordfish and two Gladiators) and a further ten destroyers. A few submarines were stretched on a patrol line across the Central

---

[1] Santoro: *L'Aeronautica Italiana nella II^a Guerra Mondiale*, p. 395, mentions 8 Italian aircraft (C.R. 42) damaged on the ground.

Mediterranean to report enemy movements. On the night of leaving harbour two submarines were attacked and probably damaged by the destroyer *Hasty*; their presence was only one of several indications that the Italians intended to harass the fleet from the moment it put to sea. Early on the 8th the submarine *Phoenix* reported two Italian battleships and four destroyers in a position half way between Benghazi and Italy steaming south, and flying-boat reconnaissance from Malta was directed to watch their movements. From this patrol the *Phoenix* did not return. Meanwhile, the *Eagle's* air patrols sighted and bombed two more submarines.

Now began a series of high-level air attacks which persisted throughout the next four or five days. During the course of one forenoon the *Warspite* counted no less than 300 bombs dropped round her in 22 attacks, the most unpleasant occasion being when 24 bombs fell close along the port side simultaneously with 12 across the starboard bow, and all within 200 yards of the ship.[1] The only hit was scored on the bridge of the cruiser *Gloucester* on the evening of the 8th, killing the Captain, six other officers and eleven men, and wounding others. The two Gladiators from the *Eagle* were in constant action and claimed to have brought down several enemy bombers.

Reports from a flying-boat late in the afternoon indicated that the enemy previously reported now consisted of two battleships, six cruisers and seven destroyers, and was about 60 miles north of Benghazi steering to the west of north. A later report stated that they had altered course to the eastward. To Admiral Cunningham this suggested that the Italian Fleet was covering a shipping movement to Libya, and this fact, coupled with the heavy air attacks he was experiencing, caused him to postpone the sailing of the convoys from Malta and move up at best speed so as to get between the enemy and his base at Taranto. It is now known that the whole Italian Fleet was returning after escorting an important convoy containing tanks and petrol to Benghazi.

At 6.0 a.m. on 9th July the *Warspite* was some 60 miles west of Navarino. In the van, eight miles ahead, were the cruisers; astern a similar distance were the slower battleships and the *Eagle*. Two hours later the enemy force appeared to be almost right ahead, about 145 miles, and flying-boats of No. 228 Squadron R.A.F. reported it consisted of two battleships, sixteen to eighteen cruisers, and twenty-five to thirty destroyers. This was a very accurate estimate: the two

---

[1] A highly coloured Rome News Bulletin of 10th July, describing the events of the 8th, spoke of 'several enemy ships being struck, some set on fire and one sunk', and an air photograph showed 'a British battleship on fire'. To the indignation of her ship's company this proved to be the *Royal Sovereign* steaming at her best speed and, because of her age, belching clouds of smoke.

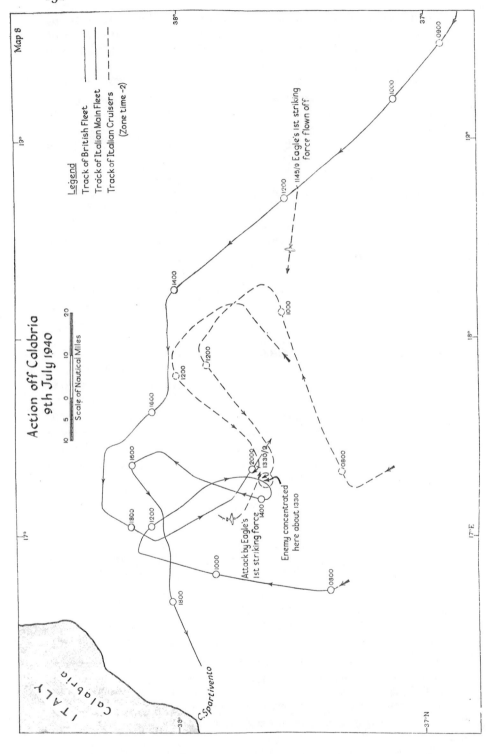

Map 8

Action off Calabria
9th July 1940

Scale of Nautical Miles

Legend
Track of British Fleet
Track of Italian Main Fleet
Track of Italian Cruisers
(Zone time -2)

ITALY
Calabria
C.Spartivento

1145/9 Eagle's 1st striking
force flown off

Attack by Eagle's
1st striking force

Enemy concentrated
here about 1330

battleships were of the *Cavour* class (12-inch); there were six 8-inch and ten 6-inch cruisers, and thirty-two destroyers. At 1.30 p.m. nine Swordfish of No. 824 Squadron made their first strike, but owing to an alteration of course they were unable to find the enemy battleships and attacked a cruiser. All torpedoes missed.

At 2.15 p.m. the fleet was between the enemy and Taranto, so course was altered due west. Contact was now imminent, and not wishing to be handicapped by the damaged *Gloucester* the Commander-in-Chief ordered her back to support the *Eagle*. The *Malaya* and *Royal Sovereign* were now racing up at their utmost speeds in a vain endeavour to join the *Warspite* before she became engaged with enemy battleships. At 2.47 the first sighting of smoke was made from the *Orion*, and fire was opened by the enemy half an hour later. The horizon became alive with a large number of ships which immediately concentrated on Admiral Tovey's four cruisers. These, owing to the shortage of 6-inch ammunition on the station, carried only half their outfits. Heavily out-numbered, out-gunned, out-ranged, and unable to control the area ahead of the battlefleet, they were saved from a precarious position by the *Warspite* coming into action at 3.26 against enemy cruisers which then turned away under smoke. A short lull followed.

At 3.50 the enemy again came into view and the *Warspite* sighted two *Cavour* class battleships at 26,000 yards. Fire was exchanged and both sides obtained straddles. A few minutes later an unmistakable hit was observed at the base of the leading battleship's foremost funnel. This was the flagship, *Giulio Cesare*. From signals made in plain language by the enemy it was learnt that the Italian Commander-in-Chief, Admiral Campioni, ordering his ships to make smoke, reported that he was constrained to retire, and the two battleships turned away. This retirement was observed by our aircraft to have been carried out in considerable confusion, and the enemy ships did not sort themselves out until after 6 p.m. Meanwhile, a second air striking force from the *Eagle* was unsuccessful.

The British destroyers, having been ordered to counter-attack, had now concentrated, and both they and the cruisers came for a time under heavy fire from enemy ships trying to cover the retirement of their battlefleet. Italian destroyers had made a half-hearted attack, but their torpedoes were fired at long range and all missed. During this period a *Bolzano* class cruiser (8-inch) received three hits from 6-inch shell and some Italian destroyers were also damaged. The Italian smoke screen was most effective. Cruisers and destroyers would dart out into the open, fire a few rounds and then disappear, which showed a clear determination on the part of the enemy to avoid close action. The targets presented were many and varied and the result was a most unusual battle in which the *Malaya* had now joined. Enemy sorties from the cover of their smoke grew fewer and by 4.50 all firing had ceased. Admiral Cunningham had no intention of plunging into this smoke screen and decided to work round to windward and northward of it, for he suspected that the enemy had intended to draw our forces over a concentration of submarines.

This was, in fact, the aim of the Italian Commander-in-Chief, who had planned a running fight for the afternoon of the 9th. He hoped that with his superior speed, the proximity of shore-based aircraft, and the laying of a submarine barrage, he might be able to inflict damage with little risk to his own forces. Admiral Cunningham had suspected a submarine trap; as events turned out, his track passed some 60 miles north of the northernmost submarine. By 5.0 p.m. not a single enemy ship was in sight and the coast of Calabria was clearly visible 25 miles to the west. More high-level bombing attacks now developed on the British Fleet and lasted for four hours, during which the Italian aircrews distributed a large number of bombs on their own fleet also, even after the ships had begun to enter the Straits of Messina. Signals were overheard indicating the fury of Admiral Campioni, who stated in his report that his ships had frequently to react with gunfire, but that none of the bombs hit them. The episode showed clearly that the co-operation between the fleet and the shore-based bombers was very far from perfect.

So ended the action off Calabria. In spite of its disappointing material results, the action undoubtedly established a moral ascendancy over the Italian Fleet. In Admiral Cunningham's opinion it must have shown the Italians that their air forces and submarines could not prevent our fleet from penetrating into the Central Mediterranean and that only their main fleet could seriously interfere with our operations there.

As soon as it was evident that the enemy had no intention of resuming the fight, the fleet turned towards Malta. That night an air striking force was launched from the *Eagle* to attack shipping in Augusta. Unfortunately the harbour was almost empty, but a tanker and a destroyer were sunk. For the next 24 hours the fleet cruised south and east of Malta while the *Royal Sovereign* and destroyers entered harbour to fuel. Meanwhile, on hearing that the fleets were engaged, the Vice-Admiral Malta had wisely sailed the convoys. During the passage back to Alexandria all forces experienced continual heavy high-level bombing attacks, but no ships were hit. On 12th July Blenheim fighters of No. 252 Wing provided fighter cover from late afternoon, after which no more was seen of the Italian bombers. Early next morning the fast convoy arrived, followed two days later by the slower.

The intention that Force H should carry out a diversionary operation has already been referred to. Admiral Cunningham had suggested that this should include air attacks on ships in Naples, Trapani, Palermo, or Messina, but owing to lack of destroyers with sufficient endurance Admiral Somerville considered that the only feasible operation would be an air attack on Cagliari. With this object Force H consisting of the *Hood, Valiant, Resolution, Ark Royal,* three cruisers and ten destroyers left Gibraltar at 7.0 a.m. on 8th July. When south of Minorca, they met with continual heavy air attacks pressed home with such determination that although no ships were actually hit Admiral Somerville considered that the risk of damage to the *Ark Royal* outweighed the advantage to be gained from a minor operation. He therefore turned back to Gibraltar, and on the way the destroyer *Escort* was torpedoed and sunk.

After these operations the Admiralty made a policy signal defining the roles of the East and West Mediterranean forces and inviting Admiral Cunningham's remarks on the composition of each as regards battleships and aircraft carriers. It was the intention to maintain a strong force in the Eastern Mediterranean as long as possible and another force at Gibraltar to control the western exit and carry out offensive operations against the coast of Italy. The Commander-in-Chief pointed out that in the Western Mediterranean the greatest danger to British interests lay in the possibility of attacks on Gibraltar and the break-out of Italian naval forces into the Atlantic. Both were unlikely while Spain remained neutral, and it was reasonable to suppose that the Italians were disinclined to proceed far from their bases. On the other hand, there were many Italian interests in the Eastern Mediterranean, where a British Fleet dominated the situation. For this reason, together with the fact that the west coast of Italy could easily be given air cover from Sardinia and Sicily, the enemy would probably base the bulk of his naval forces at Messina, Augusta, and Taranto. Hence the Eastern Mediterranean Fleet should be the stronger, and Force H should be regarded more as a raiding force.

As regards the composition of his fleet, he said that the *Royal Sovereign* class battleships were merely a source of constant anxiety and could be released at once. He wanted three, or if possible four, *Queen Elizabeth* class, including the *Valiant*, which was fitted with radar, a device not yet possessed by any of his ships: moreover she was armed with a battery of twenty 4·5-inch dual purpose guns which would be most useful in combating the air menace at sea and in harbour. He must have at least two capital ships whose guns could cross the enemy line at 26,000 yards and fast enough to have some hope of catching the enemy. It was also necessary to have two 8-inch cruisers to strengthen the forces in the van. He pointed out that he had not enough destroyers to take four battleships and the *Eagle* to sea simultaneously. The addition of the carrier *Illustrious* would be invaluable, as it would enable both an adequate striking force and a reasonable degree of fighter protection to be provided for the fleet. With the forces proposed he was certain that the Mediterranean could be dominated and the Eastern Mediterranean held indefinitely, provided that proper fighter protection was given to Malta and adequate air reconnaissance was forthcoming. He further believed that by a concerted operation from east and west it would be possible to pass the reinforcing ships through the Mediterranean. With these views Admiral Somerville generally concurred, but emphasized that the main task of Force H must be the control of the Straits of Gibraltar; raids on the Italian coast would result in losses by attrition without accomplishing much of value. The redistribution of forces was finally decided upon and it was expected that the forces for the Eastern Mediterranean would be ready to leave Gibraltar for passage through the Mediterranean about 15th August.[1] On Admiral Cunningham's urgent representation reserve ammunition and spares were to be sent in fast merchant ships round the Cape.

Meanwhile a successful action between light forces had taken place in the Eastern Mediterranean. On 19th July four destroyers of the 2nd Flotilla—*Hyperion* (Commander (D) H. St. L. Nicholson), *Ilex, Hero, Hasty*—were engaged on a routine anti-submarine sweep to the north of Crete. At 7.22 a.m., as they were passing the north-west coast of the island on a westerly course, they sighted two enemy cruisers right ahead. These cruisers—both 6-inch—were the *Bande Nere* (flag of Rear-Admiral Casardi) and the *Bartolomeo Colleoni*; they had left Tripoli on the 17th to proceed to Leros and attack British shipping in the Aegean. Making an enemy sighting report, Commander Nicholson rightly turned his division 16 points (i.e. right round, through 180 degrees), by which movement he also hoped to draw the enemy towards the Australian cruiser *Sydney* (Captain J. A. Collins, R.A.N.), who with the destroyer *Havock* was operating about 40 miles to the N.N.E. in search of Italian shipping.

The position of the destroyers was unenviable, for the superior speed of the enemy together with the range and power of their guns gave the Italians a preponderant advantage. But they threw it away. Instead of pursuing the retiring destroyers, which were now steering E.N.E., they altered course cautiously to the north under the misapprehension that because the destroyers were spread in line abreast they were forming a screen for heavier units. Fire was opened;

---

[1] The principal units of the Eastern Mediterranean Fleet were to be: battleships *Warspite, Valiant, Malaya, Ramillies* (later to be relieved by the *Barham*); carriers *Eagle, Illustrious;* 8-inch cruisers *Kent, York;* 6-inch cruisers *Gloucester, Orion, Neptune, Liverpool, Sydney;* A.A. cruisers *Calcutta, Coventry.*

The principal units of Force H were to be: battlecruiser *Renown;* battleship *Resolution;* carrier *Ark Royal;* 6-inch cruisers *Sheffield, Enterprise.* The operation began on 30th August under the code name 'Hats'.

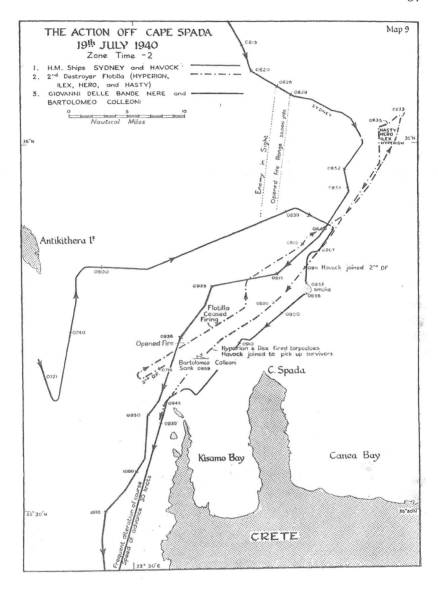

THE ACTION OFF CAPE SPADA
19th JULY 1940
Zone Time −2

Map 9

1. H.M. Ships SYDNEY and HAVOCK
2. 2nd Destroyer Flotilla (HYPERION, ILEX, HERO, and HASTY)
3. GIOVANNI DELLE BANDE NERE and BARTOLOMEO COLLEONI

0       5       10
Nautical Miles

36°N

Antikithera I.ᵈ

0800

0740

0721

36°N

0815

0820

0826

0829

SYDNEY

0833

0835

HASTY
HERO
ILEX
HYPERION

36°N

0852

0855

0830

0843

0805

0807

0911 Havock joined 2ⁿᵈ DF

0853 smoke
0855

0815

0925

0920

0800

Flotilla Ceased Firing

0936 Opened Fire

0910
Hyperion & Ilex fired torpedoes
Havock joined to pick up survivors

0715

2ⁿᵈ DF.

Bartolomeo Colleoni Sank 0959

C. Spada

0945

0950

0930

1000

1010

Frequent alteration of course
Speed of advance 30 knots

Kisamo Bay

Canea Bay

35°30′N

35°30′N

23°30′E

CRETE

Enemy in Sight

Opened fire Range 20,000 yds

the Italian shooting was erratic but the range too high for the 2nd Flotilla to respond effectively. Having increased his distance Commander Nicholson altered to a parallel course, but when the enemy eventually began to haul round to the east about 8 o'clock he turned back to a similar direction.

The *Sydney* meanwhile was steering south at full speed, acting on Nicholson's reports but observing wireless silence. Thus at 8.26 a.m. the sudden flash of her guns in the north as she entered the battle caused surprise and consternation to the enemy, who believed they were now facing two cruisers instead of one cruiser and a destroyer. The *Sydney's* firing was rapid and effective and the duel on parallel courses lasted only a few minutes. Turning to the south and west—flight to the eastward being blocked by Nicholson's division—Admiral Casardi sought to escape and at the same time avoid punishment by making smoke and violently zig-zagging. This reduced his advantage in speed and enabled the range to be closed.

The battle had now developed into a chase with the *Sydney* concentrating her fire on the rear cruiser, and the destroyers joining in as they came within range. The Italian reply was ragged; the only hit the *Sydney* received penetrated a funnel and caused one minor casualty. At 9.23 the *Colleoni* was seen to be stopped five miles to the west of Cape Spada, apparently out of action. She had been hit in the engine room and the electric power had everywhere failed. Detailing the *Hyperion, Ilex* and *Havock* to finish her off, the *Sydney* with the remaining destroyers continued to pursue the *Bande Nere* which was disappearing to the southward past the west coast of Crete. An hour later, with the range still increasing and spotting rendered impossible by the haze and smoke, the *Sydney* checked fire, abandoned the chase, and set course for Alexandria. She had only four rounds per gun left for one of the foremost turrets and one round per gun left for the other.

In the meantime, two torpedoes had finished off the *Colleoni*, which had been abandoned by the majority of her company. Having rescued over 280 survivors the *Hyperion* and *Ilex* proceeded to join the *Sydney*, leaving the *Havock* to complete the work of rescue. Shortly after noon, however, enemy aircraft came on the scene and the destroyer with a further 260 prisoners on board was forced to retire at high speed. In the course of the subsequent air attacks a near miss did slight damage to the *Havock*. As a result of this experience the Commander-in-Chief issued a warning of the unjustifiable hazards involved in the rescue of survivors from enemy ships.

When the first news of the action reached the Commander-in-Chief at Alexandria he considered it probable that other enemy units might be in support, so he arranged for flying-boat reconnaissance, ordered the fleet to sea, and postponed the sailing of an

Aegean convoy from Port Said. It was soon evident, however, that the *Bande Nere* could make the African coast before being intercepted by any of our forces, and, when by 9.0 p.m. all reports of enemy movements in the Eastern Mediterranean were negative, the fleet returned to harbour. Successful bombing attacks were, nevertheless, carried out on Tobruk by Blenheim bombers of Nos. 55 and 211 Squadrons and by torpedo carrying aircraft from the *Eagle*. Hits were scored on two destroyers, two merchant vessels, and an oiler.

It had been amply demonstrated that Malta could, if adequately defended, play an important part in naval operations. The attempt made during June to fly Hurricanes across France to Malta and Egypt had been only partially successful, but even this route was no longer available. If more fighters were to reach Malta, some other way had to be found. On 15th July the Admiralty had informed the Commander-in-Chief that twelve Hurricanes for Malta and twelve for the Middle East would shortly be shipped in a merchant vessel for Gibraltar. Was it advisable, they asked, for this ship subsequently to be routed direct to Malta? Both Admirals Cunningham and Somerville considered this to be impracticable, and the latter proposed that the aircraft should be transferred to a carrier and flown off from a position south of Sardinia. Men and stores could be transported in two submarines.

Accordingly H.M.S. *Argus* left the United Kingdom on 24th July with twelve Hurricanes to be flown to Malta (operation 'Hurry'). Postponement of the date of sailing of the *Argus* from Gibraltar to 31st July necessitated a change in Admiral Cunningham's plans for creating a diversion. Nevertheless he was able to arrange for a sweep by cruisers and destroyers in the Aegean, which included a feint to the westward through the Kithera Channel on the evening of August 1st. Two battleships and the *Eagle* would advance to a point between Crete and Libya during daylight on 1st August, and he hoped that a general impression would be given of movement into the Central Mediterranean which would deter the Italian surface forces in Sicily and Southern Italy from moving westward.

The fleet had left harbour during the early hours of the 27th to cover an Aegean convoy which had been escorted from Cape Helles by two cruisers and four destroyers. To divert attention an attack and landing on Castelorizo was simulated by two Armed Boarding Vessels supported by light forces. As the convoy encountered heavy bombing in the Aegean, it was diverted to proceed west of Crete, where it was sighted and covered during the 28th by the main fleet, which had itself been subjected to a number of air attacks. No hits had been obtained and no casualties suffered. In the course of these operations the Greek steamer *Hermione*, carrying aviation spirit for the Italians in the Dodecanese, was intercepted and sunk, her Master and crew being left in boats close to land. Ships returned to Alexandria on 30th July.

During the sweep planned for cruisers and destroyers between 31st July and 2nd August as a diversion for operation 'Hurry' no incidents occurred and there was little bombing. In the battleship force, a defect in the *Malaya* caused the squadron and the *Eagle* to return to harbour soon after they had sailed. All these movements seem to have created such uncertainty in the minds of the Italians that, unable to decide whether to move east or west, they kept their ships in harbour throughout the operation.

Admiral Somerville arranged two subsidiary operations to conceal from the Italians his aim of flying off aircraft to Malta from the *Argus*. The first was an air attack from the *Ark Royal* on the Cagliari airfields, which it was hoped would weaken enemy air effort against the *Argus*; and the second was a simulation of activity in the northern part of the western basin by the broadcasting of wireless reports by a cruiser lying off Minorca. The Force sailed from Gibraltar at 8.0 a.m. on 31st July; it consisted of the *Argus*, the *Hood*, the battleships *Valiant* and *Resolution*, the *Ark Royal*, two cruisers and ten destroyers. Italian air attacks began on the following day, but they were noticeably less determined than on the previous occasion; aircraft were seen either to jettison their bombs at a distance or to sheer off without dropping them.

That evening the *Hood* and the *Ark Royal* parted company from the remainder of the Force to carry out the attack on Cagliari, and, shortly before dawn, nine Swordfish armed with bombs and three with mines took off. Direct hits were scored on hangars, fires were started, several aircraft were hit on the ground, and the mines were successfully laid inside the gate of the outer harbour—all in the face of heavy anti-aircraft fire. One Swordfish crashed on taking off, another made a forced landing, but the remainder returned in safety. Meanwhile the *Argus* had arrived in position for flying off her aircraft at 4.45 a.m. and the operation was performed successfully. All twelve Hurricanes reached Malta, the only mishap being that one was damaged on landing. All forces then returned to Gibraltar by 4th August, without being further attacked from the air. A few days later the submarines *Pandora* and *Proteus* reached Malta with the necessary aircraft stores, thus completing a successful operation during which the weakness of the Italian reaction had been most noticeable.

Shortly afterwards Force H was ordered to the United Kingdom for reorganization in accordance with the decision to alter the composition of the two naval forces in the Mediterranean. Admiral Somerville's ships were to reassemble at Gibraltar on 20th August in preparation for the operation ('Hats') in which naval reinforcements were to be passed through to Malta and the eastern basin.[1]

The first batch of Hurricanes to reach Malta after the French collapse was of course very welcome, but it was not only fighters that were wanted. In order to locate and follow the movements of the Italian Fleet and merchant shipping there was a need of reconnaissance aircraft to keep watch on Italian harbours and search wide stretches of sea. Without adequate information attacks on the Italian communications with North Africa could only be spasmodic. Malta was clearly the base from which the majority of operations for this purpose would have to be launched. Swordfish from Malta had made a successful attack on merchant shipping in Augusta and a Sunderland had possibly damaged a merchant vessel in convoy. But that was all. Admiral Cunningham represented that the security of Malta was the key to our Mediterranean strategy, and the prospect of the island remaining so weakly defended that it could not be used as an offensive base caused him the utmost concern. Not only was there a lack of air raid shelters and underground protection for indispensable services, but he doubted whether the fortress was strong enough to defeat a determined attempt at capture. The scale of defences approved more than a year ago showed little sign of being achieved. A much more vigorous approach to the problem was required. He therefore urged on 22nd August that the aim should be to make Malta fully usable by April 1941, when he would wish light forces and submarines to be able to operate from the island, in addition to bomber and reconnaissance squadrons supported by four squadrons of fighters. The base defences should be brought as quickly as possible to a state which would allow of this. In the meantime, offensive action ought to be restricted to attacks on sea targets.

The Chiefs of Staff had not been unmindful of the importance of strengthening Malta; in fact an allotment of guns and equipment was already on its way.[2] As regards bomber squadrons, they had come to the conclusion that none could be spared to attack targets in Italy from Malta. Fighter squadrons presented a difficulty because the lack of reserves of all kinds meant that air and ground crews, aircraft and ground equipment could only be sent to Malta at the expense of Fighter Command, whose strength was still far below what was considered necessary for home defence. There were many other demands, too, for anti-aircraft guns, both at home and in the Middle East. Nevertheless the Chiefs of Staff agreed that everything

---

[1] See page 201.
[2] See page 203 footnote for the arrival of this consignment in the course of operation 'Hats'.

N

possible should be done to make Malta reasonably secure as a base for light forces, and they decided to bring the anti-aircraft defences up to the approved scale by 1st April 1941 by allocations from monthly production, and to make up the fighter strength to a total of four squadrons as soon as circumstances would permit.

On completion of operation 'Hurry' the Commander-in-Chief had in mind no large scale operation before 'Hats'. Ships needed docking, and destroyers all required boiler cleaning and minor repairs. He therefore carried out a number of local operations, including frequent anti-submarine sweeps by destroyers in the Eastern Mediterranean, sometimes combined with bombardments of the North African coast; the maintenance of pressure in the Aegean by cruiser patrols; and the cover of shipping. During the first of these operations four valuable barges and one tug which had escaped from the River Danube were encountered off Crete and escorted safely to Alexandria. In the course of three other similar sweeps no enemy forces were sighted. Even submarines were little in evidence, although eight to ten were always on patrol in the Eastern Mediterranean. In fact the only indications of their existence were the sinking of the Greek steamer *Loula* south of Crete on 31st July and the discovery of a newly laid minefield off Alexandria, which led to the sweeping of nineteen mines between 12th and 14th August. The usual air attacks were experienced, but even these showed markedly less weight and skill.

During one of these sweeps four destroyers, instead of returning to Alexandria, proceeded to Malta, where they arrived on 22nd August. After fuelling they were sailed to Gibraltar on temporary loan to Force H during the forthcoming passage of fleet reinforcements. When off Cape Bon the *Hostile* struck a mine and had to be sunk by a consort. The channel through which the destroyers were routed was the one planned for the reinforcements and therefore had to be changed.

Another of the fleet's activities was to engage concentrations of enemy troops reported near the Libyan frontier, which were possibly assembling for the advance into Egypt. On 17th August the Commander-in-Chief himself took command of a force consisting of three battleships and an 8-inch cruiser (*Kent*) screened by twelve destroyers for the purpose of bombarding Bardia in co-operation with the Army and Air Force.[1] The target area was well plastered

---

[1] The *Kent* had been transferred to the Mediterranean Station from the East Indies early in August as a first step in meeting the Commander-in-Chief's request for two 8-inch cruisers. The Fleet itself was now reorganized: the title V.A.(D) had lapsed and Vice-Admiral J. C. Tovey had assumed the title of Vice-Admiral, Light Forces, and 2nd in command Mediterranean (V.A.L.F.) All cruiser squadrons and destroyer flotillas were thus brought under the direct operational command of V.A.L.F. A Rear-Admiral flew his flag in the 3rd Cruiser Squadron.

and the opposition was weak and ineffective, but Admiral Cunningham reported that the enemy's skill in dispersion made this type of operation unjustifiable for heavy ships as long as warfare in the Western Desert remained static. It had, however, provided a useful opportunity to test methods of co-operation between the Services, and indeed the fighters had broken up air attacks on the fleet and brought down several enemy aircraft. Gladiators of the Fleet Air Arm working from Sidi Barrani destroyed others.

For further operations of this kind the gunboat *Ladybird* had now arrived on the Station. On 23rd August she carried out her first bombardment. Penetrating Bardia by night and finding no shipping, she proceeded to engage shore targets at point blank range from a few yards off the pier. It was believed that the moral effect of this action on the enemy was considerable, and it was clear that the use of gunboats off the North African coast would be of much value in conjunction with military operations ashore.

From experience so far gathered it was possible to assess the Italian menace with some accuracy. The reinforcement of the fleet by the two new battleships of the *Littorio* class (nine 15-inch, 31 knots) was believed to be imminent—in fact the *Littorio* and *Vittorio Veneto* came into service early in August—and the modernization of the battleships *Duilio* and *Doria* was almost completed. The chances of a fleet action had therefore increased. On the other hand, there was a general feeling that the Italians were unwilling to meet the British in open battle. Though they were capable of great individual gallantry, their leadership seemed poor and their training inadequate. Time and again submarines had been caught on the surface in daylight, and in spite of their numbers and their many opportunities they had achieved very little. Apart from the heavy cruisers at Calabria, ships had been handled in action with lack of skill and initiative, and the only battleships encountered had retired after receiving one hit.

The main threat was from the air, and only good fortune had enabled the fleet to escape so lightly from the intense high-level bombing to which it had been subjected, particularly just before and after the Battle of Calabria when ships were straddled again and again. As the number of bombs dropped ran into four figures, considerable damage might have been sustained. In Admiral Cunningham's opinion the accuracy of these attacks was likely to increase with experience, and this factor would have to be carefully weighed when considering the employment of valuable ships in the Mediterranean. But he believed that if the anti-aircraft armament of ships was improved and a measure of fighter protection provided, this scale of bombing could be accepted as a reasonable war risk.

On the whole therefore the naval situation in the Mediterranean could be viewed with a certain amount of satisfaction. The first ten weeks of war had provided encouragement for the future, although there was still much to cause concern. The Italian Fleet was not the menace it appeared to be on paper: it did not seriously challenge the position of the British Fleet in the Eastern Mediterranean, and Admiral Cunningham had undoubtedly acquired an ascendancy over it. But by choosing when to go to sea it could pass convoys in safety to North Africa and so increase the land threat to Egypt. This in turn would imperil the Fleet base at Alexandria.

In aircraft and submarines we were too weak to provide more than an irritant to this movement. In spite of long and arduous submarine patrols, in which five boats had been lost,[1] all that had been achieved was the destruction of three merchant vessels, apart from an Italian transport which had been sunk after striking a mine laid by the *Rorqual* off Derna. Aircraft made a number of attacks on shipping in enemy harbours; operations from Egypt—in addition to those already mentioned—included attacks on Derna, Bomba and Tobruk. On 3rd August three ships were hit by the Air Force at Derna; on the 9th, attacks were directed on naval oil tanks and vessels in Tobruk, where one ship was left on fire; and on the 22nd the three naval Swordfish operating with the Air Force from Maaten Baggush torpedoed in daylight one submarine on the surface off Bomba and a depot ship in the harbour. On August 27th bombers made another attack on Derna destroying one merchant ship. There were also attacks by single bombers on Tobruk.

The submarine sunk at Bomba, the *Iride*, had just embarked from the depot ship four underwater assault craft (human torpedoes) which were to have attempted an attack on British warships at Alexandria on the night of the 25th. This was the first attack of its kind to be planned in the Mediterranean during this war.

The enemy's air attacks on British bases had so far been singularly ineffective. In the course of nine attacks on Alexandria during July and August they had only succeeded in sinking one mooring vessel, dropping an incendiary on an ASIS (happily empty), and penetrating the netlayer *Protector* with a splinter which killed one rating. Damage ashore was negligible and casualties low. Haifa, which provided a vulnerable target, had only been attacked three times, during which the oil tanks had received some damage. The first raid on the Canal area did not occur until 28th August, and this, too, did little harm.

---

[1] *Grampus, Odin, Orpheus, Phoenix, Oswald.*

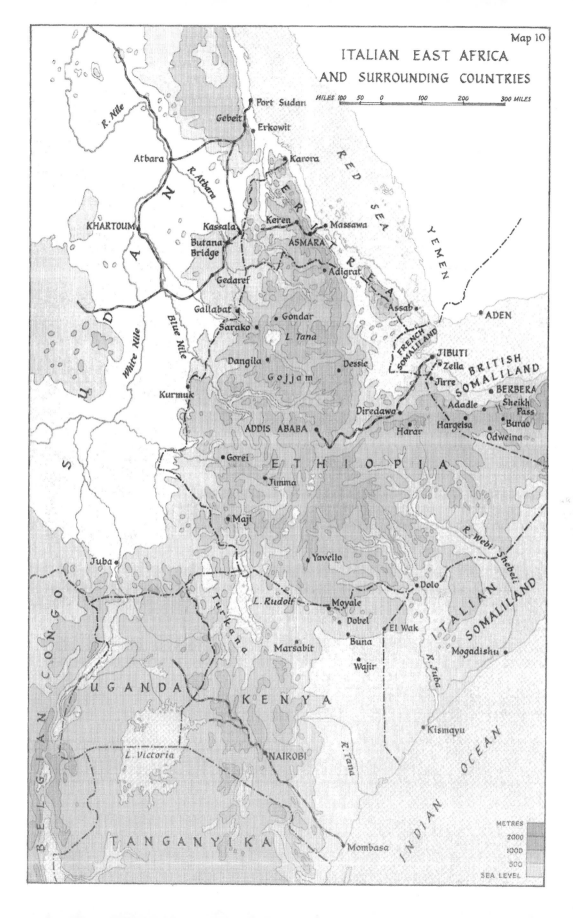

Map 10

ITALIAN EAST AFRICA
AND SURROUNDING COUNTRIES

MILES 100   50   0      100      200      300 MILES

R. Nile

Port Sudan
Gebeit
Erkowit

Atbara

R. Atbara

Karora

RED SEA

YEMEN

KHARTOUM

Kassala

Butana
Bridge

Keren

Massawa

ASMARA

ERITREA

Gedaref

Adigrat

S   U   D   A   N

Gallabat

Sarako

Gondar

L. Tana

Assab

ADEN

White Nile

Blue Nile

Dangila

Gojjam

Dessie

FRENCH
SOMALILAND

JIBUTI
Zeila

BRITISH
SOMALILAND

Kurmuk

Diredawa

Jirre

BERBERA

Adadle

Sheikh
Pass

ADDIS ABABA

Harar

Hargeisa

Burao

Odweina

Gorei

ETHIOPIA

Jumma

Maji

R. Webi Shebeli

Juba

Yavello

Dolo

ITALIAN

SOMALILAND

Turkana

L. Rudolf

Moyale

Dobel

El Wak

Mogadishu

Marsabit

Buna

R. Juba

S

Wajir

BELGIAN   CONGO

UGANDA

KENYA

Kismayu

L. Victoria

NAIROBI

R. Tana

INDIAN   OCEAN

TANGANYIKA

Mombasa

METRES
2000
1000
500
SEA LEVEL

# CHAPTER IX

# THE FIRST ENCOUNTERS ON THE BORDERS OF ITALIAN EAST AFRICA

*See Map* 10

THE UNPREPAREDNESS of Italy to face a long war was nowhere more acutely felt than in Italian East Africa. The situation of Somalia, Eritrea, and Ethiopia was strategically weak because the sea communications could easily be cut, and even the air communications were liable to be interrupted, by an enemy based in the Middle East. On land the nearest Italian post and landing ground, the oasis of Uweinat, was nearly a thousand miles away across the Sudan. It was not as if Italian East Africa had the industries, the natural resources, or the accumulated reserves to offset a prolonged interruption of the normal routes of supply. To make things worse, Ethiopia was a military liability even in peace time, because the first and ever present need was to be able to enforce internal order. It was for this, and not for operating against an external enemy, that the forces were organized.

The Duke of Aosta, Viceroy of Ethiopia and Supreme Commander of all armed forces in Italian East Africa, was so uneasy about the state of these forces that in April 1940, when Italy's intervention in the war was becoming likely, he went to Rome to represent his deficiencies to the Duce and the Ministers concerned.[1] As a result, he received an allotment of 900 million lire and a promise of reinforcements, weapons, and warlike stores. But it had been left too late, for by the time that events elsewhere had forced Italy into the war only a few officers and specialists, one company of light and one of medium tanks, 48 field guns, and some machine-guns and mortars had reached East Africa out of this consignment. Other ships were on their way, but were either recalled or were intercepted by the Royal Navy.

On May 30th the Viceroy received instructions from Marshal Badoglio that his forces were to be brought to full battle order by

---

[1] H.R.H. Prince Amedeo of Savoy, Duke of Aosta, a cousin of the King of Italy, had been Viceroy of Ethiopia since November 1937, when he succeeded the unpopular Marshal Graziani. The Duke was 42 years old in 1940 and had served in both the army and the air force. By British officials in the Sudan he was respected as an administrator and liked as a neighbour.

June 5th, and that their role was to be strictly defensive. This was, no doubt, in accordance with the Duce's belief that the impending collapse of the Allies in Europe would make unnecessary any serious fighting overseas, but the Viceroy at once enquired whether the orders precluded the operations against Jibuti which had formed an important part of the current Italian war plan, and if so whether it would be correct for him, while refraining from any large enter- prises, to undertake local frontier actions. Marshal Badoglio replied that the Viceroy's main object must be to guarantee the integrity of the Empire: he was to maintain a strictly defensive attitude but was to be ready to react swiftly and strongly to any attack; later he might be asked to study certain offensive plans. Having been informed on June 9th of the hour at which war would begin, the Viceroy asked if he might then attack the British by sea and air, in order to antici- pate them. He received a prompt reply ordering him to take no offensive action.

Within Ethiopia the needs of internal security had led to the establishment of many scattered garrisons, reasonably accessible by road, and each containing a substantial force of colonial troops, stiffened here and there by one or more Blackshirt battalions. In the colonial battalions the officers and many of the N.C.Os were Italians. The native troops varied greatly in fighting quality, and broadly speaking were armed and trained only for 'tribal' warfare; they were unaccustomed to manoeuvre on any but the smallest scale. Distributed along the frontiers were numerous groups of small irregular units or '*bande*', more lightly armed than the colonial troops and tactically rather more mobile.

But although the land forces in general lacked cohesion and flexi- bility, they were certainly strong in numbers. They consisted in the main of twenty-nine colonial brigades, mostly of three or four battalions of infantry and two batteries of pack artillery each. In addition there were seventeen independent colonial battalions, six- teen Italian battalions, and ten Italian artillery groups. Natives of all types and in all the Services, including the police, accounted for about 70% of the whole. The main reserves of troops were located at Addis Ababa, Dessie and Adigrat, the chief formations in reserve being one regular Italian division (the Savoia) and one of locally enlisted Italian nationals (the Africa). There were more than a hun- dred armoured cars manned by Italians and—from just before the start of hostilities—about 60 medium and light tanks. The 24 bomber and 4 fighter units, with a total of 183 aircraft and 61 in reserve— there were a further 81 under repair—had been accustomed to co-operate by reconnaissance and liaison in the work of policing. The ground organizations were accordingly scattered over wide distances, just as the army garrisons were.

Besides the dispersion imposed by the internal situation, a further handicap lay in the weakness of the administrative backing, which existed only on a scale suitable for the task of maintaining order and not for the support of operations against much resistance or at great distances. The shortages which caused particular concern were of anti-tank and anti-aircraft guns, ammunition of all kinds, motor and aviation fuel, aircraft and aircraft spares, and, above all, motor tyres. In short, the Duke of Aosta was by no means satisfied with his logistic situation but realized that there was little prospect of its being improved now that physical communication with Italy was cut. He resigned himself to a policy of imposing all possible economies, and of making do.

These administrative anxieties did not however prevent him from taking a balanced and sensible view of the strategical situation. He did not accept the exaggerated estimates of the British strength which were submitted to him, and did not expect to be attacked immediately. But he realized that there was a great deal of internal unrest, and in reviewing the position on June 18th he reported that in the past seven weeks there had been no less than five major disturbances, which he believed were intended to dissipate his forces and interrupt internal communications. He concluded that they were instigated by the British and supported by British propaganda and money, and he was especially concerned over the activities of the eight thousand or so Ethiopian exiles who were now scattered round the frontiers of the Empire, mostly in Kenya. The news of the Emperor's arrival in the Sudan on July 3rd reached him from Italy three weeks later and naturally increased his expectation of trouble. He thought it probable that Ethiopia would ultimately be attacked from both Kenya and the Sudan, in conjunction with an Ethiopian rising in the Gojjam and Shoa districts, which, if successful, would have the effect of cutting the country in half. But as the first two months of war passed he noted that the collapse of the French, the conquest of British Somaliland, and the various successful actions on the frontier seemed to have had a sobering effect on Ethiopian opinion. Indeed, he began to feel that the rebel elements had decided to adopt a waiting policy.

During July the Viceroy had become more and more irritated by the failure to clear up the situation in Jibuti. He had always recognized that French Somaliland presented a strategic threat to Ethiopia, but the defensive attitude imposed upon him by the Duce precluded any action being taken to reduce it. He therefore welcomed the prospect offered by the Franco-Italian armistice that the threat would be speedily removed, and viewed with increasing annoyance the successful evasions of General Legentilhomme, whom he regarded as 'an incubus sent to us by the British'. The Duce and Marshal

Badoglio shared his annoyance and did all they could to hasten matters, but it was not until July 27th that the Viceroy was able to report that the crisis had been overcome and that General Germain was in control. Even then the application of the armistice terms did not remove all his suspicions about French intentions, and he remained uneasy lest French Somaliland might yet become the bridgehead for a British invasion.

Throughout the months of June and July the Duce remained unwilling to authorize the Viceroy to undertake any offensive other than the limited attacks on Kassala and Gallabat in the Sudan, and on Moyale on the Kenya border. But he authorized the study of operations against Zeila and Berbera and plans were made to begin on any date after July 22nd. The entanglement over Jibuti, however, caused a postponement, and not until it had been unravelled was the Viceroy free to embark upon his only offensive operation of any size.

Prior to the outbreak of war with Italy an increase had been noticed in the Italian forces in Eritrea, and there were indications of concentrations towards the Sudanese frontier. It was realized that these might be defensive precautions, but they might equally well be the first signs of an intended invasion of the Sudan. In this case the choice of objectives obviously lay between Khartoum, Atbara, and Port Sudan. Khartoum was the centre of political and military control; Atbara was at the important junction of the railways to Khartoum and Port Sudan, and contained the only heavy workshops in the country; Port Sudan was the sole useful port. The distances to these objectives from the Eritrean border were very great; over 200 miles to Atbara and nearly 300 to Khartoum. This part of the country was devoid of military resources, mostly arid, and with no metalled roads, but it was traversable almost everywhere by motor transport in dry weather. With the beginning of the rains about the end of June or early July movement was liable to be severely restricted over periods of two days at a time until about the end of September. At no time, therefore, would invasion to any great distance be particularly easy.

The G.O.C. Troops in the Sudan, Major-General W. Platt, had under his command three British battalions; his only other regulars were the units of the Sudan Defence Force.[1] This Corps had been formed in 1925 from existing irregular units and certain Sudanese battalions of the Egyptian Army, and consisted of natives of the

---

[1] The Sudan Defence Force was the title of the whole Corps. Its units bore the individual titles of Camel Corps, Eastern Arab Corps, Western Arab Corps and Equatorial Corps. The Frontier Battalion is referred to on page 183.

Sudan led by British and Sudanese officers. Until 1936 its task had been to maintain internal security in the Sudan, and it was organized and lightly equipped accordingly. The conquest of Ethiopia by the Italians made it advisable to increase the scope of the force and a reorganization was begun. In June 1940 it comprised twenty-one companies, or 4,500 men in all, the most modernized units being five (later six) Motor Machine-Gun Companies—small mobile units consisting of light machine-guns carried in vans and trucks—and a number of locally constructed armoured cars. The force had as yet no artillery, though the Sudan Horse was in process of conversion into a battery armed with 3·7-inch howitzers.

General Platt's plan was to hold the three vital centres initially with his British battalions: 2nd Battalion The West Yorkshire Regiment at Khartoum; 1st Battalion The Essex Regiment at Atbara; and 1st Battalion The Worcestershire Regiment at Gebeit and Port Sudan. Upon the frontier were stationed units of the Sudan Defence Force, provincial police, and sundry irregular scouts, with the object of observing, harassing, and delaying the enemy. If a hostile thrust was clearly disclosed General Platt intended to concentrate the greatest possible force against it, relying upon distance, poor communications, and lack of supplies to absorb much of the impetus of the advance.

The tasks of the Air Force in the Sudan were the protection of shipping in the Red Sea, including anti-submarine patrols; the air defence of Port Sudan, Atbara, and Khartoum; and the close support of the Army and of the Ethiopian patriots. For these tasks there were only three bomber squadrons (Nos. 14, 47, and 223) armed with obsolescent Wellesleys, later reinforced by No. 45 (Blenheim I) Squadron from Egypt. For Port Sudan there were six Gladiator fighters of No. 112 Squadron, known as K Flight. For army co-operation No. 430 (Vincent) Flight was formed from No. 47 Squadron. These units formed No. 254 Wing, with headquarters at Erkowit, conveniently placed for controlling operations in the Port Sudan and Red Sea areas, but not those at Kassala and Gedaref or across the border. Accordingly H.Q. No. 203 Group, under the command of Air Commodore L. H. Slatter, was formed on August 17th at Khartoum, where the Air Officer Commanding was in close touch with the General Officer Commanding and in a position to supervise the Sudan sector of the Takoradi air route. No. 1 (Fighter) Squadron S.A.A.F., recently rearmed with Gladiators in Egypt, arrived at Khartoum early in August.

The first three weeks of war passed without any signs that the Italians intended to make full use of the short remaining period of dry weather, though their air forces were active and made frequent reconnaissances: bombing attacks were directed chiefly upon Kassala,

Port Sudan, Atbara, Kurmuk and Gedaref. The sole ground defence was by small-arms fire, and civilian morale suffered accordingly, but there was no military damage of any consequence. British air operations were directed chiefly against warships based on Massawa and against airfields in Eritrea. On land the Italians made no move. The Sudan Defence Force, on the other hand, was as active as possible and frequently patrolled and raided across the frontier, especially in the neighbourhood of Kassala and Gallabat. Casualties were inflicted upon the enemy, a few prisoners were taken, and the Sudanese soldiers gained in confidence. Early in July the enemy's attitude changed, and the expected attacks on the frontier posts began. Karora, Kassala, Gallabat, and Kurmuk were those chosen.

Kassala, on the long eastern loop of the Sudan Railway, was a provincial town of some importance. It was situated on the river Gash, about 20 miles from the point on the frontier to which ran the one good road—the *Via Imperiale*—from Asmara, the Eritrean capital. Kassala was an obvious first step in an advance towards either Atbara or Khartoum. At the beginning of July a concentration of the enemy was discovered near Tessenei, about twelve miles across the border, and a plan was made for attacking it on July 3rd. A failure in wireless communication led to a postponement. On July 4th the enemy advanced on Kassala from the east and along both sides of the Gash—three columns in all. Captured documents show that the force employed was two colonial brigades, four cavalry squadrons, about twenty-four light and medium tanks and armoured cars, and ten batteries of artillery of various calibres. To oppose this considerable array were two companies of the Sudan Defence Force, No. 5 Motor Machine-Gun Company and No. 6 Mounted Infantry Company, reinforced (at mid-day) by No. 3 Motor Machine-Gun Company from Butana Bridge. The action began with the bombing of the town and by 6.30 a.m. the enemy's cavalry were in contact with the defenders. The extreme disparity in numbers and weapons could lead to only one result, but though Kassala passed into enemy hands the conduct of the Sudan Defence Force gave great promise for the future. In their difficult task of causing as much loss as they could without becoming deeply involved they did in fact have 10 casualties, while the Duke of Aosta reported the Italian losses to have been 117. The three companies reassembled successfully at Butana Bridge.

On the same day an Italian colonial battalion and a *Banda* (irregular) group drove the platoon of No. 3 Company Eastern Arab Corps from Gallabat, while Karora was occupied by the enemy after the police party there had been withdrawn. On July 7th an Italian colonial battalion and irregulars, with artillery and air support, dispersed the 60 Sudanese police at Kurmuk after an hour's fight. From these successes the Italians had undoubtedly made valuable gains with which to impress the native population, to say the least. Militarily they had secured an important entrance to the Sudan at Kassala, and by capturing Gallabat they made it harder for the British to make contact with the patriots in Gojjam. The loss of Kurmuk had a bad effect on the local population, many of whom turned bandit. In contrast, and in spite of Italian boasts, the inhabitants of Kassala remained loyal throughout the six months of Italian occupation and helped the British very considerably by collecting information.

From General Platt's point of view there was no alternative to the policy of observing and harassing the enemy, while retaining the power to concentrate against renewed and deeper thrusts. In the Kassala and Gallabat areas the Sudan Defence Force continued to patrol actively. On July 5th a company of 2nd Bn. West Yorkshire Regiment was moved up to Gedaref to act as a reserve to the Sudan Defence Force. Learning that the report of this move had reached the enemy greatly exaggerated, General Platt proceeded to adopt every form of ruse to give the impression of far greater strength than he really possessed. There were good reasons for believing that these efforts were being successful, and an Italian General Staff map, of 25th July 1940, captured later, shows some 20,000 troops in or near the Kassala province of the Sudan. The situation was nevertheless not one for complacency, and when, on August 2nd, the destination of the 5th Indian Division was changed from Iraq to the Middle East, General Wavell at once ordered the leading brigade group to be disembarked at Port Sudan.

At the Anglo-French meeting at Aden in May 1939 it had been agreed that French Somaliland was of great strategic importance to the Allies. The French had been reasonably confident in their ability to hold the direct lines of approach from Ethiopia, but they had been apprehensive of an Italian advance through British Somaliland culminating in an attack on Jibuti from the direction of Zeila. It had been agreed that the French should be enabled to make the best possible tactical dispositions, moving forward, if necessary, into British Somaliland. As regards air support, the primary aim of the British air forces must be to reduce the scale of attack on Aden and the shipping. Operations to this end would be concerted from Aden and the Sudan. But if a critical situation arose in Somaliland the maximum of air support would be given to the troops, consistent with the security of any convoy that might be in the Red Sea at the time.

It had been the intention to abandon British Somaliland if invaded, but in December 1939 the Chiefs of Staff decided on General

Wavell's recommendation that in principle the policy should be to defend the territory and, in the last resort, Berbera. The troops were to come under General Wavell's Command,[1] but he was not to add to their number without the permission of the British Government. On visiting the country General Wavell came to the conclusion that a comparatively small addition to the force would make it possible to hold British as well as French Somaliland, which was very desirable for reasons of prestige and would be useful when the time came to attack the Italians. The fact that the Colonial Office, the Foreign Office and the War Office were all involved in this proposal did not make for its rapid acceptance; in fact it was March before permission to bring in one battalion was given, and it was May before the shipping was available. Financial approval for much of the intended work on defences was never given, and on June 1st General Headquarters, Middle East, took over administrative control from the Colonial Office.

On the outbreak of war with Italy the troops in British Somaliland were under the immediate command of Lieut.-Col. A. R. Chater, Royal Marines, hitherto the Commanding Officer of the Somaliland Camel Corps. In the last week of July the collapse of the opposition in French Somaliland to the terms of the armistice released large Italian forces for use against British Somaliland, but General Wavell still thought that to defend the approaches to Berbera was preferable to a withdrawal without fighting, a view which was shared by the Air Officer Commanding-in-Chief and the Commander-in-Chief East Indies. It did not seem that if the Italians occupied British Somaliland they would necessarily intensify their air attacks on Aden and on shipping, because even from well-established bases in Eritrea they had made a very poor showing.

The real issue was—to fight or not to fight; and General Wavell agreed with Lieut.-Col. Chater that nothing less than five battalions would have a reasonable chance of holding on, and these he considered could be made available. This was not to say that they could be sent at once or that Lieut.-Col. Chater could make firm plans for a force of this size, nor was it certain that any medium or field artillery would be available. By the beginning of August Brigadier Chater, who had just been promoted, had under his command 1st Bn. Northern Rhodesia Regiment, 2nd Bn. King's African Rifles and 1st East African Light Battery (four 3·7-inch howitzers) from Kenya; 1/2nd Punjab Regiment from Aden; 3/15th Punjab Regiment diverted from Aden; and the lightly armed Camel Corps, which had on mobilization received a valuable reinforcement of seventeen officers and twenty N.C.O.s from the Southern Rhodesia

---

[1] See pages 62-3 for the extension of General Wavell's responsibilities on 15th January 1940.

Regiment. 2nd Bn. The Black Watch, which had been sent to Aden from Egypt on July 1st in response to General Legentilhomme's request for a battalion to be ready to support him in French Somaliland, joined the force on August 8th, making the fifth battalion. The force therefore amounted to a last minute assemblage of units of four distinct races, each requiring different treatment and food. It lacked an organized base, a proper headquarters, and many other essentials, especially artillery, transport, and signal equipment. Air support could be provided only from the force at Aden, already committed both directly and indirectly to the protection of convoys and to the air defence of that port. Two 3-inch A.A. guns of 23rd Battery, Hong Kong and Singapore Brigade, R.A., were sent from the Aden defences. This was all that could be spared from other Middle East commitments.

The objective of any invasion would obviously be Berbera—the capital and the only port of any size, but not a suitable one for supporting a military expedition, for all unloading had to be done by lighters and a 3,000-ton ship normally took ten days to discharge. The frontier with Ethiopia was long and open, and offered no suitable positions on which to defend the main approaches to Berbera, of which there were three: one through Zeila, near the French Somaliland border, and thence eastward along the coast road; the second through Hargeisa; and the third through Burao. The main physical feature of the country is the range of rugged hills which runs parallel to the coast and about 50 miles or more from it. It was impassable by wheeled or tracked vehicles except by the roads to Hargeisa and Burao. The former and more direct road crossed the hills at a wide gap known as the Tug Argan. The road from Burao passed through a much narrower defile at the Sheikh pass. Between these hills and Berbera the ground was generally flat and open, and offered no natural position on which a smaller force could delay a determined advance for long. Brigadier Chater allotted initially two battalions and his light battery to Tug Argan and one to the other main approaches, and kept one battalion in reserve. When the fifth battalion (The Black Watch) arrived it went into reserve in place of 3/15th Punjab Regiment, which was moved up to strengthen the Tug Argan position. The Camel Corps formed a thin advanced screen for observing and delaying the enemy, and were supplemented by patrols of the Illalos, a small force of tribal levies whose normal task was rudimentary police work in the frontier areas; they showed great courage and loyalty throughout the campaign. The Camel Corps and Illalos made several bold and successful raids against enemy detachments near the frontier.

The Italian plan, as has been seen, was prevented by the ingenuity of General Legentilhomme from being put into effect sooner. The operation was under the command of Lieut.-General Nasi, General Officer Commanding Eastern Sector, who had the equivalent of an army corps made up of three Italian and twenty-three colonial battalions, three or four field howitzer batteries in addition to the pack artillery with each colonial brigade, making twenty-one batteries in all, a half-company of medium and a squadron of light tanks, some armoured cars, five groups of irregulars, and fifty-seven aircraft in support. The main column, under Major-General De Simone was to seize Hargeisa, establish a base, and then advance on Berbera. The right, or eastern column of irregulars under Brigadier-General Bertello was to move to Odweina to protect De Simone's flank, and be prepared to join him if necessary. On the extreme left Lieut.-General Bertoldi's column was to seize Zeila, seal off French Somaliland, and then send small forces eastwards. The Duke of Aosta seems to have been reasonably well informed of the British strength and dispositions, and in a written appreciation of 14th July expressed the view that the decisive encounter would take place between the Karrim and Jerato passes and that if the enemy held his ground the Italians would be able to manoeuvre so as to envelop the flanks.

The Italians crossed the frontier on August 3rd. The forward patrols of the Camel Corps fell back in touch with the advancing columns, keeping them under observation and striking when possible. On August 5th General Bertoldi occupied Zeila and began to push eastward. These movements, which seemed to threaten communications between the British force and its base, but which were not in reality vigorous, were harassed from the air and sea and by the patrols of the Camel Corps. On the eastern flank General Bertello reached Odweina on the 6th and then turned, not to Burao, but north-west towards Adadle, that is to say towards the line of advance of the centre column. General De Simone's initial advance on Hargeisa was held up by the Camel Corps, but on August 5th it was renewed in greater strength with the aid of light tanks, and the Camel Corps and a company of the Northern Rhodesia Regiment operating with them were obliged to withdraw. There was then a few days pause, except for some air reconnaissance and bombing by both sides, while the enemy stocked the Hargeisa area in preparation for a further advance. In response to the Duke of Aosta's urgings for speed General Nasi pointed out that his only road was in a very bad state, thanks to the unusual traffic and heavy rain. The advance was resumed on the 8th, and the two following days were spent in making contact with the main position and in preparing to attack it. It was during this phase that the presence of Italian medium tanks was first reported. Because there were no anti-tank guns the Captain

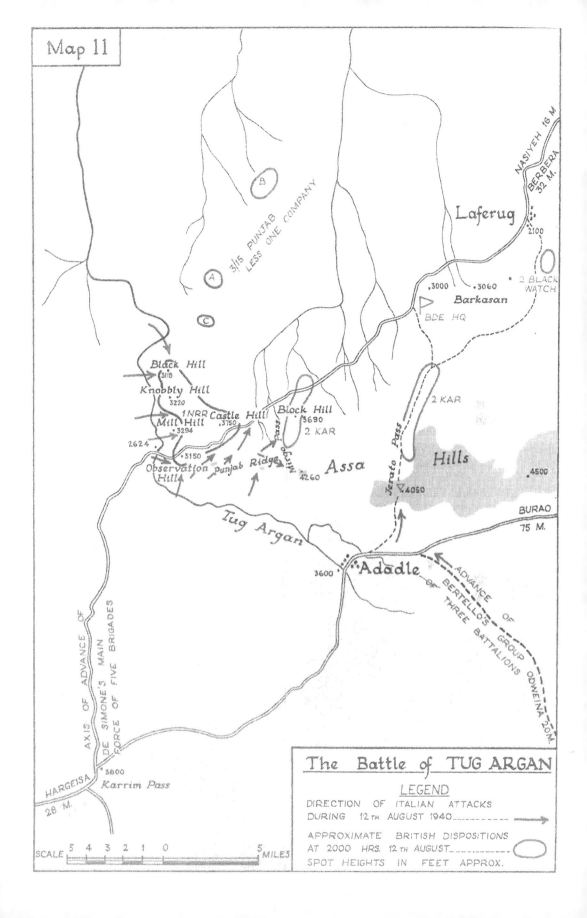

Map 11

3/5 PUNJAB LESS ONE COMPANY

B

A

C

Laferug

NASIYEH 16 M.
BERBERA 32 M.

.2100

.3000    .3060    2 BLACK WATCH

Barkasan

BDE HQ

Black Hill
.3118

Knobbly Hill
.3220

1 NRR Castle Hill
Mill Hill    .3750
.3294

2624.

.3150

Observation Hill

Punjab Ridge

Block Hill
.3690
2 KAR

2 KAR

Mirgo Pass

.4260    Assa    Hills

.4500

Jerato Pass

.4050

BURAO
75 M.

Tug Argan

Adadle

3600

ADVANCE OF BERTELLO'S GROUP OF THREE BATTALIONS ODWEINA 20 M.

AXIS OF ADVANCE OF DE SIMONE'S MAIN FORCE OF FIVE BRIGADES

HARGEISA
28 M.

.3800    Karrim Pass

SCALE 5 4 3 2 1 0                5 MILES

The Battle of TUG ARGAN

LEGEND

DIRECTION OF ITALIAN ATTACKS
DURING 12 TH AUGUST 1940 ............ ⟶

APPROXIMATE BRITISH DISPOSITIONS
AT 2000 HRS. 12 TH AUGUST ............ ⬭

SPOT HEIGHTS IN FEET APPROX.

of H.M.A.S. *Hobart* offered a 3-pdr saluting gun with 30 rounds of ammunition—an offer which was gladly accepted.[1]

When it was clear to General Wavell that the Italians were indeed intending an invasion in strength, he decided not to leave the British force entirely without field or anti-tank artillery, and ordered one field regiment (less one battery) from 4th Indian Division in the Western Desert, and one section of two anti-tank guns, to be sent by special convoy to Berbera. At the same time India was asked to load the first flight of the 5th Indian Division so that a battalion, a field battery, and a field company could be disembarked at Berbera. These reinforcements did not reach British Somaliland in time, and were sent instead to the Sudan.

It seemed to General Wavell that with all these troops under orders for Somaliland it would be appropriate to appoint a Major-General to command. Major-General A. R. Godwin-Austen, who had been temporarily commanding the troops in Palestine, had just handed over his duties and was on his way to East Africa to take command of the 2nd African Division. He was sent instead to Berbera, with instructions to prevent the Italians from advancing beyond the main position, but nevertheless to prepare, in secret, plans for evacuating the force in case this should become necessary. General Godwin-Austen arrived at Berbera on August 11th and assumed command that evening.

The same day marked the opening of the battle for the Tug Argan gap, so called from the name of a dry sandy river-bed or 'tug' which ran across the front.[2] This is the point at which the road from Hargeisa crosses the line of the Assa range and immediately turns east to pass between it and the confused mass of flat-topped hills and tugs which lie to the north. The gap consists of a flat stony floor, thinly sprinkled with thorn bush, intersected by numerous tugs and dotted with a few isolated rocky hills, 2,000 to 2,500 yards apart. These hills formed the defended localities which are named on Map No. 11 from north to south Black, Knobbly, Mill, and Observation Hills, and Castle Hill about two miles east of Mill Hill. Each had been prepared to some extent with machine-gun posts, and with a weak barbed-wire obstacle. In general, the position was a good one in that the enemy would be obliged to attack it, and it afforded good observation, although this could not be made full use of owing to the complete lack of any field artillery. (Two Bofors guns, for anti-tank use, arrived on the 13th.) The gap itself was very wide for the troops available, and the defended localities were far enough apart for infiltration to be possible between them; and except for Castle Hill

---

[1] This gun was mounted on an oil-drum and was served by a Petty Officer and two seamen who were over-run at Observation Hill and taken prisoner. They were released on the capture of Asmara on 1st April 1941.

[2] See Map 11 and Photo. 2.

they were all in the foremost line, so that most of the position had no depth. Finally—and as it turned out, this was a point of some importance—the Assa hills to the east of the bend in the Berbera road were not impassable to infantry, and there were several camel tracks such as those which crossed by the Mirgo and Jerato passes, which had the effect of widening the front still further; from the Mirgo pass to Black Hill was about eight miles.

On August 11th the enemy shelled and then heavily attacked the part of the westerly end of the Assa hills known as Punjab Ridge, employing a force estimated at not less than a brigade, which drove off the company of 3/15th Punjab Regiment holding it, and repulsed the ensuing counter-attack. Attacks on Mill Hill and Knobbly Hill failed. The next day all the principal defended localities were attacked. Towards evening the weakest, Mill Hill, was lost after severe fighting and two of the 1st East African Light Battery's invaluable howitzers had to be abandoned, having first been made useless. More serious, however, than the loss of Mill Hill was the fact that the enemy succeeded in improving his hold in the Assa hills and by nightfall was in possession of high ground dominating the southern part of the gap. The 13th saw another attack on Knobbly Hill repulsed, but small parties of the enemy began to filter down from the Mirgo pass and during the night ambushed, but failed to halt, a convoy of water and ammunition which was coming forward to Castle Hill. On the 14th Castle Hill and Observation Hill were bombed and heavily shelled and another attack on the latter was beaten off.[1] Meanwhile, in an attempt to relieve the threat to the road, a counter-attack was made towards the Mirgo pass by two companies of 2nd King's African Rifles, but after a temporary success it was thrown back.

It was now clear to General Godwin-Austen that not only was the enemy almost in a position to cut the road along which all supplies and water had to come, but that his marked preponderance in artillery, which outranged the light howitzers and so was able to fire without interference, meant that he could concentrate against each defended locality in turn. The regiment of field artillery, still on its way from Egypt, would have made all the difference in this respect. After four days of fighting the troops were becoming tired. Should Tug Argan fall there was no position behind it that could not easily be outflanked, and it would be useless simply to try to hold Berbera itself. On the 14th he therefore informed General Wilson, who was acting as Commander-in-Chief during General Wavell's absence in England, that if the present position fell he saw no alternative to evacuation, which would mean perhaps 70% of the force being

---

[1] Mussolini was not satisfied with the rate of progress and telegraphed to the Viceroy: 'Pour all available reserves into Somaliland to stimulate the operation. Order the entire Imperial air force to co-operate.' The Viceroy replied suitably on the 15th.

saved. He was of course prepared to fight to the end if this were required. After the failure to recapture the Mirgo pass it was evident that he had not the troops both for stabilizing the forward area and for covering a withdrawal, should this be necessary. The choice was therefore between fighting it out, with the loss of the whole force, and evacuating. He communicated this view early on the 15th and shortly after noon received General Wilson's order to evacuate. His plan was to hold two rearguard positions, one at Barkasan, and one at Nasiyeh, 33 and 17 miles from Berbera respectively. During three successive nights first the civilians and then the troops would be embarked. The spread over three nights was necessary because shipping had to be collected and at this season the monsoon conditions normally prevented embarkation by boat during the night and forenoon.

After being shelled for most of the day of the 15th, Observation Hill at last fell in the late afternoon to a strong attack; for extreme gallantry in its defence Captain E. C. T. Wilson, The East Surrey Regiment, attached Somaliland Camel Corps, was awarded the Victoria Cross. After dark the Northern Rhodesia Regiment was withdrawn from Black, Knobbly, and Castle Hills. The Black Watch, joined by two companies of 2nd King's African Rifles and elements of 1/2nd Punjab Regiment, took up a rearguard position at Barkasan, while another composite force occupied a second position at Nasiyeh. Through these positions the troops from Tug Argan withdrew. The Italians followed up slowly and not until August 17th did they attack at Barkasan. The brunt of the action was borne by The Black Watch, who carried out several successful counter-attacks during the day. The enemy was firmly held, though it was evident that his numbers would allow him in time to outflank the rearguard. Meanwhile embarkation had been going on with unexpected speed, so that General Godwin-Austen was able to accelerate his programme. He accordingly abandoned the Nasiyeh position and withdrew the Barkasan rearguard after dark on the 17th. Embarkation was complete by 2 p.m. on the 18th, though H.M.A.S. *Hobart* with Force Headquarters remained at Berbera until the following morning before sailing for Aden. The Italians resumed their advance on the 19th and entered Berbera that evening.

Throughout the short campaign the Royal Air Force were at a great disadvantage in that the airfields at Berbera and Laferug soon became unusable from enemy bombing; two of No. 94 Squadron's Gladiators were in fact destroyed on the ground. These airfields had only small-arm defence, since the primary task of the two 3-inch anti-aircraft guns was the defence of the port area. The bomber squadrons were therefore forced to operate from Aden, which involved a flight of 200 miles to and from the target area. Lacking

O

the protection of short-range fighters they were freely harassed by enemy fighters and suffered accordingly. The long distance also reduced the bombing effort and made it impossible to keep in touch with the army's situation. Nevertheless, in addition to distant reconnaissance, attacks were made on troops and transport, and also on enemy bases, including Addis Ababa, with the object of drawing off the fighters. Blenheim aircraft in the fighter role maintained standing patrols over Berbera for 13 days and secured for the port a reasonable freedom from air bombardment, especially during the evacuation. Air losses during the fortnight were relatively severe, seven aircraft being lost and ten others badly damaged. The Blenheim squadrons were Nos. 8, 11, and 39, all Mark I, and No. 203 (G.R.) Squadron Mark IV, recently converted to four-gun fighters. On August 14th Aden was reinforced by No. 223 Squadron from the Sudan and a flight of No. 84 from Iraq, both Blenheim Mark I's.

The Royal Navy's activities took many forms. H.M.S. *Kimberley, Auckland, Carlisle, Ceres* and H.M.A.S. *Hobart* co-operated by patrolling the coast, bombarding shore targets, and maintaining touch with and finally rescuing outlying parties of troops. In the end the Army had every reason to be grateful for the skill and speed with which 7,000 people, including civilians, were embarked.

The defence of British Somaliland cost 260 casualties, of which the majority were in the Northern Rhodesia Regiment and the machine-gunners of the Camel Corps, who together bore the brunt of the fighting in the Gap. A quantity of stores and equipment was lost because in the circumstances it could not be embarked. In spite of the safe withdrawal of the force there is no doubt that this latest set-back, and at the hands of the Italians, came as a shock to British public opinion. Yet General Wavell strongly endorsed the action that had been taken in his absence; General Godwin-Austen, he said, had judged the situation correctly and General Wilson had given a sound decision. The conduct of the troops, in very testing circumstances, had been excellent.

It may seem in retrospect that the British force had been set a task beyond its powers. On the other hand it must be remembered that in war nothing is certain, unless it be that the enemy will do what is least expected of him and that no results will ever be achieved if no risks are taken. It was not certain that the Italians intended to increase the spread of their forces still further; their internal situation was imperfectly known and might have seemed much worse to them than it did to us; their policy for all we knew might have been to conserve their reserves rigorously, realizing that until communication with Libya was opened up they could replace nothing—in itself a good reason for our not letting them have Berbera without paying for it; their colonial troops might have proved unreliable; their maintenance services might have been unequal to supporting a long advance. All these unknowns, coupled with the reflection that wars are not won by looking on but that battle experience has to be gained in battle, no doubt weighed with General Wavell in deciding that here was a risk that ought to be taken without endangering the decisive front in Egypt. In the event, the Italians used ample forces; they made a good plan, which exploited their advantages; they had supply difficulties and overcame them, at the cost of much wear and tear on their transport; and having won the battle they were unable to follow up in sufficient strength to interfere with the embarkation. They paid for their success with 2,052 casualties and an expenditure of material that they could ill afford.

The situation in Kenya in June 1940 bore many resemblances to that in the Sudan. There were very few troops for the defence of an enormous expanse of territory, but the vital areas—which were broadly those served by the Mombasa-Nairobi-Uganda railway—were a long way from the frontier. Between the escarpment marking the southern limit of Ethiopia and the foothills of the Kenya highlands stretches a flat grey landscape of 200 miles of sun-baked earth and leafless thorn trees, with occasional hills and very little water. None of the tracks across this waste remained passable during the rains, which in this district occur from April to June and from mid-October to mid-December.

Kenya's great asset was its well equipped deep-water port of Mombasa, already referred to as a potential back door to Egypt, to which it was connected by a combination of rail, road and river; not an easy or rapid line of communication, but nevertheless a slight insurance against the closing of the Red Sea. When the Italians failed to do this the need for the back door receded—at any rate for a time—and Kenya took on as its primary task the organization of a base for an advance into Italian East Africa.

Ever since the Italian conquest of Ethiopia in 1936 the Inspector-General of the African Colonial Forces, Major-General G. J. Giffard, had worked hard for an increase in the size and scope of these forces, but with only partial success as the necessary funds were not forthcoming. But he succeeded in so organizing them as to allow of efficient expansion in emergency, and, in the event, considerable headway was made with their growth and training during the eight months while Italy was hesitating. In peace time they consisted almost entirely of infantry, the men being voluntarily enlisted, with officers and senior N.C.Os seconded from British regiments. The Royal West African Frontier Force consisted of eight battalions: five in the Nigeria Regiment, two in the Gold Coast Regiment, one

Sierra Leone Battalion, and one Gambia Company. In East Africa there were the King's African Rifles, consisting of two brigades, with three battalions from Kenya and Uganda and three from Tanganyika Territory and Nyasaland; and the Northern Rhodesia Regiment of one battalion.

On the outbreak of war with Italy Major-General D. P. Dickinson, who had succeeded General Giffard as Inspector-General of the African Colonial Forces, was appointed General Officer Commanding East Africa Force, comprising only two East African brigades, an East African reconnaissance regiment and a light battery, and the 22nd Mountain Battery R.A. from India. The task given to him by General Wavell was to defend Kenya and without compromising that defence to contain as many Italians as possible on his front. He decided to hold a coastal area in front of Mombasa; to deny the enemy access to the river Tana and to the water at Wajir; and to station detachments at Marsabit, at Moyale on the frontier, and in Turkana by Lake Rudolf, which meant that the force was stretched over an arc of 850 miles. The enemy was believed to have troops at the principal centres Kismayu, Mogadishu, Dolo, Moyale and Yavello; these were in fact colonial brigades and *bande* in each case, and a further force of about two brigades near Jimma could reinforce Moyale or strike south towards Lake Rudolf and so into Uganda.[1]

The policy of the Union of South Africa in providing troops and air forces has already been referred to, and among the most valuable of their early contributions to the defence of Kenya was the 1st South African Anti-Aircraft Brigade, whose arrival enabled protection to be given to Mombasa. By the outbreak of war with Italy the air force units in Kenya comprised No. 237 Rhodesian Squadron, the Kenya Auxiliary Air Unit, Nos. 11 and 12 Bomber Squadrons S.A.A.F., armed at first with Hartbeest and German Junkers 86 aircraft respectively, followed shortly afterwards by No. 40 Squadron which took over the Hartbeests and became an Army Co-operation unit; No. 11 Squadron was then rearmed with Fairey Battles.

At first the air forces of both sides devoted most of their attention to the forward areas, while patrols of the King's African Rifles had several brushes with the enemy at points on the frontier of Italian Somaliland and at Moyale. It was only here that the Italians displayed any marked activity. Situated on the edge of the Ethiopian escarpment Moyale covered the junction of the tracks leading to Wajir and Marsabit and faced a very likely line of approach from Ethiopia. The British did not intend to hold this exposed position to the last, nor yet abandon it without a fight. The garrison of one company of the 1st King's African Rifles repulsed an attack on July 1st, and, as a precaution, reinforcements were moved up to

---

[1] Italian and British Moyale were on opposite sides of the frontier.

within supporting distance. On July 10th, after considerable shelling, a much heavier attack began for which the enemy appears to have allotted four battalions. After three days of intermittent fighting the Brigade Commander judged that to hold Moyale any longer would absorb too much of his strength. The withdrawal was successfully achieved and there was no follow up, though in due course the Italians advanced to the water-holes at Dobel and Buna. With this measure of success they appeared to be content.

At the end of June the West African contingent, which by now had been formed into two brigade groups, one from Nigeria, one from the Gold Coast, arrived by sea. A step forward in organization was taken by combining the East and West African brigades into two weak divisions, the 1st and 2nd African Divisions, later to be called the 11th and 12th. The 1st, formed of the Nigerian and 1st East African Brigade Groups, took over the coastal and Tana sector of the defences. The 2nd, formed of the Gold Coast and 2nd East African Brigade Groups, became responsible for the northern sector. At about the same time the 1st South African Brigade Group, fore-runner of the 1st South African Division, arrived from the Union by sea and continued its training in the area to the north-west of Nairobi.

With an eventual offensive in view, and with many problems of expansion and organization to be solved—the supply and training of British leaders for African troops, to mention only one—General Dickinson had a formidable task indeed. His instructions from General Wavell were that he was not to assume the offensive until he was quite certain that his administrative arrangements were adequate. In 1939 East Africa had been quite unready for war, and the *Bon Voisinage* Agreement set a severe limit on the steps that could be taken before Italy made her intentions clear.[1] Even then, the needs of Europe and Egypt left little for East Africa, and General Dickinson, with a modest staff and practically no administrative services or tradesmen or military stores or reserves of equipment of any kind, was obliged to fend very largely for himself. He was helped in every way by the Colonial Government Departments; India came to his rescue over some of the most urgent requirements, notably ammunition; but it was on South Africa that he soon came to rely for help at every turn. The Union Government were naturally interested in the country to which their forces were being sent; they understood the difficulties, and they provided invaluable equipment and skilled men of all kinds. Best of all, they supplied transport, the key to the whole problem. From early August a stream of vehicles, men and stores began to wend its way along the earthen track, or 'Great North Road', from Broken Hill in Northern Rhodesia, to which point they had been brought by rail from the Union. By the

---

[1] See page 12.

end of the year some 9,000 vehicles, mostly 1- and 3-ton trucks, many driven by inexperienced Africans, were to make the 1,500 mile trek to Nairobi over sand, stones, cotton soil, desert, and bush, up steep grades and over passes. This picturesque exploit proved to be a useful preliminary to the drive to Addis Ababa a few months later. Its importance at the time was that it met a great need without using any precious shipping space.

At the Anglo-French meeting held at Aden in May 1939 the possibility of a rebel rising in Ethiopia had been examined. There were districts where the local chieftains had never been subdued by the Italians, notably in Gojjam and to the east of Lake Tana, and it should be possible to pass arms and ammunition to them across the Sudan frontier between Kassala and the Blue Nile. It had been extremely difficult, however, to learn the true facts. The normal diplomatic channels of information had been narrowed when the consulate at Dangila, a town to the south of Lake Tana, had been closed in 1934; two others at Gorei and Maji were closed on the out-break of the Italo-Ethiopian war; and after the Italian victory the Legation at Addis Ababa was reduced to a Consulate-General. Moreover, the Italians had been taking pains to mislead observers and conceal anything that might lessen the impression of their complete and beneficent conquest. Consequently the British and French agreed that it was essential to acquire more contacts in the country. Encouragement would not be given to native uprisings before the prospect of their success could be gauged and until they could be supported by more effective means than by propaganda or the use of inadequate forces. It was recognized that premature risings would be likely to fail in view of the military superiority of the Italians; they would do more harm than good.

In July 1939, shortly after his arrival in the Middle East, General Wavell instructed his staff to study the problem of fostering rebellion in Ethiopia, but there was still not sufficient information on which to base a sound plan. In September Colonel D. A. Sandford, who had formerly settled in Ethiopia until forced out by the Italians, was appointed to direct the work. Information received during the winter from an emissary of the Emperor and from French sources indicated that the seeds of a national rebellion existed and that there was a desire for the Emperor to return to his country to unite and deliver his people. Owing to the *Bon Voisinage* Agreement the work was delicate and severely restricted, but Sandford prepared a plan for fostering and supporting revolt in the event of war with Italy, and this formed the basis of General Wavell's future policy.

In March 1940 Major R. E. Cheesman, formerly Consul at

Dangila, was appointed to deal with Ethiopian intelligence matters at Khartoum. The names of eleven Ethiopian chieftains to be approached in the event of war were chosen, and letters were prepared containing promises of arms and money if men were sent to fetch them. In May began the discreet forming of the Frontier Battalion, Sudan Defence Force, whose role would be to garrison the small bases at which these issues would be made. On June 11th, the day after the declaration of war, the letters, signed by General Platt, were sent off on their long journey. Within a fortnight the first chief arrived with his men and thereafter the arrival of similar bands was an almost daily occurrence at one point or another on the frontier.

In an instruction on policy issued on June 10th General Wavell laid down that the existing unrest was to be encouraged to spread as widely as possible, in order to force the Italians to expend their resources on internal security. The early activities were to be confined to isolated attacks by only small parties of patriots, culminating later in larger operations against important objectives, which would depend on the success already achieved and the extent to which arms and money could be introduced. He attached great importance to this step-by-step method, and insisted that the patriots were not to be led into enterprises beyond their powers by false hopes that they would be supported by troops. A small military mission (No. 101) was to be sent to give them advice and co-ordinate their efforts; its organization was entrusted to Colonel Sandford.

The Emperor, who was in England, had as yet no part in these plans. On June 18th the War Cabinet agreed to facilitate his return and six days later he was flown to Egypt in great secrecy and haste, for now that France seemed lost any delay might make the flight too dangerous. His sudden arrival incognito in Khartoum on July 3rd was the cause of some embarrassment, since the Middle East had been given no guidance on the Government's policy regarding him but now incurred a heavy responsibility for his safety and fitting treatment. The plans for assisting the revolt were explained to him with the suggestion that he should remain in Khartoum until the situation in Ethiopia could be more accurately judged. Although the Emperor was clearly disappointed, particularly at the little material help that could be offered to him, he accepted the position with dignity and understanding.

Closely connected with the Emperor's arrival was the question of the departure of 101 Mission. General Platt had directed on June 21st that it was, if possible, to be established by August 1st, and that it was on no account to allow itself to be destroyed or captured, for a bad start would be disastrous. Colonel Sandford was eager to set out, but it now had to be decided whether or not the Emperor should be invited to accompany him. Sandford urged that he should, but there were doubts whether the moment was in all ways the right one for His Majesty to re-enter his country, and the matter was referred to General Wavell, who decided that a part of the Mission was to go into Ethiopia forthwith to reconnoitre and report on the situation in the frontier provinces to the east of Gallabat. The Mission was to stimulate the first phase of the revolt—the isolation of outlying Italian garrisons by small patriot parties—and was to influence the operations in such a way as to secure an area under patriot control safe for the entry of the Emperor. On August 12th Colonel Sandford crossed the frontier on the difficult and hazardous journey to Gojjam. On the 31st Lieutenant A. Weinholt, soon to die at the hands of Italian *bande*, followed him. On September 18th Major Count Bentinck led another party of the Mission across the frontier towards the north of Lake Tana.

All this time Khartoum was the centre of much activity. An invitation had been issued to all Ethiopian refugees and exiles who wanted to fight for their country to assemble in Khartoum, where they arrived in hundreds, requiring a great deal of sorting out and organizing. Eventually four battalions, with other units, were organized, requiring a large number of British officers and N.C.Os. On September 8th General Wavell issued another instruction outlining the steps to be taken in anticipation of a favourable report by 101 Mission. Until this report was received he would be unable to decide whether to try to accelerate the revolt at once or whether to await the moment when British troops could carry the offensive into Italian territory, thereby heightening British prestige and patriot morale. In the meantime all possible preparations were to be made so that no time would be lost.

Meanwhile in Addis Ababa the Italians appear to have thought that some British enterprise was afoot at Sarako, to the north-west of Lake Tana, but it did not prevent the Viceroy from concluding that his successes in British Somaliland and at Kassala and Moyale had 'paralysed the possibility of an extension of internal rebellion'. By the end of September the Italians had heard that some Europeans were on their side of the frontier; and in October suspicion plays round a 'Mr. Rhoms', said to have once been British consul at Dangila. On December 4th it fastens upon 'a certain Colonel Sandford'.

# CHAPTER X

# ANXIETY OVER THE
# POSITION IN THE MIDDLE
# EAST

THE COLLAPSE of French resistance and the consequent wreck of Allied plans in the Mediterranean and Middle East gave rise to a grave doubt in General Wavell's mind. Could the existing machinery for the higher direction of the war be relied upon to work efficiently under the new conditions, or did it require some adjustment? The day after the announcement by Marshal Pétain that France had asked for the terms of an armistice General Wavell, strongly supported by Air Chief Marshal Longmore, telegraphed his views for the consideration of the War Cabinet.

The war, he thought, was likely to spread into large areas of Africa and Asia. Some organization situated nearer to its work than London would be needed to take control of the war effort and direct the efficient use of the resources of Africa, India, and Australia, and possibly America. Wide powers ought to be delegated to it by the War Cabinet, which seemed likely to be preoccupied with the defence of Great Britain, but which would, of course, remain responsible for general policy and ultimate control. Much time would be saved by obviating frequent reference home. The new body would consist of a Cabinet Minister and three or four other members of energy and ability chosen from the United Kingdom or the Dominions. Three Service heads (two of them being the Army and Air Commanders-in-Chief) would act as its advisers. The best place for it might be Kenya. In short, problems were going to arise which would require 'quick decision, personal touch, and resolute action', so that some form of decentralization was essential.

Admiral Cunningham agreed generally but made the comment to the Admiralty that instead of a naval adviser he would prefer to see a senior Flag Officer with full power of command over all the naval forces operating in an area corresponding to that of the Army and Air Commands. But he doubted whether decentralization to this extent by the Admiralty would be practicable. As regards material support for the war effort in the Middle East, the Commanders-in-Chief were not alone in their anxiety. British industry was already feeling the strain, and would be hard put to equip expanding forces, build up reserves, and support a campaign in the Middle East. This aspect was serious enough but was made worse by the ever-increasing shortage of shipping. In view of the likelihood of an eastward spread of hostilities, the Viceroy of India (the Marquess of Linlithgow) in June 1940 made a proposal for developing and co-ordinating the output of munitions, warlike stores, and equipment in the British Dominions and Colonies east of Suez. With the approval of His Majesty's Government, a conference of these 'Eastern Group' countries was held at New Delhi in October. Meanwhile a mission from the Ministry of Supply visited South Africa and India to study the potential capacity of both countries. The outcome of these steps was the setting up at New Delhi of an Eastern Group Central Provision Office. One of its tasks was to arrange for the requirements of the Services in the Middle East to be met as far as possible from sources under its control.

On July 1st General Wavell reported that after further consideration it seemed to him that his proposal would take so long to become effective that, far from lessening many of the delays and difficulties, it might even increase them. Events were moving so rapidly that this would be dangerous. He suggested, therefore, that it might be better to give to a sub-committee of the War Cabinet the task of keeping a close watch on the whole area from Africa to India. This was no doubt a much more welcome suggestion, and on July 11th the Prime Minister directed that a standing Ministerial Committee should be set up, consisting of the Secretaries of State for War, India, and the Colonies, to keep under review the conduct of the war in the Middle East and to report to him, as Minister of Defence. Thus the idea of setting up some form of regional War Council came to nothing—at least for a while. Exactly a year later a Minister of State was appointed to represent the War Cabinet in the Middle East; he was to give the Commanders-in-Chief political guidance, relieve them of extraneous responsibilities, and settle promptly matters within the policy of His Majesty's Government.

It was not long before the Ministerial Committee was expressing its grave concern at the shortages in the Middle East. September would mark the beginning of the most favourable season for campaigning, and it was already July. The Royal Air Force stood in urgent need of reinforcement; the 7th Armoured Division was well below strength, having two armoured brigades, each of two regiments instead of three, and needed a great deal of new equipment—in particular, cruiser tanks were required urgently; stocks of ammunition of all kinds were dangerously low. The Ministers felt that the time had come when considerable risks ought to be taken in sending material through the Red Sea and Mediterranean. They even asked when it would be possible to send another armoured division to

Egypt, to which the Chiefs of Staff replied that it ought to be sent as soon as the tactical situation in the United Kingdom would permit. As regards the 5th Indian Division, now under orders for Basra, the Chiefs of Staff and Ministers agreed that it ought to be placed at General Wavell's disposal, although this would mean providing it with a higher scale of equipment which would have to come from the United Kingdom.

On 1st July the War Cabinet had decided to send this division as part of a composite force to Iraq, but in the meantime, before it was ready to sail, General Wavell, General Cassels (the Commander-in-Chief, India), and the Viceroy in his capacity of Governor-General, all expressed their anxiety lest the move should do more harm than good. For one thing it might provoke action by Russia, and it might aggravate the trouble in Iraq. The force was not strong enough to deal effectively with these dangers if they arose, nor could it be adequately backed up. With the anti-aircraft guns no longer available from the United Kingdom, even the defence of the Anglo-Iranian oilfields could not be satisfactorily undertaken. In many respects the position was grimly reminiscent of 1914, and there was no desire to embark upon another Mesopotamian campaign if it could possibly be avoided. These arguments, together with the obvious need to increase the forces in the Middle East, led the War Cabinet to reverse its decision. Early in August they changed the destination of the 5th Indian Division from Basra to the Middle East; General Wavell thereupon decided that the leading brigade group should disembark at Port Sudan.

The Ministerial Committee reported its conclusions to the Prime Minister, who decided to invite General Wavell to London to discuss Middle East affairs. He was particularly anxious to meet this commander upon whom such a heavy responsibility rested. General Wavell accordingly flew to England and on 8th August gave the Chiefs of Staff his verbal review of the situation.

He reminded them that it had been the intention to meet an Italian advance in strength by defending Matruh and by harassing the enemy in the desert with armoured forces: it had not been intended to hold Sollum or the line of the frontier.[1] But when war came he thought it worth while to fight in the frontier zone to begin with, and the resulting operations of our small mechanized force had been very successful. Three Italian forts had been taken, with some 800 prisoners, and a quantity of guns, tanks, and lorries had been destroyed—all at small cost. The Italians had then increased their artillery strength, and had re-occupied Fort Capuzzo, and had

---

[1] See page 42.

generally established themselves in the frontier zone once more. The position now was that our patrols were losing vehicles; spare parts were very scarce; and wear and tear were beginning to reduce the efficiency of our armoured troops. In short, the point had been reached at which our advanced detachments on the frontier were ceasing to pay a dividend. If the Italians were to bring up large forces, some degree of withdrawal would be necessary, but it seemed doubtful whether they had much enthusiasm for the venture. The real danger would be the appearance of German armoured and motorized forces.

There was no evidence of the presence of German troops in Libya, but it was so difficult to obtain information of enemy movements that it would be comparatively easy for one or two armoured or motor divisions—which might be German—to reach Tripoli or even Benghazi unknown to us. The range of our available aircraft precluded adequate reconnaissance of the ports. In other respects the Intelligence Service was finding great difficulty in making up for the time lost during the 'non-provocation' period, though a certain amount of information had been obtained from prisoners. The Italians appeared to have some 280,000 troops in Libya, mostly white. There was a trend away from the Tunisian frontier eastwards, but administrative difficulties would prevent anything like the whole of this force being deployed against Egypt. At present there were four divisions and part of a fifth between Tobruk and Sollum, of which three were close to the frontier.

General Wavell estimated that the enemy might advance on a frontage of some 50 miles, thus turning the defences of Matruh, and could dispense with the use of the coastal road. He thought that their problem of maintenance would be—at any rate, partly—solved by the use of air transport. The air forces which might co-operate in such an advance would be of the order of 300 or 400 bombers, 300 fighters, and 200 troop-carrying aircraft.

Our position in Egypt would continue to be unsatisfactory until the state of the British forces could be improved. There was an urgent need for modern types of bomber and fighter aircraft. In the army not a single formation was complete. The 7th Armoured Division had 65 cruiser tanks instead of 220, while not even all these had their proper armament, and the lack of spare parts was very serious. The 4th Indian Division was short of a brigade and much of its artillery. The Australian and New Zealand troops were very short of equipment; in emergency a system of pooling would make it possible to use about one-third of their numbers for something more than internal security duties. The army had no adequate protection against low-flying attack, as the only Bofors guns in the country were the twelve at Alexandria; the heavy anti-aircraft guns were mostly manned by Egyptians. There was general shortage of anti-tank guns, and of ammunition of all kinds.[1]

Internal security was causing less anxiety now than six months before, though the presence of between forty and fifty thousand Italians and the pro-Italian attitude of certain influential Egyptians meant locking up a large number of troops on internal security duties. The Egyptian Army was comparatively well armed and well trained, and was co-operating to some extent in defending the Western Desert, but the curious fact was that Egypt and Italy were not at war. A committee of pro-British Frenchmen had been set up under M. Benois, but the French Minister was a 'Vichy-ite' and our relations with the French in Egypt were in danger of growing worse.

General Wavell gave a summary of the encounters on the Sudan border and explained that no extensive operations against the Sudan need be expected before the end of the rains in October. Meanwhile the road from Kassala to Khartoum would be impassable, though the enemy might try to capture the important bridge over the Atbara to the west of Kassala. The leading brigade group of the 5th Indian Division would disembark at Port Sudan.

Reviewing the plans for raising a revolt in Ethiopia, General Wavell commented on the scarcity of information; this was due to the pre-war policy of making no preparations for subversive activity or for obtaining secret intelligence in Italian territory. Consequently it would be some time before the arrangements for revolt would be far enough advanced to hold out a reasonable prospect of success.

It was too soon to say what would be the outcome of the Italian advance into British Somaliland. The despatch of 2nd Bn. The Black Watch from Aden to this front meant that the Italians might possibly make a move against Aden through the Yemen, though from their general lack of enterprise in the southern Red Sea it did not seem very likely that they would; in fact Aden could be regarded as reasonably secure.

In Kenya the loss of the outpost at Moyale unfortunately meant that we had now no footing on the Ethiopian escarpment. Had West African reinforcements arrived even a week sooner the outpost might have been retained. The capture of Kismayu (strategically of more importance than Mogadishu) had been studied, and the conclusion was that an overland advance presented greater prospects of success than a landing operation. General Wavell said that his administrative resources would not allow of an offensive at present.

---

[1] The artillery ammunition position was complicated by the fact that production of ammunition for 18-pdr guns and 4·5-inch howitzers, with which some units in the Middle East were armed, had ceased because of the introduction of the 25-pdr 'gun-how'. The position would be serious until rearmament with 25-pdrs could be completed. Similarly, the 37-mm anti-tank guns had only about 21,000 rounds in all; no more was being made because of the introduction of the 2-pdr gun. Rearmament with 2-pdrs was therefore an urgent requirement. See footnote to page 190.

There remained the Eastern Mediterranean. In Palestine the situation was quieter than it had been for some years. The Arabs seemed more friendly and the Jews were anxious to be armed. A contingent of each race, 1,000 strong, was being raised. In Syria it seemed that things would gradually settle down; it was certainly unlikely that the French would attack Palestine. In Cyprus the British garrison had been increased from one company to one battalion, but the French had not been satisfied with this and a French contingent had also been sent to the island. Half of these were now back in Syria, while the rest—who were pro-British—were being re-formed and re-equipped in the Canal area of Egypt. A battalion of Cypriots was being raised to help to defend the island. As regards Crete, the project for its recapture, if it were first seized by the Italians, had depended to a large extent on French co-operation. General Wavell thought that a brigade with adequate air support and anti-aircraft defences would be needed to capture and hold the island. The Air Officer Commanding-in-Chief was not in favour of the operation in present circumstances, although the Naval Commander-in-Chief was very anxious about the security of Crete. The necessary resources for its capture were not clearly available at present.

During the first eight months of the war the army's main effort had been devoted to building up the expeditionary force in France. This was why units in the Middle East remained short of much of their equipment and why their war reserves were so low. Then came the evacuation from Dunkirk, involving the loss of practically the whole of the equipment of the British Expeditionary Force. The bulk of current armament production had to be allotted to the forces required for the defence of the United Kingdom. Nevertheless, the War Office had been making great efforts to meet General Wavell's most pressing needs, and on 10th August the C.I.G.S. was able to give the Prime Minister a summary of the units and equipment which he had decided to prepare for despatch to the Middle East.[1] The provision of shipping and escorts would govern the date of sailing.

It happened that the expedition to pass naval reinforcements to the Eastern Mediterranean (*Illustrious, Valiant* and two anti-aircraft cruisers) had been planned to sail from the United Kingdom on 20th August. Subsidiary operations had been designed to cover the delivery of equipment and stores to Malta, by convoy from the east and by

---

[1] 3rd The King's Own Hussars (light tanks); 2nd Royal Tank Regiment (cruiser tanks); 7th Royal Tank Regiment (infantry tanks); 48 2-pdr anti-tank guns and 40,000 rounds; 20 Bofors light A.A. guns and 30,000 rounds; 48 25-pdr guns and 24,000 rounds; 500 Bren guns; 1 million rounds of ·303-inch tracer; 250 anti-tank rifles; 50,000 anti-tank mines; 300 tons of spare parts, wireless equipment, etc.

*Valiant* and the anti-aircraft cruisers from the west. The whole operation, known as 'Hats', required the concerted action of the naval forces in the Eastern and Western Mediterranean, that is, of the Mediterranean Fleet and of Force H. The idea of sending fast merchant ships loaded with army equipment to accompany the naval force through the Mediterranean was clearly worth looking into, but only two could be made available in time, and there would be no room for the large Matilda tanks which would therefore have to go round the Cape. The Prime Minister was most anxious to avoid parting with these fifty invaluable infantry tanks from England at such a critical time without making strenuous efforts to get them into action in the Middle East at the earliest possible moment; that is to say, by passing them through the Mediterranean. The present arrangements would merely ensure their protracted absence from both battlefields.

For several days this problem occupied the attention of Whitehall, but not of Whitehall only. On 11th August Admiral Cunningham, on whom the burden would fall, signalled his views. The practicability of passing four 16-knot ships capable of carrying mechanical transport ('M.T.' ships) through the Mediterranean in conjunction with Operation 'Hats' could, he thought, only be decided by trial. The convoy might pass unscathed, or it might become a total loss. Its presence would greatly increase the time during which Force H and the Mediterranean Fleet would be exposed to bombing attacks which might be heavy and continuous. Nevertheless, if the urgency were so great as to justify the risks of loss of the army reinforcements and of serious damage to the Fleet, he would accept the operation subject to certain conditions.

On 12th August General Wavell attended meetings of the Chiefs of Staff and of the Defence Committee.[1] The First Sea Lord placed on record that the intended operation for the reinforcement of the Mediterranean Fleet would be jeopardized to an unknown extent by the inclusion of the M.T. ships, of which it was quite possible that none would get through. In the passage of the Sicilian Narrows the speed of the *Valiant, Illustrious,* and other ships would be reduced from 21 knots to 15; their ability to avoid attacks by destroyers or M.T.B.s would thus be seriously affected. The feint which had been planned to the north of the Balearic Islands would be of no avail, for once the presence of merchant ships became known to the enemy he would know that our intention was to pass them through the Central

---

[1] The Defence Committee (Operations) of the War Cabinet was presided over by the Prime Minister as Minister of Defence. Its members, at this time, were: the Lord Privy Seal (Mr. C. R. Attlee), Lord Beaverbrook (Minister of Aircraft Production), and the three Service Ministers, with the Chiefs of Staff in attendance. Other Ministers attended as required. This Committee took decisions on military plans on behalf of the War Cabinet.

Mediterranean, where he might have up to two days in which to prepare for them. The whole character of the operation would be changed; it would become cumbersome and risky. In any event it would be definitely unsound to compromise 'Hats' to the extent of adding not two M.T. ships but four; it would also mean postponing the date of sailing, with the result that the destroyers detailed to escort the 5th Indian Division up the Red Sea to Port Sudan might not reach Aden in time. Therefore before coming to a decision it was essential to know the latest date by which the armoured reinforcements must reach Egypt.

General Wavell's considered opinion was that the risk of losing on passage through the Mediterranean a quantity of valuable equipment, much of which would take several months to replace, would not justify the gain in time. If the Italians were to attack early in September he would feel able to use his own armoured forces more boldly in the knowledge that the reinforcements were reasonably certain to arrive before the end of the month.

The Chiefs of Staff supported the naval view, and the Defence Committee accepted it also. Nevertheless it was agreed to defer the final decision on the route to be followed by the two fast ships until 26th August, when the whole expedition would be at a point to the west of Gibraltar, where it could be divided, if necessary, into two portions. To enable this decision to be taken in the light of the best possible information, the Commanders-in-Chief in the Middle East were asked to telegraph their appreciation of the present situation, paying particular attention to any indications of Italian intentions. On 16th August General Wavell left London for Cairo. On the 25th the three Commanders-in-Chief reported that reconnaissances by land, sea, and air had observed no ominous signs; they did not think that, unless the enemy had succeeded in concealing his troops and preparations with remarkable skill, he could be ready for offensive operations on a large scale for several weeks.

Acting on these expressions of opinion the War Cabinet decided on 26th August that the army convoy should go round the Cape. It had sailed on 22nd August and might be expected to reach Suez about 24th September, escorted by the cruisers *York* (8-inch) and *Ajax* (6-inch and radar) which would provide further reinforcement for Admiral Cunningham.

From the moment of taking over command in May Air Chief Marshal Longmore repeatedly reminded the Air Ministry of the inferiority of his force and, in particular, of his need for modern fighters and long-range bombers. With France out of the war, and the Mediterranean closed, it became a matter of first importance that he should know how his force was to be maintained in the future and with what types and numbers of aircraft he was to be supplied. It was not until 6th July that he was informed of the Air Ministry's plans. Twelve Hurricanes, twelve Lysanders, and twelve Blenheim IVs with an increased range, and in many other ways superior to the Blenheim Is, were to be sent out to him by sea immediately. A monthly flow of twelve Hurricanes, twelve Blenheim IVs and six Lysanders would follow. The possibility of sending him American fighters and bombers from late French orders was being investigated, but he was warned that in any case it would probably be the spring of 1941 before his squadrons could be rearmed and ready. On this information the Air Officer Commanding-in-Chief was told to base his plans for the next three months.

This programme did not meet even the immediate needs. Air Chief Marshal Longmore had already restricted air operations severely in order to conserve his resources, but even so his losses, apart from damaged aircraft, had amounted to ten Blenheims and eleven Wellesleys in three weeks. The supply of Wellesleys was dying out and they were being replaced by Blenheims. Accordingly he estimated he would require between 35 and 50 Blenheims and not less than 24 Hurricanes every month. Aircraft with suitable range and performance were required also for the reconnaissance of harbours in Italy and of the areas through which enemy convoys might pass on their way to Libya. For this purpose, and in order to provide a small striking force, he considered one torpedo-bomber/general reconnaissance ('TB/GR') squadron at Malta to be needed at once. As for the Lysander, it had proved to be unsuitable for reconnaissance duties over the great distances involved in its work with the army. It had not the necessary range, and was so vulnerable to enemy fighters that it had to be escorted, which would have been a wasteful procedure even if the Air Force had not been very short of fighters. The Air Ministry replied that they were investigating various alternatives, including an American 'attack and dive-bomber' aircraft; in the meantime they would provide extra fuel tanks to increase the range of the Lysander.

But these were not the only considerations. Now that France was out of the war, the danger had to be faced of an invasion of Egypt, preceded and supported by intense air attacks. Moreover, with the Mediterranean closed, it was more important than ever that the movements of convoys through the Red Sea, and the air reinforcement route from Takoradi in West Africa through the Sudan—described later in this chapter—should be kept free from enemy interference. If the air force was to take its proper share in the defence of the Middle East and East Africa, the Air Officer Commanding-in-Chief estimated that he must be reinforced by a minimum of $22\frac{1}{2}$

P

squadrons, viz. 12 fighter, 4 medium and 4 heavy bomber, 1 army co-operation and $1\frac{1}{2}$ G.R. squadrons. These squadrons should be armed, of course, with modern aircraft capable of reaching, in the case of the bombers, the enemy's main air bases and harbours in Libya and targets in the Dodecanese, Ethiopia, and possibly Crete, and should provide adequate support for land and sea operations, particularly long distance reconnaissance. To discuss these proposals Air Chief Marshal Longmore sent home a senior staff officer with General Wavell.

A number of factors governed the supply of aircraft to the Middle East. Aircraft had to be specially modified for tropical service by the makers before being fitted with their operational equipment at an air storage unit. In the case of Hurricanes, conversions were effected at the rate of about fifteen every week. Despatch might be by sea or by air. The former meant shipping space, not only for the aircraft but for an appropriate allotment of spares and ancillary equipment for subsequent maintenance, which had necessarily to go by sea. Thus a practical limitation to both reinforcement and rearmament was automatically set by the three months voyage. As for despatching aircraft by air, this imposed a severe drain on the trained aircrews of Bomber Command, as there were no reserves of pilots, observers, or air gunners in the Middle East. The loss of refuelling facilities on French soil made it still more difficult to deliver aircraft to the Middle East rapidly. Fighters could not fly all the way, so that unless an aircraft carrier could be used in the Mediterranean for operations like 'Hurry', all the reinforcing Hurricanes would have to be shipped either to Takoradi or round the Cape. The sea passage to Takoradi would take about three weeks and the whole voyage by the Cape route ten to twelve weeks. The medium bombers—Blenheims— could be sent by the same routes, although it was hoped that so long as Malta remained available as a refuelling base it would be possible to fly them out by night over occupied France. But the distance to Malta left a very small margin of endurance, and the flow would be affected by the weather over France and by the phases of the moon. The heavy bombers—Wellingtons—could either be refuelled at Malta or, if fitted with extra tanks, fly direct to Egypt.

Early in August the Air Ministry revised their plans. The proposal to form additional squadrons would have resulted in a number of squadrons in Bomber and Fighter Commands being immobilized until they could be built up to strength again from the output of the training organization—already stretched to the limit of. its capacity. Nor were the aircraft available for rearming the existing squadrons in addition to forming new ones. The Air Ministry concluded that the essential and most pressing requirement was to rearm the existing squadrons. The short-term plan was

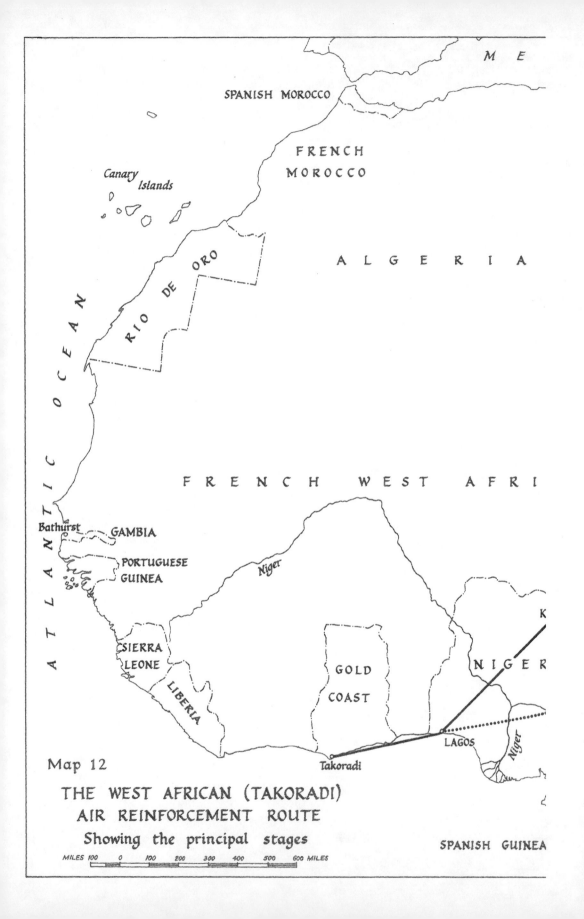

Map 12

THE WEST AFRICAN (TAKORADI)
AIR REINFORCEMENT ROUTE
Showing the principal stages

MILES 100   0   100   200   300   400   500   600 MILES

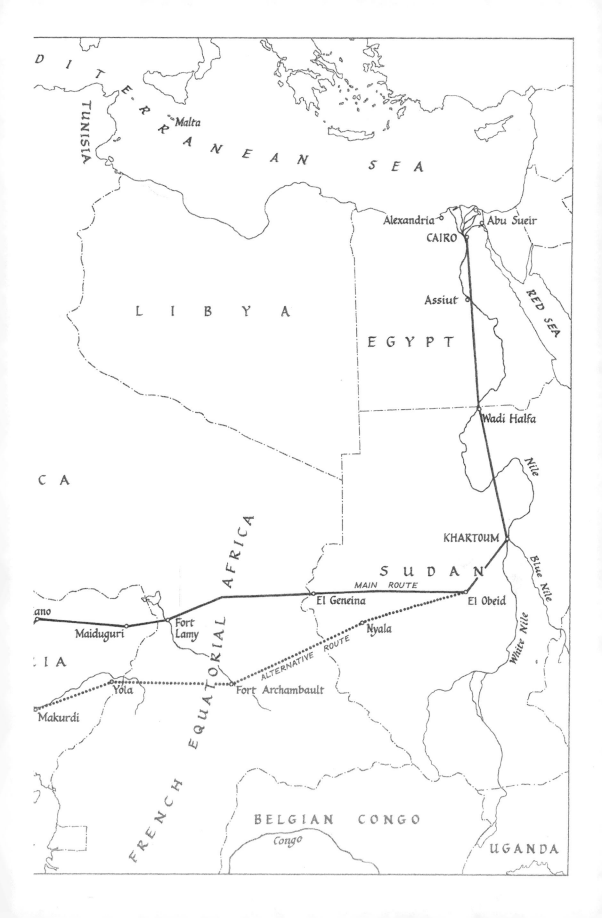

therefore to increase the allotment of bombers and fighters during August and September so that by the end of the latter month five medium bomber squadrons, three fighter squadrons, and one bomber transport squadron would be rearmed with modern aircraft: a total of 84 Blenheim IVs, 60 Hurricanes, 12 Wellingtons and a small quota of replacements. Twenty-four Hurricanes were allotted to the South African Air Force where officers and men were waiting to form new squadrons. One hundred and fifty Glenn Martin bombers, from late French orders in America, were to be divided between the Middle East Command and the South African Air Force during the forthcoming winter. For the immediate present all that could be done was to provide trained aircrews for three Glenn Martin aircraft for use on long-range reconnaissance duties over the Central Mediterranean, the men being found by disbanding the Anti-Aircraft Co-operation Unit at Malta. This was a temporary measure until a full TB/GR squadron could be provided later. As supplies of maintenance stores for Glenn Martins were very limited and as there was no way of transporting them to Malta in sufficient quantity, it was decided to supply three additional Glenn Martins to be 'cannibalised' to provide for the maintenance of the others.

A few Hurricanes and Blenheims had reached Egypt by air in a last minute attempt to reinforce the Middle East before France collapsed. Apart from these, the progress achieved by the end of August was as follows: 24 Hurricanes, shipped via the Cape, were approaching the end of their long voyage; 36 more, of which 30 were carried in H.M.S. *Argus*, were nearing Takoradi. Twenty-four Blenheim IVs had reached Egypt by air via Malta; 24 were at sea bound either for Takoradi or for Egypt round the Cape. Six Wellingtons reached Egypt on the last day of August. An initial supply of stores and spares for both Blenheims and Hurricanes had been shipped from England in June, in anticipation of rearmament, and reached Egypt during August. Further stores and ancillary equipment for Wellingtons, Blenheims, and Hurricanes were despatched after the revised plan had been issued.

Thus, by a variety of routes and methods, the process of reinforcement had indeed begun, though not at a rate which gave any cause for complacency.

The development of the Takoradi air route was a direct consequence of the French collapse, since the air route across France could no longer be used for aircraft of short endurance. A quick and safe means of reinforcing the Middle East had to be sought which would not make excessive demands on shipping. A combined sea and air route was the solution. On 20th June the Air Ministry decided to inaugurate a reinforcement route by sea to the West Coast of Africa and thence by air to Khartoum and Egypt (see Map 12 and Photo 3).

As early as 1925 the Royal Air Force had examined the strategic and commercial possibilities of an air route between northern Nigeria and Khartoum. During the following years a civil transport route was developed from the Gold Coast port of Takoradi to Khartoum, where it connected with the service running between Cairo and South Africa. By 1936 a weekly passenger and mail service across Africa had been inaugurated. Thus, in 1940, a chain of airfields existed from Takoradi through Nigeria and the Sudan to Egypt, with the necessary facilities for handling a small number of aircraft in transit. Much more than the existing organization was required, however, if large numbers of aircraft of various types were to be assembled quickly and delivered to their final destination nearly 4,000 miles away. The airfield at Takoradi—the port selected for disembarkation—had to be developed into an assembly and transit base with hangars, store-houses, workshops, offices and accommodation, capable of handling 120 aircraft and upwards every month. Along the route many of the runways needed extending; additional airfields were required; signal communications and meteorological facilities had to be improved and more accommodation built.

Briefly the plan was to ship aircraft in crates to Takoradi, erect them there, and fly them across Africa to Abu Sueir (near the Suez Canal), via Lagos (378 miles)—Kano (525 miles)—Maiduguri (325 miles)—Geneina (689 miles)—Khartoum (754 miles)—Abu Sueir (1,026 miles): a total distance of 3,697 miles. The climate along the route varied from the humid tropical heat of West Africa with its seasons of torrential rains and high winds to the desert heat (and cold) and dust storms of the Sudan. Flying in these conditions was not easy, particularly for the pilots of single-seater fighters sitting for hundreds of miles in the cramped space of their cockpits. The long hours that the ground crews had to work at Takoradi were particularly trying.

Except for a distance of about 600 miles where it crossed the Chad province of French Equatorial Africa, the route passed over British controlled territory. Had the Italians established themselves at Fort Lamy it might have become impossible to operate the route. Fortunately, before the first few of the reinforcing aircraft were ready, the Free French had taken over the administration of the province. Even so, the proximity of Vichy French territory to Takoradi, and to other places along the route, called for special defence measures against attack by sea, land and air. As an additional safeguard an alternative route farther south was organized.

A small advanced party, under Group Captain H. K. Thorold, reached Takoradi on 14th July. The first half of the unit—some 360 officers and airmen—disembarked on 21st August and the remainder arrived during the next few weeks. On 5th September the first consignment of crated aircraft arrived together with urgently needed tools, equipment, general stores and transport. There were many difficulties to be overcome owing to lack of proper equipment—from erection gear down to such necessary items as split pins! Nevertheless the first delivery flight of one Blenheim and six Hurricanes left Takoradi for Egypt on 20th September. The Air Ministry remained responsible for matters of maintenance at Takoradi, but the operational and administrative control of the route were placed under the Air Officer Commanding-in-Chief, Middle East. This additional responsibility for units on the far side of Africa was most unwelcome, since his staff at Air Headquarters was fully occupied with operations against the Italians.

From these small beginnings the route was gradually developed into an extensive and efficient organization. It was to prove a vital factor in the successful air campaigns of the Middle East. By the end of October 1943 over 5,000 aircraft (exclusive of those flown by the American Ferry Service) had been erected and despatched to the Middle East along this route. By this time the North African air route via Casablanca was in full swing and the necessity for the West African route as a reinforcement route to the Middle East had ceased.

On 16th August the Prime Minister, as Minister of Defence, issued for the comments of the Chiefs of Staff a General Directive which he had prepared for the Commander-in-Chief Middle East. It was despatched in a slightly amended form on the 22nd—just after the loss of British Somaliland—with a request for General Wavell's observations. It covered a wide range of subjects and went into considerable detail. There is no doubt that it was indicative of the deep concern that was being felt for the security of the position in the Middle East.

The theme was that a major invasion of Egypt from Libya was to be expected at any time; consequently the largest possible army must be deployed to meet it. The defence of the Sudan ranked above that of Kenya, where there was ample room to give ground. We could always reinforce Kenya faster than the Italians could pass large forces thither from Ethiopia or Italian Somaliland. Therefore two brigades, West or East African, should be moved from Kenya to the Sudan. The 5th Indian Division less one brigade should go to Egypt; one brigade could go to the Sudan. General Smuts was being asked to allow South African troops to move from Kenya to Egypt for use on internal security. One obvious criticism of the suggested moves from Kenya was forestalled by a mention of the fact that shipping possibilities in the Indian Ocean and Red Sea were being examined by the Admiralty.

There followed an exposition of the tactics to be adopted for the defence of Egypt. The invasion might be in great force, with strong armoured forces on the inner (landward) flank. If retreat were necessary, all water along the coast must be rendered undrinkable and the coastal road impassable; the suggested methods were fully described. If Matruh were successfully defended, the enemy might try to mask it. The western edge of the Delta must be diligently fortified and resolutely held; more defence works should be built and the natural obstacle of the Delta extended by broad inundations, thus providing a strong flank for the Alexandria defences. In order to attack such a position the enemy would be compelled to deploy a force which would be difficult to supply. Once deployed and seriously engaged, the enemy would be liable to harassing action by descents from the sea at Matruh, Sollum, and even much farther west. In time it was hoped to hamper the passage of enemy troops from Europe to Africa; to this end the anti-aircraft defences of Malta were to be reinforced so that the fleet could reoccupy it, and eventually air attacks would be made from it against Italy.

Although only General Wavell's observations had been asked for, the other two Commanders-in-Chief signalled theirs also. Admiral Cunningham viewed with dismay the emphasis that seemed to be laid on the defence of the Delta; would not everything possible be done to hold off the enemy from Alexandria? He feared that his base would become untenable if the Italians were to advance so close to it that their bombers could be escorted by fighters, and if this occurred it would be impossible to mount combined operations for landing behind the enemy's lines. In view of the directive he felt that he must now take energetic steps to develop the naval facilities at Port Said and Haifa, so that he could continue to operate in the Mediterranean for as long as possible if the use of Alexandria was denied to him.

Air Chief Marshal Longmore drew particular attention to the importance of preventing an Italian advance towards Port Sudan, Atbara, and Khartoum, since this would constitute a threat to our air reinforcement route from West Africa. Moreover, in order to keep down air attacks on convoys in the Red Sea it was essential to retain the use of our present airfields. He therefore strongly supported General Wavell's intention of landing the 5th Indian Division at Port Sudan. He went on to make some further comments on the subject of air reinforcements. He had to give support for the defence of the Sudan and continue his offensive against Italian East Africa. If, as the directive implied, an invasion of Egypt from Libya was now imminent, although he himself was not aware of any visible signs, it would undoubtedly be preceded by an intense air offensive, and he estimated that the Italian fighter force in Libya outnumbered his own available fighters in Egypt by more than four to one. While the Air Ministry's reinforcement plan promised a very welcome improvement in types, it did nothing to increase the number of his fighter squadrons in the near future. He had estimated his minimum requirements at eight squadrons for Egypt and four more in general Middle East reserve. Instead, he had four single-seater squadrons and one improvised Blenheim squadron. It looked as if the time had come to start improvising new squadrons, some of which could admittedly be given only obsolete aircraft, in order to meet the first onslaught. He would draw on No. 4 Flying Training School and on the Aircraft Depot at Habbaniya, and he would move No. 84 (Blenheim) Squadron from Shaibah to Egypt, although this would mean that Iraq would be left without any first-line aircraft at all.

To these proposals the Air Ministry replied that the Air Officer Commanding-in-Chief had a free hand to make the best preparations possible, realizing no doubt that it was undesirable to rearm more squadrons than could be maintained. The monthly allotment of aircraft to replace wastage might conceivably be increased, but this could not be counted upon, since a very heavy rate of wastage in the United Kingdom had already to be faced. It was important to keep up the output of pilots from No. 4 Flying Training School, for no more pilots could be sent out at present. There was a serious shortage of trained aircraft crews, and the despatch of bomber crews to the Middle East under the present plan meant a considerable drain on the resources of the Royal Air Force. With these crumbs of comfort and advice the Air Officer Commanding-in-Chief had to be content.

General Wavell, as was only to be expected, gave his views in great detail. He still considered it right to land the 5th Indian Division (less one brigade) at Port Sudan. He did not wish to transfer any African or South African troops from Kenya: the loss of British Somaliland had produced a bad effect in East Africa and retreat from the positions now held in Kenya would be deplorable. He did not agree that he could reinforce Kenya more quickly than the Italians could move to attack it. General Smuts had expressed his anxiety about the defence of Kenya, but he (General Wavell) was satisfied with the position provided that no troops were withdrawn. He emphasized that the successful defence of Egypt, and especially of the naval base, would depend on sufficient air power at least as much as on ground forces. For his own part it was material, rather than men, that he lacked. The enemy would not reach the Delta by using masses of infantry, but only by bringing up superior armoured forces. The troops now available for the defence of Egypt, not counting the Egyptian Army, were already short of something like 250 field guns, 34 medium guns, 230 anti-tank guns, 1,100 anti-tank rifles, and 500 carriers (small tracked general-purpose vehicles), and were very weak in anti-aircraft weapons. More armoured troops were essential. Even after the arrival of the reinforcements now on the way his one armoured division would still be incomplete. A second armoured division was required as soon as possible.

Thus, although the 'General Directive' never attained the status of an order, it certainly succeeded in producing a general exchange of views, which helped, no doubt, to focus attention upon essentials. In this way it contributed towards the solution of the intricate and interconnected problems with which the three Commanders-in-Chief were faced. But its main interest in retrospect lies in the fact that it was the first of a long and remarkable series of telegrams from the Prime Minister to one or other of the Commanders-in-Chief in the Middle East. Some of these telegrams were exploratory, some advisory; some were drawn in bold sweeps, some in great detail; some expressed generous praise, some were frankly admonitory. Some must have been much more welcome than others. Almost all required answers. They could have left no doubt that there was indeed a central direction of the war, and a vigorous one. There had been nothing like it since the time of the elder Pitt.

Pitt, too, had assumed office at a time of crisis. He, too, carried the nation with him and inspired all those around him with his energy, courage, and confidence. 'I can save this country, and nobody else can.' Of his new administration even Newcastle wrote: 'There had been as much business done in the last ten days as in many months before.' Pitt had advisers, it is true, but there was no question who was in executive control. Nobody knew more about war; all his life he had read and studied it. He had served in the army for four years and had always kept in touch with military affairs. In his arrangements for the campaign of 1759 'there is scarcely a single preparation, precaution, or provision, no matter how minute, which escapes the Secretary's remark. The tonnage of transport and where it is to be found. The schooners and whaleboats to be built locally by a given date. The tally of the troops and the special dispositions for the attack on Quebec. The provisions, the stores, and the battering train. Even cordage, lead, and hooks for angling during the passage, and molasses for making spruce beer, are, upon another occasion, not considered too trivial for mention'.[1] In writing to his naval and military commanders Pitt would usually take the opportunity to introduce an incentive: His Majesty, he would write, 'awaits with

---

[1] From an article by the Military Correspondent of *The Times*, 27th June 1908, reprinted by permission.

great impatience the commencement of your operations', or 'anti-cipates action of the utmost vigour'. It was his habit to state the object with the utmost lucidity and leave the manner of attaining it to the discretion of the men on the spot; indeed it could hardly have been otherwise, for his means of communication were painfully slow. He was not able, as Mr. Churchill was able, to telegraph to a distant commander and receive an answer in a matter of hours. But if he had been—and this is mere conjecture—how would Walpole's 'terrible cornet of horse' have acted? Can anyone doubt that, as the responsible Minister, he too, like Mr. Churchill, would have felt it his duty not only to direct the strategy, but also to influence the conduct of the campaign?

On the morning of 30th August the naval reinforcements for the Mediterranean Fleet left Gibraltar to make the first through passage that had been attempted since Italy entered the war. They consisted of the aircraft carrier *Illustrious* (Nos. 815 and 819 Squadrons—22 Swordfish, and No. 806 Squadron—12 Fulmars), the battleship *Valiant*, and the anti-aircraft cruisers *Coventry* and *Calcutta*. With them as escorts were four destroyers due to return to Gibraltar after refuelling at Malta, and four sent by Admiral Cunningham. In support was Admiral Somerville's Force H: *Renown*, *Ark Royal*, *Sheffield* and seven destroyers. The plan was for Force H to turn back when south of Sardinia, while the reinforcements proceeded through the Sicilian Narrows to meet the main body of Admiral Cunningham's fleet. The *Valiant* and the two anti-aircraft cruisers would enter Malta to discharge guns, stores, and ammunition for the fortress, while the destroyers would fuel. The strengthened fleet would then return to Alexandria, carrying out one or two offensive operations against Italian bases on the way. For the first time the two carriers would be operating under Rear-Admiral A. L. St. G. Lyster, who had come out in the *Illustrious* in the new appointment of Rear-Admiral Mediter-ranean Aircraft Carriers.   The operation was called 'Hats'.

Two additional destroyers accompanied Admiral Somerville; their duty was to pass between Minorca and Majorca to a position north of the Balearic Islands from where, on the morning of the day on which the main forces were to part company, they would proceed on a north-easterly course transmitting a series of wireless messages to mislead the enemy into thinking that these forces had continued towards the Gulf of Genoa during the night, and also to cover the *Ark Royal's* transmission of low-power wireless to her aircraft. Mean-while, on the night before the passage through the Narrows and during the passage itself, aircraft from the *Ark Royal* would deliver attacks on the airfield at Cagliari.

The fact that four ships with the Force were equipped with radar made it possible not only to detect the enemy's shadowing aircraft but also to direct fighters on to their targets; with the result that during the first two days fighters claimed to have shot down some of the shadowers and no bombing attacks developed. At 3.25 a.m. on 1st September the first raid on Cagliari was launched and delivered by nine Swordfish. It was generally successful, and an Italian broadcast announced that the military headquarters had been hit and aircraft destroyed on the ground. All the Swordfish returned to the *Ark Royal*.

That evening course was altered to give the impression that the Force was bound for Naples, and further shadowing aircraft were detected. After dark the ships destined for the Eastern Mediterranean with their screen of eight destroyers parted company, and Force H turned for a second attack on Cagliari. But this time the target was obscured by mist and low cloud so that the aircraft had to jettison their bombs and return to the carrier. Force H then returned to Gibraltar without encountering any opposition, although the four detached destroyers on their passage back from Malta experienced some bombing. Commenting on the operation, Admiral Somerville observed that heavy attacks had been expected during the 48 hours that the Force was within effective bombing range of Italian air bases; they were even hoped for, as he had a powerful anti-aircraft concentration and strong fighter patrols available. He ascribed the lack of opposition to the diversionary tactics adopted; had he been saddled with M.T. ships, these tactics would have been 'abortive and unconvincing'. It was subsequently learnt that, throughout the period, eleven Italian submarines were at sea in the Western Mediterranean, five of them being on patrol between Sardinia and Bône. Only one had been sighted, and this was by aircraft returning from the first attack on Cagliari.

To turn now to the movements of the Eastern Mediterranean Fleet. Admiral Cunningham in the *Warspite* with the *Malaya, Eagle, Orion, Sydney* and nine destroyers had cleared Alexandria harbour early on the morning of 30th August steaming for a position west of Crete. The 3rd Cruiser Squadron (*Kent, Gloucester, Liverpool*) and three destroyers had already sailed to make a detour through the Kaso Channel and South Aegean, and a store convoy for Malta consisting of two store ships, *Cornwall* and *Volo*, and the oiler *Plumleaf* had left on the previous evening escorted by four destroyers. At noon on the 31st the 3rd Cruiser Squadron joined up with the battlefleet south-west of Cape Matapan. No air attacks developed on the fleet, but during the afternoon a series of bombing raids was made on the convoy and one hit was scored aft in the *Cornwall*. It put her steering gear and wireless out of action, destroyed both her guns, made a hole below the waterline and started a fire. In spite of the damage the Master, Captain F. C. Pretty, steering with the engines, maintained his place in the convoy which eventually reached Malta without further mishap shortly before noon on 2nd September.

Meanwhile, on the evening of 31st August, air and submarine reports indicated that there was an enemy force of two battleships, seven cruisers and eight destroyers only 130 miles to the N.W. and steering a S.E. course. Admiral Cunningham decided to close the convoy, which was some 50 miles to the southward, and remain for the night in approximate station 20 miles to the north-west of it. Hopes of another encounter with enemy surface forces faded next day when air searches failed to locate them, and it was not until the evening that a flying-boat from Malta finally found the enemy fleet at the entrance to the Gulf of Taranto, obviously returning to base.

In the afternoon of 1st September the 3rd Cruiser Squadron proceeded ahead to make contact with the forces coming through the Sicilian Narrows. These forces, having made the passage without incident, were sighted by the main body of the Mediterranean Fleet at 9 a.m. For the rest of that day the fleet remained to the south of Malta, while destroyers refuelled and the *Valiant* and the two anti-aircraft cruisers entered harbour to discharge their men and stores for the fortress.[1] Light but unsuccessful bombing attacks were experienced during the day, and five enemy aircraft were believed to have been shot down. Shortly after midnight the whole fleet was steaming to the eastward.

The Commander-in-Chief had planned his return route north of Crete in order to carry out attacks on the Dodecanese at dawn on 4th September and provide cover for a south-bound Aegean convoy. The attacks consisted of air raids on the two airfields in Rhodes and bombardments of targets on Scarpanto by cruisers and destroyers. All achieved some measure of success, but enemy fighters caused the loss of four Swordfish. A flotilla of Italian M.T.B.s attacked ships off Scarpanto; one M.T.B. was sunk, others were damaged, and the remainder were driven off having done no harm. When south of Kaso the fleet was subjected to three air attacks, but all bombs fell wide; other formations of aircraft were driven off as they approached, and ships reached Alexandria on 5th September without damage or casualties.[2]

During the period of the operations, and especially on 31st August

---

[1] In addition to naval and R.A.F. stores there were 587 tons of army stores, including eight 3·7-inch A.A. guns, ten Bofors guns, three predictors, height finders, ten 4·5-inch A.A. barrels, sixteen Bofors barrels, 100 Bren guns and 10,000 rounds of Bofors ammunition; a most welcome addition to the defences of Malta.

[2] Apart from a quantity of naval stores, the warship reinforcements carried over 250 tons of army and R.A.F. stores, including 28 anti-tank guns and ammunition.

and 4th September, aircraft of No. 202 Group attacked Libyan airfields with the object of reducing the enemy's air effort against the fleet. Italian submarines again failed to interfere with movements of the fleet, although ten were at sea in the Eastern Mediterranean during the period. The only reminder of their existence was one faint asdic contact about noon on 4th September, and another when the fleet was about to enter the Alexandria swept channel on the following day.

As a result of this operation the Mediterranean Fleet was appreciably stronger than before, and some much needed equipment had been safely delivered at Malta and in Egypt. The Italians had been successfully attacked at places as far apart as Rhodes and Sardinia. Their own naval force which was at sea on 31st August attempted nothing, while their occasional air attacks were not so heavy or accurate as had been expected. The Italians were well aware that a British force had sailed from Gibraltar, but apparently failed to appreciate that it included ships bound for the Eastern Mediterranean. It remained to be seen whether they would profit by the experience of these few days, so as to reap the full benefit from their favourable geographical position. In a personal message of congratulation to Admiral Cunningham the Prime Minister referred to the importance of continuing to strike at the Italians during the autumn because, as time passed, Germany would be likely to lay hands on the Italian war machine. The Admiral took the opportunity to point out that for successful operations in the Central Mediterranean ample air reconnaissance was a prerequisite and that at present his operations were being drastically limited by the shortage of destroyers.

# CHAPTER XI

## THE ITALIANS MAKE A MOVE INTO EGYPT

*See Map 5*

IN HIS review of the situation in Egypt General Wavell had explained to the Chiefs of Staff that although the operations on the frontier had been highly successful the wear and tear on his armoured troops had been severe. If the enemy were to bring up large forces, some withdrawal would be necessary. A forward trend on the part of the Italians was in fact soon noticed, and their enterprise in a rather clumsy form of reconnaissance increased. At the same time their defences were being improved. It was therefore decided to arrest the harassing operations on the part of the units of the British covering force before their fighting efficiency, especially that of the tracked vehicles, fell too low for them to play a full part in more extensive operations. In other words, in order to retain the capacity to defeat a determined thrust on Matruh it was necessary not to lose heavily in defending the intervening spaces. The bulk of the armoured units were accordingly withdrawn nearer to Matruh, and the Support Group of the 7th Armoured Division, under Brigadier W. H. E. Gott, took over the front on 13th August with orders to establish a line of observation from Sollum to Maddalena, and to keep in touch with the enemy and give early warning of any changes on his dispositions.[1] If attacked, the Support Group was to impose delay without becoming seriously involved, and if necessary was to withdraw to successive lines of observation. The Support Group included three motor battalions; two 25-pdr batteries, each of twelve guns; two anti-tank batteries; a section of medium artillery; and detachments of engineers and machine-gunners. With these forces and one incomplete cruiser tank battalion the Support Group observed and patrolled its sixty miles of front and harassed the enemy as much as possible during the rest of August and early September. More distant reconnaissance on and beyond the frontier was carried out by the 11th Hussars.

The Royal Air Force, too, was feeling the strain. The problem facing the Air Officer Commanding-in-Chief was how to allocate

---

[1] The Support Group was the descendant of the Pivot Group of the Mobile Division. See page 19 footnote.

enough forces to Aden and the Sudan to keep the Red Sea secure, and at the same time conserve his resources for the expected battle for the defence of Egypt. As early as 17th July he had warned Air Commodore Collishaw that reserves of all types of aircraft in the Middle East were being rapidly consumed and that as there was no immediate prospect of receiving replacements it was necessary to exercise still greater economy. A system was introduced of attacks at night by single Bombay aircraft of No. 216 Squadron against shipping and storage tanks at Tobruk, and there were signs that these caused the Italians no little concern. But within the strict limits dictated by the need to husband resources attacks were continued on airfields and lines of communication, while the Army was asked not to call for air action, other than reconnaissance, unless an enemy attack was clearly imminent.

The lack of detailed intelligence about the Italian land forces in Libya had made it difficult to estimate their true capabilities. It had to be assumed that they would not remain inactive while the East African Empire was virtually cut off, but it would be impossible, for logistic reasons alone, for Graziani to enter Egypt with more than a fraction of his total strength: the question was, how strong and how mobile would such a force be? General Wavell had confidence in the superiority of his troops over any they had met hitherto, in evidence of which the published Italian casualties in Libya between 11th June and 9th September amounted to 3,500, while the British losses had been 150. As the intelligence mosaic took shape it gave him no indication of Italian capacity to deliver and sustain a heavy blow, though he could not rule out the possibility that armoured and mechanized units in far greater strength than his own might be brought up for the invasion. The presence of Italian medium tanks (11 or 13 ton) had already been confirmed, but the numbers were not known with any accuracy. Of the total of 85 British cruiser tanks (12½ or 14 ton) 15 were in workshops at the beginning of September, and indeed the state of the British equipment generally was such that the appearance at this moment of German mechanized units would have been particularly disturbing. It was therefore unfortunate that the sea routes to Tripoli and Benghazi could not be seriously interfered with, nor could those ports be kept under observation. In the event there might be little or no warning of German intervention.

The Italian intelligence staff, on the other hand, had for a long time enjoyed exceptional facilities for obtaining timely information about the presence of British units in Egypt; in fact, they often knew about convoys on the way and roughly what they contained. They were less well informed about shortages of weapons and equipment and the state of training—factors which are much more difficult to evaluate. Thus while they knew of the existence of the British 7th Armoured Division, and of an Indian and a New Zealand Division, they did not know how incomplete they all were. They persistently over-estimated the British strength in the Delta area, but they were well informed about the Egyptian forces and did not rate their fighting value very high.

The circumstances leading to the Italian advance across the Egyptian frontier were as follows. When Mussolini decided to enter the war there were no plans for invading Egypt and the Italian policy was to adopt a defensive attitude on both fronts in Libya. Even so, Marshal Balbo wanted the whole of June in which to build up the resources necessary for an 'honourable resistance'. With the elimination of France, however, it became possible to strengthen Cyrenaica at the expense of Tripolitania, and when at the end of June Marshal Graziani was appointed to succeed Balbo he was immediately told to make preparations for invading Egypt.[1] He lost no time in pointing out that he lacked many of the necessary resources, notably anti-tank, anti-aircraft, and medium artillery; medium tanks; and vehicles of all kinds. He awaited replacements for a number of aircraft and crews, and asked in addition for a new *Stormo* (Group) of fighters and a Reconnaissance *Gruppo* (Wing).

The Germans were already considering whether to help the Italians with equipment, and their Military Attaché in Rome, Major-General Enno von Rintelen, kept Berlin well informed of developments in Cyrenaica. He was personally acquainted with the ground, and viewed with great interest the prospect of a clash in the desert between two European Powers, each with up-to-date weapons and equipment. He understood that the Italian object was to drive the British out of Egypt and establish land communication with East Africa. Two conditions were essential to success: the safety of the sea routes and air superiority over northern Egypt. Artillery, ammunition, tanks, and aircraft were going to be more important than numbers of men. The problem of supply would loom even larger than it did in Europe, and would be greatly influenced by the available ports: if these were to drop too far behind the advance, the burden on the transport columns would become excessive; the deduction was that Matruh must be secured quickly. He reported that Graziani, as an experienced colonial fighter, well understood the need for making thorough preparations, which he was now doing with great energy.

During July Mussolini was persuaded that with more time for

---

[1] Graziani was thoroughly familiar with Cyrenaica, having been Governor in 1930–4 and commander of the punitive operations against the Senussi. During the conquest of Ethiopia he was in command of the southern front, and in 1936 became the first Viceroy. In November 1939 he was made Chief of the Army Staff, a post which he retained, at any rate in name, after his appointment to Libya.

preparations the results would be appreciably greater, but he insisted that, whether the preparations were ready or not, Graziani was to make a forward move on the day the first Germans set foot in England. To this Graziani made no objection, but he stuck to his opinion that otherwise it would be unwise to advance without the strength to carry the operations through, and gave effect to his views by postponing his date of readiness with great regularity.[1] In particular, he complained of not having received the transport necessary for motorizing the two Libyan divisions, whose role in the advance was to have been to move south of the escarpment in company with a special mechanized group under General Maletti. On September 7th Mussolini issued a peremptory order for the advance to begin in two days time, whether the Germans had landed in England or not. Graziani was now obliged to adopt a new plan, for the Libyan divisions had not enough motor transport to enable them to operate with the mechanized group. They were accordingly detailed to carry out the first phase of the advance along the coast road, their place in the lead to be taken over in due course by the 1st Blackshirt (or 23rd March) Division which was sufficiently mobile for this purpose: the Maletti Group was to retain its independent role on the southern flank. Preliminary moves began on September 9th, but on the 11th the Maletti Group lost its way to its position of assembly at Sidi Omar. Graziani, who was already disturbed by reports of massive British armoured forces to the south of the escarpment, now changed the plan again by cancelling the flanking movement altogether and placing Maletti under the orders of General Berti, commanding the 10th Army, for more intimate co-operation with the coastal advance. Two other divisions, 62nd Marmarica and 63rd Cirene, were available for the operations, making five divisions in all, and a tank group of one medium, two mixed, and four light tank battalions. Two other divisions, the 4th Blackshirt and the 64th Catanzaro, were in reserve near Tobruk.

The 5th *Squadra*, under General Porro, had been specially made up in aircraft, pilots, vehicles, and airfield equipment to enable it to support the advance.[2] Even so, its strength was much less than the British estimates of what was likely to be used for a major invasion of Egypt. It seems that there were about 300 serviceable bombers, fighters, and ground attack aircraft, apart from reconnaissance units, the Colonial Air Force, and a number of transport and air-sea rescue aircraft. The preliminary role of the air forces was to attack British

---

[1] Mussolini nevertheless wrote to Hitler on 17th July: 'The preparations for an attack on Egypt with vast objectives are now complete. In order to reach Alexandria we shall have to cross 600 km. of real desert while the thermometer registers 55 [= 131° Fahr.] in the shade. This has weakened the British units who cannot stand such temperatures.'

[2] A *Squadra* of the Italian Air Force was a balanced force of all types of flying units.

airfields, supply centres and command posts, and to cover the move to assembly positions. Subsequently they were to protect the advance, and attack enemy troops and vehicles, and objectives chosen by the High Command.

On September 9th the enemy's air activity increased appreciably. Three bomber squadrons of the Royal Air Force, Nos. 55, 113 and 211, thereupon attacked airfields, concentrations of transport, and supply dumps, one of the operations being an attack by 21 aircraft on the town airfield of Tobruk, where much transport was assembled. The enemy retaliated on the same day by carrying out a sweep by 27 fighters over the Buq Buq area, which led to further operations against Italian airfields. Air reports indicated much movement about Bardia, Sidi Azeiz, Gabr Saleh and towards Sidi Omar from the west. Evidently the long-expected invasion was about to begin, though on 11th September von Rintelen wrote that it was clear to him by now that nothing more than a tactical success was expected; there was no immediate prospect of capturing Alexandria, the Delta, or the Canal, nor of opening up the route to East Africa.[1]

The British estimate of the Italian force available for the operation was substantially correct, but it was debatable whether Graziani would attempt a wide turning movement south of the escarpment. Reports from the air suggested that something of the sort might be intended, and dispositions had to be made to deal with it, but in estimating that the Italians would not confine themselves to the vicinity of the coast road the British were crediting them with a scale of transport and a degree of desert-worthiness that they did not possess. The Italian 10th Army's intelligence summary for 19th October 1940, contained the statement: 'As is well-known, the enemy has units more manoeuvrable in the desert than ours.' The truth is that the Italians had not mastered the art of movement on a broad front. This may have been partly due to their liking for roads and their undoubted flair for making them, and partly to other causes—scanty wireless communications, for example.

Early on 13th September a spectacular artillery barrage opened on Musaid, which the enemy then proceeded to occupy. This was followed by the heavy shelling of the airfield and empty barracks at Sollum, and when the dust had cleared the enemy was disclosed to the westward with his motor-cycles, light tanks, and other vehicles drawn up as if on parade awaiting the order to advance. Opposing them in the coastal sector was a force under the command of Lieut.-Colonel J. Moubray, commanding 3rd Coldstream Guards, consisting of that battalion, C Battery and, later, part of F Battery R.H.A.,

---

[1] 'Never', wrote Ciano in his diary for 9th September 1940, 'has a military operation been undertaken so much against the will of the Commander'.

a section of 25/26th Medium Battery R.A., one company 1st K.R.R.C., and one machine-gun company 1st Royal Northumberland Fusiliers. The enemy's close formation presented excellent targets to the artillery and the air, but it was not long before the 1st Libyan Division was in possession of the barracks and was beginning to trickle down the escarpment towards Sollum.

A simultaneous movement along the plateau towards the head of the Halfaya Pass was held up by a troop of C Battery R.H.A., a company of 3rd Coldstream Guards and a platoon of the 1st Royal Northumberland Fusiliers, but this detachment became threatened by increasing infantry and tank forces and in the early afternoon began to withdraw eastward. By the evening two large columns of the enemy were converging on Halfaya Pass—they were 2nd Libyan and 63rd Cirene Divisions and the Maletti Group, all from Musaid, and the 62nd Marmarica Division from the direction of Sidi Omar —but not until next morning did any appreciable movement take place down the pass to add to the stream of vehicles coming from Sollum. In fact the Italians on the plateau above the escarpment seemed hesitant, and they were successfully harassed by C Squadron 11th Hussars, by 2nd Battalion The Rifle Brigade, and by the cruiser squadrons of 1st Royal Tank Regiment, under the control of Brigadier Gott.

Soon after noon on the 14th the commander of the coastal sector withdrew his force to a selected position just east of Buq Buq, where he was reinforced by B Squadron 11th Hussars and a French Motor Marine Company, which enabled him to keep touch with the enemy. The pattern of the ground operations along the coast road during the next two days was similar, with successive withdrawals to rearguard positions at Alam Hamid on the 15th and Alam el Dab on the 16th, during which the force inflicted as much loss as it could without becoming seriously committed. Shortly after noon on the 16th a force of some fifty Italian tanks and lorried infantry, showing more enterprise, were seen to be moving round the left flank of the Alam el Dab position, and the rearguard was withdrawn to the east of Sidi Barrani to avoid being cut off. The enemy was rapidly and successfully engaged by C and F Batteries R.H.A. and displayed no further aggressive intentions; indeed it seemed that the Italians had little idea of making use of such armoured troops as they had. However by nightfall Sidi Barrani was in the hands of the 1st Blackshirt Division.

Meanwhile there had been nothing to prevent the British force on the plateau adjusting its movements in conformity with those in the coastal sector, and it was soon clear that no particular threat was likely to develop from the southern flank. All this time the Air Force was keeping the enemy under constant observation and finding many opportunities for attacking ground concentrations. The Italian Air Force showed unusual activity; fighters in formations of up to 100 aircraft were reported operating over their advancing troops, while bombers directed their attention to the British forward airfields and troop positions.

It was believed that in occupying Sidi Barrani and Sofafi the Italians had reached their immediate objectives, and the task of observing the front passed once again to the 11th Hussars. The Support Group was withdrawn to rest, and 7th Armoured Division took up dispositions in readiness to deal with a further advance on Matruh. At first it seemed likely that this would not be long delayed: the Italian broadcasts had claimed the capture of the key to Egypt and of half the British war material, and announced that the way to the Canal was now open. The dispositions and attitude of the Italian forces, however, were soon seen to be more consistent with a policy of temporary consolidation than with any intention of maintaining their momentum. Graziani had in fact begun the laborious process of administrative development at the head of a long and difficult line of communication, and the Air Force did their best to interfere with the process by making day and night attacks on camps and transport columns. Sixty sorties were devoted to these tasks between 16th and 21st September.[1]

The rough road between the frontier and Sidi Barrani had been destroyed by demolitions and by the heavy traffic, and the water at Sidi Barrani had been rendered undrinkable. The ruling factors in the Italian time-table were the construction of a motorable road and of a water pipeline forward from the frontier. These works were only partly finished when the Duce again began to apply the spur; this time it was because he wished to attack Greece and wanted to be in possession of Matruh before doing so, thus, he thought, effectively preventing any appreciable movement of British forces to help the Greeks. But Graziani was not to be hurried, and senior German officers visiting the front reported that unless Mussolini gave a definite order there would be no resumption of the advance before mid-December. Even then it would be to Matruh and no farther.

On September 17th the Navy joined in the task of harassing Graziani's communications. Aircraft from the *Illustrious* laid mines at Benghazi and sank with torpedoes the destroyer *Borea* and the merchant vessels *Gloria Stella* and *Maria Eugenia*, both of about 5,000 tons. On the same day a second destroyer, the *Aquilone*, struck one of the mines and sank. Meanwhile Blenheims of the Royal Air Force attacked Benina airfield and destroyed three bombers on the ground[2]. The gunboat *Ladybird* shelled from close range the escarpment road

---

[1] A 'sortie' means an operational flight by one aircraft.
[2] Santoro: *L'Aeronautica Italiana nella II^a Guerra Mondiale*, p. 395.

above Sollum, and destroyers engaged targets in the Sidi Barrani area. These bombardments appeared to be effective, causing fires and explosions, and this was confirmed by prisoners who spoke of the casualties, damage, and effect upon morale. A bombardment of Bardia by the cruiser *Kent* and destroyers was unfortunately prevented by an attack on the cruiser by torpedo-bombers just as she was taking up her position. One hit with a torpedo was scored in her stern. Protected by the Royal Air Force she was brought into harbour two days later so badly damaged that she was unfit for further service in the Mediterranean. This was a serious matter, as only one other 8-inch cruiser, the *York*, had been assigned to Admiral Cunningham and she was not due to reach Suez for another week. The incident marked the beginning of a new phase in the encounter between the British Fleet and the Italian Air Force; from now until the arrival of the *Luftwaffe* the torpedo-bomber was to be the principal cause of anxiety and damage.

Other bombardments of shore targets from the sea took place during the weeks of waiting, which helped to discourage the enemy from siting his camps and depots within reach of naval guns. In addition, the *Ladybird* and *Aphis* engaged any targets that presented themselves.[1] Meanwhile on land a policy of harassing the enemy by small mobile columns was successfully adopted. Working in conjunction with the armoured car patrols they penetrated right up to the enemy's defended localities, obtaining much valuable information and establishing a local ascendancy later to be turned to good account.

The loss of the advanced landing grounds at Sidi Barrani had adverse effects on all three Services. The distance to which fighters could give protection to bombers or to which tactical reconnaissance sorties could penetrate was reduced by nearly one hundred miles, while the bombers themselves were deprived of a very useful refuelling base. Blenheims were forced to operate at extreme range to reach Benghazi. Hurricanes which could hitherto have reached Malta in emergency with the aid of extra fuel tanks could no longer be expected to do so; henceforth any reinforcing Hurricanes for Malta would have to be flown from a carrier or sent by ship in convoy. Ships engaged in bombarding the Libyan coast had formerly had fighter protection as far as Bardia; now this did not extend even to Sidi Barrani. Derna was too far for aircraft of the Fleet Air Arm to attack. The enemy, on the other hand, could give fighter escort to his bombers for attacks on the British advanced base at Matruh.

---

[1] These two gunboats formed the nucleus of Force W, later to expand and become the Inshore Squadron which followed the Army along the coast to Benghazi during the operations of December 1940 to February 1941.

This naturally made the Commanders-in-Chief more conscious than ever of the weakness of the air defence all over the Middle East. In September they set up an inter-Service body to keep the problem constantly under review and to ensure the best use being made of the available resources, but the fact remained that there were not enough fighter aircraft, or guns, or searchlights, or radar sets for all the tasks. The efforts of the Air Officer Commanding-in-Chief to build up his fighter strength have already been mentioned. As regards guns, the minimum requirements for the air defence of the ports, the base in Egypt, the Western Desert, Palestine, the Sudan, and Crete, were estimated early in November to be 174 heavy and 356 light anti-aircraft guns; the numbers available were about one-half of the heavy and less than one-third of the light. The anti-aircraft searchlight situation was worse still; apart from batteries at Aden and Malta there were no searchlights other than those manned by the Egyptian Army. General Wavell regarded this as so unsatisfactory that in October he suggested that the cargo space allotted in one of the next convoys to a heavy A.A. battery should be used instead for 24 searchlights.

An efficient warning system was of course essential if the defences were to operate successfully, but in Egypt it still consisted mainly of observer posts in the Western Desert, now of necessity deployed in new locations, and along the coast road to Alexandria and in the Nile Valley. Similar organizations existed in the Sudan, in Kenya and at Aden. At the beginning of October there were still no completed fixed radar stations anywhere in the Middle East, but there were a few mobile sets in Egypt and at Haifa, Port Sudan, Aden, and Mombasa. These were capable of giving only local warning, and in Egypt they were too far apart and too limited in performance to give much more than an indication of approach. The communications too were tenuous and uncertain, so that it is not surprising that the number of interceptions was very low.

The air defence of the fleet base caused Admiral Cunningham particular anxiety, primarily on account of the mixed nature of the organization which the Rear-Admiral commanding the fortress had to control. The guns on shore were manned by British, Maltese, and Egyptian gunners, while all the searchlights were manned by Egyptians. Low-flying aircraft armed with mines or torpedoes constituted a great threat to ships in harbour because the radar could not detect them, which meant that they were most unlikely to be intercepted before delivering their attacks. This was countered to some extent by the rigging and flying of various obstructions, but it was clearly essential for all the guns and searchlights to be most efficiently operated. During November the Italians made a number of night attacks and showed more persistence and determination than hitherto, and this, coupled with the lack of success on the part of the anti-aircraft defences at night, caused Admiral Cunningham to press strongly for the standard to be improved. Accordingly an Anti-Aircraft Defence Commander was appointed to help the Fortress Commander with the training, supervision and co-ordination of the anti-aircraft defences; eight of the searchlight positions were taken over by the Royal Wiltshire Yeomanry, who had recently been trained in this work; and British liaison officers were placed with the Egyptian units. It was decided to strengthen and extend the search-light layout as soon as more equipment and trained men were available.

The fighter aircraft allotted to the defence of the base, the Delta area, and the Canal were controlled by No. 252 (Fighter) Wing at Mex, with Sector Headquarters at Amiriya and Helwan. They included two Royal Egyptian Air Force squadrons and a variable number of Royal Air Force squadrons depending on conditions elsewhere. Indeed, on one occasion just before the British offensive in the Western Desert in December 1940, the fighter defence of the fleet base was reduced to two Sea Gladiators of the Fleet Air Arm. At each of the busy terminal ports on the Canal there was one heavy and one light battery, while there was no anti-aircraft defence other than small arms along the Canal, which meant that a big risk of damage was being taken. The situation in the whole Delta, except at Alexandria, was made worse by the unhelpful attitude of the Egyptian authorities over the air raid precautions. Had the enemy made any serious attacks on the Delta towns, especially with incendiary bombs, the Commanders-in-Chief might have had a very ugly situation to face.

The port of Haifa was attacked four times in September; some damage was done to the oil refinery, and one storage tank was set on fire. The defences consisted of one heavy battery and a few Breda light guns, with a mobile radar set of very limited performance. Early in October the observer screen was extended to give cover from north and east, and a detachment of three Blenheim fighter bombers was sent to Haifa, so that the enemy should not be entirely unopposed.

For Cyprus it had not been possible to spare any air defences at all, and up to September there were no coast defence guns either. Apart from the likelihood of air attack from the Dodecanese, the increasing importance of the exports of copper pyrites and agricultural produce made the port of Famagusta liable to be raided by light craft or bombarded from submarines; two naval 4-inch guns were accordingly installed by the Army, from equipment intended for Turkey.

In summing up the air defence position at this time it may be said that the various shortages were such as to cause grave anxiety in view of the scale of attacks which the Italians appeared to be capable of making on a number of important and widely separated objectives. As it happened, the results fell below expectation. Even so, it was not long before the situation was further complicated by the need to spread the existing resources over a still wider field, as will be described in the next chapter.

It is not to be wondered at that the Turkish Government were watching the situation with renewed interest. They had been given to expect no direct assistance from British forces until the Italian threat to British interests should have been dealt with, so they could hardly be blamed for wanting to know how matters stood now that the Italians had entered Egypt and the war was being carried to the Levant. Towards the end of September the Turkish Government asked if they might send an inter-Service delegation of senior officers to visit the British forces in Egypt. The Chiefs of Staff agreed with the Commanders-in-Chief that the suggestion should be welcomed and that the British attitude should be one of complete frankness. The declared purpose of the mission was to study air defence, but there is little doubt that they really wished to estimate the ability of the British to defend Egypt. In view of the timing of the request it was inferred—no doubt correctly—that the impression gained by the mission would have a considerable influence upon the subsequent Turkish attitude towards the Alliance. The visit took place during October; there was every reason to believe that it was a success, and that on their return the Turkish officers expressed their confidence in the eventual outcome of the war.

The fact that the Italians had made an advance into Egypt which had all the appearance of being only a first step, likely to be followed by a second and probably much more ambitious one, made it all the more important that their lines of communication should be attacked. The most suitable direct naval action was by means of destroyers and submarines, but a successful encounter with the Italian battlefleet would greatly add to the freedom of action of the light forces.

Admiral Cunningham had intended to take the whole fleet to sea on September 25th in order to pass army and air reinforcements to Malta and to engage the enemy fleet if the opportunity occurred. He was prevented from sailing by the course of events elsewhere. On the 23rd an abortive attempt was made to land Free French forces at Dakar, and for some days it was uncertain whether this would not lead to open hostilities with Vichy. Instead, the French contented themselves with bombing Gibraltar on September 24th and 25th as a reprisal. All this naturally provoked a certain restlessness in the French naval squadron at Alexandria. Admiral Cunningham's agreement with Admiral Godfroy held good unless war was declared, but if it came to the point the French ships could no doubt be seized, though in the shallow water of the harbour they might be scuttled, and bloodshed would probably result. The Commander-in-Chief was most anxious to avoid any such outcome, but for the time being he felt obliged to stand guard at Alexandria with a substantial part of his fleet.

On 26th September the Admiralty informed him that as the Dakar operation had been broken off it was unlikely that general hostilities would begin. Two days later Cunningham was able to report that Godfroy had told him that if Vichy declared war he had no personal intention of taking offensive action, but would scuttle his ships if any attempt were made to seize them. On the 27th Radio Lyons announced that as the British squadron had ceased to attack Dakar the French Admiralty had ordered reprisals against Gibraltar to be suspended, and similar information came from American sources. Thereafter the situation gradually eased and Admiral Cunningham was able to resume his postponed operation on September 29th, though on a much reduced scale. Not for another ten days did he feel justified in taking all four battleships to sea.

As regards direct naval attack on the supply lines to Libya the position in respect of both destroyers and submarines was far from satisfactory. Of destroyers there were—as an example—only twelve available for operations of all kinds on 15th September. Admiral Cunningham urged that escort vessels should be provided so that his destroyers could be released from convoy duties for more offensive operations, but escort vessels were in great demand at this time for the Battle of the Atlantic, and none could be spared for the Mediterranean.

The results of the British submarine effort had so far been disappointing. The submarines themselves had carried out their duties with courage and determination, and the lack of targets was not their fault. The main Italian supply route to Libya ran to the west of Sicily, then along the shallow waters of the Kerkenah Bank to Tripoli, and coastwise to Benghazi. The boats available in the Mediterranean up to the middle of October were too big and un-handy to operate in the confined and shallow waters of this route. Their operations had therefore been confined to the southern approaches to the Straits of Messina, the Gulf of Taranto, and the coast of North Africa as far west as Benghazi, and none of these areas covered the main route. The consequence was that submarines were led to seek targets in the highly defended areas off the south coast of Italy, and suffered casualties accordingly, while the distance from the base at Alexandria meant that even these areas could only be thinly patrolled. From the end of September some boats used Malta for refuelling by night, but this made little difference to their time on patrol, which depended mainly upon human endurance.

During October four of the more suitable 'T' class submarines arrived in the Mediterranean, but by the 23rd there was only a total of ten boats on patrol; four were refitting, and two had, unknown to the Commander-in-Chief, been sunk. One of these, the *Rainbow*, had been surprised on the surface shortly after midnight on October 12th/13th by the Italian submarine *Enrico Toti*, with a heavier gun armament; the other, the *Triad*, had been lost for an unknown reason. British losses since the outbreak of war with Italy had in fact been severe; seven boats had been destroyed in the Mediterranean, which was one-third of the number operating. Against this, the damage caused to the enemy by British submarines up to the end of October had been slight, amounting only to one submarine and six supply ships totalling 21,500 tons. Clearly there was a need for more submarines of a suitable type, and it was highly desirable to be able not only to base them at Malta, but also to provide them with enough operational intelligence from the air to increase very greatly their chances of intercepting the enemy.

The fact was that only from Malta could effective attacks of any sort be made on the sea communications to Libya. Unfortunately not only were there not enough air forces there to carry out the necessary reconnaissances and attacks but the island's defences were still too weak for naval forces to be based there. The urgency of the matter prompted the Admiralty on October 2nd to ask Admiral Cunningham what he regarded as the minimum essential requirements to justify the operation of light naval forces from Malta. He replied that he would want five additional cruisers (four 6-inch and one 8-inch) and four *Tribal* class destroyers, but that more important still was the torpedo-bomber squadron already asked for by Sir Arthur Longmore: he also supported the latter's request for a complete general reconnaissance squadron and the bringing up to strength of the two flying-boat squadrons at Alexandria. As regards air defence, he urged that the full approved scale should be provided at the earliest possible moment, but if results justified the risk he would be prepared to operate some light forces from Malta before the full scale was reached.

The Chiefs of Staff decided on October 9th to bring the Hurricanes at Malta up to a strength of one squadron and the Glenn Martins up to a total of 12 aircraft, and to accelerate the despatch of anti-aircraft guns as much as possible. Having in mind the British experience in Norway of trying to deploy and maintain forces through a port under constant air attack, they laid great stress on the need for sustained attacks on Benghazi, the enemy's only major port in Cyrenaica, particularly as they had reason to believe that

German mechanized forces were in the act of moving southwards through Italy.[1] Their further decision to increase and accelerate the supply of Wellingtons was very welcome to the Commanders-in-Chief, who had long been fully aware of the importance of Benghazi to the enemy. The Air Officer Commanding-in-Chief was already doing his utmost to attack it, but it was now only with difficulty that his Blenheims could reach there at all, while there were many calls on No. 216 Bomber Transport Squadron for its primary role of transport. In order to attack all the Cyrenaican ports as strongly as possible he was refraining from making any attacks on the Dodecanese.

A fortnight later the Admiralty was able to inform Admiral Cunningham that the additional aircraft for Malta would arrive during the next reinforcing operation in November and that two cruisers and four destroyers would accompany the battleship *Barham* as reinforcements for the fleet. No striking force of torpedo-bombers was yet available, and although the naval and air forces to be supplied were less than had been asked for it was hoped that they would enable Admiral Cunningham to operate some light forces from Malta, if only for short periods.

During the first half of October there was only one air attack on Malta, and the Hurricanes were consequently able to maintain a high rate of serviceability. This was encouraging, as was the fact that the material damage, though considerable, had not so far been serious. The Governor's chief concern was to prepare for worse to come by pressing on with all possible measures calculated to keep up civilian morale, which involved the pooling of many resources for the general good. This was achieved by the Governor, who was also Commander-in-Chief, presiding over meetings with the three Service heads and the Lieutenant-Governor, who represented the civil population. The Vice-Admiral, Malta, and the Air Officer Commanding were at the same time professionally responsible to the Commander-in-Chief, Mediterranean, and the Air Officer Commanding-in-Chief respectively, although until March 1942, the Commander-in-Chief, Middle East, had no direct responsibility for the army garrison of Malta. The position might perhaps have been open to criticism on the ground of divided allegiance, but in practice the Governor and the local Service heads were well aware of the part it was hoped that Malta would play as an offensive base; they knew that this was the reason for keeping the island secure, and that an essential step towards doing so was to maintain the morale of the population. The Services were able to help the civil

---

[1] There is no evidence that this belief was well founded.

administration in several ways: for example, the supervisory posts in the new civil Department of Shelter Construction were filled by officials of the Dockyard, and much of the general pool of structural materials had been originally ordered by the army for its own purposes.

At the end of August it was agreed with the British Government that the stocks of essential commodities in Malta should be built up to eight months, and that convoys should thereafter be run at two-monthly intervals, thus maintaining at least six months reserve. In the meantime the shipping programme was to be so planned as to build up the eight months reserve by 1st April 1941. The establishment at Alexandria of the Malta Shipping Committee has already been referred to; its task was to arrange for the despatch of the stores demanded by the Co-ordinating Committee for Supplies (COSUP) in Malta. This was not an easy matter, for Admiral Cunningham had been obliged to insist that the lowest speed he could accept for any ship in convoy to Malta was $12\frac{1}{2}$ knots, and there were very few ships suitable for the carriage of coal, cased petrol, and kerosene, capable of this speed. Kerosene was of particular importance to the civilians because the absence of trees or coal on the island had resulted in the general adoption of oil-cooking.

Towards the end of September the Chiefs of Staff reconsidered the strength of the island's army garrison. There was a grave lack of field artillery, and after allowing for the minimum scale of defence of the beaches, airfields, and vulnerable points there was virtually no infantry reserve. This was a serious matter because, as the Prime Minister wrote, the Navy did not possess command of the sea around Malta. One battalion and a field battery were accordingly put under orders to be sent to Malta from England via Gibraltar at the earliest opportunity, which would not be before the end of October. At the same time General Wavell was ordered to allot a battalion and hold it in readiness to go to Malta direct from Egypt. Meanwhile a large number of army drafts for units in Malta had arrived in Egypt and were awaiting onward passage.

It will be recalled that not until September 29th did Admiral Cunningham feel able to leave Alexandria with part of his fleet, owing to uncertainty about French reactions to the affair at Dakar. There was then nothing in the local military situation to detain him, so he resumed the operation (M.B.5) under cover of which army and air force reinforcements were to be passed to Malta, the opportunity being taken to sail an Aegean convoy also. But, as has been seen, he felt obliged to leave two battleships behind, which meant that if the Italian Fleet were to put to sea the conditions might well be unfavourable for seeking an engagement with it.

Shortly after midnight on September 28th/29th Admiral Cunningham in the *Warspite* with the *Valiant*, *Illustrious*, *Orion*, *Sydney*, *York* and eleven destroyers was clear of Alexandria harbour, to be joined later by the cruisers *Liverpool* and *Gloucester* which had embarked 1,200 troops and some airmen and air force stores for Malta. Numerous air attacks were made on the fleet during the afternoon of the 29th, but as a result of the activities of Fulmars of No. 806 Squadron they were all abortive. In fact the only loss was suffered by the Italians, for while the Australian flotilla leader *Stuart* was returning to harbour with a burst steam pipe she encountered the Italian submarine *Gondar* about 60 miles north-west of the Great Pass. After a series of depth-charge attacks during the night it was forced to the surface, where on the morning of the 30th it was bombed and sunk by a flying-boat. The *Stuart* rescued 47 of the crew of 49.

Meanwhile, unknown to Admiral Cunningham, the entire Italian battlefleet with numerous cruisers and destroyers was at sea in the Central Mediterranean. The first information he received was from a reconnaissance aircraft from the *Illustrious* shortly after noon, which reported five battleships, eleven cruisers and up to twenty-five destroyers only 80 miles to the N.N.W. of the British Fleet. They were now steering north-west, so that the only hope of forcing an engagement would have been by employing an air striking force to inflict damage. But as only nine aircraft were available for this purpose, and as the Italian Fleet had some forty ship-borne fighter-reconnaissance aircraft, apart from the powerful anti-aircraft armament of such a concentration of ships, the odds against success in daylight were so great that Admiral Cunningham decided not to launch a striking force. For the rest of the day the enemy were shadowed and, towards evening, they were reported entering Taranto and Messina. In view of the great preponderance of the Italian Fleet their behaviour on this occasion is difficult to understand. Their own shadowing aircraft had correctly reported the composition of the British Fleet, both before and after noon, as two battleships, one aircraft carrier, five cruisers and ten destroyers; yet action was refused.

That evening the *Liverpool* and *Gloucester* were detached and proceeded to Malta to disembark their troops. They rejoined the fleet in the late afternoon of October 1st, and course was then shaped to the eastward. On the return passage another Italian submarine, the *Berillo*, was surprised on the surface, surrendered and was sunk, and the cruisers *Orion* and *Sydney* carried out a sweep in the Aegean which included a bombardment of Stampalia.

A week later Admiral Cunningham staged another major operation (M.B.6) which he again hoped would entice the Italian Fleet to give battle. A store convoy (M.F.3) of four ships with supplies of all kinds was to be sailed for Malta under cover of the fleet, which was then to bring back some empty ships to Alexandria. The movement began on October 8th, and this time the Admiral was able to concentrate four battleships (*Warspite, Valiant, Malaya, Ramillies*) and two aircraft carriers, six cruisers and sixteen destroyers. Two anti-aircraft cruisers and four more destroyers provided close escort for the convoy.

The passage to Malta was uneventful: air reports indicated that the enemy fleet had not moved from Taranto; no air attacks developed, and only one or two contacts were made with submarines. During the afternoon of the 11th the convoy reached Malta; a destroyer received severe damage in the approaches in what was evidently a newly laid enemy minefield. Later in the evening three empty ships left Malta under close escort while the fleet cruised to the south and west of the island, still apparently undetected by the Italians, owing, it was believed, to the bad weather.

But this inference was wrong. A small destroyer force from Augusta had put to sea with the intention of attacking outlying units of the fleet. At 2.0 a.m. on October 12th, in position about 110 miles to the east of Malta and some 70 miles north-east of the Commander-in-Chief, the cruiser *Ajax* (Captain E. D. B. McCarthy), while proceeding to cover the eastbound convoy, reported herself in action with enemy destroyers. One, the *Ariel*, had been sighted on the starboard bow, down moon, on an opposite course. Fire was immediately opened at 4,000 yards and the destroyer blew up. At the same time a second destroyer, the *Airone*, was observed on the port bow at 2,000 yards. She was also despatched, but not before the *Ajax* had been hit twice on the bridge structure and once amidships, where a fire was started. While the *Ajax* was turning to engage the *Airone* a third destroyer, the leader *Artigliere*, came in from the starboard bow. She was also engaged at 3,000 yards, set on fire and her guns silenced, but the *Ajax* received four more hits which put one gun and her radar out of action. Torpedoes had been fired by all three destroyers, but all missed. Two more destroyers were then sighted to the north, the second of which turned to engage but after a few rounds retired behind smoke. Further touch with the enemy was then lost.

On learning of this engagement Admiral Cunningham gave orders for the 3rd Cruiser Squadron to proceed in support and for an air search to be made at dawn. Shortly after 7.0 a.m. a report was received of two destroyers, one burning and in tow of the other. As the cruisers closed, the tow was cast off and the undamaged destroyer escaped to the north-west, having been unsuccessfully attacked by a small air striking force. The other destroyer, which was the *Artigliere*, surrendered. Half an hour was given for the crew to abandon ship, and the *Artigliere* was then sunk. As Sicily was only 90 miles distant, and as submarines were believed to be in the vicinity, rescue work was restricted to throwing carley floats overboard and broadcasting the position in Italian, though some survivors were later picked up by two British destroyers. About noon a report from a flying-boat indicated three 8-inch cruisers and three destroyers in position 60 miles to the north-west of the fleet and steering north-west, but aircraft of No. 830 Squadron from Malta subsequently failed to locate them.

The Commander-in-Chief had every reason to be satisfied with the performance of the *Ajax* in her first night shoot after being newly commissioned. It happened that the enemy encountered the only British cruiser fitted with radar, but on this occasion the credit for the sightings must go to the human look-outs; the state of the moon was four days before full. The Italian destroyers had shown great gallantry, and inflicted damage on the cruiser: two British officers and ten ratings were killed and twenty wounded.

Air attacks with bombs and torpedoes developed as the fleet proceeded to Alexandria, and on the evening of October 14th the cruiser *Liverpool* was hit by a torpedo and severely damaged. With part of her bow torn off she was eventually towed safely into harbour. Meanwhile the convoy from Malta had been joined by the south-bound Aegean convoy, and on the 13th the *Illustrious* with cruisers and destroyers carried out a successful night attack on Leros.

These operations enabled the immediate needs of Malta to be met. They were shortly to be followed by co-ordinated movements from east and west to introduce reinforcements of all kinds; these are described in Chapter XIII.

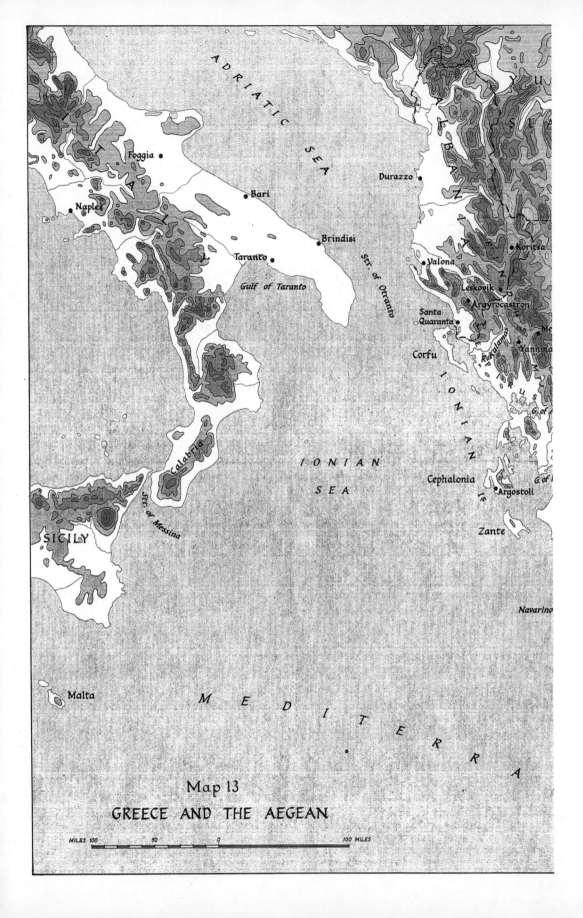

ADRIATIC SEA

*ITALY*

Foggia

Naples

Bari

Brindisi

Taranto

Durazzo

*Gulf of Taranto*

*Str. of Otranto*

Valona

Koritsa

Leskovik

Argyrocastron

Santa
Quaranta

Yannina

Corfu

*Calabria*

*Str. of Messina*

*IONIAN*

*SEA*

Cephalonia

Argostoli

Zante

SICILY

ALBANIA

YUGOSLA

EPIRUS

G. of

G. of

IONIAN

Navarino

Malta

*MEDITERRA*

Map 13

GREECE AND THE AEGEAN

MILES 100            50            0            100 MILES

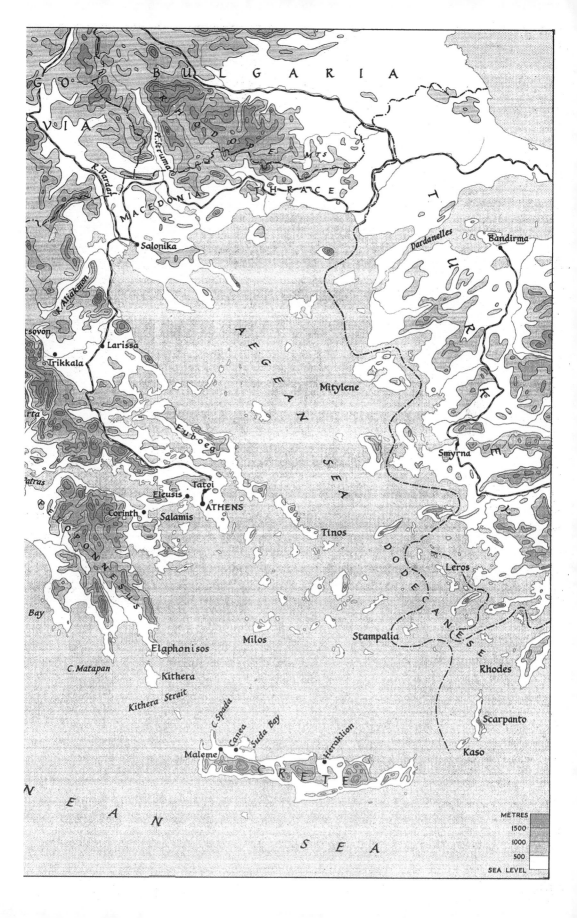

# CHAPTER XII

# THE ITALIANS CARRY THE
# WAR INTO GREECE

*See Map* 13

IN ANNOUNCING Italy's entry into the war Mussolini took the opportunity of reaffirming the assurances previously given to Greece; he had no intention, he said, of dragging her or any of Italy's neighbours into the conflict. Soon after the fall of France, however, the Italian press and radio began a campaign on well worn lines in which frontier incidents and violations of neutrality were given great prominence. In the face of these attacks the Greek Government adhered steadily to their policy of avoiding any action likely to be provocative. On 15th August 1940 the Greek cruiser *Helle* was torpedoed without warning by a submarine and sunk with heavy loss of life while she was at anchor off Tinos. The Greek Government was convinced that the submarine was Italian.[1] Even then they remained calm, and continued in their resolve to defend Greek independence with all the means at their disposal. On August 22nd the President of the Greek Council, General Metaxas, fearing that matters were coming rapidly to a head, decided to enquire what help Greece could expect from Great Britain in fulfilment of her guarantee, if—but not until—Greece should be attacked by Italy.[2] He counted upon the immediate assistance of the Fleet, and was anxious to know whether aircraft and financial help would also be forthcoming.

This was a type of question with which the British were only too familiar. On the one hand failure to help the Greeks would mean that Italian air attacks would be virtually unopposed, in which case the morale of the army and of the civil population would be dangerously weakened. The establishment of the Italians in Greece would be a severe blow to our strategic position in the Eastern Mediterranean and if it was to be easily achieved the effect on our relations with Turkey and Yugoslavia would be deplorable. On the other hand the whole position still depended upon the security of Egypt. If Egypt were lost, Greece would be beyond our help; but

---

[1] See *The Greek White Book* published in 1942 by the Royal Greek Ministry for Foreign Affairs.
[2] See page 25 for the announcement of the British guarantee to Greece.

as long as we had forces in Egypt it might be possible to afford some assistance to the Greeks. From this decisive front, however, neither land nor air forces could at present be spared. Nor could bombers, even if they were available, be sent at short notice from England; the problem was not only one of flying the aircraft to Greece but of providing the facilities for maintaining and servicing them after arrival. This was the old story: maintenance equipment and ground staff would have to go by sea all the way round the Cape. A further difficulty was the lack of airfields in Greece suitable for modern aircraft. As for naval assistance, this by itself could not prevent an invasion through Albania, though the Fleet would welcome any opportunity of engaging Italian naval forces or sea-borne expeditions: in the Aegean in particular it should be possible to interfere considerably with any Italian operation. In these circumstances the British Government felt obliged to say that no specific promises of assistance, other than by naval action, could be given to the Greek Government until the position in Egypt was secure. But they could be told that air attacks on Northern Italy would be made with the greatest strength that could be diverted from the main enemy— Germany.

The possibility of an Italian invasion of Greece naturally directed attention to Turkey, who would certainly dislike the prospect of seeing Italian troops upon her own Thracian frontier. But in view of their anxiety about German and Russian intentions in the Balkans the Turks could not be expected to send troops to Greece. If they wished to operate against the Dodecanese instead, they would need far more British help and equipment than could be spared. It seemed to the Chiefs of Staff that it would be best that Turkey should agree, in the event of an Italian invasion of Greece, to break off diplomatic relations with Italy, or at least recall her Ambassador, to place every obstacle in the way of Italian merchant shipping, and to extend a certain leniency to the British over questions of the violation of territorial air and waters.

The strategic importance of Crete had never been lost sight of, but the French troops who had been ready to go there were no longer available, and British troops were scarce. Towards the end of September the Greeks heard news of the move of three additional Italian divisions to Albania, whereupon their anxiety reached its culminating point. If an attack were coming at all, it would surely come now, during the few remaining weeks of comparatively good weather. In this atmosphere it became possible for the British to initiate discussions with a view to making a co-ordinated plan for the defence of Crete. It was hoped that the 12,000 or so Greek troops on the island would be capable of holding out until support could arrive. Little progress was made, however, because the British

Attachés could make no promises, while the Greeks would not allow any British landings before the declaration of war. As the interval before the break in the weather grew shorter and the expected attack on Greece did not begin, it seemed to General Metaxas unlikely that the Italians could be intending to act before the following spring. This was a reasonable enough deduction to make, but—as so often happens in war—the enemy thought differently.

Before the war began it had been understood between the two Dictators that the Mediterranean and Adriatic Seas were purely Italian spheres of interest, and after the armistice with France the Duce began to think seriously about improving Italy's strategic position at the expense of Yugoslavia or Greece. For an attack on Yugoslavia the Italians would need German help, and Ciano was sent to Berlin on 7th July to discuss the matter. Hitler's reply was emphatic: he had no wish to see the war spread to the Balkans. A few days later Mussolini directed that Libya was to have first call on all Italian resources, and Greece and Yugoslavia were relegated to the background for the time being, though the Duce continued to study plans for the invasion of both countries.

The Greek plan had one great attraction in that it did not depend upon German help. Indeed on 12th August Mussolini was assured by the Governor of Albania, Francesco Jacomoni, and the Military Commander, General Visconti Prasca, that there would be no difficulty in securing Corfu and the coastal sector of Epirus by a sudden surprise attack. Marshal Badoglio and the Army Staff, however, did not agree that the five divisions in Albania would be sufficient and it was decided to send three or four more from Italy. These divisions moved over in September and Visconti Prasca prepared a plan which included them. The Germans were told what Mussolini had in mind, and again their reaction was unfavourable.

During the early days of October, Mussolini seems to have wavered, but on the 13th, well knowing that the Germans would disapprove, he decided to invade Greece. He may have been influenced at this moment by the fact that Hitler had just sent a strong military mission to Rumania, a sign of German interest in the Balkans which made it unlikely that Turkey would intervene if Italy attacked Greece. At the same time Mussolini felt distinctly hurt at not having been asked to participate in the mission, for Italy and Germany had become the joint guarantors of Rumanian integrity at the time of the second 'Vienna Award' of August 30th. He may therefore have felt less inclined than usual to defer to German wishes, especially where Italy's recognized sphere of interest was concerned.

On October 15th, at a meeting of army and political chiefs,

R

Visconti Prasca claimed that the swift operation he had planned would meet with little or no resistance. The only danger was from the rains, which would be a serious handicap to movement, so that there was no time to lose. A slightly dissonant note was sounded by Marshal Badoglio who thought that the whole of Greece would have to be occupied; this would require twenty divisions whereas there were in Albania only nine. But this did not deter the Duce from approving Visconti Prasca's plan. He announced that the first objective would be Epirus; the second phase would be the march on Athens. It was generally agreed that the British would be too pre-occupied in Egypt to land any troops in Greece, though they might perhaps assist the Greeks with aircraft. Count Ciano was to stage a suitable incident, and the attack would begin on October 26th.

To the enquiries of the German Military Attaché as to the signi-ficance of the military moves taking place in Albania, Badoglio explained that preparations were being made for action in case the British should violate Greek neutrality. Von Rintelen was not taken in by this, and informed the German High Command that every-thing pointed to an attack on Greece on 28th October. On the 19th Hitler was told by Ribbentrop of the Italian preparations, but decided not to interfere. The same day the Duce wrote to him re-peating the familiar story of Greek infringements of neutrality and adding that he was determined to deal with this matter very quickly, but omitting to say when.

It is possible that Mussolini's letter did not reach Hitler at once. On the 23rd Hitler was at Hendaye, on the Spanish border, for a meeting with General Franco. He met Marshal Pétain at Montoire and then came to Florence in order to discuss with Mussolini the recent conversations with the French and Spanish Governments. This was on the 28th, and Mussolini was able, in his turn, to present a *fait accompli*, for early that morning the Italian forces had invaded Greece. The Führer did not immediately abuse him for what he had done; on the contrary, he made an offer of airborne troops for use in Crete. Not until later, when the Italian plans began to go amiss, did he see fit to point out to Mussolini how serious were the consequences of his blunder.

The Greek Government had every intention of resisting an Italian invasion but it was by no means easy for them to make full prepara-tions. There was much to be said in favour of starting to mobilize in good time, for Greece was a country with a very scattered population: it was mountainous, and the roads and railways on the mainland were few, the former mostly bad, and liable to break up under heavy traffic or extremes of weather. This meant that both the mobiliza-tion and the subsequent moves of the army were bound to be slow, and if they were still in progress when the war began they would be slower still, for much delay might be caused by the air attacks which the Italians had the strength to deliver on a large scale and against which the Greeks had very little defence. In the view of the Greek Government, however, the best chance of preserving peace lay in the continued avoidance of any action likely to provoke the Italians, a decision which saved the fragile Greek economy from bearing, unaided, the additional burden of full mobilization before war began. The outcome was that as much progress as possible was made with the less obtrusive preparations, but only three divisions and part of a fourth were mobilized before the outbreak of war.

Two of these, each augmented by an infantry brigade and other troops, were moved up close to the Albanian frontier, one on each side of the Pindus range; in the mountains themselves there was a small detachment. Of the twelve divisions not yet mobilized, five were in Eastern Macedonia and their availability was dependent upon the attitude of Bulgaria, which in the event proved to be no bar to their being moved. The remaining seven divisions were dispersed over the rest of the country. The equipment of the army was well below Italian standards, the worst shortages being anti-aircraft and anti-tank weapons and transport. The Greeks had no tanks, whereas the Italians had an armoured division—the Centauro—and, although the broken and intersected ground of Western Greece greatly restricted its use, its presence sometimes handicapped the Greeks by compelling them to avoid the more open areas.

The Greek plan was based on the certainty that the initiative would be with the Italians. The extent to which the Italian air forces would dislocate the Greek time-table was unpredictable, but their superiority was very great as they could so easily be reinforced, and even operated, from bases in Italy and the Dodecanese. The Greek air force numbered some 160 aircraft all told, and, as was usual with small nations possessing no aircraft industry of their own, it consisted of a number of different foreign types, mainly French and Polish, for which spare parts were few and difficult to replace. Squadrons were controlled operationally by the Greek General Staff, who used them almost entirely in close support of the army.

Much would depend upon the early encounters. Defensive positions had been prepared near the frontier, and it was hoped that the enemy could be held off while the concentrations were being completed. If so, the subsequent counterstroke would aim in the first place at securing the high ground about Koritsa, in order to lessen the direct threat to Salonika and deprive the enemy of the full use of his only good lateral road. It was hoped to follow this by an advance on the axis Yannina—Argyrocastron, with a view to capturing the ports of

Valona and Santa Quaranta. As it happened, this plan came within measurable distance of complete success.

At three o'clock in the morning of October 28th the Italian Minister in Athens presented to the President of the Council a note in which the Italian Government charged the Greeks with systematic violations of neutrality, by allowing their territorial waters and ports to be used by the British Navy, by giving fuelling facilities to the Royal Air Force, and by permitting a British intelligence service to be established in Greece. The note went on to demand that as a guarantee of Greek neutrality Italian troops should be given facilities for occupying certain unspecified strategic points in Greece. The Minister added that the troops would begin to cross the frontier at 6 a.m. Treating this as an ultimatum, General Metaxas promptly rejected the demands.[1] A few hours later Greece was at war with Italy through no fault of her own and, as the Prime Minister explained to the House of Commons, through no fault of Great Britain's either. 'We have most carefully abstained', he said, 'from any action likely to draw upon the Greeks the enmity of the criminal dictators. For their part the Greeks have maintained so strict a neutrality that we were unacquainted with their dispositions or their intentions.'[2]

Later in the morning the British Commanders-in-Chief met at Alexandria to determine what action to take about establishing the naval fuelling base in Crete. They decided to send by air a reconnaissance party from the three Services to report on local conditions. The fleet would sail that night, covering the passage of store ships and auxiliaries to Suda Bay. One cruiser was allotted to take the 2nd Battalion The York and Lancaster Regiment, hitherto intended for Malta, that General Wavell decided to send. In addition he agreed to make ready some anti-aircraft and other units. Having reported his action to the War Office he received a reply releasing him from the obligation to hold a battalion in readiness to go to Malta.

All other naval forces at sea in the Eastern Mediterranean were recalled to fuel, and air reconnaissance from Malta over the Ionian Sea was intensified. One British submarine was patrolling the Straits of Otranto, one was off Taranto, and two Greek submarines were off the Ionian Islands. At 1.30 a.m. on October 29th the Commander-in-Chief Mediterranean, with all available fleet units—four battleships, two aircraft carriers, four cruisers and three destroyer

---

[1] Count Ciano cynically records in his diary for 22nd October: 'Naturally it (the ultimatum) is a document that allows no way out for Greece. Either she accepts occupation or she will be attacked.'

[2] Speech of 5th November 1940.

flotillas—sailed from Alexandria and swept up into the Ionian Sea, ready for any eventuality. There was no sign of any Italian activity off Corfu. Early on the 31st the fleet was off the west coast of Crete, covering the arrival of the ships at Suda Bay. Air reconnaissance reported the Italian fleet to be at Taranto and Brindisi and, as any Italian naval activity appeared to be very unlikely, the Commander-in-Chief in the *Warspite* with the *Illustrious* returned to Alexandria on November 2nd, and other major units of the fleet followed the next day.

Early on the morning of the 29th the joint reconnaissance party arrived in Crete, and that afternoon the first convoy left Alexandria. It consisted of two Royal Fleet Auxiliaries, two armed boarding vessels, and the netlaying vessel *Protector*, escorted by destroyers and two anti-aircraft cruisers. It reached Suda Bay on November 1st at the same time as the cruiser *Ajax* arrived with 2nd Bn. York and Lancaster Regiment. By that afternoon the troops and stores had been disembarked and one anti-submarine net laid. The only Italian reactions were attacks by about fifteen bombers on Suda and Canea on November 1st and 2nd, in which no particular damage was done.

By 3rd November all the anti-submarine defences had been laid and the defences to seaward were being strengthened. Convoys arrived from the 6th onwards, carrying a brigade headquarters, one heavy and one light A.A. battery, one field company, and ancillary units, together with defence stores, and supplies for 45 days. It was hoped to be able to operate one fighter squadron for the defence of the base if required, but the only airfield on Crete was at Heraklion, some 70 miles east of Suda Bay, too far away for aircraft to give protection to the naval base. It was suitable for use by Gladiators, but by Blenheims it could be used in one direction only. Work was begun at once on making it fit for all types of aircraft, and on the preparation of another site about 11 miles west of Suda.

All this action was, of course, quite consistent with what had long been the British policy. Nothing had been said or done to encourage any expectation of intervention on the mainland of Greece. Immediately after the delivery of the ultimatum the President of the Council had invoked the British guarantee, and Mr. Churchill at once promised all the help in our power. The same evening the Defence Committee earnestly considered the matter and decided upon a number of measures, all of which were in line with previous policy. For example, they endorsed the action taken by the Commanders-in-Chief at Suda Bay, which they wished to see secured for British use. They authorized General Wavell to send up to one infantry brigade group to defend Greek islands generally and Suda Bay in particular. They decided to send a battalion to Malta via

Gibraltar to take the place of the one now going to Crete.[1] They intended to bomb towns in Northern Italy from the United Kingdom, and they ordered preparations to be made for attacking objectives in central and southern Italy from Malta.

The promptness with which the British had begun to move into Crete was encouraging to the Greeks, who were aware of the value of Suda Bay to the British Fleet, but no visible contribution was being made to the battle now in progress on Greek soil. This view was strongly put forward in a telegram from the British Minister in Athens on October 30th. Greek morale, he said, was still high, but the non-appearance of British aircraft was causing loud comment. The Greeks did not regard Crete as being in any immediate danger; and he asked whether the object of defending it could not be replaced by one of helping to defeat the Italians. The Air Officer Commanding-in-Chief had caused enquiries to be made about Eleusis airfield in connexion with the possible bombing of Taranto and Brindisi, and the Greeks had warmly welcomed the idea. The Minister thought that it was now vitally necessary to take some action or the consequences would be grave. After reading this message Air Chief Marshal Longmore immediately arranged for No. 30 Squadron (Blenheim I), whose aircraft were armed half as fighters and half as bombers, to leave for Athens as soon as the necessary preparations could be made. 'It seems', he cabled to the Chief of the Air Staff, 'that it has become politically absolutely essential to send a token force to Greece even at the expense of my forces here.' Mr. Churchill's comment was that Sir Arthur Longmore had taken a very bold and wise decision.

On October 28th the Secretary of State for War, Mr. Eden, was at Khartoum, on his way home after a visit to the Middle East. At the Prime Minister's request he returned to Cairo to discuss and report on the new situation with the Commanders-in-Chief. His views, which coincided with theirs, were that the defence of Egypt was vital to the whole position in the Middle East; if the base here was secure we could strike at Italy or help Turkey against the Germans. After much effort and risk this state, as far as the Army was concerned, was being reached, though the Air Force was still far too weak. Any land or air forces sent from the Middle East to Greece could not possibly be strong enough to have a decisive influence on the fighting there; and by dividing our resources we should risk failure in both places. Moreover we might jeopardize the plans which General Wavell was preparing, in a secrecy so great that he would not inform even the Prime Minister save by Mr. Eden's word of mouth, to attack Marshal Graziani's forces in the Western

[1]This arrived at Malta on 10th November as part of Operation 'Coat'; see pages 241, 242.

Desert. No harm came of this reticence, and the secrecy to which General Wavell attached such importance was successfully maintained, which in view of the opportunities for leakage in Egypt was a remarkable achievement. As the war expanded, the plans of Commanders in the various theatres had to be very closely related to the possibility of obtaining the necessary means, and it became normal for their intentions to be made known to the Chiefs of Staff and Minister of Defence in good time.

In London the new situation was being earnestly studied. The promise to afford all possible help to Greece was being translated into action as regards munitions, materials, and money, but the question was whether any more active assistance could be given. The War Cabinet were impressed by the turn taken by events, for there seemed a reasonable prospect of the Greeks being able to build up a front against the Italians. As no attack upon Egypt appeared to be imminent it was decided to take a risk and give the Greeks some direct help; in the circumstances this would have to consist mainly of air support, which, to be in time, must come at first from the Middle East.

The Government's instructions were received by the Commanders-in-Chiefs on November 4th. The Chiefs of Staff had fully realized that a limit would be set by the shortage of airfields in Greece. Not only were there no all-weather airfields but there were few areas on the mainland in which airfields of any size could be constructed. In the flat country about Salonika a number of dry-weather airfields existed, and in the Larissa plain there were some possible sites, but by November these were liable to serious flooding. Few other sites existed, except for an occasional flat stretch on the coast, but the heavy rainfall and the prevalence of low clouds and mist made them unsuitable during the winter months. In these circumstances the choice was limited to two airfields near Athens-Eleusis and Menidi (Tatoi), which had the disadvantage of being so far from the front that many hours would be wasted in flying to and fro. The airfields were to be properly protected before squadrons arrived to use them, and General Wavell was to send one heavy and one light battery to supplement the very limited Greek anti-aircraft resources. As soon as these preparations were complete the Air Officer Commanding-in-Chief was to send three bomber squadrons (Blenheim)—including No. 30, half bomber half fighter—and one fighter squadron (Gladiator), to be followed by a second as soon as reinforcements of Hurricanes would permit. All the necessary airmen, transport, equipment, and ancillary units for these squadrons were to be provided by the Commanders-in-Chief from their own resources.

The Chiefs of Staff fully appreciated that this would leave Egypt dangerously weak and took action to replace the withdrawals as quickly as possible. They planned to send 34 Hurricanes (No. 73 Squadron and 18 reserve aircraft) in the carrier *Furious* to Takoradi, whence they would fly to Egypt and begin to arrive there about December 2nd onwards. Squadron ground crews would arrive at about the same time via the Mediterranean. As regards bombers, 32 Wellingtons (Nos. 37 and 38 Squadrons) over and above the current replacement and rearmament programme would be sent to Egypt via Malta; their move and that of their men and stores, and of a station headquarters, would also be completed by about 2nd December. Finally, to add weight to the attacks made from Greece, the number of Wellington bombers at Malta was to be increased to 16, for which about 200 men, with stores and bombs, were to be sent by cruiser arriving at Malta on November 17th.

Mr. Eden left the Middle East on November 6th, but before doing so he cabled to say that he and Wavell and Longmore agreed that although the plan involved additional risks in the Western Desert, these must be faced 'in view of political commitments to aid Greece'. But any increase of this commitment would be a serious matter; particularly as forecasts of arrival of reinforcing aircraft had not hitherto been fulfilled. The effect in Egypt was going to be a reduction of the fighter defence by as much as one-third until mid-December, and of the striking force by a half for many weeks. The air defence of the fleet base at Alexandria and of other important targets was insufficient even before the allocations to Crete, to which were now added those for Greece.

A further consequence of the move into Crete was that on November 4th General Metaxas expressed a wish to remove the bulk of the Greek troops for use in Epirus. General Wavell was greatly concerned lest the Cretan commitment should grow, as he had no wish to draw any further on his scanty reserve of trained troops. The Chiefs of Staff, however, considered that no objection could be made to the Greek proposal, and responsibility for the security of Crete was thereupon placed upon the three British Commanders-in-Chief.

It was not only in Egypt, however, that risks were being run. There were no reserves anywhere from which the men and material could be taken, so they had to be found from forces generally accepted as being already insufficient for their probable tasks. The fighter defence of the United Kingdom would be weakened, for a time, by the equivalent of two squadrons, apart from the withdrawal of the 90 Hurricane pilots required for the rearming programme in the Middle East. A full-scale attack by the *Luftwaffe* during a spell of fine weather at this time would have found the fighter defence dangerously weak. The bomber effort against Germany would be reduced by the equivalent of two Wellington squadrons until the strength of Bomber Command could be built up again.

In order to maintain close liaison with the Greek armed forces the Chiefs of Staff established on October 31st an inter-Service Mission in Greece to keep the War Cabinet and the Commanders-in-Chief— to whom the Mission was responsible—informed of the military situation. Rear-Admiral C. E. Turle, Naval Attaché in Athens, was appointed Head of the Mission. When, on November 4th, it was decided to send an air contingent to Greece, Air Commodore J. H. D'Albiac, Air Officer Commanding in Palestine and Transjordan, was appointed to command it and act as Longmore's representative. He took up his duties on November 6th. In general his instructions were to employ his fighter aircraft to protect his airfields and important objectives in the rear area; Blenheim bombers were to be directed against targets on the enemy's lines of communication; and Wellington bombers were to attack disembarkation ports and concentration areas on the Albanian coast.[1]

Four Bombays of No. 216 Squadron conveyed the advance air party to Eleusis, and on November 4th No. 30 Squadron began operations. The ground crews, equipment, bombs and ammunition followed by cruiser on November 6th. In the middle of November Nos. 84 and 211 (bomber) Squadrons (Blenheim Mark I) and No. 80 (fighter) Squadron (Gladiator) arrived. With them came a composite force of anti-aircraft, engineer, signals, and administrative units, provided by the army, the whole under the command of the Air Officer Commanding.[2] The airfields used by the bombers were Eleusis and Tatoi, while No. 80 Squadron had to operate under conditions of great difficulty and discomfort from Trikkala and Yannina. The Wellington bombers of No. 70 Squadron based in Egypt operated on suitable nights, using Eleusis airfield for refuelling and rearming.

The Italians, as has been seen, based their plans for invading Greece on the assumption that they would meet practically no resistance. The resolute attitude of the Greeks came as a complete surprise. In Epirus the Italians succeeded in driving in the Greek covering forces and secured a bridgehead across the Kalamas river; had this success been exploited there might have been a chance for the Centauro (armoured) Division to make its weight felt. In the Pindus the 3rd (Julia) Alpini Division reached within about 12 miles of the Metsovon Pass; it was then counter-attacked by troops who

---

[1] The directive to Air Commodore D'Albiac is given in Appendix 4.

[2] The whole expedition numbered: Royal Air Force, 2,200 men and 310 vehicles; Army, 2,030 men and 400 vehicles from over 40 different units. For the voyage to Piraeus 5 cruisers, 5 transports, and 1 bulk petrol ship were used. The main convoy sailed on 15th November, and reached Piraeus next day. Disembarkation took more than four days to complete. There was no interference by Italian aircraft.

were even more suited to the mountainous country, and by November 7th was in full retreat. In the north nothing occurred save outpost skirmishes. By the 8th the Italian offensive had collapsed. On the 10th the Duce held another meeting of his Service chiefs—this time to decide how the position could be retrieved.

The weaknesses of the original plan were now apparent. Strenuous efforts were to be made to restore the shaken Italian morale. The bad weather had accentuated the lack of administrative arrangements—especially hospitals—while the available transport was quite inadequate. Fresh forces were obviously needed at once. Unfortunately the low capacity of Durazzo and Valona did not allow of cargoes of stores, animals, and vehicles being cleared rapidly. Except locally, the attitude during the winter would be defensive: the forces in the northern and Pindus sectors were to be strengthened as soon as possible, and proper preparations made for resuming the offensive in Epirus. Meanwhile the air force must increase the weight and scope of its attacks. Visconti Prasca was to remain in the field, as his removal would publicise the Italian failure, but he was replaced in command by General Soddu.

The Greeks, however, were quick to exploit their early success and had no intention of giving the Italians time to build up their strength. They had carried out their mobilization and concentration almost without interference from the air, and by November 14th were able to attack on the whole front. There followed some sharp fighting, but by the 22nd the Greeks had captured Koritsa and Leskovik, and in the south they had re-crossed the Kalamas. Thus they had thrown the enemy almost entirely out of Epirus, had secured a foothold on Albanian soil and the use of the valuable lateral road south from Koritsa, and had inflicted considerable casualties in addition to capturing much invaluable booty.

Throughout this period Air Commodore D'Albiac was convinced that his small force could best help by concentrating upon the transit ports and important centres on the lines of communication; he therefore resisted the pressure brought upon him by the Greek High Command to employ his force in close support of the troops. His attacks were mainly directed—as often as the appalling weather permitted—against Durazzo, Valona and selected Albanian towns, while Bari and Brindisi were attacked by Wellingtons from both Greece and Malta. The air position was extremely difficult, for the Greek Air Force, through casualties and lack of spares, soon became practically non-effective, leaving the Italians free to keep up constant attacks upon the Greek forward troops. The Air Officer Commanding estimated that the Italians had from 150 to 200 fighters in Albania, with which they maintained standing patrols over all the important targets, and against which his bombers had little chance. Until he

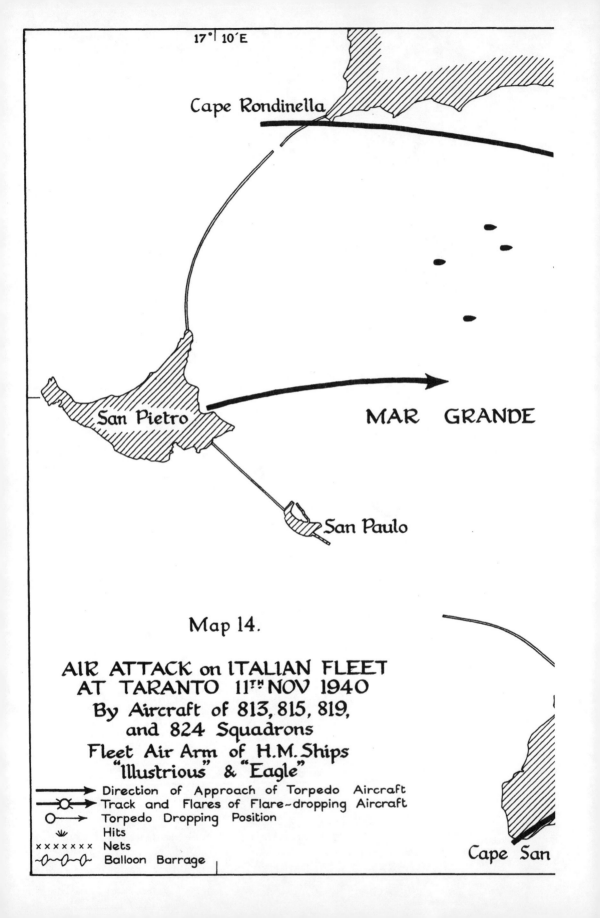

17° 10′E

Cape Rondinella

MAR   GRANDE

San Pietro

San Paulo

Map 14.

AIR ATTACK on ITALIAN FLEET
AT TARANTO 11ᵀᴴ NOV 1940
By Aircraft of 813, 815, 819,
and 824 Squadrons
Fleet Air Arm of H.M. Ships
"Illustrious" & "Eagle"

→ Direction of Approach of Torpedo Aircraft
→ Track and Flares of Flare-dropping Aircraft
○→ Torpedo Dropping Position
Hits
×××××××  Nets
Balloon Barrage

Cape San

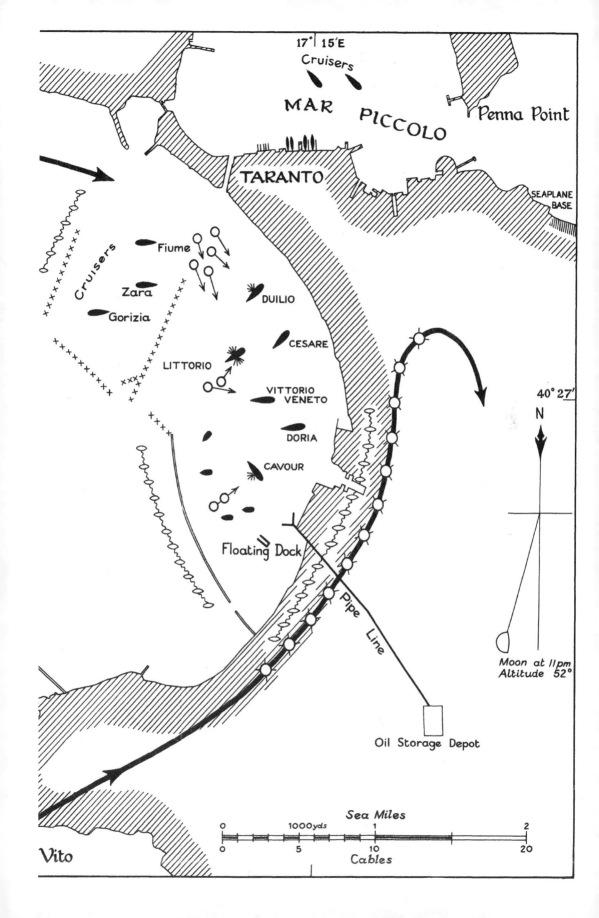

17° 15'E
Cruisers

MAR PICCOLO

Penna Point

TARANTO

SEAPLANE BASE

Cruisers

Fiume

Zara

Gorizia

DUILIO

CESARE

LITTORIO

VITTORIO VENETO

DORIA

CAVOUR

Floating Dock

Pipe Line

Oil Storage Depot

40° 27'
N

Moon at 11pm
Altitude 52°

Vito

Sea Miles

0        1000yds        1        2
0        5        10        20
Cables

was later able to operate his own fighters from airfields near the front, therefore, he was forced to apply his effort more and more to night bombing.

The speed with which the Greeks had turned to the offensive and the vigour displayed in their attacks came as an added surprise to the Italians, whose morale, already low, fell lower still. About a quarter of their force in Albania had been defeated, and they had been unable to gain any advantage from their tanks and superior transport. To their many anxieties was added the fear that the British would be able to give further assistance to the Greeks.

Meanwhile, Germany remained coldly silent and showed no signs of breaking off diplomatic relations with her ally's new enemy.

The reluctance of the Italian battlefleet to force an issue at sea had caused Admiral Cunningham to consider for some time past the possibility of attacking it in harbour. The Italian fleet was mainly concentrated at Taranto, where it was ideally situated for controlling the Central Mediterranean. As the *Littorios* came forward into service they too moved to Taranto, where by October all six battle-ships, together with numerous cruisers, destroyers, and auxiliaries, were berthed safe from surface attack. Admiral Cunningham's intention was to attack the battleships with torpedo-bomber aircraft launched from carriers. (See Map 14 and Photo 4.)

The Swordfish were to be launched from their carriers at a distance which made it necessary to fit them with extra fuel tanks. These became available when the *Illustrious* joined the Mediterranean Fleet in September, after which the crews underwent special training in night flying. It was intended to carry out the operation on the night of October 21st—Trafalgar Day—but a fire in the carrier's hangar made a postponement necessary. The outbreak of the war in Greece naturally made the project more urgent, and a chance occurred at the end of October when the fleet was operating off the west coast of Greece. At this time, unfortunately, there was no moon, and the aircrews needed more practice before they could rely entirely upon flares. The next opportunity came during the second week of November, when some intricate movements of shipping in the Central Mediterranean coincided with a suitable phase of the moon.[1] The *Eagle* was prevented from taking part in the attack by serious defects in her petrol system—the result of some near misses; so five of her Swordfish were transferred to the *Illustrious*. Three were unfortunately lost during preliminary operations, and in all only twenty-one Swordfish were available for the attack instead of the thirty originally intended.

---

[1] These movements are described on page 242.

The use of torpedoes made the operation particularly hazardous, as it forced the aircraft to come down very low. The possible dropping positions were known to be restricted by balloons and net obstructions, and for this reason not more than six torpedo-bombers were to be used at a time. The attack was planned to be delivered by two waves, about one hour apart. In each wave there would be two aircraft whose task was to illuminate the battleships by dropping a line of flares to the eastward of the anchorage. In order to distract attention and to keep the searchlights pointing upwards where they would not dazzle the torpedo droppers, bombing attacks were to be made on the ships in the inner harbour.

A great deal depended upon the detailed information about the position of the ships. For several days previously, and right up to the hour of the attack, aircraft of No. 431 Flight (Glenn Martin) and No. 228 Squadron (Sunderland) from Malta kept a close watch on the approaches to the port for any arrivals or departures. The photographs taken by the Glenn Martins showed clearly the positions of the ships and of the principal defences, including the anti-torpedo nets and the numerous barrage balloons. The postponement of the operation was therefore not without its compensations, but Admiral Cunningham signalled to the Admiralty on November 10th that in view of the strength of the defences it seemed to him that complete success was not to be expected. The latest photographs were flown to *Illustrious* in the afternoon of November 11th; they showed five battleships berthed in the outer harbour, and a flying-boat reported the sixth entering. By the time the Swordfish took off the whole Italian battlefleet was anchored in the outer harbour, and each member of the aircrews knew the position of every unit.

Shortly before 9 p.m. the first wave of twelve Swordfish from Nos. 813, 815 and 824 Squadrons, led by Lieutenant-Commander K. Williamson, was formed up and away, having been flown off from a position 170 miles to the south-east of Taranto. Two hours later, as they were approaching the target area from the south-west, the flash of anti-aircraft guns showed them that the defences were already alert. Just before 11 p.m. the flare-droppers and bombers left the formation to carry out their respective tasks, while the torpedo-bombers made off to westward to get into position for the final approach. The two sub-flights of three then dived towards the anchorage in the face of intense fire from the shore batteries supplemented by the close range weapons in the warships. The aircraft came down as low as 30 feet above the water to launch their torpedoes. The moon was three-quarters full, and to the eastward the flares were outlining the battleships perfectly. The leader attacked the southernmost battleship, the *Cavour*, and his torpedo struck home under the foc's'le as the aircraft, badly damaged, crashed near the floating dock. One minute later the *Littorio* was struck under the starboard bow by a torpedo dropped by the second sub-flight, and a few moments afterwards she was hit again on the port quarter. The other torpedoes either missed, exploded prematurely, or failed to go off, though they were all dropped from close range. Meanwhile, the flare-dropping aircraft, their main task completed, bombed the oil storage depot before making out to sea, and the other bombers attacked vessels in the inner harbour and started a fire in a hangar. In spite of the heavy fire all the aircraft of the first wave with the exception of the leader, who with his observer was made prisoner, were safely back 4½ hours after taking off.

The second wave from Nos. 813, 815, 819 and 824 Squadrons, reduced in strength to eight, led by Lieutenant-Commander J. W. Hale, appeared in the target area shortly before midnight. The tactics were the same, and once again the targets were successfully illuminated by the flares. From about 4,000 feet the five torpedo-bombers began their dive, and as before they continued it to a very low height above the water. One torpedo struck the *Duilio* on the starboard side and another hit the damaged *Littorio*, which was then hit for the fourth time by a torpedo that failed to explode. The *Vittorio Veneto* and the 8-inch cruiser *Gorizia* were unsuccessfully attacked, the latter by an aircraft which was then shot down. In the inner harbour the cruiser *Trento* was attacked, and another fire was started ashore. By three o'clock in the morning the second wave arrived back, having, like the first, lost one aircraft.[1]

During the next day, the 12th, several Italian aircraft tried to locate the British Fleet, and especially the carrier. Some were shot down or driven off by Fulmars, and no aircraft succeeded in making a sighting report. It had in fact been intended to repeat the attack on Taranto the following night, but the weather reports became too unfavourable. On the night of the 13th, however, ten Wellingtons from Malta attacked the inner harbour and naval oil tanks, and caused further fires and explosions. From the photographs taken on the 12th the success of the main operation could be judged. They showed the *Cavour* beached and apparently abandoned; in fact, though subsequently raised, she never went to sea again. The *Littorio* and *Duilio* were shown to be seriously damaged, and, in fact, they remained out of action for five and six months respectively. Results in the inner harbour were more difficult to assess: photographs suggested that two cruisers had been damaged, but it now appears from the Italian Admiral's report that two hits had been scored with bombs that failed to explode. But the main object had

---

[1] Some 13,000 rounds of various calibres up to 4-inch were fired by the shore anti-aircraft guns, apart from the close range weapons of the ships' armament. The Italian Admiral reported seven British aircraft probably destroyed.

been successfully achieved. Half the Italian battlefleet had been put
out of action, at least temporarily, by the expenditure of eleven
torpedoes and for the loss of two aircraft. The Commander-in-Chief
was guilty of no exaggeration in describing the result as an un-
surpassed example of economy of force. As *Illustrious* rejoined the
Fleet, she was welcomed with the signal '*Illustrious* manoeuvre well
executed'.

The Italian losses on the night of November 11th were not all
confined to Taranto. While the *Illustrious* and her escort were
waiting off the coast of Cephalonia for her aircraft to return, a force
consisting of the cruisers *Orion, Sydney, Ajax*, and the destroyers
*Nubian* and *Mohawk*, under the command of the Vice-Admiral, Light
Forces, was raiding the convoy route between Albania and the
Italian mainland. Keeping his force concentrated on account of the
bright moonlight, Admiral Pridham-Wippell steered up the middle
of the Straits of Otranto, crossed the Brindisi—Valona line, and at
about 1 a.m. turned to the southward.[1] A few minutes later a convoy
of four merchant vessels with two escorts was sighted about eight
miles away on the port bow, steaming in line ahead towards Brindisi.
In the short engagement which followed, all four merchant vessels
(totalling 16,938 tons) were sunk, though the escorts managed to
escape.

Admiral Cunningham's success at Taranto made a profound
impression throughout the world, for here was proof indeed that a
fleet was no longer safe in harbour. The effects in the Mediterranean
were immediate, for on November 12th every major Italian warship
capable of steaming left Taranto for more secure ports on the west
coast of Italy, thus further reducing the threat to our convoys
running to Greece and Crete. To the Greeks, who had feared that
the naval superiority of the Italians would lead to landings on Greek
coasts and islands in addition to ensuring the build-up of the army in
Albania, the whole episode was most encouraging. The Turks, for
their part, were in no immediate danger, but it was noticed that
their determination to resist a direct threat to themselves was, soon
after Taranto, appreciably increased.


It now seemed certain that Germany had secured political and
military domination over Rumania, and that as a result she was
assured of her oil supplies and of the use of the communications
through the country. She had forestalled any possible Russian move
towards the Straits, but was well placed for further action herself and

---

[1] Admiral Tovey had recently been appointed to command the Home Fleet, and
Vice-Admiral H. D. Pridham-Wippell had relieved him as V.A.L.F. and second in
command of the Mediterranean Fleet.

could make ample forces available. Whether she intended to move to the help of the Italians in Greece, or had visions of a drive to the Straits and on to Anatolia, Syria, and northern Iraq, her first step would presumably be to move into Bulgaria. But even if Bulgaria were acquiescent, which by the end of November seemed to be possible but by no means certain, it would not be easy for the Germans to move large forces over the Danube and through the country, and maintain them, without elaborate transportation arrangements. There was as yet no indication that these had been made although the amount of motor transport in the country was very small, the roads were mostly rough surfaced, and the winter was not far off, while there was no bridge over the Danube into Rumania except the one at Chernovoda in Dobrudja.

The Chiefs of Staff's view was that if after occupying Bulgaria the Germans were to help the Italians to overrun Greece the result would be a serious weakening of our naval position, but it would not be disastrous; we should hope to hold Crete although it might be difficult in the circumstances to make use of it. But Turkey was different. She could act as a barrier to a German thrust towards the south-east, and it was most important that she should resist: if she failed, our whole position in the Middle East would be jeopardized; consequently the defence of Turkey was more important than that of Greece. The War Cabinet accordingly decided to do everything possible to ensure that if Turkey were attacked she would resist, and to give her all the aid in our power; a special mission was set up to deal with questions of co-operation. The Commanders-in-Chief were warned that if Turkey were attacked in the near future any help must come, at first, from them—a formula to which they were becoming grimly accustomed. The Prime Minister made the issue quite clear by pointing out that the importance of going to the help of Turkey would far outweigh that of carrying out the Western Desert operations which General Wavell was planning; indeed, in Egypt he would be relegated to the very minimum defensive role. In spite of this discouraging prospect Wavell still hoped that there would be time to deal Graziani a heavy blow before the crisis in the Balkans occurred. On 17th November he recorded his own estimate of the probable course of events in these words: 'I am quite sure Germany cannot afford to see Italy defeated—or even held—in Greece, and must intervene. We shall, I think, see German air assistance to Italy very shortly. Germany probably does not want, at present, to push Bulgaria into war or invade Yugoslavia, but may be forced to do so. As in the last war, Germany is on interior lines and can move more quickly to attack Greece or Turkey than we can to support them.'

This forecast proved to be remarkably accurate. As early as November 4th the Führer had ordered an examination of the problem of sending German troops to support the Italians in Greece; his reasons being that the British had greatly improved their position in the Mediterranean and had obtained access to air bases from which the Rumanian oilfields, which he had taken such trouble to secure, could be bombed. On November 18th he received Count Ciano, and gave him his views on future Mediterranean strategy. He repeated the gist of them in a letter to Mussolini two days later. This letter was largely a lecture on the deplorable consequences of Italy's premature action against Greece. It would be necessary to clear up the situation during the winter and for this purpose German troops would move through Bulgaria against Greece as soon as possible. Owing to the weather this could not be before March 1941, but the Führer added pointedly that he did not imagine the Italians would be able to mount a decisive attack any sooner than that. He intended to induce Spain to enter the war so as to block the western end of the Mediterranean; he would try to reach understandings with Turkey and Yugoslavia and would encourage Russia to turn her attention eastwards rather than to the Balkans. During the winter months the main military action would have to be by air. There should be strong attacks on economic and military targets, and above all on the British fleet, which they must aim at destroying during the three or four months required for preparing the operations against Greece. He would make available a *Geschwader* of German bombers (about 100 aircraft), with the necessary reconnaissance and fighter aircraft. He emphasized the need for the Italians to capture Matruh as soon as possible, as the attack on Alexandria could then be made in overwhelming strength.

He did not tell the Duce that preparations for an attack on Russia were already in hand, but he did tell him that he would want his German forces back again in the spring—at the beginning of May at the latest. As for securing the immediate entry of Spain into the war, Hitler's approach to Franco, made on 7th December, was even less successful than had been the previous attempts by both the Axis dictators. Franco had hitherto made no promises, but he had at least kept their hopes alive, and planning for the capture of Gibraltar by German troops (operation *'Felix'*) had been in progress for the past three months. On 11th December it was abruptly cancelled. Franco was still unable to say when his country would be economically and militarily in a fit state to enter the war, but it certainly could not be so by 10th January 1941—the latest date by which Hitler could allow German troops to be committed to a campaign in Spain.

# CHAPTER XIII

# MORE REINFORCEMENTS FOR
# THE MIDDLE EAST

## (October - December 1940)

IT HAD BEEN decided at the end of September that in addition to the anti-aircraft artillery the garrison of Malta required strengthening.[1] The battalion which General Wavell had been instructed to provide had been sent instead to Crete, in circumstances which have already been described.[2] It now remained to convey the troops, stores, and equipment that were being provided from England, and it was intended that their passage should form part of a co-ordinated operation in the Mediterranean during which Force H would cover the movement of certain ships proceeding as reinforcements to the Eastern Mediterranean Fleet, and would also cover the fly-off of a number of Hurricanes to Malta from the carrier *Argus*. Delays to the *Argus* at home resulted in the operation being divided into two, the first being confined to the carriage of the troops to Malta in H.M. ships which were then to join Admiral Cunningham's fleet (operation 'Coat'). Accordingly, the men of one battalion, two 25-pdr field batteries, one tank troop, and one light and two heavy anti-aircraft batteries, in all 2,150, reached Gibraltar by liner on November 6th. They were transferred to H.M. ships after dark: 700 to the battleship *Barham*, 750 to the 8-inch cruiser *Berwick*, and 400 to the 6-inch cruiser *Glasgow*. Three destroyers carried 50 each, and three other destroyers of Force H, due to return to Gibraltar, embarked a further 150 between them. The guns, tanks and other vehicles were to follow by merchant ship later in the month.

The reinforcing ships were to be met in the neighbourhood of Malta by Admiral Cunningham's fleet, and the whole operation, which involved other important shipping moves as well, together with subsidiary operations, was known as M.B.8. The moves from the east began on November 4th with the departure first of convoy A.N.6 with coal, essential stores, and aviation spirit for Greece and Crete, and then of a convoy of five store ships for Malta (M.W.3) to which two additional ships for Suda Bay, one with eight 3·7-inch

---

[1] See page 219.
[2] See page 228.

mobile anti-aircraft guns and the other with fuel and petrol, were attached for the first part of the voyage. This convoy, under the close escort of cruisers and destroyers, was routed north of Crete while the main Mediterranean Fleet, sailing two days later, provided cover in the central basin. Another movement, also part of the general operation, was that of the cruisers *Ajax* and *Sydney* with H.Q. 14th Infantry Brigade, one light and one heavy anti-aircraft battery and administrative troops from Port Said to Suda. After disembarking their troops and stores, they were to join the Commander-in-Chief. Other movements were to be associated with the return voyage.

The fleet under the Commander-in-Chief consisted of four battleships, the *Illustrious*, two cruisers and thirteen destroyers. The passage to Malta was uneventful, such air attacks as did occur being broken up by Fulmars. On 9th November convoy M.W.3 reached Malta together with the *Ramillies* and other ships which needed to refuel. The Commander-in-Chief, meanwhile, continued to the west in order to rendezvous with the reinforcing ships coming from Gibraltar. These had sailed on the 7th with Force H, whose strength had been reduced because the *Renown* had been ordered to take part in operations against the pocket battleship *Scheer* in the Atlantic. On the morning of the 9th Admiral Somerville had directed an air attack on Cagliari by Swordfish of Nos. 810, 818 and 820 Squadrons from the *Ark Royal*. This caused damage to hangars and seaplanes, but no aircraft were observed on the ground; there was little opposition and no casualties were sustained in the British force.[1] During the forenoon the enemy had made one heavy and determined air attack. The Fulmars were unable to break up the enemy formations, and bombs had fallen unpleasantly close to several ships, including the *Barham*. But that was all. The *Ark Royal* flew off three Fulmars to Malta, for transfer to the *Illustrious*, and that evening the reinforcing ships parted company. Force H returned to Gibraltar without further incident.

On joining the Mediterranean Fleet at 10.15 a.m. on November 10th the new reinforcements proceeded to Malta and disembarked their troops. Meanwhile a convoy of four empty store ships (M.E.3) had left the island under close escort together with the monitor *Terror* which was to perform the duties of guardship at Suda Bay. By dawn on November 11th the reinforced Mediterranean Fleet was steaming to the north-eastward, and late in the day the units concerned took up positions for the Fleet Air Arm's attack on Taranto and for the cruiser raid into the Straits of Otranto which have been described in the previous chapter.

---

[1] Santoro: *L'Aeronautica Italiana nella II^a Guerra Mondiale* p. 475 refers to this as an attack by an unknown number of aircraft which dropped 15 medium-weight bombs. One hangar, two seaplanes and one other aircraft were damaged.

During all these operations the Italian Fleet showed no inclination to challenge the movements of the British forces. Air observation from November 6th onwards had confirmed that the six enemy battleships were still in Taranto, together with numerous cruisers and destroyers. The Italians were therefore in a favourable position to intercept Admiral Cunningham with a superiority of six to four in battleships, seven to one in 8-inch cruisers, ten to five in 6-inch cruisers and at least two to one in destroyers. Although no enemy aircraft seems to have reported British forces moving west until noon on 8th November, the Italians, as always, were in a position to know that the fleet had left Alexandria and in what strength. They failed, however, to make any use of their knowledge, and as a result of the raid on Taranto the numerical advantage in capital ships which they had possessed and hoped, by doing nothing rash, to retain, was lost to them for several months to come.

As the weather had prevented a repetition of the attack, Admiral Cunningham set course for Alexandria, where the fleet arrived on 14th November. The same day, at the other end of the Mediterranean, the *Argus* reached Gibraltar with twelve Hurricanes for Malta. The operation of flying them off was intended to be similar to 'Hurry', which had been so successful in August, but the result was very different. Force H, rejoined by the *Renown*, sailed early on 15th November. It was intended that the aircraft should be flown off from a suitable position south of Sardinia, but reports from Malta indicating that a force of one battleship, seven cruisers, and a number of destroyers was concentrating south of Naples decided Admiral Somerville to fly off the Hurricanes as far to the westward as the safe operational range of the aircraft would permit.

In the semi-darkness just before dawn on November 17th the aircraft took off in two flights. Each flight was led by a Skua of the Fleet Air Arm from a position between 30 and 40 miles to the west of those used for operation 'Hurry', making the distance to be flown about 400 sea miles. The *Ark Royal* provided anti-submarine patrols and fighters to cover the fly-off. Arrangements had been made for a Sunderland to meet the first flight five miles north of Galita Island; a Glenn Martin was to meet the second flight in the same position. But although it waited for over an hour at the rendezvous, the Glenn Martin failed to make contact with the second flight, none of whose aircraft reached their destination. Of the first flight two Hurricanes ran out of fuel when within 25 and 34 miles of Malta respectively, the pilot of one being rescued by the Sunderland. Four Hurricanes and one Skua succeeded in reaching Malta, with their petrol tanks almost empty when they landed. The loss of the nine aircraft was ascribed partly to faulty navigation and partly to the fact that, although the distance to be covered was well within the endurance of the aircraft, there was reason to suppose that the flights were not all made at the most economical cruising speed. The net result was that the fighter strength at Malta received only a small increase—a very disappointing result for the lives and effort expended.

The return journey of Force H to Gibraltar partly covered the movement of the cruiser *Newcastle* which had left the Straits at noon on the 17th with airmen and stores for Malta.[1] Enemy minelaying had so delayed her departure from the United Kingdom that she had been prevented from joining the *Argus* as originally intended. After a comparatively uneventful trip the *Newcastle* reached Malta safely on 19th November.


The decision taken in August 1940 to strengthen the forces in the Middle East from the United Kingdom led to the immediate despatch of one small but very important convoy.[2] This marked the beginning of a flow of men, stores, and equipment round the Cape from the United Kingdom in what were known as the 'W.S.' convoys, for which a large number of ocean-going liners were required, as distinct from the smaller or cross-channel ships which had been taken up and adapted for military service in the early stages of the war. Convoys from New Zealand and Australia—the 'U.S.' series— had already been instituted, and have been referred to in connexion with the move of the second and third contingents of troops from those countries.[3] There were also sailings from Bombay of British and Indian troops and of quantities of stores and materials provided by India; this was the 'B.N.' series, which dealt also with the large numbers of men disembarked at Bombay from the 'Monsters', as these ships could not be risked at Aden or in the Red Sea.[4] The strain on British shipping was all the greater because the Red Sea and Gulf of Aden had been declared a 'Combat Zone' by President Roosevelt, and in consequence no American ships were allowed to enter it. A complication in the 'W.S.' series was caused by the need for keeping the fastest ships on the Atlantic portion of the route, where the submarine menace was greatest; this made it necessary to disembark large numbers of men at Cape Town and Durban for onward passage in slower ships. The average time for the whole voyage was six weeks.

Except for the biggest and fastest liners, more than six months usually elapsed between the sailings of a particular ship in these Middle East convoys. This long turn-round not only limited the

---

[1] See page 232.
[2] See page 190.
[3] See page 84.
[4] The 'Monsters' were the *Queen Mary, Queen Elizabeth, Mauretania* and *Aquitania*. They were used between Australia, Malaya, and India until the beginning of 1942.

shipping available for carrying men and stores to the Middle East but it seriously affected imports into the United Kingdom, which by the end of 1940 were falling off very dangerously. Moreover, to avoid sending ships back in ballast after disembarking their military cargoes it was necessary to route them to, say, India or Australia to pick up cargo. Thus the need to supply the Middle East determined to a great extent the areas from which imports to the United Kingdom had to be found and reduced the total amounts imported.

Responsibility for providing and loading the ships rested with the home authorities. Decisions on priorities were made by an inter-Service committee, who referred when necessary to the Chiefs of Staff. Each Service in the Middle East had the chance to give its views on the urgency of the items that were offered for despatch, and the decision between conflicting bids for the available shipping space was often a matter of some difficulty. Apart from this, the technical problems involved in trying to use the ships as economically as possible were considerable. For instance, some of the very varied types of loads could only be taken by certain ships; some could only be handled quickly at certain ports; some had to be accessible for unloading at an intermediate port; some were rated as top priority by the Middle East but could only be stowed for later unloading; some would best be loaded together but were too precious to risk all in one basket. There was no satisfying everybody, but the Middle East had every reason to be grateful to the Movements, Shipping, and Transportation authorities at home and elsewhere for the efficiency with which the intricate and vital convoy problems were handled.

As the threat of invasion of the United Kingdom receded and it became possible to spare more forces and equipment for the Middle East, the W.S. convoys settled down into a regular cycle of one convoy about every six weeks. Some idea of the magnitude of the flow may be gathered from the figures for arrivals in Egypt from the last week of August 1940, to the end of the year. This includes the last convoy to sail before the opening of the British offensive in the Western Desert, the contents of which were therefore known to the Commanders-in-Chief before the fighting began. The figures are given in round numbers and for simplicity are collected into a few broad categories:—

*From the United Kingdom*

In complete British combatant units  .  .  28,000 all ranks

In administrative units (e.g. hospitals; workshops; depots; engineer, supply, ordnance and transportation units; and installations of various kinds)  .  .  .  .  .  .  .  15,500 ,,  ,,

Drafts, details and reinforcements for units of all
kinds (to bring them up to war strength and for
wastage) . . . . . . . 19,300 all ranks

Ditto for the Royal Air Force . . . . 7,500 ,, ,,

Australians . . . . . . . 5,000 ,, ,,

New Zealanders . . . . . . 700 ,, ,,

　　　　　　　Total about . . . 76,000 ,, ,,

### From Bombay and beyond

Australians, in combatant units, drafts and reinforcements . . . . . . 24,500 all ranks

Australians, administrative . . . . 3,500 ,, ,,

New Zealanders, in combatant units, drafts and
reinforcements . . . . . . 4,700 ,, ,,

New Zealanders, administrative . . . 2,600 ,, ,,

Indian troops, in combatant units, drafts and
reinforcements . . . . . . 8,400 ,, ,,

Indian troops, administrative . . . . 3,000 ,, ,,

British troops from India, in units . . . 1,000 ,, ,,

Other British troops (1,000), Royal Navy (700) 1,700 ,, ,,

　　　　　　Total about . . . 49,400 ,, ,,

Grand total nearly 126,000, which represents an average rate of
more than 1,000 men a day over the 17 weeks.

The principal combatant units and formations included in the
above figures were as follows:—

British units from the
United Kingdom　　.　2nd Armoured Division.

　　　　　　One light, one cruiser and one 'I' tank
　　　　　　regiment.

Three field artillery regiments. Two medium artillery regiments. One field survey regiment. One coast defence battery. Eight heavy and eleven light anti-aircraft batteries.

Divisional engineers for 7th Armoured Division. Two field companies. One army troops company.

A large number of signal units.

| | |
|---|---|
| British units from India | Two field artillery regiments. |
| Australian units from Australia . . | Two brigade groups of 7th Australian Division. |
| Australian units from the United Kingdom | One brigade group.[1] |
| New Zealand units from New Zealand . . | One brigade group of the New Zealand Division. |
| Indian units from India | One cavalry regiment. Four battalions.[2] |

*In addition*

From India direct to Port Sudan:

| | |
|---|---|
| British units . . | Two field artillery regiments. |
| Indian units . . | 5th Indian Division. |

From South Africa to Mombasa:

| | |
|---|---|
| South African units . | 1st South African Division. 1st South African Anti-Aircraft Brigade.[3] Two Armoured Car Companies. |

Even bigger than the problem of dealing with all these arrivals was that of receiving and distributing the vast tonnages of unit equipment, wheeled and tracked vehicles of many types, guns, cased aircraft and spares, locomotives, ammunition, bombs, explosives, engineering plant and materials, transportation equipment, and

---

[1] This had been diverted in convoy U.S.3 to the U.K. in May 1940; see page 84.
[2] Enabling 4th Indian Division to be given a third brigade.
[3] Only one battery was armed with A.A. guns (3-inch); the remainder with Lewis guns.

stores and supplies of every kind. In addition to the resulting rail and road moves from the ports there was of course a large volume of internal movement due to changes in the location of troops; from Palestine to Egypt, for instance, and from the Delta to the Western Desert, to say nothing of the assembly and despatch of expeditions for Crete and Greece. The Nile Valley route took a good deal of the traffic involved in the measures to strengthen the Sudan, while the main flow into Kenya was from, or via, South Africa.[1] Outward bound ships, mainly from Suez, were used to remove prisoners of war to India and to take evacuated British families to South Africa. They also carried various import cargoes to the United Kingdom and could sometimes be used for the long internal moves from Egypt to Port Sudan, Aden, Berbera and Mombasa.

The provision of escorts for such a large volume of shipping was a big problem for the Royal Navy. It was at this time the biggest of the problems facing the Commander-in-Chief, East Indies, whose responsibility extended as far north as the port of Suez. The early convoys in July had made the Red Sea passage without interference from Italian surface forces and the only bombing to which they were subjected was from high-level and did no damage. Thereafter the numbers of ships traversing the Red Sea steadily increased: in August there were four convoys in each direction; in September, five; in October, seven, comprising no less than 86 ships northbound and 72 southbound.

During the night of October 20th/21st Italian destroyers made their first and only attack on a convoy. B.N.7, consisting of 32 ships escorted by one cruiser, one destroyer, and five sloops, was about 150 miles to the east of Massawa when four Italian destroyers came in to attack. On being chased by the escort they quickly withdrew. At dawn action was joined, and one of the Italian destroyers, the *Francesco Nullo*, was driven ashore on an island near Massawa, where she was subsequently bombed and destroyed by three Blenheims of No. 45 Squadron. During the action the *Kimberley* came under fire from a shore battery and received a hit in the engine room which made it necessary to tow her to Port Sudan.

This encounter seems to have made the Italian surface forces less inclined than ever to take vigorous action against the stream of shipping that was bearing men and munitions to Egypt for use against their comrades—and this in spite of the fact that they could obtain exact information of every northbound convoy as it passed Jibuti. Their air attacks were few and ineffective. During October there were only six, and after November 4th they ceased altogether.

---

[1] The Palestine Railways and the Egyptian State Railways met at Kantara, on the Suez Canal. The Nile Valley route consisted of the rail link Cairo-Shellal (near Aswan); the stretch of river between Shellal and Wadi Halfa; and thence the Port Sudan and Khartoum branches of the Sudan Railways.

Between June and December the Royal Air Force escorted 54 convoys in the Red Sea, of which only one ship was sunk by air action and one damaged.

But there was no guarantee that the Italian surface forces would not suddenly be stimulated into some form of activity, so that the vigilance of the escorts had to be unceasing. The very monotony, relieved only rarely by moments of excitement, served to accentuate the discomforts of service in His Majesty's ships of the Red Sea Force. So few were the escort vessels for their many and urgent duties that it was a common occurrence for one of them, after a gruelling passage, to be ordered to turn round before reaching port and do the whole trip again. Ships were relentlessly overdriven, and it was a source of pride that the men and engines stood up as they did to the extra strain. The heat and high humidity, coupled with the difficulty of providing a suitable diet, especially fresh fruit and vegetables, led to a high incidence of prickly heat and other skin troubles. Fresh water, too, was limited. Conditions which could be made just tolerable in peace time were greatly aggravated by the need for darkening ship at night and by the constant steaming. Sleep was difficult at the best of times, and men were often called to action stations six or seven times during a night. Sometimes there was no living space in a ship at a temperature of less than 100°F., while in the engine rooms it might be as high as 170°. There were several deaths from heat stroke.

But the flow of shipping went steadily on, and on land the staffs in the Middle East responsible for Movements, Sea Transport, and Transportation were stretched to the utmost in coping with all these problems, partly because they were themselves only in the process of being built up when the big increase over normal traffic began, and partly because they did not possess complete authority over the various agencies, which were in any case not adequately equipped for the task. When the war with Italy began, the only transportation unit in Egypt was the 10th Railway Construction and Operating Company, R.E. The Egyptian State Railways were short of locomotives and rolling stock and, although co-operative, had not the flexibility to meet unusual and rapidly changing traffic problems. Not being under British control they continued to operate the whole of their system themselves, except in some of the depots where, out of the eye of the public, British troops were allowed to work, and on the Western Desert line, which in November was taken over by a New Zealand Operating Group in order to lessen the delays and interruptions due to enemy bombing. This unit, together with a Construction and Maintenance Group, had been offered by the New Zealand Government and their presence at a comparatively early date was invaluable.

It was the docks problem that grew to be the most serious of all.

There were no military docks units of any kind, and there was, unfortunately, no special branch of the Egyptian State Railways to deal with dock running. Every port had its small British contingent to watch the Forces' interests ashore, but the working was entirely in the hands of the civil authorities, who had also the commerce of the country to consider. Transports had either to be discharged by contract or by the Shipping Companies' agents. Lighters were privately owned and had to be hired as needed. Dock labourers could be hired but they could not be enlisted and put under British military discipline, and therefore were not entirely to be depended upon. In addition, the ports were neither laid out nor adequately equipped for dealing with the volume and variety of traffic that was now coming to them, so that the difficulties in securing the rapid unloading and turn-round of ships were very great. In peace time the trade of the country passed mostly through Alexandria—now under intermittent air attack; at Port Said, primarily a tranship-ment port, all cargoes were handled by lighters and the rail clearance facilities were poor; while Suez was hardly developed for general cargo and little used. Nevertheless, these three ports, and also Kantara and Haifa, could all be used for the early convoys, and ships were sometimes unloaded at all five of them simultaneously. Matters would have been improved by the early arrival of some docks units and of more transportation equipment, but these could only be allotted shipping space in the convoys in competition with units and store tonnages of a more combatant nature. Certain measures were, however, already in hand; lighterage wharves were being built at points along the Canal; a railway marshalling yard was under construction at Port Said; the rail facilities and the number of wharf cranes at Alexandria were being increased. But the only way of insuring against the risk of a breakdown due to the bombing of the Canal was by increasing the capacity to berth and clear ships at places accessible without entering the Canal. For this purpose work had begun in August on reconditioning three additional deep-water berths and two lighter jetties at Suez, and by the end of the year they were in use.

It was fortunate indeed that the Germans refrained for as long as they did from sending the *Luftwaffe* to the Mediterranean with the object of making it impossible for the British Fleet to remain there. The attempts which were made later to block the Suez Canal by aerial mining added greatly to the congestion of the port of Suez, which was already becoming a problem of the first importance.

A start had been made in August 1940 with the measures for strengthening the Air Force in the Middle East. The aim was to rearm with modern aircraft three of the four fighter squadrons, five of the twelve medium bomber squadrons, and one of the two bomber transport squadrons. It was hoped to achieve this during August and September, but it was not long before the programme received its first check. On September 5th the heavy losses during the Battle of Britain made it necessary to suspend shipment of Hurricanes indefinitely, while shipping difficulties, the weather, and the shortage of aircrews so retarded the flow of Blenheim IVs that by the end of September the only aircraft that had arrived according to programme were the Wellingtons.

The position then was that one bomber transport squadron (No. 70) had been rearmed with Wellingtons; one fighter squadron (No. 33) with Hurricanes, and one medium bomber squadron (No. 113) with Blenheim IVs. Early in October Sir Arthur Longmore took the opportunity, in a telegram of congratulation to Sir Charles Portal on his appointment as Chief of the Air Staff, to urge him to review the air situation in the Middle East Command as soon as possible. He thought it likely that the Germans would abandon their invasion plans for 1940 and turn their attention to the Middle East, and if the *Luftwaffe* were to support the Italians in a land offensive against Egypt the Air Officer Commanding-in-Chief did not feel that with his present strength he would be able to give the army all the support it would need.

At the same time Mr Eden, the Secretary of State for War and Chairman of the Ministerial Committee on military policy in the Middle East, was expressing the concern of the War Office and of his committee at the general weakness of the air situation throughout the Middle East, especially in view of the likelihood that the Italian Air Force would soon be reinforced by Germans. Fighting might break out at any moment in the Western Desert and the Sudan, and the most important weapons would be tanks, field and anti-aircraft artillery, and aircraft. Steps were being taken to increase our numbers of guns and tanks, and he represented very strongly that fresh efforts should be made to strengthen the air force also. He recalled how great, perhaps even decisive, had been the part played by the German air force against the French army during the Battle of France in May. In the desert, where concealment and cover were so much more difficult to obtain, he believed that dive-bombing attacks would be even more effective.

Although by mid-October the air situation at home could not be regarded with any complacency, the victories in the Battle of Britain combined with the approach of winter had undoubtedly reduced the likelihood of an attempt at invasion. The centre of strategic interest was now recognized to be moving south-eastwards, so that new dangers might soon appear in the Mediterranean and Middle East. The

Chiefs of Staff agreed that the time had come to increase the strength of the air forces in the Middle East as quickly as possible. There were two immediate methods by which this could be done. The first was by speeding up the rearmament of the existing squadrons with modern and more powerful types. The second was by expanding the first line strength of the two heavy and twelve medium bomber squadrons from twelve to sixteen aircraft, thus saving on the overhead establishments and reducing the delays inevitable in sending out complete units. If similar action were taken for the three South African Air Force bomber squadrons in East Africa the total first line strength in the Middle East Command would be increased by 68 bombers, or the equivalent of four squadrons. At the same time the first line strength of both Sunderland flying-boat squadrons would be raised to six.

This, in the opinion of the Air Ministry, represented the practical limit of what could be done immediately. Aircraft were to be despatched as fast as supplies, packing, shipping, and the limitations of air passage permitted; for the time being the aim would be to keep up a steady flow of replacements for aircraft and crews rather than to increase the number of squadrons.

To put these decisions into effect there was to be a monthly quota of 48 Blenheim IVs and 24 Hurricanes. Of the heavy bombers, 23 Wellingtons were to be flown out during October to rearm the second Bombay squadron and to provide a small reserve. The Air Ministry allotted to the Middle East 227 Mohawk fighters from previous French orders in the United States of America and increased from 75 to 149 the allotment of Glenn Martin bombers. A monthly flow was intended to start in October, but for various reasons the first Glenn Martin was not erected at Takoradi until December 12th; it was not until the New Year that any numbers reached the Middle East. The first four Mohawks were landed on December 17th, but a serious engine defect held up further deliveries for some months. In the meantime the performance of the Mohawks had been found to be so inferior to that of the Axis fighters that it was decided to divert them to India and to the South African Air Force for use as advanced training aircraft.

Air Chief Marshal Longmore admitted that these proposals were the quickest and most practical method of strengthening his command, but insisted that he would require three additional fighter squadrons in Egypt to meet a renewed Italian offensive in the Western Desert, which would be strongly supported by Italian—and possibly also by German—air action. By expanding the existing fighter units at Aden and in the Sudan he could produce only one additional squadron available for the Western Desert and he therefore pressed strongly for the formation of the two new ones. To this the Air Ministry agreed, and promised to increase the flow of aircraft, men, equipment, and transport accordingly, in addition to the other measures of expansion already approved.

The taking of a decision in London, however, was a very different matter from producing an aircraft in the Middle East, ready to operate, whether it went by sea round the Cape, or to Takoradi, or by air via Malta. The interval of time extended to many weeks, being dependent upon such factors as the available shipping space, the length of the voyage, the capacity of Takoradi, the extent of interference by the enemy, and the weather; thus, although the prospect of building up a stronger air force appeared much brighter, the new programme had not had any appreciable effect upon the trickle of arrivals before it became necessary to send squadrons to Greece. Towards the end of November a fresh anxiety arose. It was still possible that Graziani intended to renew his advance into Egypt, but it was hoped that the intended British operation in the Western Desert would forestall him. Great importance was attached by the Prime Minister to the launching of this operation ('Compass') early in December. The question was whether there would be sufficient air support for the army and, in particular, whether there would be enough fighters. In view of the estimated arrival in Egypt in the first week of December of 34 Hurricanes and pilots, to be landed at Takoradi from the *Furious*, General Wavell decided that he would go ahead with his plans.

Operation 'Compass' began on December 9th and is described in the next chapter. Casualties to aircraft were relatively light, but the rate of unserviceability was very high, due to the intensity of the air operations, to the climatic conditions in the desert, and to the enemy's use of explosive bullets. For example, during an attack on Bardia on December 14th, nine Blenheims of No. 55 Squadron encountered a patrol of some 50 enemy fighters and, although only one aircraft was lost, no less than seven were severely damaged by these explosive bullets. Meanwhile in Greece there were steady losses of both Gladiators and Blenheims, which the Air Officer Commanding-in-Chief was finding difficulty in replacing from his dwindling reserves in Egypt. It was obvious that, unless the flow of replacement aircraft was increased, it would be impossible to keep pace with the needs of rearmament, the offensive in Libya, the operations in Greece, and the forthcoming operations in the Sudan.

The situation had in fact been appreciated in London, and on December 17th Longmore was told that the *Furious* would sail yet again for Takoradi with forty Hurricanes and pilots, arriving there early in January. Everything possible was being done to hasten the despatch of aircraft so as to complete the present programme by the end of March 1941. But even if this was achieved it was impossible to say, so far ahead, when any further expansion would begin. But as a preliminary step about 1,200 airmen were to be sent out to the Middle East by sea, so that squadrons could be flown out as reinforcements at short notice and find on arrival a nucleus of maintenance staff.

A great deal of attention was naturally directed at about this time to Takoradi, the focal point on the West African reinforcement route. It was obviously of prime importance that the flow of aircraft through this Station should be as smooth and rapid as possible, and some doubts were felt about its capacity to deal with the increasing numbers. As it happened, Air Marshal A. W. Tedder arrived at Takoradi on December 2nd on his way to Cairo to take up the recently created appointment of Deputy Air Officer Commanding-in-Chief.[1] He was able to report that he was very much impressed by Air Commodore Thorold's 'first class improvisation'—from the devices for off-loading and erecting the crated aircraft to the accommodation for the airmen. There was evident determination to overcome difficulties and to send aircraft on their way along the route as quickly as possible.

By the end of the year the following aircraft had arrived in the Middle East (exclusive of Malta) since the beginning of September: 41 Wellingtons, 87 Hurricanes, and 85 Blenheim IVs. The heavy bomber situation was better than that of the medium bombers or fighters, whose rearmament had been greatly delayed by casualties and wastage. One squadron had been rearmed with Wellingtons, and, in addition, two complete squadrons had arrived in Egypt and one in Malta, all from England. Two fighter squadrons had been rearmed with Hurricanes, one new squadron had arrived from home and one had formed at Malta. Of the medium bombers three squadrons had been rearmed with Blenheim IVs, and there were nineteen aircraft in reserve, of which only six were serviceable. The two remaining Wellesley squadrons in the Sudan had been reduced to ten aircraft each and their reserves were exhausted. The seven Blenheim I squadrons were still armed with aircraft received before September 1939; reserves amounted to 26, of which all except two were undergoing overhaul. Far from being able to increase the first line strength of the Blenheim squadrons to sixteen, it had become difficult to maintain it at twelve.

It was not surprising, therefore, that Air Chief Marshal Longmore viewed the new year with some misgiving. The operations in Libya

---

[1] Air Marshal O. T. Boyd had been first selected for this appointment but in flying out from the United Kingdom had been forced to land in Sicily where he was made a prisoner of war.

Air Marshal Tedder had served in the Middle East (including Turkey) during 1920 to 1923 and after holding various commands and staff appointments at home became Air Officer Commanding, Far East in 1936. In 1940 he was Director General of Research and Development at the Air Ministry.

could be expected to continue on a major scale, and those in the Sudan were shortly to begin. Five of his squadrons were already in Greece, and there were signs that the Greeks would soon be pressing for more air support. Over and above these commitments he had been told that it would be his responsibility to rearm, train, and maintain the Greek Air Force.

Nor was this all, for with the possibility in mind that the main sphere of activity might move from Africa to the Balkans the Chiefs of Staff had warned the Air Officer Commanding-in-Chief to be ready for an extension of his operations in Greece and possibly in Turkey by the spring of 1941. Sufficient airfields would have to be built to enable him to operate a total force of ten fighter, ten medium bomber, and three heavy bomber squadrons in Turkey and Greece by April. The Chiefs of Staff had been tentatively considering sending him from home during the winter six fighter and six medium bomber squadrons in addition to the foregoing reinforcement programme. In the first week of January, however, he was told that circumstances at home made it unlikely that these squadrons would be sent and he must therefore make his plans to suit the forces he already had. Even this involved a large and immediate increase in the programme of airfield construction, with all the telecommunications, technical buildings, approach roads, and other necessary services. In Turkey, where construction work on airfields had been in progress during the past year, it had been beyond the capacity of the Turkish Government to undertake the whole work themselves. The same was certainly true of the Greek Government, for whom substantial aid with money and equipment would have to be provided—the latter from the already strained resources of the Middle East.

To make matters worse a political difficulty now arose. The Greek Government were prepared to allow the Air Force to survey possible airfield sites to the south of a line from Mount Olympus to the Gulf of Arta, but they were most reluctant to allow any reconnaissance farther north. The President of the Council was determined to avoid any action that might make the Germans think that the British were being given facilities for bombing the Rumanian oilfields. This attitude was perfectly understandable, but the truth is that as early as November 4th Hitler had decided that the reported British occupation of Lemnos constituted a threat to the Rumanian oilfields and a week later he had ordered preparations to be made for the occupation of northern Greece by German forces. It was obvious that if the Germans intended to attack Greece one of their earliest objectives would be Salonika; it was within easy reach by air from Bulgaria and, unless the necessary airfield sites were examined and work on them begun, it would be impossible for fighters to operate in its defence. An additional and even more urgent reason for developing airfields in northern Greece was that from here the distance to Durazzo and Valona, the base ports of the Italian forces in Albania, was shorter than from the airfields which the Royal Air Force was then using. Moreover, the northern route would avoid the worst of the mountains between Albania and Greece, an important consideration in view of the appalling flying conditions over these mountains in winter. It was emphasized that time was short and that the measure of assistance that the Greeks could expect would depend to a great extent on airfield facilities; but the Greek Government remained obdurate and refused to permit any squadrons to be based near Salonika. They allowed some very limited reconnaissance to be done, and there, for the time being, the matter rested.

As regards Turkey, the War Cabinet remained firmly determined to do everything possible to encourage her to resist aggression. War material was already being supplied to her, and there was still every intention of giving her active support if she found herself at war. The extent of this support, when the time came, would naturally depend upon the situation in the war against Italy and the progress made with the creation of a strategic reserve of land and air forces. Already the situation was very different from what it had been at the time of the conversations at Beirut in May, and the Turks agreed that the time had come to reopen discussions between the staffs. On 22nd December the Commanders-in-Chief were instructed accordingly; they were to use as their representatives the members of the British mission then in Cairo. The discussions were to cover the different circumstances in which Turkey might enter the war; Turkish plans to meet such situations; the extent of British support, particularly in the air, and the preparatory arrangements to be made to receive it; and the combined action necessary to secure communications through Syria. The Commanders-in-Chief were warned not to promise any support beyond what they could provide from their own resources. They were to impress upon the Turks that help could only be effective if it arrived quickly; to ensure this the preparations must be made well in advance. Existing airfields must be improved and new ones made; road, rail and port facilities must be developed, and fuel and munitions must be stocked at suitable points. On January 15th the talks began at Ankara.

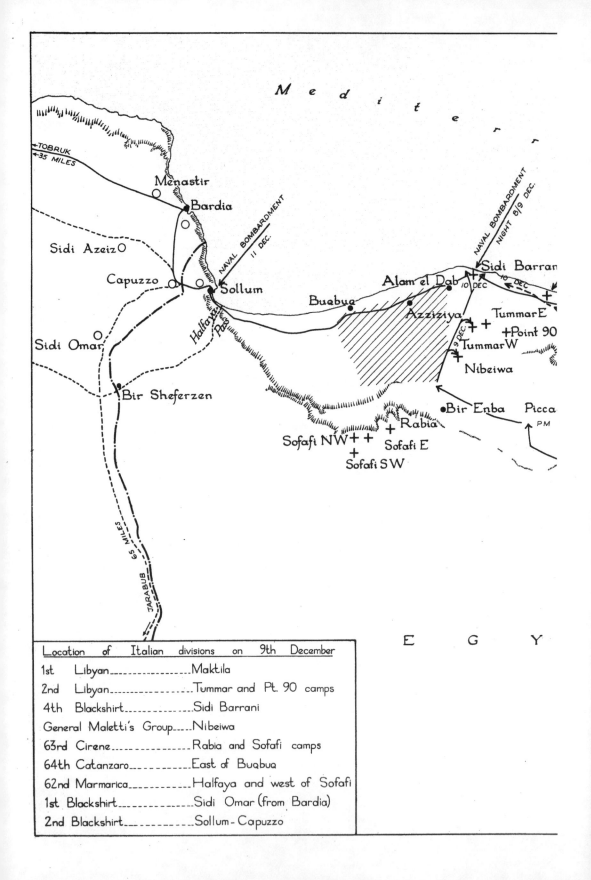

*M e d i t e r r . . .*

←TOBRUK
←35 MILES

Menastir

Bardia

NAVAL BOMBARDMENT 11 DEC.

NAVAL BOMBARDMENT NIGHT 8/9 DEC.

Sidi Azeiz

Capuzzo

Sollum

Buqbua

Alam el Dab    10 DEC    Sidi Barran

10 DEC

Azziziya

Tummar E

Halfaya Pass

Point 90

9 DEC    Tummar W

Nibeiwa

Sidi Omar

Bir Sheferzen

Bir Enba    Picca

PM

Rabia

Sofafi NW    Sofafi E

Sofafi SW

65 MILES

JARABUB

E    G    Y

Location of Italian divisions on 9th December

| | |
|---|---|
| 1st Libyan | Maktila |
| 2nd Libyan | Tummar and Pt. 90 camps |
| 4th Blackshirt | Sidi Barrani |
| General Maletti's Group | Nibeiwa |
| 63rd Cirene | Rabia and Sofafi camps |
| 64th Catanzaro | East of Buqbua |
| 62nd Marmarica | Halfaya and west of Sofafi |
| 1st Blackshirt | Sidi Omar (from Bardia) |
| 2nd Blackshirt | Sollum - Capuzzo |

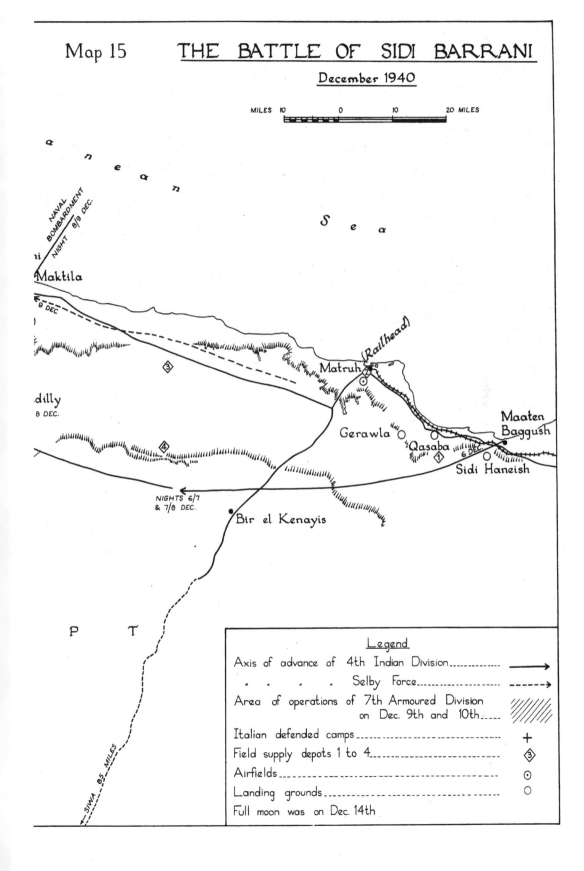

Map 15    THE BATTLE OF SIDI BARRANI

December 1940

MILES 10        0        10        20 MILES

Maktila

Matruh (Railhead)

Maaten Baggush

dilly
8 DEC.

Gerawla

Qasaba

Sidi Haneish

NIGHTS 6/7
& 7/8 DEC.

Bir el Kenayis

NAVAL BOMBARDMENT
NIGHT 8/9 DEC.

9 DEC

6 DEC.

S e a

P T

SIWA 85 MILES

Legend

Axis of advance of 4th Indian Division.............. ⟶

"    "    "    "   Selby Force..................... ⤏

Area of operations of 7th Armoured Division
on Dec. 9th and 10th......

Italian defended camps.............................. +

Field supply depots 1 to 4......................... ◈

Airfields.............................................. ⊙

Landing grounds.................................... ○

Full moon was on Dec. 14th

# CHAPTER XIV

## THE FIRST BRITISH OFFENSIVE
## IN THE WESTERN DESERT—I

*See Map* 15

FROM THE moment of entering the war the Italians had frequent occasion to represent to the Germans that they lacked many kinds of up-to-date equipment. The Germans do not seem to have made any very great efforts to meet their needs; they preferred that German equipment should be used by Germans. If help was to be given to the Italians it had better be in the form of German units. It was accordingly suggested by Hitler in July that German long-range bombers might attack the Suez Canal from Rhodes. He did not press the point and nothing came of it, but when it became necessary to look for alternatives to the invasion of England the German staffs began to consider the use of their forces in the Eastern Mediterranean. The Army proposed that a corps of one motorized and two armoured divisions might be sent to strengthen the poorly equipped Italians in Libya, an idea which the Navy supported strongly because they regarded the Suez Canal as a most important objective which the Italians alone would be very unlikely to capture. Hitler gave his approval in principle, and General von Thoma was sent to Cyrenaica to study the problem. Meanwhile, the 3rd Panzer Division was ordered to prepare itself for North Africa. On October 4th the Dictators met on the Brenner and Hitler made his offer of mechanized and specialist troops, which Mussolini received without enthusiasm. They were not wanted, at any rate for the next phase— the capture of Matruh. But for the third phase—the advance to Alexandria—he admitted that he might need heavy tanks, armoured cars, and dive-bombers.

There the matter rested until von Thoma made his report. He had found the situation thoroughly unsatisfactory. Libya was a most unpromising theatre and the supply problem was very difficult. To add German troops in the present circumstances would only make things worse. He recommended that none should be sent until the port of Matruh was firmly in Italian hands. Hitler agreed with this in the main, though he did not give up the idea of sending long-range bombers to attack the Canal. The 3rd Panzer Division thereupon

T                                   257

ceased its preparations, and was placed in reserve for the intended operation '*Felix*' against Gibraltar.[1]

Marshal Graziani was thus thrown back upon Italian resources, and, in fact, largely upon his own. He lost no opportunity of pointing out that although work on the water supply and on the road from Sollum to Sidi Barrani had made good progress, his resources were quite inadequate for an immediate advance upon Matruh. A great deal of forward stocking would be necessary, which had been impossible for want of a good road, and he had not enough transport to carry his troops across a very wide no-man's-land and at the same time supply them at an ever increasing distance from the depots. The British, on the other hand, would be fighting within a reasonable range of their railhead; unlike him they did not have to rely upon one long incomplete road. What was more, their armoured division was by now refitted and rested, and he had not the means of dealing with it. The reply to all this was that his demands could not possibly be met, and on 5th November he was told that the principal Italian front was now in Albania, and that he ought to be helping by attacking the British so as to prevent the transfer of forces to Greece. Nothing immediately came of this but the impression was gained in Rome that Graziani would attempt a forward move about the middle of December.

All this time the British intelligence staffs were finding some difficulty in assessing the state of Italian readiness to resume the advance, though on the whole the administrative preparations seemed to be fairly complete. During the latter half of October the Italian papers and radio made frequent references to the imminence of great news from Egypt, but still nothing happened. Then came the attack on Greece, and Graziani made no move—not even as a diversion. By the middle of November it seemed that he must be ready to advance, but that considerations of high policy and perhaps the course of events in Greece would decide the moment.

But General Wavell did not intend to leave the initiative with the Italians a day longer than necessary. As far back as 11th September, when their first move across the Egyptian frontier was being awaited hourly, he had initiated a study of the whole problem of advancing into Cyrenaica, with particular attention to methods of supply. At this time his orders to the Western Desert Force were to conserve its strength in the opening stages of an Italian advance, but to counterattack if the enemy extended himself so far as to try to reach the Matruh area. This counter-attack was carefully prepared, and General O'Connor had every confidence in its outcome. So had General Wavell, who had formed a very low opinion of the Italians' tactical skill and capacity to manoeuvre, and of the performance and

---

[1] See page 240.

handling of their light and medium tanks. Within a few days of the withdrawal from Sidi Barrani he gave orders that if the Italians now attempted to capture Matruh they were to be struck an extremely heavy blow which was to aim at nothing less than the complete destruction of their force. With this aim in view the bulk of the Western Desert Force was disposed in the Matruh area, while the Support Group of the 7th Armoured Division maintained contact with the enemy. The 11th Hussars carried out their familiar task of far-ranging reconnaissance, and in October received a welcome reinforcement. This was No. 2 Armoured Car Company R.A.F. from Palestine which, as D Squadron, was to work with the regiment for the next four months.

A month passed, and General Wavell judged that it was no longer necessary to await the enemy's next move before attacking him. He thought it would be within the capacity of the Western Desert Force to make a long approach march and attack one or more of the enemy's widely separated fortified camps which stretched from Maktila (east of Sidi Barrani) on the coast to Sofafi, 50 miles away to the south-west. The difficulties of supply would be great, but it ought to be possible to stage an operation lasting four or five days by making full use of the capacity of the British and Indian troops to endure hardship, manoeuvre by night, and live on short rations of food and water for a period. He was firmly convinced of their superiority over the enemy in everything but numbers, and this applied equally to the Air Force. He accordingly ordered General Wilson to make proposals for a short swift attack, after which the bulk of the forces would be withdrawn to railhead, and only covering troops left forward. The attack might perhaps be made simultaneously in the Sidi Barrani and Sofafi areas; and from the latter a force might strike north towards Buq Buq. The troops available would be 7th Armoured Division, 4th Indian Division, the Matruh garrison and the newly arrived 7th Royal Tank Regiment, equipped with heavy 'I' (Matilda) tanks.[1] Nobody was to be told of the intention as yet except General Wilson's chief staff officer; Lieutenant-General O'Connor, commanding the Western Desert Force, and Major-General O'Moore Creagh, commanding the 7th Armoured Division.

General O'Connor had already been thinking on these lines but had come to the conclusion that to attack the strongly held Sofafi group of camps simultaneously with the coastal group would involve too great a dispersion of the available forces. He proposed instead to attack first the centre group of camps, leaving those on the extreme flanks to be watched and dealt with later. The important supply

---

[1] 4th Indian Division consisted of 5th and 11th Indian Infantry Brigades and 16th (British) Infantry Brigade; 7th Indian Infantry Brigade was employed on the L. of C. For the despatch of 7th R.T.R. from England see page 190n.

and water centre of Buq Buq would be a profitable objective for raids; and when the enemy's administrative arrangements were thoroughly dislocated would be the moment to encircle Sofafi. This plan meant that the main attacking force must pass through the gap, fifteen miles wide, which existed between Nibeiwa and Rabia; from now on it would be necessary to ensure that this gap was kept open.

General Wavell agreed with General O'Connor's plan, and on 2nd November ordered the senior commanders of the Western Desert Force to be informed of it, and of his own views on the feasibility and importance of the operation. By a bold stroke the Western Desert Force was to be thrust into the heart of the enemy's position. There was a risk of discovery and heavy loss from air attack. In any case there would be much hardship and there might be heavy casualties. Great exertions would be called for, but this could be done with confidence: our troops were better trained and better equipped—especially the artillery with the new 25-pdrs; they were familiar with the ground and were better able than the enemy to adapt themselves to desert conditions. Self-confidence, *esprit de corps*, and a worthy cause were powerful assets. In short, quantity was going to be challenged by quality. There was no better way of helping the gallant Greeks than by inflicting a heavy defeat on the Italians in the desert and he was confident that it could be done. The operation, to be called 'Compass', would begin in the moonlit period at the end of November. The keynote was to be surprise, achieved by secrecy and deception.

For some days the plan looked like being wrecked by the need to despatch British forces to Greece and Crete, which entailed a serious reduction in the available numbers of fighter aircraft and the removal from the Western Desert of anti-aircraft guns, engineers, and transport, all of which were wanted for the operation. It has already been mentioned that the Secretary of State for War, Mr. Eden, was at the time on a visit to the Middle East:[1] he was informed of the 'Compass' plan and promised to do his utmost to hasten the arrival of the air reinforcements on which, in General Wavell's view, the success of the plan largely depended. This led the Prime Minister to assure General Wavell that unremitting efforts would be made to this end, and that, although the timing of 'Compass' would have to be considered in relation to the strength of the Air Force, General Wavell could count upon the full support of the Government in any well-considered resolute operation, whatever its outcome might be.

General O'Connor planned his operation in three phases. First, the 4th Indian Division and 7th R.T.R. would pass through the

---

[1] See page 230.

Nibeiwa—Rabia gap, wheel northwards, and attack in turn the camps Nibeiwa, Tummar East, and Point 90; in each case from the west —or rearward—side. The 7th Armoured Division would protect these operations from interference by any enemy from the direction of Buq Buq or Sofafi. Meanwhile, troops from the Matruh garrison were to pin down the enemy in Maktila camp, and ships of the Royal Navy would bombard Maktila and Sidi Barrani. The second phase was to be a move by the Indian Division northwards towards Sidi Barrani: meanwhile, the Armoured Division was to disrupt communications and generally play havoc in the direction of Buq Buq. Thirdly, if all had gone well, the Armoured Division might be ordered either to exploit in strength north-westwards or southwards towards Sofafi. The Navy would bombard coastal communications as far back as Sollum.

The plan for the Royal Air Force was broadly to intensify the activities which had, in varying degree, been continuous throughout October and November. During these two months frequent attacks had been made on the ports of Benghazi, Derna, Tobruk, and Bardia; on dumps, barracks, and airfields; and on coastal shipping between Derna and Sollum; the whole forming a sustained attempt to interfere with the enemy's preparations for renewing his advance and to wear down his numerical superiority in the air. Just before the beginning of 'Compass' the enemy airfields were to be systematically bombed from both Malta and Egypt. Offensive patrols would, as far as possible, protect the approach march and assembly of the attacking troops from discovery and interference by the Italian Air Force. The Air Force would then continue its programme of attacks on airfields, ports, supply depots, transport and troop concentrations.

It was an open question whether the Air Force would be able to carry out this programme in sufficient strength, and when it became necessary for the Air Officer Commanding-in-Chief to send squadrons to Greece he was very much afraid that the weakening of his force would spoil the chances of success of operation 'Compass' and, at the worst, prevent it from being launched at all. It seemed to him that every aircraft that could possibly be made available for Egypt would be needed if the Army was not to suffer severely from the Italian Air Force. He was not at all content with the state of the plan for reinforcements of aircraft, and on 21st November took the drastic step of summoning Nos. 11 and 39 Squadrons (Blenheim I) from Aden and No. 45 Squadron (Blenheim I) from the Sudan. K Flight was also moved from the Sudan to Egypt to form a slender battle reserve of Gladiator aircraft. This involved the acceptance of risks in the Red Sea area, but the other two Commanders-in-Chief agreed with him that it should be done. A further risk was taken in denuding Alexandria almost entirely of its fighter defence by moving No. 274

Squadron (Hurricane) to the Western Desert. No. 73 Squadron (Hurricane), just arrived from England, moved to Dekheila near Alexandria on 12th December, but for the previous five days the fighter defence of the naval base consisted of two Sea Gladiators of the Fleet Air Arm.

By these means the following air forces were assembled for operation 'Compass': two squadrons of Hurricanes, one of Gladiators, three of Blenheims, three of Wellingtons and one of Bombays; a total of 48 fighters and 116 bombers, all under the operational control of Air Commodore Collishaw, commanding No. 202 Group, with headquarters at Maaten Baggush.[1] In addition there was an Army/Air Component, controlled directly by General O'Connor through a senior air liaison officer at Headquarters Western Desert Force, consisting of two squadrons and one flight of mixed fighter and reconnaissance aircraft; its employment will be referred to again presently.

The problem of maintaining the attacking forces was complicated by the great distance separating them from the Italian fortified camps which were to be the first objectives. In order to achieve surprise this distance would have to be covered quickly; thereafter the force would have to be kept supplied with its essential needs for a battle to be fought at anything up to 100 miles from the present rail-head depots. It was necessary to reduce this distance somehow, because there was not enough transport to lift the attacking troops forward (and perhaps back again) and also keep up the daily maintenance of the whole force. During the preparatory period, therefore, two forward dumps or Field Supply Depots (Nos. 3 and 4) were established some forty miles to the west of Matruh, about fourteen miles apart—one each for the 4th Indian and 7th Armoured Divisions. Great pains were taken to conceal these depots and to avoid drawing attention to them in any way. They had to be specially guarded, as there was only a thin screen of troops between them and the enemy; the risk of discovery, and disclosure of British intentions, and perhaps of loss, had to be accepted. The stocking of the depots could not be done in addition to the daily maintenance work of the whole Western Desert Force without moving forward the railheads for 7th Armoured and 4th Indian Divisions; these were accordingly reopened at points nearer to Matruh, whence they had been withdrawn for better security during the period of waiting for the Italians to resume their advance.

The Field Supply Depots were stocked with five days' hard scale rations and a corresponding sufficiency of petrol and ammunition,

---

[1] Hurricanes: Nos. 33 and 274 Squadrons. Gladiators: No. 112. Blenheims: Nos. 45, 55 and 113, with detachments from Nos. 11 and 39. Wellingtons: Nos. 37, 38 and 70. Bombays: No. 216.

together with two days' supply of water at half a gallon for every man and one gallon for every radiator daily. Stocking of the depots began on 11th November and was completed by 4th December; the three M.T. companies engaged (of nearly 300 lorries in all) were then ready to lift troops of 4th Indian Division. From now onwards there was no transport at all with which to replenish the depots with anything except water, which was carried by water-tank lorries from a specially provided store. This was not ready until 7th December, the day on which the forward moves were to begin.

All these arrangements were of course not ends in themselves, though they were an essential means of giving the attack the best possible chance of success. Much thought was given to the tactics of the assault, because failure at Nibeiwa would wreck the whole plan. Valuable experience of desert fighting had been gained in the past few months, but there had been no attack on a strongly held perimeter camp, protected partly or wholly by an anti-tank ditch, mines, and barbed wire; nor had 'I' tanks yet been used in the desert. These were to be the main assaulting arm, and the line of approach and points of entry would be chosen in every case to suit them. To achieve surprise they would have to make their final approach at speed. Techniques were devised for exploding and lifting the mines and for crossing the ditches. The task of the artillery and close-support aircraft would be to demoralize the defenders and cover the approach of the tanks. Bren carriers, machine-guns and mortars would support the rifle companies whose task would be to deal with minor centres of resistance after the tanks had broken in, and generally to mop up. All this required very careful co-ordination and a high degree of tactical training, as well as a thorough mastery of dispersed movement.

To try out these methods a training exercise was held on 25th and 26th November near Matruh. Only a few officers knew that the objectives marked out on the ground were replicas of the Nibeiwa and Tummar camps. The exercise was in fact a rehearsal; as such it was of great value and led to many improvements. To the troops it was represented as merely an exercise on the attack of enemy camps in the desert; on its completion they were told that a further exercise would be held. Meanwhile, the administrative preparations —which could not pass unnoticed—were explained as precautionary measures to meet the expected Italian advance. Such deceptions were highly necessary in a spy and gossip ridden country like Egypt. But rumour has its uses, and back in the Delta it was not difficult to put about stories that routine reliefs were taking place in the desert and that the British forces were being weakened, and would be weakened still further, to provide reinforcements for Greece.

There were some novel features in the air preparations also. The

Army/Air Component adopted, for the first time, a mixed organiz-ation, with fighter and reconnaissance aircraft in the same squadron.[1] Experience in France and the Western Desert had shown that the Lysander, which was intended for army co-operation duties, was too vulnerable to carry out missions of tactical or artillery reconnaissance without fighter protection. It had been proved that co-operation with mobile forces could be undertaken with more economy and certainty by fighter aircraft, especially if the pilots had been trained in army co-operation duties. In the present case it was thought that troops in the attack might need close fighter protection from hostile aircraft and that this task and that of making low-flying attacks on a retreating enemy could most efficiently and quickly be carried out by aircraft under the direct control of the army commander. There were not enough fighters in the Middle East to replace all the Lysanders in the Army/Air Component, but the inclusion of a few made it possible for reconnaissances to be carried out by fighters and for escorts to be provided for the Lysanders when the need arose. This was the first practical application in the Middle East of the idea of Tactical Air Forces which were later to develop so greatly.

All through the preparatory period the Support Group of 7th Armoured Division was keeping up its aggressive inquisitiveness. Hardly a day or night passed in October and November without some part of the enemy's defences being visited. From time to time there were encounters between patrols or mobile columns, never far from the enemy's camps and often in the Nibeiwa-Rabia gap itself, culminating in an engagement on 19th November between the Left Column of the Support Group and a force of Italian tanks and lorry-borne infantry which emerged from Nibeiwa. Another force came out from Rabia but turned back. Five of the enemy's medium tanks were destroyed and others damaged; eleven prisoners were taken and about 100 casualties inflicted. Thereafter the Italians were even less enterprising. The British losses were three killed and two wounded, all by air action. Reconnaissance elements of 4th Indian Division were gradually introduced, under the pretext of preparing to relieve the Support Group. From all these activities, and from air photo-graphs, many of which were taken in the face of heavy fighter opposition, a fairly accurate impression was gained of the enemy's dispositions. Most important of all, the Nibeiwa-Rabia gap was kept open.

In spite of the fact that it had been necessary for administrative reasons to plan an operation lasting only five days, General Wavell had no intention of giving the Italians any respite if they showed signs of 'cracking'. In an instruction of 28th November he expressed to

---

[1] No. 208 Squadron (8 Lysanders and 4 Hurricanes); No. 3 R.A.A.F. Squadron (8 Gladiators and 4 Gauntlets); one flight of No. 6 Squadron (4 Lysanders).

General Wilson his belief that an opportunity might occur for converting the enemy's defeat into an outstanding victory. Events in Albania had shown that Italian morale after a reverse was unlikely to be high. Every possible preparation was therefore to be made to take advantage of preliminary success and to support a possible pursuit right up to the Egyptian frontier. 'I do not entertain extravagant hopes of this operation,' he wrote, 'but I do wish to make certain that if a big opportunity occurs we are prepared morally, mentally, and administratively, to use it to the fullest'.

On 2nd December General Wavell told Generals Platt and Cunningham, who had been summoned to Cairo from the Sudan and Kenya, what was about to happen. There had been a conference on future operations against Italian East Africa, the details of which are considered in Chapter XXI. One of the decisions was that in the Sudan General Platt was to further the policy of helping the Patriot movement by maintaining pressure about Gallabat, where access could best be gained to the rebel area. He was also to make plans for attacking at Kassala with the object of securing the eastern loop of the Sudan railway and gaining a gateway into Eritrea. He was to assume that as soon as the 4th Indian Division had completed its task in the Western Desert, which would be about the middle of December, it would begin to move to the Sudan and come under his orders. The 6th Australian Division would join the Western Desert Force; one brigade group by the middle of the month, the whole division by the end.

On 5th December General Wilson sent his first and only written instruction about 'Compass' to General O'Connor, who in turn issued his formal orders next day. (It could truly be said that there was the maximum of preparation and the minimum of paper.) The concentration began on December 6th with the move of 4th Indian Division from Maaten Baggush to Bir Kenayis, forty miles out from Matruh along the Siwa track. On December 7th the troops were told that this was not a second training exercise; it was the real thing. The assault would take place early on December 9th.

The information which the British had gathered about the Italian dispositions was on the whole accurate; but the picture was confused by the fact that at the end of November the enemy not only increased his strength in the forward area but also began to carry out reliefs. Actually, by 8th December the 1st and 2nd Libyan Divisions and 4th Blackshirt Division were in the Maktila, Tummar and Sidi Barrani camps; a strong mixed group under General Maletti was in Nibeiwa; 63rd Cirene Division in Rabia and Sofafi; 62nd Marmarica Division on the escarpment between Sofafi and Halfaya; while

64th Catanzaro Division had been moved up to an area east of Buq Buq, right opposite and behind the Nibeiwa—Rabia gap. Thus about seven comparatively weak enemy divisions east of the Egyptian frontier were to be attacked by one strong division and one armoured division.

The strength of the Italian air force in Libya was estimated at about 250 bombers and 250 fighters, which, it was always thought, could be supplemented from Italy at short notice. The actual numbers on December 9th were 140 bombers and 191 fighters and ground attack aircraft. Some of the bombers were based at Castel Benito near Tripoli; the others were grouped around Benghazi and Tmimi. Fighters and reconnaissance aircraft used the Tobruk, El Adem, and Gambut airfields. In order to cover the forward move of Western Desert Force the Royal Air Force had to aim at gaining temporarily complete air superiority, and the offensive against air-fields was begun on December 7th with the attack on Castel Benito by eleven Wellingtons from Malta. Twenty-nine Italian aircraft were destroyed or damaged on the ground.[1] Throughout December 8th three squadrons maintained offensive fighter patrols over the British concentration areas. That night twenty-nine Wellington and Blenheim IV bombers heavily attacked Benina, near Benghazi, and destroyed or damaged a further ten Italian aircraft; Bombays bom-barded the area of the defended camps; and Blenheims attacked the forward airfields.

On land the preliminary moves went smoothly. In the coastal sector a mixed force under Brigadier A. R. Selby made up of units and detachments from the garrison of Matruh, about 1,800 strong— the most for which transport could be provided—had moved out from Matruh with the task of preventing the occupants of Maktila from giving any help to the Tummar camps. Having stationed a brigade of dummy tanks at a harmless part of the desert to act as a decoy to the Italian Air Force, Selby Force moved into position before daybreak on 9th December a few miles to the south and east of Maktila. Maktila itself was heavily bombarded for an hour and a half in the middle of the night by the monitor *Terror* (twin 15-inch and eight 4-inch guns) and the gunboat *Aphis,* helped by flares and spotting from a Swordfish of the Fleet Air Arm. At the same time the gunboat *Ladybird* bombarded Sidi Barrani.

The camp at Nibeiwa, a rough rectangle of a mile by a mile and a half, had a perimeter wall all round, protected by a tank obstacle of a bank and ditch. It was known that mines had been laid on parts of the front, but in the north-west corner there was an entrance habitually used by the supply lorries where there might well be no minefield. A special patrol of 2nd Rifle Brigade verified this point

---

[1] Santoro: *L'Aeronautica Italiana nella II<sup>a</sup> Guerra Mondiale,* p. 396.

on the night of December 7th/8th, and it was finally decided that this was where the assault would be made. On this decision depended the selection of the final rendezvous, a point six and a half miles south-west of Nibeiwa.

The 4th Indian Division (Major-General N. M. de la P. Beresford-Peirse) halted, well dispersed, for 36 hours in the Bir Kenayis area. On December 8th it made a long move by day of over sixty miles to a rendezvous only fifteen miles from Nibeiwa. The sky was clear at first but there was a ground haze; as the day wore on it became overcast, and the visibility grew less. Everything possible was done to reduce the dust but there was of course a considerable risk of discovery. As it was, only one Italian aircraft was seen, at about mid-day, but nothing occurred to suggest that it had observed anything unusual. At dusk the force which was to capture Nibeiwa—the 11th Indian Infantry Brigade Group (Brigadier R. A. Savory) with 7th R.T.R. (Lieutenant-Colonel R. M. Jerram) under command—was again on the move and covered the thirteen miles to the final rendezvous in darkness. Farther to the south-west the 7th Armoured Division (Brigadier J. A. L. Caunter in temporary command) was assembled, with the 4th Armoured Brigade (Colonel H. L. Birks in temporary command) leading, in preparation for its task of preventing interference with the 4th Indian Division next day by any enemy from the direction of Azziziya or Sofafi. The precision with which these difficult and important night marches were done reflected great credit on the staff and troops, and was largely responsible for the subsequent success.

The night was bitterly cold. At first the Italians in Nibeiwa were alert, firing and sending up flares. This lasted until midnight, and shortly before 5 a.m. they were roused again by a diversion created by a detachment who fired into Nibeiwa from the east and generally attracted attention to that quarter. By 6 a.m. this excitement also had died down. By 7 a.m. the 4th Divisional Artillery had come into action to the south-east of the camp and although hampered by the haze began to register targets. At 7.15 a.m. 72 guns opened with concentrations on selected targets and at that moment two squadrons of 7th R.T.R. supported by 31st Field Battery R.A. bore down upon the north-west corner of the perimeter. On the flanks of the 'I' tanks were the Bren carrier platoons of 2nd Battalion The Queen's Own Cameron Highlanders and 1/6th Rajputana Rifles, firing as they advanced.

Outside the camp were about twenty medium and a few light Italian tanks, unready for action; these were quickly overrun. Not until the 'I' tanks entered the camp were they opposed or obstructed at all; but immediately afterwards the Italians opened artillery and machine-gun fire, and a few gallant but useless attempts were made to check the 'I' tanks with grenades. At 7.45 a.m. the Cameron Highlanders, who had moved up in lorries to little more than half a mile away, were ordered to advance, followed by the Rajputana Rifles. Tanks and infantry now quartered the camp methodically, helped by a section of 31st Field Battery R.A. firing at point blank range at a few stubborn and isolated centres. By 10.40 a.m. all was over. General Maletti had been killed, and some 2,000 prisoners taken. Large quantities of supplies and water were found intact. British casualties were eight officers and forty-eight men.

Meanwhile 5th Indian Infantry Brigade (Brigadier W. L. Lloyd) and 25th Field Regiment R.A.—less 31st Field Battery—were moving up west of Nibeiwa preparatory to attacking the next objective, Tummar West camp. The remainder of the divisional artillery moved up to the east of Nibeiwa into position for supporting this attack, being bombed from the air as it did so.

Tummar West camp was not unlike Nibeiwa, and of roughly the same size, with a low parapet and a tank ditch, neither of which was continuous. Air reconnaissance had shown that here too the defences were weakest at the north-west corner, and the plan for the break-in was consequently much the same as for Nibeiwa. 7th R.T.R., having lost six tanks on a minefield as they left Nibeiwa, joined the 5th Indian Infantry Brigade at 11 a.m. The day had become dull and overcast and a sand-storm was rising, which made the recognition of targets and objectives very difficult. At noon the artillery began to register. An hour later the tanks advanced and broke through the perimeter without difficulty. There was more opposition from the garrison than at Nibeiwa and again the Italian gunners fought courageously. Twenty minutes after the tank assault 1st Battalion The Royal Fusiliers, followed by 3/1st Punjab Regiment, literally drove up, for the drivers of 4th Reserve M.T. Company, New Zealand A.S.C., brought their lorries through artillery and machine-gun fire to within 150 yards of the western face of the camp. (Not to be outdone many of the drivers then joined in the fight.) By 4 p.m. all resistance was over except in the extreme north-east corner.

Six tanks of 7th R.T.R. then moved off to attack Tummar East. 4/6th Rajputana Rifles, who were to follow them, came under fire from the enemy still holding out in Tummar West, and had then to meet a counter-attack made by Italian infantry and light tanks who emerged from Tummar East. By the time they had successfully dealt with this, inflicting heavy casualties and taking many prisoners, it was too dark to press home the attack on Tummar East, though the 'I' tanks, having advanced by a different route, had already forced their way in.

All this time the left flank and rear of 4th Indian Division was being protected by 4th Armoured Brigade. Passing to the west of Nibeiwa at first light the brigade advanced north and north-west towards the Azziziya area. There was no interference from the air but there were desultory encounters and a certain amount of shelling; prisoners were taken here and there. At Azziziya the garrison of 400 surrendered and no tanks were found. Light tank patrols of 7th Hussars penetrated across the Sidi Barrani-Buq Buq road, while the armoured cars of 11th Hussars moved out farther to the west. Thus in general 4th Armoured Brigade dominated the area to the west of 4th Indian Division and was soon in a position to prevent the enemy from reinforcing Sidi Barrani. The 7th Armoured Brigade was held in reserve, while the Support Group kept the approaches from Rabia and Sofafi under observation and protected the southern flank.

News of the fall of Nibeiwa did not reach Brigadier Selby's Force until 3.20 p.m. He was unaware of the situation at the Tummars but nevertheless decided to send off a detachment in an attempt to block the westerly exits from Maktila. The difficult going and darkness prevented the accomplishment of this task, and the 1st Libyan Division made good its escape during the night.

No reports from Selby Force had reached General O'Connor when at 5 p.m. on December 9th he joined General Beresford-Peirse in Tummar West camp and decided upon plans for the next day. The 5th Indian Infantry Brigade was to clear up Tummar East, and 16th Infantry Brigade, which had been in divisional reserve and was now pushing on as far as possible to the north before nightfall, was to continue northwards and get astride the roads leading to Sidi Barrani. Two field regiments of artillery moved up during the night to support the advance and 7th R.T.R. worked hard to get as many tanks into action as possible.

The operations on December 10th bore little resemblance to the more precise tasks of the previous day, because the enemy's dispositions were unknown and there was not the same element of surprise. Shortly before 6 a.m. the commander of 16th Infantry Brigade (Brigadier C. E. N. Lomax) decided not to wait for the supporting artillery and tanks but to move forward from the very exposed position which his brigade had reached the night before. Italian artillery firing at very short range caused a certain amount of loss, but when at 8.35 a.m. the 1st and 31st Field Regiments and 7th Medium Regiment R.A. came into action the enemy's fire soon began to slacken.

Thus supported, and helped by the advance of ten tanks of 7th R.T.R. on their left flank, the brigade pressed on. They were much hampered by a dust storm, which greatly reduced the visibility, made inter-communication and co-operation very difficult, and caused the shortage of water to be felt acutely. Prisoners soon began to pour in. There was some bombing and machine-gunning from the air, and in the centre of the attack the 1st Battalion The Argyll and Sutherland Highlanders met stiff opposition about Alam el Dab, but by 1.30 p.m. the brigade had gained its objective and the exits from Sidi Barrani to south and west were barred.

General Beresford-Peirse decided not to relax the pressure, and ordered 16th Infantry Brigade to attack Sidi Barrani before nightfall. He placed the remaining 'I' tanks and the Cameron Highlanders under command of Brigadier Lomax, and arranged for 2nd Royal Tank Regiment—cruisers and light tanks—from 4th Armoured Brigade to operate on the left flank. The attack was launched just after 4 p.m., supported by the whole divisional artillery. The heart had now gone out of the enemy and in half an hour the 16th Infantry Brigade had passed through to the east of Sidi Barrani. The remains of 1st and 2nd Libyan Divisions and 4th Blackshirt Division were thus hemmed in between Selby Force and 16th Infantry Brigade, whose casualties during the day amounted to 17 officers and 260 other ranks.

On 10th December 4th Armoured Brigade, having lent its two cruiser regiments to 4th Indian Division and Selby Force, continued to operate with armoured cars across the coast road, while its artillery and light tanks engaged various Italian camps a few miles to the south and east of Buq Buq. Early on 11th December 7th Armoured Brigade (Brigadier H. Russell) moved out to deal with the enemy remaining in the Buq Buq area and made large captures of men and guns. The 4th Armoured Brigade had been ordered overnight to withdraw towards Bir Enba, but a further order to cut off the enemy from the west of Sofafi was unaccountably delayed and arrived too late to be acted on.

A patrol of the Support Group found Rabia empty on the morning of the 11th, the Cirene Division having withdrawn from there and from Sofafi during darkness. They were pursued along the top of the escarpment and contact was made by 2nd Rifle Brigade shortly after noon about ten miles south of Halfaya pass. Except for the escape of the Cirene Division, which was a great disappointment, the 11th was a day of successes. In the morning Selby Force and 6th Royal Tank Regiment (of 4th Armoured Brigade), attacked the 1st Libyan Division, which surrendered by 1 p.m. By nightfall all resistance from the 4th Blackshirt Division had also ceased.

General O'Connor now decided to pursue vigorously with the armoured division; 7th Armoured Brigade along the coast, and 4th Armoured Brigade above the escarpment. This raised an acute problem of supply which is referred to in the next chapter. It was eased by windfalls of Italian stores, but these were more than offset by the embarrassing flood of prisoners—twenty times the estimated number—to be watered, fed and removed. The attempt to supplement the overland channels of supply by sea was only partially successful; a few lighters which had come ready loaded were able to put ashore some water and rations at Sidi Barrani, but the sea was too rough for a supply ship to discharge and nothing more was possible until the harbour at Sollum became available.

The bad weather also prevented an intended Commando landing and a further shoot from seaward on December 10th. But on the 11th the *Terror* and the two gunboats bombarded the Sollum area all day and well into the night. Movements of troops and transport crowding along the coastal escape-route offered exceptional targets, which received 220 rounds of 15-inch H.E. and 600 of 6-inch, in addition to the fire of 3-inch guns and pom-poms from very close range.

By the evening of December 12th the only Italians left in Egypt were those in position blocking the immediate approaches to Sollum and a force of some strength in the neighbourhood of Sidi Omar. Passing between these, the 4th Armoured Brigade sent forward a force to cut the road between Tobruk and Bardia, and by nightfall on the 14th the armoured cars of the 11th Hussars had done so; but it soon became impossible to maintain the brigade so far forward and they were ordered instead to capture Sidi Omar, which fell on the 16th. The enemy withdrew from Sollum, Capuzzo, and the other frontier posts, and Bardia became his most forward position in the coastal sector. Farther inland he still held Siwa and Jarabub.

By 11th December General Wavell had decided to go ahead with his plan for sending 4th Indian Division to reinforce General Platt in the Sudan. This decision came as an unwelcome surprise to General O'Connor, who had not been forewarned in order not to add to his preoccupations. To the existing complications on the L. of C. were therefore added the withdrawal of this division from Sidi Barrani and the forward move of 16th Australian Infantry Brigade. This was to be followed as soon as possible by the remainder of the 6th Australian Division, whose commander, Major-General I. G. Mackay, was given the task of capturing Bardia if the enemy decided to defend it. The 16th (British) Infantry Brigade, which was not to accompany 4th Indian Division to the Sudan, would be placed under his command together with additional artillery and the 7th R.T.R. General Wavell directed that there was to be no risk of failure or of heavy casualties; subject to this, the attack was to be made as soon as possible. The 7th Armoured Division was ordered to move out between Bardia and Tobruk directly its maintenance arrangements would allow.

In reviewing the week's operation General O'Connor gave high praise to the Air Force for having dominated the Italian Air Force to the extent they did. The bomber attacks on the airfields at Derna, El Adem, Tobruk and Gambut had been very effective. The approach march was not interfered with at all, and the attacks made on Western Desert Force during the first two or three days of the battle were not serious. Thereafter the Italian Air Force became more active, doing its best to secure some respite for the disorganized army, and by the 15th it was being a decided nuisance to the troops, though it did surprisingly little damage. Meanwhile, it undertook no counter air operations, and did no bombing of Alexandria or the Delta.

Air Commodore Collishaw's policy had been to get the utmost out of his limited resources from the outset; during the peak of the first week's intensive operations some of his fighter pilots were making as many as four sorties a day. Gladiators were used for patrolling over the forward troops, while Hurricanes attacked enemy movements as far afield as fifty miles west of Bardia. The superiority of the Hurricane over the Italian fighter C.R.42 was very marked. Casualties were surprisingly light—four Blenheims and six fighters in the first half of December—but the intense activity had a big effect upon the number of fighters that could be kept serviceable. After December 13th, for instance, No. 3 Squadron R.A.A.F., which was providing close support, had to curtail its activities, and the Air Officer Commanding-in-Chief ordered forward another flight of fighters from the defences of Alexandria. At the same time he felt obliged to warn Collishaw not to go on operating at this intensity because the reserves of Gladiators were practically exhausted.

The whole 'Compass' plan showed not only great imagination but a firm determination to do the utmost with the resources available. The role of 7th Armoured Division was not, of course, a new one to them; but to 4th Indian Division the operation had several novel features, yet the confidence and enthusiasm of the troops, when they learned what they had to do, could not have been greater. The execution of the plan bore witness to sound training and good leadership, and to a fine fighting spirit in the troops. The tactics of the battle had been designed to suit the 'I' tanks, which fully justified the confidence placed in them; one of the many risks inherent in the plan was that, if the opposition had been great enough to cause the attack to be called off after four or five days, a large number of these valuable tanks would have been lost altogether, because there were no vehicles available that could transport or even tow them. More lessons are probably learned from battles which go wrong; in this battle most things went right. Even so, the difficulty of exercising control over such a large battlefield was made very clear, and pointed to the need of more reliable wireless communications.

In the three days from 9th to 11th December the Western Desert Force captured no fewer than 38,300 Italian and Libyan prisoners, 237 guns, and 73 light and medium tanks. The total of captured vehicles was never recorded, but more than a thousand were counted. The British casualties were 624 killed, wounded, and missing. This extraordinary result showed how shrewd had been General Wavell's estimate of the effect that an early success would have upon Italian morale. Everything possible had been done to ensure that the battle should be given a good start, and great emphasis had been laid upon the importance of taking the enemy by surprise. It is appropriate, therefore, to examine the extent to which surprise was really achieved.

Intelligence summaries issued by the Italian 10th Army show that throughout October and November the enemy was continually receiving reports from Egypt and elsewhere of the movements of British troops and aircraft. Some of these were accurate, some quite ludicrous; the general impression was an exaggerated one of greatly increasing strength in Egypt. From the beginning of November onwards it was assumed that many of the new arrivals would go to Greece, but it was rightly believed that the British could deploy much stronger forces in Egypt or the Sudan, or even both, than they could have done two months earlier. No very clear deduction seems to have been made from this.

Throughout November the Italian Air Force made frequent reports of concentrations of vehicles in the Western Desert, and of an increase in the movement along the lines of communication. Right up to December 5th the conclusions drawn from this were that the troops who had been so long in the forward area were being relieved, or that measures were being taken to meet the expected Italian advance, or both. The chances of a British offensive were not rated very high, though it was thought that some small enterprise might be undertaken for propaganda purposes. In this connexion it was noticed that the British were particularly active in the neighbourhood of the Nibeiwa—Rabia gap, and Marshal Graziani claims to have told the Army Commander, General Berti, on November 18th to give this matter his attention.

On December 4th the general attitude of the British was regarded as unchanged; that is to say, they were continuing to watch all Italian movements very closely. The next day an increase in the air

U

activity was noted. On the 6th some information, inaccurate in itself, drew attention to a supposed trend of movement westward from the Delta. December 7th passed without any recorded comment, but on the 8th an Italian aircraft reported having seen 400 vehicles at midday at various points about thirty to forty miles south-east of Nibeiwa. (This would have been the aircraft seen by the 4th Indian Division.) Marshal Graziani[1] also mentions this air report and says that the 10th Army was immediately notified. He thought the report particularly significant because the interrogation of a prisoner captured on December 5th had led to a verbal warning to 10th Army and 5th *Squadra* that a strong British attack might be expected in ten days or so. This warning, he states, was given on December 7th. There is no mention of it in the 10th Army's Intelligence Summary, but General von Rintelen, in an official letter dated 2nd January 1941, refers to a warning being given to Graziani by the Italian Intelligence Department on December 6th that a British attack was imminent.

The fact is that in war it is usually possible to produce some sort of evidence in support of almost every course of action open to the enemy; the art lies in knowing what to make of it all. In this case the Italian Air Force had observed and reported movements and dispositions with fair accuracy—indeed, it was often intended by the British that they should. The important point was that these reports were consistent with what the 10th Army were convinced was happening. They themselves were very much occupied with their own preparations for renewing the advance, and were only too ready to interpret the air reports as indicating that the British were actively improving their defensive arrangements. The British attempt at strategic deception was therefore successful.

But this did not alter the fact that the Italians had a very large force stationed east of the frontier. What really mattered was how competently the higher commanders would handle the defensive battle, and how well the troops would fight. In both these vital matters the Italians must be judged to have failed. They handicapped themselves from the start by failing to act on the air report of 8th December; no attack was made upon the British concentration and nothing was even done to ensure that it was kept under observation. The commanders in the forward area made no special efforts during the night to gain any information for themselves, or to increase their vigilance. The result was that at the first objective, Nibeiwa, tactical surprise was complete: the assault came at an unexpected moment from an unexpected direction, and was led by a type of tank whose presence was entirely unsuspected.

---

[1] Rodolfo Graziani: *Africa Settentrionale 1940-41*, (Rome, 1948) page 131.

The Italians in the Western Desert suffered, of course, from a great inferiority in armoured units. Neither of the armoured divisions had been made available for them; the Centauro had gone to the mountainous Albanian front and the Ariete had stayed in Italy. There was an armoured brigade near Tobruk, too far off to be of any use. Such tanks as there were in the forward area were not used on any clear plan for making a decisive contribution to the battle; thirty-five or so, for instance, were locked up in Nibeiwa camp and lost there.

In short, this three-day battle led to the conclusions that the enemy's higher commanders had little or no idea of fighting a battle in desert conditions, and that on the whole the junior leaders and men were apt to lose heart very quickly. It remained to be seen whether the Italian troops, without the Libyans, would make a better showing in the defence of an important centre, like Bardia, for which there had been ample time to construct strong permanent defences.

The Prime Minister was quick to telegraph his appreciation to General Wavell. 'The Army of the Nile has rendered glorious service to the Empire and to our cause and rewards are already being reaped by us in every quarter. . . . Pray convey my compliments and congratulations to Longmore upon his magnificent handling of the Royal Air Force and fine co-operation with the Army. . . .' He added, as his thoughts dwelt on even better things to come, 'It looks as if these people were corn ripe for the sickle'. General Wavell made a characteristic reply, giving full credit to his subordinates and to the other Services, and added that, while he and his colleagues were fully aware of the need to exploit their success, it must be realized that Bardia possessed strong permanent defences and its capture might prove to be beyond their present resources.

Mediterranean Sea

Apollonia
Cyrene
Giovan
Berta
Tocra
Barce
Slonta
Chaulan
4 FEB
Maraua
17
5 FEB
El Abiar
Akhd
Benghazi
Benina
Mech
Berka
27 JA
Jebel
14
6 FEB
6 FEB
Ghemines
Soluch
4 FEB
Msus
5 FEB
28
Sceleidima
16
El Magrun
Beda Fomm
5/7 FEB
Antelat
Sidi Saleh
Gulf of Sidra
Agedabia
Trigh el Abd
CYREN
El Agheila
Aujila
Jalo

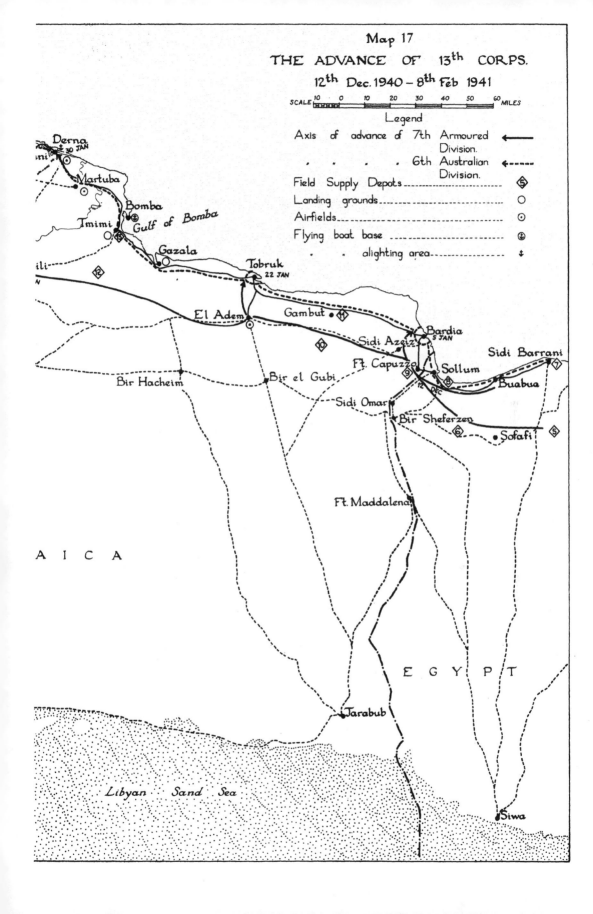

Map 17

THE ADVANCE OF 13ᵗʰ CORPS.

12ᵗʰ Dec. 1940 – 8ᵗʰ Feb 1941

SCALE  10  0  10  20  30  40  50  60 MILES

Legend

Axis of advance of 7th Armoured Division.

6th Australian Division.

Field Supply Depots

Landing grounds

Airfields

Flying boat base

alighting area

Derna
30 JAN
Martuba
Bomba
Tmimi        Gulf of Bomba
Gazala
Tobruk
22 JAN
El Adem
Gambut
Sidi Azeiz
Bardia
5 JAN
Sidi Barrani
Ft. Capuzzo
Sollum
Bir Hacheim
Bir el Gubi
Buabua
Sidi Omar
12 DEC
Bir Sheferzen
Sofafi

A I C A

Ft. Maddalena

E G Y P T

Jarabub

Libyan   Sand   Sea

Siwa

# CHAPTER XV

# THE FIRST BRITISH OFFENSIVE
# IN THE WESTERN DESERT—II

*See Map* 17

ONE OF the first reactions in London to the Italian defeat
was to consider whether the moment was favourable to invite
Egypt to enter the war. The view of the Commanders-in-
Chief was that no military advantages would be likely to accrue. In
the Ambassador's opinion it would be best to leave the Egyptian
Government to declare war of their own free will, if they so wished.
There, for the time being, the matter ended.

Within a few days the Prime Minister was expressing his wish to
see the success in the Western Desert driven well home. 'I feel
convinced', he wrote, 'that it is only after you have made sure that
you can get no farther that you will relinquish the main hope in
favour of secondary action in the Sudan or Dodecanese. The Sudan
is of primary importance and eminently desirable and it may be that
the two Indian Brigades can be spared without prejudice to the
Libyan pursuit battle. . . . The Dodecanese will not get any harder
for a little waiting. But neither of these ought to detract from the
supreme task of inflicting further defeats upon the main Italian Army'.

The Commanders-in-Chief had always been acutely aware of the
importance of the Red Sea route, and hence of the Sudan, and had
stressed the point when commenting upon the Prime Minister's
Directive of August 1940. The Dodecanese were certainly likely to
wither in Italian hands but there was always the chance of German
help. As regards the despatch of the Indian division, General Wavell
was convinced that only one division in addition to the armoured
division could be maintained in Cyrenaica without the use of Tobruk
harbour; and if the Indian troops in the Sudan were to be reinforced
for operations in Eritrea there were obvious advantages in sending
another Indian division well suited to the type of country. Finally,
on the question of driving home the initial advantage, the three
Commanders-in-Chief had already resolved to give the enemy no
respite. In the hope of inducing the garrison of Bardia to abandon
the place or surrender before the shock of defeat had worn off, they
decided to try the effect of a hammering from the sea and air while
preparations for an assault were being made.

Accordingly H.M.S. *Terror*, having replenished after bombarding Maktila, began on the 14th to engage targets systematically in the defended area of Bardia, and continued to do so for the next three days. On one night she was unsuccessfully attacked by a M.T.B., and by torpedo-bombers on another. At dawn on the 17th she supported an impertinent adventure by the *Aphis*, which entered Bardia harbour and remained inside for an hour while she engaged targets at point blank range. The *Terror* remarked that the volumes of black smoke rolling out of the harbour entrance indicated that the *Aphis* 'was having a good time'.[1] An attempt to repeat the exploit next day found the Italians on the alert, and the gunboat was pursued along the coast with fire from mobile artillery, her withdrawal being covered by the *Terror*.

The main bomber effort was also shifted on to Bardia from December 14th to 19th. More than 150 sorties were flown, the heaviest attack being made on the night 15th/16th by 36 aircraft. Wellingtons from Malta, released by bad weather in the Adriatic from their primary tasks, now joined in the attack on Italian airfields, and between the 18th and 22nd no less than 44 aircraft were destroyed or damaged at Castel Benito, Benina, and Berka, apart from other material results.[2]

By December 19th it seemed certain that the enemy intended neither to fight his way out to Tobruk nor to surrender out of hand. The attack for which General Mackay had begun to prepare, in accordance with General O'Connor's instructions, would therefore have to be carried out. The situation on December 19th was that the 16th (British) Infantry Brigade was moving up to gain contact with the southern portion of the Bardia defences, and the leading Australian Brigade—also numbered the 16th—was relieving the Support Group who had been patrolling along the south-western sector. This enabled the whole of the 7th Armoured Division to be disposed farther north, ready to deal with any attempt at reinforcement from Tobruk. The second brigade group of the 6th Australian Division could not arrive for another week, with the third a few days behind. The lines of communication were being severely strained by these movements superimposed on the tasks of maintaining the Western Desert Force and of building up resources for the attack on Bardia. It is appropriate therefore to see how the maintenance situation was developing.

In preparing for the 'five day battle' of Sidi Barrani it had been necessary to establish two Field Supply Depots (F.S.D.)—Nos. 3 and 4 on the map—far enough forward to be within daily reach of the divisional transport columns during the battle. These depots could

---

[1] See Photo. 17.
[2] Santoro, op. cit., p. 397.

not be added to (except for some water) until the reserve transport companies were released from their troop-carrying role. This occurred at the same time as the decision was taken for 7th Armoured Division to carry out the pursuit to the frontier. By December 12th the portion of this division operating south of—that is, above—the escarpment was 170 route miles from its railhead. Their F.S.D. (No. 4) had dropped nearly 100 miles behind and it was urgently necessary to form a new one. By concentrating the 4th Indian Division about Sidi Barrani it was just possible to collect enough transport to do this; the new depot was No. 5, east of Rabia. Within a few days even this was too far back, and No. 6 had to be formed half way between Sofafi and the frontier. Meanwhile for the troops in the coastal area No. 7 F.S.D. was formed near Sidi Barrani, and had the weather been better it would have been stocked by sea instead of by road from Matruh. The next to be formed were No. 8 at Sollum for the Australian Division and No. 9 at Capuzzo for the Armoured Division.

The pattern is therefore of two chains of depots, one along the coast and one following roughly the line of the escarpment; the depots in each chain being about 50 miles apart. Naturally the depots did not all exist simultaneously, for as soon as a new one was opened the previous one was eaten down and not re-stocked. This system resulted in the turn-round of the divisional transport columns being kept more or less within practical limits, but the distance covered by the transport companies employed on stocking the depots grew greater and greater.

This distance would be reduced eventually by the projected extension of the railway and water pipeline forward from Matruh, but this was no solution to the immediate problem and without additional transport there would obviously have been a breakdown. But by 12th December the men of a newly arrived Reserve M.T. Company, which hitherto had had no vehicles, had taken over 80 captured Italian 5- and 6-ton diesel trucks. On the 15th 50 heavy lorries, each with a 7½-ton desert payload, arrived with their drivers from Palestine—an invaluable addition to the transport pool. Many captured vehicles could not be used for want of drivers, though some were appropriated by units to make up their own deficiencies. By the end of December the wastage of vehicles in the Western Desert Force was nearly 40% of the establishment—the cumulative effect of several contributory causes. Most of the vehicles were already old; they had been driven unceasingly by tired drivers over rough desert tracks (even on the coast road the going was very bad) in perpetual dust, and swallowed up from time to time by sandstorms. The difficulty of ensuring routine maintenance in these conditions was aggravated by the lack of adequate workshops within easy reach.

On December 16th the small port of Sollum fell into British hands, and provided a means of alleviating the load on the overland routes. A small naval organization had existed for the purpose of supplying Matruh, should it be cut off by land, and this was now brought into use. As early as December 12th a quantity of rations, water, petrol, and stores was on passage, and owing to the bad weather most of it was still loaded when access to Sollum harbour first became possible. Until the port was working the whole Australian Division could not be maintained from No. 8 F.S.D. on the coastal axis, but unfortunately Sollum was hardly a port at all; it had only two small lighterage piers, with no equipment for handling heavy loads.[1] There were no dock or transportation troops available in the Middle East, and discharging was begun on the 18th by troops of the 16th Infantry Brigade, joined later by two Pioneer Companies of the Cyprus Regiment; the work of clearance was done by No. 4 New Zealand M.T. Company. The anchorage was very exposed to weather and to air attacks; there was also spasmodic shelling by a long-range gun from Bardia. All this caused delay and there were many casualties: on Christmas Eve 60 New Zealanders and Cypriots were killed or wounded by bombing. At the end of the month 100 stevedores from Alexandria and a detachment of the Palestine Regiment (Pioneers) were also at work. The despatch of anti-aircraft units to Crete and Greece had left only 20 heavy and 32 light A.A. guns for the Western Desert Force and the whole of the lines of communication; of these one heavy battery was allotted to Sollum. The three fighter squadrons (Nos. 33, 73 and 274) covering the forward area were formed into a fighter wing, but they were greatly handicapped by the lack of any organization for giving warning of the approach of enemy aircraft.

The lack of water was one of the worst anxieties. The storage tanks at Capuzzo, normally filled by pipeline from Bardia, were found to be very salt, and 12,000 gallons had to be sent all the way from Matruh by road. In spite of all attempts to find and use local sources it was necessary to cut the ration for several days to half a gallon. As soon as possible water was brought in by sea to Sollum, but the lack of any means of off-loading and storing in bulk made the discharge very slow. The same applied to petrol, and the wastage from the flimsy 4-gallon containers was very high. From the 21st to 23rd the *Aphis* and *Ladybird* lent a hand in landing water from the armed boarding vessel *Fiona* and delivered it straight into water-carts waiting on the beach. (Incidentally, there were not nearly enough desert-worthy water-carts.) Next day the one and only water-carrier, *Myriel*, arrived from Alexandria with over 3,000 tons, and the *Terror* assumed what was for her an unusual role and

---

[1] See Photos 14 and 16.

13. A burnt-out British tank which had become bogged in a salt marsh near Buq Buq in December 1940.

*Facing p. 280*

14. View looking down on Sollum, showing the primitive harbour. In the background is the escarpment.

15. British Matilda 'I' tank being towed up to Halfaya Pass. Sollum Bay is in the background; Sollum barracks are above the escarpment; Sollum itself to the left of the bay.

16. The river gunboat *Aphis* in Sollum harbour, where she helped the Army by landing water. December 1940.

17. View of Bardia harbour showing the damage done by
H.M.S. *Aphis* on 17th December 1940.

18. View of Bardia and its small harbour. The two abandoned
tanks are Italian.

19. Tobruk and its harbour from the west.

*Facing p. 281*   20. The Italian cruiser *San Giorgio* on fire in Tobruk harbour.

brought a further 200 tons. These efforts on the part of the Navy saved the situation, and by the end of the month the sources at Sidi Barrani and Buq Buq had been put in order and the tanks at Capuzzo were kept filled by pumping from Sollum.

It will be realized that the task of maintaining the 7th Armoured Division and the growing numbers of Australians and their supporting units was by no means easy. It was made harder still by the need to prepare for the deliberate attack on the Bardia defences. These were much more elaborate than the desert camps, and the attacking infantry would therefore need strong fire support; large quantities of ammunition had consequently to be brought forward. On top of all this the Commanders-in-Chief decided on 26th December that operations in Libya were to have priority over all others, at least as far as the capture of Tobruk. This meant that a further programme of forward stocking would have to be undertaken as soon as Bardia fell.

The Air Force too had many difficulties to overcome as its established air bases dropped farther behind. Reconnaissance and fighter aircraft were using improvised landing grounds which lacked signal communications and equipment generally. The shortage of men and the demands of the Greek campaign had made it impossible to do more than improvise additions to the Air Stores Park and to the Repair and Salvage Unit which supported the Western Desert squadrons. The frequent sandstorms rendered the task of maintaining aircraft especially difficult and trying, and kept them unserviceable much longer. A special Air Explosives and Fuel Park was formed, which made the utmost use of captured bombs and petrol, and created dumps from which the squadrons collected their requirements.

Marshal Graziani knew well enough what the pause in the British advance meant. He had given orders to General Gariboldi, the acting commander of the 10th Army in the absence on leave of General Berti, that Bardia and Tobruk were both to be held. This decision was promptly endorsed by the Duce but Graziani was not easy in his mind that it was a sound one. On 17th December he ventured to point out that it would be difficult to reinforce Bardia and that it would be only a matter of time before the British assembled enough strength to overcome the defences. Would it not be wiser to concentrate all the available forces for the defence of Tobruk, and so gain time for the arrival of the troops and air forces which he hoped were being sent from Italy? Mussolini replied that everything possible must be done to delay and exhaust the enemy, and that a prolonged resistance at Bardia would make a useful contribution. Meanwhile certain units were being prepared in Italy for despatch to Tripoli.

A similar problem, differing only in degree, had arisen in respect of the troops then holding positions on the frontier at Capuzzo and Sollum. Lieutenant-General Bergonzoli, commander of the 23rd Corps, represented to the Army Commander on December 15th that without them he had not enough troops to hold Bardia. Marshal Graziani stepped in and insisted on their withdrawal; the Italian force at Capuzzo succeeded in eluding 7th Armoured Brigade in the dark, with the result that Bergonzoli was able to collect within the Bardia perimeter the whole or part of the following divisions: 1st and 2nd Blackshirt, 62nd Marmarica, 63rd Cirene and 64th Catanzaro, in all, the equivalent of about four divisions, totalling with fortress troops and frontier guards 45,000 men and over 400 guns. The British estimate at the time was much less—only about half the true figure.

On December 21st Major-General Mackay assumed command in the Sollum area. Much had already been learned from air photographs and captured documents about the Bardia defences. These ran in a rough arc eighteen miles long round the small harbour and town. Near the coast the ground was deeply indented by *wadis*; elsewhere the perimeter ran across a flat and dusty plain. There was a main outer line of fortified posts, 500 to 800 yards apart, containing gun and machine-gun emplacements, shelters, and trenches, mostly of concrete. Each post was protected by a ditch and surrounded by barbed wire. Along part of the front there was a second line of posts, a few hundred yards back, and there were various isolated posts covering vulnerable points farther back still. Along the whole front ran a thick continuous double-apron barbed wire fence, and except where the *wadis* made it unnecessary a sheer-sided anti-tank ditch twelve feet wide or more and about four feet deep. There were six separate minefields along the front and at other points mines had been scattered inside and outside the wire. The southern corner of the defended arc had been strengthened by the provision of a second or 'switch' line of posts, which gave additional protection to the area in which were most of the artillery positions.

As soon as the 16th Australian Infantry Brigade (Brigadier A. S. Allen) took over the sector south of the Bardia—Tobruk road they set to work to secure mastery of the ground up to the Italian perimeter, and by aggressive patrolling to verify the information about the defences and discover the enemy's dispositions. Every night patrols were busy examining the Italian wire and measuring the ditches. The Italians were alert and prompt to open fire, but did little patrolling of their own. On December 27th the 17th Australian Infantry Brigade (Brigadier S. G. Savige) came up on the right of the 16th, and in the process of closing up to the enemy defences met with a certain amount of opposition; it was here that the enemy seemed to be most sensitive. From all these activities and from the latest air photographs General Mackay had obtained enough information by December 28th to make his plan.

By now it was realized that there were elements of five Italian divisions in Bardia, but it was still thought that the total strength was little more than 20,000 with over 100 guns. The attack of this force in its strong defences was to be the 6th Australian Division's first engagement. This was the first formation to be sent overseas by Australia; it was composed of early volunteers, who were proud of, and eager to rival, the fighting reputation of their forerunners of the A.I.F. of the First World War. Their training in Palestine had been vigorous and realistic, though handicapped by shortages of equipment, from which they still suffered. Part of the division had been in the convoy diverted to England in May 1940,[1] and, although a third infantry brigade—the 19th—had been formed in Palestine, some of the divisional troops were still absent. There were only two field artillery regiments instead of three; one of these had obsolete guns and howitzers, and the other had only very recently received its 25-pdrs. There was no machine-gun battalion, and no anti-tank regiment —the brigades had eleven anti-tank guns between them; carriers, mortars, and transport were all short. Only one squadron of the divisional cavalry regiment was present, the remainder being engaged farther inland, in the vicinity of the frontier posts at Jarabub and Siwa. In respect of morale, however, nothing was lacking; the chief concern of the Australians was lest they should be too late, and find the enemy gone. For the attack on Bardia the division was supplemented by two regiments and a battery of field artillery, and one medium regiment; which meant that 120 of the 154 available guns were under General Mackay's command. So were 7th R.T.R.—who, although severely handicapped by the lack of spare parts, had managed to make 23 tanks serviceable—and a machine-gun battalion, 1st Royal Northumberland Fusiliers. The 16th (British) Infantry Brigade was not to be used for the actual attack.

General Mackay chose for the point of attack the western face, about two and a half miles south of the Tobruk road. This would give access to a slight rise from which good observation would be obtained, and to gently falling ground over which the 'I' tanks could operate freely. It was opposite the junction of two defensive sectors; and it lent itself well to support by the artillery. A breakthrough here would cut the defences in half and would isolate the bulk of the Italian guns. Moreover it was thought that the Italians would hardly

---

[1] See page 84.

expect the main attack to come from the west, but from nearer to the Capuzzo road.

General O'Connor suggested to General Mackay that the plan, as at Nibeiwa, should be shaped to suit the tanks, and had also suggested a fundamental difference in the methods to be adopted to give them a good start. At Nibeiwa they suddenly appeared at dawn at a point which reconnaissance had shown was not tank-proof; and by a rapid break-in they made it possible for the infantry to follow. At Bardia, on the other hand, the way had to be prepared for the tanks to cross the ditch and get safely through the mines; therefore the first stage was an attack by the infantry to secure a bridgehead.

On December 28th General Mackay decided that zero hour should be 5.30 a.m. on January 2nd, but on the 30th he was obliged to make a postponement of 24 hours owing to the late arrival of the necessary ammunition. Between 31st December and 2nd January the Air Force made 100 bomber sorties against the Bardia area culminating in a heavy attack by Wellingtons of No. 70 Squadron and Bombays of No. 216 Squadron on the night 2nd/3rd. Throughout January 2nd H.M.S. *Terror* and the gunboats carried out harassing shoots against Bardia and the northern sector.

At 5.30 a.m. on 3rd January, when it was still dark, the artillery barrage opened on a front of about half a mile, with concentrations on selected targets north and south. The 2/1st Australian Battalion advanced from its start line to cover the 1,000 yards to the enemy's position, and met little opposition other than shell fire. The engineers blew gaps in the wire with Bangalore torpedoes; the infantry secured a bridgehead across the ditch; crossing places were made for the tanks; and nearly 100 mines were removed. In less than an hour the battalion had gained its objectives.

By 7 a.m. the tanks had moved into the bridgehead; five troops turned right and moved off to the south-east, closely followed by 2/2nd Australian Battalion. A series of sharp minor encounters now began. Some posts showed fight; others surrendered after receiving a burst of fire from the tanks. It was highly individual and very mixed fighting, in which the tanks were sometimes leading and sometimes led by the infantry. The 2/2nd Battalion soon reached the line of the Bardia-Capuzzo road. Meanwhile 2/1st had formed a flank facing north, and 2/3rd together with the divisional cavalry squadron in their Bren carriers had advanced two miles towards Bardia. While seeking to exploit this success the cavalry squadron was counter-attacked by six Italian medium tanks, which penetrated some distance among the 2/3rd Battalion before being all knocked out by two anti-tank guns.

By 8.30 a.m. the 16th Australian Infantry Brigade had occupied practically all its objectives, and had captured about 8,000 prisoners

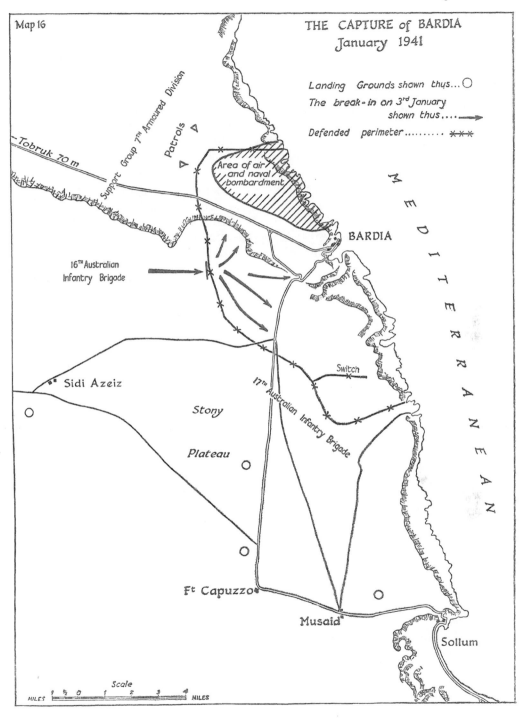

Map 16

THE CAPTURE of BARDIA
January 1941

Landing Grounds shown thus... ◯
The break-in on 3rd January shown thus....➔
Defended perimeter......... *** 

Tobruk 70 m

Support Group 7ᵀᴴ Armoured Division

Patrols

Area of air and naval bombardment

BARDIA

16ᵀᴴ Australian Infantry Brigade

Switch

17ᵀᴴ Australian Infantry Brigade

Sidi Azeiz

Stony

Plateau

Fᵗ Capuzzo

Musaid

Sollum

MEDITERRANEAN

Scale

MILES  1  ½  0  1  2  3  4  MILES

and a large quantity of weapons. There had been a good deal of shell fire, though it was somewhat wild and inaccurate and there had been very few casualties, though the tanks had been severely battered by field and anti-tank guns, and rallied very slowly to refill.

Meanwhile patrols of the Support Group demonstrated to the north of the Tobruk road, and three companies of the 2/6th Australian Battalion made a diversionary attack on posts at the extreme southern corner of the perimeter; two of the platoons came under heavy fire and were killed or wounded almost to a man.

At 8.10 a.m. the battleships *Valiant* and *Barham*, led by the Commander-in-Chief in the *Warspite*, with seven destroyers, opened fire with their main armament, and for 45 minutes a rain of 15-inch shells fell on the area north of the Bardia-Tobruk road. Shore batteries were heavily engaged by the secondary armament, and the *Illustrious* provided spotting aircraft and protective patrols. After the bombardment was over, the *Terror* and gunboats kept up intermittent fire for some hours, in which the artillery of the Support Group joined.

The main bomber effort was lifted on to the airfields at Gazala, Derna, Martuba and Tmimi. The Lysanders directing the artillery fire were covered by fighters. Other fighters of Nos. 33, 73 and 274 Squadrons patrolled the area between Tobruk and Bardia. On each homeward journey they carried out low-flying reconnaissances of Bardia. The Italian Air Force took little part in the battle. During the preliminary phase they had been busy withdrawing from the airfields in the Tobruk area to those which were now being attacked, and had been able to do little beyond making their daily attacks on Sollum and the ships anchored there.

The second phase began at 11.30 a.m. with an attack by 17th Australian Infantry Brigade against the perimeter east of the Bardia-Capuzzo road. The 2/5th Battalion, with two companies of the 2/7th under command, tired after a somewhat complicated approach march, soon came under accurate artillery fire; among the first casualties was the Commanding Officer. Six tanks took part, but delays in rallying made them late; on the left the attack was checked, and the 2/6th Battalion was pinned to its ground all day. Nevertheless, by the end of the day the attack had reached the 'switch' line, where confused fighting was still going on.

During the night 2/8th Battalion of the 19th Australian Infantry Brigade (Brigadier H. C. H. Robertson) moved up within the perimeter behind 16th Brigade. Orders had been issued during the afternoon for the 16th Brigade to renew the attack at 11 a.m. Only three tanks were available to accompany each of the two attacking battalions. The 2/2nd made progress straight towards Bardia, and 2/3rd struck northwards to the Bardia-Tobruk road. The 2/8th Australian

Battalion (19th Brigade) protected the right flank of 2/2nd Battalion. Artillery support was mainly by observed fire; the enemy's resistance was weak, and the attack made rapid progress. Thousands of prisoners were taken, and so surprised was the enemy by the speed that he failed to destroy the water supply plant or the limited harbour facilities. By the end of the day the only Italians still holding out were those in the extreme north and south.

Next morning the 2/11th Battalion, 19th Australian Infantry Brigade, supported by artillery and six tanks, attacked the remaining pocket of resistance. The tanks penetrated the gun area and fire gradually slackened. The 17th Australian Infantry Brigade was then able to move forward, and by 1 p.m. the enemy had given in. Meanwhile in the north Italians were surrendering wholesale to the Support Group.

In the three days' fighting the 6th Australian Division had 456 casualties. The 'I' tanks had again been invaluable, though they were by no means invulnerable. Many were stopped by mines, and others had their turrets jammed by direct hits from shells. Only six were still in action on the third day. The Italians lost over 40,000 officers and men, killed and captured; more than 400 guns; 13 medium and 117 light tanks—many of them serviceable; several hundred motor vehicles, and many documents of immediate value. The Corps Commander, General Bergonzoli, had escaped.

In just under a month, eight Italian divisions had been completely destroyed. It would be surprising if there had been no recriminations after a disaster of this magnitude, and, in fact, the Commander of the 10th Army, General Berti, was replaced on December 23rd by Graziani's Chief of Staff, General Tellera, so that the 10th Army had three different commanders during the battle.


No time was wasted in complying with the decision of the Commanders-in-Chief that after the capture of Bardia the advance should be continued to Tobruk. On the morning of January 5th, before all resistance at Bardia had ceased, 7th Armoured Brigade was on the move westwards to El Adem, and next day was operating to cut off Tobruk. The 19th Australian Brigade Group left Bardia on the evening of the 6th and during the next morning gained touch with the eastern sector of the Tobruk defences. The 16th Brigade came up on its left; 4th Armoured Brigade extended the investing line to the west, with the Support Group blocking the western exits and 7th Armoured Brigade operating farther west still.

These movements were almost unopposed. The offensive by air and the advance by land had seriously injured and disorganized the Italian Air Force. Many aircraft had been destroyed, the principal

airfield and repair depot in Cyrenaica—El Adem—had been captured, and the Italians were having great difficulty in maintaining
the aircraft that were left. According to Marshal Graziani, the 5th
*Squadra* had on 5th January 119 aircraft available, half of which were
fighters.[1] But as soon as Tobruk was invested the Italians abandoned
Derna airfield, and their fighters were obliged to work from Maraua,
170 miles away instead of 90, and were consequently unable to
respond to the many calls for air support from Tobruk. Meanwhile
the headquarters of No. 202 Group had advanced to Sollum,
bomber and fighter squadrons were in the area Bardia-Sollum, and
the Army Co-operation Squadrons were at Gambut; so that all were
well placed to continue the offensive.

Against this had to be set the demands of the Greek campaign,
described in Chapter XVIII, the effect of which upon the Air Force
in the Western Desert was now to deprive them of one Blenheim
squadron and one Gladiator squadron, while Alexandria had to
part with its one Hurricane squadron. In the face of the weakened
Italian Air Force these withdrawals were unwelcome but not
disastrous; they were very disturbing, however, now that the
*Luftwaffe* was known to be establishing itself in Sicily and might be
expected to come to the help of the Italians in Libya before long.

By now the Italian strength at Tobruk was known with some
accuracy. The garrison was commanded by General Pitassi Mannella,
commander of the 22nd Corps, and consisted of 61st Sirte Division, a number of medium and light tanks, two battalions, and some
frontier guards; about 25,000 men in all, and more than 200 guns.
There were no other forces nearer than Derna, where 60th Sabratha
Division had arrived from Tripoli, and an armoured brigade of
unknown quality was near Mechili. Graziani seems to have expected
no more of Tobruk than that it should gain time for resistance to
be organized on a front between Derna and Mechili, and for
further forces, principally artillery, to arrive from Tripoli. The
Ariete Armoured Division and the Trento Motorized Division were
being prepared for despatch from Italy, but could not possibly arrive
in time to be of any use.

The 7th Armoured and 6th Australian Divisions outside Tobruk
were out of reach of their Field Supply Depots at Capuzzo and
Sollum; a new depot was therefore formed for each division (Nos. 10
and 11) about 35 miles east of Tobruk. The problem this time was to
supply their daily needs; build up the requirements for the attack;
and create enough reserves to tide over the time that would be required before the port of Tobruk was in working order. This meant
another period of intense road convoy work in which captured
lorries played an important part, but even so it was a very difficult

---

[1] R. Graziani: *Africa Settentrionale* page 182.

period for the transport and there was one local crisis after another. One day it was aviation petrol; on another, rations. The worst troubles were due to the sandstorms, which upset all calculations; one convoy carrying five days' supplies for 7th Armoured Division was lost in a storm for four days. Water was a problem, as usual, and at first had to be carried from Capuzzo to fill cisterns at Gambut; once again the allowance was down to half a gallon a day.

The leap-frogging of Field Supply Depots in such a way that a division should always have one of them within reach had been on the whole very successful, but it was beginning to fail in respect of many items which the fighting troops could do without for a few days, though a flow of them was necessary if fighting efficiency was to be kept up. It will be seen later that the Field Supply Depot was to grow into the much more elaborate Field Maintenance Centre, which was practically a small advanced base containing rations, petrol, water and ammunition, as well as ordnance, engineer, and medical stores, and containing also a transit camp, army post office, and a prisoners' cage. But this was yet some way off; present conditions were distinctly hand to mouth.

The basic difficulty at such a time is to relate bulk despatches—in this case by sea from Alexandria—to the ever changing circumstances of the tactical situation. Until a reserve can be created from which detailed issues can be made (corresponding to a retail organization in civil life) it is impossible to meet a sudden demand; a shipload of ammunition is no answer to an urgent need for petrol or rations; that particular ship was so loaded in response to a forecast made several days before, and every ship is not suitable for every kind of cargo. Even when mixed cargoes arrive, the consumer will want certain items to be offloaded urgently, regardless of the effect on the general turn-round of the shipping. At Sollum the army's share of the working of the port was run by an advanced detachment of General Wilson's headquarters, largely with the object of taking some of the load off General O'Connor and his 13th Corps (as Western Desert Force was called after 1st January). Experience showed, however, that in the rapidly changing situation it was a handicap to 13th Corps not to control the working of the sea-head. It was accordingly agreed that when Tobruk was captured 13th Corps would be responsible for the working of the port, at any rate until sufficient stocks had been landed to make them independent of the arrival of bulk cargoes. The whole relationship between the three headquarters was reviewed, and General Wavell decided to relieve General Wilson of responsibility for 13th Corps, which then came directly under his own headquarters.

The port of Bardia added almost nothing to the capacity of the L. of C., and it was mainly used for sending small cargoes to Greece.

x

Sollum remained for practical purposes the only sea-head, and great efforts were made to increase its capacity. By the middle of January it was able to handle 350 tons a day and by the end over 500; in addition it was shipping prisoners away at the rate of 3,000 a day, and evacuating casualties. Even so, it was necessary to run some road convoys all the way from Matruh; only in this way were 120,000 gallons of petrol on one occasion, and 16,000 rations on another, obtained to meet an emergency.

On 5th January the ships employed off the North African coast, which since 15th December had been operating under Captain H. M. L. Waller, R.A.N., were formed into the Inshore Squadron under the command of Captain H. Hickling. They were the monitor *Terror*; gunboats *Aphis*, *Gnat*, and *Ladybird*; three minesweepers; four anti-submarine trawlers; various schooners and small motor-vessels captured and commissioned under the White Ensign; and numerous lighters and store-ships, British and Egyptian. Captain Hickling had a mobile headquarters ashore and acted as chief naval liaison officer with the Army and Air Force in the field.

Tobruk had many military features in common with Bardia. There was the same hard flat desert floor sloping down to the coast in a series of steps, with the ground near the coast deeply indented by ravines. The defences formed a rough semi-circle eight or nine miles distant from the town and harbour, giving a perimeter of over thirty miles. They consisted of a double ring of concreted posts behind a barbed wire fence, all with excellent fields of fire; an anti-tank ditch, not everywhere complete, ran the length of the front. Numerous booby-traps, worked by trip-wires, were to cause many casualties. Nearer the town, and especially around the junction of the Bardia and El Adem roads and for some distance towards Forts Pilastrino and Solaro, were other localities forming the inner defences.

As compared with Bardia, Tobruk had half the number of men to defend twice the length of front, so it was hoped that its capture would not be difficult. It was important to waste no time since the port was badly needed as a sea-head. But in order to capture the harbour and other installations intact it was necessary that the attack, once launched, should go through with the utmost speed. This in its turn meant bringing forward 1,000 tons of artillery ammunition, almost all of which came by sea to Sollum.

There was unfortunately no alternative to a deliberate attack, for the Armoured Division, though first on the scene, was not capable of forcing its way through prepared defences. To launch it against them prematurely would have had a negligible chance of success but would certainly have blunted it effectively as a weapon of pursuit. The dwindling strength of 7th Armoured Division—now down to 69 cruisers and 126 light tanks—was already a cause of anxiety. Two regiments (8th King's Royal Irish Hussars and 6th Royal Tank Regiment) were therefore withdrawn, and their tanks used to make up the remaining four regiments. Thus reconstituted, the division prepared to advance to Derna and Mechili as soon as Tobruk should fall. A second armoured division (the 2nd) had just arrived in Egypt from England; it, too, consisted of four regiments only. Its two cruiser regiments were moved up to Cyrenaica early in February though they were not in a satisfactory mechanical state.

The conduct of the attack was entrusted to General Mackay, and the plan was again based on the need for helping the 'I' tanks through the anti-tank belt. A portion of the perimeter about three miles east of the El Adem road was chosen as the narrow front on which a battalion of 16th Australian Infantry Brigade was to capture the inner and outer posts before daylight. Through this gap the remainder of the brigade and 7th R.T.R. would pass, turn east and west along the perimeter, and make a thrust towards Tobruk to give depth to the bridgehead. The 17th Brigade and the Support Group were to carry out diversionary operations on the eastern and western faces of the perimeter. An important feature of this plan was the care taken to locate hostile batteries and to neutralize them during the attack.

During the preparatory period the Air Force was seriously hampered by sandstorms; such attacks as could be made were divided between the inner defences of Tobruk and the airfields at Benina and Berka where the Italian bombers were now based. From 3 to 6 a.m. on January 21st Wellingtons of Nos. 37 and 38 Squadrons were over the Tobruk area, bombing and drowning the noise of the assembling tanks and artillery. From midnight to 2 a.m. the *Terror*, with two gunboats and a minesweeper, bombarded the inner defences, while destroyers stood ready to intercept the cruiser *San Giorgio* should she try to break out.

At 5.40 a.m. on 21st January the 2/3rd Battalion, strongly supported by the artillery, crossed their start line and advanced to the attack; meanwhile the engineers, who had disarmed the booby traps earlier in the night, cleared the mines and made passages through the wire and over the ditch. Within an hour the 16th Brigade with eighteen 'I' tanks had punched a hole a mile wide and a mile deep against resistance which varied from the negligible to the very stubborn. At 8.40 a.m., while the 16th Brigade was still fanning out to east and west, the 19th Brigade took up the advance northwards under a heavy barrage and concentrations on hostile battery positions. Most of the opposition came from the left, at the defended locality at the Bardia-El Adem road junction, and 2/8th Battalion had some stiff opposition from dug-in tanks and machine-guns. Brigadier Robertson decided to go through with his plan and at

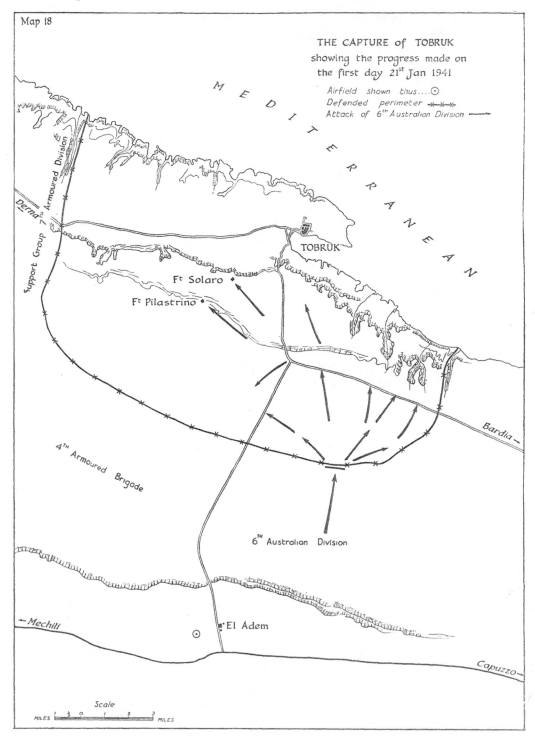

Map 18

THE CAPTURE of TOBRUK
showing the progress made on
the first day 21st Jan 1941

Airfield shown thus....⊙
Defended perimeter ✕—✕—✕
Attack of 6th Australian Division ——

M E D I T E R R A N E A N

Derna

Support Group 7th Armoured Division

TOBRUK

Ft Solaro

Ft Pilastrino

Bardia

4TH Armoured Brigade

6TH Australian Division

← Mechili

El Adem

Capuzzo →

Scale
MILES 1 ½ 0 1 2 3 MILES

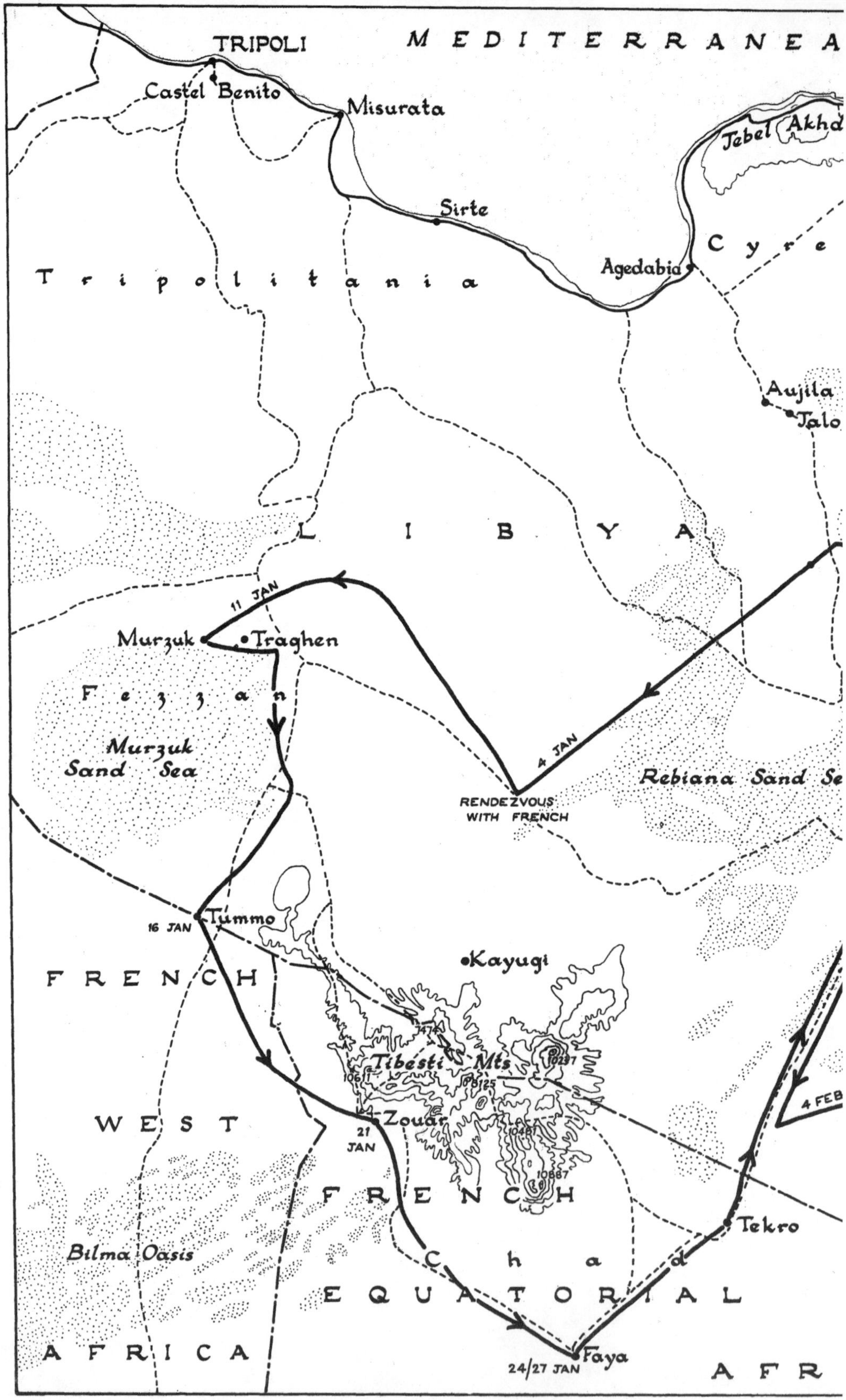
TRIPOLI
MEDITERRANEA
Castel Benito
Misurata
Jebel Akhd
Sirte
Cyre
Agedabia
Tripolitania
Aujila
Jalo
LIBYA
11 JAN
Murzuk
Traghen
Fezzan
Murzuk Sand Sea
4 JAN
Rebiana Sand Se
RENDEZVOUS WITH FRENCH
16 JAN
Tummo
Kayugi
FRENCH
Tibesti Mts
10237
10611
4 FEB
WEST
Zouar
21 JAN
FRENCH
Tekro
Bilma Oasis
Chad
EQUATORIAL
AFRICA
Faya
24/27 JAN
AFR

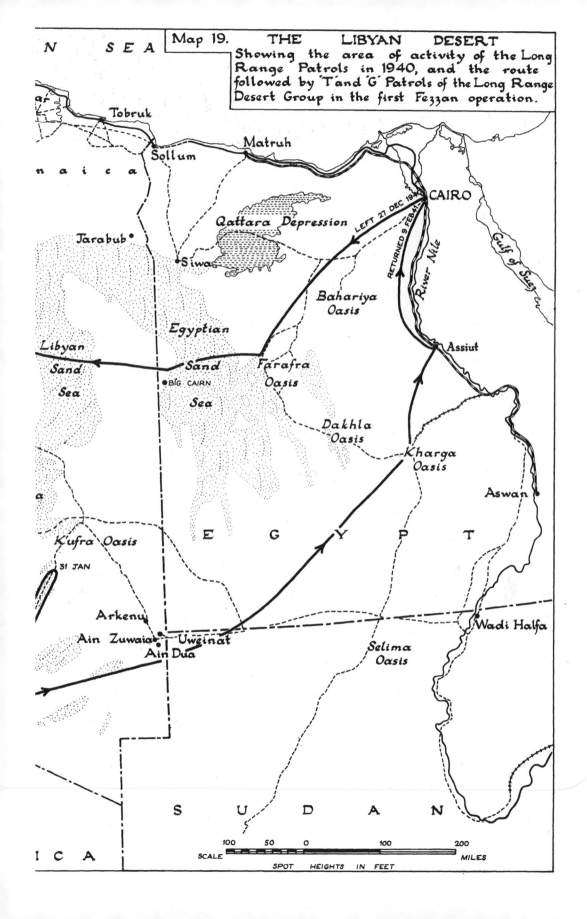

Map 19. THE LIBYAN DESERT
Showing the area of activity of the Long Range Patrols in 1940, and the route followed by 'T and G' Patrols of the Long Range Desert Group in the first Fezzan operation.

2 p.m. his brigade resumed its advance. Once more on the right and in the centre little opposition was met, but again the left battalion ran into trouble. First it met a counter-attack by seven medium tanks accompanied by some infantry covered by a barrage; this was routed by the Australians with the help of two anti-tank guns of 3rd R.H.A. and two 'I' tanks. Then there was stubborn resistance from another locality near Pilastrino which was not overcome until 9.30 p.m. Meanwhile, the Solaro area had been captured, and with it the Fortress Commander, General Pitassi Mannella. So ended a successful but very strenuous day. The 2/8th Battalion perhaps had the hardest time of all; marching 20 miles since 4.30 a.m., fighting their way for 5 of them, and losing over 100 killed or wounded. Between dawn and dusk Blenheims of Nos. 55 and 113 Squadrons had made 56 sorties against enemy positions inside the Tobruk defences, while Gladiators of No. 3 Squadron R.A.A.F. and Hurricanes of Nos. 73 and 274 Squadrons had maintained offensive patrols west of Tobruk.

By nightfall nearly half the defended area had been captured, and it was clear that the battle had been won. The rising smoke and sound of explosions told that the Italians had begun their work of destruction. During the night, therefore, General Mackay ordered a general advance next morning. It was followed by an Italian collapse. At dawn Major-General Della Mura, commanding 61st Sirte Division, surrendered with several thousand officers and men to the 2/8th Battalion. Brigadier Robertson, who had followed a small party of 6th Australian Cavalry Regiment into Tobruk, received the surrender of Admiral Vietina and the naval garrison. By 3.45 p.m. the last strong point had surrendered. The captures included 25,000 prisoners (including 2,000 sailors), 208 field and medium guns and 87 tanks. The total casualties in 13th Corps were just over 400, of which 355 were Australians.

Arrangements had been made to take over the installations as rapidly as possible, and it was a great relief to find that the demolitions had been confined chiefly to guns and ammunition. In the harbour the *San Giorgio* was beached and burning, and there were many other wrecks. A naval fuel plant had been destroyed and the floating crane sunk. The jetties were damaged but usable; the power-station was in working order, with 4,000 tons of coal; there was a complete bulk petrol storage installation; a refrigeration plant and a distillation plant were undamaged; and 10,000 tons of stored water were found. The Inshore Squadron began at once its task of sweeping for mines and on the morning of January 24th the harbour was ready to receive shipping.[1]

---

[1] See Photos 19, 20, 21.

The whole of the desert campaign so far described took place in a comparatively narrow strip, though more than wide enough for the Armoured Division to make full use of its mobility. Farther to the south, beyond the oases of Siwa, Jarabub, and Jalo, lies the inner or Libyan desert (a part of the Sahara twice the size of France) of which the Western Desert is a mere fringe. Except within the oasis depressions, to the floors of which artesian water rises, the Libyan Desert is uninhabited and utterly without life, through lack of any local rain. This was the scene of many of the exploits of the Long Range Desert Group. (See Map 19 and Photo 22).

Through this inner desert ran the eastern frontier of Libya, and within their territory the Italians had established a system of military posts and landing grounds. They had organized special colonial forces for duty in the desert; of these the motorized 'Auto-Saharan' companies had the advantage of the permanent co-operation of a few reconnaissance aircraft, but were designed to operate over comparatively good surfaces—principally between and around the posts. The French had also had special Saharan units, and at the Rabat meeting in May 1939 they had contemplated operations against Italian desert posts in Fezzan.

One series of Italian posts, linked by a well-used track, stretched south through Jalo and Kufra to Uweinat, 600 miles inland, the nearest Italian post to the East African Empire a thousand miles away across the Sudan. When war broke out the garrisons of these posts continued their watch and ward with their sense of security from ground attack undisturbed, thanks to the natural barrier formed by the great Egyptian Sand Sea which lay to the eastward.

The few people who knew by experience that sand seas were not complete obstacles to all forms of motor transport were a handful of Englishmen whose professions had taken them to the Middle East between the wars, and who had made a hobby of desert travel and exploration. Among these were W. B. Kennedy Shaw, P. A. Clayton, and G. L. Prendergast, with Major R. A. Bagnold as prime mover and usual leader. Between 1932 and 1938 they had learned much about motor travel in the inner desert, and some had actually crossed the Egyptian Sand Sea. They had acquired the skill to discern a course amidst the huge sand dunes, and had mastered the art of driving a vehicle up and across them without embedding or overturning it. They had invented 'unsticking' devices, such as the sand-channel; they had studied and adapted methods of navigation; and they had gained experience of desert surfaces of all types, from loose sand to fields of basalt.

One thing they knew was that this vast inland flank was unlikely to become the scene of operations by large forces. For one thing, the dune barrier of the sand sea could be crossed at only a few narrow places, and at these the surface would not stand up to the passage of more than twenty or thirty trucks. Parties would therefore have to be small and, because distances were vast, would have to be self-contained for a long time. They would need to have great confidence in their own powers, especially of finding their position astronomically, for the chance of being lost in almost lunar surroundings is a great deterrent to moving far away from reliable tracks.

These considerations led to the adoption of the 30-cwt. truck as a basic 'unit' of organization, carrying petrol for 1,100 miles, and food and water for three weeks for a crew of two or three, besides weapons and much other equipment. Only Major Bagnold and his few colleagues knew how to organize and train parties to carry out long patrols over the many varied types of desert; how to modify vehicles for their special purpose; what to carry; how to find the way; in short, how to eat, drink, travel, work, and fight in the severe and unusual conditions. It was not every man whose temperament and aptitude qualified him as a recruit for this sort of campaigning. For all these reasons it was judged that long-range patrol work in the desert was essentially a task for small and highly skilled detachments.

In 1939 Major Bagnold foresaw the possibility of turning his experience to good account if Italy should enter the war, by creating patrols which could reconnoitre and harry the enemy in unexpected places. He submitted proposals which appealed greatly to General Wavell's imagination and love of the unorthodox, but nothing came of them until Italy had entered the war and the French (and their Saharan troops) had dropped out. The formation of a Long Range Patrol Unit was then approved. Bagnold was present by chance and was soon joined by Shaw and Clayton. They felt that no recruits would be more suitable than men from the 'outback', like some of the Queenslanders in Palestine, but the Australian Government was opposed to its men serving outside Australian formations and General Blamey felt unable to agree. Three patrols, each of two officers and about thirty men, were chosen from the New Zealanders in Egypt and after six arduous weeks of training the small unit was inspected by General Wavell and declared fit for operations. Captain Clayton had already taken a small party on one valuable reconnaissance; he had discovered a second sand sea (the 'Libyan') to the east of the Jalo-Kufra track; and had found a way across it.

During September the new unit went out on its first long patrol. The crossings of the sand sea were further explored; several Italian landing grounds between Jalo and Kufra were visited and damaged; the exits from Kufra and Uweinat were reconnoitred, and some prisoners and transport were taken. Contact was also made with the French post at Tekro. Meanwhile quantities of petrol, food and water were dumped at points beyond the Libyan frontier for future use, and with the help of the Air Force a number of sites for landing grounds were chosen.

By now it was apparent that the Italian policy was purely defensive; there were no signs of any intention to raid the Nile valley, and there had not even been any activity in conjunction with Graziani's advance to Sidi Barrani. The initiative seemed to be left to the British, and in October the Patrol set out again, this time with more aggressive intentions. The road between Aujila and Agedabia was mined in half a dozen places; Aujila fort was attacked, and made no resistance; the Italian post at Ain Zuwaia was reconnoitred and a Savoia bomber found on the landing ground was destroyed; the track between Uweinat and Arkenu was mined; and a large dump of bombs and explosives was blown up. A landing ground was made at Big Cairn, and was used by a Valentia of No. 216 Bomber Transport Squadron fitted with long-range tanks, which co-operated with this patrol, carrying stores and first-aid equipment. Several other landing grounds were made ready for future use. The Patrol's own tracks were studied from the air and many lessons in concealment learned; valuable because Italian aircraft were their worst enemies, and were already to be seen and heard from time to time.

These successes confirmed General Wavell's opinion that the Patrol was making an important addition to the anxieties and difficulties of the enemy, and the War Office agreed with his proposal that the unit should be doubled and become the Long Range Desert Group. The right men were hard to find, however, because they were of the type which units could least well spare, and Major-General Freyberg was indeed asking for the return of his New Zealanders. A new patrol was formed from officers and men of the 3rd Coldstream Guards and 2nd Scots Guards, and in November this patrol and the New Zealanders were out in the southern and northern areas respectively. They explored the dunes between Jalo and Jarabub, and made new store and fuel dumps. In the Uweinat area they were bombed by aircraft, but attacked the Italian post at Ain Dua and inflicted several casualties.

The next step was to make touch with the Free French in the Chad Territory. It was hoped that they would join in harrying the Italians, and when Major Bagnold visited Fort Lamy in November he found that the prospect appealed to many, especially the junior officers. It was agreed that the French should send a detachment with the British patrols on a raid into Fezzan, and should also assist by transporting a small extra supply of petrol by camel to a meeting place north of the Tibesti Mountains. This plan was attractive to the British because its success would reduce the likelihood of Italian or tribal raids on the Takoradi air reinforcement route, especially in Nigeria. It was also arranged that the (British) West African

Command should send further supplies of petrol to Chad from Nigeria, if need be. Shortly afterwards Colonel Leclerc assumed military command of Chad and at once began to make preparations for the capture of Kufra by his own troops, but he asked that the British patrols, on their return from the forthcoming Fezzan operation, should join him.

Towards the end of December, while the Western Desert Force was preparing to attack Bardia, a New Zealand Patrol and the Guards Patrol left Cairo for the first Fezzan operation. With them went Sheikh Abd el Galil Seif en Nasr, a veteran of the long Arab struggle against Italian conquest, partly to act as guide and partly to remind the Italians that the Senussi had not forgotten them. A week later, having travelled 1,300 miles, the Patrols were joined, to the north of Kayugi, by the small French detachment under Lieut.-Colonel d'Ornano. The combined force then made a detour and attacked Murzuk from the north. The fort was strongly defended, but the raiders set fire to the tower, attacked the airfield—whose guards surrendered—seized the arms, wrecked the wireless, burned three aircraft, and destroyed the hangar. Five casualties were suffered, among them Lieut.-Colonel d'Ornano, whose death was a sad loss. A few Italian prisoners were carried off. The party then raided Traghen police fort, removed the arms, and destroyed the ammunition. Two other forts, which were now thoroughly alert, were fired into. Soon after this, the Italians decided to withdraw their garrison from Uweinat.

The British patrols returned by way of the French base at Faya, and were joined by a new French detachment: the whole then came under command of Colonel Leclerc for the operation against Kufra. Four days later the British force, while reconnoitring ahead of the French, was attacked from the air and by troops of an Italian Auto-Saharan Company. Captain Clayton was wounded and taken prisoner, and several men and trucks were lost. Colonel Leclerc then decided that he could not take Kufra on this occasion and released the British patrols, which reached Cairo in early February 1941, having covered 4,300 miles since they left it 45 days before. By this time Cyrenaica was almost clear of the enemy, and it was decided that for its future activities the Long Range Desert Group would need a base much farther west than Cairo. The spirited capture of Kufra on March 1st, by a French force no more numerous than the garrison, provided the new base, to which the Headquarters and three Patrols of the now enlarged Group moved in April, in readiness for further operations.

Further operations of 13th Corps, No. 202 Group, and the Inshore Squadron, which resulted in the Italians being driven out of Cyrenaica, are described in Chapter XIX, where the story is resumed at the point reached in the present chapter, namely, the capture of Tobruk. It must be remembered that the three Commanders-in-Chief had a great deal to think about apart from the Western Desert, and their conduct of the war cannot be fully understood without considering the changing situation as a whole. For this reason it is necessary now to see how the maritime war was progressing, and how it came about that, almost simultaneously with the capture of Tobruk, the encouraging naval and air situation in the Mediterranean took a violent turn for the worse. This was not the only anxiety, however, for in the middle of January there were discussions with the Greek Government to ascertain what help the Greeks would like to receive from the British. The Italian defeat in the Western Desert, the progress of the war on the Albanian front, and the prospect of German intervention in Greece formed the main background for these talks, which are described in Chapter XVIII. The result might well have been to put an end to the operations in Cyrenaica; but, as it turned out, the Greeks declined the offer of land forces, whereupon the British Government laid down that the capture of Benghazi was of the greatest importance. This intimation was received on the day of the assault on Tobruk. It necessitated no change in General O'Connor's immediate plans, for he had already ordered the 7th Armoured Division and one Australian brigade group to be ready to resume the advance westwards, and this was the most that could be done until the supply situation improved.

# CHAPTER XVI

# SUPREMACY AT SEA

THE SUCCESSFUL outcome of the operation in early September of sailing naval reinforcements right through the Mediterranean, with a call at Malta,[1] gave rise to proposals for passing merchant vessels to Malta and the Eastern Mediterranean in the same way. The Commander-in-Chief and Admiral Somerville both agreed that this should be feasible, provided that the merchant ships could make at least 16 knots. It had accordingly been proposed to combine a movement of this sort with that of the passage of the *Barham* and other ships which took place early in November,[2] but delays in the United Kingdom had prevented the merchant ships being ready. The next opportunity occurred during a complicated series of movements of the Eastern Mediterranean Fleet which included the escorting of ships to and from Malta and the passage of the *Ramillies*, *Berwick*, and *Newcastle* out of the Mediterranean westwards.

The arrival of the *Barham*, coupled with the success at Taranto, had enabled Admiral Cunningham to report that he could do without the *Ramillies*, an offer which was welcomed by the Admiralty in view of the activity of raiders in the Atlantic. Indeed, the exploits of the *Scheer* prompted them to suggest that the *Valiant* might be released also. Admiral Cunningham represented, however, that the *Valiant* and *Warspite* were the only two battleships with the necessary fuel endurance and gun range for operating against the Italian fleet, and it was decided that instead of the *Valiant* he should part with the 8-inch cruiser *Berwick*, whose high freeboard and other qualities made her suitable for service in the Atlantic. The cruiser *Newcastle*, which had made an independent passage carrying airmen and stores to Malta, was also due to return to her duties in the Atlantic.

The plan was briefly as follows. Three fast merchant ships known as 'Collar' convoy—two for Malta (*Clan Forbes* and *Clan Fraser*) and one for Alexandria (*New Zealand Star*)—would pass through the Straits of Gibraltar on the night of 24th/25th November, escorted by the 6-inch cruisers *Manchester* and *Southampton*, with Vice-Admiral L. E. Holland flying his flag in the former. In addition to a few soldiers each cruiser was to carry about 700 airmen, comprising the ground crews for air reinforcements being flown from Takoradi to

---

[1] Operation 'Hats': page 201.
[2] Operation 'Coat': page 241.

replace the squadrons sent to Greece. East of Gibraltar they would be joined by four minesweeping corvettes destined for the Eastern Mediterranean. The *Renown, Ark Royal,* two 6-inch cruisers, *Sheffield* and *Despatch,* and nine destroyers of Force H would provide general cover to the northward. On the morning of the 27th a rendezvous would be made south of Sardinia with Force D, consisting of the *Ramillies, Newcastle* and *Berwick* coming from the east supported by the *Coventry* and five of Admiral Cunningham's destroyers. Force D would then turn and accompany Admiral Somerville to a position between Sicily and Cape Bon, which they would reach at dusk. Here Force H with the *Ramillies, Newcastle* and *Berwick* would part company for Gibraltar, while Admiral Holland, reinforced by the remainder of what had been Force D, would pass through the Sicilian Narrows with the convoy. Next day he would meet the Mediterranean Fleet; the ships for Malta would break off, and the remainder would be escorted to Alexandria.

The position of the cruisers in which troops were to travel required careful consideration. With 700 extra men on board it seemed to Admiral Holland that neither ship would be in a fit condition to fight, and in case of a hit the casualties among these important reinforcements might be heavy; it might be better, therefore, for the two cruisers to proceed independently and trust to their high speed. Admiral Somerville's view was that, as the main units of the Italian fleet were now thought to be based on the west coast of Italy, having left Taranto on November 12th, the enemy might bring three battleships, seven 8-inch and several 6-inch cruisers against him; and the best deterrent to the Italians was to make as strong a show of force as possible. In addition to the safe passage of the troops he had also to consider that of the merchant ships and minesweeping corvettes; he concluded that these objects would be more likely to be achieved if he kept his own forces concentrated. But because of the possibility of an encounter later with the enemy he asked the Commander-in-Chief to say which should come first, the safety of the merchant ships or that of the troops in the cruisers. The reply was, the troops; and with this decision the Admiralty concurred, subject to the proviso that if enemy forces were in sight the action taken by warships carrying airmen and soldiers must be the same as if they were not on board.

The operations began on November 23rd with the departure from Alexandria of Vice-Admiral Pridham-Wippell in the *Orion* with the 7th Cruiser Squadron, the *Malaya, Ramillies, Eagle,* and nine destroyers, to refuel at Suda Bay. The Malta convoy (M.W.4) of four ships left Egyptian ports escorted by the *Calcutta, Coventry,* and four destroyers, routed north of Crete. Two days later the Commander-in-Chief in the *Warspite,* with the *Valiant, Illustrious,* and a further nine destroyers put to sea, and that night fifteen Swordfish from the *Illustrious* made an attack on the seaplane base at Leros in the Dodecanese. Meanwhile, aircraft from the *Eagle* attacked Tripoli, where one large ship was set on fire. Early on the 26th convoy M.W.4 arrived safely at Malta, having been attacked only by three torpedo-bombers when north of Crete. At noon the *Ramillies, Newcastle, Coventry*, and five destroyers left Malta to be joined by the *Berwick*, the whole forming Force D which was to rendezvous with Admiral Somerville next day. The main Mediterranean Fleet provided general cover to the south and east of Malta, while cruisers swept to the north-east as convoy M.E.4 of five empty ships sailed from Malta for Alexandria.

At 8 a.m. on November 27th, which was half an hour before sunrise, Admiral Somerville was about 100 miles to the south-west of Cape Spartivento. Twenty-five miles to the west-south-west were the *Manchester* and *Southampton* with the merchant ships. The minesweeping corvettes, unable to keep up, were some 10 miles astern. No reports had been received from aircraft based on Malta to suggest any aggressive move by the Italian Fleet. The visibility was excellent and the sea calm. Further reconnaissance by aircraft flown off the *Ark Royal* produced a negative report, and Admiral Somerville concluded that the most likely form of interference by the enemy would be from the air; accordingly at 9 o'clock he altered course, intending to fall back upon the convoy so as to be able to give it more effective anti-aircraft defence.

Before this alteration of course was made, however, aircraft from the carrier had transmitted two alarm reports; enemy warships were in sight to the south of Cape Spartivento, steering south-west.[1] These reports were not received by any British ship, so the *Renown*, with Force H, continued to steer away from the enemy until at 10.5 a report, made at 9.20 and transmitted from the *Ark Royal*, was received by Admiral Somerville indicating that five cruisers and five destroyers were sixty miles to the north-east of him. At first he imagined that this must refer to Force D coming from the eastward, but he never-theless began to work up to full speed on a north-easterly course. By 10.15 further reports had indicated the presence of enemy battleships and heavy cruisers, and shadowing aircraft had been detected. Admiral Somerville's first consideration now was to effect a concen-tration with Force D as quickly as possible. At this moment a Sunderland flying-boat, on reconnaissance from Malta, signalled the presence of Force D, and half an hour later the two British forces were in sight of each other.

The cruisers *Manchester, Southampton* and *Sheffield* were ordered to

---

[1] The action off Cape Spartivento is called by the Italians 'The action off Cape Teulada'. There is another Cape Spartivento off Calabria at the toe of Italy.

concentrate with the destroyers in the van, where they were later joined by the *Berwick*, *Newcastle* and the five destroyers from Force D. The convoy was directed to steer inside Galita Island, escorted by the old cruiser *Despatch* and two destroyers, to be reinforced by the *Coventry* from Force D. The *Ark Royal* was ordered to prepare an air striking force and act independently. The situation was still far from clear as the reports from the air contained many discrepancies. It seemed that five or six enemy cruisers were present, but the number of battleships was in doubt. In the circumstances Admiral Somerville decided that the best course was to show a bold front and attack the enemy as soon as possible.

At 11.15 the enemy, who had originally been seen steering to the westward, was reported as having altered course to the eastward. Thus the action seemed likely to develop into a chase, and as soon as the *Ramillies* came into sight she was ordered, on account of her low speed, to alter to a course parallel to that of the *Renown*. Shortly after this the *Ark Royal* flew off the first striking force of eleven torpedo-bomber aircraft. Just before noon the Sunderland reported an enemy force of six cruisers and eight destroyers thirty miles to the north-north-west of the *Renown*. This was much farther to the west than those previously reported and suggested the possibility that this force might work round astern and attack the *Ark Royal* and the convoy. Unfortunately communication with the flying-boat was lost before the course of the enemy just reported could be ascertained, but the Admiral considered it prudent to alter the movement of the British forces to due north.

The cruisers were now spread in line abreast about eight miles ahead, with the destroyers concentrated in a favourable position between them and the *Renown*. The flagship had developed a hot bearing in one shaft and could do no more than 27 knots, but she soon overtook the *Ramillies* which then followed astern at her best speed of 20·7 knots. The situation was still obscure, though there seemed to be a good prospect of bringing the enemy to action. The British forces had effected their concentration apparently unknown to the enemy, for the shadowing aircraft had lost touch; the sun was to the south, giving Admiral Somerville the advantage of the light; and there seemed to be a fair chance that he would be able to deliver simultaneous torpedo-bomber and surface attacks.

At this stage a reference to the report of the Italian Commander-in-Chief will make the subsequent action clear.

On November 25th Admiral Angelo Campioni, the Italian Commander-in-Chief afloat, got news that British forces had left Gibraltar. The available ships were the two battleships *Vittorio Veneto* and *Giulio Cesare*, seven 8-inch cruisers and sixteen destroyers; these left Naples and Messina at noon on the 26th, met, and steamed to the westward. The Admiral was also aware that the British Fleet had left Alexandria, and shortly after midnight he received from a torpedo boat a report of seven British warships off Cape Bon steering to the westward. This was Force D, and Campioni correctly assumed that it was on the way to join Force H. At 10.15 a.m. on the 27th, just after Admiral Somerville first became aware of the enemy, the Italian Commander-in-Chief received a report from an aircraft catapulted off one of his cruisers that one battleship, two light cruisers, and four destroyers were some 135 miles to the south-west of Cape Spartivento, steering east. This report undoubtedly referred to the *Renown* and the ships in company with Somerville, although the position given was well to the west of the real one, and no report had been made of the *Ark Royal*.

Map 20

**Action off
Cape Spartivento**
Situation shortly before noon
27th November 1940

Approx scale of Sea Miles

Having had this report confirmed, Admiral Campioni led his squadron round to the south-east at 11.28, and the cruisers conformed. He expected an encounter between the whole of his force and the *Renown*, with possibly two cruisers and a few destroyers, and he wished to bring this about in waters nearer to Sicily than to Sardinia. At a few minutes before noon he was suddenly presented with a very different picture, for a new report not only placed the *Renown's* group twenty miles nearer than was supposed, but it disclosed the presence of the aircraft carrier and showed that junction had already been made with Force D.

'A state of affairs', wrote Admiral Campioni in his official report, 'was thus created which at best was unfavourable to us both in numbers and quality'. In reality there were two capital ships on each side; seven Italian 8-inch cruisers against one 8-inch and four 6-inch British; sixteen Italian destroyers against ten. But the Italian Admiral attached particular significance to the presence of the *Ark Royal*, whose aircraft might cause much damage if their action was synchronized with that of the surface ships. He had been warned by the Minister of Marine that it was particularly important to avoid damage now that half the Italian battlefleet had been put out of action at Taranto. In view of these instructions Admiral Campioni considered that it was his duty not to become involved in battle in the existing circumstances. He admits that he ought to have been able to count on the effective intervention of shore-based aircraft, but his previous experience discouraged him from setting too much store by this. Accordingly, at 12.15 p.m. he hoisted the signal to alter course to due east, and ordered: 'Do not join action'.

But the cruisers were already in action. From the *Renown* smoke had been sighted to the northward at 12.15, and eight minutes later the Italian cruisers opened fire. The British cruisers and the *Renown* replied—the latter at 27,000 yards—and even the *Ramillies* fired a couple of salvoes. All shots from the capital ships fell short, and after six salvoes the *Renown's* target was lost in smoke. A running fight now took place between the cruisers on an east-north-east course, with the Italians gaining in distance all the time. From one of the first enemy salvoes the *Berwick* had her after turret put out of action, and fifteen minutes later she received another hit. Indeed, Admiral Holland recorded that he was very much impressed by the accuracy of the Italians' opening salvoes, compared with that of his own cruisers, and ascribed it to the superiority of their range-finding instruments.

At 12.44 the eleven aircraft from the *Ark Royal* found the two Italian battleships 25 to 30 miles to the eastward, screened by eight destroyers. The *Vittorio Veneto* was selected as the target, and all the torpedoes were dropped within the destroyer screen at distances from 700 to 800 yards. Admiral Somerville reported that one hit was

21. Damage to the wharves at Tobruk.

*Facing p. 304*

22. A Patrol of the Long Range Desert Group.

23. What the air sees of a column in the desert. Taken from just outside the perimeter of the Bardia defences.

24. The cruisers *Berwick*, *Newcastle*, and *Southampton* in action off the coast of Sardinia, 27th November 1940.

*Facing p. 305*

observed just abaft the after funnel, but Admiral Campioni records that although the attack was carried out with resolution it was effectively countered by manoeuvring and gunfire. In his turn he claimed that two British aircraft were brought down, whereas in fact they all returned safely to the carrier.

Meanwhile the action between the cruisers continued. No more hits were obtained on any British ship, but the *Manchester* was straddled several times. Smoke from the enemy made observation difficult for the British, but it was believed that, at the least, one cruiser and two destroyers were hit. According to Admiral Campioni, however, one destroyer—the *Lanciere*—was put out of action, and this was all the damage suffered by the Italians throughout the engagement. About 1 o'clock the two Italian battleships were sighted from the British cruisers, and as large projectiles began to fall round his ships Admiral Holland altered course to the south-east in order to draw the enemy towards the *Renown*. As the enemy did not conform he altered back and continued the chase. The enemy were now rapidly running out of range, and at 1.18 the action ceased.

Meanwhile Admiral Somerville was faced with the choice of continuing the chase or of falling back towards the convoy. The enemy had drawn out of range; heavy smoke had prevented accurate fire, and as far as he knew no serious damage had been inflicted that was likely to reduce the enemy's speed. To his question to Holland, 'Is there any hope of catching cruisers?' he had received the answer 'No'. He was being led towards a dense smoke screen close to the enemy's air, submarine, and light force bases at Cagliari. One of the main objects of the whole operation was the safe passage of the convoy, and it was important to give the merchant ships as much protection as possible against torpedo-bomber attacks at dusk. In addition to this, he was still without any further information of the enemy cruisers which had been reported farther to the westward by the flying-boat shortly before noon. There was the possibility that this force had worked round and would attack the *Ark Royal*, 45 miles away to the south-west, and the convoy. (As it happened, the flying-boat's report referred to the Italian cruisers which were almost due north of the *Renown* at noon, and were about to turn to the eastward.) Lastly, there were the troops in the *Manchester* and *Southampton* to be taken into account; so far both ships had escaped damage. At 1.15 p.m. he decided to abandon the chase and rejoin the convoy.

At the same time he considered the question of sending another air striking force against the Italian battleships, but decided not to do so because the attack could not take place before 3.30 or 4 p.m. by which time the enemy fleet would be well under cover of the shore defences of Cagliari. Instead, he ordered an attack to be made on an enemy cruiser which had been reported stopped and damaged some

Y

thirty miles to the north of the *Renown*. The Captain of the *Ark Royal*, correctly appreciating that Admiral Somerville had not received the report of the first air striking force, in which a certain hit had been claimed on the *Vittorio Veneto*, decided to send his nine torpedo-bombers against the enemy's main forces and seven Skuas to bomb the damaged vessel. The leader of the torpedo-bombers was given the *Vittorio Veneto* as his objective, with full liberty to change it. When he found the Italian battle squadron so well screened that an unobserved approach was impossible, he decided to attack one of the cruiser squadrons instead. All torpedoes missed. Meanwhile the Skuas, unable to find the damaged vessel (which was in fact the *Lanciere*, then being towed to Cagliari), bombed three other cruisers, but without success.

It was now the enemy's turn to attack from the air. The first formation was driven off by Fulmar fighters, but two more attacks were delivered shortly before 5 p.m. They were made from a high altitude, but were accurate nevertheless. The *Ark Royal* was straddled by about thirty bombs, two of which fell within ten yards of the ship, and many others were unpleasantly close.[1] Admiral Somerville remarked that neither fighter aircraft nor gunfire succeeded in breaking up the formations of the Italian air squadrons, and it was fortunate that these attacks were not repeated. As soon as the convoy was in sight the whole force proceeded eastward until dusk; then, led by the *Manchester*, with the *Southampton*, *Coventry*, and six destroyers, the merchant ships passed through the Narrows with the corvettes a few miles astern. Force H with the *Ramillies*, *Berwick*, and *Newcastle*, altered course for Gibraltar.

While the action off Cape Spartivento was taking place the Commander-in-Chief was some 150 miles to the east of Malta in readiness to meet any sortie of the Italian fleet in that direction. When he heard that the enemy had been sighted south of Sardinia he ordered the 3rd Cruiser Squadron to proceed to the west in order to cover the 'Collar' convoy. He himself followed later and by 8 a.m. next morning this important convoy came under the direct protection of the Mediterranean Fleet. The ships for Malta were detached under special escort; the *New Zealand Star* went on to Alexandria, and the corvettes to Suda Bay. By 30th November the fleet was back at Alexandria. There had been a little bombing to the west of Malta, but to the east not a single enemy aircraft was sighted and there was no sign of any shadowing.

Although the action off Cape Spartivento had been indecisive, the objects of the whole operation had been achieved. Convoy, troops, airmen, and minesweepers had all arrived safely at their destinations. It came therefore as a great surprise to Admiral Somerville to learn

---

[1] See Photo 25.

on his return to Gibraltar that the Admiralty had ordered an enquiry to be held into the discontinuance of the chase on November 27th and the failure of the second air striking force to attack the Italian battleships. It was remarkable that the enquiry was ordered without waiting for the Admiral's own detailed report. The Board of Enquiry was presided over by Admiral of the Fleet the Earl of Cork and Orrery, and its findings completely upheld the actions of Admiral Somerville and of the leader of the air striking force.

Before the operations to cover the 'Collar' convoy were completed the Admiralty informed Admiral Cunningham of the intention to send another convoy ('Excess') through the Mediterranean towards the end of the year. On this occasion five fast merchant vessels would leave the United Kingdom in a 'W.S.' convoy, and break away from it when they reached the latitude of Gibraltar.[1] Once more there were delays, and it was not until the second week in January that convoy 'Excess' reached the Mediterranean; its adventures there are described in the next chapter.

Admiral Cunningham fully agreed with the proposal, but drew attention once more to the danger of operating in the Central Mediterranean when air reconnaissance from Malta could not be provided on a scale commensurate with the many tasks. The Greek campaign had led to many additional calls upon the limited resources; even so, as long as the Italian Fleet was based on Taranto and Brindisi it had been possible for reconnaissance aircraft from Malta to observe it daily. But after the dispersal of the fleet along the west coast of Italy the number of reconnaissance aircraft was insufficient for keeping it under observation. Sunderland flying-boats, invaluable for reconnaissance over the sea, were very vulnerable in the vicinity of ports defended by enemy fighters. The Glenn Martins were very short of spares, and it was difficult to keep them serviceable. In addition, the weather had been bad. The net result was that the only information about the three Italian battleships which had left Taranto was that one was seen off Capri on 16th November and one at Spezia on the 20th.

In reply the Admiralty assured Admiral Cunningham that the Air Ministry was overcoming the difficulties which were holding up the Glenn Martins, and that more of these aircraft would soon be available. They also disclosed to him the intention to send three assault landing ships with convoy 'Excess'. These were converted Glen liners capable of eighteen and a half knots, which would carry about 2,000 Special Service (Commando type) troops who were to capture Pantelleria, a defended rock about 120 miles to the west of Malta.

---

[1] For W.S. convoys see page 244.

A plan for this purpose had been put forward by the Director of Combined Operations, Admiral of the Fleet Sir Roger Keyes, and was strongly supported by the Prime Minister. It would be a welcome and exhilarating example of the offensive spirit; the airfield on Pantelleria would be of great service as a staging point for aircraft arriving as reinforcements; fighters could be based upon it to give protection to our ships in the Sicilian Narrows; and bombers could attack targets in Sicily and Sardinia, as well as the Italian shipping bound for North Africa. The island was believed to be held in only moderate strength, and the idea was that, having captured it, the highly trained Special Service troops would be quickly relieved by troops from Malta. They would then proceed with their special equipment in the assault ships to the Middle East for whatever duties the Commanders-in-Chief might choose. The operation—known as 'Workshop'—would be commanded by Sir Roger Keyes in person.

The Commanders-in-Chief had long been aware that there would be scope in the Mediterranean for troops trained in landing operations and had arranged for a simple type of landing craft to be built in India. These took a long time to deliver but were eventually invaluable for port working. After Dunkirk the development of special landing equipment received great impetus in the United Kingdom, and in September 1940 the Middle East was told to expect five special ships with a full complement of landing craft and a nucleus of specially trained troops by about the middle of February 1941. A Combined Operations School was accordingly set up at Kabrit, on the shore of the Great Bitter Lake, at which the experience gained at home would be passed on.

The 'Workshop' proposal thus held out the prospect of an earlier arrival of special troops and equipment in the Middle East than had been expected, always supposing that they survived the action at Pantelleria. The Chiefs of Staff did not share the Prime Minister's enthusiasm for the project and at the end of November they asked Admiral Cunningham, alone of the three Commanders-in-Chief, for his remarks on it. Admiral Cunningham could not help admiring the spirit of adventure implicit in the plan, and had no reason to doubt that it was feasible. On the other hand he felt strongly that the Fleet had already very heavy responsibilities in the Mediterranean; it was by no means easy to keep Malta supplied, and to attempt to supply Pantelleria as well would involve an unjustified diversion of effort from the Eastern Mediterranean. There were not yet enough aircraft or anti-aircraft guns at Malta; how could it be right to spread our resources still wider? Pantelleria in the hands of the Italians had been no source of annoyance to us; it seemed very doubtful if we possessed the means of making it a source of annoyance to them. A much better plan would be to send the assaulting force direct to the

Eastern Mediterranean where it would be used for the early capture of some of the Dodecanese Islands, beginning with Stampalia and Scarpanto.

This proposal found no favour with the Prime Minister. If any of the Dodecanese Islands were attacked, it must be the big ones; this would need from ten to twenty thousand men, and the result would be to excite rivalry between the Turks and the Greeks, which was to be avoided. So in spite of the views of Admiral Cunningham and the doubts of the Chiefs of Staff the Defence Committee in London decided to proceed with 'Workshop'. In the middle of December, however, they had reason to believe that the Germans had in mind some form of action in the Western Mediterranean, and decided to keep a force in hand ready for instant action. 'Workshop' force was the most suitable, so that convoy 'Excess' had to sail without it. At the end of December the Chiefs of Staff wished to send the force to the Middle East round the Cape, but the Prime Minister preferred that it should carry out the Pantelleria operation on the way; this would be early in March.

The probability that the Italian battleships were now more of a threat in the western basin than elsewhere led Admiral Cunningham to propose on 6th December that before the passage of convoy 'Excess' the battleship *Malaya* should be sent to reinforce Force H. (The very next day air reconnaissance discovered two battleships at Naples, with five cruisers and many destroyers.) Once more there would be a series of interlocking operations: two empty merchant ships to be passed from Malta to Gibraltar; convoys to be taken into and out of Malta, and up and down the Aegean; a sweep by the main fleet into the Adriatic to bombard Valona; and carrier-borne air attacks on the Dodecanese and on the Tripoli supply route.

These operations began on December 16th. Leaving the Rear-Admiral, First Battle Squadron, in the *Barham* in operational control of the naval forces off the Libyan coast (including the Inshore Squadron, about to open Sollum) the Commander-in-Chief proceeded to sea in the *Warspite*, with the *Valiant, Illustrious, Gloucester, York*, and eleven destroyers, to be joined by the Vice-Admiral, Light Forces, with the cruisers already operating in the Aegean. The *Malaya* with three destroyers formed the close escort for the four ships comprising the Malta convoy (M.W.5). This convoy was routed south of Crete, but the main fleet went through the Kaso Strait in order to give the *Illustrious* an opportunity to strike at Stampalia and Rhodes. The weather was bad, however, and only a few aircraft could find their targets.

The fleet called at Suda Bay to refuel on the 17th and by noon the next day was off the island of Zante, steering north. That evening the 7th Cruiser Squadron parted company to sweep ahead as far as the line Bari—Durazzo while the battlefleet moved up to a position from which to bombard Valona, the principal sea-head for the Italian forces operating against the Greeks. Fire was opened shortly after 1 a.m. on the 19th and in eight minutes 100 rounds of 15-inch shell were fired, mostly at the airfield. On account of bad weather during the previous afternoon it had been decided that aircraft from the *Illustrious* would not take part, and the results of the bombardment were therefore not observed. It has since been learned that damage was done to the runways, which was soon repaired, and that twenty aircraft were damaged, nine of them badly. The enemy did not interfere, and there is no doubt that they were completely surprised.

On the following day, December 20th, Admiral Cunningham took the *Warspite* into Malta for the first time since May and received an enthusiastic welcome. The island was in great heart. The air attacks, which had started with some severity in June, had dwindled almost to nothing; which partly obscured the fact that the air defences were still far below strength. The successes at sea, the visible arrival of convoys, and the good news from the Western Desert all had an inspiring effect upon the population, and the dockyard was practically back to normal as regards repair work. Indeed, it was having a busy time: a convoy from Alexandria to be received; empty ships to be sailed to the east; and the *Malaya* to be fuelled and sailed for Gibraltar together with the two ships of the 'Collar' convoy. While the Commander-in-Chief was inspecting the naval establishments at Malta, aircraft of Nos. 815 and 819 Squadrons from the *Illustrious* sank two out of three Italian merchant ships in convoy on their way to Tripoli and attacked other shipping and the port installations at that place, while Swordfish of No. 830 Squadron from Malta laid mines in the harbour entrance. There was no reaction from Italian air or surface forces, and on Christmas Eve the fleet was safely back at Alexandria.

It was intended that Force H should co-operate in the passage of the *Malaya* and the merchant ships, but on December 14th Admiral Somerville was suddenly ordered to proceed to the Azores and prevent an expected attempt at landing by the Germans. The information proved false; he was back in Gibraltar on the 19th and able to sail eastwards next day with the *Renown*, *Ark Royal* and six destroyers. The exact dispositions of the Italian naval forces were then in doubt, but on December 21st, when the *Malaya* and the merchant ships were passing through the Sicilian Narrows, air reconnaissance from Malta found the main units of the Italian fleet at Naples and Spezia. The enemy took no action to interfere with the passage and the only mishap was that the destroyer *Hyperion* was torpedoed by a submarine off Pantelleria and had to be sunk. The next day, after Force H had joined, some shadowing aircraft were driven off by fighters of No. 808 Squadron; otherwise there was no sign of the enemy.

The next task should have been to receive convoy 'Excess', the ships of which had sailed with the large convoy W.S.5. Plans were completely upset, however, when this convoy was attacked on December 25th by the German 8-inch cruiser *Hipper*, out in the Atlantic a thousand miles from Gibraltar. In a short engagement with the *Berwick* hits were scored on either side, and the enemy was driven off, but not before one transport had been damaged and the convoy had been obliged to scatter. The Christmas festivities of Force H were interrupted and it was ordered to sea to round up the scattered ships and give them extra protection, and if possible to bring the *Hipper* to action. The first of these objects took longer than was expected, and in the bad weather the *Renown* suffered damage which reduced her speed to 20 knots and made it necessary for her to go into dock at Gibraltar. The 'Excess' ships, together with the additional escort to help them through the Narrows, were held at Gibraltar, and the operation was postponed until 6th January.

This was a very unfortunate turn of events. The various naval operations in the Mediterranean were so closely linked that a delay of this sort to one of them had its effects upon them all. As Admiral Cunningham, put it 'the trail of dislocation was progressive'; but, as will be seen, the worst effects were eventually felt during the passage of convoy 'Excess' itself.

The month of December showed clearly what a large measure of control the British Navy was able to exercise in the Mediterranean. Warships and important convoys had completed the through passage in both directions; other convoys had passed freely up and down the Aegean; places as far apart as Rhodes and Tripoli had been attacked; and the fleet had even swept into the Adriatic. Fifty-five ships (totalling over 235,000 tons) had been escorted during the month—all without damage. And yet the Italians had ample naval forces and shore-based aircraft with which to score a success against almost any of these enterprises, had they been minded to try, and they had the advantage of being well informed about the movements of shipping at Gibraltar and the Egyptian ports. Their policy, however, had given the surface ships little opportunity of coming to grips. The British Mediterranean Fleet, on the other hand, had snatched such chances as had presented themselves and had sunk one cruiser and four destroyers by gunfire. Italian gunfire had only caused minor damage to two British cruisers.

The relative strengths of the fleets were of course very different from what they had been on the outbreak of war. In particular, the arrival of the *Illustrious*, with her effective low-angle radar and her Fulmar fighters, had greatly increased the freedom of action of the fleet and had given it a high degree of local command of the air. The activities of the Fleet Air Arm were, however, not entirely confined to its primary function of operating from the carriers, for No. 830 Squadron (Swordfish) was used from Malta for attacking enemy shipping, and Swordfish of No. 813 Squadron had been operating with the Royal Air Force in the Western Desert, in attacks upon coastal shipping. Others had attacked targets in the Dodecanese from Crete.

The Italian Air Force had made repeated attacks on British ships, mostly from high-level, sometimes with great accuracy but on the whole with surprisingly little success. The chief threat to the British ships was from torpedo-bomber attacks, a type of action which the Italians had not fully developed when they came into the war, and which therefore did not figure very largely for some time. But in addition to their successes against the *Kent* and the *Liverpool*, already mentioned,[1] torpedo-bombers scored two hits on the cruiser *Glasgow* in Suda Bay early in December; all three cruisers had to leave the Mediterranean for repairs.

For reconnaissance and long-range bombing attacks the Royal Air Force had far less convenient bases than the Italian Air Force, but it was nevertheless able to make a considerable contribution. For example, the Wellington bombers of No.148 Squadron at Malta, which had followed up the Fleet Air Arm's attack on Taranto two nights later, continued during November to bomb ports in southern Italy—Brindisi, Bari, and Taranto—in order to interfere with Italian rail and sea communications carrying traffic for Albania. Naples also received attention in order to give the Italian battlefleet no respite. In December some of the effort was diverted to objectives in North Africa, notably Tripoli, in connexion with the British offensive in the Western Desert, but southern Italy also suffered. In these two months 94 sorties were flown against Italian ports.

It has been seen that the lack of reconnaissance aircraft at Malta resulted in uncertainty about the dispositions of the Italian main fleet units at the time when British convoys were to pass through the Central Mediterranean. The aircraft of all types at Malta on 31st December were as follows:

No. 830 Sqn. F.A.A. 12 Swordfish     (torpedo-bomber)
No. 261 Sqn. R.A.F. 16 Hurricanes     (and 4 in reserve)
No. 148 Sqn. R.A.F. 16 Wellingtons     (and 4 in reserve)
No. 228 Sqn. R.A.F. 4 Sunderlands     (flying-boats; and 2 in reserve)

No. 431 Flight R.A.F. 4 Glenn     (for reconnaissance: 1 in
Martins (later No. 69 Sqn.)     reserve)

---

[1] See pages 212 and 222.

Thus not only were the fighters well short of the figure aimed at, namely, four squadrons, but the number of reconnaissance aircraft was clearly much too low to keep the movements of Italian merchant ships under proper observation; opportunities for attacking them were consequently being lost. This was especially serious at a time when it was clearly necessary to harass the routes by which reinforcements would reach Graziani, and the three Commanders-in-Chief expressed to the Chiefs of Staff their grave concern over this weakness and reiterated the request of Air Chief Marshal Longmore for a Glenn Martin squadron and a long-range torpedo-bomber squadron of the Beaufort type to be stationed at Malta. In reply, the Chiefs of Staff pointed out that demands for aircraft, not only in the Mediterranean, were taxing their resources to the utmost, and could only be met at the expense of Bomber Command whose expansion was vitally important. They could make no promises about Beauforts, but hoped to send a few Glenn Martins to Malta very shortly.

This is not to say that the only shortages were in the air. The Greek campaign had thrown many extra burdens on the Fleet, and especially on the destroyers, although this was partly offset by the use of Greek destroyers as escorts for convoys and by the use of Suda Bay as a refuelling base. But there had been a great increase in tasks requiring small craft generally, and the shortage of destroyers in particular was preventing the fleet from exploiting to the full the otherwise favourable naval situation. There were not enough destroyers to enable the whole fleet to be used simultaneously on offensive operations; the same applied to Force H, whose light forces had frequently to be diverted to the interruption of inward-bound French merchant shipping suspected of trying to break the blockade. Admiral Cunningham therefore felt that, just when a highly aggressive policy against the Italians was clearly called for, the operations of the Fleet were being restricted to comparatively minor enterprises often of a defensive kind. The Admiralty was fully alive to the shortage, but the need to concentrate anti-submarine craft in the Western Approaches of the United Kingdom was vital for the country's existence and had to come first. It was hoped that it would be possible to release more destroyers for the Mediterranean by the end of February.

The difficulties under which British submarines were working have already been referred to, and the results continued to be disappointing.[1] On the outbreak of war between Italy and Greece the Adriatic was allocated at first to the Greek submarines. In the course of their first patrols they sank at least two Italian transports. It was in these waters that two British submarines—*Regulus* and *Triton*—were lost during December. In December also the Free French submarine *Narval* failed to return from patrol off the African coast. By the end of

[1] See page 216.

the year ten submarines had been lost, or nearly half the total number that had operated since the war began. Over the same period the Italians had lost twenty. In November and December only three Italian supply ships—amounting to 15,400 tons—were sunk by submarines, and the Italian naval figures for troops and supplies landed in North Africa and Albania show how trivial was this result. In North Africa between June 1940 and January 1941 47,000 troops had been landed without loss; and nearly 350,000 tons of equipment and supplies, with a loss of 2·3%. In Albania, between October 1940 and April 1941, the figures were: troops, 623,000 with a loss of 0·05%; supplies, 704,000 tons with a loss of 0·2%.

Nevertheless, the outlook was improving, for the first three of the new 'U' class of submarine arrived at Malta in December to replace three of the larger boats which then left the Mediterranean; it was confidently expected that the submarines would soon begin to achieve results. Not that the Italian submarines had done any better, though there were many more of them and they had more targets in the open sea. Since the war began they had sunk an old British cruiser, two destroyers, and one submarine. Only four merchant ships totalling 16,000 tons had been sunk; of these three were neutral and the fourth was a Norwegian tanker.

Broadly, then, the naval outlook at the end of 1940 was distinctly encouraging and the Commander-in-Chief could justly claim to be in a fair way towards achieving his first object—the control of the Mediterranean. Indeed we had taken the measure of the Italians by sea, land, and air, and the moment had come for the stronger partner of the Axis to take some of the strain off the weaker.

# CHAPTER XVII

# THE ARRIVAL OF THE
# *LUFTWAFFE*

THE FÜHRER'S letter to Mussolini of 20th November contained the proposal that German bombers should operate from bases in Italy to take part in the attack on British shipping.[1] Early in December he sent Field-Marshal Erhard Milch, the Secretary of State for Air, to make arrangements for the transfer of German air units to Italy. He wished to have them back for other duties early in February, but hoped that by that time they would have done substantial damage to the British in the Mediterranean. On December 10th a formal order was issued allotting air units to bases in southern Italy for operation '*Mittelmeer*'. (It is to be noted that there was no intention of sending any German units to Egypt or Cyrenaica until the Italians should have secured the use of Matruh.) The force selected was *Fliegerkorps X* from Norway, many of whose units had specialized in operations against shipping.[2] With its signals, transport, flak, bombs, and fuel it began to move through Italy about Christmas time. By 8th January 96 bombers were established on Sicilian airfields, joined two days later by 25 twin-engine fighters. By mid-January the figure had risen to 186 aircraft of all types.

The development was not unexpected by the British. They already knew that Italian aircraft resources were being severely taxed and that German transport aircraft were working between Italy and Albania. On January 2nd the Chief of the Italian Air Staff, General Francesco Pricolo, broadcast a message of welcome to the German air units arriving in Italy to partake in the severe air and naval struggle in the Mediterranean basin, adding, no doubt with the best intentions, that the German contingent must be considered as a great Italian unit. By this time German transport aircraft were already suspected of moving to and fro between Sicily and the mainland, but on January 5th a special reconnaissance from Malta disclosed nothing unusual on the Sicilian airfields. By this date only seven bombers had in fact arrived, but by the middle of January it was obvious that the *Luftwaffe* were present in strength; from 60 to 80

---

[1] See page 240.
[2] A *Fliegerkorps* was normally a subsidiary formation of a *Luftflotte*; *Fliegerkorps X*, however, was an independent force of all types of aircraft.

aircraft, including long-range as well as dive-bombers, were thought to be in Italy and Sicily, and it was estimated that the ultimate strength might be 250 or even more.

During the first ten days of January, by agreement between the three Commanders-in-Chief, the main air effort from Malta was devoted to the task of interfering with the enemy's sea traffic to Libya and Albania. This made big demands on the handful of reconnaissance aircraft and left little or nothing for watching Sicilian airfields; but it resulted in three very successful attacks by the Wellingtons against Tripoli, where shipping, wharves, and buildings were hit, and in the same period Palermo was successfully attacked twice, and Naples and Messina once each.

Having arrived at Gibraltar after their adventures in the Atlantic, the five ships of convoy 'Excess' were further delayed while the repairs to the *Renown* were completed. One ship, the *Essex*, was bound for Malta with 4,000 tons of ammunition, 3,000 tons of precious seed potatoes, and a deck cargo of twelve crated Hurricanes. The others—*Northern Prince*, *Empire Song*, *Clan Cumming*, and *Clan Macdonald*—were bound for Piraeus with urgent supplies for Greece, and 800 soldiers and airmen for Malta were distributed among the five ships. On the night of January 1st there was another mishap; the *Northern Prince* was driven ashore in a gale and sustained damage which rendered her unfit to proceed. Her 400 troops were accordingly transferred to the *Bonaventure*, a new type of anti-aircraft cruiser, and to the destroyers of the escort. On the evening of January 6th the four ships and their escort sailed from Gibraltar, did a feint to the westward, and reversed course under cover of darkness. Early the following morning they were followed by the main body of Force H— *Renown*, *Malaya*, *Ark Royal*, *Sheffield*, and six destroyers.

It was not possible to comply with Admiral Somerville's request for a third battleship and some more cruisers, but Admiral Cunningham did what he could in other ways to reduce the danger of an attack on Force H by the Italian battlefleet. Three submarines were sent to patrol off Sardinia; two cruisers (*Gloucester* and *Southampton*) from the Eastern Mediterranean were to join Force H while convoy 'Excess' was still slightly to the west of Sardinia; air reconnaissance from Malta was to be intensified during the critical days; and he himself would meet the convoy some 100 miles to the west of Malta.

The cruisers *Gloucester* (wearing the flag of Rear-Admiral E. de F. Renouf) and *Southampton*, having embarked between them 500 soldiers and airmen for Malta, accordingly sailed from Alexandria with two destroyers on January 6th. They reached Malta early on the 8th without incident, disembarked their troops, and sailed again for the westward a few hours later, leaving one destroyer to refit. At 9.30 a.m. next day, when about 120 miles south-west of Sardinia, Admiral

Renouf took station ahead of the 'Excess' convoy with the battleship *Malaya*, while the *Southampton* joined the *Bonaventure* astern. Just before this, an Italian shadowing aircraft closed the force and made off again, apparently undamaged.

During the forenoon of the 8th air reconnaissance from Malta had reported two Italian battleships and three cruisers at Messina, in Sicily, but there was no information of any other cruisers. Before daylight on the 9th Admiral Somerville was to the north-east of the convoy with the *Renown*, *Ark Royal*, *Sheffield*, and five destroyers. At 5 a.m. the carrier flew off five Swordfish for Malta, which all arrived safely. The Admiral then fell back on the convoy and took up a position on the port quarter to facilitate flying operations and to give close anti-aircraft support if need be. A negative reconnaissance report from a Sunderland was received at 12.26 p.m.

At 1.20 p.m. the *Sheffield's* radar detected enemy aircraft at a distance of 43 miles—the limit of its working range—and half an hour later ten S 79s made an attack out of the sun. Bombs fell very close to the *Malaya* and *Gloucester*, and a Fulmar brought down two of the bombers within sight of the *Malaya*. No further attacks took place. That evening, when about 25 miles north of Bizerta, Force H parted company and returned (with the *Malaya*) to Gibraltar. Led by the *Gloucester*, convoy 'Excess' continued to the eastward.

Meanwhile Admiral Cunningham was approaching from the east. He had sailed from Alexandria on the 7th in the *Warspite*, with the *Valiant*, *Illustrious*, and seven destroyers, while the cruisers under Vice-Admiral, Light Forces, covered movements in the Aegean and the passage of two ships (*Breconshire* and *Clan Macaulay*) to Malta. A slow convoy (M.E.6) and two fast merchant ships (convoy M.E. 5½) both left Malta on the 10th eastbound, escorted by a destroyer. Cover for these movements was provided by the Vice-Admiral, Light Forces, with four cruisers, two destroyers, the anti-aircraft cruiser *Calcutta* and four corvettes, while the Commander-in-Chief proceeded with his force to meet convoy 'Excess' coming from the west. It was known by now that the enemy had received constant air reports of the Commander-in-Chief's general movements, and on the afternoon of the 9th a force of bombers and fighters had apparently intended an attack but made an unsuccessful raid on shipping in Marsa Scirocco, Malta, instead.

Shortly after dawn on the 10th the Commander-in-Chief was about 100 miles to the west of Malta when gun flashes were sighted ahead. The *Jaguar*, of the destroyer screen, and the *Bonaventure* had simultaneously sighted two Italian torpedo boats twelve miles south-west of Pantelleria. Admiral Renouf turned the convoy away, in case these torpedo boats were the screen for heavier forces. This was evidently not so, and the incident ended with one of the Italian

Map 21

The passage of Convoy *Excess*
through the Sicilian narrows
10th January 1941

vessels, the *Vega*, being sunk by a torpedo from the *Hereward*, while
the other escaped.

The Commander-in-Chief had approached the scene by passing
close to the south of the convoy, and soon after 8 o'clock turned to
the south-east in its wake. Almost at once the destroyer *Gallant*
struck a mine and lay helpless, but in no danger of sinking, with 60
men killed and another 25 wounded on board. As the *Mohawk* took
her in tow there was an attack by Italian torpedo-bombers, but under
fire from the *Bonaventure* they dropped their torpedoes at long range,
without effect. The crippled *Gallant* made a slow and hazardous
passage to Malta, escorted by the *Bonaventure* and the destroyer
*Griffin*, and for part of the way by Admiral Renouf's force also. Air
attacks were frequent, but the *Bonaventure's* radar always managed to
give warning of them, and no more damage was caused. At 5 a.m.
next morning, within fifteen miles of Malta, the *Gloucester* and
*Southampton* left for Suda Bay and the tow struggled on and entered
harbour safely during the forenoon.

Admiral Cunningham in the *Warspite* was now left with the *Valiant*
and *Illustrious*. Only five destroyers were screening him, and three
more were with the convoy. Sixty miles to the west of Malta there

was an attack on the battleships by two Italian torpedo-bombers, but these were chased off and pursued by the four Fulmars which had been above the fleet. Immediately afterwards a strong force of enemy aircraft was reported to be approaching from the north; the Fulmars were recalled, and the *Illustrious* turned to fly off fresh aircraft.

This was still being done when between thirty and forty Ju 88s and 87s (Stuka dive-bombers) came into sight. There was just time to turn back to the south-easterly course before the attacks began, but the fighters were not yet in a position to intervene. The enemy split up into three groups and attacked from astern and from either beam; two formations concentrated on the *Illustrious* while the other engaged the battleships. The attacks were made with great skill and determination and were quite unlike anything the fleet had experienced at the hands of the Italians. The Fulmars had been unable to intervene in time, but they had some success in the later stages, and together with the anti-aircraft guns they accounted for some of the enemy.[1] By this time, although the battleships had escaped injury, the *Illustrious* had suffered severely. She had been hit six times. Bombs had wrecked the flight deck, destroyed nine aircraft, put half the guns out of action, and set the ship on fire fore and aft. She hauled out of line grievously stricken, with many of the ship's company killed or wounded.

As the *Illustrious* was now useless as a carrier, her Captain (D. W. Boyd) was ordered to make for Malta. For three hours the *Illustrious* remained out of control with her steering gear disabled, before she was able to proceed by steering with her main engines. There had been another air attack while she was still turning circles; this time by high-level bombing upon the convoy and the escorts. No damage was done. But just after 4 p.m. thirteen dive-bombers made an attack on the *Illustrious* herself; this was not as formidable as the previous one, and the ship was able to manoeuvre. Nevertheless, she was hit by one bomb and more damage was done.

An hour later it was the turn of the battleships when fourteen aircraft attacked them. The ships were well prepared and there were no hits. As the enemy made off, three Fulmars from the *Illustrious'* original patrol came out from Malta to attack. By this time the *Illustrious* was close under the southern shore of the island, and the Fleet, which had manoeuvred to try to afford her the support of its anti-aircraft fire, now parted company. Finally, an hour after sunset, when the *Illustrious* was within five miles of the entrance to Valletta harbour, she was attacked again by torpedo-bombers. They were driven off by gunfire and at 9 p.m. the carrier entered harbour, her troubles by no means over. She had suffered in casualties 126 killed and 91 wounded.

---

[1] The German figure is six destroyed and one damaged.

All this time the convoy was proceeding unhindered on its way. The *Essex*, bound for Malta, had been escorted into harbour shortly before the arrival of the *Illustrious*, and the other merchant vessels had been joined by the two ships of M.E.5½. Owing to the afternoon's air attacks, the battleships were still some distance away by nightfall; Vice-Admiral, Light Forces, away to the eastward, was therefore ordered to take up a position during the night to the north of the convoy in order to meet a possible attack by surface ships. By daylight next day Admiral Cunningham was himself some twenty-five miles to the north of the convoy. That afternoon the ships for Alexandria parted company, and the 'Excess' ships reached Piraeus safely next morning.

Meanwhile the six ships of the slow convoy M.E.6 had only the *York* and four corvettes as escort, so the Commander-in-Chief sent his Swordfish aircraft with a message to Admiral Renouf telling him that instead of making for Suda Bay he was to overtake and support convoy M.E.6. It was shortly after noon on January 11th when the *Gloucester* and *Southampton* altered course, and three hours later they were some thirty miles astern of the convoy. Neither ship was fitted with radar, and the approach of a dozen dive-bombers out of the sun was undetected; the first indication of attack was the whistle of falling bombs. Two or three struck the *Southampton*, and caused severe damage. One hit the *Gloucester* and penetrated five decks without exploding. For an hour the *Southampton* struggled on, continuing to make 20 knots, and a high-level bombing attack made during this period was beaten off. But the loss of boiler water gradually reduced her speed, and at 4.40 p.m. she stopped. For another two hours the fires that were raging on board were fought, but without success. The damage made it impossible to flood the magazines and the position became hopeless. Permission was given by the Commander-in-Chief to abandon ship, and at 10 p.m., when Vice-Admiral, Light Forces, had arrived on the scene in the *Orion*, three torpedoes were fired into her. Five minutes later she sank. Her casualties were 80 killed and 87 wounded.

Next morning, January 12th, the *Orion*, *Perth*, and *Gloucester*, with their accompanying destroyers, joined the Commander-in-Chief off the west end of Crete, where they were met by Rear-Admiral Rawlings, who had sailed from Alexandria in the *Barham* with the *Eagle*, *Ajax*, and destroyer screen. The Commander-in-Chief's intention had been, after the safety of the convoy was assured, to carry out a series of strikes against the enemy's naval forces and shipping. The disabling of the *Illustrious* made most of the plan impracticable, so Admiral Cunningham with the *Warspite*, *Valiant*, and *Gloucester* shaped course for Alexandria. Bad weather prevented Admiral Rawlings from carrying out his share of the operations in the

25. Bombs dropping all round H.M.S. *Ark Royal* during the action off Cape Spartivento, 27th November 1940.

26. Walrus amphibian aircraft about to be catapulted. This was one of the spotting aircraft used at the bombardment of Genoa.

*Facing p. 320*

28. Vertical air photograph of Benghazi harbour, showing a large ship on fire, another on fire and sinking, a sunken destroyer, another ship partly submerged, and several other ships damaged. Leaking oil is clearly visible on the surface of the water.

*Facing p. 321*            27. Destruction at the Italian seaplane base at Bomba.

Dodecanese. The *Orion* and *Perth* proceeded to Piraeus, embarked the troops who had taken passage in the 'Excess' ships, and carried them safely to Malta.

Not one ship of the fourteen in the four convoys had been damaged, and all the troops had been safely landed at their destinations. The Navy had therefore succeeded in what they set out to do, but at a very heavy cost to themselves.

The serious damage to the *Illustrious* meant the loss of the fleet's essential air support, for even if she could be made sufficiently seaworthy at Malta to steam to Alexandria she would still need several months' work in a properly established dockyard. The Admiralty made a quick decision on January 12th, before Admiral Cunningham had even arrived back at Alexandria, and ordered the carrier *Formidable*, which was about to replace the *Ark Royal* in Force H, to join the Mediterranean Fleet instead. She was to come round the Cape, which would take her more than a month. As for the *Eagle*, she was very old and constantly in need of repair; with dive-bombers in the Mediterranean Admiral Cunningham regarded her as too much of an anxiety and was prepared to part with her when the *Formidable* arrived.

To make good his other losses Admiral Cunningham was allowed to keep the *Bonaventure* and the destroyer *Jaguar*, which would otherwise have returned to other duties. The *Bonaventure*, with her radar and modern anti-aircraft armament was very suitable for service in the Mediterranean, though there were as yet no stocks of her special 5·25-inch ammunition. To avoid having ships lying unnecessarily at Malta while the *Illustrious* was present, these two and the *Orion* sailed on January 14th for Alexandria, leaving only the *Perth*, which was under repair.

It was only too obvious that *Fliegerkorps X* would renew their attacks on the *Illustrious* as soon as they knew she was still at Malta. To reduce the intensity No. 148 Squadron R.A.F. attacked the airfield at Catania on the night of January 12th. Thirty-five aircraft had been seen on this airfield, but bad weather prevented any reconnaissance until the 15th, when photographs showed about 100 aircraft to be present, of which 25 appeared to be Junkers; about 30 others were burnt out or badly damaged. Hangars and buildings had also been hit. That night the Wellingtons struck again, but by this time *Fliegerkorps X* was established in strength, not only at Catania but on several other airfields, and could not be subdued by the weight of any attack that Malta could deliver.

On January 16th came the first of the heavy attacks on the harbour and in particular on the *Illustrious* as she lay under repair. Much damage was done in the dockyard and neighbourhood; the wireless station was put out of action; and there were about a hundred civilian casualties. The *Illustrious* received one hit on the quarter deck, which did little harm. The *Perth* was severely shaken by a near miss, but was nevertheless able to sail for Alexandria the same evening. The *Essex*, which was unloading, was hit by a heavy bomb. Fortunately her large cargo of ammunition did not explode, but fifteen of her crew were killed and twenty-three wounded and seven Maltese stevedores were killed. This was the first time that unloading had been interrupted by bombing, and the local stevedores refused to go on working. Gangs of soldiers and sailors took their place, but inexperienced workers are not as quick as trained stevedores and unloading was not completed until the 29th.

The heavy attacks were renewed on the 18th by a large force of Stukas escorted by fighters. The main targets this time were the airfields at Hal Far and Luqa; the latter was rendered unserviceable for several days, six British aircraft were destroyed on the ground, and many others were damaged. The Vice-Admiral, Malta, Sir Wilbraham Ford, had hoped to have the *Illustrious* ready to sail by the 20th, but another heavy attack on the dockyard on the 19th resulted in more under-water damage and made further delay inevitable. Indeed it almost looked as if the *Illustrious* might never go to sea again. But the dangerous and difficult work of repair went doggedly on, in spite of set-backs, and Admiral Ford was finally able to report that the ship would be ready for sea on the evening of the 23rd.

During the time the *Illustrious* was in harbour only about six Hurricanes, three Fulmars (too slow to engage the dive-bombers), and one Gladiator, could be sent up at any one time to oppose the raiders, whose numbers varied from forty to eighty. Nevertheless a certain toll was taken of the enemy, either by fighters or by the anti-aircraft guns of the fortress and of the carrier herself. German records show that sixteen of their aircraft were destroyed in attacks on Malta while the carrier was in harbour.

The enemy was not likely to let the *Illustrious* go without making a determined effort to sink her. She had none of her own aircraft to defend her, because she was not in a state to use them; she would therefore have to rely upon speed and evasion. Since January 20th cruisers and destroyers had been assembling in the vicinity of Suda Bay ready to move out and cover her passage, but the weather was too bad for any destroyers to go to Malta for the purpose of forming her escort. In fact, if the *Illustrious* had been ready any sooner she would have had to wait for the destroyers.

At dusk on the 23rd she crept out of harbour unobserved by the enemy. Just before she left, two large empty merchant vessels, *Clan*

*Macaulay* and *Breconshire*, left also, to take advantage of the same cover. That night the *Illustrious* was able to make 24 knots, which was a higher speed than had been expected, and next morning neither V.A.L.F. with his cruisers nor the reconnoitring aircraft from Malta were able to locate her. But she was sighted and joined by Rear-Admiral, First Battle Squadron, during the forenoon. The force was observed and reported by enemy aircraft on two occasions, but no attack resulted, perhaps on account of the poor visibility. The cruisers to the north were attacked, however, by dive- and torpedo-bombers, as well as by aircraft from high-level, with no result worse than some near misses. At noon on the 25th, cheered by every ship present, the *Illustrious* steamed slowly into Alexandria habour. To the Vice-Admiral, Malta, the Commander-in-Chief expressed his warm appreciation of the work of the dockyard officers and men. He also acknowledged with gratitude the contribution made by the Royal Air Force to the *Illustrious'* safe passage by their attacks on enemy airfields in North Africa. The Governor of Malta, in a characteristic message, expressed his sympathy for the Navy's losses and his appreciation of the efforts made on the island's behalf.

The arrival of the German *Fliegerkorps* marked, in the Prime Minister's words, the beginning of evil developments in the Mediterranean. The German aircraft could be easily maintained and reinforced. They already possessed enough bases on land for operations over the Central Mediterranean, and from these and from bases in the Dodecanese they could cover all the coasts of Libya and the Levant.

The Navy had enjoyed great freedom of movement in the Central Mediterranean, and almost complete freedom elsewhere, when the only opposition had been from the Italians; but it had been quickly shown that the movement of ships within the range of German dive-bombers in daylight was very expensive. This at once affected the passage of the single ship *Northern Prince*, with her badly needed cargo for Greece. There could be no question now of sending her through the Mediterranean, and at the end of January she left Gibraltar to join a convoy routed round the Cape. (The sequel was that on the last stage of her long journey she was sunk by air attack in the Kithera Channel.)

If freedom of movement in the Central Mediterranean was to be restored, the first requirement would be to gain a measure of air superiority. This would need more fighters—both shore-based and carrier-borne—more bombers, and more bases. But aircraft of all kinds were scarce and the line of supply was long. The importance of Malta as a base had become greater than ever; but it was not merely a matter of sending in more aircraft, for the capacity of the island to receive them was strictly limited. It was therefore very encouraging that the airfields in the bulge of Cyrenaica were being secured for British use; from them it would be possible to extend air operations over the Central Mediterranean, provided that the necessary aircraft could be devoted to this purpose. At the moment it looked as if the demands of the Greek campaign would cancel out this advantage.

The insistence of the Naval and Air Commanders-in-Chief upon the paramount importance of Malta was supported by the Chiefs of Staff, who ruled on January 21st that the Air Officer Commanding-in-Chief's first duty was to maintain a sufficient air force at Malta to sustain its defence: a consignment of forty fighters was to be taken by H.M.S. *Furious* to Takoradi as soon as possible.[1] Every opportunity was being taken of using Malta as a base for attack, a policy which, to their credit, was never lost sight of by the Governor or the Service commanders. Consequently the Wellingtons continued to attack the Sicilian airfields whenever they could, and great efforts were made to find and attack Italian shipping. An initial success was scored on January 27th, when a Sunderland of No. 228 Squadron reported three merchant vessels steering south off the Tunisian coast. Six Swordfish of No. 830 Squadron were called up and sank one of the ships by torpedoes—a good example of combined action by searching and striking forces at a distance of 165 miles from their base.

The importance of basing submarines at Malta if they were to operate effectively against the traffic between Italy and North Africa had long been recognized.[2] At the beginning of February it became possible to concentrate small boats of the 'U' class (*Unique, Usk, Utmost, Upright, Upholder*) off the Tunisian coast, and these, together with the larger submarines, which kept, as a rule, to the deeper water, caused increasing loss and damage to enemy shipping supplying North Africa.

It had to be recognized that the German Air Force might spread also into the Dodecanese, where they would be a menace to the Aegean traffic and be able to attack the Suez Canal. The only sure way of preventing this would be for British forces to capture the Dodecanese Islands first. The Commanders-in-Chief had always had this on their list, as it were, but now it became more urgent. In the middle of January they asked the Chiefs of Staff for the Glen (Assault) ships to be sent out as soon as possible round the Cape in order that they could be used against the Dodecanese. Meanwhile, they planned a sea-borne assault, with forces already available, against the small island of Kaso which lies just east of Crete. To agree with this request would have meant cancelling operation 'Workshop' (the capture of

---

[1] One such consignment had reached Takoradi early in January. See page 253.
[2] See page 217.

Pantelleria), and the Prime Minister, far from wishing to do this, held the view that 'Workshop' was of greater importance than ever.[1] Thus the Chiefs of Staff could only reply on January 16th that the question of the employment of the Glen ships was still undecided, but that in any case it was undesirable to stir up any of the Dodecanese by pin-pricking sea-borne raids until the programme for the whole of the action against the islands had been settled.

This veto arrived after the expedition to Kaso had sailed, and Admiral Cunningham at once signalled that the intention was not to raid the island but to capture it. Lying as it did at one side of the Kaso Strait there were good reasons for occupying it, and to cancel the expedition at this late stage would be bad for morale. Could it not be allowed to proceed? But the Chiefs of Staff were adamant, and their order to cancel the operation arrived a few hours before the assault was to have been made.

On January 20th the Defence Committee agreed that the presence of the *Luftwaffe* in strength in Sicily meant that operation 'Workshop' was impracticable. The three Glen ships were to sail at the end of the month round the Cape, carrying their Special Service troops and equipment to the Middle East. They would be followed a fortnight later by the Mobile Naval Base Defence Organization (M.N.B.D.O.), which consisted of over 5,000 officers and men of the Royal Marines, with anti-aircraft and coast defence equipment, the whole specially designed for the rapid defence of captured bases. They were to be used in any way the Commanders-in-Chief might decide.

While it seemed to the Commanders-in-Chief that no major enterprises against the Dodecanese could therefore be undertaken before the beginning of April, they remained firmly opposed to the idea of leaving the islands undisturbed for so long, and requested the Chiefs of Staff to reconsider their ban on raids and the capture of small objectives. They argued that the possession of Kaso would enable Scarpanto airfield to be shelled and that the capture of Scarpanto would be of great value in the later attack on Rhodes. They thought also that it would be as well to test the enemy's strength and especially his morale, which after his recent reverses on land might be very low. To this the Chiefs of Staff replied that the Glen ships should arrive in time to operate in the middle of March and that any smaller enterprises must be timed in relation to the larger ones; they must, in fact, be all part of one plan. The rejoinder to this was that the Commanders-in-Chief's plan was to capture Kaso immediately and then Castelorizo. After the Glen ships arrived they would capture Scarpanto as a necessary preliminary to Rhodes.

An attempt was accordingly made to land on Kaso on February 17th, but it failed owing to lack of information about the landing

---

[1] See page 308.

places and the exits from them. A week later a force of 200 Commando troops and some naval parties were landed at Castelorizo from H.M.S. *Decoy* and *Hereward*, with only slight opposition. A detachment of Royal Marines was put ashore in the harbour from H.M.S. *Ladybird*, which was then damaged by air attack and had to withdraw. It had been intended to land a permanent garrison of troops from Cyprus, but after a series of misunderstandings and mishaps they were diverted to Alexandria. Another attempt was made, but meanwhile the Italians appear to have acted promptly and landed some 300 men themselves. The resulting encounters caused the British about 50 casualties, and in the face of almost unopposed air attack it was decided to withdraw. It was evident that there was much to be learned about the conduct of this sort of operation, and that the enemy's morale in this quarter was not as low as had been hoped.

The Glen ships duly arrived in the Great Bitter Lake on March 9th, by which time the capture of any Dodecanese Islands had to be set aside owing to the march of events in Greece.

It was not long before the anxiety of the Commanders-in-Chief lest the *Luftwaffe* should establish itself at Rhodes was shown to be well founded. Towards the end of January aircraft began to lay mines in the Suez Canal, using Rhodes for refuelling. This quickly looked like having a serious effect upon the whole conduct of the war in the Middle East. The through passage of the Mediterranean was already denied, and now the sole remaining link with the outer seas was in danger of being blocked.

After the first night of minelaying one ship was sunk, and all traffic had to be stopped while the Canal was swept. A few days later, as no more mines had been dropped, the Canal was deemed safe and was reopened. Next day a ship blew up, although twelve others had passed safely over the spot, so that traffic had again to be stopped. The same thing happened again: the Canal was swept and reopened; several ships passed safely, and then a transport blew up in the middle of the channel. Next day two hoppers, one towing a sweep, were also mined, and the Canal was blocked to shipping of every size.

The deduction from these events was that not only magnetic but also acoustic mines were being dropped, and there was no gear available for dealing with these. There was no possibility of making any substantial increases in the fighter and anti-aircraft defences along the Canal, for already there were not enough anywhere; the newly captured ports of Sollum and Tobruk, for instance, were inadequately defended, although the maintenance of the Western Desert Force depended on their use. All that could be done along the Canal was to try to prevent aircraft from flying low enough to lay their mines with accuracy; if a mine did fall in the water it was necessary to mark the exact spot so that it could be destroyed deliberately with no danger to shipping. Various obstructive devices were tried, including balloons, of which there were very few available; smoke screening was tried, without success; searchlights were multiplied; and by deploying large numbers of troops—British, Indian, and Egyptian—along the banks it was possible to meet a raider with fairly intense small-arms fire. At the same time the troops were used for spotting the fall of mines—no small undertaking, as the posts needed to be not more than fifty yards apart in the dark, and the Canal was ninety miles long. At a few places, where a sunken ship would be especially troublesome, huge nets were stretched between the banks every night to indicate the point where a mine had broken through. (Not, as some have supposed, to catch the mines!)

So began a long and intensely irritating period. The Navy had the anxiety of keeping the shipping moving, and apart from the heavy routine traffic, including their own tankers, there were some very important movements of H.M. ships; in particular, there was the *Formidable* shortly to be passed through in order to change places with the *Illustrious*. To the Air Officer Commanding-in-Chief nothing could have been more unwelcome than the growth of the Canal commitment at this moment. He was trying hard to spare fighters for Greece; he was supporting the army's operations in Cyrenaica and the Sudan, and had now to reinforce the fighter strength at Malta. (He had just sent six Hurricanes.)

For the Army, as the Service principally concerned with transportation, the blocking of the Canal had very serious implications. As soon as Italy entered the war it had been obvious that Suez would be overloaded, and in the past eight months the improvements to the jetties, and to the rail and road communications, had doubled the capacity of the port.[1] At the same time, wharves had been built at points along the Canal where ships could unload and have their cargoes cleared by road and rail. Now that mining had begun it became even more urgent to increase the capacity at, or south of, Suez so that as many ships as possible could be cleared without entering the Canal. To pass traffic into Palestine it was decided to build a road and rail link northwards from the primitive port of Aqaba, but except for this small alleviation there was the grim prospect that everything for the forces, and for Egypt, might have to be cleared through Suez; and cargoes for Greece and Turkey might have to be taken across Egypt by rail and reloaded at Port Said or Alexandria. The immediate decisions were to develop the port of Suez to its utmost capacity; to double the railway between Suez and Ismailia; to develop Ataqa as a lighterage port for

---

[1] See page 250.

vehicles; and to lay a pipeline the whole length of the Canal so that, naval fuel oil could be pumped from near Suez to Port Said. These projects called for the provision of large quantities of stores and of technical units, all of which would have to be brought from overseas, and compete for shipping space with more warlike cargoes.

Thus within the short space of three weeks the *Luftwaffe* had made its presence felt in areas as far apart as the Sicilian Narrows and the Gulf of Suez. It had, for the time being at any rate, closed the Mediterranean to through traffic. Its arrival meant that convoys to Malta and in the Aegean and supply ships to ports in Cyrenaica would require greatly increased protection—more than could be provided by the carrier-borne fighter aircraft. There was an urgent need for more defensive measures of all kinds: for fighters, shore-based and carrier-borne; for ships fitted with radar, since the value of receiving early warning of attack had been clearly proved; for anti-aircraft equipment and devices of all kinds on shore; and also for guns with which merchant vessels and small craft could defend themselves. Malta, Greece, Crete, and Cyrenaica were suitable· locations for bases from which aircraft could play an effective part in the Mediterranean war, but it seemed to the Commanders-in-Chief that they had insufficient resources for the vigorous action that would be necessary if this new menace was to be mastered before it could do much greater damage. This task, together with the other enterprises to which the British forces were already committed, would not allow of the simultaneous creation of the strategic reserves which the Defence Committee had ordered to be formed, in circumstances to be related in the next chapter.

Ever since the attack on Taranto had driven the main units of the Italian Fleet to the west coast ports, Admiral Somerville had been considering which of these ports could profitably be attacked from the sea. Information early in December suggested that one of the *Littorio* class battleships was being repaired at Genoa, and Genoa was a place which lent itself to bombardment from waters too deep to be mined, a place moreover whose defences were thought to be almost negligible.

To bombard Genoa meant accepting the risk of damage to the *Ark Royal* and *Renown* at a distance of 700 miles from their base,[1] and the extrication of a damaged ship might well be impossible. Also there might be no Italian battleship in harbour to form the primary target. On the other hand, it was the sort of action that might have a big moral effect; it might draw off Italian naval and air forces

---

[1] See Map 22.

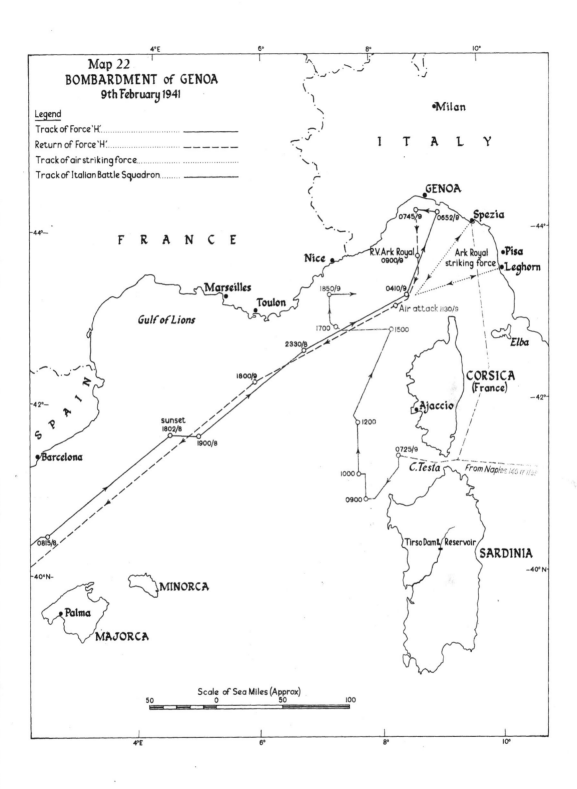

Map 22
BOMBARDMENT of GENOA
9th February 1941

Legend
Track of Force 'H'..................... ─────────
Return of Force 'H'..................... ─ ─ ─ ─ ─
Track of air striking force................... ·············
Track of Italian Battle Squadron........ ─────────

ITALY

•Milan

FRANCE

Nice •

Marseilles

Toulon

Gulf of Lions

GENOA
•
0745/9    0652/9    Spezia
•Pisa
R.V.Ark Royal        Ark Royal
0900/9              striking force    Leghorn •

0410/9          Air attack 1130/9

1850/9

1700        1500

2330/8

1800/9                    CORSICA
(France)

Ajaccio
sunset        1200
1802/8
1900/8        0725/9
SPAIN                    C.Testa    From Naples 1400 17 11/38
•Barcelona    1000
0900

Elba

Tirso Dam & Reservoir
0815/8                    SARDINIA

MINORCA

•Palma

MAJORCA

Scale of Sea Miles (Approx)
50    0    50    100

from other fronts, cause damage to the war industry and to shipping, and, in short, give the Italians something new to worry about. After the discouraging turn of events caused by the arrival of the *Luftwaffe*, Admiral Cunningham expressed himself strongly in favour of the idea of offensive action in the Gulf of Genoa and the Admiralty agreed that Admiral Somerville's operation should take place as soon as certain repairs to the *Malaya* were completed. They also suggested a subsidiary operation. The Tirso dam in Sardinia was believed to be vulnerable to attack by torpedo aircraft, and it supplied one third of the island's electric power and was also of great importance for irrigation. A successful attack upon it would be well rewarded.

A point may be mentioned here which illustrates the importance of exact information. If any Italian battleships were present at Genoa, they would of course be the primary targets and the type of shell to be used against them would be armour-piercing. For shore targets high explosive would be much more effective. To change from one type to the other would take the *Renown* ten minutes, a delay which was not acceptable in the bombarding position. It was necessary to know in advance what to expect. On 23rd January the information was that the *Littorio* might be in dry dock with the *Giulio Cesare* alongside. A Spitfire, specially modified for long-range photographic reconnaissance, was by chance at Malta at the time and was sent to verify the information. Unfortunately, it was shot down.

Force H—*Renown*, *Malaya*, *Ark Royal*, *Sheffield* and ten destroyers—sailed from Gibraltar on the evening of January 31st with the intention of attacking the Tirso dam on February 2nd and bombarding Genoa the next day. Meanwhile Admiral Cunningham sailed westward from Alexandria with a portion of his fleet to create a diversion. At 6 a.m. on 2nd February eight aircraft of No. 810 Squadron armed with torpedoes were flown off from a position west of Sardinia. Over the land it was raining, and the aircraft experienced severe icing; as they approached the target they came under heavy anti-aircraft fire. No explosions were seen and the dam appeared unharmed; a very disappointing result which incidentally supported the view of the Air Ministry that torpedoes would be useless against dams.

By 8.45 a.m. all the aircraft except one had returned to the carrier. (This one was shot down and its crew made prisoners.) The weather was getting worse, and the wind from the north-east reached gale force. This would have meant the final approach to Genoa being made in daylight, a risk which the Admiral considered unjustifiable. He therefore abandoned the operation and returned to Gibraltar.

The earliest date on which the operation could now be begun was February 6th. Conditions would not be ideal, for the final approach would be in bright moonlight, but the Admiralty had reason to believe (wrongly) that an expedition against the Balearics was about to be launched from Genoa and no delay could be accepted. Malta was asked to repeat the special reconnaissance, but unfortunately no suitable aircraft was now available.

On February 6th Force H sailed from Gibraltar in two groups, one east, one west, and the whole force concentrated early on the 8th to the north of Majorca. Aircraft, which may have been French or Spanish, were occasionally detected by radar, and course was then immediately altered to the south-east to give the impression of a move towards Sardinia. Bogus wireless signals were made by two destroyers off Minorca during the final approach of the force to Genoa, also to focus attention on Sardinia.

At 4 a.m., after a calm and moonlit passage, the *Ark Royal* was detached with three destroyers for her tasks of bombing the oil refinery at Leghorn and laying magnetic mines off Spezia. Two hours later the spotting aircraft were catapulted from the bombarding ships, *Renown*, *Malaya* and *Sheffield*.[1] Shortly before 7 a.m. a land fix was obtained and ships altered to the bombarding course, west-north-west. So far, so good; but were there any battleships in harbour? At 7.11 the *Renown's* spotting aircraft made the eagerly awaited report; no battleship could be seen. (It is now known that this report was wrong: the *Duilio*, damaged at Taranto, was in dry dock.)

A low haze hid the foreshore, and as the mountains beyond turned from grey to pink in the rising sun the *Renown* opened fire. The range was from ten to fourteen miles, so not much of Genoa could be seen from the ships, but the *Renown's* salvoes were quickly directed by the aircraft on to the Ansaldo works, marshalling yards, and factories. The battlecruiser's secondary armament pounded the waterfront, while the *Malaya* engaged targets around the dry docks. (Even so, the *Duilio* was not hit.) The *Sheffield* directed her fire at industrial installations. Fires and explosions were seen, and the smoke billowing from a fired oil tank made spotting difficult. One shore battery opened up and there was a certain amount of anti-aircraft fire. Two of the inshore destroyers made smoke to hamper the coast artillery and conceal the composition of the squadron. At 7.45 a.m. fire ceased, and the spotting aircraft withdrew to the *Ark Royal*. Two hundred and seventy-three rounds of 15-inch shell had been fired, apart from large quantities of smaller calibres.

Meanwhile the *Ark Royal* had been carrying out her share of the programme. Shortly after 5 a.m. she launched her striking force of fourteen Swordfish, each armed with four 250-lb. bombs, and

[1] See Photo 26.

incendiaries, and four more carrying magnetic mines. The target for the bombers was the Azienda oil refinery at Leghorn; one explosion was seen, but from subsequent reports the damage was slight. The minelayers made a gliding approach to Spezia, which was only partially blacked out, and laid their mines successfully in both entrances to the harbour. Before 9 a.m. all the aircraft were back in the *Ark Royal,* except one which had been shot down. Ten minutes later the carrier had rejoined Force H now steaming south at 22 knots.

In expectation of air attack six fighters were maintained over the force throughout the day, but the Italians made no attempt to close. A number of isolated aircraft were detected on the radar screen, and two of them dropped a few bombs well astern of the *Ark Royal.* Our fighters claimed two. After 1 p.m. low visibility assisted the withdrawal and Force H reached Gibraltar on 11th February without further incident.

There can be no doubt that the nature of the attack came as a surprise to the enemy, as no precautions had been taken to guard against an incursion into the Gulf of Genoa. According to Admiral Bernotti the Italians had reason to expect another raid on Sardinia and an attack on the Ligurian coast.[1] News of the sailing of Force H on February 6th was duly received. On February 8th Admiral Iachino, who had replaced Admiral Campioni as Commander-in-Chief of the Fleet, was ordered to sea from Spezia with three battleships and seven destroyers, to be joined by three 8-inch cruisers and three more destroyers from Naples.[2] Instead of concentrating in the Ligurian Sea, Admiral Iachino was sent through the Straits of Bonifacio. The Italians were uncertain of the destination of Force H and chose a position from which they might hope to intervene either to the north or to the south. This resulted in Admiral Iachino's force being about forty miles west of Cape Testa at the moment when the first shells were falling on Genoa. The only information he had received was that the lookouts at Tirso had been alarmed by the sound of aircraft overhead, and he did not turn north until the action at Genoa was over.

He was well placed, however, to head off the retreat of Force H, but he received highly conflicting reports, and his own catapulted aircraft made no contacts. Not until the afternoon, when his force had turned westward and had rescued the crew of one of the aircraft shot down by the *Ark Royal's* fighters some hours before, did he realize

---

[1] R. Bernotti: *La Guerra sui Mari nel Conflitto Mondiale 1939-41* (Leghorn, 2nd edition. 1948) p. 280.
[2] Admiral Campioni's appointment had been as commander of the Battle Squadron only. As the senior officer present he had commanded the Fleet during the operations that had led to the actions off Calabria and Cape Spartivento. But until Admiral Iachino was appointed there was no Commander-in-Chief responsible for the training of the Fleet as a whole.

that he was much too late. Admiral Bernotti attributes the failure to intercept not so much to the poor visibility as to the faulty liaison between the Naval and Air High Commands.

The official Italian naval historian, Captain Bragadin, records that the bombardment did grave damage in Genoa and in the harbour, although the *Duilio* was not hit. The moral effect was serious, all the more because the action of the Italian aircraft, though obviously ineffective, was praised, while there was no mention of the naval sortie; as a result, the Italian people thought the Navy had let them down.[1]

It was indeed remarkable that a British fleet, with no chance of sailing unobserved from its base, could penetrate to the extreme north of the Gulf of Genoa, inflict damage, and return without being attacked. Once more good fortune had favoured a bold plan prepared with great thoroughness and resolutely carried out. It was a disappointment to Admiral Somerville to find no big ships at Genoa, and the *Duilio* must be deemed very lucky. The action did not have the effect of causing any diversion of Italian air forces, and the dislocation of war industry cannot have been very serious. Far more important were the shock to Italian morale, already weakened by the reverses in Albania and Cyrenaica, and the feeling that no Italian port was safe from attack. It also showed that the British had no intention of taking the arrival of the *Luftwaffe* lying down; and that Italy's troubles were by no means over.

---

[1] *Che ha fatto la Marina?* p. 120

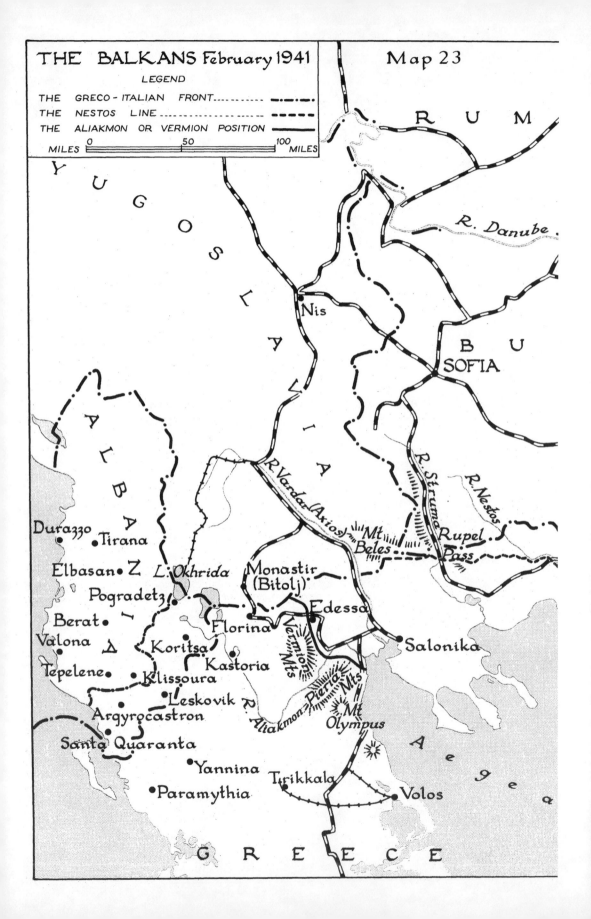

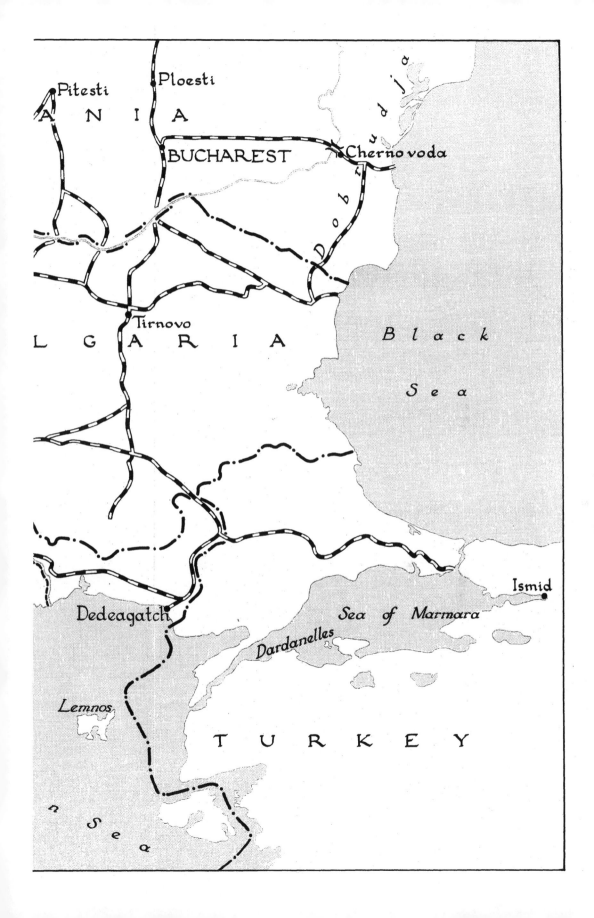

# CHAPTER XVIII

# GERMANY TURNS TO THE BALKANS

*See Map 23*

EARLY IN November the Greeks had successfully taken the shock of the initial Italian attacks; by the middle of the month they were striking back and quickly regained much of the lost ground. The Commander-in-Chief, General Papagos, naturally wished to exploit these successes before fresh forces from Italy—which were sure to come and indeed were already reported to be arriving—could intervene effectively. Being severely handicapped by the shortage of all kinds of transport, the Greek High Command planned first to press forward in the northern and central sectors so as to gain plenty of depth in front of the invaluable lateral road running from Koritsa to Leskovik. In the south they hoped to ease the heavy administrative burden by securing the small port of Santa Quaranta, and using it for the discharge of sea-borne supplies brought through the Gulf of Corinth. After these preliminary moves the main advance was to be made along the axis Argyrocastron-Tepelene, and was to culminate in the capture of Valona. The Italians would then have Durazzo as their only port, and the size of the forces that they could then keep in the field would be severely limited.

By the second week in December the Greeks had reached Pogradetz at the southern point of Lake Okhrida, and had penetrated deep into the mountains to the north-west of Koritsa; their northern flank was thus secure. In the centre they had made good progress in the direction of Berat, and in the south they had captured Santa Quaranta and Argyrocastron. The next step was to secure the important road-centres of Klissoura and Tepelene. By 10th January Klissoura had been captured but Tepelene was still in Italian hands. On the rest of the front it had been necessary to call a halt while communications were improved and the supply and transport organizations over-hauled. Some sharp counter-attacks were made at various points by the Italians, but they were repulsed without great difficulty.

Although they were held up at Tepelene, the Greeks had every reason to be proud of their achievements. General Papagos had felt able to transfer troops from opposite the Bulgarian frontier, and by the end of the year had succeeded in making about thirteen divisions available for the Albanian front. Meanwhile the Greeks had identified elements of some fifteen Italian divisions in the fighting. The Italians had the advantage of having been on a war footing for much longer than the Greeks, but when it came to fighting in the mountains they felt an acute lack of infantry, their divisions having been reduced from three infantry regiments to two.[1] Against this, the Greeks had not the vehicles and mobile equipment with which to exploit the successes that they gained in the mountain fighting. Their lack of tanks and anti-tank weapons compelled them to keep away from the more open ground, so that their progress was slow and the strain on men and pack animals was very great.

During December, January, and the early part of February Air Vice-Marshal D'Albiac's three bomber squadrons were directed almost entirely against ports, airfields and points on the Italian lines of communication, principally Valona, Durazzo, Berat and Elbasan. The weather could hardly have been worse; the heavy falls of snow, the prevalence of low cloud, and the severe icing conditions made flying difficult and hazardous. Based, as the bombers were, on air-fields near Athens, every raid into Albania meant a preliminary flight of some 200 miles to the frontier, and later 200 miles back, over mainly mountainous country which made the navigational aids unreliable and added to the strain on the aircrews. In order to keep down the losses from the enemy fighters that were being encountered over the targets in increasing numbers, it was necessary to provide escorts for the bombers.[2] This was not easy to do, on account of the distance between the bomber and fighter airfields, the unreliable communications, and the constant changes of weather. Moreover, the squadrons were falling below strength and were handicapped by the shortage of spares, of ground equipment, and of transport. The salvage of any aircraft larger than a fighter along the narrow winding roads was almost impossible. All this tended to reduce the effectiveness of the small bomber force, and the determination of the pilots and aircrews to carry out their arduous tasks in spite of all difficulties deserves the highest praise.

Throughout January it became increasingly probable that the Germans intended to enter Bulgaria with a view to attacking the Greeks, who would then be faced with a war on two fronts. If this happened, the Greek situation would indeed be desperate. As it was, they had a great many difficulties to contend with on the Albanian front alone. Their battle casualties had not been excessive, in view of what they had achieved, but the weather was causing great hard-ship. Blizzards had been frequent, and large numbers of men were disabled by frostbite. Clothing and boots were woefully scarce,

[1] See page 38.
[2] See page 234.

and so were vehicles and pack animals. And unless something drastic was done there would be no gun ammunition left in two months' time.

The three ships of convoy 'Excess', whose eventful passage was described in the last chapter, had brought a welcome contribution of vehicles and stores of all kinds, and some field and anti-aircraft guns and ammunition. But the whole problem of arranging for the supply of war materials to Greece was very complicated. The Greeks had started the war with a large variety of weapons mainly of French and German make. In England there was no ammunition for these types; in the United States of America the small remaining stocks of French ammunition had either been delivered to Greece or were on their way. Further orders on the United States of America would affect the British armaments programme and in any case could not be met in time for Greece to receive supplies before the end of 1941. The only satisfactory solution would be to re-equip the Greek forces with British weapons. This, however, would take a long time because there were no reserve stocks; it would also seriously delay the equipping of our own troops. All that could be done immediately was to try to meet the essential needs of the Greek arsenal and supply the Greek forces with as much as possible of the Italian equipment and transport captured in Libya.

One effect of the Albanian war had been to add very greatly to the amount of shipping requiring escort in the Eastern Mediterranean and Aegean. During December and January seven convoys, of 63 ships in all, carried supplies to Greece from Alexandria and Port Said without loss. One of these convoys was escorted by Greek destroyers, as were several smaller convoys to Piraeus from Suda Bay and the Aegean ports.

Greek submarines had had some successes against the Italian supply line across the Adriatic, and had sunk a 12,000 ton transport and (according to the Italians) one other merchant vessel, but the lack of maintenance facilities caused this effort to fade out. Meanwhile continuous patrols of the Elaphonisos and Kithera Channels—north and south of the island of Kithera respectively—were maintained by British minesweeping corvettes and trawlers, sometimes supported by cruisers and destroyers. On February 3rd Greek patrol boats took over the Elaphonisos Channel, and two days later the enemy's mining at Tobruk made it necessary for the British to relinquish responsibility for the Kithera Channel also. By this date no anti-torpedo baffle was in place at Suda Bay, so that, although this anchorage could be used as a base for operations by destroyers and light craft, cruisers and bigger ships could use it only as a quick fuelling base. The airfield at Maleme was taken into use by fighters of the Fleet Air Arm towards the end of January.

In view of the growing likelihood during January that troops would have to be moved back to the Bulgarian frontier, General Papagos decided to resume the offensive as soon as possible in a determined attempt to take Valona. A great deal depended upon the outcome of this operation, and the greatest single obstacle to a Greek success was deemed to be the supremacy of the Italian Air Force. The Greek Air Force had virtually ceased to exist and the Italian Air Force held undisputed mastery over the forward areas, where their continual air attacks had begun to tell on the morale of the Greek troops. Moreover the weight of the air attacks on the enemy's rearward organizations was, in the circumstances, so small that it could hardly have interfered seriously with the flow of Italian reinforcements. The Greek High Command therefore appealed at this moment for more air reinforcements, and urged the Air Officer Commanding to change his bombing policy and use his squadrons in close support of the Greek troops. The success of the whole operation might depend upon the stimulus afforded by the sight of friendly aircraft overhead and by the satisfaction of seeing the Italians receive the punishment that the Greeks had endured for so long. Air Vice-Marshal D'Albiac recognized the force of these arguments and acceded to General Papagos' request. Sir Arthur Longmore afterwards wrote, 'There is no doubt that this departure from the orthodox was a great stimulant to morale',[1] and the Greeks were generous in their praise of the willingness of the Royal Air Force to take great risks in order to give as much encouragement as possible to the troops.

Further help was forthcoming from the Middle East Command. Six Wellingtons of No. 37 Squadron left Egypt for Greece on February 12th, and on the same night, making a special effort, they successfully attacked the airfields at Durazzo and Tirana. No. 33 Squadron (Hurricane) was also ordered to Greece; their ground crews sailed on the 15th, and the aircraft followed a few days later. For the better control of the air operations a Wing Headquarters was now formed at Yannina. All serviceable Blenheim I aircraft were moved forward to the landing strip at Paramythia, which was dry enough to take them, but which had to be provisioned by air for some days until communication by road could be established. A second fighter squadron was also sent forward, together with a few Hurricanes which had just arrived for the rearming of No. 80 Squadron. By the end of February the Wing had provided nearly 200 sorties in support of the Greek army. Since the Greek campaign began the Royal Air Force had lost 30 aircraft and the Italians 58.

To the great disappointment of the Greeks the weather became very bad soon after they had begun their attack on 13th February to

---

[1] *From Sea to Sky*, 1946, page 253.

capture Tepelene, and although they met with some success at first the operation had to be suspended. By this time it had become evident that a big Italian offensive against the central sector was being prepared. It was not destined to succeed, but it marked the end of the Greek hopes of capturing Valona.

As might be expected, the complete failure of the Italian plans for the rapid occupation of Greece caused much recrimination in political and military circles in Rome. It was obvious to everybody that not enough forces had been assigned to the task; in von Rintelen's view the arrangements were suitable only for a military entry without any fighting, while the logistic organization was rudimentary and from the outset quite unequal to the strain. Marshal Badoglio was in the not entirely enviable position of being able to remind the Duce that the General Staff had estimated twenty divisions as the size of the force required. This he duly did, and on November 26th resigned his post as Chief of Staff. His place was taken by General Cavallero, an officer with a reputation for organizing ability. General Visconti Prasca had already been replaced in command of the Albanian front by General Soddu, the former Under-Secretary of State for War, but in December Soddu was removed in turn and Cavallero himself went to Albania. As if this was not enough for the bewildered Italian public, Admiral Cavagnari, the Chief of the Naval Staff, was replaced by Admiral Riccardi.

Having thus pinned the blame on his professional advisers Mussolini made great efforts to restore the Italian fortunes. Graziani and his troubles were forgotten, and the Albanian front assumed overriding importance. Mussolini announced to Hitler in a letter of 22nd November that no less than thirty divisions were being made ready for Albania. (By the middle of March 1941 a total of twenty-eight had indeed been sent there.) Hitler had been following the progress of events with some attention, and by 9th December a German Air Transport Group—the first unit of the *Luftwaffe* to be stationed in Italy—had begun to work between Foggia and Albania. Early in January he decided that further action on his own part was called for, and directed that a strong German contingent was to be put under orders for Albania. (Operation '*Alpenveilchen*'.) The Italians were not enthusiastic about this offer and succeeded in getting the proposed force whittled down to one mountain division, by stressing the difficulty of supplying a German force along the already over-loaded line of communication. By the middle of February it seemed to the Germans that the Italians—with twenty-one divisions—were now capable of holding their own and were unlikely to lose Valona. As the German General Staff had come to the conclusion that no decisive success could be achieved in Albania at that time of year, even by German troops, the proposal to send the mountain division

AA

was dropped and the Italians were left to themselves to pin down as many Greek and British forces as they could.


By the first week in January the prospects in Libya and Albania were distinctly encouraging. On both fronts the Italians had suffered serious reverses, while their irresolute defence of Bardia had confirmed the impression, gained during the fighting in December, that there were many Italians whose hearts were not in the war. It was at this moment that Germany's intention of going to the help of her failing ally became apparent. Information was reaching London which showed that the Germans were busily making preparations in Rumania with the ultimate purpose of attacking Greece. There was little doubt that the move would be made through Bulgaria, where the Government appeared to have lost control of events and where the Press had become little more than a mouthpiece of Axis propaganda. Would Greece stand firm under this added threat? '. . . Although perhaps by luck and daring', wrote the Prime Minister to the Chiefs of Staff on January 6th, 'we may collect comparatively easily most delectable prizes on the Libyan shore, the massive importance of the taking of Valona and keeping the Greek front in being must weigh hourly with us'.

These anxieties were reflected in the instructions sent to the Commanders-in-Chief by the Chiefs of Staff on January 10th, a week after the capture of Bardia. The German advance into Bulgaria might be expected to begin in perhaps ten days time, and would probably be directed upon Salonika through the Struma valley. One armoured and two motorized divisions and parachute troops, supported by some 200 dive-bombers might be used; three or four more divisions might be added after March. The easterly route from Bucharest to Dedeagatch would probably not be used, being too near to the Turkish frontier; nor was an advance through Yugoslavia thought to be likely. Bulgaria was not expected to offer any resistance. In these circumstances His Majesty's Government had decided that it was essential to afford the Greeks all possible help, in order to ensure that they would resist German demands by force. The extent and effectiveness of our help might well determine the attitude of Turkey, and it would have an influence upon opinion in the United States of America and Russia.

As soon as Tobruk had been captured, assistance to Greece was to take priority over all operations in the Middle East, though this decision was not to be taken as forbidding an advance to Benghazi 'if the going is good'. But the Commanders-in-Chief were told once again that any immediate help provided must come from their resources. Wavell and Longmore were to go and confer with General

Metaxas in order to exchange views and to determine the size of force to be sent. The Chiefs of Staff in London were obviously not in a position to lay this down, but they expressed the view that assistance would have to take the form of furnishing specialist and mechanized units and air forces with which to support the Greek divisions. They specified various types of tank and artillery units that might be sent, in addition to three Hurricane and two Blenheim IV squadrons.

Before this decision on policy reached the Commanders-in-Chief, they had a good idea of what was in the wind from an Air Ministry telegram, warning Longmore of the scale of air assistance to Greece that was being contemplated. He pointed out that this would mean, in effect, the transfer of perhaps all three of his Hurricane squadrons from Libya; that even if they were sent there were no airfields large enough for them in the Salonika area, and none at present available within reach of the Italians in Albania; that his only two Blenheim IV squadrons—other than those on convoy escort along the Red Sea route—were supporting the advance of the Army in Libya. To withdraw these bombers and fighters would not only severely handicap all the Libyan operations, but would give the Italian Air Force time to reorganize and be reinforced from Italy. General Wavell's reaction was to urge the Chiefs of Staff to consider most earnestly whether the German concentration in Rumania was not a bluff to induce us to disperse our force in the Middle East, to stop our advance in Libya when it was going so well, and to play upon the Greek morale. On the other hand, if the reports were accurate and if a determined German advance was about to begin, nothing that we could send from Egypt would arrive in time to stop it.

Although these expressions of doubt crossed, in transmission, the Chiefs of Staff's instructions, they drew from the Prime Minister an immediate rejoinder, amplifying the reasons for the Government's decision. The German concentration in Rumania was certainly no bluff, nor was it a move in the war of nerves. The force might not be large but it would be of deadly quality. If not stopped it might play the same part in Greece as the breakthrough of the German Army on the Meuse played in France. All the Greek divisions in Albania would be fatally affected. The destruction of Greece would eclipse the victories gained in Libya and might affect the Turkish attitude decisively, especially if we had shown ourselves callous of the fate of an ally. Large interests were therefore at stake. The matter had been earnestly weighed by the Defence Committee of the Cabinet. 'We expect and require prompt and active compliance with our decisions for which we bear full responsibility.'

By this time General Wavell had already made his arrangements to go to Athens and was preparing to send to Greece such units as could be made immediately available. He had learnt from Major-General T. G. G. Heywood, the Army member of the military mission, that the Greeks would be unlikely to ask for field or medium artillery for the Albanian front, but would probably want transport and anti-aircraft artillery. These were two of his own worst shortages: the former was wanted everywhere, and in particular for maintaining the momentum of the advance in Libya; the latter was already stretched to the utmost, and any despatches to Greece would be at the expense of the naval and air bases and the troops in the forward areas. The appearance of the *Luftwaffe* within the last few days increased the need for strengthening the anti-aircraft defences; it was certainly an inopportune moment for weakening them.

General Wavell left for Athens on 13th January. Air Chief Marshal Longmore was visiting his units in Libya at the time, and followed two days later. Meetings took place with the President of the Council, General Metaxas, the Commander-in-Chief, General Papagos, and their staffs. Admiral Cunningham was represented by the British Naval Attaché, Rear-Admiral C. E. Turle.

As regards the Albanian front General Papagos explained that his worst shortages were of transport, clothing, and anti-tank and anti-aircraft artillery. General Wavell at once decided to divert to Greece a shipload of transport vehicles which had just reached Egypt, and to follow this up with as many captured Italian lorries as possible as soon as they could be got back to Alexandria and shipped. He had very few pack animals and none to spare. He had already sent 180,000 pairs of boots, 350,000 pairs of socks, large numbers of blankets and much clothing from his reserve stocks. He mentioned his own acute shortage of anti-aircraft artillery, but having understood that the Greek advance in Albania was being much hampered by low-flying attacks, he offered to send a combined anti-aircraft and anti-tank regiment for use on that front. This was politely but quite definitely refused as was the offer of a company of light tanks, on the ground that it would be too difficult to maintain them.

As for the provision of further air support, Air Chief Marshal Longmore could make no definite promises, in view of his many commitments, but asked that the work on the airfields in the area south and west of Mount Olympus should be pressed on with all speed in order that fourteen squadrons could be handled. The provision of these, in a serviceable state, would be the limiting factor in sending squadrons from Egypt. His considered opinion was that two fighter squadrons and one Blenheim squadron were the most that could be accommodated in Greece at present, in addition to the four squadrons already there, and they would be sent at once.

Discussion on the German preparations in Rumania showed that the Greeks did not regard an advance to be immediately practicable, on account of the bad state of the roads and the lack of bridges. This did not mean that they questioned the facts; indeed, they estimated six German divisions, including one armoured division, to be in southern Rumania. Bulgaria had four divisions on the Greek frontier and five opposite Turkey, and could mobilize nine more. General Papagos explained that the concentration of the Greek forces against the Italians had left only about four weak divisions on the Bulgarian front. He estimated that for the defence of Eastern Macedonia and Salonika a further nine divisions with appropriate air forces would be needed.

A wide divergence was now apparent between the British and Greek views. The army units offered by General Wavell amounted to two regiments of field artillery, and one or two of medium artillery; one anti-tank regiment; one cruiser tank regiment; and one or two batteries of anti-aircraft artillery. General Metaxas considered that the arrival of such a force would have none of the desired results. It was likely to provoke an attack by the Germans, and possibly by the Bulgarians also, which the British and Greeks would not be strong enough to check. The effect on Yugoslavia would be very different from what the British expected: he had a categorical assurance that Yugoslavia was resolved to oppose the passage of German troops through her territory, but that this assurance would be withdrawn if the German aggression were provoked by the presence of British forces in Salonika.

The most important step, in the President's opinion, was to clear up the situation in Albania; this would release large Greek forces for the Bulgarian front. As soon as these were available he would welcome British assistance. The best plan therefore was to make all possible secret preparations for landing a British expedition at Salonika and the neighbouring ports, but to send no troops at all until they could arrive in sufficient numbers to act offensively as well as defensively. General Metaxas therefore proposed that a joint study should be made by the staffs; the Greeks themselves would then make the necessary preparations. The move of British troops to Greece should take place only if German troops crossed the Danube (or the frontier of Dobrudja) and penetrated into Bulgaria. General Wavell, loyally supporting his instructions, maintained the British view 'with all the arguments I could command', but without success. The President added that this should not be interpreted as a final refusal, but as a request for postponement. Finally, and with great emphasis, he said that if Salonika were attacked the Greeks would fight to the last; the British could rest assured that the Greeks would be with them to the end whether Germany came in or not; there would be no question of a separate peace.

The refusal to accept the immediate offer of British Army units applied also, as far as the Salonika area was concerned, to units of the Royal Air Force. General Metaxas agreed, however, that this area should be used for the re-forming of the Greek Air Force. Air Chief Marshal Longmore welcomed this decision, as it offered an opportunity of developing the appropriate airfields; these would be available in emergency as advanced landing grounds and re-fuelling bases. Permission was given for officers of the British Air Mission to visit them, and also to reconnoitre airfields on the islands of Lemnos and Mitylene. Longmore had already been told that aircraft for the reconstituted Greek Air Force would come out of his own reinforcements, and some 30 of the first Mohawk fighters to arrive had been promised to Greece. Unfortunately, a defect had been found in the engines of these aircraft, which made a major modification necessary, so that further delays would occur before they could reach the Middle East. He was now told that 500 Toma-hawk fighters had also been purchased from the United States of America and that 300 of these would reach Takoradi during the next five months. Little was known of their operational charac-teristics; but as they were fitted with American guns they would be useless until supplies of American ammunition could also reach the Middle East. As it was not known when this would happen, it was impossible for the Air Officer Commanding-in-Chief to make a firm plan for rearming his own squadrons or those of the South African or Greek Air Forces. He could only urge the Air Ministry to keep up the supply of Hurricanes at the highest possible rate because the question of the supply of American aircraft had not yet been clarified.

On hearing the result of the discussions the Chiefs of Staff replied that the Defence Committee had noted the Greek Government's refusal of British units for the Albanian front and that there could be no question of forcing our aid upon them. As regards Salonika it was assumed that General Metaxas was fully aware of the information which had prompted His Majesty's Government to make their offer; if so, we must submit to his judgment. But Wavell and Long-more were instructed before leaving Athens to make it quite clear that, if the special force proposed by the British was not despatched until after the German advance had begun, it would certainly be too late. For their own information the Commanders-in-Chief were told that there could be no question of sending to Salonika, either now or later, an expedition strong enough to act offensively as well as defensively. It was even possible that British forces might have to be sent to Turkey instead of to Greece. Therefore no preparations for the reception of British troops at Salonika and neighbouring ports were to be made except for those units needed for the maintenance of any air squadrons operating from that area.

General Wavell arrived back in Cairo on the evening of the 17th, having visited Crete and having had a discussion with Admiral Cunningham at Alexandria on the way. He immediately cabled his own views on what had occurred. He thought that the British proposal was a dangerous half-measure. The help suggested would not be enough to give the weak Greek forces at present holding the Bulgarian front the support they would need if the Germans were really determined to capture Salonika. Almost inevitably we should be compelled to send further troops in haste or become involved in retreat or defeat. If valuable technical troops were now sent to Salonika and Germany made no move, they would be locked up to no purpose. Meanwhile, the advance into Libya would come to a halt and the Italians would be given time to recover. Both from the naval and air points of view there would be great advantages in securing Benghazi, but air protection during the advance and afterwards would be essential, and he regarded the shortage of fighter aircraft and anti-aircraft equipment as the most serious factor in the present situation. The result of dispersing resources still farther—to cover Salonika, for instance—would be weakness everywhere, with no port, base, or other vulnerable point properly defended. The arrival of the German Air Force in the Mediterranean increased the gravity of this matter. General Wavell added that he thought Germany might well hesitate to violate Bulgarian neutrality, because this would expose the Rumanian oilfields to air attack. Finally, he was of course ready to send the strongest force available if the War Cabinet ordered him to do so, but he felt it his duty to communicate the foregoing views and to state his conclusions: that the Greek refusal should be accepted; that reconnaissances and preparations of the Salonika front should go ahead; but that no promise should be given to send troops at any future date.

On 21st January the Commanders-in-Chief received the British Government's conclusions reached in the light of the Greek refusal and of the appearance of the *Luftwaffe* in the Central Mediterranean. First, the capture of Benghazi was clearly of the greatest importance. It ought to become a strongly defended naval and air base, and its use should enable the long overland line of communication to be dropped, with a great saving of men and transport. Secondly, the German Air Force must be expected to spread into the Dodecanese Islands and threaten Alexandria, the Canal, and the sea communications with Turkey and Greece. It was therefore important to capture these islands, particularly Rhodes, as soon as possible. The troops for this expedition would have to be found from Middle East resources, to which would soon be added the Special Service troops about to sail in the Glen ships.[1] Thirdly, it was confirmed that No. 11 (Blenheim) Squadron and No. 112 (Gladiator) Squadron were to go to Greece. The Air Officer Commanding-in-Chief was now to regard as his first duty the maintenance at Malta of 'a sufficient air force to sustain its defence', and to help in this H.M.S. *Furious* was shortly to take a third consignment of Hurricanes to Takoradi. Finally, a strategic reserve should be created, with the primary object of rendering assistance to Turkey and Greece within the next two months. It was hoped that this force would soon attain the equivalent of four divisions. The arrival of these instructions from the Chiefs of Staff coincided with the welcome news of the capture of Tobruk.

Having been asked for their comments, the three Commanders-in-Chief replied agreeing that the capture of Benghazi and Rhodes was of urgent importance and 'noting' the need for forming a strategic reserve. They thought that the reinforcements and equipment which General Wavell was expecting to receive would go some way towards enabling the Army to carry out its various tasks, but the sort of risks which the Navy and Air Force had been taking with weak forces against an unenterprising enemy would not be justified against the Germans. It was fully intended to push on to Benghazi, but the subsequent development and defence of this port would be governed primarily by the arrival of equipment from England. More supply ships would be essential; in the meantime, by using men-o'-war and by continuing to run light craft long after they were due for a refit, a limited supply line by sea could be kept going, but only as far as Tobruk; so that the need for a land route would not disappear. The Navy had not enough light craft and escort vessels to safeguard a sea supply line stretching as far as from John-o'-Groat's to Land's End, and at the same time cover the convoys to Malta and the increasing traffic in the Aegean—not to mention any other operations. As it was, traffic between Cyprus, Palestine, and Egypt had to run unescorted. Admiral Cunningham required, first, a flotilla of destroyers and two modern cruisers with good anti-aircraft armament; next, a number of small merchant ships of about 2,000—3,000 tons and a speed of at least ten knots. These were not to be found in the Mediterranean; he had already been compelled to take three ships off the feeder service to Greece and Turkey in order to run a supply service even to Sollum.

The capture of Rhodes was obviously an urgent requirement and would be done as soon as possible after the arrival of the Glen ships. If the *Luftwaffe* began to operate from the Dodecanese the whole coast from Haifa in Palestine to Apollonia in Cyrenaica would be within range of German bombers. Even if Benghazi were in our

---

[1] See page 325.

hands, the air threat to Egypt would remain until Rhodes had been taken, so that fighters would have to be kept in Egypt for the present for the defence of the naval base and the Canal. There seemed to be no signs of the men and equipment for the three fighter squadrons which the Air Officer Commanding-in-Chief had been authorized to raise. As regards Malta, the Air Chief Marshal pointed out that it was not easy to fly fighters to the island even from Libyan airfields at this time of year.

To these comments the Chiefs of Staff replied that Admiral Cunningham's naval requirements would be met during the next three months; the necessary merchant ships would be collected from other areas as soon as possible. Once again they stressed the need for abolishing the overland line of communication in Cyrenaica; when Benghazi became a well-filled base with substantial reserves of supplies there would be no need for coastal convoys to run continuously. They hoped that the coastal and anti-aircraft defences of the port would be largely provided by captured Italian guns and equipment. As regards the Dodecanese, the Glen ships would arrive early in March and it was hoped that the first major operation would be undertaken by the middle of March at the latest.[1] Finally, Sir Arthur Longmore was given authority to form as many new squadrons as his resources permitted; a concession which, in the circumstances, he could not regard as very helpful. In short, the impression left upon the Commanders-in-Chief was that they would have to live for some time largely upon what General Wavell called their 'leanness'.

Towards the end of January the Chiefs of Staff became convinced that preparations were being made for a German move into Bulgaria, and His Majesty's Government turned its attention to the increasing danger threatening Turkey. At the staff talks the Turks had accepted the idea of a single Allied front in the Balkans.[2] They realized that Greece had first claim to British aid both in men and materials, but if their own country were attacked they would certainly want, above everything else, aircraft—especially fighters—and anti-aircraft artillery. They were dissatisfied at the inability of the British to work to a firm programme, even for the supply of aircraft which had long been on order for the Turkish Air Force. Many of their squadrons were therefore grounded, and training was being delayed. They had promised to hasten the preparation of ports, airfields and communications to which the British attached so much importance, but they naturally hesitated to do anything which might plunge them into war against the Axis before their own formations were suitably

[1] See page 325.
[2] See page 256.

trained and equipped. The report of the staff talks reached London on 22nd January, and on the 31st the Prime Minister addressed a personal appeal to the President of the Turkish Republic.

He pointed out that the Bulgarian Government were allowing the Germans to establish themselves on Bulgarian airfields, and drew attention to the consequent grave danger to Turkey. The remedy was to adopt similar measures. The British Government would send to Turkey at least ten squadrons of fighters and bombers apart from those now in action in Greece, as soon as they could be received. They were also prepared to send 100 anti-aircraft guns from Egypt. More air forces would follow. Together we should be able to threaten to bombard the Rumanian oilfields if the Germans were to advance into Bulgaria. At the same time the threat to Baku might well restrain Russia from giving any help to the Germans.[1]

This message caused the Chiefs of Staff to change the emphasis in their recent instructions to the Commanders-in-Chief. The 'Graeco-Turkish situation' was now to have first place in their thoughts, and steps to counter German infiltration into Bulgaria were to be given the highest priority. Benghazi was to be captured as quickly as possible, provided this could be done without prejudice to the European interests. Action against the Dodecanese was more urgent than ever because of the need for good communications with Turkey. Air Chief Marshal Longmore was warned that if the Turkish Government accepted the Prime Minister's proposals the ten squadrons referred to were to be found by him. He expressed astonishment that squadrons should be sent to Turkey, where they might be locked up doing nothing, at a time when operations against the Italians in Cyrenaica and Eritrea were in full swing and there was an urgent need to oppose the *Luftwaffe* in the Mediterranean. The reply was that they must try to deter Germany from absorbing in turn Bulgaria, Greece, and Turkey, thus dominating the Eastern as well as the Central Mediterranean. When he restated his many shortages and pointed out that his replacements of aircraft were barely keeping pace with current wastage, he was told that by the end of March he might expect to have received a further 100 Hurricanes, 120 Blenheim IVs, 45 Glenn Martins and 35 Wellingtons, so that by careful planning and by taking risks—particularly against the Italians—it might be possible to meet all his commitments. It was admitted, however, that the Air Force would be stretched to the utmost.

The Prime Minister's message was not, however, received with much enthusiasm by the Turkish President. The presence of British army and air units in Turkey would inevitably mean the entry of Turkey into the war, which, in the opinion of the President, would

---

[1] The text of this message is given in full in Appendix 5.

not be in the best interests of either Britain or Turkey. Turkey was still very short of military equipment and supplies, and until her state of preparedness was much improved she was not prepared to take any action likely to provoke the Germans.

Meanwhile, the Greeks had suffered a grievous loss in the sudden death, on January 29th, of General John Metaxas, whose resolute leadership had been an inspiration to the whole nation. It can never be easy to succeed a dictator, and there were obvious difficulties in store for the new President, M. Alexander Koryzis, Governor of the National Bank of Greece and former Minister of Public Assistance. On February 8th—two days after the British had entered Benghazi —M. Koryzis reaffirmed the determination of Greece to resist a German attack at all costs, and repeated the declaration made by General Metaxas that no British troops were to be sent to Macedonia unless the Germans crossed the Rumanian frontier into Bulgaria. Staff talks had been taking place during the past three weeks to investigate the possible composition of a British force to be sent in that event, and M. Koryzis now suggested that this matter should be settled, in order to determine whether the British and Greek forces together would be sufficient to check the German attack and encourage Yugoslavia and Turkey to take part in the struggle. He added his conviction that the premature despatch of an insufficient force would be treated by the Germans as a provocation; it would destroy even the faint hope that the attack might be avoided.


The programme outlined by Hitler in his letter to Mussolini of November 20th could not, in the event, be carried out in full.[1] Mention has already been made of General Franco's refusal to receive German troops in Spain early in January 1941. Bulgaria was invited to follow the example of Hungary and Rumania by adhering to the Tripartite Pact between Germany, Italy, and Japan, but declined to be hurried, principally because she was nervous of Russia and Turkey. But although she was unwilling to side openly with Germany, she promised to give secret support for the German preparations for an attack upon Greece; when the time came she would offer no resistance to the passage of German troops through her territory but she would make no promise of active support.

By about the end of the year the results of Germany's further diplomatic activities were broadly as follows. She could not be certain that Yugoslavia would stand aside while Greece was attacked, but had to assume that the passage of German troops through Yugoslavia would not be permitted. Action by Turkey against Bulgaria was unlikely, but would have to be guarded against; the

---

[1] See page 240.

Bulgarians would therefore have to mobilize in time to protect themselves. The attempts to divert Russia's attention from the Balkans had been singularly unsuccessful; she had continued to watch German activities very closely and had even made a cautious attempt to influence Bulgaria herself. When the Russians enquired the meaning of the German concentration in Rumania and the preparations for moving into Bulgaria, they were told that the British were to be driven out of Greece but that the Germans had no intention of violating Turkish neutrality unless Turkey herself intervened.

The main German forces began to move into Rumania through Hungary early in January, the arrangements for their reception having been made by the strong Army and Air Missions ostensibly set up to organize and train the Rumanian forces. The directive for operation '*Marita*' was issued by Hitler on 13th December, in confirmation of plans already well advanced. The object was to move through Bulgaria and occupy Grecian Macedonia, and possibly the whole mainland of Greece as well, in order to prevent the British from establishing under the protection of a Balkan front an air base which would be a threat to Italy and to the Rumanian oilfields. The forces allotted were the 12th Army, then in Vienna under Field-Marshal List, supported by *Fliegerkorps VIII*, under General Frh. von Richthofen. Field-Marshal List was to have five army corps headquarters; one group of four armoured divisions; and one motorized, two mountain, and eleven other divisions. *Fliegerkorps VIII* would consist of 153 bombers (39 Ju 88, 114 Ju 87) and 121 fighters (83 Me 109, 38 Me 110). There would be a liberal allotment of anti-aircraft (flak) units.

The 12th Army was told to be ready to start moving into Bulgaria any time after 7th February, but the severity of the weather made it impossible to keep to the programme of train moves, and the preparations for crossing the Danube were held up by the treacherous ice. On 6th February the date was postponed a fortnight. Meanwhile the bad weather had interfered with the moves of the air forces, and a thaw in the middle of February made most of the Rumanian airfields unusable. On the 17th Hitler ordered a further postponement: the bridging of the Danube was to start on February 28th, and the first crossing on March 2nd. The attack on Greece was to be made in the first few days of April.

Thus the information which led His Majesty's Government to offer help first to Greece and then to Turkey was timely and accurate. In the circumstances this is not surprising, for Hitler could only allay the suspicions of Russia, Turkey, and Yugoslavia, by creating the impression that Germany's intervention in the Balkans was directed only against Britain and her ally, Greece. The time factor was of great importance to him, for there seemed no likelihood of the Italians being able to clear up the Greek situation unaided, and he particularly did not wish German military intervention to drag on in such a way as to interfere with the preparations for the attack on Russia. For it was this attack—'*Barbarossa*'—that really mattered; everything else was subsidiary and he had laid down in his Directive of 18th December that preparations for '*Barbarossa*' must be completed by 15th May. In deciding that there would be time to carry out '*Marita*' first, Hitler was staking heavily on the correctness of his political judgment. For if Turkey should turn hostile in consequence of German military activity so near her frontier, the German General Staff estimated that '*Barbarossa*' could not begin on the intended date. Nor would it be wise to begin '*Marita*' unless Yugoslavia, whose frontier lay so close to the approaches to Salonika, could be relied upon to remain passive. The risk was accepted, however; but on the day of the Yugoslav *coup d'état*, 27th March 1941, Hitler postponed '*Barbarossa*' about four weeks.

# CHAPTER XIX

# GRAZIANI IS SWEPT OUT OF CYRENAICA

## (January - February 1941)

*See Map* 17

ON JANUARY 21st, the day of the assault on Tobruk, the Chiefs of Staff informed the Commanders-in-Chief that the capture of Benghazi was now of the greatest importance. General O'Connor had already arranged for 7th Armoured Brigade to press on towards Derna, and for 4th Armoured Brigade to begin its 100-mile move to Mechili. By the next evening the former was in contact with the enemy 20 miles from Derna, while the latter had patrols astride the tracks leading west, south, and south-east from Mechili.

The advanced troops were now approaching a type of country quite unlike any of the previous battlefields of the desert war. The change from the familiar desert takes place roughly along a line between the Gulf of Bomba, which is midway between Tobruk and Derna, and Soluch, which is just south of Benghazi. To the north of this line the bulge of Cyrenaica rises to over 2,500 feet above sea level to form the Jebel Akhdar, or Green Mountains. Together with its foothills this range forms a district of fairly fertile soil, with a temperate climate and a rainfall sufficient for the needs of cultivation. It had become an important centre of Italian colonization. In Benghazi, with its 65,000 inhabitants, one third were Italians; and large numbers of Italian families had been planted in the smaller towns and villages. In contrast to the desert it was a settled district with an administrative and social existence.

The communications within the Jebel area were moderately good. The port of Benghazi was linked by rail through Benina northwards to Barce, and southwards to Soluch. The main coastal road which linked Tripoli with Cyrenaica turned inland just north of Benghazi and was duplicated for most of the way along the Jebel, regaining the coast at Derna. Secondary roads were few and of poor quality, and the winter rains were apt to turn the heavy red soil into thick mud. On the airfields in the region, such as Barce, Benina, and Berka (Benghazi), this meant that vehicles were apt to be bogged and aircraft unable to take off—a serious disadvantage which did not apply in the Derna region or farther east, where the airfields had hard desert surfaces.

Fifty miles inland from Derna is Mechili, where tracks from all directions converge. One of these runs due west to Benghazi, right across the grain of the southern foothills of the Jebel. In fact, an arc stretching from Derna to Mechili and round to Soluch embraces broken and difficult country all the way, and higher up the slopes of the Jebel the ground becomes more rugged still, with steep rocky outcrops, presenting severe, and often complete, obstacles to wheeled or tracked vehicles. The Jebel area thus lends itself to defence against an advance from the east or south.

In the desert which lies to the south of the line Mechili—Soluch ran various caravan tracks, ill-defined, mostly waterless, and affording every variety of 'going' from vile to good. Together they formed a tenuous connexion between the Tobruk—Bomba coast and the Gulf of Sidra. From Tobruk to Agedabia is 250 miles by air, and a great deal more by the desert tracks. The Italians were content to leave to nature the task of opposing any move by these routes, and themselves prepared to impose as much delay as possible in the Jebel area.

The information at 13th Corps headquarters was that Derna and Mechili were probably being held as advanced localities, the 60th Sabratha Division being at Derna, less one regiment which was at Mechili together with General Babini's armoured brigade. The composition of this brigade, which had so far been kept in reserve, was not accurately known; still less was known about its efficiency. It was certain, however, that it contained medium tanks—probably two battalions—and was clearly to be reckoned with. Of the dispositions farther back in the Jebel the information was rather vague, but it seemed that Headquarters, 10th Army, was at Cyrene and 20th Corps at Giovanni Berta, and there were thought to be units of the 17th Pavia and 27th Brescia Divisions around Cyrene and Slonta. The enemy's response to patrol activity showed that he intended to fight; he seemed to be plentifully supplied with mines; and the inference was that he would make full use of the natural delaying power of this piece of country.

The Italian Air Force had now been forced back to its last group of airfields in Cyrenaica and was finding the greatest difficulty in maintaining its remaining aircraft. The numbers serviceable on January 20th were about 46 bombers and 34 fighters; of the ground attack aircraft only a handful remained. The Royal Air Force, too, were feeling the effects of nearly two months' hard fighting in desert conditions, and they had the additional complication of establishing new airstrips in step with the advance of the Army. To make the squadrons properly mobile much more motor transport would have been required—a need that could not be met by transport aircraft, of which by this time there were very few. It was indeed, fortunate that the Italians had abandoned large quantities of aviation petrol and bombs which the Air Force were able to use.

After the fall of Tobruk Nos. 73 and 274 Fighter Squadrons moved to Gazala and the Army Co-operation Squadrons to Tmimi. Air Commodore Collishaw opened his own headquarters at Tobruk, and from January 25th, with the agreement of the Army, directed his whole bomber effort against the tottering Italian Air Force. The airfields at Apollonia, Barce, Maraua, Soluch and El Magrun were attacked with increasing intensity, with results which contributed greatly to the collapse of the enemy's air effort.

On January 24th the 19th Australian Brigade Group took over from the 7th Armoured Brigade south of Derna and began to work forward across very difficult ground to probe the enemy's defences. The same day a large force of the enemy, including about fifty medium tanks, was encountered by 4th Armoured Brigade to the north of Mechili. A tank *v.* tank fight ensued, in which the enemy lost eight medium tanks destroyed and one captured; the British losses were one cruiser and six light tanks.

It seemed to General O'Connor that, although the enemy's forces at Mechili appeared to be strong in tanks and artillery, there was a weakness in the general dispositions owing to the distance between Mechili and Derna. This offered a chance of inflicting a defeat in detail and, of the two forces, he decided to destroy or capture General Babini's first. He accordingly gave orders for the 6th Australian Division to apply pressure on the Derna front and to send one brigade to join the 7th Armoured Division which, strongly reinforced by artillery, would carry out the Mechili operation. He gave explicit orders that the Armoured Division was on no account to allow the enemy to escape from the Mechili area.

To General O'Connor's great disappointment, General Babini succeeded in withdrawing his force northwards during the night of January 26th. It was attacked on the way to Slonta by fighter aircraft next day, and pursued fruitlessly by 4th Armoured Brigade until the 28th. The bad going, heavy rain, numerous mechanical breakdowns, and shortage of petrol then combined to bring the pursuit to a stop.

Although the Italians had succeeded in keeping their armoured brigade intact, they were disappointed with the result of the encounter of the 24th at Mechili, and Marshal Graziani was disturbed by a report by Babini on the weakness of his tanks and on the greatly superior numbers of the British, which made it necessary to withdraw. (The dummy tank regiment may have contributed to this impression.) The truth is that the Italians had in all about 100 medium and 200 light tanks, of which perhaps rather more than half were serviceable, while the British had reached the stage where many of their vehicles were on their last legs, and on January 27th only 50 of the cruisers were able to run.

As if the situation in Cyrenaica were not bad enough, Graziani now began to receive disquieting news from Rome of sinister stirrings in Algeria and of a possible British intention to attempt a landing in French North Africa. Mussolini himself sent him a warning against French dissidents. The presence of Weygand, although he was not a follower of de Gaulle, was regarded with great misgivings. Added to this was the unwelcome news of the exploits of the Long Range Desert Group and the French Patrols, which had lost nothing in the telling. The fact that they had been accompanied to Murzuk by the old Senussi Chief and bitter opponent of the Italians, Abd el Galil Seif en Nasr, suggested that more trouble might be brewing in the inner desert.

As Commander-in-Chief of the Armed Forces Graziani must have realized that a withdrawal from Cyrenaica was almost inevitable, though as Governor-General of Libya he must have found the prospect very unwelcome. When it seemed clear to him that the British would not be content with securing the use of Tobruk, but meant to conquer the whole of Cyrenaica, he decided that delaying action in the Jebel would only result in the loss of the remaining elements of 10th Army and that the right course was to save what he could from the wreck as quickly as possible. On February 1st he reported to the Duce that he intended to withdraw the remains of 10th Army to the vicinity of Sirte, where General Gariboldi, commanding in Tripoli, had been instructed to organize the defences. The next day he ordered General Tellera to take over command of all forces in eastern Libya from 3rd February, with the task of withdrawing from Cyrenaica and reassembling in Sirtica. Graziani himself left Benghazi early on February 3rd by road.

Meanwhile General O'Connor was considering what to do after the mishap which left at large the strong force of Italian tanks that he had hoped to isolate and destroy. The enemy's withdrawal from Mechili was followed on January 29th by the evacuation of Derna, with the result that the Italian forces were now more concentrated than before. The detachments high up on the Jebel to the north-west of Mechili showed every sign of resisting strongly. There was a report, later shown to have been wrong, that German troops— probably anti-aircraft units—had arrived at Benghazi. If this were true it was unlikely that the Italians would give up their positions in the Jebel without a fight and they probably intended to resist at, and to the east of, Benghazi. Therefore an advance towards Benghazi by the direct track from Mechili would be likely to meet opposition in country which was correctly judged to be unfavourable for tanks; and it would not turn the flank of the enemy's probable position.

An advance south-west across the desert to Msus, on the other hand, was far less likely to be expected and would open up attractive possibilities. General O'Connor therefore proposed that the Australian Division (less one brigade) should continue to exert pressure in the coastal region and that 7th Armoured Division and one infantry brigade should advance to Msus. If the enemy stood at Benghazi, this force would continue its move westwards to Soluch, cut the road to Tripoli, and attack Benghazi from the south. If, however, the enemy had begun to withdraw, the British force would move farther south through Antelat and strike at the line of retreat from that direction. This outline plan was submitted on January 31st and was approved by General Wavell next day.

The timing depended upon two main factors. The first was the maintenance situation which was difficult, but improving. Since January 27th the forward troops had been drawing from Nos. 12 and 13 Field Supply Depots, both about 60 miles west of Tobruk. Water had become less of a problem, at least in the coastal zone, thanks to the resources of Tobruk and of a few places to the west of it. There were serious shortages of petrol from time to time, and maintenance generally continued to be an anxiety for some days. Tobruk harbour was swiftly cleared by the Royal Navy and the unloading of the first ship began on January 28th—several days earlier than was expected. By February 1st the port was handling 900 tons of cargo a day, which greatly eased the strain on the transport which had hitherto been lifting nearly everything from Sollum. The new plan for advancing across the desert made it absolutely essential to have sufficient reserve stocks well forward at the outset; another Field Supply Depot (No. 14) was therefore formed 25 miles south-west of Mechili, into which ten days' stock of food and petrol and two refills of ammunition were to be put—nearly 3,000 tons in all—with special arrangements for water. To do this over and above the daily routine running was estimated to require twelve days. The only way of reducing this time was to use the port of Derna, which was much nearer than Tobruk, but it was so poorly equipped as to be useless except for cased petrol.

The second limiting factor was the state of the vehicles of 7th Armoured Division, most of whose fifty remaining cruiser tanks were due for a major overhaul. While General O'Connor was prepared to employ the Armoured Division as long as it had a tank that could run, it seemed to him necessary to await the two fresh cruiser regiments of 2nd Armoured Division, which were expected to join him between February 7th and 9th. In the meantime he decided to make up 4th Armoured Brigade with all the best cruiser and light tanks at the expense of 7th Armoured Brigade.

Taking everything into account it was hoped to begin the new advance between February 10th and 12th. On January 30th, in reply to an urgent enquiry by the Chief of the Imperial General Staff, General Wavell said that, as a rough forecast, he expected to capture Benghazi by the end of February.

On 31st January the 19th Australian Infantry Brigade gained touch with the enemy six miles west of Derna; fifteen miles or so inland was the 17th Australian Infantry Brigade. Farther to the left, opposite Chaulan, patrols of the 11th Hussars were also in contact. On 1st February, there were reports from the air of westward movement between Giovanni Berta and Barce, but it was not clear whether this indicated a retirement from the coastal sector or the start of a general withdrawal. By the afternoon of February 2nd reports from air and ground led General O'Connor to think that a withdrawal might be in progress on a much larger scale than the events of the last few days had suggested. Clearly no time was to be lost, and in this new situation three questions in particular required immediate answers: Could he afford to wait for the two fresh cruiser regiments? Could the 7th Armoured Division be launched in its mechanically doubtful condition across 150 miles of unreconnoitred desert? If so, could it be maintained?

General O'Connor's mind was soon made up. He would not await the armoured reinforcements, and 7th Armoured Division must move until it could move no longer. As for maintenance, the first convoys loaded at Tobruk were beginning to arrive at Mechili, and by February 4th it would be just possible for 7th Armoured Division to set out with its supply vehicles full; it could be followed by a convoy containing two days' supplies, water, petrol, food and two refills of ammunition. No other convoy would be able to reach Msus before these amounts were exhausted.

These were the plain facts; and whatever the tactical fortunes of the advance might be, the risks of such a close-run administrative situation were clear enough. General O'Connor accepted them, and as it turned out the Armoured Division was kept supplied—but only just—until it had achieved its object.

The warning order to 7th Armoured Division was issued that evening and was followed next morning by an instruction to start the move to Msus at first light on February 4th, with a view to making a further advance to Soluch and Ghemines as soon as the administrative arrangements permitted. The stated objects were to prevent any Italian forces south of Soluch and Ghemines from joining those around Benghazi, and equally to prevent these from with-drawing southwards. The 6th Australian Division was to press on with all speed; this they certainly did, and before nightfall had entered Cyrene.

Air reports during the 3rd provided definite evidence of a general withdrawal from Cyrenaica. Columns of transport were seen moving westward in the Jebel area, and were constantly attacked by the Blenheims. Sixty tanks were seen, and bombed, on rail at Barce. Retreating columns were moving south from Benghazi, and the inactivity of the Italians in the air indicated that their Air Force was quitting its southern airfields. To supplement the Blenheims a detachment of six Wellingtons of No. 70 Squadron reached El Adem from the Canal, and Tripoli harbour and the airfield at Castel Benito were attacked by Wellingtons from Malta.

As opposition in the air gradually diminished, the fighter squadrons were able to devote more and more of their efforts to harassing the retreating enemy. Marshal Graziani refers to the grievous losses caused by these attacks, and to the severe strain on morale already sorely tried by the vicissitudes and fatigues of the past few days.[1] But on February 3rd the shortage of Merlin engines put a stop to this activity. (There were no spare Merlin engines in Egypt nor any spare parts; 32 engines awaited overhaul in the depots.) Air Com-modore Collishaw had certainly used his force to the limit; he could now look forward to the prospects of being able to reach Tripoli with his bombers, and of the Nile Delta being out of range of any Italian aircraft in North Africa. For the immediate task of supporting the advance to Msus he ordered forward a flight of Lysanders and Hurricanes from No. 208 Army Co-operation Squadron to Mechili to co-operate with 7th Armoured Division.

General Wavell flew up to Tmimi on February 4th and gave his approval to General O'Connor's plan. At first light that morning the 11th Hussars[2] had left Mechili to lead the advance over ground which had purposely not been visited, lest the intention should be disclosed. Low-flying aircraft had reported to General O'Connor that the 'going' looked possible, though very difficult. It proved, over the first fifty miles, to be the worst of any yet encountered in the desert. Rocks and steep wadis caused much delay, especially to the light tanks. By 3 p.m. the armoured cars had covered the ninety-four miles to Msus, from which a small Italian garrison fled on their approach. Some of the armoured cars then drove on a further 30 miles towards Antelat. The night was moonlit, and by daybreak on the 5th the whole division was just east of Msus.

---

[1] *Africa Settentrionale*, page 223.
[2] 11th Hussars, in the advance to Msus, consisted of Regimental Headquarters and C Squadron, with B Squadron 1st King's Dragoon Guards attached from 2nd Armoured Division. The other squadrons of 11th Hussars were detached to work with 6th Australian Division and the Support Group.

General Creagh had been told that the enemy were in full retreat, attempting to escape. The Air Force would do all they could to harass and delay them, and General O'Connor made it very clear that General Creagh was to press forward with the utmost vigour in order to head the enemy off. Accordingly he decided in the first place to form a small column on wheels only, to push ahead of the slower tracked units and cut the Benghazi—Agedabia road as quickly as possible. Secondly, acting on information from the air, he decided to move his main body south-west from Msus instead of west towards Soluch. To this decision General O'Connor afterwards gave the credit for the completeness of the ultimate success.

Next morning, February 5th, the force on wheels (a squadron each of 11th Hussars and 1st K.D.G., C Battery R.H.A., some anti-tank guns of 106th Regiment R.H.A., and the 2nd Rifle Brigade) reached Antelat and came under command of Lieut.-Colonel J. F. B. Combe, 11th Hussars.[1] By about 12.30 p.m. patrols of 11th Hussars were observing the main road between points west of Beda Fomm and Sidi Saleh. The remainder of the force soon followed and even as it was arriving an Italian column came in sight and was engaged by C Battery R.H.A., the leading anti-tank guns of 106th R.H.A. and B Squadron K.D.G. It was thrown into confusion and many prisoners were taken. In the afternoon the Rifle Brigade, commanded by Lieut.-Colonel J. M. L. Renton, established themselves astride the main road against some opposition. During the rest of the day the Italian columns kept piling up, without making any co-ordinated attacks, which suggests that the enemy had no idea how small was the force which barred the way. But small as it was it repelled all attempts to break through, destroyed many vehicles, and continued to take prisoners.

The 4th Armoured Brigade had succeeded in reaching Antelat by 4.30 p.m. and heard from the air and from Combe's Force the news that the enemy were piling up along the road. Colonel Combe advised that there was good tank going close to Beda Fomm, and the brigade, moving off at once past that place, began to attack the enemy column on the main road at two points three miles apart, to destroy its cohesion. The first attack caught the enemy halted, as a result of the way being barred to the south by Combe's Force. By dusk, when the action was broken off, many more vehicles had been destroyed and about 1,000 more prisoners taken. But it was evident from the continual movement of guns and lorries that the strength of the enemy was building up in this area, and large numbers of vehicles were reported from the air to be moving south of Ghemines, on the main road.

The coastal plain which stretches from Benghazi towards Agedabia

[1] See Map 24.

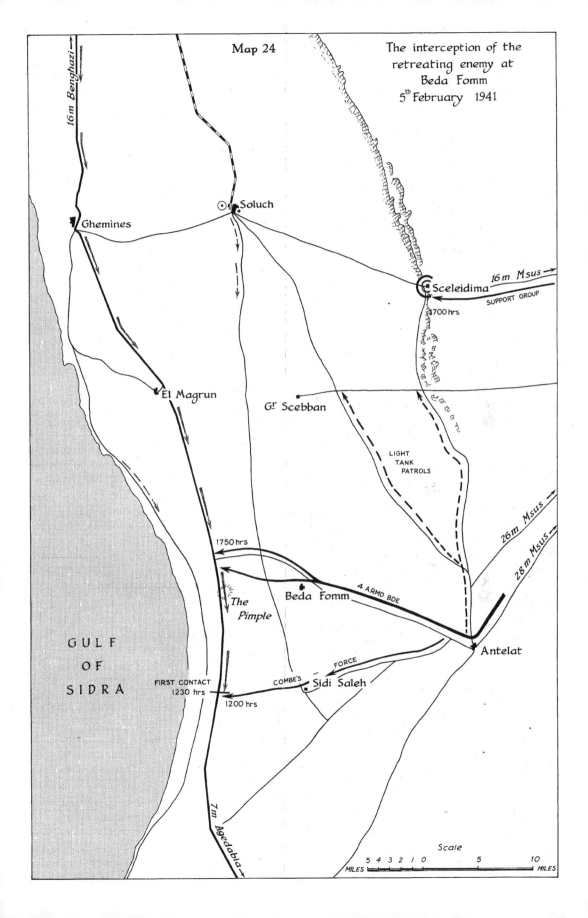

Map 24

The interception of the
retreating enemy at
Beda Fomm
5th February 1941

16m Benghazi

Soluch

Ghemines

Sceleidima          16m Msus →

SUPPORT GROUP

1700 hrs

El Magrun

Gr Scebban

LIGHT
TANK
PATROLS

26m Msus →

28m Msus →

1750 hrs

Beda Fomm          4 ARMD BDE

The
Pimple

Antelat

GULF

OF

SIDRA

FORCE

COMBE'S          Sidi Saleh

FIRST CONTACT
1230 hrs              1200 hrs

7m Agedabia

Scale

5 4 3 2 1 0          5          10

MILES                          MILES

is bounded on the east by an escarpment. North of Sceleidima this is an almost complete obstacle to vehicles but to the south it becomes progressively less steep until, in the neighbourhood of Antelat, it is no obstacle at all. The 7th Armoured Brigade, now reduced to only one regiment of tanks, and the Support Group (less the Rifle Brigade) had been directed westward from Msus with the initial object of capturing Sceleidima. Contact had been made with Sceleidima fort when General Creagh received the information that large columns were already south of Ghemines. He thereupon ordered the 7th Armoured Brigade to move with all speed to Antelat, leaving the tasks in the northern area to be carried out by the Support Group. Early on February 6th the fort at Sceleidima was attacked, and in three hours the garrison was driven out. The Support Group then went on to occupy Soluch and sent out patrols towards Ghemines and Benghazi, preparatory to chasing the enemy southwards along the coast road next morning.

Meanwhile in the Jebel Akhdar area the 6th Australian Division was pressing on as hard as it could. The 17th Brigade, with its own few vehicles, contrived to leap-frog its leading battalion as far as Slonta, where it was passed by 19th Brigade mounted on transport collected from the rest of the division and running entirely on captured petrol. Hampered by mines and road blocks this brigade reached Barce on February 5th, and next day, in spite of heavily mined roads and rain which turned the ground into a morass of red mud, pressed on to Benghazi and reached it before nightfall.

The scene of the decisive actions of February 6th was the country bordering a 14-mile stretch of main road between Beda Fomm and the sea. It was sandy but firm, and generally flat with small hummocks and a number of long low ridges running north and south which provided some cover for the armoured vehicles of both sides without being obstacles to their movement. A low round hillock, the 'Pimple', which was crossed by the main road to the west of Beda Fomm, gave observation up and down the road, and was the scene of much fighting. West of the main road the flat sandy tract stretched for two miles before merging into the coastal sand dunes. Thus it was by no means an ideal battlefield for a delaying action by a small force if the enemy were suitably disposed for dealing with opposition.

Throughout the morning of February 6th the Italians tried to force their way down the main road. The object of 4th Armoured Brigade was to prevent this, and to attack and destroy the enemy wherever encountered. The vital task of Colonel Combe's force was to continue to block the road to the south. The 2nd Royal Tank Regiment started the day in possession of the 'Pimple' area, and in general their role was to stop the head of the enemy's column and attack it from the east. Their fit tanks numbered nineteen cruisers and seven light.

Farther north the 7th Hussars (with one cruiser and twenty-nine light tanks) tried repeatedly to locate the enemy's tail and attack it from both sides of the road. One light tank squadron of the 3rd Hussars was watching the tracks leading north towards Soluch and Sceleidima from Antelat, and only one squadron of six light tanks and one of seven cruisers were available for operating against the enemy from eastward, to the north of 2nd R.T.R. The fact that the Italians had groups of medium tanks distributed along their columns made it difficult for the British light tanks to approach, but they managed to do a good deal of damage and added to the general confusion.

From 7.30 a.m. onwards 2nd R.T.R. was continually in action against repeated attempts by groups of tanks to break out, all of which were stopped. A number of Italian vehicles left the road and made towards the dunes, but they were engaged and destroyed and 350 prisoners were taken. During the morning the weather deteriorated and the visibility was greatly reduced from time to time by squalls and scudding rain. All this time the enemy columns were coming on, repeatedly attacked by the cruisers while the light tanks snapped at the column and bit it when the escorting medium tanks permitted. Some of these encounters were local, others broadened into a general *mêlée*. By noon forty of the enemy's medium tanks had been accounted for, but there still seemed to be fifty or more in action, which was a serious matter because the cruiser strength of 4th Armoured Brigade was now reduced to fifteen.

In the afternoon the Italians showed no signs of giving up the contest and brought fresh troops and tanks into action against the weary British crews. The only reserve of cruiser tanks in the whole of 7th Armoured Division was eleven in 1st Royal Tank Regiment. Unfortunately the overnight move of this unit from near Msus had been much delayed for want of petrol, but it was ordered forward from Antelat after replenishing and reached the battlefield in the early afternoon. By this time the enemy had succeeded in occupying the Pimple and was threatening to broaden the front by breaking out to the east. His great superiority in numbers of tanks made this situation dangerous, but it was restored, first, by the action of 2nd R.T.R. who, supported by F Battery R.H.A. (the results of whose shooting was plainly to be seen next day), reoccupied the Pimple; secondly, by the arrival of 1st R.T.R. who appeared just in time to head off a number of Italian tanks breaking out eastwards from the road a little farther north. But in the meantime a number of enemy vehicles with at least thirty tanks had succeeded in passing through to the south of the Pimple, and warning was sent to Combe's Force to expect attack.

While the day-long battle had been swaying about the Pimple, Combe's Force had resisted a series of attacks. These varied in strength and cohesion but most of them were supported by artillery and tanks. The Rifle Brigade, admirably supported by C Battery R.H.A. and nine Bofors guns of 106th R.H.A., repulsed them all, preventing the breakthrough which the enemy might well have achieved at any moment by sheer weight of numbers. As the day wore on, the country became littered with derelict vehicles, under cover of which some groups of Italians exchanged fire with the Rifle Brigade; many others, more demoralized, surrendered. After dark the enemy made his last bid of the day, when some of the tanks which had escaped from the Pimple appeared and tried to find a way through. Four were destroyed by mines and gunfire; four and a number of lorries broke right through; the remainder lost heart and abandoned the attempt.

At daybreak on February 7th the enemy made a final determined attempt to escape, when thirty tanks heading a column of lorries advanced straight down the road. The tanks broke through the forward companies of the Rifle Brigade, and so tense was the moment that the officer commanding C Battery R.H.A. asked for, and received, permission to engage targets in the areas occupied by the infantry. The anti-tank guns, which now numbered eleven, gradually knocked out the advancing tanks, the last one being stopped a stone's throw from the Officers' Mess. Meanwhile the forward companies had stood firm, and their fire and that of the guns brought the Italian infantry to a standstill. White flags then began to appear. The Rifle Brigade and the supporting artillery had splendidly accomplished their task.

Farther to the north the 4th Armoured Brigade had hemmed in another large mass of enemy and by about 9 a.m. all resistance ceased. The leading Australian troops were now approaching El Magrun (fifteen miles south of Ghemines and the same distance from the Pimple), with the rest of a whole brigade group about two hours behind. This was the result of a message from General O'Connor to General Mackay asking him to press on against the retreating enemy; the speed with which the 19th Brigade Group was ferried forward would have soon settled the issue if the enemy had not collapsed when he did.

The battlefield was an astonishing scene of wreckage and confusion—fifteen miles of lorries, guns, and tanks in abandoned jumble. Everywhere were herds of prisoners, reckoned at 25,000, amongst them the mortally wounded General Tellera, commander of the 10th Army, his entire staff, and General Bergonzoli, commander of the 23rd Corps, who, having long avoided capture, surrendered at last to the Rifle Brigade. More than 100 medium tanks and well over 100 guns were destroyed or captured. The success of the plan to cut off the 10th Army, as it retreated from Cyrenaica, could not have been more complete; hardly a man or a vehicle escaped.

Yet there was a great disparity between the forces, and particularly in the armour, for the Italian medium tanks outnumbered the British cruisers by about four to one, and most of them had run only a few hundred miles whereas the British tanks had covered over 1,000 miles in the last two months' campaigning. It was the speed of the final dash across the desert that came as a surprise to the Italians, although they knew that such a move was possible. Even if their air force failed to keep 7th Armoured Division under observation, the danger of being intercepted on the coast road ought to have been apparent once the British armoured cars had appeared at Msus, which they did on the early afternoon of February 4th. If on February 5th the retreating Italian columns had been on the alert, in expectation of finding the road barred by a weak British force, and if they had been properly disposed so that their guns and tanks could be used on a co-ordinated plan, instead of piecemeal, the result might have been very different.

As for the British plan, it was fully realized that only the boldest and most vigorous action would be likely to succeed and that it would be very difficult to ensure the timely deliveries of petrol, food and ammunition for anything but a short encounter. There were several anxious moments during the battle on this account, and the margin could not have been narrower.

The campaign which began at Nibeiwa and Sidi Barrani and ended ten weeks later at Beda Fomm was the first in which two modern armies, with comparable air forces, had met and fought over undeveloped country. The result exceeded all expectations. A British force of never more than two divisions—one of them armoured —with a proportion of Corps troops, advanced 500 strenuous miles and totally destroyed an army of ten divisions, for a loss of 500 killed, 1,373 wounded, and 55 missing. The captures were 130,000 prisoners; 180 medium tanks and more than 200 light; and 845 guns of the size of field guns and above.

The 5th *Squadra*, whose first line strength early in December was about 380 aircraft, also suffered crippling losses. Apart from the wrecks of the many aircraft destroyed by the continual attacks of the Royal Air Force, 91 aircraft were abandoned intact on the enemy's main airfields. To these losses must be added those aircraft destroyed in combat, shown by the Italian records to have been 58 of all types. In fact, the 5th *Squadra* was so completely mastered by the Royal Air Force that it made no effective contribution to the campaign. The British had always assumed that reinforcements of aircraft would be sent from Italy if the need should arise, though the opening of a new front in Greece obviously affected the number that could be spared.

During December and January some aircraft did in fact arrive in Libya from Italy, but in the confusion of constant withdrawals the ground organizations were quite unable to deal with the aircraft already in the country, so that the reinforcements achieved very little, and in the final stages the retreating army was left practically without air support.

Many reasons contributed to the Italian failure. In the first place the nation was not ready for a war in 1940 and was only pitch-forked into it by the Duce, who judged that there were valuable prizes to be won without any serious fighting and that the shortcomings of the Italian war machine would therefore not be noticed. For the particular war in which he soon found himself involved there were no comprehensive plans and no clear military objectives, and there was no competent central direction capable of reaching sound strategic conclusions in a new situation. The direction was in the hands of Mussolini, with a Chief of Staff, Marshal Badoglio, who was nominally a co-ordinator but in reality a fifth wheel. (It will be seen that General Cavallero, who succeeded Badoglio, later made some radical changes in the central direction.) The instructions to Marshal Graziani were more the expression of political hopes than the outcome of careful consideration by the Service Chiefs. Thus he was forced against his will to sprawl forward to Sidi Barrani—a move which was obviously unsound unless followed by the capture of Matruh. Having placed him in this position the Duce seems to have been unable to decide whether to order the next step or not. Instead, for reasons which were other than military, he opened up a rival front in Greece, a singularly ill-judged enterprise for which the Italians were even less well prepared than they were for the invasion of Egypt.

Marshal Graziani's position, then, was not a happy one, and his frigid relations with Marshal Badoglio made it no better. There was much truth in his complaints about the material deficiencies of his forces, but it is impossible to avoid the conclusion that with better leadership they would have been able to achieve much more than they did. Their own experience of supplying a large force by road over a long distance should have shown the Italians that the surest way of putting a brake on the British advance would be to deny them the port of Sollum. Instead of making every effort to do this they let it go, and locked up most of their resources in the defence of Bardia, whereas, after Sollum, the next place worth denying to the British was Tobruk. When it came to defending Tobruk there were not enough forces left.

Graziani never ceased to protest that he had no means of dealing with the British armour, although this was an exaggeration. It was, of course, true in general that in the desert the army with the superior mobile troops possessed the means of turning the enemy's flank, and whereas the British had an organized armoured formation the Italians had not; they habitually used their tanks in penny packets. But the number of British cruisers was persistently over-estimated, and was in fact far less than the total of captured Italian medium tanks.[1] Moreover, all tanks were vulnerable to artillery fire, as the Italian gunners had shown on more than one occasion, and they were also extremely sensitive to minefields. What was really lacking was a clear appreciation by the higher commanders of the nature of mechanized desert warfare, and the determination to do everything possible with the means available. Perhaps the most generous and not the least accurate view of the attitude of most of the Italian junior leaders and soldiers is that they had no heart for this particular war.

This in no way alters the fact that the British thoroughly deserved their success. They had formed a much more accurate estimate of the type of force required in the desert, and in spite of the threat of invasion of England and of many difficulties and set-backs they persevered in building it up; it was comparatively small, below strength, and short of equipment, but it was nevertheless well suited to the task, imbued with a fine spirit, well trained, and resolutely led. Throughout this campaign its employment was a model of well-judged adjustment of means to suit the end. Deception and surprise —especially by the choice of the unorthodox course—were sure to be essential ingredients of any plan of General Wavell's, but their use was not confined to the opening phase, where, naturally, there was great scope for it; at Bardia and Tobruk, and on other occasions where an attack was obviously to be expected, the enemy was kept guessing as to the time, the place, and the method.

Reviewing the factors that had contributed to this remarkable victory—the first British success on land over either of the Axis powers—and after giving credit to the unfailing response of officers and men to every call made upon them, General Wavell referred to the good workmanship that had enabled heavy—indeed, almost outrageous—demands to be made also upon the endurance of British-made vehicles. These had withstood great strains over a long period in appalling conditions, and yet were capable of the final and protracted effort which proved decisive.

When Tobruk had fallen and the capture of the Jebel area was in sight, General Wavell decided to create a Cyrenaica Command, as distinct from the Egypt Command, the fundamental difference being that Cyrenaica was Italian territory, and its occupation involved

---

[1] Captured Italian M. 13 tanks were taken into use by the British in default of enough of their own cruisers. The M. 13 was, by comparison, slow, unhandy, and uncomfortable, but its 47-mm gun was an efficient and hard-hitting weapon.

setting up an organization to replace the civil administration. On February 4th Lieut.-General Sir H. Maitland Wilson became Military Governor and General Officer Commanding-in-Chief, Cyrenaica, and Lieut.-General O'Connor shortly afterwards took over command in Egypt. The 1st Australian Corps (Lieut.-General Sir Thomas Blamey) was ordered to take over from 13th Corps, and the 7th Armoured Division, which had now been in contact with the enemy for nearly eight months without rest, was to be relieved by the 2nd. In conformity with the Chiefs of Staffs' policy of 'no serious operation beyond Benghazi' the attitude in the forward area was to be generally defensive. Should the enemy try to advance he was to be stopped west of El Agheila, at the southernmost point of the Gulf of Sidra, which British troops had occupied on February 8th. The present indications were that there were no enemy troops, except stragglers, any nearer than Sirte. There were four Italian divisions in Tripolitania, most of whose artillery had been sent to Cyrenaica and lost.

The Air Force set up a corresponding Headquarters in Cyrenaica, with No. 3 Squadron R.A.A.F. (rearming with Hurricanes) and No. 73 Squadron, for the defence of Benghazi and Tobruk respectively; No. 6 Army Co-operation Squadron; and No. 55 Bomber Squadron (Blenheim); and the necessary ancillaries. Headquarters, No. 202 Group, and Nos. 45, 113 and 274 Squadrons were withdrawn to Egypt for refit, in readiness to meet further calls for help to Greece.

It has been related how the first lorries loaded at Tobruk only reached Mechili two days before the departure of 7th Armoured Division on its dash to Beda Fomm. Tobruk was gradually replacing Sollum as the sea-head for supplies, though the discharge of ships was hampered by heavy weather, sandstorms, and Italian air attacks. On the night of February 4th the German Air Force joined in by mining the harbour; the next day a petrol ship struck a mine, caught fire, and set alight an ammunition ship. This was a serious turn of events, as the two minesweepers were under repair. Owing to bad weather the force detailed to clear Benghazi harbour could not sail from Tobruk until February 12th, and no sooner had it arrived than the *Luftwaffe* began to make regular attacks on Benghazi. The Army's slender resources did not allow of a reasonable anti-aircraft defence to be provided here in addition to Tobruk, and this fact coupled with the shortage of small ships made it impossible for Admiral Cunningham to accept the commitment of building up Benghazi as an advanced base; all that he could undertake was to send an occasional small convoy there, perhaps once a fortnight. The first supply convoy of four ships arrived on the 17th but was so heavily attacked that it could not be unloaded and had to return to Tobruk.

The upshot was that the possession of Benghazi did almost nothing to relieve the Army's long overland haul from Tobruk, which to the farthest post, El Agheila, was as much as 450 miles by the coastal road.

The German aircraft did not, however, confine themselves to the persistent bombing and mining of Benghazi. They also attacked lorry convoys, airfields, and the troops in the forward area, though not without loss to themselves. As the intervention of the Germans in this theatre was soon to be attended by a violent reversal of fortunes, it is pertinent to see how it came about.

After the chilly report by General von Thoma on his visit to the Italian 10th Army in October, the Führer had lost interest in North Africa.[1] The disasters of December caused Mussolini to remind him that Italy was very short of many essential weapons and raw materials and was bearing the brunt of the war against Britain; but Hitler still appeared to treat the matter as if it were no concern of his. On December 31st he informed the Duce that he did not believe that a counter-attack on a large scale could be made at present; preparations would take some months, and it would then be the wrong time of year. The best course was to improve all the measures for defence against tanks, and weaken the British sea power by every means other than by offensives on land.

It was not long before Hitler changed his mind, largely as the result of the views of his naval staff, who regarded the latest development in the Mediterranean with grave misgiving. The Italian defeat had removed at a stroke the threat to Egypt and hence to Britain's entire position in the Eastern Mediterranean, which had now been firmly consolidated. The British would be able to send strong forces from Egypt to Greece—in fact the process had already begun. The naval staff considered that the British had gained a great strategic success; their fleet could not now be driven from the Mediterranean, although this was a step which, in the opinion of Admiral Raeder, was vital to the favourable outcome of the war.

On the heels of this report came von Rintelen's views from Rome on the causes of the Italian misfortunes. The army in Libya had not been properly equipped, especially in tanks and anti-tank weapons. The Italian soldier, though patriotic, enduring, and brave in attack, had not the temperament to enable him to resist to the last. As for the generals, he considered their ideas to be so out-of-date that they were unable to do even such things as their limited means made possible. The Italians were now asking for forces and weapons, and von Rintelen suggested that if these were sent it would be advisable for the Germans to be given a share in the conduct of operations.

---

[1] Page 257.

Shortly after the fall of Bardia Hitler decided that it was important for the Axis that an Italian collapse should be prevented, and made up his mind to do everything in his power to avert the loss of North Africa. He realized that the opportunities of sending German aid were limited by the need to use the few available ports for handling Italian supplies and reinforcements. He did not consider it possible for the Italians or the Germans to reopen the offensive against Alexandria with any prospect of success. He could not force German leadership too brusquely upon the Italians; nor did he wish to have to inform them of his operational plans. He had decided, however, to support them with German anti-tank, anti-aircraft, and tank units, which he insisted were on no account to be lost.

On January 11th Hitler issued his instructions—Directive No. 22 —on the assistance to be given by German forces in the Mediterranean area. He laid down that this assistance had become necessary 'for strategic, political and psychological reasons'. Tripolitania must be held, and the German General Staff was therefore to prepare a special blocking detachment (*Sperrverband*) for early despatch to Tripoli. *Fliegerkorps X* was to operate from Sicily with the chief task of attacking British naval forces and the sea communications between the Western and Eastern Mediterranean; it was also to be prepared to support Marshal Graziani's army by attacking British ports and coastal supply bases in Cyrenaica and Egypt.

Meanwhile the Italian General Staff had arranged to send the Ariete Armoured Division and the Trento Motorized Division to Tripoli between January 17th and February 20th. General Guzzoni, the new Deputy Chief of Staff, had given von Rintelen a written statement of the General Staff's views on January 9th. Briefly, they expected Tobruk to fall, and recognized that this would ease the administrative problem for the British, so that, even if the further advance were slow, it would be difficult to bring it to a halt entirely. But the British supply line was becoming very long, and a pause would be forced upon them either at Tobruk or Benghazi. In any case, the reinforcements being sent to Graziani would enable him to attack the British, whether they halted in Cyrenaica or continued their advance into Tripolitania.

Hitler showed no inclination to discuss his intentions with the Duce. The subject of Libya was scarcely mentioned at the meeting between the dictators at Obersalzberg on January 18th, and the Führer even remarked that he could see no sense in committing German troops to months of inaction in Tripoli. The details of the intended assistance were given by Jodl to Guzzoni: the 5th German Light Motorized Division was being specially constituted and was to be despatched about the middle of February. It was particularly strong in anti-tank units, and its role was foreseen not as a reserve but as a force to be committed at the point where the British armoured forces were expected to appear or where the final defence was to be organized. The code name for the move was '*Sonnenblume*' (Sunflower).

On January 29th von Rintelen reported that Guzzoni thought it unlikely that any of the 10th Army would be saved for the defence of Tripolitania and that it would only be possible to hold a fortified camp at Tripoli itself. Von Rintelen was far from satisfied with this defeatist outlook, and was instructed to obtain further information, for if nothing more than a local defence of Tripoli were intended it would be useless to send German troops to Africa at all. It then transpired that Graziani was about to withdraw from Cyrenaica in view of the threat of encirclement from the south. There was no intention of using naval forces to delay the formation of British bases along the coast, but the Italian Air Force in North Africa had been reinforced and had now 90 bombers and 130 fighters. In answer to the question whether the allotted forces would be enough to defend Tripolitania if the British had not already broken through before they could arrive, Guzzoni replied that they would.

On February 5th, the first day of Beda Fomm, Hitler wrote to Mussolini expressing displeasure at the conduct of the campaign, and offering advice on what ought to have been done. He had come to the conclusion that the anti-tank formation that he had had in mind would now be insufficient, because it was essential that the defence should be conducted aggressively; a complete armoured division would therefore be necessary in addition, but he would only send it on condition that the Italians held on, and did not retreat to Tripoli. Malta must be bombed incessantly to reduce the scale of attack on shipping, and the British fleet must be prevented from establishing any new bases to support the advancing forces; combined naval and air operations would therefore have to be carried out against the British sea communications. On February 10th von Rintelen was able to report that the Duce had accepted the German advice and had ordered a forward policy for the defence of Tripolitania. Marshal Graziani was about to resign, and would be replaced by General Gariboldi.[1]

The same day the German General Staff issued their orders for '*Sonnenblume*', and gave instructions for the conduct of German troops in Italian theatres of war. The principal points were that for tactical purposes, but in no other way, the German troops would be subordinated to the Italian Commander-in-Chief. Save in exceptional circumstances they were to be used as a formation under a German commander and not split up over the front. Should the

---

[1] Marshal Graziani left Tripoli on 11th February and his resignation was accepted on 25th March.

German commander receive an order which would, in his opinion, lead to failure and so prejudice the reputation of the German troops, it was his right and duty to appeal to his German superiors. *Flieger-korps X* was to remain responsible to Marshal Göring.

On February 11th Lieut.-General Erwin Rommel, the commander designate of the enlarged German contingent, was received in Rome by Guzzoni, who assured him that the Duce's orders complied in every way with the Führer's views. The first line of defence in Tripolitania was to be at Sirte, and the main defence at Misurata: General Roatta was going to Tripoli next day to ensure that the Duce's orders were carried out. Moreover, it had been decided that the Italian mobile formations—so far only the Ariete Division—would be placed under Rommel's command.

Rommel left for Tripoli on the 12th to judge matters for himself. The first German troops for the lines of communication had already disembarked, and by the 16th a reconnaissance unit and an anti-tank unit had been pushed forward to Sirte. On the same day Rommel submitted to Gariboldi his suggestions for the conduct of the defensive battle at, and to the west of, Sirte. Shortly afterwards Hitler announced that the German forces under General Rommel would be known as the *Deutsches Afrika Korps* (D.A.K.). The Panzer Division to reinforce the 5th Light Division would be the 15th, and it would probably cross to Africa about March 20th. Such were the measures taken by the Germans to stiffen Italian resistance and to keep the British at a distance from Tripoli. Of 220,000 tons of cargo loaded for North Africa at Italian ports in February and March, only 20,000 failed to arrive.

# CHAPTER XX

# THE GREEKS ACCEPT THE BRITISH OFFER

WHEN, ON February 8th, M. Koryzis reaffirmed his country's determination to resist a German attack at all costs, he suggested that the time had come to decide whether the size of the British force that would be sent to Greece if the Germans entered Bulgaria would be sufficient, together with the Greek forces, to check the German attack and encourage Yugoslavia and Turkey to take part in the struggle.[1] This suggestion came just after the unexpectedly early fall of Benghazi, and after the Turkish Government had declined Mr. Churchill's offer of British air and anti-aircraft units.[2] The attitude of Japan was becoming so menacing that it looked as if she might intend to enter the war before very long, and it was still possible that the Germans might attempt an invasion of the British Isles. As regards the flow of supplies from the United States, the Lend-Lease Bill had passed the House of Representatives two days before, and was now to come before the Senate. In this general setting the Defence Committee met on February 10th to review their policy for the Middle East.

A point which required instant decision was whether the Italians should be chased back to Tripoli. It was certain that if Tripoli were not captured at once the Germans and Italians would reinforce it. Its capture would remove the last of the Italian troops from North Africa and make it impossible for the enemy to invade Egypt again without first undertaking a sea-borne operation. Tripoli would provide another base from which bombers could attack Sicily, though it would not enable fighters to provide cover for convoys passing through the Narrows. At Tripoli the British forces would find themselves close to the French, which might be useful at some future date. Thus there would be advantages in possessing the place, and it was quite possible that the Army could go forward on the crest of the wave and take it, for Italian morale and fighting power were at a very low ebb and resistance was likely to be weak. But, even if Tripoli were captured at once, its defence would make heavy demands on the resources with which it was hoped to oppose a German occupation of the Balkans, especially the already stretched fighter

[1] See page 347.
[2] See page 346.

371

aircraft and anti-aircraft artillery. The Navy, too, would find it very difficult to safeguard a supply line to Tripoli in addition to its other commitments, to which might soon be added a greatly increased scale of movement to Greece or Turkey. The Defence Committee were firmly convinced that they must retain the ability to intervene in the Balkans and came to the conclusion that they ought to adhere to their previous policy of halting when a secure flank for Egypt had been gained after the capture of Benghazi. No serious operations, therefore, were to be undertaken beyond this. The garrison of Cyrenaica was to be reduced to the minimum, and the largest possible land and air force concentrated in Egypt in preparation for movement to Europe.

In previous examinations of the Balkan problem the Chiefs of Staff had consistently maintained that our first aim should be to make certain of Turkey, and that support to her should rank before any other commitment in the Balkans. But the question now facing the Defence Committee was how to reply to the Greek Government's request. Obviously there were many political aspects to be considered. Would Turkey regard a German invasion of Bulgaria or an ultimatum to Greece as reasons for entering the war? If the Greeks received no help from us, would they submit to Germany's greatly superior strength—and who could blame them if they did? If this happened, Turkey could be expected to fight only in defence of her own territory; Yugoslavia would be lost; and any hope of forming a Balkan front against the Germans would vanish. The best way of encouraging Turkey to fight would probably be to give effective support to Greece; but without knowing the Greek plan for the defence of the Bulgarian front it was impossible to judge whether our support could be effective or not. If the Greeks had a good plan, the right course would be to back it as strongly as possible. A full and frank exchange of views with the Greek leaders was clearly necessary, and in order that the intricate military and diplomatic measures should be concerted as completely as possible the Prime Minister decided to send the Foreign Secretary, Mr. Eden, and the Chief of the Imperial General Staff, General Sir John Dill, to the Middle East. Before going to Athens to confer with the Greeks they were to have preliminary discussions in Cairo; meanwhile, the Commanders-in-Chief were to initiate such plans and preparations as they could, including the collection of shipping, for the move of the maximum forces to Greece at the earliest possible moment.

The Commanders-in-Chief shared the opinion of the Defence Committee that highest priority should be given to countering German moves in the Balkans. They had gained the impression, however, that in assessing the ability of the forces in the Middle East to meet the many and varied commitments there was a tendency at home to over-estimate their actual resources. They now felt it right to say so.

The Navy was already fully extended in covering the long lines of sea communications on the Libyan coast and in protecting the Libyan ports in addition to the Mediterranean bases. The cruisers and light craft being sent out would not all have arrived until May, but the despatch of strong army and air forces to the Balkans would create a heavy commitment in safeguarding lines of supply through the Aegean and in establishing new bases on Greek islands and perhaps in Turkey. If the Balkan operation began before the present acute shortages in light craft, escorts, local defence vessels, and men for shore bases had been met, the situation might well become critical.

Nor was this all, for the German Air Force was obviously preparing to operate from Bulgarian airfields, and shipping in the North Aegean would be under a grave threat of bombing. Adequate fighter protection for troop and supply convoys against the probable scale of German air attacks would be very difficult to provide with the few aircraft and airfields available, and casualties to troops and ships must be expected. Even more serious would be the danger from magnetic and acoustic mines laid by aircraft in the Aegean ports, and in the approaches to them. With his existing resources Admiral Cunningham would not be able to keep clear yet more areas, and he was doubtful if he could do so even with the additional craft and gear on its way. He regarded it as imperative that he should be sent at once more sweepers for dealing with all types of mines, as well as extra gear to fit into local craft. If he knew that more anti-mine equipment was on its way he could take greater risks in Egypt and Libya in order to release something for Greek ports. As it was, air mining was restricting the use of Sollum and Tobruk, and had caused the Canal to be temporarily closed. It was necessary to face the fact that the risks from mines were great, while the resources to combat them were slender.

Air attacks on Egypt from the west were now unlikely, but it was necessary to provide for the air defence of Benghazi and the lines of communication through Cyrenaica, against which German aircraft were already active. It would be necessary to leave some bombers and at least three fighter squadrons in Cyrenaica. Moreover, until the threat from Rhodes had been removed, it would be necessary to provide for the continued protection of Alexandria, the Delta, and the Canal. The deliveries of medium bomber aircraft to the Middle East had fallen a long way short of expectations, and as regards equipment of all kinds there was a long interval between the date of despatch from home and the time when it was fit to use and in the hands of the users. This was very marked in the case of new types of aircraft. The Air Ministry were doing what they could to improve matters; 19 Blenheim IVs and 23 Glenn Martins had just reached Takoradi, and 79 Blenheim IVs and 6 Glenn Martins were at sea.

The War Office were well aware of the incomplete state of all General Wavell's formations, and, prompted by the Prime Minister, suggested that a complete division—the 50th—should be sent out in the next convoy. In this way they hoped to make a useful contribution to the strength of the strategic reserve, but it would mean the exclusion of nearly 15,000 corps troops, drafts, and administrative units, for which, they suggested, the need was now less, as the capture of Benghazi might be expected to release many units for service elsewhere. General Wavell replied that he would have been very glad of the 50th Division, but not at this cost. In the first place, it had not been possible to abolish the overland L. of C. to Benghazi, as the German air attacks had prevented the use of that port as a sea-head.[1] Secondly, he wished to have his existing fighting formations brought up to strength; they were particularly short of artillery, engineers, and signallers. Thirdly, experience had shown the absolute necessity for a strong administrative backing of base, L. of C. and transportation units, if the efficiency and striking power of the fighting troops was to be maintained. The outcome was that the convoy sailed without the division, and the Prime Minister instructed Mr. Eden to address himself to the problem of ensuring that the many valuable military units in the Middle East were fitting into a coherent scheme and were immediately pulling their weight. This seemed to the Prime Minister very far from being the case.

Mr. Eden was anxious to reach the Middle East at the earliest possible moment, and he and his party left London on February 12th, only to be delayed by bad weather at Plymouth and again at Gibraltar; they did not reach Cairo until late on the 19th, having lost five valuable days. The principal object of the Foreign Secretary's mission was to send speedy succour to Greece against a German attack; secondly, he was to encourage the Turks and Yugoslavs to fight, or at least to do the best they could for the Allied cause, bearing in mind that the interests of Turkey were no less important to us than those of Greece. Mr. Eden's powers were very wide; he was to represent His Majesty's Government in all diplomatic and military matters, and to initiate any action he thought necessary with the Commanders-in-Chief and with the Governments of Egypt, Greece, Yugoslavia and Turkey. The Chief of the Imperial General Staff would act as his military adviser, and in extreme urgency Mr. Eden was to act upon his own initiative without reference home.

---

[1] See page 365.

The Foreign Secretary lost no time in exchanging views with the Commanders-in-Chief and members of the military missions to Turkey and Greece. Hitherto General Dill had held that forces sent to Greece would inevitably be lost and that it would be better to concentrate on helping Turkey, but after thorough discussion in Cairo both he and Mr. Eden agreed that the fullest measure of help ought to be offered to Greece at once, although if this were accepted there would be nothing left for Turkey. The Greeks were already fighting, and fighting well, and seemed determined to oppose the Germans with or without any outside help. General Dill was now satisfied that all evidence indicated that Greece, and not Turkey, was to be Hitler's next victim. The Turks were unlikely to fight at our bidding, although they would defend themselves if attacked and might enter the war if we were successful in helping the Greeks to stem the German advance. Yugoslavia would not fight unless Turkey fought, and the converse might well be true. Hence the only chance of preventing the Balkans being devoured piecemeal was to go to the help of Greece with everything we could. This would certainly be risky, but not so risky as doing nothing. It was obviously necessary to learn what plans the Greeks had made, and the Greek Government immediately welcomed the proposal for a secret meeting on February 22nd.

The question to be settled at once was the composition of the forces to be offered. Mr. Eden's instructions from the War Cabinet required him to consider the slowing down of operations in the various Middle Eastern theatres in order to collect the largest possible force for Greece, bearing in mind that Eritrea ought to be cleared up and that the capture of Rhodes was still of great importance. He consulted General Wavell, who recommended that Cyrenaica should be garrisoned by one of the less well trained and equipped Australian divisions, an Indian motor brigade under training, and one armoured brigade group which was all that could be found from the 7th Armoured Division. The 4th and 5th Indian Divisions were committed in Eritrea, where there was a hold-up at Keren, and could not be drawn upon until their operations were successfully completed. In Kenya some reduction could be accepted, and the South African Division would be moved to Egypt when shipping could be made available. The 6th (British) Division, which was being formed from the 16th Infantry Brigade, the Matruh garrison, and miscellaneous units, was to be used for the operation against Rhodes.

The forces available were therefore as follows: first contingent, ready to sail, one armoured brigade group and the New Zealand Division (whose third infantry brigade had not yet arrived from England), together with two medium artillery regiments and some anti-aircraft artillery; to be followed by the Polish brigade group and an Australian division; with a third contingent consisting of a second armoured brigade, if required, and another Australian division. Disembarkation of the first contingent could be completed about thirty days after the decision to send it; and that of the second and third contingents at intervals of three weeks.[1] The maintenance of a force of this size would strain the administrative resources of the Middle East to the utmost, and would call for a large amount of improvisation. At least fifty ships would be needed for the passage, which meant that many of the ships arriving at Suez in convoys would have to be diverted to the Mediterranean through the Canal, which was liable to be closed by mining. The retention of these ships would of course have its effect upon the United Kingdom's imports and upon the subsequent flow of men and material to the Middle East.

The most unsatisfactory aspect of all was the shortage of aircraft. Coupled with the weakness in anti-aircraft units, it made the possibility of using Salonika as a port for disembarkation and maintenance seem almost out of the question. The Royal Air Force had three fighter and four bomber squadrons in Greece; another bomber squadron was to go there at the end of February, and two more, with an army co-operation squadron, by the end of March. Three night bomber Wellington squadrons based in Egypt, but operating from Greek airfields during moonlight periods, would be available for long distance raids by night. There was no immediate prospect of withdrawing any squadrons from the operations in Eritrea and Italian Somaliland. The arrival of the *Luftwaffe* in the Mediterranean had created new problems for the Air Force at Malta, in the Central Mediterranean, and in western Cyrenaica, and wastage had inevitably increased in fighting the Germans, who were more highly skilled and better equipped than the Italians. Moreover, squadrons were tired after their long chase across Cyrenaica, and needed to rest and rearm with modern aircraft. Air Chief Marshal Longmore was hoping to raise two fighter squadrons during March, but this depended upon the arrival of equipment and ammunition for the American Tomahawks. The flow of modern aircraft to the Middle East was still below expectations, and the net result was that the number which could be sent to Greece—and nothing but the best would be good enough against the Germans— was smaller than had been estimated in London before the Mission left. The conclusion was that if effective support were to be given to Greece there would be nothing left for Turkey.

This conclusion made it difficult to decide what the British attitude to the Turks should be. The arguments for and against inducing

---

[1] The total strength of British army forces in Greece would then be about 100,000 men, 32 medium guns, 240 field guns, 200 anti-tank guns, 192 heavy and light A.A. guns, and 142 tanks.

29. The South Africans' pontoon bridge over the river Juba at Yonte, 19th February 1941.

*Facing p. 376*

30. Unloading stores at Kismayu, 19th February 1941.

32. An aircraft dropping a message for the troops just before
the entry into Addis Ababa.

31. Bridge built over the river Awash to replace the bridge
destroyed by the Italians.

33. The Emperor Haile Selassie arrives by air at the frontier
of Ethiopia. The officer holding the paper is Colonel Wingate.

34. Mount Belaya, the Emperor's first headquarters on returning to his country.

35. The camel train taking stores and ammunition to Gojjam, February 1941.

36. 'A way up the Ethiopian escarpment has been found.'

Turkey to enter the war were fairly evenly balanced, but the feeling was that on the whole it would be best if she would agree to do so. The advantages were that the Germans would be further extended; the Yugoslavs might be encouraged to declare war also; and we should acquire bases from which to bomb the Rumanian oilfields. On the other hand, we should not be able to comply with the inevitable requests for assistance, and the Turks might be defeated by the Germans while the only available British forces were in Greece. The one certain conclusion was that it would be wrong to divide our effort between the two, and it seemed that the proper course was to tell the Turks frankly that we were determined to support the Greeks and that this would be the best way of helping all our friends, including the Turks.

Before Mr. Eden left for Athens he was told that the Prime Minister approved of his proposal to make contact with the Greek leaders before going to Ankara. Mr. Churchill added: 'Do not consider yourselves obligated to a Greek enterprise if in your hearts you feel it will only be another Norwegian fiasco. If no good plan can be made, please say so. But of course you know how valuable success would be.'

Mr. Eden, Sir John Dill, General Wavell, Air Chief Marshal Longmore, and Captain R. M. Dick, R.N. (representing Admiral Cunningham), with their staffs, arrived secretly by air in Greece on February 22nd, and were made the guests of the King of the Hellenes at Tatoi Palace. Meetings were held lasting all day, and before they began the President of the Greek Council handed to Mr. Eden a written declaration of Greece's determination to go on fighting the Italians and if necessary to defend herself against the Germans, even if she had to do so alone.[1]

Mr. Eden began by explaining the views of the British War Cabinet. These were that the Germans intended to subdue Greece and immobilize Turkey, hoping thus to strike a decisive blow at the British position in the Middle East. They would occupy Bulgaria, and then either attack Greece or try to intimidate her into coming to terms with Italy. These terms would include a German occupation of Greece on the Rumanian model. At this M. Koryzis intervened to say categorically that Greece would resist any attempt at invasion.

Mr. Eden went on to say that the War Cabinet had decided, with the full agreement of the Chiefs of Staff and of the Commanders-in-Chief at Cairo, that the maximum of help should be offered to the Greeks as soon as possible. He then gave a summary of the land and air forces that could be sent, and when. It was of course essential to

---

[1] This statement is given in full at Appendix 6.

be able to guarantee a reasonable degree of safety for the convoys against attack from both surface craft and submarines, and at the same time continue to protect the west coast of Greece. This would impose a heavy additional strain on the Royal Navy, but Admiral Cunningham was confident that he could meet it. What we were now offering represented the most we could do; the troops were well trained, well equipped, and would acquit themselves well. The force would be commanded by General Wilson, with all the experience of the Desert campaign behind him—an announcement which was received with evident pleasure by General Papagos.

M. Koryzis, in reply, emphasized once more that Greece was determined to defend herself against attack from any quarter, and any aid from Great Britain would be warmly welcomed. At the same time they had to remember the danger of precipitating a German invasion. He thought that the military representatives should examine together the adequacy of the combined Anglo-Greek forces to resist German attack, bearing in mind the uncertain attitude of Yugoslavia and Turkey. Mr. Eden agreed with the President's suggestion, but pointed out that if avoidance of provoking Germany was carried too far it would mean that no effective help would reach Greece in time. Their decisions ought to be made without waiting to find out what Turkey and Yugoslavia would do.

The first military consideration was that owing to the steady reinforcement of the Italian forces in Albania it had been necessary to withdraw Greek troops from eastern Macedonia, where there now remained only three weak divisions, with another thirteen battalions and a few batteries of artillery in western Thrace. The defence of the Bulgarian frontier presented a difficulty, for, although an enemy would have very few lines of approach through the mountains, the strip of country between the frontier and the Aegean Sea would be very difficult to defend because of the lack of depth and the fact that the main communications ran parallel to the front. Work had, nevertheless, been begun upon a position running from the Yugoslav frontier on the Beles mountains to the mouth of the river Nestos, and upon another which followed roughly the line of the river Struma. The purpose of these lines was to cover Salonika, which was the only port through which munitions and supplies could be sent to Yugoslavia. As long, therefore, as there was any chance that the Yugoslavs would fight by the side of the Greeks, there was a strong desire not to give up Salonika. But it would be useless for the Greeks to attempt to stand on either the Nestos or the Struma, for their forces in northern Greece were quite insufficient to hold such long fronts.

A much shorter position, and one of some natural strength, could be found forty miles to the west of the line of the river Vardar (or Axios). It would run along the northern slopes of the Olympus—

Pieria mountains and follow the line of the Vermion range northwards to the Yugoslav border—over seventy miles in a straight line.
Through this front there were only four major gaps; one on each
side of Mount Olympus; one which formed the valley of the river
Aliakmon; and one, much wider, at Edessa, through which passed
the road and railway from Florina to Salonika. Except for these gaps
the lower forward slopes were generally steep and rugged, and formed
an obstacle to vehicles.

If the attitude of Yugoslavia remained doubtful, as it now was,
General Papagos considered that the proper military course would
be to withdraw everything except light covering detachments from
Thrace and eastern Macedonia to the Aliakmon position. This
would take about twenty days to do. Simultaneously, by drawing
back to a shorter line on the Albanian front he would be able to
spare some forces from there also. In all, he could find thirty-five
Greek battalions for the Aliakmon position, with one or two divisions in reserve. If they were joined by the British contingent, the
position should be quite formidable. It would have been better still
if it covered the important approach from Monastir, but there would
only be a danger of this route being used by the Germans if they had
traversed a large part of Yugoslavia, in which case the Yugoslavs
would presumably be fighting in defence of their own country.

With these views Generals Dill and Wavell agreed, and made the
point that the difficulty of defending Salonika against air attack from
Bulgarian airfields meant that the British expedition would have to
land at Piraeus and Volos. Also, that as the British had no pack
animals it would be necessary to start at once on the improvement of
communications to enable their mechanized forces, especially the
medium artillery, to be used to the best advantage. But, if the plan
for the occupation of the Aliakmon position required mobile forces
to delay the enemy by operating out in front, this was a role for
which some of the British units would be very suitable.

At the final plenary session, late on 22nd February, the military
representatives announced their complete agreement that in view of
the uncertain attitude of the Turks and Yugoslavs it was not possible
to contemplate holding a position covering Salonika; the only sound
military course was to occupy the Aliakmon position. Mr. Eden then
referred to the political problems, namely, whether to approach the
Yugoslav Government in the hope of ascertaining their intentions,
and whether their reply should affect the withdrawal of the advanced
Greek troops. On the first point it was decided that Mr. Eden should
make an approach to the Regent of Yugoslavia, drawing his attention to the danger to Salonika presented by current German activities
in the Balkans and asking for Prince Paul's views on the subject. On
the second point the decision recorded was 'that preparations should

at once be made and put into execution to withdraw the Greek advanced troops in Thrace and Macedonia to the line which we should be obliged to hold if the Yugoslavs did not come in'. There is no doubt whatever that General Dill and General Wavell were left with the firm impression that the withdrawal was to take place as soon as the necessary preparations could be made. General Papagos, however, was later to argue that it was to have been contingent upon the result of the approach to Yugoslavia.

On the matter of the forthcoming British approach to the Turks it was agreed that Mr. Eden should inform them of the decision to give as much help as possible to the Greeks, and should try to persuade them to reaffirm their intention of coming into the war if Greece were invaded or even if German formations entered Bulgaria. The Greek Government had no great hopes, however, of any offensive action by the Turks in any event, because of their repeated protestations of unreadiness.

Finally the Foreign Secretary asked to be assured that the Greek Government accepted the offer of British help of their own free will, and that the arrival of British troops in the numbers and on the conditions proposed would be sincerely welcomed by the Greek Government. The British did not wish to give the impression that they were forcing their offer on the Greeks; but wanted to be sure that they were anxious to accept it of their own free will. The President of the Council, without hesitation and showing some emotion, stated formally that the Greek Government accepted with deep gratitude the offer of His Majesty's Government and entirely approved the military plan on which the military representatives had agreed. Greece would do her duty by herself and by her ally, Great Britain.

The Mission returned to Cairo next day, 23rd February, greatly impressed by the frank, friendly, and courageous attitude of the Greek leaders. Mr. Eden reported to the Prime Minister that he was sure of their determination to resist with all their strength, and that His Majesty's Government had no alternative but to back them whatever the consequences. He added that 'we are all convinced that we have chosen the right course'. The risks, he thought, were indeed great, but there was a fair chance of stopping the Germans before the whole of Greece was overrun. It meant accepting difficulties which would make heavy demands upon the Middle East's resources of aircraft; it was particularly important to hasten the flow of fighters.

That evening the Chiefs of Staff considered very seriously whether to endorse the Foreign Secretary's proposal. They came to the conclusion that it had undoubted military attractions, although the risks of failure were serious. But the disadvantages of leaving Greece to her fate—deserting, in fact, a small ally already engaged in a fight against one aggressor and willing to defy another—would be certain and far-reaching. Even the complete failure of an honourable attempt to help Greece need not be disastrous to our future ability to defeat Germany, and it was better to make the Germans fight for what they wanted than let them have it by default. On balance, they recommended that the enterprise should go forward, and that everything possible should be done to ensure the participation of Turkey and Yugoslavia; for without the support of one or the other our help to Greece was unlikely in the long run to have a favourable effect on the war as a whole.

Next day the War Cabinet decided to approve the despatch of a military force to Greece on the basis of the Foreign Secretary's proposals. The Governments of Australia and New Zealand and the Polish Government in London would of course have to be consulted.[1] In communicating this decision to Mr. Eden the Prime Minister wrote: 'Therefore while being under no illusions we all send you the order "Full steam ahead".'

Having thus attained the first object of his mission, and having made the agreed approach to the Regent of Yugoslavia, the Foreign Secretary had now to sound the Turks. Accompanied by his advisers, he continued his strenuous round and reached Ankara by air on 26th February for an official visit. A series of meetings, interspersed with many ceremonies, was held with the heads of the Turkish Government and Services, and finally one with President Inönü himself. Mr. Eden told the Turkish leaders in confidence of his recent secret visit to Greece, of the determination of the Greeks to resist the Germans, of the intention of the British to help to the limit of their ability, and of the decision to bar the enemy's advance west of Salonika.

This news was on the whole well received, and the Turks agreed with the view that it would be wrong to divide the British forces between Greece and Turkey. But it might be Turkey's turn to be attacked after Greece or even before. If attacked, she would defend herself, but having no offensive power her best contribution to the common cause would be to remain out of the war if she could. When her deficiencies, especially in aircraft and armoured and motor vehicles, were remedied, she could enter the war as an effective combatant and not as a military liability. She intended to remain loyal to her alliance with Great Britain, and sooner or later she would be certain to enter the war; but she did not wish to precipitate a German attack upon herself and she could not say in advance what

---

[1] See page 387, footnote.

her action would be if Germany attacked Greece. The Turkish Government had recently made an appeal to the Yugoslav Government, and was disappointed by the evasive nature of the reply, but was still willing to concert common action with Yugoslavia in view of the danger to that country from the German threat to Greece.

The problem of making good the Turkish deficiencies of equipment and war material, to which the Turks attached very great importance, led to a long and detailed discussion at which General Dill promised that everything possible would be done to meet the Turkish requirements, though he qualified his promise by referring to the many other demands that the British had to meet, including the needs of their own troops.

All this time Mr. Eden had been anxiously awaiting a reply to his message to the Regent of Yugoslavia which he had sent from Athens on 23rd February. Late on the evening of 27th February, after the meetings with the Turkish leaders were over, the Yugoslav Ambassador at Ankara delivered a communication from his Government. It was to the effect that, although Yugoslavia would defend herself against any aggression and would not permit the passage of foreign troops across her territory, it was impossible for her to say what her reaction would be to a German move across Bulgaria. The Ambassador begged that His Majesty's Government would not insist on a more definite attitude for the present. It is easy to imagine what a disappointment it was to Mr. Eden to receive such a negative reply; he decided in the circumstances to summon the British Minister at Belgrade to Athens for consultation.

Next day his party left Ankara for Ismid on the Sea of Marmara, there to waste twenty-four hours while grounded by bad weather. They eventually reached Athens during the afternoon of 2nd March, by which time German troops had crossed the Danube and Bulgaria had aligned herself openly with the Axis.

On arriving at the British Legation in Athens Mr. Eden's party was astonished to learn that no order had as yet been given by General Papagos for the withdrawal of the Greek troops from Thrace and Eastern Macedonia, nor from the Albanian front, although it was on the assumption that these withdrawals would be carried out that the British had set in train the move of their own forces to Greece. The news that nothing had been done was disturbing indeed, and profoundly affected the whole problem. Attempts to resolve this new difficulty lasted until late on March 4th; three intensely anxious days of plain speaking and searching argument in a very different atmosphere from that of the meetings of the previous week.

The negative attitude of Turkey and Yugoslavia came as a great disappointment to the Greek leaders, but M. Koryzis reiterated that they were determined as ever to oppose the Germans and continue the struggle against the Italians. He expressed doubt, however, whether the resistance that could be offered to a German attack would be effective, and Mr. Eden pointed out that they had already come to an agreed conclusion on this question; the uncertain attitude of Turkey and Yugoslavia had led to the decision to occupy the Aliakmon position, and the knowledge that the intervention of these countries was now more uncertain than ever did not constitute a new factor in the problem. The point for decision was whether there was still time to occupy the Aliakmon position in sufficient strength.

Discussion of this military problem disclosed a very unsatisfactory state of affairs. It appeared that General Papagos had not already given the order for the withdrawal from Thrace and eastern Macedonia because he was waiting to know whether Yugoslavia would enter the war. He was unwilling to give it now because there was a danger that the withdrawing troops would be caught on the move by the Germans, and because of the consternation that would be caused among the Greek population of Macedonia. He now proposed that, after all, the Greeks should attempt to defend the Nestos-Rupel line—the more easterly of the two positions covering Salonika—but admitted that there were not enough troops available to do so with any hope of success. His information of the German preparations pointed to the likelihood of operations against Greece beginning in about ten days.

General Dill, who had summoned Generals Wavell and Wilson for consultation, thought that the Germans could not begin operations anything like so soon. He nevertheless believed that it was out of the question to try to land the British force at Salonika, a port which was very liable to be mined and which would be much more difficult to defend from air attack than Piraeus or Volos. There was in any case no point in trying to hold with three weak Greek divisions the Nestos line which was estimated to require nine. The British force could not be expected to arrive before the Greeks had been overrun, and even if they did the united forces would still be less than the required nine divisions. This proposal therefore merely invited defeat in detail. If, however, withdrawal were to begin at once, some Greek troops might be lost but others would get back; given luck, none would be lost. This was surely the lesser of the two evils. The proper course, in his view, was to adhere to the existing plan for the disembarkation of the British force, and to occupy the Aliakmon position with the full intention of operating forward of it with armoured troops. The question was: could the Greeks now make enough forces available from anywhere, including Albania, to ensure, together with us, the security of that position?

General Papagos replied emphatically that they could not. The Greek troops on the Albanian front had been fighting for four months without any rest; they had suffered heavily, and were now at the limit of their endurance against an enemy who was steadily growing stronger. They could therefore make no contribution to the Aliakmon position, and, as it was too late to withdraw from the Bulgarian front, the only feasible plan was for the British to come forward to Salonika.

It is not difficult to understand General Papagos's distress. The national spirit of the Greeks had been roused in October by the wanton Italian attack and their morale had been sustained by successes won against heavy odds. And now a new and even stronger enemy was coming to attack them from another direction. To meet this threat by withdrawing before the Italians would have had a disastrous effect on the morale of the Greeks. They could hardly be blamed if they saw little chance of success against both enemies at once and if, rather than be beaten on both fronts, they preferred to be stabbed in the back by the Germans while still facing the Italians.

The Chief of the Imperial General Staff, too, was in an unenviable predicament. The Foreign Secretary had been given the task of sending speedy succour to Greece, and his instructions enjoined him to act, if need be, without referring home. Consequently, General Dill, as his military adviser, bore a great responsibility; in the present crisis of the negotiations, when time was obviously all too short, the decision lay, to all intents and purposes, with him. Nothing could be more distasteful than to desert an ally—and a very deserving one—and General Dill paid generous tribute to the magnificent fight made by the Greeks against the Italians. He said, however, that he was quite unable to recommend that the only British reserves in the Middle East should be committed to a plan which he believed to be unsound—a plan which amounted to the gradual dribbling forward of forces into battle.

Next morning, March 4th, General Papagos continued to advocate the use of all available forces on the Nestos line, but in the light of the British refusal to attempt to concentrate their forces as far forward as eastern Macedonia he explained that certain reinforcements already on their way to the Nestos Line could be diverted to the Aliakmon. General Dill was unable to agree that the seven or eight battalions thus offered were sufficient.

At the next meeting His Majesty the King of the Hellenes was present. General Dill restated his view that the object should be to establish ourselves in adequate strength on the Aliakmon position, and General Papagos then announced that he could make available two infantry divisions, one motorized division, and perhaps seven other battalions, although he regarded this as an undesirable dispersion of forces. It was not the best plan, but if it commended itself to the British he would accept it and do his utmost to see it through.

The British were thus faced with the choice of withdrawing their offer altogether or of occupying a position on which practically no work had been done, with the help of perhaps about twenty Greek battalions instead of the expected thirty-five. Shortly before midnight they decided, with some misgivings, to adhere to their plan. It meant that the British force would be engaged upon a task which was more hazardous than it had seemed a week before. But, while recognizing the dangers and difficulties, General Dill considered the prospects of checking and holding the German advance by no means hopeless; the position was naturally strong, with few approaches, and at the worst it should be possible to make a fighting withdrawal from it through country eminently suitable for rearguard action. The Greek forces allotted to the Aliakmon position were to be concentrated there with all speed under a Greek commander responsible to General Wilson, who would command all the forces on the position and be responsible in turn to General Papagos. Details of preparations to hasten the occupation of the position were examined and approved. To avoid further misunderstanding the agreed French version of the decisions was signed by General Papagos and General Dill.[1]

All preparations for the despatch of the British force from Egypt had gone ahead on the original plan. On March 4th, as the first ships were about to sail, Admiral Cunningham informed the Admiralty that, while he was convinced that the right policy was being followed, he wished to make it clear that a big risk was being taken, principally on account of the weakness of the convoys and of the ports of disembarkation against air attack. A convoy would have to be run to Malta when the *Formidable* arrived, but otherwise the moves to Greece would absorb the whole energies of the Fleet for the next two months—and even longer if the Germans continued to close the Canal by mining. Meanwhile, the Cyrenaican supply line would go practically unprotected and the operations against the Dodecanese would have to be postponed.

Even if there were no delays to the shipping programme the margin of time was dangerously narrow. The armoured brigade and one New Zealand brigade could not be in position until the third week of March, and the whole New Zealand Division and one Australian brigade not before the end. The timing of the German moves through Bulgaria would depend largely on the weather, which

---

[1] The text in English is given in Appendix 7.

might be bad until the second week of April, and upon the delay caused by air action, demolitions, and the resistance of the advanced Greek troops; it was estimated that if all went smoothly for the Germans two divisions might possibly reach the Aliakmon by mid-March, and five before the end, one of which might be armoured and three motorized.

In the light of these figures and of Admiral Cunningham's remarks the Chiefs of Staff made a searching analysis of the situation, laying great stress on the twelve wasted days during which not even the preparatory steps had been taken to carry out the original plan. They came to the obvious conclusion that the hazards of the enterprise had greatly increased. The delay to the operations against the Dodecanese was a most unfortunate turn, for it meant that some of our air effort would have to be used to reduce the scale of attack from these islands against our sea lines of communication to Greece. But in spite of their misgivings they did not feel as yet in a position to question the military advice of the men on the spot, who had described the enterprise as not by any means hopeless.

On receiving this lukewarm approval the Prime Minister immediately prepared Mr. Eden for an adverse decision by the War Cabinet, for it was difficult, he wrote, to see how we had now any power to avert the fate of Greece unless Turkey or Yugoslavia or both came in, which seemed most improbable. We had done our best to promote a Balkan combination against Germany, and Greece must not be urged against her better judgement into making a hopeless resistance alone. Grave Imperial issues were raised in committing New Zealand and Australian troops to an enterprise which had become even more hazardous; the assent of their Governments to this new proposition could not be forecast.

Mr. Eden's reply to this message was to reaffirm the decision, to which he, General Dill, and the three Commanders-in-Chief adhered. This steadfast attitude greatly impressed the Prime Minister, who emphasized once more that the British must not take on their shoulders the responsibility of urging the Greeks against their better judgement to fight a hopeless battle; if, however, with the full knowledge of the help that we could send they resolved to fight to the death, then obviously we must share their ordeal. A large proportion of the troops would be from the Dominions, and the War Cabinet would have to be able to tell their Governments that this hazard was being undertaken, not because of any commitment entered into by a British Cabinet Minister at Athens, but because the Chief of the Imperial General Staff and the Commanders-in-Chief were convinced that there was a reasonable fighting chance.

It says much for the sense of urgency which possessed the War Cabinet that a decision was reached without waiting for any further information from Mr. Eden. On March 7th they authorized the operation to proceed, and in so doing accepted full responsibility. They undertook to communicate with the Governments of Australia and New Zealand.[1]

News of this decision crossed Mr. Eden's final appreciation. He and his advisers had been fortified in their views by a meeting with General Smuts, who had just arrived in Cairo. There had never been any question, he wrote, of coercing the Greeks to resist the Germans; on the contrary, the Greeks had consistently declared that this was their intention, with or without help from outside. Squadrons of the Royal Air Force and anti-aircraft units had been in action in Greece for nearly four months, and to desert the country now, when it was well known that British forces had become available after the Libyan victories, would be a calamity. Yugoslavia would certainly be lost and Turkey's resolution might waver. Our prestige would no doubt suffer if we were ejected ignominiously, but this would be less damaging than leaving Greece to her fate. They were all agreed that the decision was the right one although they were under no illusions about its gravity.

The references in the appreciation to more strictly Service matters made it very clear that the risks had not been overlooked; indeed, the views of the Commanders-in-Chief as expressed on this occasion show that while in no doubt as to the proper strategic course they were very anxious about their ability to carry it out. General Wavell thought that, if his forces could be concentrated upon the Aliakmon position in time, there might be a good chance of holding the enemy's advance. Admiral Cunningham, however, felt that the naval situation had deteriorated; the mining of the Canal was serious, and if the Germans were to mine the Greek ports he could not guarantee to clear them. Air Chief Marshal Longmore was particularly anxious about our relative weakness in the air and was by no means confident of giving adequate air support to the operations. German air forces working on interior lines were increasing the weight of their attacks from Sicily, Tripoli, the Balkans and the Dodecanese. No corresponding increase in Royal Air Force reinforcements was being made, and the promised allotment of Tomahawks had just been reduced. Unless his reinforcements could be speeded up he faced his commitments on the Albanian and Macedonian fronts, added to those in Africa and Malta, with the gravest misgivings. As for the enemy, it was to be expected that they would be hampered by the weather and by long and bad communications through countries whose friendship was doubtful, but this was almost the only

---

[1] The communications from the United Kingdom Government to the Governments of Australia and New Zealand, and their replies expressing agreement, are referred to in the forthcoming volume in this series by J. R. M. Butler on *Grand Strategy*.

encouraging aspect of the military situation which Mr. Eden and his advisers could suggest. However, they declared themselves convinced that there was a 'reasonable fighting chance' and, given good fortune, an opportunity 'of perhaps seriously upsetting the German plans'.

It has been seen how Great Britain's active assistance to Greece grew from a very small beginning—the sending of one squadron of the Royal Air Force in the first flush of admiration for the defiant contempt with which the Greeks had received the Italian ultimatum. The Greek President, General Metaxas, invoked the British guarantee of April 1939, and Mr. Churchill responded by promising all the help in our power. The British contribution was gradually increased, but was confined to squadrons and their necessary adjuncts, limited as much by what could be usefully accepted as by what could be spared. Early in January 1941 came information of the move of German army and air forces into Rumania, and the British offered to help by providing some of the specialist troops that the Greek Army lacked. This offer was declined, but the Greek Government declared that if German military formations entered Bulgaria the despatch of a British force to Greece would be welcomed. On February 8th, the day following the total defeat of the Italians in Cyrenaica, the new Greek President, M. Koryzis, asked for the particulars of the British force to be settled.

The outcome of this request was the tour of the Eden Mission, which led to complete military agreement upon a plan that was independent of the help of Turkey or Yugoslavia. It seems almost incredible that an opening should have been left for genuine doubt as to what exactly was decided, but the fact remains that the preliminary action upon which the British were counting was not taken. On returning to Athens after their exploratory visit to Ankara the British representatives found themselves faced with a military situation of which the best that could be said was that it was not hopeless. There was not a moment to lose, for German troops were on the move into Bulgaria and the expedition from Egypt was on the point of sailing. One way or another the decision had to be taken— to go ahead or to back out. There was no question of being pressed from London; on the contrary, the Prime Minister had shown that he would back up his emissaries if they chose to abandon the venture now.

To the Chief of the Imperial General Staff and the three Commanders-in-Chief the military dangers were all too clear; we might be bundled out of Greece as we had been out of Norway, and we might lose heavily in the process, especially in equipment. But the cause for which we stood might suffer an even greater blow if at this critical moment we shrank from our obligations to our Ally, whatever the circumstances that caused us to change our plans. Which course would put heart into the freedom-loving nations: to attempt and fail, or not to attempt at all? Which course would show the United States, 'the arsenal of democracy', that we deserved their all-out help? As for the Turks, they had agreed that it was right for us to give all the help we could to Greece; their reaction to a *volte-face* might well be unfavourable. By doing nothing we should certainly lose any chance of winning over the Yugoslavs, and the Germans would be free to take whatever they wanted in Greece and spill over into the Aegean Islands. Our strategic reserve would still be intact, but in these circumstances would be unable to move quickly to the help of Turkey.

Mr. Eden and his advisers must have felt, like General Wolfe, that war is indeed an option of difficulties. In this particular dilemma they decided to take what seemed to them to be the big view, and accept the short-term consequences. The war, in fact, was more important than the battle. They agreed unanimously that the proper course was to go forward with the enterprise and 'engage the enemy more closely'.

The resulting campaigns in Greece and Crete were by no means the only ones in which the Middle East Command was involved in the spring of 1941. Before the German invasion of Greece had even begun, the British had lost a large part of Cyrenaica. Malta had been suffering heavy attacks from the air—possibly as the prelude to an attempt at capture. Iraq showed signs of unrest. In Italian East Africa there had been many rapid successes, but there had also been a long, anxious, and bloody contest at Keren.

It is difficult to turn at this moment from events in the Balkans to follow the progress of the campaign in East Africa without sharing to some extent the feeling of the Commanders-in-Chief that this war was not 'one damned thing after another': it was everything in all directions at once.

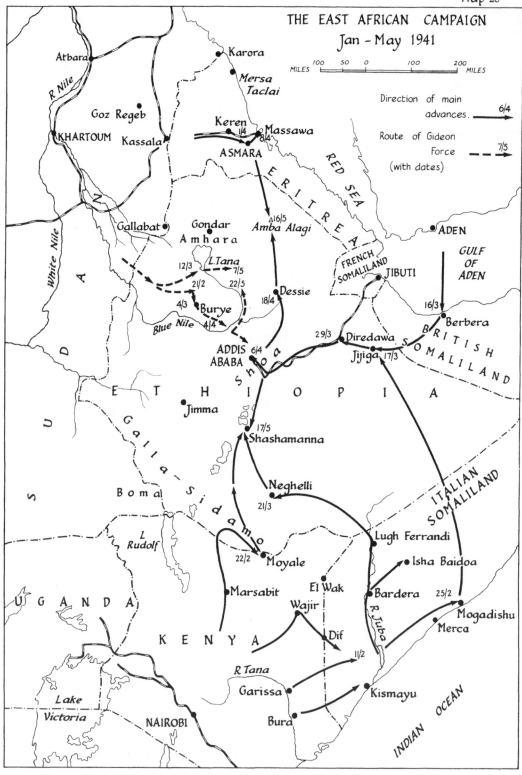

Map 25

THE EAST AFRICAN CAMPAIGN
Jan – May 1941

MILES 100 50 0 100 200 MILES

Direction of main
advances.                                    6/4

Route of Gideon
Force                                        7/5
(with dates)

Atbara
R Nile
Karora
Mersa
Taclai
Goz Regeb
KHARTOUM   Kassala
Keren   1/4   Massawa
ASMARA   8/4
RED SEA
Gallabat   Gondar   △16/5
Amhara   Amba Alagi   ADEN
12/3   L.Tana   7/5   GULF
White Nile   21/2   22/5   FRENCH   OF
4/3   SOMALILAND   JIBUTI   ADEN
Burye   18/4   Dessie   16/3
Blue Nile   4/4   29/3   Diredawa   Berbera
ADDIS   6/4   Jijiga   17/3   BRITISH
ABABA   Shoa   SOMALILAND
ETHIOPIA
Jimma
17/5
Shashamanna
Boma   Neghelli
21/3   ITALIAN
SOMALILAND
L   Lugh Ferrandi
Rudolf   22/2   Moyale   Isha Baidoa
UGANDA   Marsabit   El Wak   Bardera   25/2
Wajir   R Juba   Mogadishu
KENYA   Dif   Merca
R Tana   11/2
Lake   Garissa   Kismayu
Victoria   NAIROBI   Bura   INDIAN OCEAN

SUDAN
ERITREA
Galla-Sidamo

# CHAPTER XXI

# THE ITALIANS LOSE THE
# INITIATIVE IN EAST AFRICA

*See Maps 10 and 25*

THE GENERAL situation on the borders of Italian East Africa at the end of August 1940 was as follows. In the Sudan the British had lost the town of Kassala and the frontier posts of Gallabat and Kurmuk, but reinforcements were arriving in the country. In Ethiopia the Patriot movement was gaining strength, and Colonel Sandford had entered Gojjam to meet certain leaders and collect first-hand information, while in Khartoum the Emperor was eagerly waiting to enter his country. British Somaliland had just been lost, as had the post of Moyale on the Kenya border. In Kenya the organization and training of the British forces were going steadily forward, with much help from the Union of South Africa.

The three following chapters describe the ensuing campaign against Italian East Africa until the surrender at Amba Alagi in May 1941. The main events are General Platt's pursuit from Kassala in January; the long fight for Keren on the edge of the Asmara plateau, and its capture in March; the advance down to Massawa, on the Red Sea, and the destruction of the remaining Italian warships; and the encirclement of the Duke of Aosta's forces at Amba Alagi. All this time squadrons of the Royal Air Force from Aden and the Sudan were escorting the Red Sea convoys, attacking the Italian Air Force, supporting the Army's operations, and penetrating deep into Ethiopia. In Kenya, General Cunningham, supported by the South African Air Force, began his advance a little later; in February he captured Kismayu and Mogadishu, and then conducted a rapid pursuit of over 1,000 miles right up to Addis Ababa itself. Meanwhile in Ethiopia, after Colonel Sandford's successful exploration, Colonel Wingate and the Ethiopian Patriots, with support from the air, had been working their way eastward through Gojjam. They were followed by the Emperor, who entered his capital on May 5th.

In order that these events may be viewed in their correct perspective it is first necessary to trace the development of the policy behind the various military operations. For although the pattern of conquest

seemed to be a wide pincer movement through Eritrea and Somaliland combined with a direct thrust through western Ethiopia, it
was not so designed. The campaign grew gradually from the progress
of events and was, as General Wavell later wrote, 'an improvisation
after the British fashion of war'. Thus it was that in September 1940,
when he was beginning to consider the implications of an advance
from Egypt into Cyrenaica, he gave orders to the commanders in
Kenya and the Sudan for step by step action and not for a general
offensive. General Platt was to prepare local attacks on Gallabat
and at a few other points, to be carried out when the dry weather
came again. In Kenya General Dickinson was to concentrate for
the present upon an active defence, but was to submit plans for a
future offensive.

In October Mr. Eden, then Secretary of State for War, was visiting
the Middle East, and General Smuts was inspecting the South
African forces in Kenya. The opportunity was taken to arrange a
meeting between the two at Khartoum, beginning on October 28th
—the day of the Italian attack on Greece. General Wavell's view at
this time was that the British forces in Kenya and the Sudan were
sufficient for defensive purposes and should soon be capable of
attacking. After retaking the frontier posts and thus securing an
entry into Ethiopia through which to foster the spread of the revolt,
it should be possible to make things very difficult for the Italians,
who were virtually cut off and would soon be running short of petrol
and supplies of all kinds. The interest therefore lay in the state of the
offensive plans and preparations. General Platt intended to retake
Gallabat about mid-November and open the frontier in that
important area, after which he proposed to gain control of the exits
from Eritrea in the Kassala area and recover the use of the eastern
loop of the railway and of the Kassala landing ground; for this he
would need certain extra troops—infantry, armour, and artillery.
General Dickinson intended to operate to the east of Lake Rudolf;
he had studied the capture of Kismayu but had not the resources—
especially in transport—to undertake it as yet. General Smuts
thought that the attack on Kassala should be accompanied by
others, particularly from Kenya, and pointed to the need for removing the threat presented to the base at Mombasa by the Italian
forces at Kismayu; he undertook to give General Dickinson all
possible help with his preparations.

The meeting was not one at which the responsible Commanders-
in-Chief could take a formal decision, but Mr. Eden expressed the
general feeling when he proposed that Gallabat should be attacked
early in November and Kassala early in January. As for Kismayu,
General Cunningham was to examine the possibility of taking it in
January also. (Lieut.-General A. G. Cunningham was on the point

of relieving Lieut.-General Dickinson, who was in poor health and worn out by his exertions in Kenya.) Mr. Eden took home the outline plans, and he, rather than the Chiefs of Staff, had the task of explaining them to the Prime Minister, who was dissatisfied with the number of troops 'virtually out of action' in Kenya and was pressing for one of the brigades from West Africa to be returned, so as to make it unnecessary to send British troops to defend the important convoy-collecting station of Freetown.

A fortnight later General Cunningham reported on the Kismayu operation. He advised postponing it until after the end of the spring rains in May, basing his opinion on the strength of the Italians in southern Somalia and on the great difficulty that he himself would have in moving and supplying enough troops to secure success across the wide stretch of desert; during the rains this would be impossible. At present his African soldiers were insufficiently trained and there were no grounds for assuming that Italian morale had deteriorated. He suffered from a general shortage of equipment and of the means of carrying the necessary water; he thought that the risk of administrative failure was so great that to make the attempt in February could be justified only by the gravest strategical necessity. When informing the War Office of General Cunningham's conclusions General Wavell announced that in Kenya he wished to carry out minor operations on the northern front in December, for which both West African brigades would be required. The news was not well received in London. Mr. Churchill was 'shocked' and demanded a further report, and the C.I.G.S. telegraphed hoping that the attack on Kismayu need not be thus postponed, because reports of declining Italian morale made it desirable 'to hit them whenever and wherever we can'.

The hard fact remains that General Platt's operation at Gallabat, carried out early in November, failed of its object. On 1st and 2nd December General Wavell again reviewed the whole field at a meeting of commanders held at Cairo, and informed them of the forthcoming offensive in the Western Desert. He decided that as much help as possible was to be given to the Patriot movements, and that pressure was to be maintained on the enemy at Gallabat. Kassala was to be attacked early in 1941, though the Air Officer Commanding-in-Chief was very doubtful of his ability to meet the heavy call on fighter aircraft that would probably result. The 4th Indian Division would probably be sent to General Platt from Egypt, starting towards the end of December. In Kenya General Cunningham was to gain control of the country up to the frontier of Italian Somaliland as soon as possible, so as to enable administrative arrangements to be made for a further advance in May. West of Moyale and in the vicinity of Lake Rudolf there were to be operations to harass the enemy and encourage the Patriots in southern Ethiopia. The idea behind these orders was that the Patriot movement offered the best prospect of making the position of the Italians untenable; the reason for the capture of Kassala and Kismayu was to deprive the enemy of likely lines of advance and so make it possible to withdraw troops from Kenya and the Sudan for use farther north.

Communicating these decisions to the War Office General Wavell asked to be allowed to keep both West African brigades at least until the end of February, and on December 11th the C.I.G.S. sent him tentative approval subject to any developments which might arise from the battle of Sidi Barrani (which had begun two days before) or from events in the Balkans. He added that the time had come when risks could be accepted in order to undertake the most energetic operations against the Italians in all quarters.

The rapid expulsion of the Italians from Egypt led the Chiefs of Staff to conclude at the end of December that operations to clear up Ethiopia should take priority next after those in the Western Desert, and that the growing probability of a German advance through Bulgaria made it very desirable that the victory in Italian East Africa should be a speedy one. The Prime Minister indeed expressed the hope that by the end of April the Italian Army in Ethiopia might have submitted or been broken up. No one was more eager than General Smuts, who showed particular interest in the removal of any threat to Kenya, and was ready to supply a second South African division to hasten matters. The Chiefs of Staff, however, having in mind the general balance of forces and tasks, were doubtful whether the strength of the forces already in Kenya was entirely justified. But when all these opinions had been expressed, it was the Commander-in-Chief who had to decide upon the allotment of means to ends; to estimate the pace of the various operations; and to judge the value of their probable results.

The Italians helped to make matters easier for him by withdrawing from Kassala without waiting to be attacked—an indication that the disaster to Graziani might be having effects beyond the borders of Libya. The experience of the past month had shown a tendency on the part of the Italians to melt away in adversity. It would therefore be right to take risks against them, and it might even be possible to sweep them, as they retreated, over the mountain passes of Eritrea and on to the Asmara plateau. General Wavell therefore ordered General Platt to press on to Asmara.

The same thoughts had occurred to General Cunningham. He had now enough transport to lift four brigades and a bare sufficiency of supplies and had fortunately succeeded in finding water on the routes leading to Italian Somaliland. In the circumstances he felt that there was a reasonable chance of taking Kismayu with this force and on 28th January he asked permission to try. General Wavell agreed, and the date was fixed for 11th February.

At this moment the Commanders-in-Chief in the Middle East were to feel the pressure of events not only in the Balkans but also in the Far East, for on February 10th the Chiefs of Staff issued a warning about the possibility of aggressive action by the Japanese in the near future, and followed it by pointing out that the early destruction of the Italian forces in East Africa might have a very good deterrent effect upon another would-be aggressor. At the same time the Commanders-in-Chief were told that the War Cabinet's policy was to be ready to help Greece, and perhaps Turkey as well, and that consequently they must be able to send the largest possible land and air forces from Africa to the Balkans. The decision facing General Wavell was whether to continue operations against Italian East Africa or to start withdrawing troops to meet this new commitment. He decided that it would be best to continue operations for the time being, but he ordered General Platt to limit himself to occupying Eritrea and not to advance into Ethiopia; he warned him that two or three of his brigade groups would be withdrawn as soon as Eritrea was taken. General Cunningham was told that if Kismayu fell he could advance on Mogadishu but that he might soon have to part with the South African Division.

The position was well summed up by Mr. Eden (now Secretary of State for Foreign Affairs) when he met the Commanders-in-Chief in Cairo on the occasion of his Balkan mission. He pointed out that it was urgent to complete the operations in Eritrea but that it might be necessary to leave Ethiopia to rot by itself. The urgency was due to the need for concentrating army and air forces farther north and also for making the Red Sea route safe, as this, it was hoped, might result in the United States Government permitting their ships to proceed to Suez, and so ease the severe strain on British shipping. The Commanders-in-Chief informed the Chiefs of Staff that they were equally anxious to be rid of military commitments in East Africa but that they could go no faster, for in view of the policy of preparing help for Greece they could spare no more troops or aircraft for the East African theatre.

Towards the end of February General Platt appeared to be committed to a long and difficult operation at Keren, occupying two divisions. By this time the British were deeply involved in the provision of forces for Greece, so that General Wavell had to decide whether to stop the battle at Keren or not. In view of General Platt's opinion that a renewal of the attack might very well succeed, and seeing that the admission of failure might encourage an Italian counter-stroke, he decided to continue the operations. He had already authorized General Cunningham to advance from Mogadishu to Harar, and was arranging for the recapture of Berbera by a force from Aden in order to shorten his line of communication. After that he intended that this advance should cease and that some of the troops and much of the transport should be withdrawn. He doubted whether the capture of Addis Ababa would achieve any great strategical purpose, and it was not until General Cunningham asked to be allowed to go on because he thought the capture of the capital would be quite easy, and that coupled with the success in Eritrea it might lead the Italians to capitulate, that General Wavell approved the further advance.

Keren fell on 27th March, and Massawa on 8th April, just after General Cunningham's forces had entered Addis Ababa. On 11th April President Roosevelt announced that the Gulf of Aden and Red Sea were no longer combat zones; they were therefore open to American ships. By this time General Rommel had recaptured most of Cyrenaica, and General Wavell decided that no major operations in Eritrea or Ethiopia could be allowed to interfere with the removal of troops to Egypt. He accordingly ordered General Cunningham to move north and help to secure the use of the main road from Addis Ababa to Asmara, along which reinforcements of troops and transport could then pass on their way to Egypt. This resulted in the Duke of Aosta becoming pinned between General Cunningham's force and General Platt's—the latter now greatly reduced by withdrawals to Egypt—and on 16th May he surrendered at Amba Alagi.

Strong Italian forces still remained in Ethiopia, requiring to be rounded up later, and they kept the two African divisions occupied all through the summer. Nevertheless, one country at least had been liberated from Fascist domination and had had its rightful ruler restored. The main operations in East Africa had therefore succeeded beyond all expectations, and had ended just in time. This was largely due to the steadiness of purpose of General Wavell and Air Chief Marshal Longmore, who had to achieve a workable and appropriate balance of forces while doing their best to comply with a rapid succession of instructions and suggestions, such as to part with forces from Kenya, to capture Kismayu quickly, to capture Eritrea quickly, to deter the Japanese by 'liquidating Italian East Africa', to treat as a 'first duty' the air defence of Malta, to be prepared to send ten squadrons to Turkey, to regard the capture of Rhodes as 'of first importance', and to 'let their first thoughts be for Greece'.

*See Map* 26.

Reinforcements from various sources had been reaching the Sudan towards the end of the summer of 1940: the 5th Indian Division (Major-General L. M. Heath) from India; a mixed squadron of cruiser and light tanks from Egypt; a field regiment and a troop of anti-tank guns which had been intended for British Somaliland, but were too late; and an Indian battalion from Aden. The 5th Indian Division contained only six battalions, all Indian, and on its arrival General Platt used the three British battalions already in the Sudan to form three brigades each of one British and two Indian battalions. During September No. 203 Group received No. 45 Squadron (Blenheim I) from Egypt, to join the three bomber squadrons in the Port Sudan area; and from Kenya came No. 237 (Rhodesian) Army Co-operation Squadron, armed with obsolescent Hardy and Vincent aircraft. In all Air Commodore Slatter had a first line strength of 54 bombers and 19 Gladiator fighters, and at Aden there were three bomber squadrons, and one Blenheim and one Gladiator fighter squadron, or 38 bombers and 19 fighters in all. The Italian Air Force in East Africa had about 160 aircraft serviceable out of a total of 260.

In and around Kassala the Italians appeared to have two cavalry groups, three colonial brigades, two mechanized groups of medium artillery, and two companies of tanks—in all some 13,500 men, 60 medium, pack, and field guns, and 30 medium and light tanks. Farther south, at Um Hagar, there were believed to be a colonial brigade and a group of pack artillery, say, 3,000 men and 12 guns, and in the Gallabat area a colonial battalion and a group of *bande*. In all these areas the Italians were inactive, but were suspected of intending to seize bridgeheads over the river Atbara as preliminaries to a later advance.

General Platt retained one brigade of the 5th Indian Division—the 29th[1]—under his own command in the Port Sudan area, and the division, less this brigade, with certain units of the Sudan Defence Force attached, was given the task of preventing any Italian advance towards Khartoum from Goz Regeb on the river Atbara to about Gallabat—a front of over 200 miles. A mobile force—'Gazelle'—was formed near Kassala to probe deeply into enemy territory and be prepared to delay any advance. Its main units were Skinner's Horse and No. 1 Motor Machine-Gun Group of the Sudan Defence Force, with a variable amount of artillery and other units, the whole under the command of Colonel F. W. Messervy. The 10th Indian Infantry Brigade (Brigadier W. J. Slim) was at Gedaref, on its way to Gallabat, and the 9th (Brigadier A. G. O. M. Mayne) in a central position at Butana Bridge. The Baro salient, at the most westerly point of Ethiopia, was patrolled by Sudan Police, and the Boma area by the Equatorial Corps of the Sudan Defence Force. In the back areas administrative preparations went busily on. By the end of October there were 28,000 troops in the Sudan, a figure well below the enemy's estimate.

---

[1] Previously numbered 21st.

The main tasks of the Air Force were to co-operate with the Navy in keeping open communications in the Red Sea, to neutralize and destroy the Italian Air Force, and to support the Army. Air Commodore Slatter's principal bomber effort was directed against warships based on Massawa, against the Italian Air Force, and against land communications. Many valuable flying hours were spent in escorting ships and on anti-submarine patrols, but the sustained attack on aircraft, airfields, fuel and bomb dumps, and maintenance installations caused damage which the enemy was unable to replace or repair, and steadily wore down the effectiveness of his air force.

On 15th October the Italians made their first enterprising move since August. A Colonel Rolle, with over 1,000 irregulars, made a sortie from near Kurmuk to a distance of nearly fifty miles. They were attacked from air and ground, and after a week withdrew exhausted and suffering greatly from hunger and thirst. The raid caused some anxiety in the Sudan, but had no other effect.

The attack on Gallabat and Metemma, which had been decided upon at the Khartoum conference of 28th October, was entrusted to 10th Indian Infantry Brigade with B Squadron 6th R.T.R. under command. Gallabat Fort itself is in the Sudan, and beyond a dry river bed with steep banks which marks the frontier lies the neighbouring post and village of Metemma. Both posts had good field defences; the first was held by a colonial battalion, the second by two colonial battalions and a group of *bande*. The plan was to capture Gallabat by a tank and infantry assault, and then, if crossings for the tanks over the river bed could be found, to capture Metemma. Six Wellesleys, nine Gladiators, and the army co-operation aircraft, working from temporary landing strips, were to carry out reconnaissance, bombing, and close support, and provide defensive fighter patrols. About seventeen Italian fighters and thirty-two bombers were thought to be within range of the area.

The attack began early in the morning of 6th November and the resistance at Gallabat was quickly overcome, but by this time four of the six cruisers and five of the six light tanks were out of action, mainly through the damage done to their tracks by mines and boulders in the long grass: the attack on Metemma was postponed until they could be repaired. Meanwhile the Italian air forces reacted strongly. Five Gladiators—of inferior performance to the Italian fighters—were quickly shot down and a sixth forced to land. Deprived of fighter cover the troops were subjected to a series of deliberate and accurate bombing attacks. There was no cover to be had in the open rocky ground, and Gallabat Fort itself was particularly heavily bombed. By the middle of the afternoon there had been many casualties, the sight of which, as they made their way back, caused some demoralization. By ill-chance the lorry carrying the spare parts for the tanks was destroyed, which made it all the longer before the attack could be renewed. The bombing began again next morning, and during the afternoon Brigadier Slim decided that he must withdraw to less exposed ground about three miles west of Gallabat. This was done without any interference. The British had lost forty-two killed and 125 wounded, but though the result was disappointing the effect on the Patriots was on the whole good; to them the fact that the Italians had been attacked by forces armed with modern weapons was a welcome sign.

Efforts were now concentrated on active preparations for the attack on Kassala. The Italians were constantly harried by aggressive patrolling, in which Gazelle Force was particularly active, so much so that the Duke of Aosta himself directed General Frusci not to submit to this shepherding. The result was that Gazelle and two Italian battalions had an encounter about thirty miles to the north of Kassala, lasting on and off for over a fortnight, before the enemy withdrew and became passive again. Meanwhile, the British preparations went on.

It will be recalled that on the third day of the battle of Sidi Barrani—December 11th—General Wavell gave orders for the 4th Indian Division to move to the Sudan. It has been seen that this decision could have been taken no earlier, and by taking it when he did General Wavell was able to make use of shipping which was in the process of turning round at Suez.[1] The move was completed during December and early January by sea, rail, road, and river. At this time it was General Platt's intention to attack at Kassala on 8th February, with 4th Indian Division on the north and the 5th on the south. Each division would have two infantry brigades only, as the 4th Indian Division was leaving one—the 7th—in the Port Sudan area and the 9th Indian Infantry Brigade would be at Gallabat.

Since early in January there had been indications that the enemy was thinning out his troops on the Sudan frontier, and it soon seemed that a withdrawal from the Kassala area was about to take place. General Platt's troops were not yet deployed for the attack: 4th Indian Division had in hand only Gazelle Force and the 11th Indian Infantry Brigade; 5th Indian Division had its 10th and 29th Indian Infantry Brigades, but sufficient transport was not yet present to allow of a general pursuit at short notice. Air Commodore Slatter too had not yet completed the preparations which he had been making as best he could without stopping his other operations, hampered as he was by shortages of aircraft, signal equipment, and vehicles.

---

[1] See page 271.

Kassala has already been referred to as a focal point of communications between Eritrea and the Sudan, which was the reason for its seizure by the Italians on the outbreak of war. It was connected to Agordat by two routes; on the north an indifferent dry-weather track through Keru and Biscia, on the south a good motorable road—the *Via Imperiale*—through Tessenei, Aicota and Barentu. A cross-track connected Aicota, on the southern route, with Biscia, the western terminus of the Eritrean narrow-gauge railway. After Biscia the northern route improved, and was metalled in parts. From Agordat, where the two routes joined, there was no practicable way to Asmara save by the main road through Keren.

General Platt decided to begin his advance on 19th January, by which time he hoped to catch the enemy on the move. The 4th Division (Major-General N. M. de la P. Beresford-Peirse) was to secure Sabderat and Wachai (about forty miles east of Kassala) and to advance as far towards Keru as the supply arrangements would permit. The 5th Indian Infantry Brigade, from Gedaref, was to join its division as quickly as possible. B Squadron 4th R.T.R. ('I' tanks), on its way from Egypt, was also to join 4th Indian Division. The task of 5th Indian Division was to secure Aicota and be prepared to move either east on Barentu or north-east on Biscia.

The information about the enemy proved to be substantially correct, and on January 18th he was found to have withdrawn from Kassala. The pursuit began next day. Gazelle Force was attacked from the air but met no serious opposition until January 21st, when a strong Italian rearguard of 41st Colonial Brigade checked the pursuit at Keru. The 5th Indian Division sent off the 10th Indian Infantry Brigade from Aicota to cut the enemy's line of retreat from Keru, and on the night of 22nd/23rd January the 41st Colonial Brigade withdrew; the Commander, his staff, and over 800 others were captured.

Gazelle Force reached Biscia on the 24th, and pressed on at once towards Agordat. The brigades of 4th Indian Division arrived in the area by dint of great exertions, the 11th on the following day and the 5th (from Gedaref) on January 27th. Meanwhile 10th Indian Infantry Brigade, its task with 4th Indian Division done, set out across country to approach Barentu from the north, and cut the motor road joining Agordat to Barentu, at both of which places the Italians evidently intended to make a stand.

The position at Agordat taken up by 4th Colonial Division was a naturally strong one which had been improved by field defences. It faced generally south-west, covering the approaches from both Biscia and Barentu. The northern flank was protected by the sandy bed of the Baraka river; to the front was a broken plain on which the defenders held a prominent hill, while farther east, beyond the

Barentu road, another rugged hill rose to 2,000 feet. General Beresford-Peirse first tried to outflank the position from the north, but found no practicable route. He then decided to seize the eastern hill and advance north to cut the main Keren road. A hard mountain battle ensued, lasting three days, during which the Italians, seeing the danger, brought up strong reinforcements; but on 31st January the hill was finally occupied by the 11th Indian Infantry Brigade. The same morning 5th Indian Infantry Brigade and the newly arrived 'I' tanks struck northward across the plain, carried the defences, and destroyed a number of Italian tanks concealed for counter-attack. By 4.30 p.m. they had taken their objective and cut the Keren road, but most of the enemy's 4th Colonial Division escaped by a track farther north. It had lost about two battalions, twenty-eight field guns and a number of light and medium tanks. Gazelle took up the pursuit at dawn next day, greatly delayed by heavy mining and demolitions.

The enemy's position at Barentu was held by the 2nd Colonial Division, less its 12th Brigade most of which had gone north to Agordat. It was left with nine battalions, 32 guns, and about 36 light tanks and armoured cars. The 10th Indian Infantry Brigade, on its way to rejoin its own division, was the first to gain contact and attacked from the north, meeting determined resistance. Meanwhile 29th Indian Infantry Brigade was approaching as fast as it could from the west, much delayed by rearguards and mining. Both brigades continued to attack until 1st February, the day of the Italian defeat at Agordat. That night the 2nd Colonial Division withdrew from the Barentu position, and the motor road between Tessenei to Agordat became available as a British supply route. The Italians retreated by the only track open to them, towards Tole and Arresa, pursued through difficult country by No. 2 Motor Machine-Gun Group. By February 8th it was found that the Italians had abandoned their vehicles and taken to the hills.

Farther to the south the 43rd Colonial Brigade had withdrawn from Um Hagar on 26th January and was pursued by a small mounted force of Indian troops, Sudan Defence Force, and Spahis recently arrived from Syria. Fighters and bombers of the Royal Air Force found good targets and the retreat became a rout. The brigade at Wolkait withdrew towards Adowa, and by February 3rd the whole Um Hagar area was under British control.

At Gallabat the Italians stood firm until the night of January 31st, when they withdrew towards Gondar, pursued by a mobile detachment from 9th Indian Infantry Brigade. The withdrawal was well conducted and was covered by a lavish use of mines. For his part in detecting and clearing fifteen minefields in the space of fifty-five miles 2nd Lieut. P. S. Bhagat, Royal Bombay Sappers and Miners, was awarded the Victoria Cross. The enemy succeeded in breaking away, and the 9th Indian Infantry Brigade concentrated at Gedaref, with a detachment at Metemma to patrol forward.

Such were the immediate consequences of the Italian with-drawals from the Sudan frontier. These withdrawals were deliberate and were followed up as speedily as the limited mobility of the British forces would allow. Squadrons of the Royal Air Force were forced to work from airfields too far back for them to make their full contribution to the enemy's difficulties at the outset. The necessary re-dispositions were made and the Italian airfields at Sabderat and Tessenei were taken into use as quickly as possible. Their targets were enemy columns and the lines of communication, especially the rail-way, while the Eritrean airfields were kept under constant attack. The first Hurricanes for No. 1 (Fighter) Squadron S.A.A.F. arrived when the pursuit was beginning and helped to gain air superiority. In the month from mid-January to mid-February the Italians recorded the loss of 61 aircraft, of which 50 were lost by enemy action, either in combat or on the ground.

While the action at Keru was only that of a rearguard, the Duke of Aosta had ordered 'resistance to the end' at Agordat and Barentu, for he felt that in the rocky foothills of the Eritrean plateau the British would not be able to exploit their supposed superiority in mechanical vehicles, as they could in the Sudan plain. On February 3rd General Wavell signalled to General Platt 'Now go on and take Keren and Asmara . . .'

In the middle of August 1940 Colonel Sandford had started on his hazardous journey into Ethiopia with the objects of stimulating local opposition to the Italians and of finding a secure place to which the Emperor could move.[1] Eighty miles of desert scrub and foothills had to be crossed, the Ethiopian escarpment climbed, and the Italian garrisons and patrols evaded, for Sandford's Mission was not a fighting force but one which relied for its safety upon secret move-ment and Patriot protection. In a month, after many adventures, including a narrow escape from capture, he reached Sakala, south-east of Dangila, and there set up his headquarters. On the way he had collected much information about affairs in Ethiopia, and he now signalled his recommendations to Khartoum. He considered it of first importance to open up a route from the Sudan into Gojjam in order to send in arms, ammunition, and money before the rains ended and the Italians perhaps became more active. He favoured the route through Sarako which he himself had followed, and suggested that early action might be taken to clear certain Italian

[1] See page 184.

posts from it; he suggested also that routes should be established eastward from Roseires, and into Armachaho, to the north of Lake Tana. Finally, he urged that the Emperor should enter Ethiopia early in October because the Patriots' first question was always of his whereabouts, and they clearly regarded his presence and leadership as a necessary condition for a widespread rising. 'When the dagna (judge) comes no one will be afraid', they would say, 'but until he comes who will not be afraid?'

As an advanced base, and as a first headquarters for the Emperor, Sandford favoured Belaya, an isolated table-mountain rising to 7,000 feet above sea-level and standing about thirty miles west of the main Ethiopian escarpment. A rapid and successful reconnaissance by Captain R. A. Critchley confirmed his opinion. It was a natural fortress-base, safe from surprise, well placed for a further advance into Gojjam or, if things went badly, for an escape by the valley of the Blue Nile. It would not, however, be accessible by transport until the beginning of the dry season in November, but this was no drawback in General Platt's estimation, as he had no wish for risings to occur until he was in a position to take the offensive against the Italians in Eritrea.

The success of any plans for loosening the enemy's grip on Gojjam depended largely upon penning in the Italian garrisons which were spaced along the main Gojjam road in a wide arc from Bahrdar Giorgis, at the southern end of Lake Tana, through Dangila and Debra Markos, and on to Addis Ababa. As long as the Italians could move freely along this road they could easily concentrate their forces at any threatened point. During October some of the garrisons were reinforced, and the Italian troops became more active, at a time when Patriot enterprises were being handicapped by dissensions which the Emperor was not present to reconcile. In particular, the two leading Gojjam chieftains, Dejesmach Mangasha and Dejesmach Nagash,[1] though firm and bitter enemies of the Italians, were mutually suspicious and antagonistic. Their co-operation was, however, plainly essential, and Colonel Sandford achieved one of his most striking successes when he induced them to fraternize publicly and agree to act together.

While the ground was thus being prepared, the preliminary arrangements in Khartoum received a fresh stimulus from General Wavell, when he decided that the Patriots were to play a large part in his operations against Italian East Africa. Together with Mr. Eden he twice met the Emperor, who was not satisfied with the deliveries of equipment which he considered had been promised to him in England before the fall of France, nor with the number and quality of the rifles which had reached the Patriots, nor with the progress in

---

[1] The title 'Dejesmach' means literally 'Commander of the Main Body'.

the training of his bodyguard. The British losses in France had, of course, greatly lessened the supplies available for the Middle East, but General Wavell gave orders for improving matters, so far as he could, in keeping with the importance now attached to the Patriot revolt. Rifles were taken from the Polish Brigade in Palestine and given to the Patriots. A few Bren guns were issued. The 2nd Ethiopian and 4th Eritrean Battalions (of refugees) were brought from Kenya to join the battalion at Khartoum. More British instructors were provided and the training speeded up. Special units, called Operational Centres, were formed, each consisting of a British officer, five N.C.Os, and a few picked Ethiopians; the units were to be specially trained in guerrilla warfare and their role was to provide skilled leadership for Patriot bands. A million pounds was allotted to financing the Patriots, and two officers were appointed to General Platt's staff with the special duty of organizing support for them. The senior was Major O. C. Wingate, chosen by General Wavell because of an impression, gained in Palestine in 1939, that he might make a valuable leader of unorthodox enterprises in war. Wingate lost no time in applying his ruthless energy to his new task.

To co-ordinate their activities it was clearly necessary for Wingate and Sandford to meet. The latter had seen most of the leading chiefs of western Gojjam, and in mid-November he returned to Sakala from an arduous journey into eastern Gojjam where he had been trying to counter the growing Italian strength by personally telling of the Emperor's presence in the Sudan and of British support to the Patriot cause—news which the inhabitants had previously been disinclined to believe. On 20th November Flight Lieutenant Collis in a Vincent of No. 430 Flight successfully landed Wingate on the roughest of clearings at Sakala. From what he saw of the country between Belaya and the frontier during the flight Wingate was satisfied that this was a suitable line of approach for the Emperor. For two days he and Sandford discussed the plans they would submit to General Platt. Wingate then flew back to Khartoum. His visit made a big impression in Gojjam, for the Ethiopians had had bitter experience of Italian air power. The landing of a British aircraft was therefore in itself an event, but better still were the visible signs of air support that followed, for the Royal Air Force managed with its scanty resources to bomb many Italian posts—notably Dangila, to drop money and supplies on 101 Mission, and to scatter propaganda leaflets to subvert the Italian native troops. News of these doings spread from mouth to mouth through the countryside and did much to raise Patriot morale. One of the conclusions to which Sandford and Wingate came was that no more arms and ammunition should be spared for Armachaho, the district to the north of Lake Tana where Major Count A. W. D. Bentinck of 101 Mission had arrived in September. His principal task was to induce the rival chieftains in this neighbourhood to unite in resisting the Italians. For a long time his patient uphill work met with no success in this respect, though a few chiefs, who had received British arms, took some aggressive action, and several successful ambushes were brought off along the road between Metemma and Gondar. When in February the Italian garrison of Wolkait was withdrawn, the local patriots were sufficiently encouraged to help Bentinck, who was then almost single-handed, to create difficulties for the Italians to the north-west of Gondar.

After Wingate's return to Khartoum General Platt quickly decided upon his plan. The objects were to seize a stronghold in Gojjam, perhaps at Dangila; to install the Emperor; and to widen the area of revolt. The Frontier Battalion of the Sudan Defence Force[1] was first to secure Belaya, which was to be the advanced base from which the Operational Centres would pass into Gojjam and begin work with the various Patriot bands. To Belaya Colonel Sandford was to send recruits to be trained for the Emperor's body-guard, and he was to collect 3,000 mules to supplement the camels being provided by the Sudan. The Emperor would move to Belaya as soon as possible.

Preparations went forward accordingly, with both Sandford and Wingate constantly advising speed. The Italians had met with some success in dividing and weakening the Patriots by bringing back to Gojjam the hereditary governor, Ras Hailu, who still had much local influence.[2] Nevertheless Sandford thought the outlook favourable and by mid-December he was advising immediate action without waiting for every preparation to be completed. By early January the Frontier Battalion had opened two routes to Belaya, though both were difficult and not suitable for motors, and they had safely delivered there large quantities of stores. Only two Operational Centres were ready; the training of the bodyguard was backward; and the Gojjam chieftains were proving reluctant to weaken themselves by providing recruits for the Emperor. Worst of all, Sandford had been unable to provide any mules; a very serious matter, for if the camels could not climb the escarpment and then work in an unaccustomed climate on unfamiliar food the operations in Gojjam would be paralysed for lack of transport.

By now the success in the Western Desert had led to a sharpening of the pace of operations against the Italians everywhere. The Emperor was becoming more impatient than ever to return to his country, and appealed to the Prime Minister. General Platt, with the impending operation at Kassala in mind, was equally anxious

---

[1] See page 183.
[2] The title 'Ras' is equivalent to Commander-in-Chief.

for his entry, and on 31st December it was agreed that he should enter in the middle of January. He eventually crossed the border on 21st January, and reached Belaya a fortnight later.

With the Italians withdrawing from the Sudan frontier, the British organization for dealing with the Patriots was changed. The normal responsibility of a commander for administering territory previously occupied by the enemy now fell upon General Wavell, and on 15th February he informed the Emperor of the steps being taken. These were in line with Mr. Eden's statement in the House of Commons on February 4th, that military operations would be guided and controlled in joint consultation with the Emperor. Sir Philip Mitchell, Chief Political Officer at Middle East Headquarters, was to make the administrative, economic, financial, and judicial arrangements appropriate to a temporary military occupation. His deputies were being appointed to the staffs of Generals Cunningham and Platt. To ensure full consultation with the Emperor, Colonel Sandford, now promoted Brigadier, was to be the Emperor's personal adviser on military and political matters, and was to act as liaison officer between him and Generals Wavell, Platt, and Cunningham. Lieut.-Colonel Wingate was to be the new head of 101 Mission, working in close collaboration with the Emperor through Brigadier Sandford.

In his new role of Commander in the field Lieut.-Colonel Wingate had at his disposal the Frontier Battalion (less the fifth company), the 2nd Ethiopian Battalion, and Nos. 1 and 2 Operational Centres. The whole force, with his fondness for scriptural allusion, he christened Gideon. The immediate task given to him by General Platt was to secure a stronghold in Gojjam to which the Emperor could move. This would entail clearing Dangila and Burye of the enemy—there was about one colonial brigade at each—and gaining control of the road between those places and Bahrdar Giorgis. The efforts of the Patriots were to be directed to harrying the main roads leading from Gondar and Addis Ababa, and forcing the Italians to commit as many troops as possible to the defence of the capital. The adventures of Gideon Force are described towards the end of the next chapter.

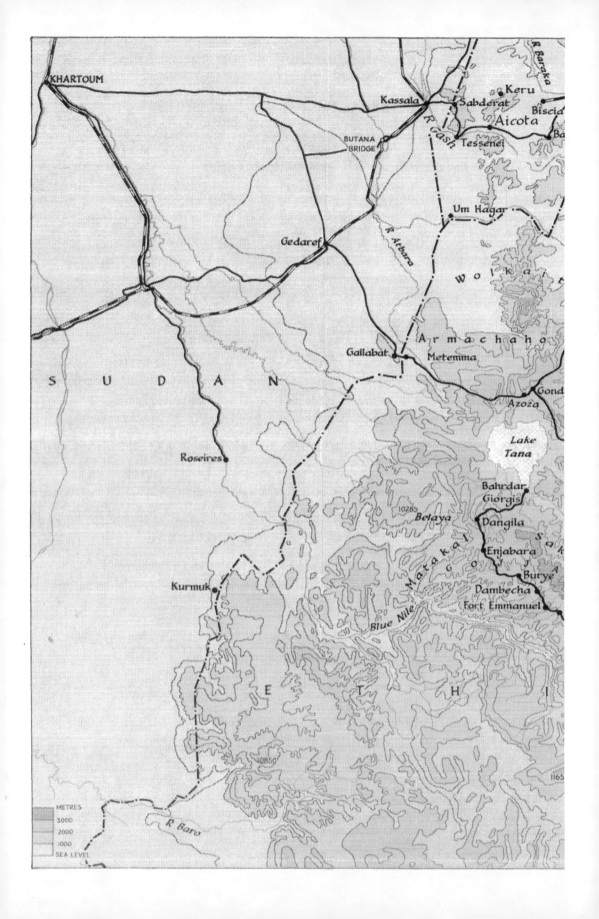

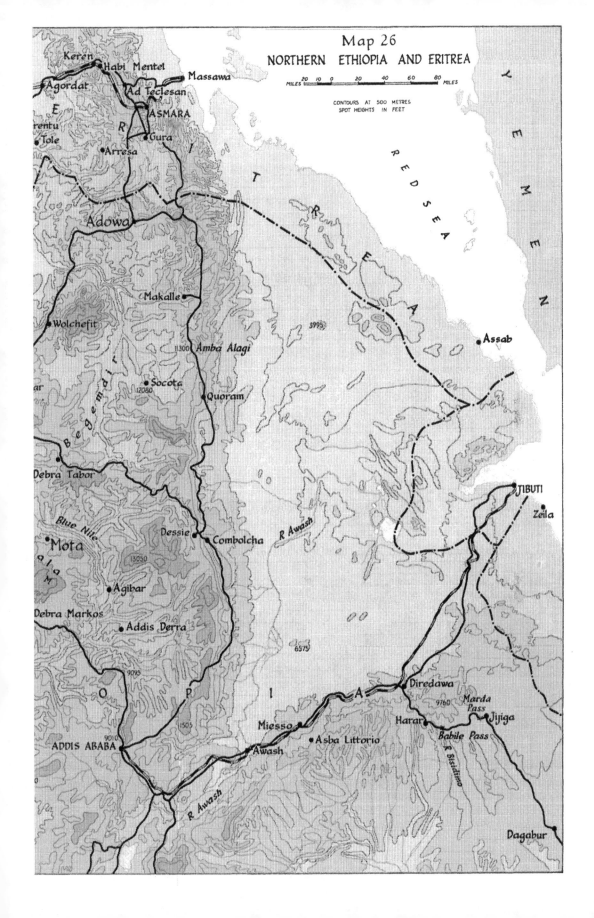

Map 26
NORTHERN ETHIOPIA AND ERITREA

CONTOURS AT 500 METRES
SPOT HEIGHTS IN FEET

# CHAPTER XXII

# THE ADVANCE ON ADDIS ABABA THROUGH SOMALIA AND GOJJAM

*See Maps 25 and 26*

LIEUTENANT-GENERAL Dickinson had achieved much
in the fourteen months during which he commanded
East Africa Force in Kenya. It is true that the Italian policy
had been defensive, but the British were now well established in
localities stretching from the sea to Lake Rudolf and their patrols
were masters of the wide no-man's-land before them—so far as there
could be mastery in so huge an area. On the administrative side, the
foundations of the supply and transport systems had been laid; the
procuring and production of war stores had been organized;
administrative units of all types were in training; and the financial
and legal difficulties that had hampered the raising of local forces
had been overcome. Over more detailed matters an immense amount
remained to be done.

The British strength had steadily risen and at the end of November
1940 was, in round numbers, 77,000. Of these roughly 27,000 were
South Africans, 6,000 were Europeans serving with the East and
West African forces, 33,000 were East Africans, and 9,000 were
West Africans. Among them were the 1st Northern Rhodesia
Regiment, 2nd King's African Rifles, and 1st East African Light
Battery, all of which had returned in September from British
Somaliland via Aden. The principal additions to the South African
forces during October and November included Headquarters 1st
South African Division (Major-General G. L. Brink), the 2nd and
5th Infantry Brigades, a regiment of field artillery, and many
engineer, transport, and other technical units.

After No. 237 (Rhodesian) Squadron had been transferred to the
Sudan in September, the air units remaining in Kenya, with the
exception of the Communication Squadron, Royal Air Force, all
belonged to the South African Air Force. They were Nos. 2 and 3
Fighter Squadrons (Fury, Gauntlet and Hurricane), Nos. 11 and
12 Bomber Squadrons (Battle and Ju. 86), Nos. 40 and 41 Army
Co-operation Squadrons (Hartbeest). The maintenance of so many

different types of aircraft disposed over a very wide area was a most difficult problem. Squadrons were administered by the South African Army, but by agreement with the Government of South Africa operational control was exercised on behalf of the Air Officer Commanding-in-Chief Middle East by Air Commodore W. Sowrey, R.A.F., with Brigadier H. Daniel, S.A.A.F., as his senior air staff officer. The air operations had three objects: to neutralize the Italian air forces in southern Ethiopia and Italian Somaliland; to defend Mombasa and Nairobi and other vulnerable points; and to co-operate directly with the army. A limit was set on operations of all types by the small numbers of aircraft, the scarcity of spare parts, and the great distances to be flown, but the Italians were lacking in enterprise and completely failed to take advantage of their numerical superiority. The South African squadrons, by their pugnacity, resource and endurance, soon won ascendancy over the Italian Air Force and never lost it.

General Cunningham's first task on relieving General Dickinson early in November was to examine the project for capturing Kismayu, and as a result he advised its postponement until after the spring rains.[1] General Wavell supported this view and General Cunningham gave orders for the forward movement of part of his force to the frontier during January; in the meantime, the moral ascendancy of his troops over the Italians was to be secured by various enterprises. The first raid was entrusted to 12th African Division, and its commander, Major-General Godwin-Austen, suggested as its objective the frontier post of El Wak, which lay north-west of Wajir across 110 miles of very indifferent going. It consisted of five defended localities held by colonial infantry and *bande*, perhaps 2,000 men in all with a few light guns. General Godwin-Austen decided to attack it with 1st South African Brigade, 24th Gold Coast Brigade, and 1st South African Light Tank Company, not because he over-estimated the opposition but because he wished to encourage his unseasoned troops with a success, and to give them experience in an operation involving the use of a large number of vehicles, including a long move by night. On December 16th—Dingaan's Day—after a successful approach march, the attack was delivered with the support of five fighter aircraft, three bombers and nine army co-operation Hartbeests. The Italian troops dispersed rapidly into the bush and their aircraft made little attempt to intervene. Next day the raiding force was withdrawn, having accomplished all it set out to do and having captured 13 guns and 44 prisoners. A British radio communiqué referred somewhat contemptuously to the Italian resistance, and Mussolini ordered the Duke of Aosta to hold an enquiry: as a result Lieutenant-General

---

[1] See page 393.

Pesenti, Governor of Italian Somaliland and Commander of the Juba sector, was replaced by Major-General De Simone.

General Cunningham's next object was to open up the Galla-Sidamo province of Ethiopia, where it was hoped to start a revolt among the Patriot leaders with whom contact had been made. This entailed operating both east and west of Lake Rudolf, and the task was given to the 1st South African Division, comprising its own 2nd and 5th Infantry Brigades and the 25th East African Brigade, with six Ethiopian irregular companies under command.[1] At the end of December the South African brigades were at Marsabit and the 25th East African Brigade was at Lokitaung near the Sudan border, 200 miles away across Lake Rudolf.

From the mountain oasis of Marsabit there were two possible routes into Ethiopia. The one by Moyale passed through the easily defensible country of the Ethiopian escarpment and was correctly believed to be strongly garrisoned. The other led across the lava rock and dust of the Chalbi desert and through Dukana, and was expected to be only lightly watched. This was the route chosen. On 16th January the 1st Natal Mounted Rifles of the 2nd Brigade (Brigadier F. L. A. Buchanan) and two irregular companies attacked El Yibo, whose garrison of *bande* held out for two days before slipping away. The 5th Brigade (Brigadier B. F. Armstrong) then moved up to Dukana and on 31st January both brigades crossed the frontier; the 2nd captured Gorai and the 5th Hobok. The division had thus achieved its first object with little difficulty other than that due to the great distance—400 miles from railhead—and the terrible heat.

This penetration of the fringe of the Italian defences did not produce a Patriot rising, and General Brink's next thought was to secure a better line of communication, for the approaching rains would make the Chalbi desert impassable. This entailed the capture of Moyale, and General Cunningham agreed with the proposal to take Mega first and then advance on Moyale from the north. General Brink intended to attack Mega with both brigades simultaneously on 16th February, but for various reasons the 2nd South African Brigade did not make its attack until two days later, and that afternoon the garrison surrendered. Twenty-six officers, 972 Italian and African soldiers, and seven guns were captured. On 22nd February one of the irregular companies acting with 2nd Brigade entered Moyale unopposed, and found a large quantity of war material abandoned. Throughout these operations the supply of water had been a vital factor; some had to be carried over 200 miles, and more than 300 wells were developed. Moreover the troops had to endure sharp contrasts of climate from the heat and dust of the shadeless Chalbi desert, where the lava rock blistered the flesh, to the rain,

---

[1] See pages 393-4.

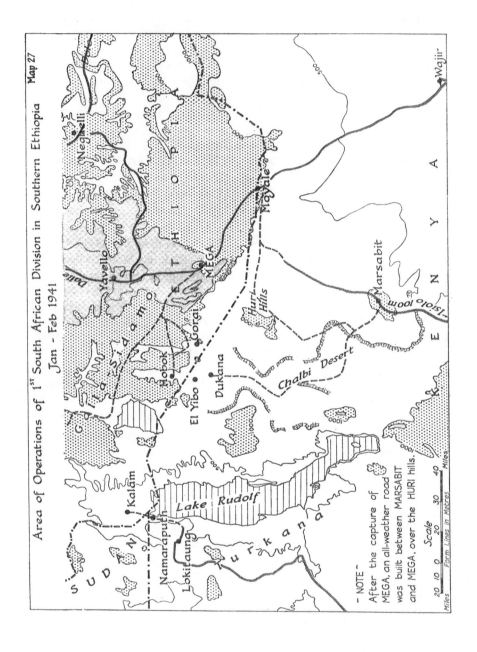

Area of Operations of 1ST South African Division in Southern Ethiopia   Map 27
Jan - Feb 1941

- NOTE -
After the capture of
MEGA, an all-weather road
was built between MARSABIT
and MEGA, over the HURI hills.

Scale
Miles 20 10 0    20    30    40    Miles
Form Lines in Metres

mud, and cold of the Ethiopian escarpment. Once again the Italian
Air Force failed to intervene, no doubt as the result of the attacks
made by Nos. 11 and 12 Squadrons on the airfields at Shashamanna,
Yavello and Neghelli.

On the western side of Lake Rudolf, the 25th East African Brigade
(Brigadier W. Owen), of two newly formed battalions of the King's
African Rifles, had advanced to Namaraputh with the eventual
object of capturing Kalam. But the wild Merille tribesmen of that
area showed themselves to be so hostile that it would first have been
necessary to operate against them. In General Cunningham's view
this would have been unprofitable at this stage, and he directed that
the brigade should act defensively.

By the time that Mega and Moyale were captured, the advance
into Italian Somaliland, now to be described, had reached Mogadishu. General Cunningham expected that he would require the
2nd and 5th South African Brigades for the coming thrust into
Ethiopia, and, having been told by General Wavell that the South
African Division might have to be taken from him at short notice,
he relieved these brigades by the 21st East African Brigade (Brigadier
A. McD. Ritchie) from Wajir, and moved them back to Kenya.

Meanwhile preparations for closing up to the frontier of Italian
Somaliland had been steadily going forward. Since the raid on
El Wak it had been apparent that the Italians had been withdrawing
to the river Juba, leaving west of it only *bande* and a single colonial
battalion at the landing ground and wells of Afmadu and a garrison
at Kismayu. On the lower Juba was the 102nd Colonial Division of
two brigades with some *bande*, in all about 14,000 men, and on the
upper Juba the 101st Colonial Division also of two brigades with
*bande*, in all only just over 6,000 men. At the end of January General
Cunningham, correctly judging from events on other fronts that
great risks could be taken against the Italians, asked for, and received,
General Wavell's permission to aim at capturing Kismayu[1]. On
2nd February he issued his orders.

The difficulties to be overcome were mainly due to distance,
shortage of equipment, lack of water, and the bad routes leading
forward. From railhead near Nairobi to the line of the river Tana
was nearly 250 miles, and it was another 250 miles to the river Juba.
The routes running eastward from Bura and Garissa on the Tana
were bush tracks of unstable surface, unfit to stand the passage of
many vehicles. Between the Tana and the Juba water was believed
to be very scarce. The administrative problem might well have been
insoluble had not the declining Italian morale encouraged General
Cunningham to believe that he could succeed with a smaller force
than he had originally thought necessary—four brigade groups

---

[1] See page 395.

instead of six. Thanks to the unceasing help of the Union Government there was now enough transport to move and maintain this force for the time thought necessary for the capture of Kismayu. Stocks of ammunition, stores, and supplies of all kinds had been built up at Bura and Garissa. Under a light protective screen the South African Engineers improved the main routes forward of these places; on both they discovered and developed limited amounts of water. Depots of all kinds were made as far forward as the frontier, and preparations were begun to deliver stores and supplies by sea from Mombasa to Kismayu.

General Cunningham's plan was for 12th African Division (1st South African, 22nd East African and 24th Gold Coast Infantry Brigades) to capture Afmadu on February 11th. The South African Brigade was then to turn south, capture the airfield at Gobwen, and seize a bridgehead over the river Juba at Jumbo. Meanwhile, the Gold Coast Brigade was to move east to Bulo Erillo and Jelib to prevent the reinforcement of the Gobwen area from the north. The 23rd Nigerian Brigade of 11th African Division, on the southern route from Bura, was to advance on Kismayu a little later when the enemy's attention would already be occupied by the 12th African Division. The Royal Navy was to provide a force of six warships (Force T) under Captain J. H. Edelsten, R.N., to bombard Brava and the coastal road during the early stages of the operation, and also to bombard Kismayu if necessary.[1] In order to preserve secrecy no written orders were issued, and an attempt was made, with some success, to persuade the enemy, by bogus wireless activity, that there was an Australian division in the Wajir area. The orders only covered the capture of Kismayu and the Jumbo bridgehead, and it was calculated that if Kismayu were not captured by the tenth day the troops would have either to be maintained across the open beaches, or to be withdrawn. General Cunningham informed his commanders that, if the Italian resistance broke, his next aim would be to advance to Mogadishu, Isha Baidoa and Lugh Ferrandi. Much would depend upon the administrative situation.

For the Air Force to be ready to support these operations a general move forward of squadrons was necessary, in some cases as much as 200 miles. In order to provide as many aircraft as possible Air Commodore Sowrey withdrew all the fighters from the defence of Nairobi and nearly all from Mombasa. The system of command was one fighter squadron direct under Air Headquarters; the other fighter squadron with both bomber squadrons under No. 2 Wing; with the two army co-operation squadrons apportioned to the three

---

[1] H.M.S. *Shropshire, Hawkins, Hermes* (No. 814 Squadron, Swordfish), *Capetown, Ceres, Kandahar.*

divisions. This made a total, including reserves, of 94 aircraft, in addition to which all the obsolete aircraft from the Operational Training Unit were made available as further reserves for the army co-operation squadrons, while every other possible aircraft was pressed into service for ambulance and communication tasks. The Italian strength, apart from reserves, was estimated on February 10th at 123, of which only 14, mostly bombers, were thought to be in Italian Somaliland and 26 others in southern Ethiopia. The true figures were a total of 188 in the whole of Italian East Africa, of which 78 were in workshops and depots.

Air attacks were made from 2nd February onwards by Nos. 3, 11 and 12 Squadrons S.A.A.F. on the Italian airfields at Gobwen, Afmadu and Dif, and a particularly heavy one on the Afmadu defences on the 10th; this was too much for the garrison, which melted away, so that the 22nd East African Brigade (Brigadier C. C. Fowkes) moved in next morning unopposed. The 24th Gold Coast Brigade (Brigadier C. E. M. Richards) had then 60 miles to cover in reaching Bulo Erillo, where it overcame fairly strong resistance and captured 141 prisoners, 4 armoured cars and much equipment. In the 2nd Gold Coast Regiment, which led the assault with great gallantry, eight of the white officers and N.C.Os were killed or wounded. Meanwhile, the 1st South African Brigade (Brigadier D. H. Pienaar) had reached a position ten miles from Gobwen, where they were to remain under cover throughout the day. Brigadier Pienaar had strict orders not to patrol and not to break wireless silence, so that his attack next day should come as a surprise. When, therefore, he heard explosions which suggested that the enemy might be preparing to evacuate Kismayu there was nothing he could do. His brigade with twelve light tanks advanced by night through the thick bush, colliding occasionally with fugitives from Kismayu, and secured Gobwen early on February 14th but not in time to intercept the garrison of Kismayu. On the previous evening, however, the information reaching General Cunningham from the air and from Force T, which was keeping a close watch on the coast, had suggested that the enemy was withdrawing. As the Nigerian Brigade was not yet within reach he ordered the 22nd East African Brigade from Afmadu to move at once on Kismayu, which it occupied by the evening of February 14th—six days ahead of the critical date.

Realizing that the enemy was considerably disorganized, General Cunningham determined to force the Juba with all speed. At Gobwen the pontoon bridge was destroyed, the river was 200 yards wide, any movement drew heavy fire, and it was clear that an attempt to cross here would be very costly. Brigadier Pienaar soon found a more suitable place ten miles upstream at Yonte where a company

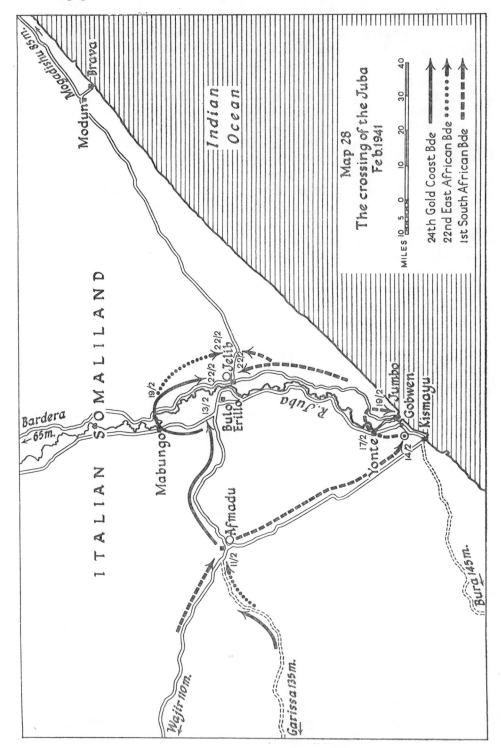

Map 28
The crossing of the Juba
Feb.1941

MILES 10 5 0 10 20 30 40

24th Gold Coast Bde
22nd East African Bde
1st South African Bde

*Indian Ocean*

ITALIAN SOMALILAND

Mogadishu 85m.

Brava

Modun

Bardera
← 65m.

Mabungo

19/2
22/2
22/2
13/2
Jelib
22/2
22/2

Bulo
Erillo

R. Juba

Yonte
17/2

Jumbo
Gobwen
19/2
Kismayu
14/2

Afmadu
11/2

Wajir 110m.

Garissa 135m.

Bura 145m.

of the Royal Natal Carbineers crossed in assault boats on the afternoon of the 17th. Next morning the Transvaal Scottish, which had taken over the bridgehead, beat off a counter-attack with heavy loss to the Italians. On the 19th a pontoon bridge was completed, and the brigade swooped down on Jumbo, capturing most of the garrison and fourteen guns.[1] The same day the Gold Coast Brigade crossed at Mabungo. It now remained to capture Jelib, in order to open the Mogadishu road. A converging movement was made with the Gold Coast Brigade moving down the thirty miles from Mabungo while the South Africans came up fifty miles and attacked from the south. The 22nd East African Brigade was sent south-east from Mabungo to cut the Mogadishu road. On February 22nd Jelib fell, and the Italian forces then disintegrated.

Thus ended the first phase. Casualties had been light, for the enemy had nowhere offered any systematic opposition, though sharp local clashes had been frequent. The troops had shown determination and endurance, having had to move far and fast in extreme heat, with little water, along dusty tracks or else through dense unfriendly bush. The passage of even a brigade column did grievous damage to the tracks, and it was largely due to the South African Road Construction and Maintenance Companies that the advance did not come to a dead stop.

The Air Force had given very effective support of all kinds and had practically driven the enemy out of the air, with the result that General Cunningham was able to lift the restriction he had placed on daylight movement of vehicles, thus speeding everything up and greatly relieving the strain on drivers. A large number of prisoners had been taken, many Italian colonial units had vanished into the bush, and the enemy were clearly in great confusion. They had concentrated their efforts on defending the Juba, and it seemed to General Cunningham that there was now nothing to stop him securing Mogadishu, and further that by denuding troops in Kenya of transport he could carry three brigade groups to Harar and maintain them. On February 22nd he suggested that, if General Wavell approved of this, the port of Berbera should be captured and opened so as to shorten his overland line of communication. He was informed in reply that this would be done by a force from Aden, but that he would have to provide the base units himself.

The first convoy by sea from Mombasa arrived at Kismayu on February 19th, and was unloaded with great difficulty from lighters, there being only one jetty that could be used, and even that was almost inaccessible from the landward side, since all the roads broke up at once under lorry traffic.[2] The power plant, the ice factory, and

[1] See Photo 29.
[2] See Photo 30.

the bulk oil stores were all out of action. There were great difficulties therefore in developing the place as an advanced base for all troops on or east of the Juba, as intended. Although the port was invaluable, it was necessary to keep the overland line of communication from Kenya in being for a long time.

The 23rd Nigerian Brigade (Brigadier G. R. Smallwood) had meanwhile moved up via Kismayu and Afmadu to the bridgehead at Mabungo, where they repulsed an attack made from the north on the evening of 22nd February. The 22nd East African Brigade from east of Jelib led the pursuit to Modun, where the Navy assisted with a bombardment which, according to the Viceroy, caused heavy losses. Next day the 23rd Nigerian Brigade took over the lead; they reached Mogadishu unopposed on the 25th, having advanced 235 miles in three days. The 1st South African Brigade was withdrawn into reserve. The 12th Division, now consisting of 21st East African and 24th Gold Coast Brigade Groups, was ordered to move northwards on Bardera and Isha Baidoa, but the difficulties at Kismayu prevented their doing so until the end of the month.

At Mogadishu there was a pause. Some of the harbour facilities were damaged, but the main cause of delay in opening the port was that apparatus was not immediately available for sweeping the magnetic mines which had been dropped there by the British. Meanwhile stores were coming forward by road from Kismayu, and the small lighterage port of Merca was quickly brought into use with the expert help of officers and men of the Merchant Navy who had been discovered in captivity at Mogadishu. Great quantities of stores of all kinds were found in Mogadishu, the most valuable items being 350,000 gallons of motor fuel and 80,000 gallons of aviation spirit. On the airfield were the remains of 21 aircraft. A particularly useful find was a handbook of every airfield and landing ground in Italian East Africa.

The 102nd Colonial Division was of no further account as a fighting formation, and the Duke of Aosta ordered General De Simone to withdraw what he could towards Jijiga. He was to send the 101st Division from the Upper Juba to Neghelli, where it would come under General Gazzera, the commander of the southern sector. General Cunningham instructed Generals Brink and Godwin-Austen to encourage the enemy to believe that the main British advance would be through Neghelli, his real intention being to exploit his advantage by pushing on as rapidly as possible to Harar. This was a large undertaking, although little opposition was expected, because there was no time to make forward depots, as there had been before the advance to the Juba. The first objective of importance was Jijiga, the junction of the roads from Harar and

Berbera. Of the 660 miles of single road from Mogadishu to Jijiga about one-third was very good and the remainder very rough, while north and south of Dagabur there were two stretches where there was no road at all. A small mobile force from the Nigerian Brigade with parties for road, water, and airfield reconnaissance was pushed boldly ahead to Dagabur.

On 11th March the 1st South African Brigade Group and 22nd East African Brigade at Brava were placed under command of the 11th African Division (Major-General H. E. de R. Wetherall), which now comprised 1st South African, 22nd East African, and 23rd Nigerian Brigades, while a large part of the divisional troops, including all the field and medium artillery, were South African. On the 13th the administrative situation permitted the remainder of the Nigerian brigade to move up to Dagabur. The division was then strung out on a single road, with its groups moving at about 48-hour intervals to permit the passage of the necessary supply columns. The Air Force, too, was moving up as quickly as it could. Advanced Air Headquarters and No. 2 Wing and its squadrons were in the Mogadishu area by March 2nd, and No. 41 Army Co-operation Squadron followed the moves of 11th African Division Headquarters as closely as possible. Full use was made of captured transport and all the workshop equipment that was found intact on the main Italian airfields; this made it necessary, as the advance went on, to send forward for repair work only airmen and stores. The opportunity was taken to send seven bomber aircraft back to Nairobi for overhaul.

At this stage air operations consisted mainly of offensive reconnaissances, from which it was clear that the enemy was withdrawing at least as far as Jijiga. The airfield at Dagabur was found abandoned and a detachment of No. 3 Fighter Squadron moved there close behind the leading troops; but the speed of the advance and the state of the road made the supply of bombs and petrol difficult and it was necessary to curtail operations by short-range aircraft accordingly. When it became clear that most of the Italian squadrons were now using the Diredawa airfields, it was decided to attack them heavily with the object of helping both the advance on Jijiga and the landing in British Somaliland. The attacks were made by No. 8 Squadron R.A.F. from Aden on two successive nights, and twice by low-flying fighters of the S.A.A.F. by day, and were very successful in destroying and damaging Italian aircraft.

The landing in British Somaliland began on March 16th with the arrival off Berbera of H.M. ships *Glasgow*, *Caledon*, *Kandahar* and *Kingston* with transports containing two battalions and supporting units from the garrison of Aden. After a short naval bombardment the landing was accomplished with little opposition, and the 70th Colonial Brigade melted away. The primitive port was quickly brought into working condition in the face of many difficulties—shortage of lighters, no cranes, no electric light, extreme heat, and frequent interruptions by the Kharif wind which scattered the sand and stirred up the surf. Yet within a week the 11th African Division was being partly maintained through Berbera, at a saving of 500 road miles. On 23rd March the 2nd South African Brigade, less one battalion, arrived by sea from Mombasa, and the third battalion, with all the transport, arrived a fortnight later, having come all the way by road. On April 8th Brigadier A. R. Chater was appointed Military Governor of British Somaliland and under his direction the country was rapidly re-settled.[1]

On March 17th patrols of the Nigerian Brigade entered Jijiga and next day found the enemy to be holding the Marda Pass, through which the road climbs out of the flat bush country straight into the tangle of steep hills of the Ethiopian highlands. This road was the only route through the first barrier of hills practicable for vehicles, and it was heavily blocked at the Pass. Of the three brigades known to be in the Harar area, it seemed that three battalions with two *bande* groups and pack artillery were holding the Pass, disposed over a wide front on each side of it. There was no question here of making the quick frontal thrust accompanied by an outflanking movement before which Italian resistance had hitherto always collapsed; General Wetherall decided to await the arrival of the South African Brigade and more artillery, which meant postponing his attack until 23rd March. Bombing attacks were made on the position itself, upon troop movements on the roads behind it and upon the railway between Diredawa and Awash. As operations were now within range of Italian fighters it was necessary to provide fighter escort for the bombers.

Early on 21st March reports reaching General Wetherall from patrols and deserters indicated that the enemy intended to withdraw. He decided that the Nigerian Brigade, supported by all the available artillery (three field batteries and one light battery), should attack as soon as possible, in spite of the fact that the ground to be covered was in full view of the enemy. The attack began at noon, the main thrust being made towards a prominent hill on the right, from which it was hoped to advance along the crest to the Pass itself. Fairly heavy small-arms and mortar fire was encountered, but by nightfall a secure lodgement had been made and during the night the enemy withdrew. British casualties had been seven killed and thirty-seven wounded.

The advance was held up by road demolitions until the afternoon of 22nd March, and next day the Italians were found in another

---

[1] For an account of the military government and re-settlement of this and other territories see Lord Rennell of Rodd: *British Military Administration in Africa 1941 to 1947* (1948).

strong position at the rocky Babile Pass; but after a brisk engagement they withdrew to a position on the Bisidimo river where they were attacked by the Nigerian Brigade on the morning of 26th March. The same morning General Cunningham learned from a B.B.C. broadcast that Harar had declared itself an open town. He at once had a message dropped on Harar stating that it would not be considered an open town unless the Italian troops withdrew from it. By noon the Nigerian Brigade had driven the enemy from the Bisidimo, whereupon an Italian civil official came out to parley, declaring that General Cunningham's message implied that the Italian troops would be permitted to withdraw unhindered. General Wetherall quickly disillusioned him and sent forward his armoured cars to Harar, where 572 prisoners and 13 guns were taken. At this point the 23rd Nigerian Brigade had advanced just under 1,000 miles in the last thirty-two days.

The lie of the roads now had an important bearing on the pursuit. A few miles south of Diredawa the road from Harar divided; one branch led steeply down to Diredawa itself and then followed the railway to Miesso, Awash and Addis Ababa, while the southern road led to Miesso through Asba Littorio. The 1st South African Brigade was called forward to take the lead through Diredawa and force the passage of the river Awash at the place of that name. But so badly obstructed was the Diredawa road that General Wetherall decided to divert the South Africans to the tortuous southern road, although there were demolitions here too. On March 29th an urgent request for help came from the Italians in Diredawa, where native deserters were attacking the white civilians. Two companies of the Transvaal Scottish entered Diredawa on foot, drove out the rebels in a street fight, and finally restored order next morning. Meanwhile the block on the main road was cleared much sooner than was expected, and the advance continued by both roads for about 100 miles to Miesso, at which point the brigade was held up for lack of petrol.

The 22nd East African Brigade (which had covered 910 miles in 12 days) then passed through, drove in an enemy rearguard, and made for the river Awash. This was a formidable obstacle, with the road and railway bridges both destroyed, and the enemy in position on the far bank. The 5th King's African Rifles, supported by 22nd Mountain Battery R.A. and 7th South African Field Brigade, quickly forced a crossing a little distance upstream, captured Awash village, and established a bridgehead under cover of which a new road bridge was built.[1] The speed of this move to the Awash had important results, for the Italians, relying on the road demolitions to hold up pursuit for several days, had withdrawn most of their forces through Asba Littorio with the intention of approaching

[1] See Photo 31.

Awash from the south. The advance of the British by the northern road outstripped them, and their way northwards was barred. There was no passable road to the west, so the remnants of the 13th and 14th Colonial Brigades were cut off, and a few days after the capture of Addis Ababa they surrendered.

Towards the end of March the Italian Air Force began to play a rather more active part. Their fighters, working from the Addis Ababa area and refuelling at intermediate landing grounds, began to attack our forward airfields, and although every effort was made to disperse aircraft on the ground a few were destroyed in these attacks and others damaged. The South African bomber squadrons were now very short of serviceable aircraft and had to be reinforced from Nairobi. A welcome reinforcement of twelve Gladiator fighters was received from No. 94 Squadron at Aden, whose airmen were being transferred to Egypt to be rearmed. As contact with the enemy was becoming more frequent, a system of close support was organized in the form of a 'close support flight' of four Gladiators from No. 3 Squadron, and four Hartbeests from No. 41 Squadron operating as bombers. This flight responded to calls from the forward troops for immediate help in clearing away light opposition.

The Aden Air Command had for months past been carrying out reconnaissance and escort tasks over the Red Sea and Gulf of Aden and successfully attacking Italian supply, fuel and ammunition depots and airfields. Among their principal targets were Assab, Dessie, and the railway through Diredawa. The withdrawal at the end of November of the two bomber squadrons to Egypt left the striking force at Aden very weak.[1] From February No. 203 Squadron was used, half as bombers, half as fighters, against targets in the Addis Ababa and Awash areas and traffic on the roads through Dessie. The necessary operational zones were decided upon by arrangement with No. 203 Group in the Sudan.

By 30th March General Cunningham felt certain that he would soon capture Addis Ababa. The Italian forces had just suffered a major disaster at Keren, and on his own front it was evident that the enemy's morale was deteriorating rapidly. The disorders at Diredawa had made him apprehensive of what might happen on a much larger scale in the capital after the Italian troops had withdrawn. He therefore suggested that touch should be made with the Duke of Aosta, whereupon General Wavell sent a message for the Duke which was dropped on Addis Ababa from the air on April 2nd. This stated that General Wavell was anxious to co-operate in ensuring the safety of Italian women and children so far as would be consistent with his military duty in continuing action against those of the Duke of Aosta's forces still in arms. General Cunningham would

---

[1] See page 261.

receive and report any proposals. The Viceroy replied that he would send an emissary to visit General Cunningham on 3rd April, while he pointed out to Rome that a pause in hostilities would be very useful in enabling troops in the Addis Ababa area to be transferred elsewhere.

Early on 3rd April General Cunningham received from General Wavell a telegram containing further instructions, but so corrupt as to be unintelligible. The Italian envoy arrived and was given General Cunningham's proposals: the Italians were to be responsible for protecting the women and children in Addis Ababa until the British could arrange to do so; essential services and staffs were to be left intact, with stores of food and fuel; and the railway between Awash and Addis Ababa was to be handed over with rolling stock and staff complete. The written Italian reply stated that the security and maintenance of the population of Addis Ababa had been provided for; that the British would be responsible for order as soon as they entered the city; and that Italian officers would assist with all necessary information. The Italian military command would under-take nothing further. However, the Duke of Aosta sent a verbal message by his envoy expressing his appreciation of the British initiative in the matter.

At this moment the Defence Committee in London, which had been kept informed by General Wavell, signalled to say that they disagreed with the instructions he had given to General Cunningham, and wished the terms to cover unconditional surrender and the handing over of the ships in Massawa harbour. General Cunningham, who was unaware of what General Wavell had written, could only ask for further guidance in view of the fact that his own lesser pro-posals had not been fully accepted by the Italians. Having received no reply by the time the road bridge over the Awash was ready, he ordered the advance to continue, but decided not to let his troops enter the city until General Wavell had had 24 hours in which to reply.

On April 4th, 5th and 6th bombers of Nos. 11 and 12 Squadrons S.A.A.F. and fighters of No. 3 Squadron S.A.A.F. attacked the airfield at Addis Ababa and reduced it to a shambles. About thirty aircraft were later found burnt out, damaged or crashed, a sight which, in General Cunningham's words, further increased the confidence of the troops in the efficiency of the support they had had from the Air Force. In the early hours of 5th April, as soon as the bridge was ready, the 22nd East African Brigade crossed the Awash and resumed its pursuit of the enemy known to be withdrawing not to Addis Ababa but to the south-west. At the same time there was much movement northwards from Addis Ababa towards Dessie. At 7.40 a.m. an Italian police officer arrived to ask that Addis Ababa should be occupied as soon as possible, as looting had begun. Brigadier Fowkes thereupon sent part of his force towards Addis Ababa, but General Cunningham stopped him short of the city and directed that a representative force should enter next morning. Early on April 6th, therefore, Major-General Wetherall, Brigadier Pienaar and Brigadier Fowkes, escorted by East African armoured cars, entered the city and drove to the Duke of Aosta's palace for the ceremony of formal surrender.

In southern Ethiopia the relief of the 2nd and 5th South African Brigades at Moyale and Mega in the first week of March had left the 21st and 25th East African Brigades under General Brink's command, while the 24th Gold Coast Brigade (12th African Division) was clearing up the area to the north-west of Mogadishu. On 17th March a small column from the latter brigade left Dolo for Neghelli, which it entered on the 21st after overcoming some opposition. Operations had to be undertaken to quell inter-tribal disturbances and to restore order generally, for the overthrow of the Italians had had an unsettling effect, and many fugitive native soldiers, as they scattered to their homes, readily turned bandit. General Godwin-Austen was, however, soon able to make a semblance of a threat from Neghelli and Yavello, though nothing on a large scale was administratively possible.

Early in April the 21st and 25th East African Brigades passed to the command of the 12th African Division, and later in the month the Headquarters, 1st South African Division, and the 5th South African Brigade sailed from Mombasa for Egypt. The 2nd South African Brigade, which had been moved to British Somaliland in the middle of March, was awaiting shipping to take it north also.

In a campaign of eight weeks the British had covered the 1,700 miles from the Tana to the enemy's capital and had destroyed, captured, or dispersed a large proportion of his total land and air forces at a cost of 501 battle casualties and the loss of eight aircraft. It is evident that the Italian commanders lost control of the battle at a very early stage, and that thereafter the resistance was piecemeal. There were many occasions when the ground greatly favoured the defence, but the unreliability of the colonial troops and the general lack of the will to fight prevented the most being made of these opportunities for imposing delay. With the rains and the monsoon approaching, delay was what the British had most to fear.

The Italian Air Force were never allowed to work to any methodical or practical plan—even if they had one. There were plenty of vulnerable targets, such as the port of Mombasa, the Kenya railway, the crossings of the Tana, the interminable columns of motor traffic, and the airfields, but the South African Air Force allowed the enemy little or no opportunity of attacking them, and, instead, the Italians lost numbers of aircraft destroyed in the air and on the ground. It is true that the Italian Air Force played a rather more active part in the close country of the Ethiopian Highlands, but here again they were prevented from making the most of the great opportunities for imposing delay.

The quantity of war material abandoned intact points to a failure to appreciate the difficulties that would face the British in the course of a long advance; otherwise the Italians would have taken care that the ports were thoroughly destroyed before being evacuated and that no stocks of petrol, food, machinery, engineer stores, and motor spares were left for the British to use.

Nevertheless, the British must be given credit for carrying out their plan with energy and determination. The squadrons of the South African Air Force took the initiative from the outset, and never lost it, and their success removed one of the Army's biggest anxieties. On land there was no lack of the offensive spirit, and all the contingents of this very mixed force showed great fortitude and adaptability. The efficiency of the administration, on which everything depended, was largely due to the help that General Dickinson and his successor received from the South African Government, who provided most of the transport and ancillary services by which their own troops and the East and West Africans were maintained and rendered mobile.

Mobility was in fact the keynote of the whole campaign; it gave formations the ability to manoeuvre and to take the opportunities offered of thrusting boldly forward regardless of what was happening on the flanks. To keep up the momentum of such a rapid advance it was necessary for the administrative staffs and services to exercise great foresight and resource; the campaign is full of examples of both.

Some idea of the size and difficulty of the struggle against the climate and the conditions is given by the following figures, which are for the whole of East Africa Force from June 1940 to May 1941: battle casualties, 1,154; cases of sickness or accidents, 74,550, of which over 10,000 were due to dysentery and the same to malaria; 744 of these died. These figures serve as a reminder not only of the medical implications of campaigning in an under-developed country but also of the organization necessary to provide the trained men with which to keep up the effective strength of the force. The very varied composition of East Africa Force made these problems no easier.

When General Cunningham was beginning the advance that led from Kenya to Addis Ababa, the Emperor of Ethiopia had entered his country and was waiting at Belaya, 70 miles from the Sudan border. Lieutenant-Colonel Wingate, the new head of 101 Mission, then went ahead in command of Gideon Force to clear the way for the Emperor's advance to the capital. It quickly became known that the Italians, alarmed by the nearness of supposedly numerous British and Ethiopian troops, the increasing hostility of the inhabitants, and the withdrawals on other fronts, were about to quit western Gojjam and retire to Bahrdar Giorgis and the neighbourhood of Debra Markos, thus releasing the very road that General Platt wished to secure. By 19th February Gideon Force reached the top of the escarpment at Matakal, by a route which was in a friendly area and by remarkable good fortune was found passable by the all-important camels. Hearing that Colonel Torelli's brigade from Dangila had retired towards Bahrdar Giorgis, Wingate sent Major A. C. Simonds with one company of the Frontier Battalion and one Operational Centre in pursuit, and decided to use the rest of Gideon against the Italian garrisons which remained on the main road. His intention was that Gideon should turn guerrilla; it would attack secretly and often, and so create in the minds of the Italians the same erroneous impression of strength that had led them to quit Dangila.

The Italian Commander of the brigade in Burye and Enjabara, Colonel Natale, withdrew from the latter place before Wingate could arrive, but he deferred the evacuation of Burye so long that Gideon Force was able to get into position to operate at points on the road east of Burye; the result was that Natale's withdrawal was made in distinctly difficult circumstances, and by 4th March, when he was hustled out of Burye, he had lost nearly 400 killed and wounded, 2,000 prisoners, 4 guns, and many vehicles and stores. The losses were not confined to the enemy, however, for the 2nd Ethiopian Battalion in a sharp engagement lost 100 men and so many animals that little more than a company played any useful part in subsequent operations.

The whole of the western loop of the important Gojjam road was now clear of the enemy, and with Colonel Torelli's brigade rendered passive by Major Simonds's small force the way was open for the Emperor to enter Gojjam. He climbed the escarpment at Matakal and was given a ceremonial reception by Dejesmach Mangasha at Enjabara on 12th March. Two days later he entered Burye.

The precipitate withdrawal of the Italians from Burye left them with the Debra Markos group of forts as their most advanced position. Colonel Wingate decided to push ahead to the Blue Nile with a part of his force, leaving the remainder under Lieutenant-Colonel J. E. H. Boustead, commanding the Frontier Battalion, to

37. Ras Hailu's army comes to surrender to the Emperor at Debra Markos, April 1941.

38. The bombing of the Caproni workshops at Mai Edega, near Gura, by the R.A.F. on 16th February 1941, showing hits on hangars and buildings.

*Facing p. 424*

lway bridge | Cameron Ridge | Brig's Peak | Sanchil | Dongolaas Gorge | Pinnacle | Fort Dologorodoc | Pimple | Zebar

39. Panorama of the Italian position in front of Keren, looking north-east from the main road just before it bends to enter the Dongolaas Gorge. The scar on the hillside below Sanchil and Cameron Ridge is the railway. On the right of the gorge the road is seen climbing the lower slopes of Pinnacle.

40. A Wellesley of the R.A.F. on its way to Keren.

41. Battle of Keren: site of the road-block in the Dongolaas Gorge. One of the first armoured cars to pass through.

42. Middle Hill, Little Alagi, and Amba Alagi from the southern slopes of Elephant.

*Facing p. 425*

43. Amba Alagi: view looking north from near the Dessie road. On the left Amba Alagi; farther to the right, Triangle.

invest Debra Markos. He had begun his march when Ras Hailu appeared with several thousand men, presenting a danger to Wingate's small force and exerting a bad influence on the local leaders who were sitting watchfully on the fence. Disregarding Wingate's peremptory order to surrender, Ras Hailu joined the Italians at Debra Markos. By this time General Nasi had realized how weak were the forces before which the Italians had retreated; he visited Debra Markos, replaced Colonel Natale by Colonel Maraventano, and announced that the Italians would return to Burye. As an earnest of their intentions they reoccupied Fort Emmanuel, half way back to Burye, while Torelli launched a simultaneous attack on the small force opposite Bahrdar Giorgis.

Wingate was thus faced with a crucial decision. He had the choice between falling back on Burye to afford closer protection to the Emperor and to his own stores and communications, and taking the initiative against the greatly superior forces at Debra Markos. Choosing the bolder course, he began a series of small sudden onslaughts and raids on the Italian positions. They were made by night, now here, now there, after very careful preparation, and required much of the Sudanese troops, whose skill, discipline, and dash were nevertheless equal to the occasion. When Wingate himself had to leave the forefront in order to resolve some acute problems on his line of communication, the battle was continued with such success by Colonel Boustead that on 4th April the Italians withdrew from Debra Markos and Ras Hailu surrendered.[1] Meanwhile Colonel Torelli's attack, made by five battalions supported by pack artillery, had been repulsed. On 6th April, the day of the fall of Addis Ababa, the Emperor entered Debra Markos and the first task of Gideon Force was accomplished.

General Cunningham's capture of Addis Ababa and General Platt's success in Eritrea placed the Patriot movement in a new setting. It was no longer a matter of fostering a stubborn revolt against unyielding Italians. Italian rule was crumbling and it was already possible to aim at getting the Emperor to his capital, there to take charge of his own forces, which, it was hoped, would play an increasing part in overcoming the remaining Italian resistance.

The new conditions brought about a dispersion of Gideon Force to a variety of tasks. General Platt's instructions to Wingate were to operate against roads over a wide area in order to prevent the Italian forces at Amba Alagi, Gondar, Dessie, and those in the south-west around Jimma, from reinforcing each other. Major Simonds and two Operational Centres had already set out for Begemdir, to the east of Lake Tana, with the object of keeping cut the main road through Debra Tabor. This small and very isolated force had many

---

[1] See Photo 37.

hardships to contend with, but it made several effective ambushes and succeeded in rousing a large number of Patriots to action, so that the Italians were firmly penned in their posts. Towards the end of April the company of the Frontier Battalion in front of Bahrdar Giorgis beat off another attack, and a few days later the Italian brigade retired along the eastern side of Lake Tana. Ras Hailu was still at Debra Markos, and, as his local prestige was high and his relations with the Emperor cool, it was necessary for part of the Frontier Battalion to remain there; it accompanied the Emperor to Addis Ababa and then followed the 1st South African Brigade north to Asmara. Part of the battalion went north from Debra Markos to Lake Tana (a march which took the Sudanese plainsmen in their cotton uniforms over a 14,000 foot pass in a blizzard) and by enterprise and deception they persuaded an Italian colonial battalion at Mota—the last remaining garrison in Gojjam—to surrender.

On 5th May General Platt handed over control of Patriot operations east and south of the big curve of the Blue Nile to General Cunningham, who exercised it largely through the Emperor and Brigadier Sandford. Colonel Wingate disliked this turn of events, for he was always happier giving orders than receiving them. Appropriately enough, however, it was he who completed the downfall of the Italian force he had chased through Gojjam.

When, in the middle of March, Wingate made his decision to deal with Debra Markos, he arranged for the chieftain, Lij Belai Zalleka, supported by Bimbashi W. Thesiger and Captain T. M. Foley of 101 Mission with a platoon of the Ethiopian Battalion, to block the escape route to the Blue Nile. Unfortunately Belai Zalleka, who had an understanding with Ras Hailu, did nothing, and the Italians crossed almost unhindered and turned north-east to Addis Derra. Bimbashi T. C. Johnson, with three platoons of the Frontier Battalion and one of the Ethiopian Battalion, had clung grimly to their heels, and continued to do so though his men were well-nigh starving and out of ammunition. By the last week in April two Operational Centres had joined the force in order to work on the Patriots, and Major D. H. Nott of 101 Mission took command of the whole.

By the end of the month, in spite of disappointments over Patriot help, Major Nott was pressing the enemy as they climbed the Addis Derra escarpment. By ingenuity and great activity by day and night he kept them in a state of unrest, and a successful raid followed by the repulse of a counter-attack stimulated the somewhat hostile local population to offer help and, better still, to bring in food. There seemed little hope, however, of dislodging the Italians.

On 15th May Colonel Wingate himself arrived from Addis Ababa, determined to settle with Colonel Maraventano. By coincidence the

Italians left their strong fort that night and made north for Agibar and the road to Debra Tabor and Gondar. Disregarding orders calling him to other tasks, Wingate followed like a bloodhound. He sent part of his force to cut the Italians off, and he himself was joined by 300 chosen Patriots and various others who came in to snap at the retreating enemy. On 19th May Maraventano was called upon by Wingate to surrender; he refused, but admitted that he had asked his superiors what he should do. The Italians continued to resist, and even made a counter-attack, but Wingate repeated his demand and added that as his troops were needed elsewhere he would have to leave the Italians to the mercy of the large Ethiopian force which had now collected. This was a bluff, for the Ethiopians were almost out of ammunition, but it worked. Colonel Maraventano duly received permission to negotiate, but what he did was to surrender, and 1,100 Italian and 7,000 colonial troops with their arms, equipment and transport were made prisoners, and were passed in review by the Emperor.

So ended the campaign of Gideon Force.[1] At its strongest it had numbered 50 officers, 20 British N.C.Os, 800 trained Sudanese, and 800 partly trained Ethiopians. It had a few mortars, no artillery, and no direct support from the air—though it was helped by the occasional bombing of enemy centres. It operated in wild and often hostile country, at the end of an immensely long line of communication along which nearly all the 15,000 camels died. With help from the local Patriots Gideon chased General Nasi's forces out of Gojjam in six weeks. Its total captures amounted to 1,100 Italians and 14,500 colonial troops, 12 guns, large quantities of machine-guns, rifles, and ammunition, and more than 200 transport animals.

In this remarkable achievement the honours were mostly to the Sudan Frontier Battalion. It was vital for Colonel Wingate to have a trained and disciplined unit as the hard core of his very mixed force, and this battalion showed great spirit and endurance, and responded to every call that his exacting and highly individual leadership made upon it. The amount of help from the local Patriots varied greatly, swayed as they were by tribal jealousies and internal politics; but the fact remains that from the first they presented a threat to the Italians, who had been having trouble from intractable chieftains like Mangasha and Nagash long before the British took a hand. As the impression of British strength grew, so did Patriot influence increase. With the news of the Emperor's triumphant return the number of desertions of Italian colonial troops mounted at a rate which no army could endure for long.

---

[1] The part played by Patriots and irregulars in the subsequent mopping-up of the Italian forces will be described in Volume II.

The outstanding feature of the whole enterprise was the success of the timing. The idea of turning the internal situation in Ethiopia to good account was not in itself remarkable; indeed, after French Somaliland had gone over to Vichy there seemed little else to be done. What is remarkable is the good fortune and the ability to make use of it which enabled the spadework of Sandford and his colleagues to produce its results, Gideon to take the field as a force capable of deep penetration, and the Emperor to enter his country as a conqueror—all these at the moment when General Platt had just become strong enough to attack the enemy's main forces in Eritrea, and General Cunningham was on the point of turning a success in Italian Somaliland into a threat to Addis Ababa. The combined effect of Gideon and the Patriots cannot be precisely assessed, but there is no doubt that it was considerable and that it reached its climax at exactly the right moment.

# CHAPTER XXIII

# VICTORY ON THE NORTHERN
# FRONT IN EAST AFRICA

*See Maps 25 and 26*

IT IS appropriate at this stage to glance back at events as they had appeared to the Duke of Aosta. After the capture of the frontier posts in Kenya and the Sudan in July 1940, and their success in British Somaliland in August, the Italian High Command in East Africa settled down to a defensive policy, qualified only by Marshal Badoglio's request that the Viceroy should study the possibility of moving into the Sudan at the same time as Graziani resumed his offensive and advanced to the Suez Canal. The arrival of the 5th Indian Division in Port Sudan and its move forward were of course noted by the Italian Intelligence, who greatly overrated the numbers of 'Anglo-Indians'. The British attack on Gallabat early in November made no particular impression on the Viceroy, nor, in his view, on Ethiopian opinion either, but by the end of the month he judged that further British attacks were imminent: from Gallabat towards Gondar, and from the Kassala area towards Agordat and Keren. He expected that these would begin almost simultaneously, and be followed later by offensives into Galla-Sidamo and against Kismayu, and perhaps also by an attempted landing in British Somaliland as a preliminary to an advance on Harar.

Faced with all these threats the Viceroy decided that the system of holding the reserves centrally would have to be modified, for although the Italians were on interior lines the distances were very great and motor fuel and tyres were already seriously short. He decided therefore to send forward some of his reserves nearer to the northern front, where he expected the first attacks to occur. If other fronts were also attacked they would have to look after themselves as best they could, playing for time and avoiding decisive engagements; he hoped that if the main attack were held, the lesser ones could be dealt with later. He accordingly allotted four colonial brigades and various other units from his reserve to General Frusci's northern sector and brought two more brigades to a central position at Dessie.

He then ordered the commanders in Eritrea, Amhara, and Gojjam —Generals Frusci and Nasi—to organize areas of resistance which were to be defended to the end. Mobile forces, chiefly colonial brigades, were to be concentrated between these areas and the frontier and were to hold positions from which they might issue to attack the enemy's flanks and rear. A retreat would have a very bad effect on the loyalty of the native troops and their conduct could not be foreseen, whereas the effect of checking the enemy's advance early would undoubtedly be encouraging and would mean that resistance might be prolonged for some months—into the rainy season. General Pinna was to continue to control the Air Force, but his units were to be dispersed throughout the sectors in order to be in close touch with the sector commanders.

The dispositions in the vital areas at the end of December were broadly as follows. In Eritrea General Frusci had three colonial divisions, three colonial brigades, and garrison and other troops. At Gallabat and Metemma he had three colonial brigades, and in and north of Gondar five Blackshirt battalions and numerous native *bande*. In Gojjam, General Nasi had four colonial brigades (twenty-three battalions in all) and several *bande*. In Shoa, around Addis Ababa, were the Savoia and Africa Divisions, which with other units amounted to twelve Metropolitan and Blackshirt battalions and twelve colonial battalions. Two more colonial brigades were in reserve at Harar. The ten colonial brigades, and Blackshirts and *bande* in the southern and Juba sectors, were regarded as a necessary minimum and could not be drawn upon.

By now the Viceroy was becoming increasingly pessimistic. He felt that his power to defend the Empire was declining; resources were being used up without being replaced, while economic difficulties were causing widespread discontent and a large part of the forces had to be ready to keep internal revolt in check. The morale of the British, on the other hand, had been stimulated by the success of their offensive in Cyrenaica, and their forces in the Sudan and Kenya were being rapidly strengthened. They were sure to attack before long, and the Viceroy expected the first blow to fall in the northern sector. He had confidence in General Frusci, however, and felt that he would be able to resist successfully; if he gave way 'everything would crumble'.

On 11th January the Viceroy explained that the British mechanized troops would have such an advantage on the flat ground that he wished to withdraw most of his forces from the Sudan-Eritrea frontier to the eastward of Tessenei, Sabderat, and Keru; none of the ground west of Agordat and Barentu would hamper mechanized action sufficiently. Next day Mussolini approved the Viceroy's proposals, expressed confidence in his leadership, and reminded him that the destiny of Africa would be decided by events in Europe. The Viceroy thereupon gave orders for the evacuation of Kassala,

Tessenei, and Gallabat-Metemma. These operations were to be supported by the Air Force.

The withdrawal was, on the whole, successful, though the 41st Brigade's action at Keru was disappointing. A disquieting feature was that continual retreating had greatly disheartened the forces, especially the native troops, and the Viceroy ordered that there was to be no withdrawal from Agordat and Barentu, and that a regiment of his best troops—the Savoia Grenadiers—was to be sent from Addis Ababa to Keren to help 'to close the gap absolutely'. On the other fronts all was comparatively quiet. An attack on Kismayu might soon occur, but he decided not to hold this place and ordered everything of use to the enemy to be removed from it. At the same time he ordered General De Simone to hold the line of the Juba to the last; however, after General Cunningham's first successful attack he told him to disengage and fall back to cover the Jibuti railway. In the west, the front between Lake Rudolf and the Blue Nile was quiet. In Gojjam there was always the chance of a flare-up if the Italians suffered many reverses, and the Viceroy decided to simplify the system of command by creating a new western sector under General Nasi to include the whole of Amhara and Shoa, thus leaving General Frusci responsible only for meeting the British advance in Eritrea, while General Nasi dealt with the Patriots.

By the middle of February the Duke of Aosta thought he had discerned the aims of the British, which were to capture the Italian colonies of Eritrea and Somalia and reconquer British Somaliland with their own forces, while helping the ex-Emperor with money, arms and aircraft to recapture Ethiopia. He protested to Rome that the forecasts which had been thought so pessimistic were being proved accurate. He had sent all the reinforcements he could spare to the northern sector, and realized that nothing could now reach the Empire from outside except aircraft, and for these he asked, if only to enable him to carry out essential reconnaissance. Out of 188 aircraft at the middle of February, only 67 were serviceable; a month later these figures had dwindled to 39 out of 150.

The Duke believed that so long as any Italians held out anywhere the Empire could not be called lost. He proposed therefore to give ground where resistance would be useless and gradually to concentrate his troops and Italian civilians in districts whose inhabitants were loyal, and to hold out there until the end of the war. He himself would fight and govern to the end. These plans were approved generally by Mussolini, who laid down that the Viceroy's object should be to gain time and await the outcome of events in Europe; he was not to abandon the capital unless absolutely compelled, because this would be politically equivalent to losing the Empire. As for aircraft, the loss of Benghazi had made it more difficult to fly them to East Africa, but they would continue to be sent. In the past two months 20 aircraft had arrived in this way, of which eight were fighters.

The Viceroy could now do little more than scrape up reinforcements for Keren and Massawa and hope for the best. On 16th March he wrote to Mussolini bemoaning his many difficulties, notably the lack of transport, anti-tank weapons, and aircraft, and the poor quality of the Italian officers serving in the Empire. The white troops varied—when led by good officers they were excellent —but the bulk of his forces were natives, who would follow strong masters for the sake of prestige and reward, and only the simplest could now believe that the Italians were stronger than the British. They regarded an order to retreat as a proof of weakness, and would desert sooner than obey if retreat meant leaving their own countryside and abandoning their families to unknown dangers. He commented bitterly on the poor spirit of the Italian civilians, who seemed unwilling to make the sacrifices imposed on them by the war. In response to his request for a forecast of the probable course of the war elsewhere, he was informed that the Axis powers would probably occupy Egypt by autumn 1941 and that the existence of organized forces in the Empire would obviously be a help towards conquering the Sudan and British East Africa. Therefore everything possible should be done to prolong the resistance of the remaining forces.

On 24th March the Viceroy ordered De Simone to resist as long as possible on the Awash, while Nasi's forces in Gojjam were to prevent the rebels from advancing into Shoa. Everything useful was to be removed from Addis Ababa, and all troops (other than those required for protecting the Italian civilians from the natives) were to move north and create a southern front for General Frusci. There would be three fortified areas of final resistance, in Eritrea, Gondar, and Galla-Sidamo. Once more the Duce approved, and exhorted the Viceroy to resist to the utmost.


As soon as Gazelle Force could get clear of the mines and demolitions to the east of Agordat, they pressed on boldly along the Keren road.[1] On the afternoon of February 2nd the leading troops reached the foot of the wall of hills that shuts off the Keren plateau from the valley below; a barrier pierced only by the Dongolaas gorge, which carries on its eastern slopes the road, and on its western the light railway. A length of the road, well inside the gorge, was found to be completely blocked, and Gazelle was brought to a halt. It took the British nearly eight weeks to break through this barrier of hills, which was resolutely defended by some of the best Italian troops.

---

[1] See page 401, Map 29 and Photo 39.

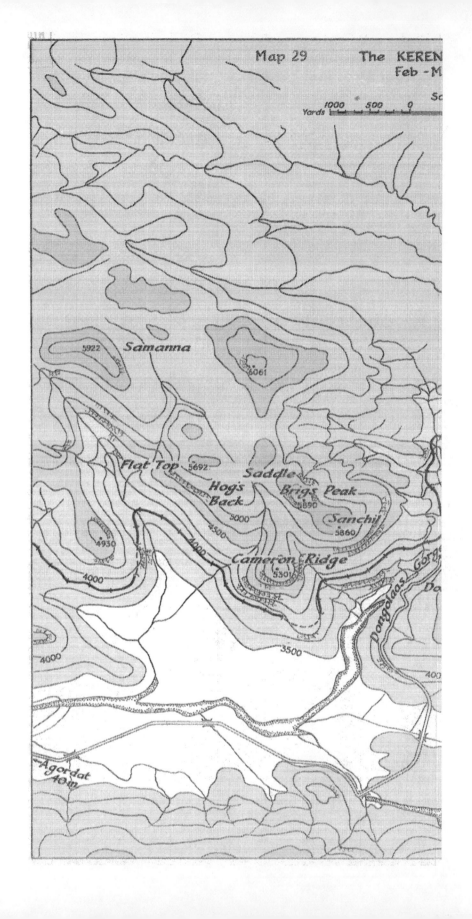

Map 29    The KEREN
Feb - M

Yards 1000    500    0    Sc

Samanna
5922
6061
Flat Top    5692    Saddle
Hog's    Brigs Peak
Back    5890
5000    Sanchil
4500    5860
4930
4000    Cameron Ridge
5301
4000
3500    Dongolaas Gorge    Do
4000
Agordat
4m

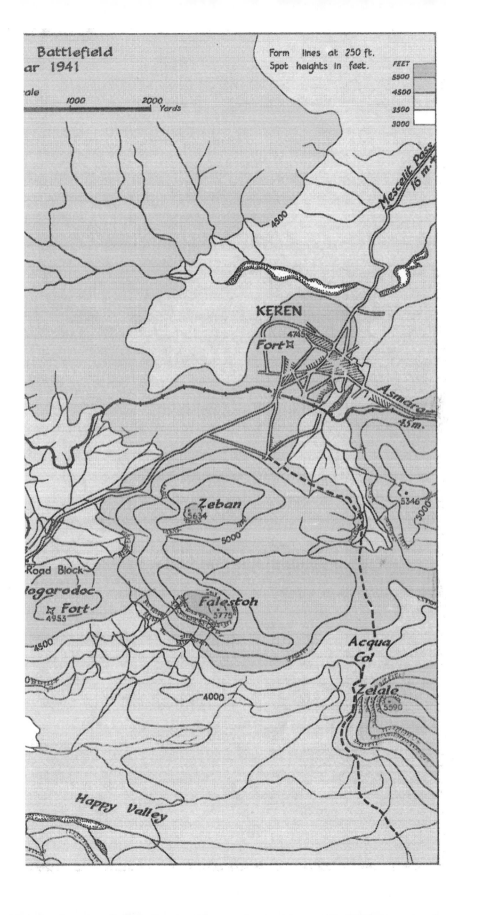

Battlefield
ar 1941

Form lines at 250 ft.
Spot heights in feet.

FEET
5500
4500
3500
3000

ale

1000          2000
                    Yards

Mescelit Pass
16 m.

4500

KEREN

4745
Fort ⌂

Asmara
45 m.

Zeban
5634

5346
5000

5000

Road Block
Dogorodoc
⌂ Fort
4953

Falestoh
5775

4500

Acqua
Col

Zelale
5390

4000

Happy Valley

To east and west of the gorge a number of peaks rise steeply to more than 2,000 feet above the floor of the valley. The names given to the features on the west were, in turn, Sanchil, Brig's Peak, Saddle, Hog's Back, and so on westward to Samanna. To the east the hills were slightly lower, though no less severe. Dologorodoc stood on a jumble of under-features and was surmounted by a concrete field-work—Fort Dologorodoc; farther east, Falestoh, joined to its northern neighbour, Zeban; eastward again, Zelale, or The Sphinx; and between Falestoh and Zelale was a tangle of rugged ridges across which a track led northwards to Keren over the precipitous Acqua Col. Sanchil and Brig's Peak were of particular importance because they gave observation all the way to Keren. Cameron Ridge was a halfway house to Sanchil and the other peaks to the westward.

On this formidable position the Italians had already deployed one colonial brigade and the three battalions of 11th Grenadier Regiment of the Savoia Division from the general reserve at Addis Ababa, a sure sign that the High Command fully intended to hold the plateau. In addition, on the route from Karora were the two brigades of the 1st Colonial Division, whose commander, General Carnimeo, was placed in command of the whole front. In the back area were the remains of three brigades that had been at Keru and Agordat. One brigade arrived next day from the general reserve at Addis Ababa, and in the Arresa area were the two brigades which had withdrawn through Barentu, and the one from Um Hagar.

Much as General Platt disliked the idea of a head-on collision, there was no other practicable way of reaching Asmara. The track through Arresa was useless for vehicles, while the route through Karora, which approached Keren from the north, might be of use for a diversionary move, but would not support the traffic of a large force. Therefore, although the 7th Indian Infantry Brigade Group from the Port Sudan area was ordered to advance by this route, it was imperative to try to open the main road through the Dongolaas gorge.

The commander of the leading brigade of the 4th Indian Division, Brigadier R. A. Savory, failed to find any way round to right or left of the position and decided to go for Sanchil and Brig's Peak, whose capture would have obvious advantages. From the afternoon of 3rd February the 11th Indian Infantry Brigade, with increasing artillery support, struggled hard for three days to secure a footing.[1] They actually reached both peaks, but lost them to counter-attacks, and after stiff fighting were left in possession of Cameron Ridge and some features to the west of it. Meanwhile 'I' tanks had probed the gorge and confirmed that the road-block was impassable.

---

[1] 11th Indian Infantry Brigade consisted of 2nd Cameron Highlanders, 1/6th Rajputana Rifles, 3/14th Punjab Regiment, with 3/1st Punjab Regiment attached.

GG

There is a sameness in the result of these early attacks, and of many later ones, which is understandable in the light of the conditions. The British artillery could bring down observed fire on the forward slopes of the hills, but targets beyond the crest were much more difficult to hit unless observation parties could establish themselves on the top. Aircraft were used for directing artillery fire, but they were not always available, the flying conditions were bad, and the technique was not highly developed. Moreover, if the targets were close behind the crest they were very difficult for guns, or even bomber aircraft, to hit. On the other hand, the whole of the British area was in full view from one point or another on the hills, so that to avoid observed artillery fire or to preserve secrecy it was necessary to move almost entirely by night.

The attack demanded great exertions of the infantryman, for the weather was hot and the hillsides waterless, and he had to clamber up rocks and over huge boulders, plod across shale, and often tear a way through thorn scrub and spear grass. Weapons, ammunition, and the minimum of other necessary equipment made, on a steep slope, an oppressive load. During the last hundred feet or so of rocky scramble the supporting artillery had to lift its fire, and an alert defender could man the crest from a covered position behind it and throw showers of small grenades among the exhausted climbers. When, in spite of all this, the attacking troops reached the crest, they were often too exhausted and depleted in numbers to withstand the counter-attacks which were usually made promptly and boldly, supported by the accurate fire of hidden mortars. Moreover, it was a laborious and costly task to supply the foremost troops with rations, ammunition, and water, for everything had to be carried up by men, so that perhaps a quarter of a battalion's numbers might be acting as porters at a time when every infantryman was badly needed. Perhaps worst of all was the heart-breaking labour of bringing the wounded off the hillside.

By 7th February, however, although the task was obviously hard, there was still no reason to doubt that the 4th Indian Division would be able to capture Keren, for on many previous occasions the Italians had started by resisting stoutly, only to give way when hard pressed. In any case, there was not enough transport to maintain both the 4th and 5th Indian Divisions in their present positions. The 5th, less its 29th Indian Infantry Brigade, was therefore withdrawn from the Barentu area to within easy reach of railhead at Kassala, and given the task of training intensively for mountain warfare.

The next phase of the battle was conducted by General Beresford-Peirse, who had now two Indian Infantry Brigades—the 5th and the 11th. He started with a night attack by the 5th (Brigadier W. L. Lloyd) against a new part of the front, Acqua Col. Desertions by

Italian colonial troops in this area had suggested that it might be a weak spot, and a rapid success here might lead to cutting off all the enemy west of the gorge. The difficulties were great, for no one knew the ground in detail, although it was clear that bad going, as well as the need for secrecy, would prevent the use of vehicles, and this meant a very long carry for the men.

The attack was made by the 4/6th Rajputana Rifles, and the other two battalions stood ready to push through along the track that led to Keren.[1] The leading companies gained their objectives, but with such losses that they were too weak to defeat the counter-attacks which followed. To the inevitable confusion of a battle in the dark in wild country was added a breakdown of signal communications. Next day the plan was given up, though covering positions on this eastern flank continued to be held.

General Beresford-Peirse decided, with General Platt's approval, to renew the attack on February 10th, this time on both fronts. The 11th Indian Infantry Brigade was first to capture Brig's Peak; then the 5th was to take Acqua Col, and if they were successful the 29th (Brigadier J. C. O. Marriott)—on loan from the 5th Indian Division—would pass through and exploit towards Keren. The outcome was that on the left Brig's Peak was twice taken and twice lost, while Saddle and Hog's Back were won and had to be given up. On the right, a gallant attempt to capture Acqua Col just failed, in the course of which Subedar Richpal Ram of the 4/6th Rajputana Rifles won a posthumous Victoria Cross. This battalion suffered 123 casualties from a strength already depleted by the previous attempt, while the other battalion engaged, the 4/11th Sikhs, lost over 100. General Beresford-Peirse considered that with this rate of losses he was not justified in renewing the attack; the enemy was fighting extremely well in a strong position, and seemed to be lavishly equipped with mortars and machine-guns. General Platt agreed with him and had further reconnaissances made to see whether the road to Arresa could be made into a main route. He came to the conclusion that its best use would be to support a small force which might divert a much larger enemy force from the Keren front. The main effort would still have to be made at Keren and both divisions would have to be used. The 4th Indian Division, in spite of steady daily losses, would have to maintain its present positions while the preparations for the large operation were being made.

The time required for these preparations depended mainly upon the number of vehicles that could be put on to the 180 mile journey forward of railhead, after the needs of troop-carrying and current daily maintenance had been met. The plan was to deliver into the

---

[1] 1st Royal Fusiliers and 4/11th Sikhs.

forward area enough petrol, food and stores for fourteen days, and a large quantity of ammunition. Railhead was pushed forward to Tessenei, to reduce road distance, but even so every possible vehicle was used to its utmost. In the forward area, too, there was much to be done; dumps of all kinds to be stocked, tracks to be made, signal communications to be laid, and the light railway put into running order, principally for removing the wounded; these tasks were all the harder for having to be done by night.

All this time the 7th Indian Infantry Brigade Group had been making its way south from Karora. Brigadier Briggs had now under his command one field battery diverted from Keren, one British and one Indian battalion, and the Free French *Brigade d'Orient*, formed of the 14th Battalion of the Foreign Legion from Egypt and the 3rd Battalion of the Chad Regiment from French Equatorial Africa. This force had occupied Mersa Taclai on the Red Sea, through which was established an improvised sea line of communication, and on 23rd February fought a successful engagement with the enemy at Cub Cub about 45 miles north-east of Keren.

With the capture of Agordat and Barentu, British fighter aircraft were able to reach the enemy's main air bases in Eritrea; attacks were at once made on Gura and Azoza airfields, and others were reconnoitred. During the first half of February efforts were mainly concentrated on supporting 4th Indian Division by offensive patrols, tactical and photographic reconnaissances, and bombing attacks on gun areas, dumps and communications—especially the railway between Asmara and Keren. Italian bomber activity was confined to the forward area, but fighters made several low-flying attacks on British airfields and at Agordat they destroyed or damaged thirteen aircraft.

From mid-February to mid-March, the period of preparation for the attack by both divisions, determined efforts were made to weaken the enemy in the Keren area and to cripple his Air Force. Eight Wellesleys of No. 223 Squadron one night dropped 10,700 lb of bombs on the Caproni workshops at Mai Edega;[1] two days later Wellesleys and Hurricanes attacked them again by day, after which all the main buildings had been extensively damaged. Hurricanes carried out several offensive patrols as far as Gura and Asmara, meeting little opposition. Asmara and its airfield were heavily attacked on 19th February, Massawa airfield on the 21st, and Makalle on the 23rd. The last was a particularly successful attack, made at the long range of 150 miles, and caused eight aircraft to be burnt out and others damaged. This sustained offensive practically drove the Italian Air Force out of Eritrea, and reduced it to almost complete inactivity. In addition, as H.M.S. *Formidable* (Nos. 826

---

[1] See Photo 38.

and 829 Squadrons, Albacores) passed up the Red Sea[1] her aircraft made several attacks on Massawa, and as a pendant to all these operations British aircraft dropped thousands of pamphlets in Amharic and Tigrean script, which, according to prisoners' statements, caused many Italian colonial troops to desert.

By 1st March General Platt had decided upon his outline plan. The attack was to be begun by 4th Indian Division to the left of the Dongolaas gorge, followed by 5th Indian Division on the right. The objective on the left was the line of peaks from Sanchil to Samanna; and for the 5th Indian Division Fort Dologorodoc was eventually chosen, with exploitation towards Falestoh and Zeban. General Heath elected to attack from west of the gorge, because only there could any covered assembly positions be found. An important point was that the bulk of the artillery could support first one division and then the other without changing position, and it was thought that the gently falling ground behind Fort Dologorodoc promised good fire effect to the artillery and aircraft. Particular attention was paid to providing good communications between the various Army headquarters and the Royal Air Force. Finally, in order to keep the enemy stretched as much as possible, the 7th Indian Infantry Brigade Group, now only fourteen miles north-east of Keren, was to make a further advance, while on the Arresa front a mobile detachment consisting of Skinner's Horse and units of the Sudan Defence Force was set up with orders to simulate a much larger force.

On 8th March the 5th Indian Division—now rejoined by its third Brigade, the 9th (Brigadier F. W. Messervy)—began to move into the forward area as unobtrusively as possible. Though the Italians must have expected a renewal of the attack they do not seem to have had any particular suspicions, for they did nothing to interfere; their chief concern at the time was with the harassing effect of the British air attacks. Their patrols showed some enterprise to the west of the main positions, and the newly arrived 51st (Middle East) Commando was sent up to counter their activities.

Early on the morning of 15th March a stream of Blenheims, Wellesleys and Hardys of Nos. 14, 47, 223 and 237 Squadrons began an intense bombardment of Italian gun areas and infantry positions, and at 7 a.m. the artillery of both divisions and 212th and 233rd Medium Batteries R.A. opened fire in support of 4th Indian Division's attack. This was made by 11th Indian Infantry Brigade reinforced by two battalions of the 5th Indian Infantry Brigade and 2/5th Mahratta Light Infantry. Sanchil and Brig's Peak were taken —but not for long; Hog's Back and Flat Top were taken and held; and on the extreme left the weakened 5th Indian Infantry Brigade

---

[1] On her way to replace H.M.S. *Illustrious*.

won a foothold on Mount Samanna and was then checked. Nevertheless General Platt and General Heath considered that a sufficient diversion had been caused, and at 10.30 a.m. 2nd Battalion The Highland Light Infantry, under command of the 9th Indian Infantry Brigade, attacked across the gorge towards Dologorodoc. They were soon stopped by fire, which was especially severe in enfilade from the lower slopes of Sanchil, and it was decided not to renew the attack until after dark. That night the 4th Indian Division made another attempt to take Brig's Peak and Sanchil without success, and Hog's Back and Flat Top were held against counter-attacks. On the right of the gorge, however, 3/5th Mahratta Light Infantry and 3/12th Frontier Force Regiment of 9th Indian Infantry Brigade secured the outlying features on the south-west of Mount Dologorodoc soon after midnight. Brigadier Messervy took the opportunity to send his reserve battalion, 2nd West Yorkshire Regiment, at the Fort from the south, and by 6.30 a.m. they had captured it with very slight loss. The enemy made several counter-attacks, which were all repulsed.

The next night, March 16th/17th, General Platt put in his last reserve—4/10th Baluch Regiment and 3/18th Royal Garhwal Rifles —to make yet another attempt on Sanchil and Brig's Peak; once again the Italian resistance was too strong. The same night, on 5th Indian Division's front, an attempt to exploit the success at Fort Dologorodoc was made by passing the 29th Indian Infantry Brigade (1st Worcestershire Regiment, 3/2nd Punjab Regiment and 6/13th Frontier Force Rifles) through to assault Falestoh and Zeban. The ground proved to be very difficult, the barrage was lost, and during the morning the leading troops were pinned down short of their objectives by intense fire and virtually isolated. The Royal Air Force came to the rescue at very short notice by dropping ammunition and rations packed in improvised containers. During the night these troops were withdrawn from their untenable position.

There was, however, one encouraging outcome. The attack had made it possible for the engineers to examine the road block, and they estimated that 48 hours' work would be required to clear it for tracked vehicles.[1] The task, viewed from a distance, had seemed much more formidable, and the idea of attempting it had been discarded. Even now it could not be done until covering positions had been secured on each side of the gorge. General Platt ordered 5th Indian Division to seize these positions, clear the block, and then pass a force of 'I' tanks and Bren carriers through to Keren. The date was fixed as 25th March, to give time for the necessary preparations.

Between 18th and 22nd March the Italians attacked Fort Dologorodoc no less than seven times and suffered damaging losses.

---

[1] See Photo 41.

General Lorenzini, who was respected by both sides as an inspiring leader, was killed on this front. General Frusci reported daily to the Viceroy that his troops were suffering heavily, especially from air attacks and artillery fire. By 20th March the strength of units had been reduced by a third, and thereafter Frusci's reports show increasing anxiety. General Platt's forecast was being amply borne out, for he had said: 'It is going to be a bloody battle . . . against both enemy and ground. It will be won by the side which lasts longest.'

Early on 25th March the attack up the gorge took place: 9th Indian Infantry Brigade on the right, 10th on the left. A good deal of artillery, mortar, and machine-gun fire was met but both brigades reached their objectives beyond the block and captured nearly 500 prisoners, many of them Bersaglieri. The Sapper and Miner Field Companies of 5th Indian Division, working in rotation and hampered by mortar and shell fire, cleared a passage through the road-block by the afternoon of the 26th. A force of 'I' tanks and Bren carriers, known as Fletcher Force, was ordered to make its way through to Keren at dawn.[1]

During the afternoon there had been a marked lessening of Italian activity. The Italians had seen with anxiety their failure to prevent the clearing of the road, and on 26th March General Frusci reported that the situation was critical and that it would no longer be possible to stop the British tanks. That night the Italians gave up the struggle and skilfully withdrew the bulk of their troops and guns, leaving only a screen. Next morning, as the British tanks picked a way across the road-block, white flags appeared on Sanchil and soon the 4th Division's patrols were moving forward across the ground they had fought so hard to gain. By 7 a.m. the air reported that the enemy was clearing Keren, and Colonel Fletcher was ordered to pursue. The tanks entered Keren an hour later and moved on to the Habi Mantel gorge where they awaited the other vehicles which had been delayed by the difficulties of passing the Dongolaas gorge.

At Keren the British had 536 killed and 3,229 wounded; the Italians, according to General Frusci, had 3,000 killed. The battle was not the last of the campaign, but it was decisive, for although the Italians managed to withdraw a large amount of their artillery, and some of their infantry, they never fought with the same determination again. They had seen that General Platt could not manoeuvre

---

[1] One squadron less one troop of 4th Royal Tank Regiment, and about 50 Bren carriers of units of 4th and 5th Indian Divisions, all under the command of Lieutenant-Colonel B. C. Fletcher, Highland Light Infantry, who had been in temporary command of 10th Indian Infantry Brigade until March 21st, when Brigadier T. W. Rees took over.

them out of Keren, and, although his diversionary action was as successful as could be expected, they can never have doubted that the vital point was at Keren. They knew that they must hold the hills astride the Dongolaas gorge and retake any that they lost. This simple plan succeeded until their casualties became more than they could bear.

It is not possible to say when General Frusci felt that the battle was lost, but it is worthy of note that he seems to have judged that the last two battalions of the Savoia Grenadiers arrived from the general reserve too late to influence the action. They were used in rearward positions where they achieved nothing. It is remarkable, too, that the Italians never tried to drive the British from Cameron Ridge or to interfere with their preparations for the set battle. Even a limited counter-attack or one or two raids might have caused a lot of delay, and General Platt expected that they would attempt something of the sort.

An active hostile Air Force would have immeasurably increased the hazards and difficulties facing the British. The Army had therefore good reason to be grateful to the Royal Air Force, which by its bold and sustained operations drove the enemy's air bases farther and farther back and caused heavy losses in aircraft, results to which the squadrons from Aden and the South African squadrons farther south contributed their share. The consequence was that Italian aircraft interfered very little during the vulnerable stages of the build-up and deployment, and played a negligible part in the critical phase of the battle. By 22nd March the Italians had only 37 serviceable aircraft in the whole of East Africa, which is the measure of the Air Force's success.

To General Wavell belongs the credit for allotting to the Eritrean front the two divisions most likely to adapt themselves quickly to the conditions and the best able to work in double harness. Many of the commanders and troops had had experience of mountain warfare, but not against an enemy who possessed aircraft and artillery and numerous mortars, machine-guns, and grenades. This formidable weight of fire made progress very slow, but the enemy, though fighting with determination, was suffering heavily also. And as in every hard fought battle there were many instances of great gallantry and tenacity on both sides.

The British commanders, having seized the initiative, never lost it and stuck doggedly to their task, supported by the resolution, endurance, and courage of the regimental officers and men. They were devotedly served by the whole administrative machine: food, water, and ammunition were sufficient—nearly 200,000 rounds were delivered to the batteries during March—and the arduous task of evacuating the wounded and sick was well done. The achievements of the 4th and 5th Indian Divisions, who formed the bulk of the British force, drew a generous tribute from the Prime Minister.

As soon as Keren was captured the Air Force began to harass the Italian columns retreating to Asmara and towards Gondar. The winding road from Keren to Asmara was well suited to delaying tactics, and the enemy had made ready to oppose the British advance near Ad Teclesan. He realized that this was the last ditch before Asmara, and that when Asmara fell Eritrea was lost.

On 31st March, after a day-long fight, the Teclesan position fell to the 9th Indian Infantry Brigade, with 460 prisoners and 67 guns. Next day the Italian authorities in Asmara surrendered the town.

Our naval and air forces were at last rewarded for the long watch on Massawa. On the evening of 31st March three of the remaining six large Italian destroyers had put to sea. Their plan, it is believed, was to raid the Gulf of Suez and then scuttle themselves. The *Leone* grounded shortly after sailing; next morning she sank and the operation was cancelled. Aircraft had reported the stranded *Leone* and had seen another destroyer returning to Massawa; the third reached port unseen. On 2nd April all five remaining destroyers sailed in company to attack Port Sudan and then sink themselves. Their departure was reported by aircraft from Aden and at dawn on the 3rd four of them were seen some twenty miles east of Port Sudan by Swordfish of Nos. 813 and 824 Squadrons, which had flown from the *Eagle* at Alexandria to Port Sudan a few days before. These Swordfish, reinforced by five Blenheims of No. 14 Squadron, sank the *Sauro* and *Manin*. The hunt went on, and the *Pantera* and *Tigre* were next found close inshore south of Jeddah, where they were being abandoned. Here Wellesleys of No. 223 Squadron from Port Sudan and H.M.S. *Kingston* destroyed them. The missing destroyer *Battisti* had developed a defect during the previous night and had been scuttled. All six destroyers were thus accounted for. The Italians, however, had one success before Massawa fell. The cruiser *Capetown* was torpedoed by one of the remaining Italian motor torpedo boats, and after being towed to Port Sudan she had to go to Bombay for permanent repairs.

The 4th Indian Division was already under orders to go back to Egypt, leaving the 7th Indian Infantry Brigade Group under the command of General Heath. On General Platt's orders he sent light mobile forces southward to Adowa and Adigrat, and turned to his main task of capturing Massawa. His first action was to send an ultimatum to Admiral Bonetti, commanding at Massawa, by the unusual means of ringing up his headquarters on the undamaged telephone line. If the ships in Massawa were scuttled, the British would take no responsibility for feeding or evacuating the Italian population in Eritrea or Ethiopia, to which the reply was that the Duke of Aosta had ordered resistance and no guarantee could be given regarding the ships.

The 7th Indian Infantry Brigade Group soon reached the northern part of the Massawa defences, and by 5th April the ring was closed by 10th Brigade and the *Brigade d'Orient*. Admiral Bonetti was called upon to surrender, but after consulting Rome he refused. Early on 8th April an advance by 7th Indian Infantry Brigade Group was resolutely opposed, but a simultaneous attack by 10th Indian Infantry Brigade and B Squadron 4th Royal Tank Regiment bit deeply into the western defences and the Free French troops broke into the south-western sector. Bombers of Nos. 47 and 223 Squadrons co-operated throughout, principally by attacking the Italian guns, which were very active. Early in the afternoon Admiral Bonetti surrendered with 9,590 men and 127 guns. Much damage had been done to the harbour, all the ships had been scuttled, and a great deal of equipment and supplies had been dumped in the sea. Nevertheless a sea supply line was quickly organized; by 27th April the Massawa-Asmara railway was cleared for traffic; and by 1st May the main line of communication for 5th Indian Division was running through Massawa.

All organized opposition in Eritrea was now over; all the Italian warships had been accounted for, and the handful of aircraft remaining in Ethiopia presented no danger. The strategic object of the East African campaign, which was to remove the threat to shipping through the Red Sea, had thus been attained. It was not long before this victory had a most valuable sequel, for on 11th April President Roosevelt declared the Red Sea and Gulf of Aden to be combat zones no longer. This meant that ships of the United States could now enter these waters and lighten the task of the overtaxed British shipping.

A few days after the loss of Keren the Viceroy saw that there was no longer any hope of retaining a hold on Eritrea, and decided upon a centre of resistance at Amba Alagi instead. On the 30th he telegraphed to Mussolini that the very rapid crumbling, forecast a long time ago, had set in. 'It only remains for us to resist wherever we can and for as long as we can for the honour of the flag.' The Italian forces in Ethiopia were now concentrating in three centres; one in Galla-Sidamo, under General Gazzera, one at Gondar under General Nasi, and one on the Asmara-Dessie road at Amba Alagi, to which the Duke himself went on 3rd April, and where he united the remainder of his own reserve troops with the remnants of General Frusci's Eritrean Army.

General Platt had only enough troops to fight one serious engagement at a time, and in order to remove all threat to the Sudan frontier he proposed to deal first with General Nasi. He began, therefore, to consider how to tackle the formidable Wolchefit Pass on the road to Gondar, but at this moment came General Wavell's order to clear the Dessie-Asmara road as quickly as possible, so that it could be used for the transfer of forces northward. General Platt accordingly gave the task of watching Wolchefit to a Motor Machine-Gun Group of the Sudan Defence Force and a host of Patriots under Major B. J. Ringrose, and ordered 5th Indian Division to destroy the enemy force at Amba Alagi.

The commander of the 5th Indian Division was now Major-General A. G. O. M. Mayne, who had replaced General Heath on his promotion to command a Corps in Malaya. In spite of the prompt arrival of a nucleus of the British Military Administration,[1] there were many duties in Asmara and Massawa for which troops were still required, and the force available for further operations against the Italians was no more than the mobile Fletcher Force, the 29th Indian Infantry Brigade, two battalions (one from 9th Indian Infantry Brigade, one from 10th), one Commando, two field regiments and one medium battery. In the air there was No. 237 (Rhodesian) Squadron (Gladiator, Lysander and Hardy), supplemented by a detachment of Wellesleys of No. 47 Squadron. A large force of Ras Seyoum's Patriots, led by Lieutenant-Colonel W. Rankin of the Sudan Defence Force, was sent to work round behind Amba Alagi, and by 27th April had captured Socota.

Approaching from the south was the 1st South African Brigade Group, which had left Addis Ababa on 13th April in consequence of General Wavell's order to General Cunningham to help to secure the use of the road between Addis Ababa and Asmara. After making its way past extensive demolitions the Brigade came under shell fire from a prepared position at Combolcha, a few miles south of Dessie. Here a strong force, with ample artillery and good observation, was holding a line of hills to the east of the road and roughly at right angles to it. To the west of the road the ground was exposed and marshy. Running towards the enemy's position was another line of hills, roughly parallel to the road. Brigadier Pienaar decided to establish himself on these hills and then make a plan for attacking the main position.

This entailed a methodical advance by the infantry, while the twelve field guns of 4th Field Brigade and one section of 1st Medium

---

[1] For a full account see Lord Rennell of Rodd: *British Military Administration in Africa 1941 to 1947.*

Brigade S.A.A. proceeded to gain the mastery over the far more numerous Italian guns. Progress by the infantry was slow, for everything had to be manhandled over steep and rough going, but by the afternoon of 19th April the 1st Duke of Edinburgh's Own Rifles completed their long advance by occupying a hill which overlooked the main Italian position. The enemy at once tried to retake this hill, but failed with considerable loss, and many deserters began to come in. Early on the 22nd Brigadier Pienaar made his attack. He had been joined by a large band of Patriots under Lieut. A. G. S. Campbell, of The Black Watch, which proved most useful in locating and harrying the enemy's flanks. The 1st Royal Natal Carbineers moved across country and attacked the enemy's left flank, which they proceeded to roll up, and the 1st Transvaal Scottish captured the remaining hills. Much was due to the efficiency of the artillery support. By the early afternoon the enemy was in full retreat.

The results of this successful action were remarkable. Dessie fell after little further opposition. In all over 8,000 prisoners, of which a large proportion were Italians of the Africa Division, were captured together with 52 guns and large quantities of other weapons, lorries, stores, and petrol. Nineteen burnt-out aircraft were found on Combolcha airfield. The South African casualties were nine killed and thirty wounded, a tribute to Brigadier Pienaar's careful plan and a proof of the saying that hard work saves casualties. The physical exertion of carrying heavy loads up steep hills at an altitude of well over 6,000 feet was very great, especially for men who had been lorry-borne for so long. The further advance towards Amba Alagi was delayed for some days by elaborate road blocks, but Campbell's scouts were able to push ahead, and at Quoram joined forces with Rankin's Patriots.

Meanwhile General Cunningham was finding that his operations were being continually hampered by requests from Italian civilians for protection against marauders. He therefore invited the Duke of Aosta to receive another communication about the safety of Italian women and children. The Duke agreed, and General Cunningham explained to an envoy that only if the Italian forces unconditionally laid down their arms could he be responsible for the protection, feeding, and evacuation of Italian nationals. The Duke considered this proposal to be an attempt to extort surrender by threats, and on 20th April rejected it.

The stronghold in which the Duke had installed his headquarters was situated halfway between Asmara and Dessie, where the road climbs by a series of hairpin bends to cross a steep mountain barrier at the Toselli Pass, nearly 10,000 feet high.[1] To right and left of the road stretched a tangle of precipitous rocky heights, dominated by

---

[1] See Map 30 and Photos 42 and 43.

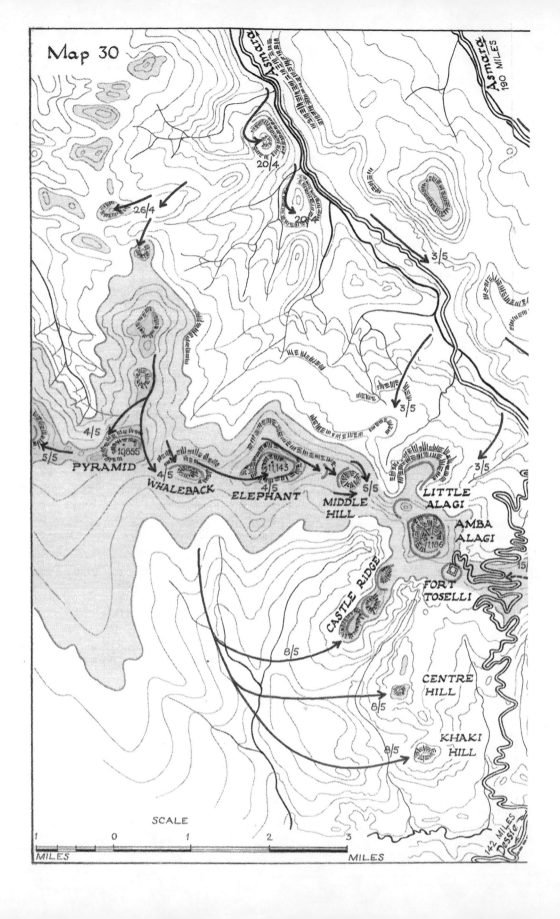

Map 30

Asmara

Asmara
190 MILES

20/4

26/4

20/4

3/5

3/5

3/5

3/5

4/5
10855
5/5
PYRAMID
4/5
WHALEBACK
4/5
11,143
ELEPHANT
4/5
5/5
MIDDLE
HILL
LITTLE
ALAGI

AMBA
ALAGI
11,186
15/

CASTLE RIDGE
FORT
TOSELLI

8/5
CENTRE
HILL
8/5

8/5
KHAKI
HILL

142 MILES
Dessie

SCALE

1          0          1          2          3

MILES                                      MILES

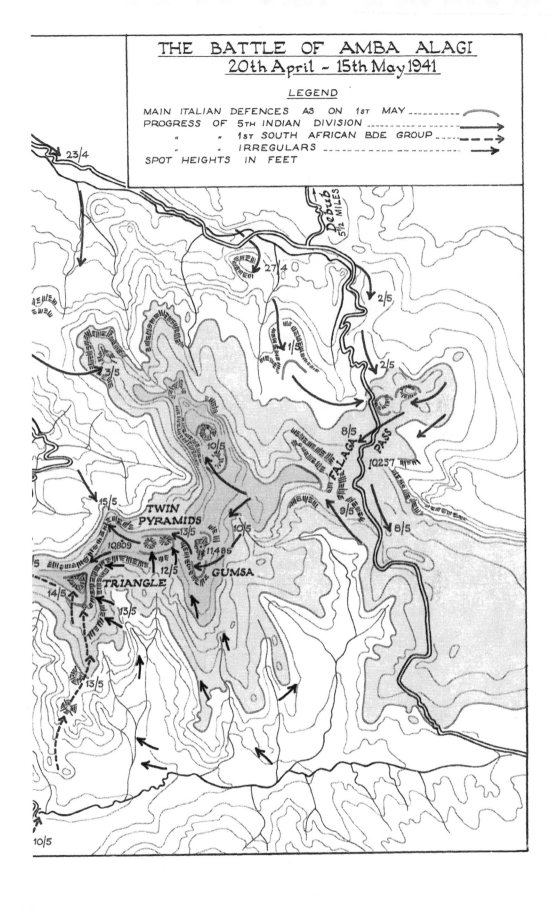

# THE BATTLE OF AMBA ALAGI
## 20th April ~ 15th May 1941

### LEGEND

MAIN ITALIAN DEFENCES AS ON 1ST MAY
PROGRESS OF 5TH INDIAN DIVISION
      "      "   1ST SOUTH AFRICAN BDE GROUP
      "      "   IRREGULARS
SPOT HEIGHTS IN FEET

Amba Alagi—11,186 feet—less than a mile from the Pass itself. It was here that General Frusci had assembled a force estimated at four or five thousand men, with perhaps thirty guns. (This was in fact an under-estimate.) The neighbouring peaks had been fortified, a quantity of barbed wire put up, and cave shelters and gun pits constructed; water was sufficient but not abundant, and there was food for three months.

While his troops were moving forward, General Mayne made his plan. He thought the Italian position to be very wide for the number of its defenders, and by stretching them hoped to create a weak spot. There were two possible lines of advance apart from the main road. On the east a track led to the rugged Falaga Pass, seven miles from the Toselli Pass; between them were the features Gumsa, Twin Pyramids and Triangle—all fortified. On the west a spine of defended hills (Pyramid, Whale Back, Elephant, Middle) led to Little Alagi and Amba Alagi itself. General Mayne decided to demonstrate against the centre and east and to attack from the west, a decision which showed great confidence in his troops, for it committed them to a long approach over almost pathless hills. He considered that the enemy would be unlikely to expect a force of any size to attack from this direction.

Fletcher Force, which had been probing towards Falaga Pass, made such good progress, and was receiving so many deserters from Italian colonial troops, that on May 2nd General Mayne ordered Colonel Fletcher to increase the pressure. An attempt was accordingly made to capture the Pass, but without success. The same day, 3rd May, 3/18th Royal Garhwal Rifles made the demonstration against the centre, and early on 4th May 6/13th Frontier Force Rifles and 3/2nd Punjab Regiment of 29th Indian Infantry Brigade, supported by timed artillery concentrations, took Pyramid, Whale Back and Elephant. A further advance over the bare ridge to Middle Hill was deferred until dawn next day. This hill was duly taken under a barrage, but daylight disclosed strong wire obstacles across the narrow neck which led onward, and 1st Worcestershire Regiment were pinned down by machine-gun fire.

There seemed little chance of further progress from Middle Hill, but as Fletcher Force had discovered that the enemy's eastern flank did not extend far beyond the Falaga Pass, General Mayne decided to transfer his main effort to that side. He quickly organized a brigade group, gave Colonel Fletcher the headquarters of 9th Indian Infantry Brigade, and ordered him to work round the eastern flank on May 7th with a view to attacking Falaga Pass.

To add to the enemy's uncertainties, 6/13th Frontier Force Rifles (29th Brigade), after a long advance by night in the rain, made a surprise attack, and occupied two outlying hills (Khaki and Centre) to the south of the Toselli Pass. The same day, May 8th, General Cunningham placed the 1st South African Infantry Brigade Group (less one battalion) at General Platt's disposal, retaining responsibility only for its supply. By May 10th the leading South African troops were only twenty miles away, with Rankin's Patriots and Campbell's scouts close by. These irregulars proved to be a rather mixed blessing, because they were joined by many who were not amenable to control and whose main object was loot—British or Italian. By this time the 3/12th Frontier Force Regiment (9th Brigade) had taken the Falaga Pass and had reached Gumsa, capturing a large number of prisoners and obtaining excellent observation for the artillery. The net was tightening, but the way from Gumsa to Amba Alagi was seen to lie along a saw-tooth ridge, of which each tooth was defended—a very uninviting prospect. Rain added its difficulties, particularly to the exacting business of supplying the troops on the heights. The nights were bitterly cold.

General Mayne now decided to attack the features Twin Pyramids and Triangle from the south, and on 11th May he flew to arrange with Brigadier Pienaar for the operation to begin on the 13th. While the preparations were going forward the Patriots made a private and independent attack on Twin Pyramids, and most gallantly and astonishingly captured them. Encouraged by this, they tried, again independently, to storm Triangle, but this time were bloodily repulsed. Nevertheless, the attempt assisted the South Africans, whose attack, methodically pressed against stiff opposition throughout 14th May, together with pressure by the 9th Indian Infantry Brigade, induced the Italians to abandon Triangle that night. It was not necessary to attack Fort Toselli, for the enemy's endurance was exhausted.

Negotiations for an armistice began on the 16th and were conducted at Amba Alagi by Colonel D. Russell of the divisional staff, after the Italian envoy, General Volpini, had been murdered by marauders while on his way to General Mayne's headquarters. The Italians were anxious to escape humiliation and asked that the Viceroy and his troops should be allowed to remain at Amba Alagi, under arms but non-belligerent. This novel form of parole was refused, and a little later the Italians had to accept surrender with the honours of war. On 19th May the garrison, about 5,000 strong, marched past a Guard of Honour and was then disarmed, and next day the Duke with his personal staff made his formal surrender to General Mayne before being conducted to General Platt.

Amba Alagi differed from Keren in that there was far more scope for manoeuvre. The features of the battle were the flexibility of the British plan and the cross-country mobility of the troops over very difficult ground and in appalling weather. After the ring was closed the only question was how long it would take to overcome the defence, but as the perimeter shrank and the bombardment by air and artillery became more concentrated the morale of the garrison seems to have sunk rapidly. The Viceroy's anxiety about the recovery and care of the wounded (which he reported to Rome on 13th May) was no doubt shared by his men, who were alarmed also by the activities of the irregulars. Indeed, many Italians surrendered in order to avoid falling into their hands.

Of the 325 Italian aircraft in East Africa when the war began, and the 75 which were flown in at various times, there now remained a negligible number in a serviceable state. The Italian records show 250 as lost on all the East African fronts by the middle of March; the corresponding British losses were 138. Of the 350,000 or so men with which the Italians entered the war there now remained the garrisons of the defended posts in and around Gondar, swollen by fugitives from the north, and seven colonial divisions in Galla-Sidamo which included the remains of General De Simone's force. These would have to be rounded up, but everything else had been destroyed, captured, or dispersed.

The main reasons for this catastrophe are easily seen. First and foremost is the fact that in June 1940 Italy was not ready for war, but was thrown into the conflict as a matter of political expediency. It was assumed that the Axis had practically won the war already and were certain to do so before very long. There was no strategic plan for the sort of war in which Mussolini, to his surprise, soon found himself engaged. The results of this miscalculation upon the campaign in the Western Desert have already been seen; in East Africa they were much more serious, because the territory was cut off from Italy by sea and land and became a wasting asset, since steps had not been taken in time to build up enough stocks.

The Duce's initial instructions to the Viceroy were perfectly consistent with the basic idea of a short war. There was no need to attack French Somaliland, for France was on the verge of collapse. It was good defensive strategy to deprive the British of the main gateways into the Empire and it was tactically easy to do so. And when, after a few exasperating weeks, French Somaliland passed safely into Vichy hands, the opportunity of seizing the weakly held British Somaliland was too attractive to miss, even though no strategic advantages were to be gained. The truth is that with the exception of French Somaliland there were no worth-while objectives within easy reach of the Italian land forces, and for a venture farther afield there was not the necessary administrative backing, nor, with the possible exception of the Savoia Division, were the higher formations sufficiently well trained.

For these reasons it was no doubt sound to adopt a defensive strategy on land, although this must have been a disappointing decision because it was known that the British had very few forces in Kenya and the Sudan, and the time to strike at them was before they became stronger. This strategy would have been still sounder had it included the intention of making determined air attacks upon British shipping in the Red Sea. But virtually nothing was done to interfere with the arrival of British reinforcements in convoys, at the ports of Mombasa and Port Sudan, or on the railways leading from them. Moreover it was not long before dwindling stocks of spares, fuel, and reserve aircraft were acting as a brake on all enterprise, which was further curbed by the inability of the ground organization to maintain the number of aircraft in the country. A quarter of these indeed were in workshops when the war began. Lack of enterprise in the air was matched at sea, and the destroyers and submarines based at Massawa were inactive. Thus the strategic asset of Italian East Africa's geographical position on the flank of Britain's vital sea-route was thrown away.

In these circumstances the role of the Italian forces in East Africa could only be to hold out against the British for as long as possible. To do this it was of course necessary to keep internal unrest in check, which was a commitment that grew with every British success. The Duke of Aosta was certainly in an unenviable position, not made any better by the knowledge that whatever he did the war would be decided somewhere else. He maintained a realistic outlook, kept his head, and as was to be expected set a good example, but the Italian failures in Greece and the Western Desert made it all the harder for him to keep up the morale of the Italian nationals, and through them that of the loyal population and the native troops. By early February 1941 the local situation had become much worse, for the simultaneous British advances into Eritrea, Somalia and Gojjam had shown up the weaknesses of the Italian colonial forces, and the danger of internal disorder had greatly increased. There were not enough Italian national troops to stiffen all the fronts, and it cannot have been easy to decide where best to use them. For instance, while one of the regiments of Savoia Grenadiers took part in the whole of the decisive battle of Keren, the other was used neither there nor in the difficult country in front of Harar, but was held back at Addis Ababa until it was too late to use it effectively anywhere.

But, although the Italian forces were not equal to the dual task of resisting the British and maintaining internal order, the military commanders should have appreciated that the British too had their difficulties and that these could be turned to good account to impose delay. For example, the Italians might have known that the British advance on Kismayu would involve administrative problems which the capture of an undamaged port would greatly ease. Yet the port facilities at Kismayu were not destroyed, although there was plenty of time and the High Command had ordered it to be done. A huge stock of petrol was left at Mogadishu as a gift, and another British problem was solved. It was well known that a landing from the sea could be a very hazardous undertaking, yet the British were allowed to land and take Berbera almost unopposed. The impression of British speed and invincibility led to a general loss of heart, which was manifested by wholesale desertions by the colonial troops.

Even when allowance is made for the inferiority of the Italian equipment, and for the depressing effect of being always on the defensive, there remains the impression that on many occasions positions were abandoned before they had caused anything like the maximum of delay, and that a more aggressive defence would have achieved far better results. In Gojjam the Italians were actually the better equipped—for example, Gideon Force had no artillery at all —but here also there was a failure to grasp the military essentials; the colonial brigade at the south of Lake Tana should never have allowed itself to be contained by a small detachment, leaving Wingate free to attack Debra Markos against big odds and open the way to Addis Ababa from the north. Weakness of purpose of this sort more than offset some very gallant acts of junior leadership.

The British succeeded largely because they exploited the enemy's weaknesses. Until these were disclosed, the British commanders, though they saw clearly what had to be done, were inclined to doubt whether they had the resources or the time to do it. Once they began, they sought and took their opportunities, and showed firm purpose coupled with sound judgment in matters of time, space, and resources. Above all they were ready to take risks.

The campaign involved men of many races in a wide variety of operations, in the course of which they had to advance vast distances over all sorts of country, in extremes of climate, with seldom even the barest of amenities. Not only must the administration have been excellent, but the training which enabled plans to be quickly translated into action had obviously been carried out on sound lines.

The British forces in East Africa, their main task over, were drastically reduced. The 5th South African Infantry Brigade had already sailed from Mombasa for Egypt; the 2nd was awaiting shipping at Berbera; the 1st was on its way to Massawa—also for shipment to Egypt. The 4th Indian Division had gone; the 5th was under orders to follow. Withdrawals of air forces began directly after the capture of Massawa, and during April three fighter, three

HH

bomber, and one general reconnaissance squadron left for Egypt. These were Nos. 94 and 203 Squadrons R.A.F. from Aden, No. 1 Squadron S.A.A.F., and Nos. 14 and 223 Squadrons R.A.F. from the Sudan, and Nos. 2 and 24 Squadrons S.A.A.F. from Kenya. No. 237 (Rhodesian) Squadron and No. 12 (Bomber) Squadron S.A.A.F. followed at the end of May. For the present, Ethiopia was under British military guidance and control, while British Somaliland, Italian Somaliland, and Eritrea were under British Military Government. The forces remaining behind to deal with the Italian armies were the 11th and 12th African Divisions. To support them were: in the Sudan, No. 47 (Bomber) Squadron; at Aden, No. 8 (Bomber) Squadron; and in Kenya No. 3 (Fighter), No. 11 (Bomber) and Nos. 40 and 41 (Army Co-operation) Squadrons of the South African Air Force.

With the collapse in East Africa, Italy suffered the third of the major defeats which followed her disastrous decision to enter a war for which she was not ready and for which there was by no means universal enthusiasm. By early in February 1941, Cyrenaica had been lost, and with it a vast number of men and a mass of material. By the middle of March the last unaided attempts to defeat the Greeks had failed. On both these fronts the Germans were preparing to intervene, and the British were soon to learn—if they did not know it already—that the means and methods that had done so well against the Italians were not good enough against the Germans.

| 1940 | General | Mediterranean Sea |
|---|---|---|
| June | 11 Italy enters the war<br>22 Franco-German armistice<br>24 Franco-Italian armistice<br>28 His Majesty's Government recognizes General de Gaulle | 23 Admiral Somerville's Force H begins to assemble at Gibraltar |
| July | 1 Rumania denounces Anglo-French guarantee<br>Battle of Britain begins | 3 Action against French warships at Oran<br>4 French ships at Alexandria demilitarized<br>9 Fleet action off Calabria<br>19 Action off Cape Spada |
| August | 26 French Equatorial Africa declares for de Gaulle<br>30 Second 'Vienna Award' announced | 1 H.M.S. *Argus* flies Hurricanes to Malta |
| September | 23/25 General de Gaulle's unsuccessful expedition to Dakar<br>27 Germany, Italy and Japan sign a ten-year Pact | 5 Naval reinforcements including H.M.S. *Illustrious* reach Alexandria |
| October | 23 Meeting between Hitler and Franco | |
| November | 4 Spain assumes control of Tangier | 11 Fleet Air Arm's attack at Taranto<br>17 H.M.S. *Argus* flies Hurricanes to Malta<br>27 Action off Cape Spartivento, Sardinia |
| December | Several changes in Italian High Command<br>11 Hitler's plans to capture Gibraltar cancelled<br>18 Hitler issues directive for invasion of Russia | |

# EVENTS FROM JUNE 1940

| Egypt and the desert | Red Sea and East Africa | Balkans |
|---|---|---|
| Frontier action | Success against Italian submarines | |
| | Frontier operations:<br>*Sudan:* 4 Loss of Kassala and Gallabat<br>*Kenya:* 15 Loss of Moyale<br>*Khartoum:* 3 Emperor Haile Selassie arrives from England | |
| | 5 General Legentilhomme leaves Jibuti<br>5-19 Loss of British Somaliland<br>*Sudan:* 12 Sandford's Mission enters Ethiopia | 15 Loss of Greek cruiser *Helle* |
| 13/18 Italian advance into Egypt<br>20 First aircraft leave for Egypt along the Takoradi reinforcement route | | |
| 16 Mr. Eden's three-weeks tour begins | | German troops enter Rumania<br>28 Italians invade Greece<br>29 British advanced parties reach Crete |
| | *Sudan:* 6/9 Action at Gallabat | 4 Royal Air Force begin to operate in Greece<br>8 Italian offensive collapses<br>18 Greek counter-stroke begins; British Liaison Mission to Turkey |
| 9 First British offensive begins<br>16 Capture of Sollum | *Kenya:* 16 Raid on El Wak | |

| 1941 | General | Mediterranean Sea |
|---|---|---|
| January | 10 Lend-Lease Bill before Congress | 11 First attack by the *Luftwaffe* from Sicily<br>12/23 H.M.S. *Illustrious* at Malta |
| February | 12 Mr. Eden and General Dill leave England for the Middle East | 9 Bombardment of Genoa<br>17 Attempted landing on Kaso<br>25 Landing on Castelorizo |
| March | 1 Bulgaria joins the Axis | |
| | 11 Lend-Lease Act signed by President Roosevelt<br>27 Yugoslav *coup d'état* | 28 Battle of Matapan |
| April | 3 *Coup d'état* in Iraq | 21 Bombardment of Tripoli |
| May | 2 Iraq forces attack Habbaniya | Successful passage of 'Tiger' convoy |

Thick line denotes end of the present volume.

| Egypt and the desert | Red Sea and East Africa | Balkans |
|---|---|---|
| 4 Capture of Bardia<br>11 Long Range Desert Group raids Murzuk<br>22 Capture of Tobruk<br>29 Aerial mining of the Suez Canal begins | British offensive begins:<br><br>*Sudan:* 19 Capture of Kassala<br>*Kenya:* Capture of<br>18 Mega and<br>22 Moyale | 13 British offer of troops to Greece declined<br>29 Death of General Metaxas<br>31 Mr. Churchill's appeal to the Turkish President |
| 6 Capture of Benghazi<br>5/7 Battle of Beda Fomm<br>12 General Rommel arrives at Tripoli | *Sudan:* Actions at<br>1 Agordat and<br>2 Barentu<br>3 Battle of Keren begins<br>23 Emperor enters Ethiopia<br>*Kenya:* 19 Crossing of River Juba<br>Capture of<br>14 Kismayu and<br>25 Mogadishu | 22 The Eden Mission in Athens;<br>26 Ankara |
| 1 Capture of Kufra by the Free French<br><br>30 Axis offensive begins | 27 Capture of Keren | 2 The Eden Mission returns to Athens<br>5 Sailing of the British forces for Greece begins<br>9/16 Italian offensive in Albania |
| 10 Tobruk cut off and besieged | Capture of<br>1 Asmara<br>8 Massawa and<br>5 Addis Ababa<br>11 Red Sea opened to United States shipping | 6 Germans invade Greece<br>23 Greek Government goes to Crete<br>27 Germans enter Athens |
| Fighting at Sollum and Halfaya | 16 Duke of Aosta surrenders at Amba Alagi | 20 Germans invade Crete |

# APPENDIX I

*(See page 32)*

# Army Council Instructions to the General Officer Commanding-in-Chief in the Middle East

0143/3108

1. You are appointed General Officer Commanding-in-Chief in the Middle East.

2. The area over which your command extends in *peace* comprises:—
> Egypt
> The Sudan
> Palestine and Transjordan
> Cyprus

3. In these areas you will exercise general control over all British land forces in matters of high policy in peace and will, in particular, be responsible for the review and co-ordination of war plans and plans for reinforcements in emergency, including the distribution of available land forces and material between these areas.

4. In addition you will be responsible for the preparation of all war plans, in co-operation with the local military or air force commanders, for the employment of land forces in British Somaliland, Aden, Iraq and the shores of the Persian Gulf.

5. In carrying out these tasks you will where appropriate consult and co-operate with the Naval Commander-in-Chief, Mediterranean, the Naval Commander-in-Chief, East Indies Station, the Commander-in-Chief in India, the Inspector General, African Colonial Forces, and the Air Officer Commanding-in-Chief in the Middle East.

6. You will maintain close touch with His Majesty's Ambassador in Egypt; His Majesty's Ambassador in Iraq; the Governor General in the Sudan; the High Commissioner for Palestine and Transjordan; the Governors of Cyprus, Aden and British Somaliland; and the Political Resident in the Persian Gulf.

7. The policy of His Majesty's Government with regard to the Egyptian Forces is that they shall be developed into efficient modern forces capable of co-operating with the British Forces in the defence of Egypt. You will maintain close touch with His Majesty's Ambassador in Egypt, the Head of the British Military Mission, and the Egyptian General Staff in all matters of high policy affecting the development and employment in war of the Egyptian Army, with due regard to the existing responsibilities of the General Officer Commanding-in-Chief, Egypt, in such matters as local defence co-operation between British and Egyptian troops, and training. You will delegate to the General Officer Commanding-in-Chief,

the British Troops in Egypt, such matters as are, in your opinion, best arranged by him direct with the appropriate Egyptian authorities and, subject to the agreement of the Egyptian Government at the time, command of the Egyptian Army in war.

The agreement of the Egyptian Government to place the Egyptian Army under the command of the General Officer Commanding-in-Chief in Egypt will be obtained by His Majesty's Ambassador through whose intermediation all demands on the Egyptian Government will be made.

8. You should bear in mind that His Majesty's Ambassador must retain in all circumstances his existing position *vis-à-vis* the Egyptian Government. This does not exclude direct communication between the General Officer Commanding-in-Chief, British Troops in Egypt, and the Egyptian authorities on routine matters agreed by His Majesty's Ambassador.

The same considerations will apply as regards your relations with His Majesty's Diplomatic Representatives in the other countries included in the area over which your command will extend in war. In the case of Iraq, this will not preclude direct communication with the Inspector General of the Iraq Army on such matters as may be agreed by His Majesty's Ambassador to Iraq.

9. You will visit all areas which are included in war in your Command (vide paragraph 14 below) to study local situations and inform yourself of local problems.

10. Subject to the direction of the Chiefs of Staff, and of the War Office in respect of the land forces, you are responsible, in conjunction with the Naval Commander-in-Chief, Mediterranean, the Naval Commander-in-Chief, East Indies Station, and the Air Officer Commanding-in-Chief, Middle East, for co-ordinating the British war plans with the war plans of Allies of His Majesty's Government in the Near and Middle East and North Africa.

This will involve at present co-ordination with the French military authorities in North Africa, Syria and French Somaliland; the Turkish General Staff; and possibly ultimately the Greek and Rumanian General Staffs.

You will arrange to exchange visits with these authorities as may be required.

11. To assist you in these tasks you will be provided with a staff for your own use. Of this Staff, the Senior General Staff Officer will also be a member of the Joint Planning Staff for the Middle East, which will include the Chief Staff Officers of the Commander-in-Chief, Mediterranean, and the Air Officer Commanding-in-Chief, Middle East.

The Joint Planning Staff will be responsible for inter-service co-ordination of all war plans as may be directed by the Commanders concerned, namely, the Commander-in-Chief, Mediterranean, the Commander-in-Chief, East Indies, the Air Officer Commanding-in-Chief, Middle East, and yourself.

The composition of the staffs of your headquarters and of the Joint Planning Staff is shown in the Annexure to these instructions.

12. Your requirements as regards intelligence will be provided by the Middle East Intelligence Centre, which is being established in Cairo.

The charter for this Centre, as approved by the Committee of Imperial Defence, was issued to all concerned under War Office letter No. 0160/2133 (M.I.2) dated 30th June 1939.

13. Your headquarters will be located at Cairo.

14. Should war break out the area of your Command will be extended to include all military forces in British Somaliland, Aden, Iraq and the shores of the Persian Gulf, with the exception of those which are normally under the control of the Royal Air Force.

15. Your tasks in *war* are to co-ordinate (in consultation with the Air Officer Commanding-in-Chief, Middle East, for matters affecting Iraq and Aden) the action of the land forces in the areas under your command and the distribution of available resources between them. You will be guided by the policy for the conduct of operations which will be communicated to you from time to time.

You will co-ordinate the operations of the forces under your command with the operations of the various allied forces in the areas mentioned in paragraph 10.

For this purpose you will work in direct co-operation with allied military commanders concerned.

By command of the Army Council,
(Sgd.) H. J. CREEDY.

The War Office,
24th July 1939.

ANNEXURE

1. *Staff of the General Officer Commanding-in-Chief, Middle East.*

   1 Brigadier, General Staff.
   1 General Staff Officer, Grade 2.
   2 General Staff Officers, Grade 3 (including 1 for Joint Planning Staff).
   1 Administrative Staff Officer.

2. *Joint Planning Staff.*

   Chief Staff Officer to Commander-in-Chief, Mediterranean.
   1 Naval Staff Officer.
   Brigadier, General Staff, Middle East.
   1 General Staff Officer, Grade 3.
   Senior Air Staff Officer, Middle East.
   1 Air Staff Officer.

# APPENDIX 2

*(See page 94)*

# Directive to Air Officer Commanding-in-Chief, Middle East

To—H.Q., R.A.F., M.E.
From—Air Ministry.
X.540.   11 June 1940.

Personal to Sir Arthur Longmore.   Your 493 May 13.

Following are the instructions of the Air Council as to your responsibilities.

1. You will command all Royal Air Force Units stationed or operating in the following areas. Egypt, Sudan, Palestine and Transjordan, East Africa, Aden and Somaliland, Iraq and adjacent territories, Cyprus, Turkey, Balkans (Yugoslavia, Roumania, Bulgaria, Greece), Mediterranean Sea, Red Sea, Persian Gulf.

2. The Air Officers Commanding Aden, Iraq and the Mediterranean[1] will continue to exercise local administrative control in direct communication with the Air Ministry. You will, however, be responsible for general administrative control of these commands so far as operational requirements dictate. You may also draw on, or interchange, the resources of these commands as circumstances may require.

3. You will be responsible, in conjunction with the Naval Commander-in-Chief, Mediterranean, Naval Commander-in-Chief, East Indies and the Commander-in-Chief, Middle East, as may be appropriate for the preparation of plans for the employment of the units under your Command.

4. In so far as your other commitments permit you will, after consultation with the Commander-in-Chief, Middle East, place under the command of the General Officer Commanding, British Forces in Palestine and Transjordan such air forces as are from time to time required by him to meet the local situation.

5. The Commander-in-Chief, Middle East will assume command of the land forces in Aden, Iraq and the shores of the Persian Gulf in the event of major land operations in or beyond the borders of those territories. This in no way affects the responsibilities of the Air Officers Commanding, British Forces in Iraq or Aden, in the conduct of purely local operations of a minor character.

6. You will, where appropriate, maintain touch with His Majesty's representatives in Egypt, Iraq, Turkey, Greece, Roumania and Yugoslavia; the Governor-General in the Sudan; the High Commissioner for

---

[1] See page 31.

Palestine and . Transjordan; the Governors of Aden, Malta, Cyprus, British Somaliland, Kenya, Uganda, Tanganyika, Northern Rhodesia and Nyasaland; the British Resident in Zanzibar and the Political Resident in the Persian Gulf.

7. You will keep H.E. the Commander-in-Chief in India in touch with operational matters which may concern or be of interest to him.

8. The Air Officers Commanding, Aden and Iraq will continue to maintain direct communication with the political and diplomatic authorities in their Commands.

9. Subject to the direction of the Chiefs of Staffs and of the Air Ministry you are responsible in consultation with the Naval Commander-in-Chief, Mediterranean, the Naval Commander-in-Chief, East Indies and the Commander-in-Chief, Middle East for co-ordinating the operations of Royal Air Force units in your area with those of the Air Forces of the Allies of His Majesty's Government. In addition, you are responsible for the co-ordination of the operations of the units under your command with those of the French Air Forces in North Africa and in West Africa should operations extend to these areas.

10. The primary role of the forces under your command is the defence of Egypt and the Suez Canal, and the maintenance of communications through the Red Sea. This does not, however, preclude the possibility of air forces from your Command being employed in the execution of such other plans as may be approved by the Chiefs of Staff from time to time.

11. The policy of His Majesty's Government with regard to the Egyptian forces is that they shall be developed into efficient modern forces capable of co-operating with the British forces in the defence of Egypt. You will maintain close touch with His Majesty's Ambassador in Egypt, the head of the British Military Mission and the Senior Air Force Officer attached to that Mission in all matters affecting the development and training of the Royal Egyptian Air Force and the employment of that Force in War.

12. The agreement of the Egyptian Government to place the Royal Egyptian Air Force under your command will be obtained by His Majesty's Ambassador, who will be the intermediary for all requests to the Egyptian Government. This does not exclude direct communication between yourself and the Egyptian authorities on routine matters agreed by His Majesty's Ambassador.

# APPENDIX 3

*(See page 138)*

# Admiral Darlan's signal of 24th June 1940

### AMIRAL OUEST — SUD — AFRIQUE — F.N.E.O. — ANTILLES — 3ème ESCADRE — FORCE X — D.N.L. — MARINE TOULON — MARINE BIZERTE

7030

5143–44–45

CLAUSES ARMISTICE: vous sont notifiées en clair par ailleurs. Je profite dernières communications que je peux transmettre en chiffre pour faire connaître ma pensée sur ce sujet.

PRIMO: Les navires guerre démobilisés doivent rester français avec pavillon français équipage réduit français séjournant port français metropolitain ou colonial.

SECUNDO: Précautions secrètes de autosabotage doivent être prises pour que ennemi ou étranger s'emparant d'un bâtiment par force ne puisse s'en servir.

TERTIO: Si commission armistice chargée interpréter texte décidait autrement que dans paragraphe PRIMO, au moment exécution cette décision nouvelle navires guerre seraient sans nouvel ordre soit conduits Etats-Unis soit sabordés, s'il ne pouvait être fait autrement, pour les soustraire à ennemi. En aucun cas ils ne devront être laissés intacts à l'ennemi.

QUARTO: Navires ainsi réfugiés à l'étranger ne devront pas être utilisés à opérations guerre contre Allemagne ou Italie sans ordre du C.E.C. F.M.F. -Stop-

XAVIER 377.

1245/24/6

Amirauté Française

---

*Notes*  
F.N.E.O.  Force Navale Extrême Orient.  
C.E.C.  Commandant-en-Chef.  
D.N.L.  Division Navale du Levant.  
F.M.F.  Force Maritime Française.

# APPENDIX 4

(*See page* 233)

# Directive to the Air Officer Commanding, British Air Forces in Greece

To:—Air Commodore J. H. D'Albiac, D.S.O.

1. The Cabinet have decided to give Greece the greatest possible material support at the earliest moment. In consequence the British Air Forces now in Greece are to be strengthened.

2. You have been selected to act as representative of the Air Officer Commanding-in-Chief and to command all Royal Air Force Units and ancillary British Army Units supporting them in Greece. You will take over command from Wing Commander A. H. Willetts on arrival in Athens.

3. The Air Forces under your command will be known as 'British Air Forces in Greece'.

4. In addition to No. 30 Blenheim Squadron—composite fighter-bomber squadron already established in Greece—the following Units will join your Command at an early date:—

2 Blenheim Bomber Squadrons
1 Gladiator Fighter Squadron

A second Gladiator Fighter Squadron will follow later.

5. It is further intended to use Eleusis Aerodrome as a refuelling and rearming base for Wellington bombers operating against suitable strategic objectives in the Adriatic and, subject to general directives issued by the Air Officer Commanding-in-Chief, these bombers will also operate under your Command while in Greece.

6. The necessary Royal Air Force administrative and maintenance units will accompany the above units and you are aware generally of their composition.

7. The Greeks are being asked, through the British Minister, Athens, to provide anti-aircraft defence for the aerodromes used by the Royal Air Force. In addition one battery of H.A.A. guns (8) and one battery of L.A.A. guns (12) are being despatched forthwith from Egypt to supplement what the Greeks are able to supply. You will be responsible for the siting of the A.A. Defences and should signal your decisions as soon as possible.

8. The Army are responsible for establishing the normal ancillary services. Appropriate military advisers will be added to your staff.

9. On arrival at Athens you will report to the British Minister by arrangement with the Assistant Air Attaché, Wing Commander R. J. Legg (whose office is in the British Embassy).

10. You will have the status of an independent Air Force Commander but, although not under the control of the Greek General Staff, the conduct of air operations by the Royal Air Force should, as far as practicable and subject to the general instructions issued in para. 11, conform as closely as possible to the Greek plan for the defence of the country.

11. Wing Commander Willetts has had preliminary discussions with the Greek General Staff on the general conduct of operations and the manner in which the Royal Air Force can most profitably assist the Greek military plan and a copy of his report is attached.

In general, the fighters are being provided primarily for the defence of your aerodromes and vulnerable objectives in the rear area. The attacking of selected points in the enemy lines of communication and his concentrations in the rear areas appear to be suitable tasks for the Blenheim bombers. You are not to allow bombers to be used as artillery or to participate in the actual land operations unless the military situation becomes so critical as to justify the temporary diversion of our bombers from strategic bombing to support of the Greek land forces. Appropriate objectives for the Wellington bombers are the points of disembarkation and concentration areas on the Albanian coast, but further guidance on these operations will be signalled to you from time to time.

12. Bombing is to be confined to military objectives and must be subjected to the following general principles:—

(*a*) Intentional bombardment of civil population as such is illegal.

(*b*) It must be possible to identify the objective.

(*c*) The attack must be made with reasonable care to avoid undue loss of civil life in the vicinity of the target.

(*d*) The provisions of the Red Cross conventions are to be observed.

The term 'Military' may be interpreted in its widest sense and includes all enemy merchant shipping whether in port or on the high seas. Provided the principles set out above are observed, all objectives, the destruction of which is of immediate military necessity, may be attacked for particular reasons. For the present, targets in Rome may not be attacked unless special instructions are issued. For special reasons also, targets in Taranto should not be attacked until after the 11th November.

In the event of it being decided to carry out attacks against targets on the Italian mainland you should, whenever possible, give prior warning to Air Officer Commanding Mediterranean, repeated this Headquarters, as aircraft from Malta are also operating against these targets and, on occasion, it may be necessary for you to co-ordinate bombing operations with Air Officer Commanding Mediterranean.

13. You are empowered to refuse to undertake any operation which, in your opinion, would jeopardize the security of the air forces under your Command. In such an event you are to report the circumstances direct to this Headquarters.

14. You should signal the results of any important discussions with the Greek General Staff and keep the Air Officer Commanding-in-Chief informed from time to time of your general intentions and progress of operations.

15. You are to refrain from committing the Royal Air Force to any

further assistance, but you will naturally be in a position to advise the Air Officer Commanding-in-Chief as to the form any air reinforcements should take in the event of further assistance being forthcoming at a later date.

16. A British Liaison Mission will be formed in Greece at an early date and you are also to keep the air representative, Wing Commander Forbes, fully informed of the conduct of operations.

17. The future trend of events in Greece cannot be appreciated, but the possibility of a sudden and complete collapse of Greece must not be lost sight of when making your decisions on the location of the squadrons. If time does not permit prior reference to the Air Officer Commanding-in-Chief you are to use your discretion as to the appropriate moment to evacuate the Royal Air Force from Greece, and, in the absence of any further instructions from this Headquarters, you are to retire to Crete.

18. You are to deal solely with this Headquarters in all matters concerning the Royal Air Force in Greece.

(Sgd.) R. M. Drummond,
*Air Vice-Marshal*
for Air Chief Marshal Commanding-in-Chief
Royal Air Force, Middle East.

5th November 1940.

II

# APPENDIX 5

*(See page 346)*

## Message from the British Prime Minister to the President of the Turkish Republic,
### for delivery by His Britannic Majesty's Ambassador in Ankara

31st January 1941

'The rapidly growing danger to Turkey and to British interests lead me, Mr. President, to address you directly. I have sure information that the Germans are already establishing themselves upon Bulgarian aerodromes. Hutments are being prepared, and advance servicing personnel numbering several thousands have arrived. This has been done with the full connivance of the Royal Bulgarian Air Force and undoubtedly of the Bulgarian Government. Very soon, perhaps in a few weeks, the movement into Bulgaria of German troops and Air Squadrons will begin. The Air Squadrons will only have to fly from their stations in Roumania to the bases they are preparing in Bulgaria, and will immediately be able to come into action. The Germans would then be in a position to summon you to stand aside, under threat that they will immediately bombard Istanbul and your great cities, and dive-bomb your troops in Thrace. No doubt they would hope either to reach Salonika unopposed or to compel the Greeks to make peace with Italy and yield them air bases in Greece and in the Islands, thus endangering the communications between our Armies in Egypt and the Turkish Army. They would deny the use of Smyrna to our Navy, they would completely control the exits from the Dardanelles, and thus complete the encirclement of Turkey in Europe on three sides. This would also facilitate their attacks upon Alexandria and Egypt generally.

Of course, I know, Mr. President, that, confronted with these mortal dangers, Turkey would fight for her life. But why is it necessary to hand over to the enemy the enormous advantage of being able to secure the mastery of the Bulgarian airfields without a word being said or a single effective counter-measure being taken?

The Germans are, in fact, preparing to repeat on the frontiers of Turkey exactly the same kind of manoeuvre as they accomplished on the frontiers of France in April and May 1940. But in this case, instead of having hesitating and terrified neutrals like Denmark, Holland and Belgium, she has in Bulgaria a confederate and former ally who has beyond all doubt abandoned the will, and never had the power, to resist.

All this, I repeat, may fall upon us in February or in March, and will be open to the Germans even without moving any large masses of troops from the moment when the Bulgarian airfields have been fitted to receive the German Air Force and are occupied by the advanced aircraft personnel and ground staff. Do we propose to sit still with folded hands and watch the steady preparation of this deadly stroke?

It seems to me that we should be held gravely blameworthy by our respective nations if we were to fail in ordinary prudence and foresight. Even now we have waited too long.

I therefore propose to you, Mr. President, that our two countries should repeat in defence of Turkey the same kind of measures which the Germans are taking on the Bulgarian airfields. My Government wish to send to Turkey at the earliest moment when accommodation can be provided at least ten squadrons of Fighter and Bomber aircraft apart from the five now in action in Greece, which we intend to maintain to help her in her fight. And further we will fight the air war from Turkish bases with ever-increasing air forces of the highest quality. Thus we shall help to give the Turkish Army the additional air support which they need to sustain their famous military qualities.

But, more than that, we shall place Turkey in a position, once our squadrons are on the Turkish airfields, to threaten to bombard the Roumanian oilfields if any German advance is made into Bulgaria, or better still, if the air personnel already in Bulgaria is not speedily withdrawn. We will undertake not to take such action from Turkish airfields except by agreement with you.

There is more to come. The attitude of Russia is uncertain and it is our hope it may remain loyal and friendly. Nothing will more restrain Russia from aiding Germany, even indirectly, than the presence of powerful British bombing forces, which could attack the oilfields of Baku. Russia is dependent upon the supply from these oilfields for a very large part of her agriculture, and far-reaching famine would follow their destruction. We are assured that the whole soil around the oilwells is impregnated with petroleum, making it possible to start a conflagration on a scale not hitherto witnessed in the world.

Thus Turkey, once defended by air power, would have the means perhaps of deterring Germany from overrunning Bulgaria, and quelling Greece, and of counterbalancing the Russian fear of the German armies. If this decisive position is to be saved, there is not an hour to lose, and on receipt of your assent His Majesty's Government will immediately give the necessary orders for our advanced personnel, either in uniform or in plain clothes, as you prefer, to start at once for Turkey.

Further, we are prepared to send you a hundred A.A. guns which are now either in or on their way to Egypt. These would be complete with personnel either in uniform, if you so desire, or in the guise of instructors. All other measures which have been discussed with Marshal Chakmak and also the naval measures will, at the right moment, be brought into operation.

The victories we have gained in Libya will enable us to give a far more direct and immediate measure of aid to Turkey in the event of our two countries becoming allied in war, and we will make common cause with you and use our growing strength to aid your valiant armies.'

# APPENDIX 6

*(See page* 377)

# Declaration handed by the Greek President of the Council to the Secretary of State for Foreign Affairs, at Tatoi, 22nd February 1941.
## *(Translated from the French.)*

At the outset of our meeting I wish to repeat in the most categorical manner the declaration I made to the British Government when I succeeded the late General Metaxas as President of the Council. It represents the firm basis of Greek Policy.

Having been given a spontaneous guarantee by Great Britain and having received valuable help from her on the occasion of Italy's unprovoked aggression, Greece is now her faithful ally, and is firmly resolved to continue the war to a victorious conclusion with all her strength at the side of her great ally in whom she has complete confidence.

This determination on the part of the King and Government is shared by the entire Greek nation, and in this complete unity lies the explanation of the brilliant victories gained by the Greek army against an incomparably stronger and better equipped enemy.

You are aware that this resolve on the part of Greece to defend her liberty and integrity is not limited to Italy but applies equally to aggression by Germany. Indeed, Greece is fighting for both liberty and honour.

As for Italy, Greece has been able not only to resist the invader successfully but also to gain a succession of victories over a period of four months, and to penetrate deeply into the enemy's territory in spite of the rigours of winter and the great difficulty of the country.

But in this struggle she has been compelled to use almost all her forces and has only three divisions in Macedonia facing Bulgaria. Therefore the problem—and it is a purely military one—is to decide the size and composition of the force with which the Greek army must be reinforced to make it capable of offering effective resistance to a German invasion. The Greek Government possesses more or less accurate information about the German armies in Rumania, which are being continually reinforced (there are twenty-five divisions according to the most recent reports), and about the Bulgarian forces, but they only know the help the British might be able to give within the space of two months.

They do not even know the intentions of Turkey or Yugoslavia, nor what military aid these countries could give, nor when and how it would be sent. This question is not only exceptionally important but also extremely urgent.

In these circumstances your Excellency's arrival in the Middle East is most opportune, for it will serve not only to clarify the situation but also to turn it to the common advantage of Great Britain and Greece. But let me repeat once again that whatever the future holds in store, and whether there is any hope of repelling the enemy in Macedonia or not, Greece will defend her national soil, even if she has to do so alone.

# APPENDIX 7

*(See page 385)*

## Agreement signed at Athens on 4th March, 1941 by the Chief of the Imperial General Staff and the Commander-in-Chief of the Greek Army.
### *(Translation from the French.)*

'The following decisions were taken as a result of the discussions between the Greek and British High Commands held at Athens on the 2nd, 3rd and 4th March 1941:—

    1. The Greek Army will leave in Macedonia three divisions to defend the prepared positions on the Nestos-Rupel line.

    2. The Greek Army will concentrate, with all possible speed, on the position Mt. Olympus-Veria-Edessa-Kajmakcalan (called the Haliacmon position[1]) the following forces:—

        (*a*) 12th Division from Western Thrace, already moving towards the west by train;

        (*b*) 20th Division from Florina;

        (*c*) 19th Motorized Division from Larissa;

        (*d*) Seven battalions from Western Thrace, provided that the Turkish Government agree to release them as requested by the Greek and British Governments.

    3. A separate Greek Commander will be appointed forthwith for these forces.

    4. The British forces will be despatched as rapidly as shipping will permit to Piraeus and Volos.

    5. The British forces will concentrate on the Haliacmon position, on which it is intended that the Graeco-British forces should give battle.

    6. The command of all forces on the Haliacmon position will be entrusted to Lieutenant-General Sir H. M. Wilson under the High command of General Papagos. The date on which General Wilson assumes his command will be settled by General Papagos in consultation with him, and will depend on the arrival of General Wilson's Headquarters and the establishment of his communications.

N.B.—As regards paragraph 6, it had already been agreed during the conversations held at the Royal Palace at Tatoi on 22nd February that in the event of the General Officer Commanding the British troops finding himself in disagreement with General Papagos, he would have the right to refer to the Commander-in-Chief, Middle East. If the Commander-in-Chief, Middle East, was unable himself to settle the matter with General Papagos, he would similarly have the right to refer to His Majesty's Government.'

---

[1] or Aliakmon.

# APPENDIX 8

## Some particulars of British and Enemy Aircraft in use in the Middle East and Mediterranean Theatre during the period of this volume

The figures in these tables are no more than a general guide to the characteristics and capabilities of each type of aircraft. The performance is affected by the climate, the skill of the pilot, the accuracy of navigation, and by the uncertainties of flying in the presence of the enemy. For these reasons the operational range—not to be confused with the radius of action—is always much less than the still air range. Broadly speaking, after allowing for the running of the engines on the ground and for the climb to the height quoted, the still air range is the distance that can be flown in still air until the tanks are empty.

NOTES:  (i) The most economical cruising speed is the speed at which the greatest range is achieved.
        (ii) The height given in column IV is the optimum height for the maximum speed.

## FIGHTER AIRCRAFT
### BRITISH

| I | II | | III | IV | V | VI |
|---|---|---|---|---|---|---|
| Aircraft | Fuel and Still Air Range at Most Economical Cruising Speed | | Most Economical Cruising Speed in Miles Per Hour | Maximum Speed in Miles Per Hour | Gun Armament | Remarks |
| | Galls. | Miles | | | | |
| Blenheim Mk. IV F Twin engine monoplane Crew 2 | 466 | 1,615 | 170 at 15,000 ft. | 266 at 11,800 ft. | 6×·303 | |
| Fulmar Single engine monoplane Crew 2 | 155 | 820 | 170 at 10,000 ft. | 253 at 10,000 ft. | 8×·303 | Fleet Air Arm. |
| Fury Single engine biplane Crew 1 | 50 | 440 | 127 at 15,000 ft. | 205 at 15,000 ft. | 2×·303 | |
| Gauntlet Single engine biplane Crew 1 | 79 | 626 | 118 at 15,000 ft. | 225 at 15,000 ft. | 2×·303 | |
| Gladiator Single engine biplane Crew 1 | 83 | 523 | 142 at 15,000 ft. | 245 at 15,000 ft. | 4×·303 | Sea Gladiators of the Fleet Air Arm were a modified version. |
| Hurricane Mk. I Single engine monoplane Crew 1 | 97 | 600 | 180 at 15,000 ft. | 316 at 17,750 ft. | 8×·303 | |
| Tomahawk Single engine monoplane Crew 1 | 132 175 | 695 825 | 185 at 15,000 ft. | 340 at 16,000 ft. | 2×·50 4×·303 | American design and manufacture. First operated in the Middle East (in the Western Desert) in April, 1941. |

## BOMBER AIRCRAFT

(including bomber transport, bomber reconnaissance, and torpedo-bomber)

### *BRITISH*

| Aircraft | Still Air Range with Associated Bombload | | Most Economical Cruising Speed in Miles Per Hour | Maximum Speed in Miles Per Hour | Armament | Remarks |
|---|---|---|---|---|---|---|
| | Miles | Bombload | | | | |
| Albacore Single engine biplane Crew 2 or 3 | 521 | 1 Torpedo or 1,500 lb. | 105 at 6,000 ft. | 163 at 4,800 ft. | $2 \times .303$ | Figures relate to use as torpedo-bomber. Fleet Air Arm. |
| Battle Single engine monoplane Crew 2 | 1,050 | 1,000 lb. | 148 at 15,000 ft. | 241 at 13,000 ft. | $2 \times .303$ | |
| Blenheim Mk. I Twin engine monoplane Crew 3 | 920 | 1,000 lb. | 165 at 15,000 ft. | 265 at 15,000 ft. | $2 \times .303$ | |
| Blenheim Mk. IV Twin engine monoplane Crew 3 | 1,457 | 1,000 lb. | 170 at 15,000 ft. | 266 at 11,800 ft. | $5 \times .303$ | |
| Bombay Twin engine monoplane Crew 4 | 1,500 330 | (a) (b) | 120 at 10,000 ft. | 159 at 10,000 ft. | $2 \times .303$ | Transport aircraft (a) With 10 troops. (b) With 24 troops. Could carry up to 2,000 lb. bombs. |
| Glenn Martin (Maryland) Twin engine monoplane Crew 3 | 1,210 1,080 | 1,500 lb. 2,000 lb. | 176 at 15,000 ft. | 278 at 11,800 ft. | $8 \times .303$ | American design and manufacture |
| Hardy Single engine biplane Crew 2 | 477 | 500 lb. | 115 at 10,000 ft. | 156 at 10,000 ft. | $2 \times .303$ | |
| Hartbeest Single engine biplane Crew 2 | 450 | 568 lb. | 110 at 11,000 ft. | 145 at 11,000 ft. | $3 \times .303$ | Figures given are for East African conditions. |

# BOMBER AIRCRAFT

(including bomber transport, bomber reconnaissance, and torpedo-bomber)

## *BRITISH*

| Aircraft | Still Air Range with Associated Bombload | | Most Economical Cruising Speed in Miles Per Hour | Maximum Speed in Miles Per Hour | Armament | Remarks |
|---|---|---|---|---|---|---|
| | Miles | Bombload | | | | |
| Ju. 86 Twin engine monoplane Crew 6 | 700 | 1,160 lb. | 120 at 8,000 ft. | 140 at 6,000 ft. | 6×·303 | Figures given are for East African conditions. Performance differs from that of the German Ju. 86 (military version). |
| Lysander Single engine biplane Crew 2 | 1,410 | 500 lb. | 123 at 10,000 ft. | 212 at 4,500 ft. 197 at 15,000 ft. | 4×·303 | |
| Skua Single engine monoplane Crew 2 | 980 | 500 lb. | 157 at 15,000 ft. | 212 at 15,000 ft. | 5×·303 | Fighter dive-bomber. Fleet Air Arm. |
| Sunderland Flying-Boat Four engine monoplane Crew 10 | 1,850 2,425 | 1,900 lb. Nil. | 142 at 5,000 ft. | 188 at 6,500 ft. | 7×·303 | |
| Swordfish Single engine biplane Crew 2 | 528 | 1,500 lb. | 103 at 5,000 ft. | 139 at 5,000 ft. | 2×·303 | Torpedo-bomber. Fleet Air Arm. |
| Valentia Twin engine biplane Crew 2 | 367 | (a) | 104 at 6,500 ft. | 111 at 6,500 ft. | None | Transport aircraft (a) With 22 troops. |
| Vincent Single engine biplane Crew 2 | 726 | 500 lb. | 95 at 10,000 ft. | 141 at 10,000 ft. | 2×·303 | |
| Wellesley Single engine monoplane Crew 2 | 2,250 | 1,060 lb. | 133 at 15,000 ft. | 206 at 15,000 ft. | 2×·303 | |
| Wellington Mk. I Twin engine monoplane Crew 6 | 2,550 1,200 | 1,000 lb. 4,500 lb. | 165 at 10,000 ft. | 225 at 4,700 ft. 235 at 15,500 ft. | 6×·303 | |

## FIGHTER AIRCRAFT

### *ITALIAN*

| Aircraft | Fuel and Still Air Range at Most Economical Cruising Speed | | Most Economical Cruising Speed in Miles Per Hour | Maximum Speed in Miles Per Hour | Armament | Remarks |
|---|---|---|---|---|---|---|
| | Galls. | Miles | | | | |
| C.R. 32<br>Single engine biplane<br>Crew 1 | 80 | 790 | 130 at 10,000 ft. | 233 at 10,000 ft. | 2 × 12·7 mm. | |
| C.R. 42<br>Single engine biplane<br>Crew 1 | 77 | 535 | 150 at 13,100 ft. | 270 at 13,100 ft. | 2 × 12·7 mm. | |
| G. 50<br>Single engine monoplane<br>Crew 1 | 69 | 530 | 170 at 14,500 ft. | 300 at 14,500 ft. | 2 × 12·7 mm. | |
| M.C. 200<br>Single engine monoplane<br>Crew 1 | 70 | 570 | 170 at 15,000 ft. | 310 at 15,000 ft. | 2 × 12·7 mm. | |

### *GERMAN*

| Aircraft | Fuel and Still Air Range at Most Economical Cruising Speed | | Most Economical Cruising Speed in Miles Per Hour | Maximum Speed in Miles Per Hour | Armament | Remarks |
|---|---|---|---|---|---|---|
| Me. 110<br>Twin engine monoplane<br>Crew 2 | 280 | 930 | 200 at 18,000 ft. | 360 at 20,000 ft. | 6 × 7·9 mm.<br>2 × 20 mm. | |

## BOMBER AIRCRAFT

(including bomber transport, bomber reconnaissance, and torpedo-bomber)

### *ITALIAN*

| Aircraft | Still Air Range with Associated Bombload | | Most Economical Cruising Speed in Miles Per Hour | Maximum Speed in Miles Per Hour | Armament | Remarks |
|---|---|---|---|---|---|---|
| | Miles | Bombload | | | | |
| Ba. 65 Single engine monoplane Crew 1 to 2 | 590 | 880 lb. | 160 at 13,500 ft. | 255 at 16,400 ft. | 2 × 12·7 mm. 3 × 7·7 mm. | Ground attack aircraft. |
| B.R. 20 Twin engine monoplane Crew 4 | 1,350 | 2,200 lb. | 175 at 13,000 ft. | 255 at 13,500 ft. | 1 × 12·7 mm. 2 × 7·7 mm. | |
| Ca. 133 Three engine monoplane Crew 4 | 750 | 2,000 lb. | 105 at 5,500 ft. | 174 at 5,500 ft. | 4 × 7·7 mm. | Used mainly for transport. |
| Ca. 310 Twin engine monoplane Crew 3 | 1,060 | 880 lb. | 115 at 5,500 ft. | 212 at 5,500 ft. | 3 × 7·7 mm. | Used mainly for reconnaissance. |
| Ca. 311 Twin engine monoplane Crew 3 to 4 | 1,315 | 880 lb. | 120 at 13,000 ft. | 260 at 13,000 ft. | 4 × 7·7 mm. | |
| Cant. Z. 501 Single engine flying-boat Crew 4 to 5 | 2,450 | 1,100 lb. | 85 at sea level | 152 at sea level | 4 × 7·7 mm. | |
| Cant. Z. 506 Three engine seaplane Crew 4 to 5 | 1,130 | 1,750 lb. | 140 at 13,000 ft. | 230 at 13,000 ft. | 1 × 12·7 mm. 3 × 7·7 mm. | |
| Cant. Z. 1007 b Three engine monoplane Crew 4 to 5 | 1,650 | 1,100 lb. | 160 at 15,000 ft. | 280 at 15,000 ft. | 2 × 12·7 mm. 2 × 7·7 mm. | |

# BOMBER AIRCRAFT

(including bomber transport, bomber reconnaissance, and torpedo-bomber)

## *ITALIAN (Contd.)*

| Aircraft | Still Air Range with Associated Bombload | | Most Economical Cruising Speed in Miles Per Hour | Maximum Speed in Miles Per Hour | Armament | Remarks |
|---|---|---|---|---|---|---|
| | Miles | Bombload | | | | |
| Ghibli Twin engine monoplane Crew 3 to 4 | 530 1,210 | 740 lb. Nil | 100 at 3,000 ft. | 158 at sea level | 3 × 7·7 mm. | Reconnaissance and light bombing |
| Ro. 37 Single engine biplane Crew 2 | 1,100 1,295 | 400 lb. Nil | 120 at 14,000 ft. | 200 at 14,000 ft. | 2 × 12·7 mm. 1 × 7·7 mm. | |
| S. 79 Three engine monoplane Crew 4 to 5 | 1,190 | 2,750 lb. | 155 at 13,000 ft. | 255 at 13,000 ft. | 3 × 12·7 mm. 2 × 7·7 mm. | Used, when modified, as a torpedo-bomber. |
| S. 81 Three engine monoplane Crew 4 to 5 | 1,030 | 2,200 lb. | 130 at 15,000 ft. | 210 at 15,000 ft. | 6 × 7·7 mm. | |
| S. 82 Three engine monoplane Crew 4 to 5 | 1,250 | Nil | 155 at 10,000 ft. | 205 at 7,000 ft. | 1 × 12·7 mm. 4 × 7·7 mm. | Transport aircraft. Freight: 5,000 lb. |

## BOMBER AIRCRAFT
(including bomber transport, bomber reconnaissance, and torpedo-bomber)

### *GERMAN*

| Aircraft | Still Air Range with Associated Bombload | | Most Economical Cruising Speed in Miles Per Hour | Maximum Speed in Miles Per Hour | Armament | Remarks |
|---|---|---|---|---|---|---|
| | Miles | Bombload | | | | |
| Do. 17<br>Twin engine monoplane<br>Crew 4 | 890 | 2,200 lb. | 180 at 15,000 ft. | 255 at 15,000 ft. | 7 × 7·9 mm.<br>1 × 20 mm. | Used mainly for reconnaissance. |
| He. 111<br>Twin engine monoplane<br>Crew 5 to 6 | 1,510 | 2,200 lb. | 180 at 17,000 ft. | 240 at 14,000 ft. | 7 × 7·9 mm.<br>2 × 20 mm. | |
| Ju. 52<br>Three engine monoplane<br>Crew 3 to 4 | 530–790 | Nil | 132 at sea level | 165 at sea level | 5 × 7·9 mm. | Transport aircraft.<br>Freight: 4,000–5,060 lb. |
| Ju. 87 (Stuka)<br>Single engine monoplane<br>Crew 2 | 360 | 1,100 lb. | 160 at 15,000 ft. | 245 at 15,000 ft. | 3 × 7·9 mm. | Dive-bomber. |
| Ju. 88<br>Twin engine monoplane<br>Crew 4 | 1,310 | 2,200 lb. | 194 at 16,400 ft. | 295 at 14,000 ft. | 7 × 7·9 mm.<br>1 × 20 mm. | |

# APPENDIX 9

# Principal Commanders and Staff Officers in the Mediterranean and Middle East

(The ranks given are in some cases 'acting' ranks)

## ROYAL NAVY

*Commander-in-Chief, Mediterranean:* Admiral Sir Andrew B. Cunningham

*Chief of Staff:* Rear-Admiral A. U. Willis

*Additional Chief of Staff R.N., at Middle East H.Q., Cairo (also represented Commander-in-Chief East Indies):* Commodore H. G. Norman (from Sept. 1940)

[1]*V.A. Light Forces and Second-in-Command Mediterranean Fleet:* Vice-Admiral J. C. Tovey; Vice-Admiral H. D. Pridham-Wippell (from Oct. 1940)

*R.A. 1st Battle Squadron:* Rear-Admiral H. D. Pridham-Wippell; Rear-Admiral H. B. Rawlings (from Oct. 1940)

*R.A. Mediterranean Aircraft Carriers:* Rear-Admiral A. L. St. G. Lyster

*Admiral Commanding 3rd Cruiser Squadron:* Rear-Admiral E. de F. Renouf

*Vice-Admiral in charge, Malta:* Vice-Admiral Sir Wilbraham T. R. Ford

*Senior British Naval Officer, Suez Canal Area:* Vice-Admiral (retd.) Sir James Pipon

*R.A. Alexandria:* Rear-Admiral (retd.) F. Elliott

*Flag Officer Force H:* Vice-Admiral Sir James F. Somerville

*Commander-in-Chief, East Indies:* Vice-Admiral R. Leatham

*Senior Officer, Red Sea Force:* Rear-Admiral A. J. L. Murray

## THE ARMY

*Commander-in-Chief:* General Sir Archibald Wavell

*Principal Staff Officers*

    *General Staff branch:* Major-General A. F. Smith.

    *Quarter-Master-General's branch:* Major-General B. O. Hutchison

    *Adjutant-General's branch:* Brigadier R. M. Scobie (from 13th May 1940) Major-General N. W. Napier-Clavering (from 11th Sept. 1940)

### British Troops in Egypt

Lieutenant-General Sir H. Maitland Wilson (to 4th Feb. 1941)
Lieutenant-General R. N. O'Connor (from 4th Feb.-Apr. 1941)

### Western Desert Force (became 13th Corps on 1st Jan. 1941)

Lieutenant-General R. N. O'Connor (to 4th Feb. 1941)

---

[1] The title V.A.L.F. replaced that of A.C. 7th Cruiser Squadron and V.A. Destroyers on 20th August 1940.

*Cyrenaica Command*

Lieutenant-General Sir H. Maitland Wilson (Feb. 1941)
Lieutenant-General P. Neame (Feb.-Apr. 1941)

*Palestine, Transjordan and Cyprus*

Lieutenant-General M. G. H. Barker
Lieutenant-General P. Neame (Aug. 1940-Feb. 1941)

*Sudan*

Lieutenant-General W. Platt

*East Africa Force*

Lieutenant-General D. P. Dickinson
Lieutenant-General A. G. Cunningham (from 1st Nov. 1940)

*Formations*

*7th Armoured Division:* Major-General M. O'Moore Creagh

*1st Cavalry Division:* Major-General J. G. W. Clark

*4th Indian Division:* Major-General P. Neame; Major-General N. M. de la
P. Beresford-Peirse (from Aug. 1940)

*5th Indian Division:* Major-General L. M. Heath; Major-General
A. G. O. M. Mayne (from Apr. 1941)

*1st Australian Corps:* Lieutenant-General Sir Thomas Blamey

*6th Australian Division:* Major-General I. G. Mackay

*1st South African Division:* Major-General G. L. Brink

*11th African Division:* Major-General H. E. de R. Wetherall

*12th African Division:* Major-General A. R. Godwin-Austen

*New Zealand Division:* Major-General B. C. Freyberg

*2nd Armoured Division:* Major-General J. C. Tilly (to 16th Jan. 1941)

*Malta*

*Governor and Commander-in-Chief:* General Sir Charles Bonham-Carter (until
Oct. 1940); Lieutenant-General Sir William Dobbie (from 11th Oct.
1940; acting from May-Oct. 1940)

## ROYAL AIR FORCE

*Command Headquarters*

*Air Officer Commanding-in-Chief:* Air Chief Marshal Sir Arthur M. Longmore

*Deputy Air Officer Commanding-in-Chief:* Air Marshal A. W. Tedder (from
29th Nov. 1940)

*Senior Air Staff Officer:* Air Vice-Marshal R. M. Drummond

*Air Officer-in-Charge of Administration:* Air Vice-Marshal A. C. Maund

*Egypt and the Western Desert*

Air Commodore R. Collishaw   No. 202 Group.
Group Captain H. W. G. J. Penderel   No. 201 Group, Alexandria

*Cyrenaica*

Group Captain L. O. Brown   (from 19th Feb. 1941)

*Greece*

Air Vice-Marshal J. H. D'Albiac (from 5th Nov. 1940)

*Palestine and Transjordan*

Air Commodore J. H. D'Albiac (until 4th Nov. 1940)
Air Commodore J. W. B. Grigson (from 1st Dec. 1940)

*Iraq*

Air Vice-Marshal H. G. Smart

*Aden*

Air Vice-Marshal G. R. M. Reid (also Commander of all British Forces)

*East Africa*

Air Commodore W. Sowrey

*Sudan*

Air Commodore L. H. Slatter   No. 203 Group.

*Malta*

Air Commodore F. H. M. Maynard

# APPENDIX 10

# Operational Code Names

## BRITISH

COAT — Passage of reinforcements for the Fleet and of troops for Malta; November 1940.

COLLAR — Convoy of fast merchant ships for Malta and Alexandria; November 1940.

COMPASS — Operations against the Italians in the Western Desert beginning in December 1940.

EXCESS — Convoy of fast merchant ships for Greece and troops for Malta; January 1941.

HATS — Passage of naval reinforcements into the Mediterranean; September 1940.

HURRY — Fly-off of Hurricanes to Malta from H.M.S. *Argus*; August 1940.

WORKSHOP — Plan for the capture of Pantelleria early in 1941.

## GERMAN

ALPENVEILCHEN (Cyclamen) — Plan for sending German forces to help the Italians in Albania.

BARBAROSSA — The attack on Russia.

FELIX — Plan to capture Gibraltar and close the Straits.

MARITA — Invasion of Greece through Bulgaria.

MITTELMEER (Mediterranean) — Order for units of the *Luftwaffe* to operate from Italian bases in the Mediterranean.

SONNENBLUME (Sunflower) — Move of German forces to Libya.

193

# INDEX

Ships of all nationalities are in their alphabetical places *in italics*. Groups, Wings, Squadrons and other units of the R.A.F. are under Royal Air Force. Squadrons of the F.A.A. are under Fleet Air Arm. Squadrons of the R.A.A.F. and S.A.A.F. are under Royal Australian Air Force and South African Air Force. Corps, Divisions and Brigades of the British Army are under those headings. Formations of the German and Italian Armies are under the headings German Army and Italian Army. All army units are in their alphabetical places in the index.

S.O. Code No. 63-111-21-3*

# HISTORY OF
# THE SECOND WORLD WAR
## UNITED KINGDOM MILITARY SERIES

Reprinted by the Naval & Military Press in twenty two volumes with the permission of the Controller of HMSO and Queen's Printer for Scotland.

## THE DEFENCE OF THE UNITED KINGDOM

*Basil Collier*

Official history of Britain's home front in the Second World War, from the Phoney War, through the Battle of Britain and the Blitz to victory in Europe.
ISBN: 1845740556
Price £22.00

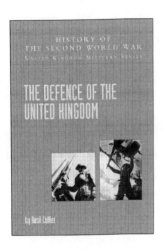

## THE CAMPAIGN IN NORWAY

*T. H. Derry*

The catastrophic 1940 campaign which caused the downfall of Neville Chamberlain and brought Winston Churchill to power.
ISBN: 1845740572
Price: £22.00

## THE WAR IN FRANCE AND FLANDERS 1939-1940

*Major L. F. Ellis*

The role of the BEF in the fall of France and the retreat to Dunkirk.
ISBN: 1845740564
Price £22.00

## VICTORY IN THE WEST
### Volume I: The Battle of Normandy

*Major L. F. Ellis*

The build-up, execution and consequences of D-Day in 1944.
ISBN: 1845740580
Price: £22.00

### Volume II: The Defeat of Germany

*Major L. F. Ellis*

The final stages of the liberation of western Europe in 1944-45.
ISBN: 1845740599
Price £22.00

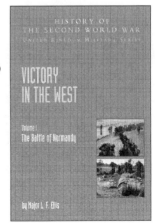

# THE MEDITERRANEAN AND MIDDLE EAST

## Volume I: The Early Successes against Italy (to May 1941)

*Major-General I. S. O. Playfair*

Britain defeats Italy on land and sea in Africa and the Mediterranean in 1940.
ISBN: 1845740653
Price: £22.00

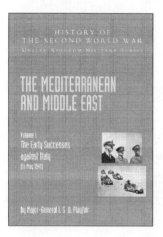

## Volume II: The Germans Come to the Help of their Ally (1941)

*Major-General I. S. O. Playfair*

Rommel rides to Italy's rescue, Malta is bombarded, Yugoslavia, Greece and Crete are lost, and Iraq and Syria are secured for the Allies.
ISBN: 1845740661
Price: £22.00

## Volume III: (September 1941 to September 1942) British Fortunes reach their Lowest Ebb

*Major-General I. S. O. Playfair*

Britain's darkest hour in North Africa and the Mediterranean, 1941–42.
ISBN: 184574067X
Price: £22.00

## Volume IV: The Destruction of the Axis Forces in Africa

*Major-General I. S. O. Playfair*

The battle of El Alamein and 'Operation Torch' bring the Allies victory in North Africa, 1942–43.
ISBN: 1845740688
Price: £22.00

## Volume V: The Campaign in Sicily 1943 and the Campaign in Italy – 3rd Sepember 1943 to 31st March 1944

*Major-General I. S. O. Playfair*

The Allies invade Sicily and Italy, but encounter determined German defence in 1943–44.
ISBN: 1845740696
Price: £22.00

## Volume VI: Victory in the Mediterranean Part I: 1st April to 4th June 1944

*Brigadier C. J. C. Molony*

The Allies breach the Gustav, Hitler and Caesar Lines and occupy Rome.
ISBN: 184574070X
Price: £22.00

## Volume VI: Victory in the Mediterranean Part II: June to October 1944

*General Sir William Jackson*

The 1944 Italian summer campaign breaches the Gothic Line but then bogs down again.
ISBN: 1845740718
Price: £22.00

## Volume VI: Victory in the Mediterranean Part III: November 1944 to May 1945

*General Sir William Jackson*

The messy end of the war in Italy, Greece, and Yugoslavia.
ISBN: 1845740726
Price: £22.00

# THE WAR AGAINST JAPAN

## Volume I: The Loss of Singapore

*Major-General S. Woodburn Kirby*

The fall of Hong Kong, Malaya and Singapore in 1941–42.
ISBN: 1845740602
Price: £22.00

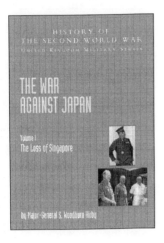

## Volume II: India's Most Dangerous Hour

*Major-General S. Woodburn Kirby*

The loss of Burma and Japan's threat to India in 1941–42.
ISBN: 1845740610
Price: £22.00

## Volume III: The Decisive Battles

*Major-General S. Woodburn Kirby*

Turning the tide in the war against Japan at the battles of Kohima, Imphal and the Chindit campaigns.
ISBN: 1845740629
Price: £22.00

## Volume IV: The Reconquest of Burma

*Major-General S. Woodburn Kirby*

The reconquest of Burma by Bill Slim's 'forgotten' 14th Army.
ISBN: 1845740637
Price: £22.00

## Volume V: The Surrender of Japan

*Major-General S. Woodburn Kirby*

Victory in South-East Asia in 1945 – from Rangoon to Nagasaki.
ISBN: 1845740645
Price: £22.00

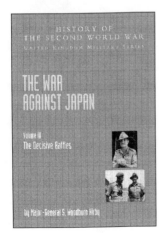
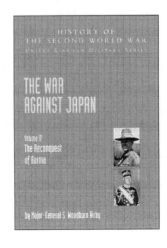
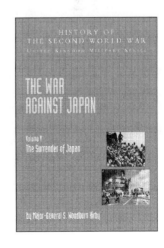

# THE WAR AT SEA - 1939—1945

Captain Roskill has long been recognised as the leading authority on The Royal Navy's part in the Second World War. His official History is unlikely ever to be superceded. His narrative is highly readable and the analysis is clear. Roskill describes sea battles, convoy actions and the contribution made by technology in the shape of Asdic & Radar.

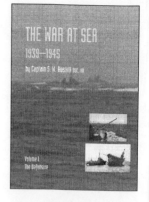

## Volume I: The Defensive

*Captain S. W. Roskill, D.S.C., R.N.*

2004 N&MP reprint (original pub 1954).
SB. xxii + 664pp with 43 maps and numerous contemporary photos.
ISBN: 1843428032
Price: £32.00

## Volume II: The Period of Balance

*Captain S. W. Roskill, D.S.C., R.N.*

2004 N&MP reprint (original pub 1956).
SB. xvi + 523pp with 42 maps and numerous contemporary photos.
ISBN: 1843428040
Price: £32.00

## Volume III: Part I The Offensive
## 1st June 1943-31 May 1944

*Captain S. W. Roskill, D.S.C., R.N.*

2004 N&MP reprint (original pub 1960).
SB. xv + 413pp with 21 maps and numerous contemporary photos.
ISBN: 1843428059
Price: £32.00

## Volume III: Part 2 The Offensive
## 1st June 1944-14th August 1945

*Captain S. W. Roskill, D.S.C., R.N.*

2004 N&MP reprint (original pub 1961).
SB. xvi + 502pp with 46 maps and numerous contemporary photos.
ISBN: 1843428067
Price: £32.00

35076274R00375

Made in the USA
Lexington, KY
29 August 2014